W9-AEM-331

PLOT SUMMARY INDEX

Second Edition,
Revised and Enlarged

compiled by

CAROL KOEHMSTEDT KOLAR

PN
44
.K64
1981

The Scarecrow Press, Inc.
Metuchen, N.J., & London
1981

INDIANA-PURDUE LIBRARY

WITHDRAWN

FORT WAYNE

Library of Congress Cataloging in Publication Data

Kolar, Carol Koehmstedt, 1931-
    Plot summary index.

    1. Literature--Stories, plots, etc.--Indexes.
I. Title.
Z6514.P66K64 1981 [PN44]   809   80-27112
ISBN 0-8108-1392-0

Copyright © 1981 by Carol Koehmstedt Kolar

Manufactured in the United States of America

Dedicated to my husband, Jim,
for his support and his patience.

ACKNOWLEDGMENTS

I wish to extend my appreciation to the staffs of the Parmly Billings Library, Eastern Montana College Library, and Rocky Mountain College Library (all of Billings, Montana), but in particular to Gene M. Robson and her staff, Interlibrary Loan, and Chris Liggett-Eicholz, Reference, of Parmly Billings Library for their generous and gracious assistance over many months.

My appreciation is also extended to my mother who often assisted in the voluminous task of card-sorting.

iv

CONTENTS

PREFACE

The symbols for the books indexed are the last names of the authors of the collections. Using the author's name rather than an arbitrary symbol should prove to be a time-saver allowing the librarian to go directly to the shelf for a familiar collection.

This index is in two sections: title and author. The title entry serves as the main entry listing the sources for the plot summaries. Title cross-references are listed only in the title section; author cross-references are listed only in the author section. Works are listed under a pseudonym if that is the name commonly used; e. g. works are listed under Twain, Mark, with a cross-reference from Clemens, Samuel Langhorne.

Literary works of all types have been included in this second edition including fiction, non-fiction, musical comedy, narrative poetry and epic poetry. Inclusion has been dictated by the contents of the collections chosen for indexing. Collections have been indexed exhaustively except for summaries of short poems; collections not completely indexed have been so noted in the Symbols for Collections Indexed list.

Titles are listed under the English title wherever possible. Variant titles are listed in parentheses following the English title. If a plot summary is located in a collection under a variant title or out of the general order of that collection, such will be noted following the author symbol, e. g. Shank p. 26.

It will be noted that Latin titles are not capitalized uniformly. Using A Manual of Style for Authors, Editors and Copywriters (12th ed. rev. , Univ. of Chicago Press, 1969) as the authority, titles of authors prior to the Middle Ages are not capitalized, whereas titles of authors after the Middle Ages are capitalized as are English titles.

Author entries are for joint and individual authors. Where joint authors share the same surname, a cross-reference has been made from one given name to the other, e. g. Spewack, Samuel, see Spewack, Bella and Samuel. In the case of musical comedies or literary works with four or more authors, the title or main entry will list all authors, but the individual author entries will read "et al.," e. g. Hammerstein, Oscar, II et al.

Alphabetizing is word by word (nothing comes before something). In a title, Mrs. is filed m-r-s, but Dr. is filed d-o-c-t-o-r. Designations such as Mrs., Honorable, Count, Saint are overlooked in filing; e. g. Patrick, Saint comes before Patrick, John.

English titles and foreign titles beginning with an article of speech are alphabetized according to the first significant word; e. g. A View from the Bridge is alphabetized under "V," L'Aiglon, under "A."

Summaries vary in length from collection to collection and within collections. In general all summaries were indexed under the rationale that a brief summary is better than none. Major reference works which generally have excellent summaries--McGraw-Hill Encyclopedia of World Drama, New Century Classical Handbook, New Century Handbook of English Literature, the Oxford Companions, Benet's Reader's Encyclopedia--have been omitted because of sheer volume, and one or the other will generally be available in all but the smallest libraries. Collections that include only very brief annotations (Baker's Guide to the Best Fiction and Logasa's Historical Fiction) have been omitted.

There are the purists who do not approve of plot summaries --but plot summaries do have their place. When the Reference Librarian is approached by a student fifteen minutes before examination time, being able to quickly and affirmatively assist that patron is justification for this listing.

C. K. K.

viii

SYMBOLS FOR COLLECTIONS INDEXED

Anderson   Anderson, Michael J. Crowell's Handbook of
Contemporary Drama, by Michael Anderson
... and others. New York, Crowell, 1971.

Armstrong   Armstrong, Spencer, ed. 101 of the World's
Greatest Books; with illus. by Rockwell Kent.
New York, Greystone Press, 1950.

Baker   Baker, Arthur Ernest. A Shakespeare Commentary. New York, F. Ungar Pub. Co.,
1957.

Benedict   Benedict, Stewart H. A Teacher's Guide to
Contemporary Teenage Fiction. New York,
Dell Pub. Co., 1973.

Berry-1   Berry, Thomas E. Plots and Characters in Major Russian Fiction; vol. I Pushkin, Lermon-
tov, Turgenev, Tolstoi. Hamden, Conn.,
Archon Books, 1977. (Plots and Characters
Series).

Berry-2   Berry, Thomas E. Plots and Characters in Major Russian Fiction; vol. II Gogol', Goncharov,
Dostoevskii. Hamden, Conn., Archon Books,
1978. (Plots and Characters Series).

Best 'yr.   The Best Plays. New York, Dodd, Mead, 1894/
99-1978/79.

Bonin   Bonin, Jane F. Prize-Winning American Drama:
A Bibliographical and Descriptive Guide. Metuchen, N.J., Scarecrow Press, 1973.

Campbell   Campbell, Oscar James, ed. The Reader's Encyclopedia of Shakespeare. Assoc. ed. Ed-
ward G. Quinn. New York, Crowell, 1966.

Carrington   Carrington, George C., Jr. Plots and Characters in the Fiction of William Dean Howells,
by George C. Carrington, Jr., and Ildiko de
Papp Carrington, with a foreword by George

Arms. Hamden, Conn., Archon Books, 1976. (Plots and Characters Series). [N. B.: Indexed the novels only.]

Cartmell Cartmell, Van Henry, ed. Plot Outlines of 100 Famous Plays. Philadelphia, Blakiston Company, New Home Library. n. d.

Chapman '53-'56 Theatre. Edited by John Chapman. New York, Random House, 1953-1956. 4 vols.

Chapman '57, '59 Chapman, John Arthur. Broadway's Best; the Complete Record of the Theatrical Year. Garden City, N. Y., Doubleday, 1957, 1959.

Chute Chute, Marchette G. Stories from Shakespeare. Cleveland, World Pub. Co., 1956.

Clark Clark, Sandra, ed. The New Century Shakespeare Handbook. Englewood Cliffs, N. J., Prentice-Hall, 1974.

Cohen Cohen, Sam D. The Digest of the World's Great Classics. New York, Daily Compass, 1950.

Downs F Downs, Robert Bingham. Famous Books, Ancient and Medieval. New York, Barnes & Noble, 1964.

Downs FG Downs, Robert Bingham. Famous Books: Great Writings in the History of Civilization. Totowa, N. J., Littlefield, Adams, 1975.

Downs M Downs, Robert Bingham. Molders of the Modern Mind. New York, Barnes & Noble, 1961.

Drinkrow Drinkrow, John. The Vintage Musical Comedy Book. Reading, Osprey Publishing, 1974.

Drury Drury, Francis Keese Wynkoop. Drury's Guide to Best Plays, by James M. Salem. 3d ed. Metuchen, N. J., Scarecrow Press, 1978.

Feder Feder, Lillian. Crowell's Handbook of Classical Literature. London, Barker, 1964.

Fleming Teaching the Epic. Margaret Fleming, editor. Urbana, Ill., National Council of Teachers of English, 1974.

French French, Samuel, Firm, Publishers. The Guide to Selecting Plays. London. n. d.

Gale-H   Gale, Robert L.   Plots and Characters in the
Fiction and Sketches of Nathaniel Hawthorne.
Hamden, Conn. , Archon Books, 1968.   (Plots
and Characters Series).

Gale-J   Gale, Robert L.   Plots and Characters in the
Fiction of Henry James.   Hamden, Conn. ,
Archon Books, 1965.   (Plots and Characters
Series).

Gale-M   Gale, Robert L.   Plots and Characters in the
Fiction and Narrative Poetry of Herman Melville.   With a foreword by Harrison Hayford.
Hamden, Conn. , Archon Books, 1969.   (Plots
and Characters Series).

Gale-P   Gale, Robert L.   Barron's Simplified Approach
to Edgar Allan Poe.   Woodbury, N. Y. , Bar-
ron's Educational Series, Inc. , 1969.   [N. B. :
Indexed short stories only.]

Gale-PP   Gale, Robert L.   Plots and Characters in the
Fiction and Poetry of Edgar Allan Poe.   With
a foreword by Floyd Stovall.   Hamden, Conn. ,
Archon Books, 1970.   (Plots and Characters
Series).

Gale-T   Gale, Robert L.   Plots and Characters in the
Works of Mark Twain.   With a foreword by
Frederick Anderson.   Hamden, Conn. , Archon
Books, 1973.   (Plots and Characters Series).
[N. B. :   Indexed only works identified by Gale
as 50, 000 words or more in length.]

Gassner   Gassner, John.   Reader's Encyclopedia of World
Drama,   edited by John Gassner and Edward
Quinn.   New York, Crowell, 1969.   [N. B. :
Indexed only literary works having separate
title entries, and indexed selectively from
country entries.)

Gerber   Gerber, Philip L.   Plots and Characters in the
Fiction of Theodore Dreiser.   Hamden, Conn. ,
Archon Books, 1977.   (Plots and Characters
Series).

Gerould   Gerould, Winifred Gregory.   A Guide to Trollope.
Princeton, N. J. , Princeton University Press,
1948.

Goodman   Goodman, Roland Arthur, ed.   Plot Outlines of
100 Famous Novels: The First Hundred.
Garden City, N. Y. , Doubleday, 1962.

Grozier	Grozier, Edwin Atkins, ed. Plot Outlines of 101 Best Novels: Condensations Based on Original Works. New York, Barnes & Noble, 1962.
Guerber-SC	Guerber, Hélène Adeline. Stories of Shakespeare's Comedies. New York, Dodd, Mead, 1910.
Guerber-SH	Guerber, Hélène Adeline. Stories of Shakespeare's English History Plays. New York, Dodd, Mead, 1912.
Guerber-ST	Guerber, Hélène Adeline. Stories of Shakespeare's Tragedies. New York, Dodd, Mead, 1911.
Halford	Halford, Aubrey S. The Kabuki Handbook, by Aubrey S. Halford and Giovanna M. Halford. Tokyo; Rutland, Vt., C. E. Tuttle Co., 1956.
Halliday	Halliday, Frank Ernest. A Shakespeare Companion. New York, Funk & Wagnalls Company, 1952.
Halperin	Halperin, John. Plots and Characters in the Fiction of Jane Austen, the Brontës, and George Eliot. John Halperin and Janet Kunert. Hamden, Conn., Archon Books, 1976. (Plots and Characters Series).
Hardwick	Hardwick, John Michael Drinkrow. The Bernard Shaw Companion, by Michael and Mollie Hardwick. New York, St. Martin's Press, 1974, c1973.
Hardwick CD	Hardwick, John Michael Drinkrow. The Charles Dickens Companion, by Michael and Mollie Hardwick. New York, E. P. Dutton, 1968.
Hardwick SH	Hardwick, John Michael Drinkrow. The Sherlock Holmes Companion, by Michael and Mollie Hardwick. Garden City, N. Y., Doubleday, 1963.
Hathorn	Hathorn, Richmond Yancey. Crowell's Handbook of Classical Drama. New York, Crowell, 1967. [N. B.: "Lost" plays have been indexed only when listed as a separate title entry (some exceptions).]
Haydn	Haydn, Hiram. Thesaurus of Book Digests; Digests of the World's Permanent Writing from the Ancient Classics to Current Literature,

compiled under the editorial supervision of
Hiram Haydn and Edmund Fuller. New York,
Crown, 1949.

Heiney   Heiney, Donald W. Essentials of Contemporary
Literature. Great Neck, N. Y., Barron's Educational Series, Inc., 1955, c1954. [N. B.:
Indexed "chief works" section under each author; chapter "Tradition and Revolt in Poetry"
indexed as "Poetry of..." rather than by individual title.]

Hix   Hix, Melvin. Fifty English Classics Briefly Out-
lined. New York, Noble and Noble, 1925.
[N. B.: Partially indexed.]

Holzknecht   Holzknecht, Karl Julius. Outlines of Tudor and
Stuart Plays, 1497-1642. London, Methuen,
1963, c1947.

Johnson   Johnson, Rossiter. Authors Digest; the World's
Great Stories in Brief. Metuchen, N. J.,
Mini-Print Corp., 1970, c1909. 5 vols.

Johnson-18th   Johnson, Clifford R. Plots and Characters in the
  -18th/2   Fiction of Eighteenth-Century English Authors.
Vols. 1 and 2. Hamden, Conn., Archon
Books, 1977. (Plots and Characters Series).

Jolliffe   Jolliffe, Harold Richard. Tales from the Greek
Drama. Philadelphia, Chilton Books, 1962.

Kaye   Kaye, James R. Historical Fiction. Chicago,
Snowdon Pub. Co., 1920.

Keller   Keller, Helen Rex. The Reader's Digest of
Books. New York, Macmillan, 1929.

Keller suppl.   ---Supplement. (Within same volume).

Kienzle   Kienzle, Siegfried. Modern World Theater; a
Guide to Productions in Europe and the U. S.
Since 1945. Translated by Alexander and
Elizabeth Henderson. New York, Frederick
Ungar Pub. Co., 1970.

Lamb   Lamb, Charles The Complete Tales from Shake-
speare, All Those Told by Charles & Mary
Lamb, with 12 Others Newly Told by J. C.
Trewin. New York, F. Watts, 1964.

Lass AN   Lass, Abraham Harold. A Student's Guide to

	50 American Novels. New York, Washington Square Press, 1966.
Lass AP	Lass, Abraham Harold. A Student's Guide to 50 American Plays, edited by Abraham H. Lass and Milton Levin. New York, Washington Square Press, 1969.
Lass BN	Lass, Abraham Harold. A Student's Guide to 50 British Novels. New York, Washington Square Press, 1966.
Lass EN	Lass, Abraham Harold. A Student's Guide to 50 European Novels, edited by Abraham H. Lass and Brooks Wright. New York, Washington Square Press, 1967.
Lovell	Lovell, John. Digests of Great American Plays; Complete Summaries of More Than 100 Plays from the Beginnings to the Present. New York, Crowell, 1961.
McCutchan-SC	McCutchan, J. Wilson. Plot Outlines of Shakespeare's Comedies, Scene by Scene. New York, Barnes & Noble, 1965.
McCutchan-SH	McCutchan, J. Wilson. Plot Outlines of Shakespeare's Histories, Scene by Scene. New York, Barnes & Noble, 1965.
McCutchan-ST	McCutchan, J. Wilson. Plot Outlines of Shakespeare's Tragedies, Scene by Scene. New York, Barnes & Noble, 1965.
McSpadden-D	McSpadden, Joseph Walker. Synopses of Dickens's Novels. New York, T. Y. Crowell & Co., 1909.
McSpadden-DH	Dickens, Charles. Stories from Dickens, by J. Walker McSpadden. Intro. by Veronica Hutchinson; illus. by Virginia Grilley. New York, T. Y. Crowell & Co., 1949.
McSpadden S	McSpadden, Joseph Walker. Shakespearean Synopses; Outlines or Arguments of All the Plays of Shakespeare. New York, T. Y. Crowell & Co., 1902.
McSpadden W	McSpadden, Joseph Walker. Waverley Synopses; a Guide to the Plots and Characters of Scott's "Waverley Novels." New York, T. Y. Crowell & Co., 1909.

Magill I-IV	Magill, Frank Northen. Masterpieces of World Literature in Digest Form. 1st-4th series. Edited by Frank N. Magill, with the assistance of Dayton Kohler and staff. New York, Harper, 1952-69. 4 vols.
Magill '54-'76	Masterplots Annual. New York, Salem Press, 1954-1976.
Magill '77-'79	Magill's Literary Annual. Englewood Cliffs, N. J. , Salem Press, 1977-1979. Continues: Masterplots Annual.
Magill CAL	Magill, Frank Northen. Masterpieces of Catholic Literature in Summary Form, edited by Frank N. Magill with associate editors A. Robert Caponigri and Thomas P. Neill. New York, Harper & Row, 1965.
Magill CE	Magill, Frank Northen. 1,300 Critical Evaluations of Selected Novels and Plays: Offprints of All the New Material from the 12-Volume Revised Edition of Masterplots. Englewood Cliffs, N. J. , Salem Press, 1978. 4 vols.
Magill CHL	Magill, Frank Northen. Masterpieces of Christian Literature in Summary Form, edited by Frank N. Magill with Ian P. McGreal. New York, Harper and Row, 1963.
Magill M1	Magill, Frank Northen. Masterplots; Eighteen Hundred and Ten Plot-Stories and Essay-Reviews from the World's Fine Literature, edited by Frank N. Magill with story editor Dayton Kohler. New York, Salem Press, 1971. 18 vols.
Magill M2	Magill, Frank Northen. Masterplots: 2010 Plot Stories and Essay Reviews from the World's Fine Literature, edited by Frank N. Magill with story editor Dayton Kohler. Rev. ed. , including the four series and further critical evaluations. Englewood Cliffs, N. J. , Salem Press, 1976. 12 vols.
Magill MAF	Magill, Frank Northen. American Fiction Series; 262 Plots in Story Form from the Best American Fiction. Story editor: Dayton Kohler. New York, Salem Press, 1961. (Masterplots [Categories ed. , 2])
Magill MAL1-5	Magill, Frank Northen. Masterplots of American Literature: The Nineteenth Century. New York, Harper & Row, 1970+. 5 vols.

Magill MB   Masterplots Annual. Masterplots; Best Master-
                     plots, 1954-1962: 175 Essay-Reviews from
                     Masterplots Annuals Since 1954, edited by
                     Frank N. Magill with associate editor Dayton
                     Kohler. New York, Salem Press, 1963.

Magill MC   Magill, Frank Northen. Masterplots; Compre-
                     hensive Library Edition: Two Thousand and
                     Ten Plot Stories and Essay Reviews from the
                     World's Fine Literature, edited by Frank N.
                     Magill with story editor Dayton Kohler. Defin-
                     itive ed. New York, Salem Press, 1968. 8
                     vols.

Magill MD   Magill, Frank Northen. Drama Series; 366 Plots
                     in Story Form from the World's Fine Drama.
                     Story Editor: Dayton Kohler. New York,
                     Salem Press, 1964. (Masterplots. [Categories
                     ed. , 1])

Magill MEF   Magill, Frank Northen. English Fiction Series;
                     337 Plots in Story Form from the Best English
                     Fiction. Story editor: Dayton Kohler. New
                     York, Salem Press, 1964. (Masterplots.
                     [Categories ed. , 3])

Magill MEUF   Magill, Frank Northen. European Fiction Series;
                     287 Plots in Story Form from the Best Euro-
                     pean Fiction. Story editor: Dayton Kohler.
                     New York, Salem Press, 1964. (Masterplots.
                     [Categories ed. , 4])

Magill MNF   Magill, Frank Northen. Non-Fiction Series; 117
                     Essay-Reviews of the World's Fine Non-Fiction.
                     Story editor: Dayton Kohler. New York, Sa-
                     lem Press, 1964. (Masterplots. [Categories
                     ed. , 6])

Magill MP   Magill, Frank Northen. Poetry Series; 141 Essay-
                     Reviews of the World's Fine Poetry. Story
                     editor: Dayton Kohler. New York, Salem
                     Press, 1964. (Masterplots. [Categories ed. ,
                     5])

Magill S   Magill, Frank Northen. Survey of Contemporary
                     Literature; Updated Reprints of 1500 Essay-
                     Reviews from Masterplots Annuals, 1954-
                     1969, edited by Frank N. Magill with associate
                     editor Dayton Kohler. New York, Salem Press,
                     1971.

Magill Ss   ---Supplement. Englewood Cliffs, N. J. , Salem
                     Press, 1972.

Magill SF   Magill, Frank Northen. Survey of Science Fic-
                     tion Literature; Five Hundred 2, 000-Word
                     Essay Reviews of World-Famous Science Fic-
                     tion Novels with 2, 500 Bibliographical Refer-
                     ences.   Englewood Cliffs, N. J. , Salem Press,
                     1979. 5 vols.

Magill WP   Magill, Frank Northen. Masterpieces of World
                     Philosophy in Summary Form. Associate
                     editor: Ian P. McGreaL New York, Harper,
                     1961.

Matlaw   Matlaw, Myron. Modern World Drama; an Ency-
                     clopedia. New York, Dutton, 1972. [N. B. :
                     Partially indexed.]

Morehead   Morehead, Albert Hodges. 100 Great American
                     Novels; synopses edited by Albert H. More-
                     head, Harold J. Blum and others. New York,
                     New American Library, 1966.

Mudge   Mudge, Isadore Gilbert. A Thackeray Dictionary;
                     the Characters and Scenes of the Novels and
                     Short Stories Alphabetically Arranged, by Isa-
                     dore Gilbert Mudge and Minnie Earl Sears.
                     New York, Humanities Press, 1962, c1910.

NBC 1-3   National Broadcasting Company, Inc. National
                     Broadcasting Company Presents Great Plays,
                     a Drama Guide, by Blevins Davis. New York,
                     Pub. by Columbia Univ. Press for the NBC,
                     1937-1939.

NCTE   National Council of Teachers of English. Guide
                     to Play Selection; a Selective Bibliography for
                     Production and Study of Modern Plays. 3d
                     ed. Urbana, Ill. , National Council of Teach-
                     ers of English, and R. R. Bowker Co. , N. Y. ,
                     1975. [N. B. : Indexed only full-length plays
                     and musical plays.]

Olfson   Olfson, Lewy, ed. Plot Outlines of 100 Famous
                     Novels: The Second Hundred. Garden City,
                     N. Y. , Doubleday, 1966.

Pinion   Pinion, F. B. A Hardy Companion; a Guide to
                     the Works of Thomas Hardy and Their Back-
                     ground. New York, St. Martin's Press; Lon-
                     don, Macmillan, 1968.

Reinhold   Reinhold, Meyer. Classical Drama Greek and
                     Roman. Woodbury, N. Y. , Barron's Educa-
                     tional Series, Inc. , 1959.

Ruoff   Ruoff, James E. Crowell's Handbook of Eliza-
bethan and Stuart Literature. New York,
Crowell, 1975. [N. B.: Indexed only literary
works having separate title entries.]

Sabater   Sabater, José. Human Monuments. New York,
Greenwick Bk. Pub. , 1959.

Saxelby   Saxelby, F. Outwin. A Thomas Hardy Dictionary.
New York, Humanities Press, 1962, c1911.

Shank   Shank, Theodore J. A Digest of 500 Plays; Plot
Outlines and Production Notes. New York,
Collier Books; Collier-Macmillan Ltd. , 1963.

Shipley   Shipley, Joseph Twadell. Guide to Great Plays.
Washington, Public Affairs Press, 1956.

Smith   Smith, Guy E. American Literature; a Complete
Survey with Plot Summaries of Major Works
and Dictionary of Literary Terms. Ames,
Iowa, Littlefield, Adams, 1957.

Sobel   Sobel, Bernard, ed. The New Theatre Handbook
and Digest of Plays. New York, Crown, 1959.

Sprinchorn   Sprinchorn, Evert, ed. 20th Century Plays in
Synopsis. New York, Crowell, 1966.

Stade   Stade, George, comp. Six Modern British Nov-
elists. New York, Columbia University Press,
1974. [N. B.: Partially indexed.]

Thomas   Schnittkind, Henry Thomas. Stories of the Great
Dramas and Their Authors. New York, Gar-
den City Pub. Co. , Inc. , 1939.

Walker   Walker, Warren S. Plots and Characters in the
Fiction of James Fenimore Cooper. Hamden,
Conn. , Archon Books, 1978. (Plots and
Characters Series).

Ward   Ward, Alfred Charles. Longman Companion to
Twentieth Century Literature. Harlow, Long-
man, 1970. [N. B.: Indexed only literary
works having separate title entries.]

Wilson   Wilson, Barbara Logan. Capsule Classics; with
an introduction by David Appel. Cleveland,
World Pub. Co. , 1952.

A la recherche du temps perdu see
Remembrance of Things Past
A 1-12. Louis Zukofsky. Magill
'68, S
Aaron Slick from Punkin Crick.
Beale Cormack. Shipley
Aaron Trow. Anthony Trollope.
Gerould
Aaron's Rod. D. H. Lawrence.
Ward
Abadon. Janez Mencinger. Ma-
gill SF
Abasement of the Northmores, The.
Henry James. Gale-J
Abba Eben: An Autobiography. Ab-
ba Eben. Magill '78
Abbé Constantin, The. Ludovic
Halévy. Cohen; Grozier; Keller;
Magill I, CE, M1&2, MEUF,
MC
Abbe Mouret's Transgression see
Faute de l'Abbé Mouret, La.
Abbess of Vlaye, The. Stanley J.
Weyman. Kaye
Abbey Grange, The. Sir Arthur
Conan Doyle. Hardwick SH
Abbot, The. Sir Walter Scott.
Johnson; Kaye; Keller; McSpad-
den W
Abdallah. Edouard Laboulaye.
Johnson
Abe Lincoln in Illinois. Robert E.
Sherwood. Best '38; Bonin;
Drury; Haydn; Lovell; Magill I,
CE, M1&2, MC, MD; Matlaw;
Shipley; Sobel
Abencerraje, The. Antonio de
Villegas. Haydn
Abie's Irish Rose. Anne Nichols.
Cartmell; Drury; Lovell; Mat-
law; NCTE; Shipley; Sobel
Abinger Harvest. E. M. Forster.
Ward
Able McLaughlins, The. Margaret
Wilson. Keller suppl.
About the House. Wystan Hugh
Auden. Magill '66, M1, S

Above the Battle: War-Making in
America from Appomattox to Ver-
sailles. Thomas C. Leonard.
Magill '79
Abraham. Roswitha. Shipley
Abraham and Isaac. Unknown.
Haydn; Magill III, CE, M1&2,
MC, MD; Shank; Wilson
Abraham Lincoln. Lord Charnwood.
Keller (Lincoln)
Abraham Lincoln. John Drinkwater.
Best '19; Drury; French; Keller
suppl.; Matlaw; Shipley; Sobel;
Ward
Abraham Lincoln. Carl Sandburg.
Haydn; Keller suppl. (Lincoln);
Magill III, '54, M1, MB, MC,
MNF, S
Abraham Lincoln; a History. John
G. Nicolay and John Hay. Kel-
ler (Lincoln)
Abraham Lincoln, the True Story of
a Great Life. William Henry
Herndon. Keller (Lincoln)
Absalom, Absalom! William Faulk-
ner. Heiney; Magill I, CE, M1&
2, MAF, MC
Absalom and Achitophel. John Dry-
den. Haydn p. 216; Keller; Ma-
gill III, M1, MC, MP
Absence of a Cello, The. Ira Wal-
lach. Drury; NCTE
Absences; New Poems. James Tate.
Magill '73
Absent-Mindedness in a Parish Choir.
Thomas Hardy. Saxelby
Absentee, The. Maria Edgeworth.
Johnson; Magill II, CE, M1&2,
MC, MEF
Absolute at Large, The. Karel
Čapek. Magill SF
Abuelo, El (The Grandfather). Beni-
to Pérez Galdós. Drury (Grand-
father); Sobel
Abuse of Power. Theodore Draper.
Magill '68, M1, S
Abyss, The. Marguerite Yourcenar.

Admirable Crichton, The. Sir
James M. Barrie. Cartmell;
Drury; French; Keller; Magill
I, CE, M1&2, MC, MD;
Matlaw; NCTE; Shank; Ship-
ley; Sobel; Sprinchorn; Thomas;
Ward
Adolescence. G. Stanley Hall.
Keller
Adolescent, The see Raw Youth,
A
Adolf Hitler. John Toland.
Magill '77
Adolphe. Benjamin Constant.
Keller; Magill III, CE, M1&2,
MC, MEUF
Adonais. Percy Bysshe Shelley.
Haydn (a)
Adopted, The. Anna Eliza Bray.
Kaye
Adornment of the Spiritual Mar-
riage, The. John of Ruys-
broeck. Magill CHL
Adrea. David Belasco and John
Luther Long. Matlaw
Adria. Alexander N. Hood. Kaye
Adrienne. André Maurois.
Magill '62, M1, S
Adrienne Lecouvreur. Augustin
Eugène Scribe and Ernest
Légouvé. Keller; Shipley;
Sobel
Adrift in New York. Addison
Aulger. Drury
Advancement of Learning see
Of the Proficience and Advance-
ment of Learning, Divine and
Human
Advantage of Lyric: Essays on
Feeling in Poetry, The. Bar-
bara Hardy. Magill '78
Advent, a "Mysterium." August
Strindberg. Matlaw
Adventure, An. Anne Moberly
and Eleanor Jourdain. Ward
Adventure, The. Paul Zweig.
Magill '75
Adventure Story. Terence Ratti-
gan. French; Ward
Adventurer, The. Alfred Capus.
Drury
Adventurer and the Singer, The.
Hugo von Hofmannsthal.
Heiney
Adventures in Arabia. W. B.
Seabrook. Keller suppl.
Adventures in Criticism. Sir
Arthur Thomas Quiller-

Couch. Keller
Adventures in the Skin Trade.
Dylan Thomas. Magill '55, S
Adventures of an Aide-de-Camp,
The. James Grant. Kaye
Adventures of Augie March, The.
Saul Bellow. Lass AN; Magill
IV, MC; Morehead
Adventures of Caleb Williams,
The see Caleb Williams
Adventures of Conan Doyle, The.
Charles Higham. Magill '77
Adventures of François, The.
Silas Weir Mitchell. Keller
(François)
Adventures of Fred Pickering,
The. Anthony Trollope.
Gerould
Adventures of Gil Blas of Santil-
lane, The see Gil Blas de
Santillane
Adventures of Girard. Sir Arthur
Conan Doyle. Kaye
Adventures of Guzman d'Alfarache
see Guzman d'Alfarache
Adventures of Huckleberry Finn,
The see Huckleberry Finn
Adventures of Master F. J., The.
George Gascoigne. Ruoff
Adventures of Mr. Verdant Green,
an Oxford Freshman, The.
Cuthbert Bede. Johnson; Kel-
ler (Verdant)
Adventures of Obadiah Oldbuck.
Rodolphe Töpffer. Keller
(Obadiah)
Adventures of Philip, The. Wil-
liam Makepeace Thackeray.
Johnson; Mudge
Adventures of Sherlock Holmes
see Sherlock Holmes
Adventures of Telemachus. Féne-
lon. Keller (Telemachus)
Adventures of the Black Girl in
Her Search for God, The.
George Bernard Shaw. Ward
Adventures of Thomas Jefferson
Snodgrass, The. Mark Twain.
Gale-T
Adventures of Timothy, The.
Edith C. Kenyon. Kaye
Adventures of Tom Sawyer, The
see Tom Sawyer
Advice to a Prophet. Richard
Wilbur. Magill '62, S
Advice to a Son. Francis Osborn.
Ruoff p. 81
Advise and Consent. Allen Drury.

ADVISE

4

(See also adaptation by Loring
Mandell.) Magill '60, M1, S
Advise and Consent. Loring
Mandell. (Based on the novel
by Allen Drury.) Drury;
NCTE
Advisors, The. Herbert F. York.
Magill '77
Aelita. Count Alexei Tolstoy.
Magill SF
Aemilius. Augustus David Crake.
Kaye
Aeneid, The. Vergil. Armstrong;
Cohen; Downs M, FG; Feder;
Fleming; Grozier; Johnson;
Keller; Magill I, CE, M1&2,
MC, MP; Sabater; Wilson
Aeolosicon. Aristophanes.
Hathorn
Aeolus. Euripides. Hathorn
Aesop's Fables. Aesop. Downs
F, FG; Haydn (Fables); Keller
(Fables); Magill III, M1, MC,
MEUF
Aesthetics, as Science of Expres-
sion and General Linguistics.
Benedetto Croce. Keller;
Magill IV, MC, WP
Aeterni Patris. Pope Leo XIII.
Magill CAL
Aethiopica. Heliodorus of Emesa
in Syria. Keller; Ruoff
Aetnaeans, The. Aeschylus.
Hathorn
Affair, The. Ronald Millar.
(Based on the novel by C. P.
Snow.) French
Affair, The. C. P. Snow. (See
also adaptation by Ronald
Millar.) Magill IV, '61, MB,
MC, S; Ward
Affaires de Rome (Roman Affairs).
Félicité Robert de Lamennais.
Keller (Roman)
Affairs of State. Louis Verneuil.
Best '50; Drury; French;
Kienzle
Affinities. Vernon Watkins.
Magill '64, S
Affluent Society, The. John Ken-
neth Galbraith. Magill '59,
M1, S; Ward
Afloat and Ashore. James Feni-
more Cooper. Johnson; Walker
African Queen, The. C. S.
Forester. Ward
African Witch, The. Joyce Cary.
Magill '63, S; Ward

After Babel. George Steiner.
Magill '76
After Borges. R. H. W. Dillard.
Magill '73
After Experience. W. D. Snod-
grass. Magill '68, S
After Many a Summer. Aldous
Huxley. Magill SF; Ward
After My Fashion. Diana Morgan.
French
After Our War. John Balaban.
Magill '75
After Strange Gods. T. S. Eliot.
Magill IV, MC; Ward
After the Fall. Arthur Miller.
Anderson; Best '63; Drury;
Kienzle; Magill '65, S; Matlaw
After the Pardon. Matilde Serao.
Keller
After the Pleasure Party: Lines
Traced Under an Image of
Amor Threatening. Herman
Melville. Gale-M
After the Rain. John Bowen.
Best '67; Drury
After the Trauma. Harvey Curtis
Webster. Magill '71
After Worlds Collide. Edwin
Balmer and Philip Wylie.
Magill SF
Afterlife, The. Larry Levis.
Magill '78
Aftermath. James Lane Allen.
Keller (Kentucky)
Afternoon at the Seaside. Agatha
Christie. French
Afternoon Men. Anthony Powell.
Magill '64, S
Afternoon of an Author. F. Scott
Fitzgerald. Magill '59, S
Afternoon of Pocket Billiards, An.
Henry Taylor. Magill '76
Against Eunomius. Saint Basil.
Magill CAL
Against Heresies. Saint Irenaeus.
Magill CAL, CIIL
Against Interpretation. Susan
Sontag. Magill '67, S
Against Our Will. Susan Brown-
miller. Magill '76
Against the American Grain.
Dwight MacDonald. Magill '63,
S
Against the Grain. Joris Karl
Huysmans. Haydn; Magill II,
CE, M1&2, MC, MEUF
Agamemnon. Aeschylus. Arm-
strong; Drury; Hathorn (Ores-

teia); Haydn; Feder (Oresteia);
Jolliffe; Keller; Reinhold;
Shank; Sobel
Agamemnon.   Lucius Annaeus
Seneca.   Feder; Hathorn; Rein-
hold
Agamemnon's Death.   Gerhart
Hauptmann.   Matlaw
Agape and Eros.   Anders Nygren.
Magill CHL
Age of Anxiety, The.   Wystan
Hugh Auden.   Haydn p. 59;
Kienzle; Ward
Age of Chivalry or The Legends
of King Arthur, The.   Thomas
Bulfinch.   Keller
Age of Discontinuity, The.   Peter
F. Drucker.   Magill '71
Age of Fable or The Beauties of
Mythology, The.   Thomas Bul-
finch.   Keller
Age of Innocence, The.   Edith
Wharton.   Haydn; Heiney;
Keller suppl.; Magill I, CE,
M1&2, MAF, MC; Morehead;
Olfson
Age of Louis XIV, The.   Will and
Ariel Durant.   Magill '64, S
Age of Louis XIV, The.   Voltaire.
Haydn
Age of Napoleon, The.   Will and
Ariel Durant.   Magill '77
Age of Reason, The.   Thomas
Paine.   Haydn p. 149; Keller;
Magill IV, MC
Age of Reason, The.   Jean-Paul
Sartre.   (See also trilogy title
Roads to Freedom.)   Heiney
Age of Reason Begins, The.   Will
and Ariel Durant.   Magill '62,
M1, MB, S
Age of Reform, The.   Richard
Hofstadter.   Magill Ss
Age of Revolution, The.   Winston
S. Churchill.   Magill '58, MB,
S
Age of Roosevelt, The, Vol. I.
Arthur Meier Schlesinger, Jr.
Magill '58, S
Age of Roosevelt, The, Vol. II.
Arthur Meier Schlesinger, Jr.
Magill '60, S
Age of Roosevelt, The, Vol. III.
Arthur Meier Schlesinger, Jr.
Magill '61, S
Age of the Despots, The.   John
Addington Symonds.   Keller
(Renaissance)

Age of Uncertainty, The.   John
Kenneth Galbraith.   Magill '78
Age of Voltaire, The.   Will and
Ariel Durant.   Magill '66, S
Agen.   Python.   Hathorn
Agincourt.   George Pain Rainsford
James.   Kaye
Agnes Bernauer.   Christian Fried-
rich Hebbel.   Drury
Agnes Grey.   Anne Brontë.   Hal-
perin; Johnson; Keller; Magill
III, CE, M1&2, MC, MEF
Agnes of Sorrento.   Harriet
Beecher Stowe.   Johnson; Kaye;
Keller
Agnes Surriage.   Edwin Lassetter
Bynner.   Johnson
Agriculture.   Columella.   Keller
Agriculture.   Rosset.   Keller
Agriculture.   Terentius Varro.
Keller
Agriculture (Book of Ibn-el-Awam).
Mullet, Clément, trans.   Keller
Ah King.   W. Somerset Maugham.
Ward
Ah Sin.   Mark Twain.   Gale-T
Ah, Wilderness.'   Eugene O'Neill.
(See also adaptation Take Me
Along by Joseph Stein et al.)
Dest '33; Drury; Haydn; Lass
AP; Lovell; Matlaw; NCTE;
Shank; Shipley; Sobel; Ward
Aias   see   Ajax
Aids to Reflection.   Samuel Taylor
Coleridge.   Keller; Magill CHL
Aiglon, L'.   Edmond Rostand.
Drury; Haydn; Keller; Magill
II, CE, M1&2, MC, MD;
Matlaw; NBC3; Shipley; Sobel
Aimee.   Agnes Giberne.   Kaye
Aino Folk-Tales.   Basil H.
Chamberlain.   Keller
Ain't Supposed to Die a Natural
Death.   Melvin Van Peebles.
Best '71
Air-Conditioned Nightmare, The.
Henry Miller.   Ward
Air for Murder, An.   Falkland L.
Cary and Philip King.   French
Air Raid.   Archibald MacLeish.
Sobel
Airships.   Barry Hannah.   Magill
'79
Airy Fairy Lilian.   Mrs. Hunger-
ford.   Keller
Ajax.   Sophocles.   Feder; Gass-
ner; Hathorn; Haydn; Jolliffe;
Keller; Magill II, CE, M1&2,

liene and Florida Friebus.
(Based on the story by Lewis
Carroll.) Drury
Alice of Old Vincennes. Maurice
Thompson. Keller
Alice Sit-by-the-Fire. Sir James
M. Barrie. Drury; Keller
suppl. ; NCTE; Sobel
Alice's Adventures in Wonderland
see Alice in Wonderland
Alicia's Diary. Thomas Hardy.
Pinion
Alien Corn. Sidney Howard.
Best '32; Drury; Sobel
Alison's House. Susan Glaspell.
Best '30; Bonin; Drury; Haydn
(Glaspell); Matlaw; Shipley;
Sobel
Alkahest, or The House of Claës.
Honoré de Balzac. Keller
Alkestis see Alcestis
All About Eve. Mary Orr.
(See adaptation Applause by
Betty Comden et al.)
All Fall Down. James Leo Her-
lihy. Magill IV, '61, MC, S
All Fools. George Chapman.
Holzknecht; Keller; Magill III,
CE, M1&2, MC, MD; Ruoff;
Shipley
All for Love, or, The World
Well Lost. John Dryden.
Drury; Gassner; Haydn;
Keller; Magill II, CE, M1&2,
MC, MD; Shank; Shipley;
Sobel; Thomas
All for the Best. Luigi Piran-
dello. Matlaw; Sobel
All God's Chillun Got Wings.
Eugene O'Neill. Keller suppl. ;
Matlaw; Shipley; Sobel; Ward
All God's Dangers: The Life of
Nate Shaw. Theodore Rosen-
garten. Magill '75
All Good Children. Donald
Howarth. French
All Green Shall Perish. Eduardo
Mallea. Magill '67, S
All Hallows Eve. Charles Wil-
liams. Magill IV, MC
All in the Family. Marc-Gilbert
Sauvajon. French
All Men Are Brothers. Shih
Nai-an. Haydn (Shui Hu
Chuan); Magill III, CE, M1&2,
MC, MEUF
All Men Are Enemies. Richard
Aldington. Ward

All My Friends Are Going to Be
Strangers. Larry McMurtry.
Magill '73
All My Sons. Arthur Miller.
Best '46; Bonin; Drury; Kienzle;
Matlaw; NCTE; Shank; Sobel
All Our Yesterdays. H. M. Tom-
linson. Ward
All over Town. Murray Schisgal.
Best '74; Drury
All Passion Spent. Hon. Victoria
Mary Sackville-West. Ward
All Quiet on the Western Front.
Erich Maria Remarque. Good-
man; Haydn; Heiney; Lass EN;
Magill II, CE, M1&2, MC,
MEUF; Ward
All Said and Done. Simone de
Beauvoir. Magill '75
All Sorts and Conditions of Men.
Sir Walter Besant. Johnson;
Keller
All Summer Long. Robert Ander-
son. (Based on the novel by
Donald Wetzel.) Drury
All Summer Long. Donald Wetzel.
(See adaptation by Robert Ander-
son.)
All the King's Men. Robert Penn
Warren. Drury; Lass AN;
Magill II, CE, M1&2, MAF,
MC; Morehead; Olfson; Shank
All the Little Live Things. Wal-
lace Stegner. Magill '68, S
All the President's Men. Carl
Bernstein and Bob Woodward.
Magill '75
All the Way Home. Tad Mosel.
(Based on A Death in the Fam-
ily by James Agee.) Best '60;
Bonin; Drury; Kienzle; NCTE
All the Years of American Popular
Music. David Ewen. Magill
'78
Allan Quatermain. Henry Rider
Haggard. Keller
Allegory of Love, The. Clive
Staples Lewis. Magill IV, MC;
Ward
Allegory of the Cave, The. Plato.
(AUU MIUU Fili Magilli) Arm-
strong
Allegro. Richard Rodgers and
Oscar Hammerstein II. Best
'47
Allegro, L', and Il penseroso.
John Milton. Hix; Ruoff
Allies of a Kind: The United

States, Britain and the War
Against Japan, 1941-1945.
Christopher Thorne. Magill '79
Alligator Bride, The. Donald
Hall. Magill Ss
All's Lost by Lust. William Row-
ley. Sobel
All's Well That Ends Well. Wil-
liam Shakespeare. Campbell;
Chute; Clark; Gassner; Guer-
ber-SC; Halliday; Haydn; Kel-
ler; Lamb; McCutchan-SC; Mc-
Spadden S; Magill II, CE, M1&2,
MC, MD; Ruoff; Shank; Shipley;
Sobel
Almagest. Ptolemy of Alexandria.
Haydn; Keller
Almanac for Moderns, An. Donald
Culross Peattie. Magill IV, MC
Almayer's Folly. Joseph Conrad.
Keller; Magill II, CE, M1&2,
MC, MEF; Stade p. 140; Ward
Alone. Marion Harland. Johnson
Alone. Mrs. Mary Virginia Ter-
hune. Keller
Alp. William Hjortsberg. Magill
'70
Als der Krieg zu ende War (When
the War Was Over). Max
Frisch. Kienzle
Altar of the Dead, The. Henry
James. Gale-J
Alteration, The. Kingsley Amis.
Magill SF
Altiora Peto. Laurence Oliphant.
Johnson
Alton Locke, Tailor and Poet.
Charles Kingsley. Johnson;
Kaye; Keller
Altrurian Romances, The. Wil-
liam Dean Howells. Carrington
Alzire or the American. Voltaire.
Keller
Ama (The Fisher Girl). Seami.
Sobel
Amadís de Gaul. Vasco de
Lobeira. Keller; Magill III,
CE, M1&2, MC, MEUF
Amateur Means Lover. Dodie
Smith. French
Amateur Poacher, The. Richard
Jefferies. Keller
Amateurs. Donald Barthelme.
Magill '78
Amazing Doctor Clitterhouse, The.
Barré Lyndon. Drury; French
Amazons, The. Arthur Wing
Pinero. Drury

Ambassadors, The. Henry James.
Gale-J; Haydn; Keller; Magill
II, CE, M1&2, MAF, MAL3,
MC; Morehead; Ward
Ambassador's Journal. John Ken-
neth Galbraith. Magill '70
Amber Gods, The. Harriet Pres-
cott Spofford. Keller
Ambitious Guest, The. Nathaniel
Hawthorne. Gale-H
Ambitious Woman, An. Edgar
Fawcett. Keller
Ambrose Applejohn's Adventure.
Walter Hackett. French
Ambush. Arthur Richman. Best
'21; Drury
Amédée or How to Get Rid of It.
Eugene Ionesco. Kienzle; Mat-
law; Shank; Sprinchorn
Amelia. Henry Fielding. Haydn;
Johnson; Johnson-18th/2; Kel-
ler; Magill I, CE, M1&2, MC,
MEF
Amen. Yehuda Amichai. Magill
'78
Amen Corner, The. James Bald-
win. Drury; NCTE
Amenities of Literature. Isaac
Disraeli. Keller
America As a Civilization. Max
Lerner. Magill '58, S
America Comes of Age. André
Siegfried. Keller suppl.
America Finding Herself. Mark
Sullivan. Keller suppl. (Our
Times)
America Hurrah. Jean-Claude van
Itallie. Best '66; Drury; Ki-
enzle
America in Vietnam. Guenter
Lewy. Magill '79
America Is Worth Saving. Theo-
dore Dreiser. Gerber
American, The. Howard Fast.
Haydn
American, The. Henry James.
Gale-J; Haydn p. 25; Keller;
Lovell; Magill I, CE, M1&2,
MAF, MAL3, MC; Morehead
American Adventure, The. David
Saville Muzzey. Keller suppl.
American Buffalo. David Mamet.
Best '76; Magill '78
American Caesar: Douglas Mac-
Arthur, 1880-1964. William
Manchester. Magill '79
American Catholic Crossroads.
Walter J. Ong, S. J. Magill

IV, MC
Amoretti. Edmund Spenser.
Haydn; Ruoff
Amorosa Fiammetta, L'. Giovanni
Boccaccio. Johnson; Magill I:I,
CE, M1&2, MC, MEUF
Amorous Goldfish, The. Michael
Voysey. French
Amorous Prawn, The. Anthony
Kimmins. French
Amos Judd. J. A. Mitchell.
Keller
Amour, L'. Jules Michelet.
Keller
Amphitryon. Titus Maccius
Plautus. Feder; Gassner;
Hathorn; Haydn; Magill II, CE,
M1&2, MC, MD; Reinhold;
Shank; Shipley
Amphitryon, or The Two Sosias.
John Dryden. Sobel
Amphitryon 38. Jean Giraudoux.
Best '37; Drury; Heiney;
Magill III, M1, MC, MD;
Matlaw; NCTE; Shank; Ward
Amrita. Ruth Prawer Jhabvala.
Magill '57, S
Amulet. Carl Rakosi. Magill
'69, S
Amyas Egerton, Cavalier.
Maurice H. Hervey. Kaye
Anabasis. St.-John Perse.
Magill III, M1, MC, MP
Anabasis, The. Xenophon.
Downs M; Haydn; Keller;
Magill III, MC, MNF
Anagyrus. Aristophanes. Hathorn
Analects of Confucius, The.
(Lun Yü) Confucius. Downs
F; Magill WP
Analogue Men. Damon Knight.
Magill SF
Analogy of Religion, The. Joseph
Butler. Keller. Magill CHL
Analysis of Beauty, The. William
Hogarth. Keller
Analysis of Knowledge and Valua-
tion, An. Clarence Irving
Lewis. Magill WP
Analysis of the Sensations, The.
Ernst Mach. Magill WP
Anastasia. Guy Bolton. (Based
on the play by Marcelle Maur-
ette.) Chapman '55; Drury;
French; NCTE
Anastasia. Marcelle Maurette.
(See also adaptation by Guy
Bolton.) French

Anastasius, or Memoirs of a
Modern Greek Written at the
Close of the Eighteenth Cen-
tury. Thomas Hope. Keller
Anathema. Leonid N. Andreyev.
Drury; Haydn; Keller; Matlaw;
Shipley; Sobel
Anatol. Arthur Schnitzler. Cart-
mell; Drury; Heiney; Keller;
Matlaw; Shank; Shipley; Sobel
Anatole France Himself. Jean
Jacques Brousson. Keller
suppl. (France)
Anatomical Exercise on the Motion
of the Heart and Blood in Ani-
mals (De motu cordis et san-
guinis). William Harvey.
Downs M, FG; Haydn (De motu)
Anatomie of Abuses. Philip
Stubbes. Keller
Anatomist, The. James Bridie.
Drury; French; Matlaw; Ward
Anatomy of a Murder. Robert
Traver. (See also adaptation
by Elihu Winer.) Magill '59, S
Anatomy of a Murder. Elihu
Winer. (Based on the novel by
Robert Traver.) Drury
Anatomy of Melancholy, The.
Robert Burton. Haydn; Keller;
Magill III, M1, MC, MNF;
Ruoff p. 50
Anatomy of Wit, The see
Euphues, The Anatomy of Wit
Anaxagoras: Fragments. Anaxa-
goras of Clazomenae. Magill
WP
Anaximander: Fragments. Anaxi-
mander of Miletus. Magill WP
Ancestral Footstep, The. Nathan-
iel Hawthorne. Gale-H
Ancient Law. Henry Sumner
Maine. Keller
Ancient Régime, The. Hippolyte
Adolphe Taine. Keller
Ancient Rome in the Light of Re-
cent Discoveries. Rodolfo
Lanciani. Keller
Ancient Stone Implements, Weap-
ons, and Ornaments of Great
Britain, The. Sir John Evans.
Keller
Ancrenriwle, or Rule of Nuns.
Unknown. Haydn
And Chaos Died. Joanna Russ.
Magill SF
And Even Now. Max Beerbohm.
Ward

- And I Worked at the Writer's
Trade: Chapters of Literary
History, 1918-1978. Malcolm
Cowley. Magill '79
And Light Shines in Darkness see
Light That Shines in Darkness,
The
And Miss Reardon Drinks a Little.
Paul Zindel. Drury
And Never Said a Word. Heinrich
Böll. Magill '79
"And No Birds Sing. " Jenny Laird
and John Fernald. French
And Other Stories. John O'Hara.
Magill '69, S
And Pippa Dances! Gerhart
Hauptmann. Matlaw
And Quiet Flows the Don. Mikhail
Sholokhov. (See also series
title The Silent Don.) Lass
EN; Magill I, CE, M1&2, MC,
MEUF
And So Ad Infinitum see Insect
Comedy, The
And So It Will Be. Konstantin
Simonov. Matlaw
"And So to Bed. " James Bernard
Fagan. Drury; French
And Suddenly It's Spring. Jack
Popplewell. French
Andere Jehanné, De (The Other
Joan). Herwig Hensen. Kienzle
Andersen's Fairy Tales (Selections).
Hans Christian Andersen.
Haydn (Fairy); Magill II, CE,
M1&2, MC, MEUF
Andersonville. MacKinlay Kantor.
Magill '55, S
Andersonville Trial, The. Saul
Levitt. Best '59; Drury;
Kienzle; NCTE
Andes and the Amazon, or Across
the Continent of South America,
The. James Orton. Keller
Andorra. Max Frisch. Anderson;
Best '62; Kienzle; Matlaw
André. William Dunlap. Drury;
Lovell; Shipley
André Malraux. Jean Lacouture.
Magill '77
Andrea del Sarto. Alfred de
Musset. Sobel
Andreas Hofer. Louise Muhlbach.
Kaye
Andrée de Taverney. Alexandre
Dumas (father). Johnson; Kaye
Andrew Goodfellow. Helen H.
Watson. Kaye

Andrew Jackson and the Course of
American Empire, 1767-1821.
Robert V. Remini. Magill '78
Andrey Satchel and the Parson and
Clerk. Thomas Hardy. Saxel-
by
Andria (Woman of Andros).
Terence. Feder (Woman);
Hathorn; Magill II, CE, M1&2,
MC, MD; Reinhold; Shank;
Shipley (Woman)
Androcles and the Lion. George
Bernard Shaw. Drury; Hard-
wick; Haydn; Matlaw; NCTE;
Shank; Shipley; Sobel; Ward
Andromache. Euripides. Feder;
Gassner; Hathorn; Haydn; Kel-
ler; Magill III, CE, M1&2,
MC, MD; Reinhold; Shank;
Shipley
Andromache. Jean Baptiste Ra-
cine. Drury; Gassner; Haydn;
Keller; Magill II, CE, M1&2,
MC, MD; Shank; Sobel
Andromeda. Euripides. Hathorn
Andromeda. Sophocles. Hathorn
Andromeda. Ivan Yefremov.
Magill SF
Andromeda Strain, The. Michael
Crichton. Magill '70, SF
Anecdotes of Destiny. Isak Dine-
sen. Magill '59, S
Aneroestes the Gaul. E. M.
Smith. Kaye
Angel Comes to Babylon, An.
Friedrich Dürrenmatt. Kienzle;
Matlaw
Angel Guerra. Benito Pérez
Galdós. Magill III, CE, M1&2,
MC, MEUF
Angel in the House, The. Coven-
try Patmore. Keller
Angel of Montparnasse, The.
Jean Giltene. French
Angel of the Odd, The. Edgar
Allan Poe. Gale-PP
Angel of the Revolution, The.
George Griffith. Magill SF
Angel Pavement. J. B. Priest-
ley. Ward
Angel Street (Gaslight). Patrick
Hamilton. Best '11, Drury,
French (Gaslight); NCTE;
Shipley (Gaslight)
Angle of Ascent. Robert Hayden.
Magill '77
Angler, The Compleat see Com-
pleat Angler, The

Anglo-Saxon Attitudes. Angus
Wilson. Magill '57, S; Ward
Anglo-Saxon Chronicle, The.
Unknown. Haydn
Anglomaniacs, The. Constance
Cary Harrison. Johnson
Angry Young Man. Leslie Paul.
Ward
Aniara. Harry E. Martinson.
Magill SF
Animal Farm. Nelson Bond.
(Based on the novel by George
Orwell.) Drury; NCTE
Animal Farm. George Orwell.
(See also adaptation by Nelson
Bond.) Heiney; Ward
Animal Grab (Catch As Catch
Can). Jean Anouilh. Kienzle
Animal Kingdom, The see
Règne animal, Le
Animal Kingdom, The. Philip
Barry. Best '31; Drury; Lass
AP; Matlaw; NCTE; Shipley;
Sobel
Animal Symbolism in Ecclesiastical
Architecture. E. P. Evans.
Keller
Animals in That Country, The.
Margaret Atwood. Magill '70
Animula. T. S. Eliot. Ward
Ann Veronica. H. G. Wells.
Haydn; Ward
Ann Vickers. Sinclair Lewis.
Ward
Anna and the King of Siam. Mar-
garet Landon. (See adaptation
The King and I by Oscar Ham-
merstein II and Richard Rod-
gers.)
Anna Christie. Eugene O'Neill.
Best '21; Bonin; Drury; Haydn;
Heiney; Keller suppl. ; Lovell;
Magill II, CE, M1&2, MC,
MD; Matlaw; NCTE; Shank;
Shipley; Smith; Sobel; Ward
Anna K. Eugenie Leontovich.
(Based on Anna Karénina by
Leo Tolstoy.) NCTE
Anna Karénina. Count Leo Tol-
stoy. (See also, adaptation
Anna K. by Eugenie Leontovich.)
Armstrong; Berry-1; Cohen;
Goodman; Grozier; Haydn;
Johnson; Keller; Lass EN;
Magill I, CE, M1&2, MC,
MEUF; Wilson
Anna Kleiber. Alfonso Sastre.
Matlaw

Anna, Lady Baxby. Thomas
Hardy. Pinion; Saxelby
Anna Lucasta. Philip Yordan.
Best '44; Drury
Anna of the Five Towns. Arnold
Bennett. Magill II, CE, M1&2,
MC, MEF; Ward
Anna on the Neck. Anton Chekhov.
Keller suppl. (Party)
Anna Sophie Hedvig. Kjeld Abell.
Drury; Matlaw; Shank
Annajanska, the Bolshevik Em-
press. George Bernard Shaw.
Hardwick; Ward
Annals of a Fortress. E. Viollet-
le-Duc. Keller
Annals of a Quiet Neighborhood.
George Macdonald. Keller
Annals of a Sportsman. Ivan
Turgenev. Keller
Annals of Rural Bengal. Sir Wil-
liam Wilson Hunter. Keller
Annals of Tacitus, The. Publius
Cornelius Tacitus. Downs M;
Feder; Haydn; Magill III, M1,
MC, MNF
Annals of the Parish. John Galt.
Keller; Magill II, CE, M1&2,
MC, MEF
Annals of the Roman People.
Livy. Magill III, M1, MC,
MNF
Anne. Constance Fenimore Wool-
son. Keller
Anne of Geierstein. Sir Walter
Scott. Johnson; Kaye; Keller;
McSpadden W
Anne of the Thousand Days. Max-
well Anderson. Best '48; Drury;
Kienzle; Matlaw; NCTE; Shank
Anne Pedersdotter. Hans Wiers-
Jenssen. Sobel
Anne Scarlett. Mary Imlay Taylor.
Kaye
Anne Sexton: A Self-Portrait in
Letters. Anne Sexton. Magill
'78
Anneau d'amethyste, L'. Anatole
France. Keller (Histoire)
Annie. Thomas Meehan, Charles
Strouse and Martin Charnin.
Best '76
Annie Get Your Gun. Herbert and
Dorothy Fields and Irving Berlin.
Drinkrow; Drury; Kienzle; NCTE
Annie Kilburn. William Dean
Howells. Carrington; Keller
Anniversaries: From the Life of

Gesine Cresspahl. Uwe Johnson. Magill '76
Anniversary, The. Anton Chekhov. Matlaw
Anniversary Waltz. Jerome Chodorov and Joseph Fields. Drury
Anonymous Sins and Other Poems. Joyce Carol Oates. Magill '70
Another I, Another You. Richard Schickel. Magill '79
Another Language. Rose Franken. Best '31; Drury
Another Part of the Forest. Lillian Hellman. Best '46; Drury; Haydn p. 324; Matlaw; NCTE; Shank
Another World, 1897-1917. Anthony Eden. Magill '78
Anpao: An American Indian Odyssey. Jamake Highwater. Magill '78
Answer from Limbo, An. Brian Moore. Magill '63, S
Ante-Nicene Library, The. Dr. J. Donaldson and Dr. A. Roberts. Keller
Antenoridae. Sophocles. Hathorn
Anthia and Habrocomus, or The Ephesiaca. Xenophon of Ephesus. Keller
Anthologia Planudea. Maximus Planudes. Feder (Greek Anthology)
Anthology of Korean Poems see Shijo-Yuchip
Anthony Adverse. Hervey Allen. Haydn; Magill I, CE, M1&2, MAF, MC; Morehead
Anthony Comstock, Roundsman of the Lord. Heywood Broun and Margaret Leech. Keller suppl. (Comstock)
Anthony Trollope. Michael Sadleir. Keller suppl. (Trollope)
Anthony Wilding. Rafael Sabatini. Kaye
Anthropology. Sir Edward Burnett Tylor. Keller
Anthropos, or the Future of Art. E. E. Cummings. Kienzle
Antic Hay. Aldous Huxley. Haydn; Ward
Anticipations of the Reaction of Mechanical and Scientific Progress upon Human Life and Thought. H. G. Wells. Ward
Antidosis, or Exchange of Properties. Isocrates. Keller
Antidote, The. Count Vittorio Alfieri. Shipley (One, Few...)
Antigone. Jean Anouilh. Best '45; Drury; Heiney; Matlaw; NCTE; Shank; Sprinchorn; Ward
Antigone. Euripides. Hathorn
Antigone. Sophocles. Armstrong; Downs M, FG; Drury; Feder; Gassner; Hathorn; Haydn; Jolliffe; Keller; Magill I, CE, M1&2, MC, MD; NBC 3; Reinhold; Shank; Shipley; Sobel; Thomas
Antigone of Sophocles, The. Bertolt Brecht. Matlaw
Anti-Intellectualism in American Life. Richard Hofstadter. Magill Ss
Anti-Memoirs. André Malraux. Magill '69, S
Antinous. Adolph D. Hausrath. Kaye
Antiope. Euripides. Hathorn
Antiquary, The. Sir Walter Scott. Johnson; Keller; McSpadden W; Magill II, CE, M1&2, MC, MEF
Antique Ring, The. Nathaniel Hawthorne. Gale-H
Antiquities of the Jews. Flavius Josephus. Haydn; Keller (Jews)
Antiquity of Man. Sir Charles Lyell. Haydn
Antiworlds. Andrei Voznesensky. Magill '67, S
Antonin Artaud. Antonin Artaud. Magill '77
Antonin Artaud. Martin Esslin. Magill '78
Antonina. Wilkie Collins. Johnson; Kaye; Keller
Antonio and Mellida. John Marston. Keller; Shipley
Antonio's Revenge. John Marston. Keller (Antonio and Mellida); Shipley (Antonio and Mellida)
Antony and Cleopatra. William Shakespeare. Campbell; Chute; Clark; Gassner; Halliday; Haydn; Johnson-18th/2; Keller; Lamb; McCutchan-S1; McSpadden S; Magill II, CE, M1&2, MC, MD; Ruoff; Shank; Shipley; Sobel; Wilson
Ants, Bees, and Wasps. Sir John Lubbock. Keller
Anxiety and the Christian. Hans

Urs von Balthasar. Magill CAL
Anxiety of Influence, The. Harold
Bloom. Magill '74
Any Number Can Die. Fred Car-
michael. Drury
Any Other Business. George Ross
and Campbell Singer. French
Any Wednesday. Muriel Resnick.
Drury; NCTE
Anything Goes. Cole Porter, Guy
Bolton and P. G. Wodehouse.
Drinkrow
Aoi-no-ue. Seami. Gassner
Apartment, The. Billy Wilder
and I. A. L. Diamond. (See
adaptation Promises, Promises
by Neil Simon et al.)
Apartment in Athens. Glenway
Wescott. Haydn
Ape and Essence. Aldous Huxley.
Magill SF
Apes, Angels, and Victorians.
William Irvine. Magill '55,
MB, S
Aphorisms. Hippocrates. Downs
F, FG; Haydn
Aphrodite. Pierre Louys. Arm-
strong; Haydn; Heiney
Aphrodite in Aulis. George
Moore. Ward
Apocalypse. D. H. Lawrence.
Ward
Apocryphal Gospels, and Other
Documents Relating to the His-
tory of Christ. B. H. Cowper,
trans. Keller
Apollo. Salomon Reinach. Keller
Apollo de Bellac, The. Jean
Giraudoux. French
Apologia pro Vita Sua. John
Henry Cardinal Newman.
Haydn; Keller; Magill III,
CAL, CHL, M1, MC, MNF
Apology. Plato. Downs FG;
Feder; Haydn; Magill WP
Apology for Poetry, An see
Defence of Poesie
Apology for Raimond Sebond.
Michel Eyquem de Montaigne.
Magill WP
Apology for the Life of Colley
Cibber, Comedian, An. Col-
ley Cibber. Haydn; Keller
(Apology for His Life); Magill
III, M1, MC, MNF
Apology for the True Christian
Divinity, An. Robert Barclay.
Magill CHL

Apology of Aristides, The. Aris-
tides. Magill CAL, CHL
Apology of Athenagoras, The.
Athenagoras. Magill CHL
Apology of Tertullian, The. Ter-
tullian. Haydn (Apology);
Magill CAL, CHL
Apostle, The. Sholem Asch.
Magill I, CE, M1&2, MAF, MC
Apostolic Fathers, The. J. B.
Lightfoot. Keller
Apostolic Tradition, The. Saint
Hippolytus. Magill CHL
Apparition of Mrs. Veal, The.
Daniel Defoe. Johnson-18th
Appearance and Reality. Francis
Herbert Bradley. Magill WP
Appius and Virginia. John Web-
ster. Sobel
Applause. Betty Comden, Adolph
Green, Charles Strouse and
Lee Adams. (Based on Ail
About Eve by Mary Orr.)
Best '69
Apple, The. Jack Gelber. Ki-
enzle
Apple Cart, The. George Bernard
Shaw. Drury; Hardwick; Mat-
law; Shipley; Sobel; Ward
Apple of the Eye, The. Glenway
Wescott. Magill I, CE, M1&2,
MAF, MC
Apple Tree, The. Sheldon Har-
nick, Jerry Bock and Jerome
Coopersmith. Best '66; NCTE
Apple-Tree Table, The. Herman
Melville. Gale-M
Applesauce. Barry Conners.
Drury
Appointment in Samarra. John
O'Hara. Haydn; Lass AN;
Magill II, CE, M1&2, MAF,
MC; Morehead
Appointment with Death. Agatha
Christie. French
Appreciation: Painting, Poetry
and Prose. Leo Stein. Haydn
Appreciations, with an Essay on
Style. Walter Pater. Haydn
Approaching Simone. Megan
Terry. Bonin
April Hopes. William Dean
Howells. Carrington; Keller
Arabella Stuart. George Pain
Rainsford James. Kaye
Arabesque and Honeycomb.
Sacheverell Sitwell. Magill '59,
S

Arabesques. Nikolai V. Gogol.
Berry-2
Arabian Nights' Entertainments,
The (Selections; A Thousand and
One Nights). Unknown. Downs
F (Thousand); Grozier; Haydn;
Keller; Magill II, CE, M1&2,
MC, MEUF; Wilson
Arabian Sands. Wilfred Thesiger.
Magill '60, S
Arabs, Israelis, and Kissinger,
The. Edward R. F. Sheehan.
Magill '77
Arachne. Georg Moritz Ebers.
Kaye
Araucanaid, The. Alonso de Er-
cilla y Zuñiga. Haydn
Arbitration, The. Menander.
Feder; Hathorn; Magill III, CE,
M1&2, MC, MD; Reinhold
Arcades. John Milton. Ruoff
Arcadia. Sir Philip Sidney.
Haydn; Keller; Magill III, CE,
M1&2, MC, MEF; Ruoff
Arcadians, The. Lionel Monckton,
Howard Talbot, Mark Ambient,
Alexander M. Thompson, Robert
Courtneidge and Arthur Wim-
peris. Drinkrow; Shipley
Arcana coelestia see Heavenly
Arcana
Arch of Triumph, The. Erich
Maria Remarque. Heiney
Archibald Malmaison. Julian Haw-
thorne. Johnson
Archipel Lenoir ou il ne faut pas
toucher aux choses immobiles,
L' (The Lenoir Archipelago,
or One Must Not Touch Im-
mobile Things). Armand Sala-
crou. Kienzle
Architecte et l'empereur d'Assyrie,
L' (The Architect and the Em-
peror of Assyria). Fernando
Arrabal. Anderson; Gassner;
Matlaw
archy and mehitabel. Don Mar-
quis. Haydn; Ward
Arctic Boat Journey, An. Isaac
Israel Hayes. Keller
Arctic Explorations. Elisha Kent
Kane. Keller
Arcturus Adventure, The. William
Beebe. Keller suppl.
Ardèle (The Cry of the Peacock).
Jean Anouilh. Anderson; Ki-
enzle; Matlaw; Shank
Arden Massiter. William Barry.

Kaye
Arden of Feversham. Attributed
to Thomas Kyd. Clark; Gass-
ner; Holzknecht; Ruoff; Shipley;
Sobel
Aren't Men Beasts! Vernon Syl-
vaine. French
Aren't We All? Frederick Lons-
dale. Drury
Areopagitica. John Milton.
Downs M, FG; Haydn; Magill
IV, MC; Ruoff
Argenis. John Barclay. Magill
III, CE, M1&2, MC, MEF;
Ruoff
Argent, L'. Emile Zola. Keller
(Rougon)
Argonautica. Apollonius of
Rhodes. Feder; Haydn; Keller
Argonautica. Valerius Flaccus.
Feder
Argonauts, The see Golden
Fleece
Aria da Capo. Edna St. Vincent
Millay. Haydn p. 488; Matlaw
Ariadne. Gabriel Marcel. Shank
Ariadne on Naxos. Paul Ernst.
Heiney
Arichandra. Anonymous. Gass-
ner
Ariel. Sylvia Plath. Magill '67,
S
Ariel, the Life of Shelley. André
Maurois. Keller suppl.; Ward
Aristocrat, The. Louis Napoleon
Parker. Drury
Aristocrat, The. Conrad Richter.
Magill '69, S
Aristocrats. Nikolai Fyodorovich
Pogodin. Matlaw
Arithmetical Researches see
Disquisitiones Arithmeticae
Arizona. Augustus Thomas.
Drury; Sobel
Armada, The. Garrett Mattingly.
Magill '60, MB, S
Armadale. Wilkie Collins. John-
son; Keller
Armadin. Alfred Bowker. Kaye
Armageddon in the Middle East.
Dana Adams Schmidt. Magill
'75
Armageddon 2419 A.D. Philip
Francis Nowlan. Magill SF
Arme Heinrich, Der. Hartmann
von Aue. Magill III, CE,
M1&2, MC, MP
Arme Mann Luther, Der (The

Sophocles.   Hathorn
Assignation, The.   Edgar Allan
Poe.   Gale-PP
Assistant, The.   Bernard Malamud.
Lass AN; Magill '58, S; More-
head
Assommoir, L'.   Emile Zola.
Goodman; Haydn (Dram Shop);
Keller (Rougon)
Assumption of Hannele, The   see
Hannele's Journey to Heaven
Assyrian Bride, The.   William
Patrick Kelly.   Kaye
Astonished Heart, The.   Noel
Coward.   French
Astoria, or Anecdotes of an Enter-
prise Beyond the Rocky Moun-
tains.   Washington Irving.
Keller
Astrée.   Honoré d'Urfé.   Haydn;
Keller
Astronomer and Other Stories,
The.   Doris Betts.   Magill '67,
S
Astronomia Nova (New Astronomy,
The).   Johannes Kepler.   Downs
M; Haydn
Astrophel and Stella.   Sir Philip
Sidney.   Haydn; Ruoff
Asylum Christi.   E. Gilliat.
Kaye
At Isella.   Henry James.   Gale-J
At Lady Molly's.   Anthony Powell.
Magill '59, MB, S
At Midnight on the 31st of March.
Josephine Young Case.   Magill
SF
At Mrs. Beam's.   C. K. Munro.
Drury; Keller suppl.
At Odds.   Baroness Tautphoeus.
Kaye
At Odds with the Regent.   Burton
E. Stevenson.   Kaye
At Play in the Fields of the Lord.
Peter Matthiessen.   Magill '66,
S
At Sea Under Drake.   C. H. Eden.
Kaye
At Sunwich Port.   William Wymark
Jacobs.   Johnson
At the Bottom   see   Night's
Lodging, The
At the Crossroads.   Evan S. Con-
nell, Jr.   Magill '66, S
At the Earth's Core.   Edgar Rice
Burroughs.   Magill SF
At the Exit.   Luigi Pirandello.
Matlaw

At the Fall of Montreal.   Edward
Stratemeyer.   Kaye
At the Fall of Port Arthur.   Ed-
ward Stratemeyer.   Kaye
At the Hawk's Well.   William
Butler Yeats.   Gassner; Matlaw
At the King's Right Hand.   Mrs.
E. M. Field.   Kaye
At the Mountains of Madness.   H.
P. Lovecraft.   Magill SF
At the Point of the Bayonet.
George A. Henty.   Kaye
At the Red Glove.   Katharine
Sarah Macquoid.   Johnson;
Keller
At the Siege of Quebec.   James
O. Kaler.   Kaye
At the Sign of the Golden Fleece.
Emma Leslie.   Kaye
At the Sign of the Reine Pédauque.
Anatole France.   Magill II, CE,
M1&2, MC, MEUF
Ataka.   Kwanze Kojiro Nobumitsu.
Gassner
Atala.   François René de Chateau-
briand.   Haydn; Johnson; Keller;
Magill II, CE, M1&2, MC,
MEUF
Atalanta in Calydon.   Algernon
Charles Swinburne.   Haydn;
Keller; Magill II, CE, M1&2,
MC, MP; Ward
Ataturk.   Patrick Balfour, Lord
Kinross.   Magill '66, S
Athalie.   Jean Baptiste Racine.
Drury; Gassner; Haydn; Keller;
Shank; Sobel
Atheistic Communism.   Pope Pius
XI.   Magill CAL
Atheist's Tragedy, The; or The
Honest Man's Revenge.   Cyril
Tourneur.   Holzknecht; Ruoff;
Sobel
Atlantis.   Gerhart Hauptmann.
Keller
Atomic Energy for Military Pur-
poses.   Henry De Wolf Smyth.
Haydn
Atomic Quest.   Arthur Holly
Compton.   Magill '57, S
Atomic Theory and the Description
of Nature.   Niels Bohr.   Haydn
Atrides-Tetralogy, The.   Gerhart
Hauptmann.   Matlaw
Atsumori.   Seami.   Gassner;
Shipley (Seami)
Attachments.   Judith Rossner.
Magill '78

Attack on Christendom. Søren
Kierkegaard. Magill CHL
Attic Philosopher, An. Emile
Souvestre. Keller
Attila. George Pain Rainsford
James. Kaye
Attila and His Conquerors. Eliza-
beth R. Charles. Kaye
Attilas Nächte (Attila's Nights).
Julius Hay. Kienzle
Au bonheur des dames. Emile
Zola. Keller (Rougon)
Aubrey's Brief Lives. Oliver
Lawson Dick, Editor. Magill
'58, S
Aucassin and Nicolette. Unknown.
Haydn; Keller; Magill I, CE,
M1&2, MC, MEUF; Wilson
Audrey. Mary Johnston. Keller
Audubon: A Vision. Robert
Penn Warren. Magill '70
August for the People. Nigel
Dennis. French
August 1914. Aleksandr I. Solz-
henitsyn. Magill '73
Augustus. John Williams.
Magill '73
Augustus Does His Bit. George
Bernard Shaw. Hardwick;
Ward
Auld Licht Idylls. Sir James M.
Barrie. Keller
Aulularia see Pot of Gold, The
Aunt Edwina. William Douglas
Home. French
Aunt Urikke. Gunnar Heiberg.
Sobel
Auntie Mame. Patrick Dennis.
(See also adaptation by Jerome
Lawrence and Robert E. Lee.)
Magill '55, M1, S
Auntie Mame. Jerome Lawrence
and Robert E. Lee. (Based
on the novel by Patrick Den-
nis; see also adaptation Mame by
Jerome Lawrence et al.)
Drury; NCTE
Aunt's Story, The. Patrick White.
Ward
Aurelian. William Ware. Keller
Aureng-Zebe. John Dryden.
Gassner
Aurora Leigh. Elizabeth Barrett
Browning. Haydn; Keller
Australasia. Alfred Russel.
Keller
Authentic Anecdotes of "Old
Zack." Herman Melville.

Gale-M
Author of Beltraffio, The. Henry
James. Gale-J
Auto de los reyes magoes, El
(The Play of the Three Wise
Men). Unknown. Sobel
Autobiography. Edward Gibbon.
Haydn; Keller (a)
Autobiography. Máxim Górky.
Haydn
Autobiography. John Stuart Mill.
Haydn; Keller (a)
Autobiography. Lincoln Steffens.
Haydn
Autobiography, An. Anthony
Trollope. Magill IV, MC
Autobiography of a Hunted Priest,
The. John Gerard. Magill
CAL
Autobiography of a Pocket Hand-
kerchief see Mouchoir, Le.
Walker
Autobiography of a Slander, The.
Edna Lyall. Keller
Autobiography of a Super-Tramp,
The. W. H. Davies. Ward
Autobiography of Alice B. Toklas,
The. Gertrude Stein. Haydn;
Heiney; Ward
Autobiography of an Ex-Coloured
Man, The. James Weldon
Johnson. Haydn; Magill Ss
Autobiography of Benjamin Frank-
lin, The. Benjamin Franklin.
Armstrong; Downs M; Haydn;
Keller; Magill III, M1, MC,
MNF
Autobiography of Benjamin Robert
Haydon, The. Benjamin
Robert Haydon. Magill IV, MC
Autobiography of Benvenuto Cel-
lini, The. Benvenuto Cellini.
Armstrong; Haydn; Keller (a);
Magill II, CE, M1&2, MC,
MNF
Autobiography of Bertrand Rus-
sell: 1872-1914, The. Bert-
rand Russell. Magill '68, M1,
S
Autobiography of Bertrand Rus-
sell: 1914-1944, The. Bert-
rand Russell. Magill '69, M1,
S
Autobiography of Bertrand Rus-
sell: 1944-1969, The. Bert-
rand Russell. Magill '70
Autobiography of Edward, Lord
Herbert of Cherbury, The.

strong; Haydn; Heiney; Keller
suppl.; Lass AN; Magill I,
CE, M1&2, MAF, MC; More-
head; Olfson; Smith; Ward
Babel-17.   Samuel R. Delany.
Magill SF
Babes in the Wood.   Unknown.
Shipley (end section)
Babylonian Captivity of the Church,
The.   Martin Luther.   Magill
CHL
Babylonian Influence on the Bible
and Popular Beliefs.   A.
Smythe Palmer.   Keller
Babylonian Talmud.   Michael L.
Rodkinson, ed.   Keller (Tal-
mud)
Babylonians, The.   Aristophanes.
Hathorn
Bacchae, The.   Euripides.
Downs F, FG; Feder; Gassner
(Bacchants); Hathorn; Haydn;
Magill II, CE, M1&2, MC,
MD; Reinhold; Shank; Shipley
(Bacchants); Sobel
Bacchides (The Two Bacchides).
Titus Maccius Plautus.   Feder
(Two); Hathorn; Reinhold;
Shipley
Bacchus.   Jean Cocteau.   Kienzle;
Matlaw
Bachelor of the Albany, The.
Marmion W. Savage.   Johnson
Bachelors, The.   Henry de
Montherlant.   Magill '62, S
Bachelors, The.   Muriel Spark.
Magill IV, '62, MC, S
Bachelor's Establishment, A.
Honoré de Balzac.   Johnson
Back Country, The.   Gary Snyder.
Magill Ss
Back to Methuselah.   George
Bernard Shaw.   Drury; Hard-
wick; Haydn; Heiney; Keller
suppl.; Magill III, M1, MC,
MD, SF; Matlaw; NBC 2;
Shipley; Sobel; Sprinchorn;
Ward
Background.   Warren Chetham-
Strode.   French
Background to Glory.   John Dake-
less.   Magill '58, S
Bad Habits.   Terrence McNally.
Best '73; Drury
Bad Lands, The.   Oakley Hall.
Magill '79
Bad Man, The.   Porter E. Browne.
Best '20; Drury

Bad Man, A.   Stanley Elkin.
Magill '68, S
Bad Mouth: Fugitive Papers on
the Dark Side.   Robert M.
Adams.   Magill '78
Bad Seed, The.   Maxwell Ander-
son.   (Based on the novel by
William March.)   Best '54;
Chapman '55; Drury
Bad Seed, The.   William March.
(See also adaptation by Maxwell
Anderson.)   Magill '54, S
Bad-Tempered Man, The see
Dyskolos
Bad Times, The.   G. A. Birm-
ingham.   Kaye
Baden-Baden Didactic Piece on
Acquiescence, The.   Bertolt
Brecht and Paul Hindemith.
Matlaw
Badger's Green.   Robert Cedric
Sherriff.   French
Balcony, The.   Jean Genet.
Drury; Kienzle; Matlaw; Shank
Balcony, The.   Gunnar Heiberg.
Drury; Sobel
Bald Eagle, The.   Attributed to
Nathaniel Hawthorne.   Gale-H
Bald Prima Donna see Bald
Soprano, The
Bald Soprano, The.   Eugene
Ionesco.   Andersen; French
(Bald Prima Donna); Gassner;
Kienzle; Matlaw; Shank
Baldur's Gate.   Eleanor Clark.
Magill '71
Ball of Tallow see Boule de
Suif and Other Tales
Ballad of East and West, The.
Rudyard Kipling.   Ward
Ballad of Peckham Rye, The.
Muriel Spark.   Kienzle; Magill
'61, S
Ballad of Reading Gaol.   Oscar
Wilde.   Haydn
Ballad of the Sad Cafe, The.
Edward Albee.   (Based on the
novel by Carson McCullers.)
Kienzle; NCTE
Ballad of the Sad Cafe, The.
Carson McCullers.   (See adapta-
tion by Edward Albee.)
Ballade vom Eulenspiegel, vom
Federle und von der dicken
Pompanne (The Ballad of Eulen-
spiegel, Federle and Fat Pom-
panne).   Günther Weisenborn.
Kienzle

Ballades and Verses Vain. Andrew
Lang. Keller
Balloon-Hoax, The. Edgar Allan
Poe. Gale-PP
Balmoral. Alexander Allardyce.
Kaye
Balthazar. Lawrence Durrell.
Magill '59, M1, MB, S
Bambi. Felix Salten. Haydn;
Magill I, CE, M1&2, MC,
MEUF
Bamboo Bed, The. William East-
lake. Magill '70
Band of Angels. Robert Penn
Warren. Magill '55, S
Bankruptcy, A. Bjørnstjerne
Bjørnson. Drury; Matlaw
Banner of St. George, The. Miss
Mary Bramston. Kaye
Banquet, The. Plato. Keller
Banquet, The. Xenophon. Keller
Banquet of Jests, The see Cena
delle beffe, La
Banqueters, The. Aristophanes.
Hathorn
Banzuin Chobei Shoin Manaita.
Sakurada Jisuke. Halford
Bar Sinister, The. Richard Hard-
ing Davis. Haydn (a)
Barabbas. Marie Corelli. Kaye;
Keller
Barabbas. Michel de Ghelderode.
Matlaw; Shank
Barabbas. Pär Lagerkvist.
Magill III, CE, M1&2, MC,
MEUF
Barbar, Der (The Barbarian).
Julius Hay. Kienzle
Barbara Frietchie, the Frederick
Girl. Clyde Fitch. Best '99;
Drury; Shipley
Barbara of the House of Grebe.
Thomas Hardy. Pinion; Saxelby
Barbara's History. Amelia Ann
Blanford Edwards. Keller
Barber of Seville, The. Pierre
A. Caron de Beaumarchais.
Cartmell; Drury; Haydn; Keller;
Magill II, CE, M1&2, MC,
MD; Shank; Shipley; Sobel;
Thomas
Barchester Towers. Thomas Job.
(Based on the novel by Anthony
Trollope.) Sobel
Barchester Towers. Anthony
Trollope. (See also adaptation
by Thomas Job.) Gerould;
Goodman; Haydn; Johnson;

Keller; Lass BN; Magill I, CE,
M1&2, MC, MEF
Bare Souls. Gamaliel Bradford.
Keller suppl.
Barefoot in Athens. Maxwell
Anderson. Best '51; Drury;
Kienzle; Shipley
Barefoot in the Park. Neil Simon.
Best '63; Drury; Kienzle; NCTE
Bargain, The. Michael Gilbert.
French
Bargaining for Supremacy: Anglo-
American Naval Collaboration,
1937-1941. James R. Leutze.
Magill '78
Barke von Gawdos, Die (The Bark
of Gavdos). Herbert Meier.
Kienzle
Barlaam and Josaphat. St. John
of Damascus. Keller
Barlasch of the Guard. Henry S.
Merriman. Kaye
Barley Fields, The. Robert
Nathan. Haydn (a)
Barnaby Rudge. Charles Dickens.
Hardwick CD; Haydn; Johnson;
Kaye; Keller; McSpadden-D;
Magill II, CE, M1&2, MC,
MEF
Barnavelt, Sir John Van Olden
see Sir John Van Olden Barna-
velt
Barnum. M. R. Werner. Keller
suppl.
Baron Munchausen's Narrative.
Rudolph Erich Raspe. Cohen
(Marvelous Adventures ...);
Keller (Travels); Magill II,
CE, M1&2, MC, MEUF
Baronet in Corduroy, The. Al-
bert Lee. Kaye
Baron's Heir, The. Alice W.
Fox. Kaye
Barrack-Room Ballads and Other
Verses. Rudyard Kipling.
Haydn; Heiney; Keller (Ballads
and Barrack ...)
Barren Ground. Ellen Glasgow.
Haydn; Keller suppl. ; Magill I,
CE, M1&2, MAF, MC; More-
head
Barrett Wendell and His Letters.
Barrett Wendell. Edited by
Mark Antony De Wolfe Howe.
Keller suppl. (Wendell)
Barretts of Wimpole Street, The.
Rudolf Besier. Best '30;
Drury; French; Matlaw; NCTE;

Beatrijs. Unknown. Haydn
Beatrix. Honoré de Balzac.
  Johnson
Beatrix of Clare. John Reed
  Scott. Kaye
Beau Brummell. Clyde Fitch.
  Drury; Sobel
Beauchamp's Career. George
  Meredith. Keller; Magill II,
  CE, M1&2, MC, MEF
Beautiful and Damned, The. F.
  Scott Fitzgerald. Heiney
Beautiful Despot, The. Nikolai
  Nikolaevich Yevreinov. Mat-
  law; Sobel
Beautiful People, The. William
  Saroyan. Drury; NCTE; Shank
Beautiful Rebel, A. Wilfrid Camp-
  bell. Kaye
Beauty and Love. Sheyh Galib.
  Haydn
Beauty and Sadness. Yasunari
  Kawabata. Magill '76
Beauty and the Beast. Keller
  (Fairy Tales)
Beautyful Ones Are Not Yet Born,
  The. Ayi Kwei Armah. Magill
  '69, S
Beaux' Stratagem, The. George
  Farquhar. Cartmell; Drury;
  Gassner; Haydn; Keller; Magill
  II, CE, M1&2, MC, MD;
  Shank; Shipley; Sobel
Beaver Coat, The. Gerhart Haupt-
  mann. Magill III, CE, M1&2,
  MC, MD; Matlaw; Shank; Sobel
Beaverbrook. A. J. P. Taylor.
  Magill '73
Bech: A Book. John Updike.
  Magill '71
Becket. Alfred, Lord Tennyson.
  Drury; Shipley; Sobel
Becket, or The Honor of God.
  Jean Anouilh. Anderson; Best
  '60; Drury; French; Kienzle;
  Matlaw; NCTE; Shank;
  Sprinchorn
Bed Bug, The. Vladimir Maya-
  kovsky. Magill SF; Matlaw;
  Shank; Shipley
Bed of Rose's. Falkland L.
  Cary. French
Bedford Forrest and His Critter
  Company. Andrew Lytle.
  Magill '61, S
Bedford Row Conspiracy, The.
  William Makepeace Thackeray.
  Mudge

Bedroom Farce. Alan Ayckbourn.
  Best '78
Before Adam. Jack London.
  Magill SF
Before Breakfast. Eugene O'Neill.
  Matlaw
Before Dawn (Before Sunrise).
  Gerhart Hauptmann. Gassner;
  Heiney; Matlaw
Before My Time. Maureen
  Howard; Magill '76
Before My Time. Niccolò Tucci.
  Magill '63, S
Before Sunrise see Before Dawn
Before the Dawn. Joseph A. Alt-
  sheler. Kaye
Before the Dawn. John Taine.
  Magill SF
Before the Party. Rodney Ack-
  land. French
Beggar, The. Rheinhard Johannes
  Sorge. Matlaw; Sprinchorn
Beggar on Horseback. George S.
  Kaufman and Marc Connelly.
  Best '23; Drury; Keller suppl. ;
  Lovell; Matlaw; NCTE; Shipley;
  Sobel
Beggars' Bush, The. John
  Fletcher and Philip Massinger.
  Holzknecht; Magill III, CE,
  M1&2, MC, MD; Ruoff; Sobel
Beggar's Opera, The. John Gay.
  (See also adaptation The Three-
  penny Opera by Bertolt Brecht
  and Kurt Weill.) Cartmell;
  Drury; Gassner; Haydn; Keller;
  Magill I, CE, M1&2, MC, MD;
  NBC 3; Shank; Shipley; Sobel;
  Thomas
Beginners, The. Dan Jacobson.
  Magill '67, S
Beginners of a Nation, The. Ed-
  ward Eggleston. Keller
Beginning Again. Leonard Woolf.
  Magill '65, S
Beginning with O. Olga Broumas.
  Magill '78
Beginnings of New England, The.
  John Fiske. Keller
Begum's Daughter, The. Edwin
  Lassetter Bynner. Kaye;
  Keller
Begum's Fortune, The. Jules
  Verne. Magill SF
Behaviourism. John B. Watson.
  Keller suppl.
Behold the Bridegroom. George
  Kelly. Best '27

Behold the Man. Michael Moorcock. Magill SF
Being and Having. Gabriel Marcel. Magill CHL
Being and Nothingness. Jean-Paul Sartre. Magill WP
Being and Time. Martin Heidegger. Magill WP
Being with Children. Phillip Lopate. Magill '76
Bel-Ami. Guy de Maupassant. Johnson; Magill I, CE, M1&2, MC, MEUF
Beldonald Holbein, The. Henry James. Gale-J
Belief and Faith. Josef Pieper. Magill CAL
Belinda. Maria Edgeworth. Keller
Belinda. A. A. Milne. Drury
Bell, The. Irish Murdoch. Magill IV, '59, M1, MB, MC, S
Bell, Book, and Candle. John van Druten. Best '50; Drury; French; Kienzle; Matlaw; NCTE
Bell for Adano, A. John Hersey. (See also adaptation by Paul Osborn.) Magill I, CE, M1&2, MAF, MC
Bell for Adano, A. Paul Osborn. (Based on the novel by John Hersey.) Best '44; Drury; NCTE
Bell of St. Paul's, The. Sir Walter Besant. Keller
Bell-Tower, The. Herman Melville. Gale-M
Bellamy. Anthony Armstrong and Arnold Ridley. French
Bellavita. Luigi Pirandello. Matlaw
Belle of New York. Gustav Kerker and Hugh Morton. Drinkrow; Sobel
Belle-Rose. Louis Achard. Johnson
Bellerophon. Euripides. Hathorn
Belle's Stratagem, The. Mrs. Hannah Cowley. Sobel
Bellman of London, The. Thomas Dekker. Ruoff
Bells. Nathaniel Hawthorne. Gale-H
Bells Are Ringing. Betty Comden, Adolph Green and Jule Styne. NCTE

Bell's Biography, A. Nathaniel Hawthorne. Gale-H
Bells in Winter. Czeslaw Milosz. Magill '79
Beloved Returns, The. Thomas Mann. Heiney
Beloved Vagabond, The. William J. Locke. Keller
Belshazzar. William Stearns Davis. Kaye
Belshazzer's Feast. Pedro Calderon de la Barca. Drury
Belton Estate, The. Anthony Trollope. Gerould
Belvedere. Gwen Davenport. NCTE
Ben Hur. William Young. (Based on the novel by Lew Wallace.) Sobel
Ben Hur: A Tale of the Christ. Lew Wallace. (See also adaptation by William Young.) Goodman; Grozier; Haydn; Johnson; Kaye; Keller; Magill I, CE, M1&2, MAF, MC; Morehead
Bench of Desolation, The. Henry James. Gale-J
Benefactor, The. Susan Sontag. Magill '64, M1, S
Beneficent Bear, The. Carlo Goldoni. Drury
Benefits Forgot. Wolcott Balestier. Johnson
Benito Cereno. Herman Melville. Gale-M; Magill III, CE, M1&2, MAF, MAL4, MC
Benjamin Franklin. William Cabell Bruce. Keller suppl. (Franklin)
Benjamin Franklin. Philips Russell. Keller suppl. (Franklin)
Benjamin Franklin: A Biography in His Own Words. Benjamin Franklin. Magill '73
Benjamin Jowett. Evelyn Abbott and Lewis Campbell. Keller (Jowett)
Benjamin Major. Richard of St. Victor. Magill CAL
Benjamin Minor. Richard of St. Victor. Magill CAL, CHL
Bent Twig, The. Dorothy Canfield Fisher. Haydn (a)
Benten Kozo. Kawatake Mokuami. Halford
Benvolio. Henry James. Gale-J
Beowulf. Hygeberth. Cohen

Beowulf. Unknown. Fleming;
Haydn; Keller; Magill I, CE,
M1&2, MC, MP

Berenice. Edgar Allan Poe.
Gale-PP

Bérénice. Jean Baptiste Racine.
Drury; Gassner; Magill III,
CE, M1&2, MC, MD; Shank;
Sobel

Berg, The. Herman Melville.
Gale-M

Berge, Meere und Giganten. Alfred Döblin. Magill SF

Beritten hin und Zuruck (There
and Back on Horseback).
Günter Grass. Kienzle

Berkeley Square. John L. Balderston and J. C. Squire.
Best '29; Drury; French;
Matlaw; NCTE; Shank; Shipley; Sobel; Ward

Berlin. Theodor Plievier.
Magill '58, S

Berlin and Sans-Souci. Louise
Muhlbach. Johnson

Berlin Stories, The. Christopher
Isherwood. Heiney; Magill
'54, S

Bernadette. Noël Woolf and
Sheila Buckley. French

Bernard Shaw. George Bernard
Shaw. Magill '66, M1, S

Bernard Shaw: Collected Letters,
1898-1910. George Bernard
Shaw. Magill '73

Bernardine. Mary Coyle Chase.
Best '52; Chapman '53; NCTE

Berryman's Sonnets. John Berryman. Magill '68, S

Berserker. Fred Saberhagen.
Magill SF

Bertrams, The. Anthony Trollope. Gerould

Bertrand of Brittany. Warwick
Deeping. Kaye

Beryl Coronet, The. Sir Arthur
Conan Doyle. Hardwick SH

Beside the Bonnie Briar Bush.
Ian Maclaren. Keller

Bessy Conway. Mary Ann Sadlier. Johnson

Best and the Brightest, The.
David Halberstam. Magill '73

Best Foot Forward. John Cecil
Holm. Drury

Best Man, The. Gore Vidal.
Best '59; Drury; Kienzle;
Magill '61, S; NCTE

Best of C. L. Moore, The.
Catherine L. Moore. Magill
SF

Best of C. M. Kornbluth, The.
Cyril M. Kornbluth. Magill
SF

Best of Cordwainer Smith, The.
Cordwainer Smith. Magill SF

Best of Henry Kuttner, The.
Henry Kuttner. Magill SF

Best of Philip K. Dick, The.
Philip K. Dick. Magill SF

Besuch aus der Zone (A Visit
from the Other Side). Dieter
Meichsner. Kienzle

Bête dans la jungle, La (The
Beast in the Jungle). Mar-
guerite Duras and James Lord.
Kienzle

Bête humaine, La. Emile Zola.
Keller (Rougon)

Bête noire, La (The Black Beast).
Jacques Audiberti. Kienzle

Betrothal, The. Maurice Maeterlinck. Keller suppl.; Matlaw;
Sobel

Betrothed, The. Alessandro Man-
zoni. Haydn; Johnson; Kaye;
Keller; Magill II, CE, M1&2,
MC, MEUF

Betrothed, The. Sir Walter Scott.
Johnson; Kaye; McSpadden W

Betty Alden. Jane Goodwin Austin. Keller

Between the Acts. Virginia Woolf.
Magill III, CE, M1&2, MC,
MEF

Between the Dark and the Daylight. William Dean Howells.
Carrington

Between Two Empires. Theodore
Friend. Magill Ss

Between Two Thieves. Richard
Dehan. Kaye

Between Two Thieves (Man on
Trial). Diego Fabbri. Kienzle;
Shank

Beverly of Graustark. George
Barr McCutcheon. Keller

Bevis of Hampton. Unknown.
Magill III, CE, M1&2, MC,
MP

Beyond Apollo. Barry N. Malz-
berg. Magill SF

Beyond Good and Evil. Friedrich
Wilhelm Nietzsche. Downs M;
Magill III, M1, MC, MNF, WP

Beyond Human Power I. Bjørnst-

jerne Bjørnson. Matlaw; Sobel
Beyond Human Power II.
Bjørnstjerne Bjørnson.
Drury (Beyond Our Power);
Haydn; Magill II, CE, M1&2,
MC, MD; Shank; Shipley; Sobel
Beyond the Aegean. Ilias Venezis.
Magill '57, S
Beyond the Bedroom Wall. Larry
Woiwode. Magill '76
Beyond the Bridge. Jack Matthews.
Magill '71
Beyond the Fringe. Alan Bennett,
Peter Cook, Jonathan Miller
and Dudley Moore. Drury
Beyond the Horizon. Eugene
O'Neill. Best '19; Bonin;
Drury; Gassner; Haydn; Heiney;
Keller suppl. ; Matlaw; NCTE;
Shank; Shipley; Smith; Sobel
Beyond the Pale. B. M. Croker.
Keller
Beyond This Horizon. Robert A.
Heinlein. Magill SF
Bhagavadgita. Unknown. Arm-
strong; Haydn; Keller (Sacred
Books)
Bhowani Junction. John Masters.
Magill '54, S
Bible, The. Downs F; Haydn;
Keller
Bible and Sword. Peter H.
Hunter. Kaye
Bible in Spain, The. George
Henry Borrow. Haydn; Keller;
Magill IV, MC
Bibliotheca. Attributed to Apol-
lodorus. Feder
Bibliothekar, Der. Gustav von
Moser. (See adaptation The
Private Secretary by Charles
Hawtrey.)
Bid for Loyalty, A. James
Blythe. Kaye
Bid Me to Live. Hilda Doolittle.
Magill '61, S
Biedermann and the Firebugs.
Max Frisch. Gassner (Fire-
bugs); Kienzle; Matlaw
Big Ball of Wax. Shepherd Mead.
Magill Ul'
Big Fish, Little Fish. Hugh
Wheeler. Best '60; NCTE
Big House, The. Brendan Behan.
Kienzle
Big Knife, The. Clifford Odets.
NCTE
Big Money, The. John Dos

Passos. (See also trilogy title
U. S. A.) Haydn p. 773
Big Sky, The. A. B. Guthrie,
Jr. Magill I, CE, M1&2,
MAF, MC; Morehead
Big Steamers. Rudyard Kipling.
Ward
Big Time, The. Fritz Leiber,
Jr. Magill SF
Big Woods. William Faulkner.
Magill '55, M1, S
Biglow Papers, The. James Rus-
sell Lowell. Keller; Magill
III, M1, MAL4, MC, MP
Bijou. David Madden. Magill '75
Bill of Divorcement, A. Clem-
ence Dane. Best '21; Drury;
Ward
Bill, the Galactic Hero. Harry
Harrison. Magill SF
Billiards at Half Past Nine.
Heinrich Böll. Magill Ss
Billy Budd. Louis O. Coxe and
Robert Chapman. (Based on
the novel by Herman Melville.)
Best '50; NCTE; Shank
Billy Budd, Foretopman. Herman
Melville. (See also adaptation
by Louis O. Coxe and Robert
Chapman.) Gale M; Lass AN;
Magill II, CE, M1&2, MAF,
MAL4, MC; Morehead; Olfson
Billy Liar. Keith Waterhouse.
(See also adaptation by Keith
Waterhouse and Willis Hall.)
Magill '61, S
Billy Liar. Keith Waterhouse
and Willis Hall. (Based on the
novel by Keith Waterhouse.)
Kienzle
Bimbi: Stories for Children.
Ouida. Keller
Biographia Literaria. Samuel
Taylor Coleridge. Haydn;
Keller; Magill IV, MC
Biographical Stories. Nathaniel
Hawthorne. Gale-H
Biography. S. N. Behrman.
Best '32; Drury; Lass AP;
Lovell; Matlaw; Shank; Shipley;
Wilmt
Biography. Max Frisch. Mat-
law; NCTE
Birch Dene. William Westall.
Keller
Birch Interval. Joanna Crawford.
Magill '65, S
Bird, The. Jules Michelet.

Keller
Bird in Hand. John Drinkwater.
Drury; French; Matlaw; Sobel;
Ward
Bird of Time, The. Peter Mayne.
French
Birds, The (Aves). Aristophanes.
Downs F, FG; Drury; Feder;
Gassner; Hathorn; Haydn;
Keller; Magill II, CE, M1&2,
MC, MD; NBC 1; Reinhold;
Shank (Aves); Shipley; Sobel
Birds, Beasts, and Relatives.
Gerald Durrell. Magill '70
Birds Fall Down, The. Rebecca
West. Magill '67, M1, S
Birds of America. John James
Audubon. Haydn; Keller
Birth. Zona Gale. Keller suppl.
Birth and Growth of Religion,
The. George Foot Moore.
Keller suppl.
Birth of Britain, The. Winston
S. Churchill. Magill '57, M1,
MB, S
Birth of God, The. Verner von
Heidenstam. Sobel
Birth of Merlin. Attributed to
William Rowley. Sobel
Birthday Honours. Paul Jones.
French
Birthday King, The. Gabriel
Fielding. Magill '64, S
Birthday Party, The. Harold
Pinter. Anderson; French;
Kienzle; Matlaw; Shank
Birthday Party, or, The Ladies'
Tea, The. Hjalmar Berg-
ström. Sobel
Birthmark, The. Nathaniel Haw-
thorne. Gale-H
Birthplace, The. Henry James.
Gale-J
Bishop Misbehaves, The. Fred-
erick Jackson. Drury
Bishop's Bonfire, The. Sean
O'Casey. Kienzle; Magill
'55, S; Matlaw
Bishop's Wife, The see Barley
Fields, The
Bismarck. Werner Richter.
Magill '66, S
Bismarck; Some Secret Pages
of His History. Moritz Busch.
Keller
Bismarck, the Story of a Fighter.
Emil Ludwig. Keller suppl.
Bitter Honeymoon. Alberto

Moravia. Magill '57, S
Bitter Lemons. Lawrence Dur-
rell. Magill '59, S
Bitter Sweet. Noel Coward.
Drinkrow
Bitter-Sweet. Josiah Gilbert Hol-
land. Keller
Black April. Julia Peterkin.
Keller suppl.
Black Arrow, The. Robert Louis
Stevenson. Johnson; Kaye;
Magill I, CE, M1&2, MC,
MEF
Black Beauty. Anna Sewell.
Haydn; Keller
Black Cat, The. Edgar Allan
Poe. Gale-P, PP
Black Cloud, The. Fred Hoyle.
Magill SF
Black Cloud, White Cloud. Ellen
Douglas. Magill '64, S
Black Comedy. Peter Shaffer.
Best '66; Drury
Black Crook, The. Charles M.
Barras. Shipley; Sobel
Black Cuirassier, The. Philip
L. Stevenson. Kaye
Black Diamonds. Maurice Jókai.
Keller
Black Disc, The. Albert Lee.
Kaye
Black Douglas, The. Samuel
Rutherford Crockett. Kaye
Black Dwarf, The. Sir Walter
Scott. Johnson; McSpadden W
Black Easter. James Blish.
Magill SF
Black English. Joey Lee Dillard.
Magill '73
Black Family in Slavery and
Freedom, 1750-1925, The.
Herbert G. Gutman. Magill
'77
Black Feast, The. Jacques
Audiberti. Anderson (Fête)
Black Flame, The. Stanley G.
Weinbaum. Magill SF
Black Friday. Frederick S.
Isham. Kaye
Black Glove, The. August Strind-
berg. Matlaw
Black Jack: The Life and Times
of John J. Pershing. Frank
E. Vandiver. Magill '78
Black Lamb and Grey Falcon.
Rebecca West. Magill I, CE,
M1&2, MC, MNF
Black Like Me. John Howard

Griffin. Magill Ss
Black Limelight. Gordon Sherry.
  French
Black Mask, The. Gerhart
  Hauptmann. Matlaw
Black Maskers, The. Leonid N.
  Andreyev. Drury; Sobel
Black Obelisk, The. Erich Maria
  Remarque. Magill '58, M1, S
Black Orchid. Nicholas Meyer
  and Barry Jay Kaplan. Magill
  '78
Black Oxen. Gertrude Atherton.
  Keller suppl.
Black Pearl, The. Victorien
  Sardou. Drury
Black Peter. Sir Arthur Conan
  Doyle. Hardwick SH
Black Prince, The. Shirley Ann
  Grau. Magill '55, S
Black Prince, The. Iris Murdoch.
  Magill '74
Black Sheep, The. Edmund Yates.
  Keller
Black Shilling, The. Amelia
  Edith Barr. Kaye
Black Sun. Geoffrey Wolff.
  Magill '77
Black Swan, The. Thomas Mann.
  Magill IV, '54, MC, S
Black Tulip, The. Alexandre
  Dumas (father). Johnson; Kaye
Black Ulysses. Jef Geeraerts.
  Magill '79
Black Valley. Hugo Wast.
  Magill III, CE, M1&2, MAF,
  MC
Blackberry Winter. Margaret
  Mead. Magill '73
Blacks. The. Jean Genêt.
  Anderson (Nègres); Drury;
  Kienzle; Matlaw; NCTE; Shank;
  Sprinchorn
Blair of Balaclava. Escott Lynn.
  Kaye
Blaise. Claude Magnier. Kienzle
Blanched Soldier, The. Sir
  Arthur Conan Doyle. Hard-
  wick SH
Blanchette. Eugène Brieux.
  Drury, Matlaw
Blancs, Les. Lorraine Hans-
  berry. Magill '73
Blast of War, The. Harold Mac-
  millan. Magill '69, S
Bleak House. Charles Dickens.
  Hardwick CD; Haydn; Johnson;
  Keller; McSpadden-D; Magill

I, CE, M1&2, MC, MEF
Blennerhassett. Charles Felton
  Pidgin. Kaye
Bless the Beasts and Children.
  Glendon Swarthout. Magill Ss
Bless the Bride. Vivian Ellis and
  A. P. Herbert. Drinkrow
Bless This House. Norah Lofts.
  Magill '54, S
Blessed Damozel, The. Dante
  Gabriel Rossetti. Haydn
Blind, The. Maurice Maeterlinck.
  Haydn; Heiney; Keller; Matlaw;
  Sobel
Blind Ambition. John W. Dean
  III. Magill '77
Blind Date. Jerzy Kosinski.
  Magill '78
Blind Goddess, The. Ernst Tol-
  ler. Drury
Bliss. Katherine Mansfield.
  Keller suppl.
Blithe Spirit. Noel Coward.
  Best '41; Drury; French; Mat-
  law; NCTE; Shank; Shipley;
  Sprinchorn
Blithedale Romance, The. Nathan-
  iel Hawthorne. Gale-H; John-
  son; Kaye; Keller; Magill II,
  CE, M1&2, MAF, MAL2, MC
Blockade Busters. Ralph Barker.
  Magill '78
Blockade of Phalsbourg. Emile
  Erckmann and Alexander Chat-
  rian. Kaye
Blockhead, The. Ludwig Fulda.
  Drury
Blood, Hook & Eye. Dara Wier.
  Magill '78
Blood in My Eye. George L.
  Jackson. Magill '73
Blood Mountain. John Engels.
  Magill '78
Blood, Sweat and Stanley Poole.
  James and William Goldman.
  NCTE
Blood, Sweat and Tears. Winston
  S. Churchill. Haydn
Blood Wedding. Federico García
  Lorca. Drury; Gassner;
  Heiney; Magill II, CE, M1&2,
  MC, MD; Matlaw; Shank;
  Shipley; Spinchorn
Bloodfire. Fred Chappell. Ma-
  gill '79
Bloodline. Ernest J. Gaines.
  Magill '69, S
Bloodshed and Three Novellas.

Cynthia Ozick. Magill '77
Bloody Brother; or, Rollo, Duke
of Normandy, The. John
Fletcher and Ben Jonson.
Sobel
Bloody Conquests of Mighty Tam-
burlaine (Part II), The. Chris-
topher Marlowe. Holzknecht
Bloody Mary. Carolly Erickson.
Magill '79
Bloody Tenent of Persecution,
The. Roger Williams.
Magill CHL
Bloomers, The see Pair of
Drawers, A
Bloomsday. Allan McClelland.
(Based on Ulysses by James
Joyce.) Kienzle
Blot in the 'Scutcheon, A.
Robert Browning. Drury;
Haydn; Keller; Magill II, CE,
M1&2, MC, MD; Shipley;
Sobel
Blue and Green. Henry Pottinger.
Kaye
Blue Bird, The. Maurice Maeter-
linck. Drury; Haydn; Heiney;
Keller; Matlaw; NBC 2; Ship-
ley; Sobel
Blue Boy. Jean Giono. Heiney
Blue Carbuncle, The. Sir Arthur
Conan Doyle. Hardwick SH
Blue Denim. James Leo Herlihy
and William Noble. Magill
Ss; NCTE
Blue Estuaries, The. Louise
Bogan. Magill '69, S
Blue Garden, The. Barbara
Howes. Magill '73
Blue Goose, The. Peter Black-
more. French
Blue Hammer, The. Ross Mac-
donald. Magill '77
Blue Juniata. Malcolm Cowley.
Magill '09, S
Blue Nile, The. Alan Moorehead.
Magill '63, S
Blue Skies, Brown Studies. Wil-
liam Sansom. Magill '62, S
Bluebeard. Keller (Fairy Tales)
Bluebeard's Ghost. William
Makepeace Thackeray.
Mudge
Blues for Mr. Charlie. James
Baldwin. Drury; Kienzle; Mat-
law; NCTE
Boarder, The see Parasite, The
Bob Hampton of Placer. George

Randall Parrish. Kaye
Bob, Son of Battle. Alfred Olli-
vant. Keller
Bodas de sangre see Blood
Wedding
Body Rags. Galway Kinnell.
Magill '68, S
Boeing-Boeing. Marc Camoletti.
Kienzle
Boesman and Lena. Athol Fugard.
Best '70; Drury
Bohemian Life see Scènes de la
vie de Bohème
Bohemians of the Latin Quarter,
The. Henri Murger. Keller;
Magill II, CE, M1&2, MC,
MEUF
Bohn's Libraries. Henry George
Bohn. Keller
Boke Named the Governour, The
see Book Named the Governor,
A
Bold Stroke for a Wife, A. Mrs.
Susannah Freeman Centlivre.
Shipley; Sobel
Bolsheviks Come to Power, The.
Alexander Rabinowitch. Magill
'77
Bomb, The. Frank Harris.
Kaye
Bonaparte in Jaffa (Napoleon in
Jaffa). Arnold Zweig. Kienzle
Bonaventure. Charlotte Hastings.
French
Bon-Bon. Edgar Allan Poe.
Gale-PP
Bond, The. August Strindberg.
Matlaw
Bondage of the Will, The. Martin
Luther. Magill CHL
Bondman, The. Hall Caine.
Keller
Bondman, The. Philip Massinger.
Magill III, CE, M1&2, MC,
MD; Ruoff
Bonds of Interest, The. Jacinto
Benavente y Martínez. Cart-
mell; Drury; Haydn; Heiney;
Keller suppl.; Magill II, CE,
M1&2, MC, MD; Matlaw;
Shank; Shipley; Sobel
Bonduca. John Fletcher. Sobel
Bone-Gatherers, The. Aeschylus.
Hathorn
Bonjour Tristesse. Françoise
Sagan. Magill '55, M1, S
Bonnie Prince Charlie. George
A. Henty. Kaye

Book About Myself, A. Theodore Dreiser. Gerber

Book Named the Governor, A. Sir Thomas Elyot. Haydn (Boke); Ruoff (Governor)

Book of Autographs, A. Nathaniel Hawthorne. Gale-H

Book of Changes, The. R. H. W. Dillard. Magill '75

Book of Christopher Columbus, The. Paul Claudel. Matlaw

Book of Common Prayer, The. Thomas Cranmer. Ruoff

Book of Common Prayer, A. Joan Didion. Magill '78

Book of Days, The. Robert Chambers. Keller

Book of Divine Love, The. Juan Ruiz de Alarcón y Mendoza. Haydn

Book of Job, The. Unknown. Armstrong (Job); Drury; Shank (Tragedy of); Shipley (end section); Sobel

Book of Martyrs, The see Acts and Monuments of These Latter and Perilous Days, Touching Matters of the Church

Book of Merlyn, the Unpublished Conclusion to The Once and Future King, The. Terence Hanbury White. Magill '78

Book of Mormon, The. Joseph Smith. Haydn; Keller (Mormon)

Book of Nonsense. Edward Lear. Keller

Book of Proverbs. Otloh of St. Emmeram. Magill CAL

Book of Salvation, The. Avicenna. Magill WP

Book of Sand, The. Jorge Luis Borges. Magill '78

Book of Sentences, The. Peter Lombard. Magill CAL

Book of Sir Thomas More, The. William Shakespeare (?). Ruoff (Sir Thomas More)

Book of Snobs, The. William Makepeace Thackeray. Keller; Mudge

Book of Songs. Heinrich Heine. Magill III, M1, MC, MP

Book of the Body, The. Frank Bidart. Magill '78

Book of the Courtier, The. Baldassare Castiglione. Haydn (Courtier); Keller; Magill IV,

MC; Ruoff (Courtier)

Book of the Dead, The. Unknown. Downs F, FG; Haydn

Book of the Duchess, The. Geoffrey Chaucer. Haydn

Book of the Small Souls see Small Souls

Books and Bookmen. Andrew Lang. Keller

Books and Culture. Hamilton Wright Mabie. Keller (Essays... Mabie)

Books and Their Makers. George Haven Putnam. Keller

Boomerang. Winchell Smith and Victor Mapes. Drury

Boon Island. Kenneth Roberts. Magill '57, M1, S

Boots and Saddles: or Life in Dakota with General Custer. Elizabeth B. Custer. Keller

Boris Godunov. Alexander Pushkin. Drury; Gassner; Haydn; Keller; Magill II, CE, M1&2, MC, MD; Shank; Shipley; Sobel

Boris Lensky. Ossip Schubin. Keller

Boris the Bear Hunter. Frederick J. Whishaw. Kaye

Born Free. Joy Adamson. Magill '61, M1, S

Born on the Fourth of July. Ron Kovic. Magill '77

Born Yesterday. Garson Kanin. Best '45; Drury; Lass AP; NCTE; Shank

Borough: A Poem in Twenty-Four Letters, The. George Crabbe. Magill IV, MC

Borstal Boy. Brendan Behan. Drury; Magill '60, M1, S; Ward

Boscobel: or The Royal Oak. William Harrison Ainsworth. Kaye

Boscombe Valley Mystery, The. Sir Arthur Conan Doyle. Hardwick SH

Bosnian Chronicle. Ivo Andrić. Magill '64, S

Boss, The. Edward Sheldon. Drury; Lovell; Matlaw

Bostonians, The. Henry James. Gale-J; Haydn (a); Keller; Magill IV, MAL3, MC

Boswell. Stanley Elkin. Magill '65, S

Boswell for the Defence, 1769-1774. James Boswell. Magill

'60, MB, S
Boswell in Search of a Wife, 1766-
1769. James Boswell. Magill
'57, MB, S
Boswell: Laird of Auchinleck,
1778-1782. James Boswell.
Magill '78
Boswell on the Grand Tour.
James Boswell. Magill '55,
MB, S
Boswell: The Ominous Years.
James Boswell. Magill '64, S
Boswell's London Journal: 1762-
1763. James Boswell. Magill
IV, MC
Botanic Garden, The. Erasmus
Darwin. Keller
Both Ends Meet. Arthur Macrae.
French
Both Sides of the Border. George
A. Henty. Kaye
Both Your Houses. Maxwell Ander-
son. Best '32; Bonin; Drury;
Matlaw; NCTE; Shipley; Sobel
Bothwell. James Grant. Johnson;
Kaye
Boudicca. C. H. Dudley Ward.
Kaye
Boule de Suif and Other Tales.
Guy de Maupassant. Haydn
Bound East for Cardiff. Eugene
O'Neill. (See also series title
S. S. Glencairn.) Matlaw;
Sobel
Bourgeois Gentleman, The (The
Would-Be Gentleman). Molière.
(See also adaptation The
Prodigious Snob by Miles
Malleson.) Drury; Gassner;
Haydn; Magill II, CE, M1&2,
MC, MD; NBC 2; Shank; Sobel
Bouvard and Pécuchet. Gustave
Flaubert. Magill III, CE,
M1&2, MC, MEUF
Dow of Odysseus, The. Gerhart
Hauptmann. Matlaw
Bow of Orange Ribbon, A.
Amelia Edith Barr. Johnson
Bowge of Court, The. John Skel-
ton. Ruoff
Box and Cox. John Maddison
Morton. (See adaptation by
Francis Cowley Burnand and
Arthur Sullivan.)
Boy and the Baron, The. Adeline
Knapp. Kaye
Boy David, The. Sir James M.
Barrie. Drury; French; Mat-

law; Ward
Boy Friend, The. Sandy Wilson.
Best '54; NCTE
Boy Meets Girl. Samuel and Bella
Spewack. Best '35; Drury;
Lass AP; NCTE; Sobel
Boy Who Could Make Himself Dis-
appear, The. Kin Platt. Bene-
dict
Boy with a Cart, The. Christopher
Fry. Ward
Boyar of the Terrible, A. Fred-
erick J. Whishaw. Kaye
Boyne Water. John Banim. John-
son; Kaye
Boys from Syracuse, The. George
Abbott, Lorenz Hart and Richard
Rodgers. (Based on The Come-
dy of Errors by Shakespeare.)
NCTE
Boys in the Band, The. Mart
Crowley. Best '67; Drury;
Magill '69, S
Boys of the Light Brigade. Her-
bert Strang. Kaye
Bracknels, The. Forrest Reid.
Magill II, CE, M1&2, MC,
MEF
Braggart Soldier, The (Miles
gloriosus; Braggart Warrior).
Titus Maccius Plautus. Drury;
Feder (Braggart); Gassner
(Miles); Hathorn (Miles); Magill
III, CE, M1&2, MC, MD;
Shank (Braggart); Reinhold
(Miles); Shipley (Braggart)
Brain Wave. Poul Anderson.
Magill SF
Braintree Mission, The. Nicholas
E. Wyckoff. Magill '58, S
Brand. Henrik Ibsen. Haydn;
Heiney; Magill III, CE, M1&2,
MC, MD; Matlaw; Shank; Ship-
ley; Sobel
Brass Butterfly, The. William
Golding. Drury
Brautigan's. Richard Brautigan.
Magill '70
Brave African Huntress, The.
Amos Tutuola. Magill Ss
Brave Lady, A. Dinah Maria
Mulock. Johnson
Brave New World. Aldous Huxley.
Haydn; Heiney; Lass BN; Magill
I, CE, M1&2, MC, MEF, SF;
Olfson; Ward
Bravest Gentleman in France, The.
Herbert Hayens. Kaye

Bravest of the Brave, The.
George A. Henty. Kaye
Braving the Elements. James
Merrill. Magill '73
Bravo, The. James Fenimore
Cooper. Johnson; Keller;
Walker
Brazenhead the Great. Maurice
Hewlett. Kaye
Breach of Marriage. Dan Suther-
land. French
Bread and Wine. Ignazio Silone.
Haydn; Heiney; Lass EN; Magill
I, CE, M1&2, MC, MEUF
Bread of Those Early Years, The.
Heinrich Böll. Magill '77
Breadwinner, The. W. Somerset
Maugham. Drury; French
Bread-Winners, The. John Hay.
Johnson; Keller
Break of Noon. Paul Claudel.
Gassner; Matlaw; Shank;
Sprinchorn
Breakfast at Tiffany's. Truman
Capote. Magill Ss; Morehead
Breakfast for One. James Daran.
French
Breakfast of Champions. Kurt
Vonnegut, Jr. Magill '74
Breaking Open. Muriel Rukeyser.
Magill '74
Breasts of Tiresias, The. Guil-
laume Apollinaire. Gassner;
Matlaw
Breath of Spring. Peter Coke.
French
Brecht on Brecht. Bertolt Brecht.
Drury; NCTE
Bred in the Bone and Other Stories.
Elsie Singmaster. Keller suppl.
Brewster's Millions. George
Barr McCutcheon. Haydn
Brian Fitz Count. Augustus David
Crake. Kaye
Bricks Without Straw. Albion
Winegar Tourgee. Kaye
Bride and the Bachelor, The.
Ronald Millar. French
Bride Comes Back, The. Ronald
Millar. French
Bride from the Bush, A. Ernest
William Hornung. Keller
Bride of Lammermoor, The. Sir
Walter Scott. Haydn; Johnson;
Keller; McSpadden W; Magill
III, CE, M1&2, MC, MEF
Bride of the Innisfallen, The.
Eudora Welty. Magill '55, S

Bride of the Lamb, The. William
Hurlbut. Best '25
Bridegroom Dick. Herman Mel-
ville. Gale-M
Brideshead Revisited. Evelyn
Waugh. Heiney; Magill I, CE,
M1&2, MC, MEF; Stade p. 70;
Ward
Bridge, The. Hart Crane. Magill
III, M1, MC, MP
Bridge at Andau, The. James A.
Michener. Magill '58, S
Bridge of San Luis Rey, The.
Thornton Wilder. Grozier;
Haydn; Heiney; Keller suppl. ;
Lass AN; Magill I, CE, M1&2,
MAF, MC; Morehead; Olfson;
Ward
Bridge of Sighs. Thomas Mus-
champ. French
Bridge on the Drina, The. Ivo
Andrić. Magill IV, '60, M1,
MC, S
Bridge over the River Kwai, The.
Pierre Boulle. Magill '54, M1,
S
Bridge Too Far, A. Cornelius
Ryan. Magill '75
Bridgewater Treatises, The.
Keller
Brief Lives. John Aubrey. Magill
IV, MC
Brief Moment. S. N. Behrman.
Best '31; Drury; Sobel
Briefing for a Descent into Hell.
Doris Lessing. Magill SF
Briefträger kommt, Der (The
Postman Arrives). Hans
Joachim Haecker. Kienzle
Brigadier and the Golf Widow, The.
John Cheever. Magill '65, S
Brigadoon. Alan Jay Lerner and
Frederick Loewe. Best '46;
Drinkrow; NCTE; Shipley
Brigham Young. M. R. Werner.
Keller suppl. (Young)
Brighton Rock. Graham Greene.
Ward
Brignol and His Daughter. Alfred
Capus. Drury; Sobel
Drinking Cup, The. Dorothy
Canfield Fisher. Keller suppl.
Bring the Jubilee. Ward Moore.
Magill SF
Britannicus. Jean Baptiste Racine.
Gassner; Magill III, CE, M1&2,
MC, MD; Shank; Shipley; Sobel
British History in the Nineteenth

Century. George Macaulay Tre-
velyan. Keller suppl.
British Legion, The. Herbert
Hayens. Kaye
British Revolution, 1880-1939,
The. Robert Rhodes James.
Magill '78
Broad and Alien Is the World.
Ciro Alegría. Magill II, CE,
M1&2, MAF, MC
Broad Highway, The. Jefferey
Farnol. Keller
Broadway. Philip H. Dunning and
George Abbott. Best '26;
Drury; Keller suppl.; Shipley;
Sobel
Brockenbrow see Hinkemann
Broken Dishes. Martin Flavin.
Drury
Broken Ground, The. Wendell
Berry. Magill '65, S
Broken Heart, The. John Ford.
Holzknecht; Ruoff; Sobel
Broken Jug, The. Heinrich von
Kleist. Gassner; Magill III,
CE, M1&2, MC, MD; Shank;
Shipley
Broken Wings. Henry James.
Gale-J
Broker of Bogota, The. Robert
Montgomery Bird. Drury
Brontës, The. Alfred Sangster.
French
Bronx Express. Ossip Dymov.
Shipley
Bronze Horseman: A Petersburg
Tale, The. Alexander Push-
kin. Magill IV, MC
Brook Kerith, The. George
Moore. Keller; Ward
Brooklyn Bridge: Fact and Sym-
bol. Alan Trachtenberg.
Magill '66, S
Brooksmith. Henry James.
Gale-J
Brother Ass. Eduardo Barrios.
Magill IV, MC
Brother Goose. William Davidson.
Drury
Brother Jacob. George Eliot.
Halperin
Brother Rat. John Monks, Jr.
and Fred F. Finklehoffe.
Drury; Sobel
Brotherly Love. Gabriel Fielding.
Magill '62, S
Brothers. Herbert Ashton, Jr.
Drury

Brothers, The. Richard Cumber-
land. Sobel
Brothers, The (Adelphoe). Ter-
ence. Drury; Feder; Gassner
(Adelphoe); Hathorn (Adelphoe);
Magill III, CE, M1&2, MC,
MD; Reinhold; Shank (Adelphi);
Shipley; Sobel
Brothers Ashkenazi, The. Israel
Joshua Singer. Haydn; Magill
II, CE, M1&2, MC, MEUF
Brothers Five. Violet T. Kirke.
Kaye
Brothers in Arms. F. Bayford
Harrison. Kaye
Brothers in Law. Ted Willis and
Henry Cecil. French
Brothers Karamazov, The. Fyo-
dor Mikhailovich Dostoevskii.
Berry-2; Goodman; Haydn; Kel-
ler; Lass EN; Magill I, CE,
M1&2, MC, MEUF; Wilson
Brothers Reuther, The. Victor
G. Reuther. Magill '77
Brown Decades, The. Lewis
Mumford. Magill IV, MC
Brown Mask, The. Percy J.
Brebner. Kaye
Brown of Moukden. Herbert
Strang. Kaye
Brown on Resolution. C. S.
Forester. Ward
'Browne's Folly.' Nathaniel Haw-
thorne. Gale-H
Browning Version, The. Terence
Rattigan. French; Matlaw;
Shank
Bruce-Partington Plans, The.
Sir Arthur Conan Doyle. Hard-
wick SH
Brunhilde. Pedro Antonio de
Alarcón. Johnson
Brush with a Body. Maurice Mc-
Loughlin. French
Brushwood Boy, The. Rudyard
Kipling. Magill II, CE, M1&2,
MC, MEF
Brut, The. Layamon. Haydn;
Keller; Magill III, M1, MC,
MP
Brutal Friendship, The. F. W.
Deakin. Magill '64, S
Brutus. Marcus Tullius Cicero.
Feder; Keller
Brutus; or, The Fall of Tarquin.
John Howard Payne. Drury;
Sobel
Buckdancer's Choice. James

Dickey. Magill '66, S
Bucktails; or, Americans in Eng-
land, The. James Kirke
Paulding. Lovell
Bucky. Hugh Kenner. Magill '74
Bucolics see Eclogues
Buddenbrooks. Thomas Mann.
Haydn; Heiney; Keller suppl.;
Lass EN; Magill I, CE, M1&2,
MC, MEUF
Buddhist Mahâyâna Texts. Un-
known. Keller (Sacred Books)
Buddhist Suttas. Unknown. Kel-
ler (Sacred Books)
Buds and Bird Voices. Nathaniel
Hawthorne. Gale-H
Buenos Aires Affair, The. Manuel
Puig. Magill '77
Bug Jack Barron. Norman Spin-
rad. Magill SF
Builders of the Bridal Chamber,
The. Aeschylus. Hathorn
Builders of the Waste. Thorpe
Forrest. Kaye
Bulfinch's Mythology. Thomas
Bulfinch. Haydn
Bull from the Sea, The. Mary
Renault. Magill '63, S
Bullet Park. John Cheever.
Magill '70
Bulwark, The. Theodore Dreiser.
Gerber; Magill III, CE, M1&2,
MAF, MC
Bundle of Letters, A. Henry
James. Gale-J
Bunsen's Biblical Researches.
Rowland Williams. Keller
(Essays and Reviews)
Bunty Pulls the Strings. Graham
Moffat. French
Buoyant Billions. George Bernard
Shaw. Hardwick; Matlaw
Burgomaster, The. Gert Hofmann.
Kienzle
Burgomaster of Stilemonde.
Maurice Maeterlinck. Sobel
Burgomaster's Wife, The. Georg
Moritz Ebers. Kaye
Buried Alive. Arnold Bennett.
Ward
Buried Alive: The Biography of
Janis Joplin. Myra Friedman.
Magill '74
Buried Land, A. Madison Jones.
Magill '64, S
Burlesque. George M. Watters
and Arthur Hopkins. Best '27;
Sobel

Burning Bright. John Steinbeck.
(Drama based on his novel.)
Kienzle
Burning Glass, The. S. N. Behr-
man. Magill '69, S
Burning Glass, The. Charles
Morgan. Magill '54, S; Matlaw
Burning of Rome, The. Alfred
John Church. Kaye
Burnt Flower-Bed, The. Ugo
Betti. Matlaw; Shank
Burnt House, The. August Strind-
berg. Matlaw
Burnt Ones, The. Patrick White.
Magill '65, S
Burnt-Out Case, A. Graham
Greene. Magill IV, '62, MC,
S
Burr: A Novel. Gore Vidal.
Magill '74
Bury the Dead. Irwin Shaw.
Lass AP; Matlaw; Shipley;
Sobel
Bus Stop. William Inge. Best
'54; Chapman '55; Drury; Ki-
enzle; Magill Ss; Matlaw; NCTE
Bushido. Takeda Izumo. Shipley
(Takeda)
Business in Great Waters, A.
Julian Corbett. Kaye
Business Is Business. Octave
Henri Marie Mirbeau. Shipley;
Sobel
Business Man, The. Edgar Allan
Poe. Gale-PP
Business of Being a Woman, The.
Ida M. Tarbell. Keller
Bussy D'Ambois. George Chap-
man. Gassner; Holzknecht;
Keller; Magill II, CE, M1&2,
MC, MD; Ruoff; Shipley; Sobel
But for Whom Charlie. S. N.
Behrman. Drury
But Not in Shame. John Toland.
Magill '62, MB, S
But Yet a Woman. Arthur Sher-
burne Hardy. Keller
Butcher Rogaum's Door see
Old Rogaum and His Theresa
Butley. Simon Gray. Best '72;
Drury; NCTE
Butter and Egg Man, The.
George S. Kaufman. Best '25;
Drury; Matlaw
Butterflies Are Free. Leonard
Gershe. Best '69; Drury;
NCTE
Butterflies of the Province, The.

Honor Tracy. Magill '71 Butterfly's Evil Spell, The. Federico García Lorca. Matlaw

Buying a Horse. William Dean Howells. Carrington

By Conduct and Courage. George A. Henty. Kaye

By Daylight and in Dream. John Hall Wheelock. Magill '71

By Dulvercombe Waters. Harold Vallings. Kaye

By England's Aid. George A. Henty. Kaye

By Love Possessed. James Gould Cozzens. Magill '58, S

By Neva's Waters. John R. Carling. Kaye

By Right of Conquest. George A. Henty. Kaye

By Sheer Pluck. George A. Henty. Kaye

By the North Gate. Joyce Carol Oates. Magill '64, M1, S

Bye Bye Birdie. Michael Stewart, Lee Adams and Charles Strouse. NCTE

Byron. Leslie A. Marchand. Magill '58, M1, MB, S

-C-

CIA and the Cult of Intelligence, The. Victor Marchetti and John D. Marks. Magill '75

C. S. Lewis: A Biography. Roger Lancelyn Green and Walter Hooper. Magill '74

Cab at the Door, A. V. S. Pritchett. Magill '69, S

Cabala, The. Thornton Wilder. Magill I, CE, M1&2, MAF, MC

Cabaret. Joe Masteroff, John Kander and Fred Ebb. (Based on I Am a Camera by John van Druten.) Best '66; NCTE

Cabbages and Kings. O. Henry. Morehead (under author Porter, William Sydney)

Cabbalah. Unknown. Haydn

Cabin, The. Vicente Blasco Ibáñez. Magill II, CE, M1&2, MC, MEUF

Cabin Road, The. John Faulkner. Magill '70

Cable, The see Rudens (The Rope)

Cabot Wright Begins. James Purdy. Magill '65, S

Cactus Flower, The. Abe Burrows. (Based on Fleur de cactus by Pierre Barillet and Jean-Pierre Gredy.) Best '65; Drury; NCTE

Cadmus. Unknown. Magill I, CE, M1&2, MC, MEUF; Morehead

Caedwalla. Frank Cowper. Kaye

Caesar: A Sketch. James Anthony Froude. Keller

Caesar and Cleopatra. George Bernard Shaw. Drury; Gassner; Hardwick; Haydn; Heiney; Keller; Magill III, M1, MC, MD; Matlaw; Shank; Shipley; Sobel; Ward

Caesar or Nothing. Pío Baroja y Nessi. Heiney; Magill I, CE, M1&2, MC, MEUF

Caesar's Column. Ignatius Donnelly. Magill SF

Caesars Witwe (Caesar's Widow). Franz Theodor Csokor. Kienzle

Cage for Loulou, A. Rudolph von Abele. Magill '79

Caged Lion, The. Charlotte Mary Yonge. Kaye

Caged Panther, The. Harry Meacham. Magill '68, S

Cages. Lewis John Carlino. Kienzle

Cain. George Gordon, Lord Byron. Magill II, CE, M1&2, MC, MD; Shipley

Caine Mutiny, The. Herman Wouk. (See adaptation The Caine Mutiny Court Martial.)

Caine Mutiny Court Martial, The. Herman Wouk. (Based on his novel The Caine Mutiny.) Best '53; Chapman '54; Drury; Kienzle; NCTE; Shank

Cakes and Ale. W. Somerset Maugham. Heiney; Magill I, CE, M1&2, MC, MEF; Ward

Calandria, La. Bernardo Dovizi, Cardinal da Bibbiena. Gassner

Calcutta, May 4. Lion Feuchtwanger and Bertolt Brecht. Matlaw

Cale. Sylvia Wilkinson. Magill '71

Caleb Williams. William Godwin. Haydn; Johnson; Keller; Magill

I, CE, M1&2, MC, MEF
California Suite. Neil Simon.
Best '76
Caligula. Albert Camus. Anderson; Best '59; Gassner; Matlaw;
Shank
Call Home the Heart. Clemence
Dane. French
Call It a Day. Dodie Smith.
Best '35; Drury; French
Call It Sleep. Henry Roth. Magill
IV, '65, M1, MC, S
Call Me Madam. Irving Berlin,
Howard Lindsay and Russel
Crouse. Drinkrow
Call of All Nations, The. Saint
Prosper of Aquitaine. Magill
CAL
Call of the Blood, The. Robert
S. Hichens. Keller
Call of the Wild, The. Jack London. Haydn; Heiney; Hix;
Keller; Lass AN; Magill I,
CE, M1&2, MAF, MC; Morehead; Olfson; Smith; Ward
Call to Honour, The. Charles
de Gaulle. Magill '55, S
Called Back. Hugh Conway.
Johnson; Keller
Callista. Cardinal John Henry
Newman. Kaye; Keller
Calvary. William Butler Yeats.
Matlaw
Camberwell Beauty and Other
Stories, The. V. S. Pritchett.
Magill '75
Cambises, King of Persia.
Thomas Preston. Gassner;
Holzknecht (Life of...); Ruoff
Cambridge Described and Illustrated. Thomas Dinham Atkinson. Keller
Camel Through the Needle's Eye.
Frantisek Langer. Drury
Camelot. Alan Jay Lerner and
Frederick Loewe. (Based on
The Once and Future King by
T. H. White.) NCTE
Camel's Back, The. Arnold Helsby. French
Camera obscura. Hildebrand.
Haydn
Camicans, The. Sophocles.
Hathorn
Camille; the Lady of the Camellias. Alexandre Dumas (son).
Armstrong; Cartmell; Cohen;
Drury; French (Lady); Gassner;

Goodman; Grozier; Haydn; Johnson; Keller; Magill I, CE,
M1&2, MC, MD; NBC 2; Shank;
Shipley; Sobel
Camino Real. Tennessee Williams. Drury; Kienzle; Matlaw;
Sprinchorn
Camp Concentration. Thomas M.
Disch. Magill SF
Camp of Refuge, The. Charles
MacFarlane. Kaye
Camp on the Severn, The. Augustus David Crake. Kaye
Campaign in the Jungle, The.
Edward Stratemeyer. Kaye
Campaspe. John Lyly. Holzknecht (Alexander, Campaspe...);
Magill III, CE, M1&2, MC,
MD; Ruoff; Sobel
Can-Can. Cole Porter and Abe
Burrows. Drinkrow; Kienzle
Can Such Things Be? Ambrose
Bierce. Magill SF
Can You Forgive Her? Anthony
Trollope. Gerould; Johnson
Cancer Ward, The. Aleksandr I.
Solzhenitsyn. Magill '69, M1,
S
Candelaio, Il (The Candle-Maker).
Giordano Bruno. Gassner
Candida. George Bernard Shaw.
Drury; Hardwick; Haydn;
Heiney; Keller; Magill III, M1,
MC, MD; Matlaw; NCTE;
Shank; Shipley; Sobel; Sprinchorn; Ward
Candide. Lillian Hellman, Leonard Bernstein, Richard Wilbur,
John Latouche and Dorothy
Parker. (Based on the novel
by Voltaire.) Best '56; Chapman '57
Candide. Voltaire. (See also
adaptation by Lillian Hellman
et al.) Armstrong; Goodman;
Grozier; Haydn; Keller; Lass
EN; Magill I, CE, M1&2, MC,
MEUF
Candied Peel. Falkland L. Cary.
French
Candle in the Wind. Maxwell
Anderson. Best '41
Candle-Maker, The see Candelaio, Il
Cane. Jean Toomer. Magill S
Cannibal, The. John Hawkes.
Magill IV, MC
Canon of Medicine. Avicenna.

Downs; Haydn

Canterbury Pilgrims, The. Nathaniel Hawthorne. Gale-H

Canterbury Pilgrims, The. Percy MacKaye. Drury; Keller

Canterbury Tales, The (Selections). Geoffrey Chaucer. Downs F, FG; Haydn; Keller; Magill II, CE, M1&2, MC, MP; Wilson

Canterbury Tales. Martin Starkie, Nevill Coghill, Richard Hill and John Hawkins. Drury; NCTE

Canti. Giacomo Leopardi. Haydn

Cántice. Jorge Guillén. Magill '66, S

Canticle for Leibowitz, A. Clark Fuller. (Based on the novel by Walter M. Miller, Jr.) Drury

Canticle for Leibowitz, A. Walter M. Miller, Jr. (See also adaptation by Clark Fuller.) Magill SF

Canticle of the Sun. Saint Francis of Assisi. Haydn

Cantos. Ezra Pound. Haydn (a); Magill III, M1, MC, MP; Ward

Canzoniere, Il. Francesco Petrarch. Haydn

Cap and Bells. Luigi Pirandello. Matlaw

Capable of Honor. Allen Drury. Magill '67, M1, S

Cape Cod. Henry David Thoreau. Keller

Cape Cod Folks. Sarah Pratt McLean Greene. Johnson

Cape Cod Lighter, The. John O'Hara. Magill '63, S

Capitaine Bada. Jean Vauthier. Anderson; Kienzle

Capital see Kapital, Das

Capital Punishment. Charles L. Black, Jr. Magill '75

Caponsacchi. Arthur Goodrich and Rose A. Palmer. Keller suppl.; Shipley; Sobel

Caprice. Sil-Vara. Sobel

Caprices of Marianne, A. Alfred de Musset. Shank (Un Caprice); Shipley

Captain, The. Churchill Williams. Kaye

Captain Applejack. Walter Hackett. Sobel

Captain Blackman. John A. Williams. Magill '73

Captain Brassbound's Conversion.

George Bernard Shaw. Drury; Hardwick; Matlaw; Shank; Shipley; Sobel; Ward

Captain Carleton. Daniel Defoe. Johnson-18th

Captain Carvallo. Denis Cannan. French

Captain Cook and the South Pacific. John Gwyther. Magill '55, S

Captain Courtesy. Edward Childs Carpenter. Kaye

Captain Fracasse. Théophile Gautier. Johnson; Keller

Captain from Köpenick. Carl Zuckmayer. Matlaw; Shank; Shipley; Sprinchorn

Captain Horatio Hornblower. C. S. Forester. Magill I, CE, M1&2, MC, MEF

Captain Jinks of the Horse Marines. Clyde Fitch. Matlaw; NBC 3; Shipley

Captain of Irregulars, A. Herbert Hayens. Kaye

Captain of the Guard, The. James Grant. Kaye

Captain of the Janizaries, The. J. M. Ludlow. Johnson; Kaye

Captain of the Wight, The. Frank Cowper. Kaye

Captain Pantoja and the Special Service. Mario Vargas Llosa. Magill '79

Captain Singleton. Daniel Defoe. Johnson-18th; Magill III, CE, M1&2, MC, MEF

Captain Steele. Calhoun Winton. Magill '65, S

Captain Veneno. Pedro Antonio de Alarcón. Keller

Captains All. William Wymark Jacobs. Keller

Captains Courageous. Rudyard Kipling. Grozier; Haydn; Johnson; Keller; Magill I, CE, M1&2, MC, MEF

Captain's Daughter, The. Alexander Pushkin. Berry-1; Haydn; Johnson; Kaye; Keller; Magill I, CE, M1&2, MC, MEUF

Captain's Doll, The. D. H. Lawrence. Keller suppl.

Captive, The. Edouard Bourdet. Keller suppl.; Shipley; Sobel

Captive, The. Marcel Proust. (See also series title Remembrance of Things Past.) Haydn

p. 631; Heiney
Captive and the Free, The. Joyce
Cary. Magill '60, S
Captive of the Corsairs, A.
John Finnemore. Kaye
Captive Women, The. Sophocles.
Hathorn
Captives, The. Titus Maccius
Plautus. Drury; Feder;
Gassner (Captivi); Hathorn;
Magill II, CE, M1&2, MC,
MD; Reinhold (Captivi);
Shank; Shipley
Captives, The. Hugh Walpole.
Keller suppl.
Car Cemetery, The. Fernando
Arrabal. Gassner
Car Thief, The. Theodore
Weesner. Magill '73
Caractères, ou moeurs de ce
siècle. Jean de La Bruyère.
Keller
Caravan. John Galsworthy.
Keller suppl.
Card, The. Arnold Bennett.
Ward
Card Index, The. Tadeusz
Rozewicz. Anderson (Karto-
teka); Kienzle
Cardboard Box, The. Sir Arthur
Conan Doyle. Hardwick SII
Cardillac. Robert Barr. Kaye
Cardinal, The. James Shirley.
Holzknecht; Ruoff; Sobel
Cardinal and His Conscience, A.
Miss Graham Hope. Kaye
Cardinal of Spain, The. Henry
de Montherlant. Kienzle
Cardinal's Pawn, The. K. L.
Montgomery. Kaye
Cardinal's Snuff-Box, The.
Sidney Luska. Johnson
(under author Harland,
Henry)
Cards of Identity. Nigel Dennis.
Magill '55, S
Career of a Nihilist, The. S.
Stepniak. Johnson
Careless Husband, The. Colley
Cibber. Sobel
Caretaker, The. Harold Pinter.
Best '61; Gassner; Kienzle;
Magill IV, MC; Matlaw;
NCTE; Shank; Ward
Carians, The. Aeschylus.
Hathorn
Caricature and Other Comic Art.
James Parton. Keller

Carissima, The. Lucas Malet.
Keller
Carlotta's Intended. Ruth McEn-
ery Stuart. Johnson
Carlyles, The. Constance Cary
Harrison. Kaye
Carmelites, The. Georges Ber-
nanos. Anderson (Dialogues);
Kienzle; Shank (Dialogues)
Carmen. Henri Meilhac, Ludovic
Halévy and Georges Bizet.
(Based on Prosper Merimée's
novel.) Shipley
Carmen. Prosper Mérimée.
(See also adaptation by Henri
Meilhac et al.) Armstrong;
Cohen; Haydn; Johnson; Keller;
Magill I, CE, M1&2, MC,
MEUF
Carmen Deo Nostro. Richard
Crashaw. Magill CAL
Carmen saeculare. Horace.
Feder
Carmina. Gaius Valerius Catul-
lus. Magill III, M1, MC, MP
Carnival! Michael Stewart and
Bob Merrill. NCTE
Carnival: Entertainments and
Posthumous Tales. Isak Dine-
sen. Magill '78
Caroline, O Caroline. Paul van
Herck. Magill SF
Carousel. Richard Rodgers and
Oscar Hammerstein II. (Based
on Liliom by Ferenc Molnár.)
Matlaw; NCTE
Carrington, V. C. Dorothy and
Campbell Christie. French
Carrying the Fire: An Astronaut's
Journeys. Michael Collins.
Magill '75
Carson of Venus. Edgar Rice
Burroughs. Magill SF
Carthaginian, The see Poenulus
Casa Braccio. Francis Marion
Crawford. Keller
Casanova's Chinese Restaurant.
Anthony Powell. Magill '61,
MB, S
Case, The. Alexander Sukhovo-
Kobylin. Gassner (Krechin-
sky's)
Case-Book of Sherlock Holmes,
The. Sir Arthur Conan Doyle.
Hardwick SH
Case Is Altered, The. Ben Jon-
son. Ruoff; Sobel
Case of Conscience, A. James

Blish. Magill SF
Case of Identity, A. Sir Arthur
Conan Doyle. Hardwick SH
Case of Libel, A. Henry Denk-
er. (Based on My Life in
Court by Louis Nizer.)
Drury; NCTE
Case of Rebellious Susan, The.
Henry Arthur Jones. Best
'94; Drury; Matlaw
Case of Sergeant Grischa, The.
Arnold Zweig. Haydn; Magill
I, CE, M1&2, MC, MEUF
Casey Agonistes and Other Sci-
ence Fiction and Fantasy
Stories. Richard McKenna.
Magill SF
Cashel Byron's Profession.
George Bernard Shaw. Johnson
Casina. Titus Maccius Plautus.
Feder; Hathorn; Reinhold;
Shipley
Cask of Amontillado, The. Edgar
Allan Poe. Gale-P, PP
Casket, The see Cistellaria
Caso clinico, Un (A Clinical
Case). Dino Buzzati. Kienzle
Caso Pinedus, Il (The Pinedus
Case). Paolo Levi. Kienzle
Caspar Hauser. Jacob Wasser-
mann. Haydn
Cass Timberlane. Sinclair Lewis.
Magill I, CE, M1&2, MAF,
MC
Cassandra Singing. David Madden.
Magill '70
Cassilis Engagement, The. St.
John E. C. Hankin. Drury;
Sobel
Caste. Thomas William Robert-
son. Cartmell; Drury; Magill
II, CE, M1&2, MC, MD;
Shank; Shipley; Sobel
Castel Del Monte. Nathan Gal-
lizier. Kaye
Casti Connubii. Pope Pius XI.
Magill CAL
Castilian Days. John Hay.
Keller
Casting Away of Mrs. Lecks and
Mrs. Aleshine, The. Frank
R. Stockton. Johnson; Keller
Castle, The. Franz Kafka.
(See also adaptation Das
Schloss by Max Brod.)
Heiney; Lass EN; Magill I,
CE, M1&2, MC, MEUF
Castle Daly. Annie Keary.

Kaye; Keller
Castle Dangerous. Sir Walter
Scott. Johnson; Kaye; McSpad-
den W
Castle in Sweden. Françoise
Sagan. Kienzle
Castle Keep. William Eastlake.
Magill '66, S
Castle of Fratta, The. Ippolito
Nievo. Magill III, '59, CE,
M1&2, MC, MEUF, S
Castle of Indolence, The. James
Thomson (1700-1748). Haydn
Castle of Otranto, The. Horace
Walpole. Haydn; Johnson;
Keller; Magill I, CE, M1&2,
MC, MEF
Castle of Perseverance, The.
Unknown. Sobel
Castle Omeragh. F. Frankfort
Moore. Kaye
Castle Rackrent. Maria Edge-
worth. Haydn; Johnson; Keller;
Magill I, CE, M1&2, MC,
MEF
Castle Richmond. Anthony Trol-
lope. Gerould
Casuals of the Sea. William Mc-
Fee. Magill I, CE, M1&2,
MC, MEF
Casuarina Tree, The. W. Somer-
set Maugham. Ward
Cat Among the Pigeons. Duncan
Greenwood. French
Cat and Mouse. Günter Grass.
Magill IV, '64, MC, S
Cat of Bubastes. George A.
Henty. Kaye
Cat on a Hot Tin Roof. Tennes-
see Williams. Anderson; Best
'54; Bonin; Chapman '55;
Drury; Kienzle; Magill IV,
'55, MB, MC, S; Matlaw;
NCTE; Sobel; Sprinchorn; Ward
Catch Me If You Can. Robert
Thomas. (See adaptation by
Jack Weinstock and Willie Gil-
bert.)
Catch Me If You Can. Jack
Weinstock and Willie Gilbert.
(Based on the play by Robert
Thomas.) Drury
Catch-22. Joseph Heller. Magill
IV, '62, M1, MC, S; NCTE;
Olfson
Catcher in the Rye, The. J. D.
Salinger. Lass AN; Magill S;
Morehead; Ward

Catechetical Lectures, The. Saint Cyril, Bishop of Jerusalem. Magill CAL, CHL

Catharine. Jules Sandeau. Keller

Catharine Furze. Mark Rutherford. Keller

Cathedral, The. Hugh Walpole. Keller suppl.

Catherine. William Makepeace Thackeray. Johnson; Mudge

Catherine Carmichael. Anthony Trollope. Gerould

Catherine Carmier. Ernest J. Gaines. Magill S

Catherine de Medici. Honoré de Balzac. Johnson

Catherine Douglas. Rachel Willard. Kaye

Catherine, Empress of All the Russias. Vincent Cronin. Magill '79

Catherine the Great. Katherine Anthony. Keller suppl.

Catherine the Great. Joan Haslip. Magill '78

Cathleen ni Houlihan. William Butler Yeats. Gassner; Matlaw; Sobel

Catholicism. Henri de Lubac, S. J. Magill CAL

Catiline. Henrik Ibsen. Matlaw

Catiline. Ben Jonson. Magill III, CE, M1&2, MC, MD; Sobel

Cato. Joseph Addison. Haydn; Keller; Shipley; Sobel

Cat's Cradle. Maurice Baring. Keller suppl.

Cat's Cradle. Kurt Vonnegut, Jr. Magill S, SF

Caucasian Chalk Circle, The. Bertolt Brecht. Anderson; Drury; Gassner; Kienzle; Matlaw; NCTE; Shank; Sprinchorn; Ward

Caught in That Music. Seymour Epstein. Magill '68, S

Caught in the Web of Words. K. M. Elisabeth Murray. Magill '78

Cause for Wonder. Wright Morris. Magill '64, S

Causeries de Lundi. Charles Augustin Sainte-Beuve. Haydn; Keller

Cautionary Tales. Hilaire Belloc. Ward

Cautionary Tales. Miguel de

Cervantes Saavedra. Haydn

Cavalcade. Noel Coward. Matlaw; Thomas

Cavalier, The. George W. Cable. Keller

Cavalier and Covenant. George Eyre Todd. Kaye

Cavaliers, The. Samuel R. Keightley. Kaye

Cavalleria Rusticana. Giovanni Verga. Keller; Magill II, CE, M1&2, MC, MEU

Cave, The. Robert Penn Warren. Magill '60, S

Cave Dwellers, The. William Saroyan. Drury; Kienzle; NCTE

Cavern, The. Jean Anouilh. Kienzle

Caves of Steel, The. Isaac Asimov. Magill SF

Cavour. Countess Evelyn Martinengo-Cesaresco. Keller

Cawdor. Robinson Jeffers. Heiney; Magill I, CE, M1&2, MC, MP

Caxtons, The. Lord Edward Bulwer-Lytton. Johnson; Keller

Cecè. Luigi Pirandello. Matlaw

Cecil Dreeme. Theodore Winthrop. Keller

Couile, or the School for Fathers. Jean Anouilh. Kienzle

Cecilia. Fanny Burney. Keller; Magill III, CE, M1&2, MC, MEF

Celebration. Tom Jones and Harvey Schmidt. Best '68; NCTE

Celebration. Harvey Swados. Magill '76

Celestial Omnibus, The. E. M. Forster. Ward

Celestial Railroad, The. Nathaniel Hawthorne. Gale-H

Celestina. Fernando de Rojas. Haydn; Magill II, CE, M1&2, MC, MEUF; Shipley; Sobel

Céline. Patrick McCarthy. Magill '77

Celles qu'on prend dans ses bras (Women One Takes in One's Arms). Henry de Montherlant. Kienzle

Cellular Pathology. Rudolf Virchow. Haydn

Celtic Twilight. William Butler Yeats. Ward

Celts: The People Who Came Out of the Darkness, The. Gerhard

Herm. Magill '78
Cena delle beffe, La (The Banquet of Jests). Sem Benelli. Gassner
Cenci, Les. Antonin Artaud. Gassner
Cenci, The. Percy Bysshe Shelley. Haydn; Keller; Magill I, CE, M1&2, MC, MD; Shipley; Sobel
Cent nouvelles nouvelles, Les. Unknown. Haydn; Keller; Kienzle
Centaur, The. John Updike. Magill '64, M1, S
Centennial. James A. Michener. Magill '75
Central and Eastern Arabia. William Gifford Palgrave. Keller (Arabia)
Centuries of Santa Fe, The. Paul Horgan. Magill '57, S
C'era una volta un planeta. L. R. Johannis. Magill SF
Ceremonies in Dark Old Men. Lonne Elder, III. Magill '70; NCTE
Ceremony in Lone Tree. Wright Morris. Magill IV, '61, MB, MC, S
Certain Notes of Instruction. George Gascoigne. Ruoff p. 90
Certain Rich Man, A. William Allen White. Keller suppl.; Smith
Certain Smile, A. Françoise Sagan. Magill '57, S
Cervantes: A Biography. William Byron. Magill '79
César Birotteau. Honoré de Balzac. Haydn p. 355; Johnson; Keller; Magill II, CE, M1&2, MC, MEUF
Cesta kolem svĕta za 80 dní (Around the World in Eighty Days). Pavel Kohout. (Based on the novel by Jules Verne.) Kienzle
Chainbearer, The. James Fenimore Cooper. Johnson; Magill III, CE, M1&2, MAF, MC; Walker
Chains. Elizabeth Baker. Drury; Sobel
Chains (Love). Theodore Dreiser. Gerber; Keller suppl.
Chairs, The. Eugene Ionesco. French; Gassner; Kienzle; Mat-

law; Shank; Sprinchorn
Chaldee Ms., The. Unknown. Keller
Chalk Circle, The. Unknown. Drury
Chalk Garden, The. Enid Bagnold. Best '55; Chapman '56; Drury; French; Kienzle; Matlaw; NCTE; Shank
Chamber Music. Arthur L. Kopit. Kienzle
Champion of the Faith, A. J. M. Callwell. Kaye
Chance. Joseph Conrad. Olfson; Ward
Chance Acquaintance, A. William Dean Howells. Carrington; Keller
Chance and Circumstance: The Draft, the War and the Vietnam Generation. Lawrence M. Baskir and William A. Strauss. Magill '79
Chance Meetings. William Saroyan. Magill '79
Chance to Shine, A. Elaine Morgan. French
Chances, The. John Fletcher. Sobel
Chandalika. Rabindranath Tagore. Matlaw
Change for the Better. Juan Ruiz de Alarcón y Mendoza. Shipley
Change of Air, A. Philip Johnson. French
Change of Skin, A. Carlos Fuentes. Magill '69, S
Change of Weather. Winfield Townley Scott. Magill '65, S
Changed Man, A. Thomas Hardy. Pinion
Changeling, The. Thomas Middleton and William Rowley. Gassner; Holzknecht; Magill III, CE, M1&2, MC, MD; Ruoff; Shank; Sobel
Changelings, The. Lee Wilson Dodd. Best '23; Drury
Changing Room, The. David Storey. Best '72; Drury; Magill '74
Changing Winds. St. John G. Ervine. Keller suppl.
Chanson de Roland see Song of Roland
Chanticleer. Edmond Rostand. Drury; Keller; Matlaw; Shank; Shipley; Sobel

Chesapeake. James A. Michener. Magill '79
Chest, The see Vidularia
Chester Plays, The. Unknown. Gassner
Chetvĕrty (The Fourth). Konstantin Simonov. Kienzle
Chevalier d'Harmental, The. Alexandre Dumas (father). Kaye
Chevalier of the Maison Rouge, The. Alexandre Dumas (father). Johnson; Kaye; Magill III, M1, MC, MEUF
Chevalier of the Splendid Crest, The. Herbert E. Maxwell. Kaye
Chez Torpe. François Billetdoux. Anderson (Va); Kienzle
Chicago. Fred Ebb, Bob Fosse and John Kander. (Based on the play by Maurine Dallas Watkins.) Best '75
Chicago. Maurine Dallas Watkins. (See also adaptation by Fred Ebb et al.) Best '26; Drury
Chicago Poems. Carl Sandburg. Magill IV, MC
Chickamauga. Glenn Tucker. Magill Ss
Chicken Feed (Wages for Wives). Guy Bolton. Best '23; Drury
Chicken Soup with Barley. Arnold Wesker. Kienzle; Matlaw
Chico the Jester. Alexandre Dumas (father). Johnson
Chief Thing, The. Nikolai N. Evreinov. Drury; Shipley
Chiefly about War Matters, by a Peaceable Man. Nathaniel Hawthorne. Gale-H
Chieko's Sky. Kotaro Takamura. Magill '79
Child Buyer, The. John Hersey. (See also adaptation by Paul Shyre.) Magill '61, S, SF
Child Buyer, The. Paul Shyre. (Based on the novel by John Hersey.) Drury; NCTE
Child Christopher. William Morris. Johnson
Child of Montmartre, The. Paul Léautaud. Magill '60, S
Child of Our Time. Michel del Castillo. Magill '59, S
Child of the Ball, The. Pedro Antonio de Alarcón. Keller
Child of the Jago, A. Arthur Morrison. Keller

Child-Who-Was-Tired, The. Katherine Mansfield. Heiney
Childe Cycle, The. Gordon R. Dickson. Magill SF
Childe Harold's Pilgrimage. George Gordon, Lord Byron. Haydn; Keller; Magill IV, MC
Childhood, Boyhood, Youth. Count Leo Tolstoy. Magill IV, MC
Childhood's End. Arthur C. Clarke. Magill SF
Children and Fools. Thomas Mann. Keller suppl.
Children at the Gate, The. Edward Lewis Wallant. Magill '65, S
Children from Their Games. Irwin Shaw. Drury
Children Is All. James Purdy. Magill '63, M1, S
Children of Darkness. Edwin Justus Mayer. Matlaw; Shank
Children of Dune. Frank Herbert. Magill '77, SF
Children of Gibeon. Sir Walter Besant. Keller
Children of God. Vardis Fisher. Magill I, CE, M1&2, MAF, MC
Children of Heracles, The see Heraclidae
Children of Herakles, The. Euripides. Feder; Gassner; Magill III, CE, M1&2, MC, MD; Reinhold; Shipley
Children of Pride, The. Robert Manson Meyers. Magill '73
Children of Sánchez, The. Oscar Lewis. Magill '62, MB, S
Children of the Abbey, The. Regina Maria Roche. Johnson; Keller
Children of the Atom. Wilmar H. Shiras. Magill SF
Children of the Center Ring. Gerald Sanford. Bonin
Children of the Ghetto. Israel Zangwill. Johnson; Keller; Magill II, CE, M1&2, MC, MEF
Children of the Moon. Martin Flavin. Drury
Children of the Soil. Henryk Sienkiewicz. Keller
Children of the Sun. Martin Green. Magill '77
Children of the World. Paul Heyse. Keller

Children of Violence: Vols. I and II. Doris Lessing. Magill '65, S

Children of Violence: Vols. III and IV. Doris Lessing. Magill '67, S

Children to Bless You. G. Sheila Donisthorpe. French

Children's Hour, The. Lillian Hellman. Best '34; Drury; Haydn (a); Matlaw; NCTE; Shank; Sobel; Sprinchorn

Child's Garden of Verses. Robert Louis Stevenson. Haydn

Child's Play. Robert Marasco. Best '69; Drury

Child's Play. David R. Slavitt. Magill '73

Child's Story, The. Charles Dickens. Hardwick CD

Childwold. Joyce Carol Oates. Magill '77

Chilly Scenes of Winter. Ann Beattie. Magill '77

Chiltern Hundreds, The. William Douglas Home. French

Chimera. John Barth. Magill '73

Chimes, The. Charles Dickens. Hardwick CD

Chimes of the Kremlin, The. Nikolai Fyodorovich Pogodin. Matlaw

Chin P'ing Mei. Hsu Wei. Haydn

Chinese Classics, The. Unknown. Haydn

Chinese Communist Party in Power, 1949-1976, The. Jacques Guillermaz. Magill '78

Chinese Foreign Policy After the Cultural Revolution, 1966-1977. Robert G. Sutter. Magill '79

Chinese Honeymoon, A. Howard Talbot and George Dance. Drinkrow

Chinese Lantern, The. Laurence Housman. Drury

Chinese Prime Minister, The. Enid Bagnold. Drury; NCTE

Chinese Wall, The. Max Frisch. Kienzle; Matlaw; Shank

Chippinge. Stanley J. Weyman. Kaye

Chippings with a Chisel. Nathaniel Hawthorne. Gale-H

Chips Are Down, The. Jean-Paul Sartre. Kienzle

Chips from a German Workshop. F. Max Müller. Keller

Chips with Everything. Arnold Wesker. Best '63; Drury; Kienzle; Magill IV, MC; Matlaw; NCTE; Ward

Chita. Lafcadio Hearn. Magill II, CE, M1&2, MAF, MAL2, MC

Chitra. Rabindranath Tagore. Shipley

Chocolate Soldier, The. Rudolf Bernauer, Leopold Jacobson, Oscar Straus. (Based on Arms and the Man by George Bernard Shaw.) Matlaw

Choephori (Libation Bearers). Aeschylus. Feder (Oresteia); Hathorn (Oresteia); Reinhold; Shank; Sobel

Choice of Books, The. Frederic Harrison. Keller

Choir Invisible, The. James Lane Allen. Johnson; Keller

Choral Lyrics. Bacchylides. Feder

Choral Lyrics. Pindar. Feder

Chorus Girl, The. Anton Chekhov. Keller suppl.

Chorus Line, A. Michael Bennett, James Kirkwood, Nicholas Dante, Marvin Hamlisch and Edward Kleban. Best '74

Chosen, The. Chaim Potok. Magill '68, M1, S

Chouans, The. Honoré de Balzac. Johnson; Kaye; Keller; Magill II, CE, M1&2, MC, MEUF

Christ and Culture. H. Richard Niebuhr. Magill CHL

Christ and Society. Charles Gore. Magill CHL

Christ and Time. Oscar Cullmann. Magill CHL

Christ in the Concrete City. Philip Turner. NCTE

Christ of Faith, The. Karl Adam. Magill CAL

Christabel. Samuel Taylor Coleridge. Haydn

Christian, The. Hall Caine. Keller

Christian Directory, A. Richard Baxter. Magill CHL

Christian Discourses. Søren Kierkegaard. Magill CHL

Christian Doctrine. J. S. Whale. Magill CHL

Christian Doctrine of Justification and Reconciliation, The. Al-

brecht Ritschl. Magill CHL
Christian Dogmatics. Hans Lassen Martensen. Magill CHL
Christian Education of Youth,
The. Pope Pius XI. Magill
CAL
Christian Faith, The. Friedrich
Schleiermacher. Magill CHL
Christian Humanism. Louis
Bouyer. Magill CAL
Christian Message in a Non-Christian World, The. Hendrik
Kraemer. Magill CHL
Christian Mysticism. William
Ralph Inge. Magill CHL
Christian Nurture. Horace Bushnell. Magill CHL
Christian Pastor, The. Washington
Gladden. Magill CHL
Christian Science. Mark Twain.
Gale-T
Christian System, The. Alexander
Campbell. Magill CHL
Christian Theology: An Ecumenical Approach. Walter Marshall
Horton. Magill CHL
Christian Theology in Outline.
William Adams Brown. Magill
CHL
Christian Understanding of God,
The. Nels Ferré. Magill CHL
Christian Woman, A. Emilia
Pardo-Bazán. Keller
Christian Year, The. John Keble.
Haydn
Christianity Among the Religions
of the World. Arnold Toynbee.
Magill '58, S
Christianity and Liberalism.
John Gresham Machen. Magill
CHL
Christianity and Paradox. Ronald
W. Hepburn. Magill CHL
Christianity As Old As the Creation. Matthew Tindal. Magill
CHL
Christianity in China, Tartary,
and Thibet. Abbé Evariste
Régis Huc. Keller
Christianity Not Mysterious. John
Toland. Magill CHL
Christianity, Past and Present.
Charles Guignebert. Keller
suppl.
Christianopolis. Johann Valentin
Andreae. Ruoff p. 448
Christians and the State. John
Coleman Bennett. Magill CHL

Christie Johnstone. Charles
Reade. Johnson; Keller
Christmas at Thompson Hall.
Anthony Trollope. Gerould
Christmas Banquet, The. Nathaniel Hawthorne. Gale-H
Christmas Carol, A. Charles
Dickens. (See also adaptation
by Shaun Sutton.) Cohen; Hardwick CD; Haydn; Magill I, CE,
M1&2, MC, MEF; Olfson; Wilson
Christmas Carol, A. Shaun Sutton. (Based on the story by
Charles Dickens.) French
Christmas Day at Kirkby Cottage.
Anthony Trollope. Gerould
Christmas Every Day and Other
Stories Told for Children.
William Dean Howells. Carrington
Christopher. Richard Pryce.
Keller
Christopher and His Kind, 1929-
1939. Christopher Isherwood.
Magill '77
Christopher Blake. Moss Hart.
Best '46; Drury
Christopher Columbus, Mariner.
Samuel Eliot Morison. Magill
'55, MB, S
Christ's Tears over Jerusalem.
Thomas Nash. Ruoff p. 309
Christus Victor. Gustaf Aulén.
Magill CHL
Chronica majora. Matthew Paris.
Magill CAL
Chronicle History of Perkin Warbeck, The see Perkin Warbeck
Chronicle of the Conquest of Granada, A. Washington Irving.
Magill III, M1, MC, MNF
Chronicle of Young Satan, The.
Mark Twain. Gale-T
Chronicles of Carlingford. Margaret Wilson Oliphant. Keller
Chronicles of Clovernook, The.
Douglas Jerrold. Keller
Chronicles of Denmark, The.
Saxo Grammaticus. Haydn
Chronicles of England, Scotland
and Ireland. Raphael Holinshed,
editor. Haydn
Chronicles of Froissart. Jean
Froissart. Haydn; Keller;
Magill III, M1, MC, MNF
Chronicles of Hell. Michel de

Ghelderode. Matlaw; Sprinchorn
Chronicles of the Schonberg-Cotta
Family. Elizabeth R. Charles.
Johnson; Kaye; Keller
Chronique. St.-John Perse.
Magill IV, '62, MB, MC, S
Chroniques d'une planète provisoire
(Reports from a Provisional
Planet). Armand Gatti. Kienzle
Chrysal. Charles Johnstone.
Keller
Chthon. Piers Anthony. Magill
SF
Chu Chin Chow. Oscar Asche and
Frederic Norton. Drinkrow;
Shipley
Chuang Tzu. Chuan Chou. Magill
WP
Chunhyang Chun. Unknown. Haydn
Chuntokyo Kyochi. Choi Jewu,
Choi Siyung, and Son Pyunghi,
et al. Haydn
Church, The. Giovanni Battista
Cardinal Montini (Pope Paul
VI). Magill CAL
Church and State. Luigi Sturzo.
Magill CAL
Church Dogmatics. Karl Barth.
Magill CHL
Church of the Word Incarnate,
The. Charles Journet. Magill
CAL
Churchills, The. A. L. Rowse.
Magill '59, S
Chushingura. Takeda Izumo.
Gassner
Cicely. Sarah B. Kennedy.
Kaye
Cicero and His Friends. Gaston
Boissier. Keller
Cicero's Orations. Marcus Tul-
lius Cicero. Downs F, FG;
Magill III, M1, MC, MNF
Cid, The. Pierre Corneille.
Cartmell; Drury; Haydn;
Keller; Magill I, CE, M1&2,
MC, MD; NBC 2; Shank;
Shipley; Sobel; Thomas
Cid, The. Unknown. Fleming;
Haydn (Poem of the Cid);
Johnson; Keller; Magill III,
CE, M1&2, MC, MP (Poem
of the Cid)
Cincinnati, The. Herman Mel-
ville. Gale-M
Cinderella. Keller (Fairy Tales)
Cingalee, The. Lionel Monckton,
Paul A. Rubens, James T.

Tanner, Adrian Ross and Percy
Greenbank. Drinkrow
Cinna. Pierre Corneille. Drury;
Gassner; Magill III, CE, M1&2,
MC, MD
Cinq-Mars. Alfred de Vigny.
Haydn; Johnson; Kaye; Keller;
Magill II, CE, M1&2, MC,
MEUF
Cipolla, La (The Onion). Aldo
Nicolaj. Kienzle
Circle, The. W. Somerset
Maugham. Best '21; Drury;
French; Gassner; Haydn; Keller
suppl.; Matlaw; NCTE; Shank;
Sobel; Sprinchorn; Ward
Circle in the Ring. Gerda Red-
lich. French
Circle of Chalk, The. Unknown.
Drury (Chalk Circle); Gassner;
Magill III, CE, M1&2, MC,
MD; Shipley (end section)
Circles: A Washington Story.
Abigail McCarthy. Magill '78
Circuit Rider, The. Edward Eg-
gleston. Johnson
Circular Staircase, The. Mary
Roberts Rinehart. (See adapta-
tion The Bat by M. R. Rine-
hart and Avery Hopwood.)
Circus Parade. Jim Tully.
Keller suppl.
Ciris. Attributed to Vergil.
Feder
Cistellaria (The Casket). Titus
Maccius Plautus. Feder
(Casket); Hathorn; Reinhold;
Shipley (Casket)
Citadel of Learning, The. James
Bryant Conant. Magill '57, S
Cities in Flight. James Blish.
Magill SF
Cities of Northern and Central
Italy. Augustus J. C. Hare.
Keller
Cities of the Plain. Marcel
Proust. (See also series title
Remembrance of Things Past.)
Haydn p. 631; Heiney
Citizen Hearst. W. A. Swanberg.
Magill '62, M1, S
Citizen of the Galaxy. Robert A.
Heinlein. Magill SF
Citizen of the World, The. Oliver
Goldsmith. Haydn; Keller
Citizen Tom Paine. Howard Fast.
Haydn
Citizens of Calais, The. Georg

Kaiser. Gassner (Burghers); Matlaw
Citoyenne Jacqueline. Sarah Tytler. Keller
City, The. Clyde Fitch. Cartmell; Drury; Matlaw; Shipley; Thomas
City. Clifford D. Simak. Magill SF
City and the Stars, The. Arthur C. Clarke. Magill SF
City Heiress, The. Mrs. Aphra Behn. (See also adaptation Dorothy by Alfred Cellier and B. C. Stephenson.) Sobel
City in History, The. Lewis Mumford. Magill '62, S
City Life. Donald Barthelme. Magill '71
City Madam, The. Philip Massinger. Gassner; Sobel
City of Dreadful Night, The. James Thomson (1834-1882). Haydn
City of God. Saint Augustine. Downs; Haydn; Keller; Magill CAL, CHL, WP
City of Joy and Confidence, The. Jacinto Benavente y Martínez. Matlaw
City of the Sun, The. Tommaso Campanella. Ruoff p. 447
City of Truth, The. Lev Lunts. Magill SF
City Wit, or, Woman Wears the Breeches, The. Richard Brome, Sobel
City Without Walls and Other Poems. Wystan Hugh Auden. Magill '71
Ciudad, La. Mario Levrero. Magill SF
Civil War. Henry de Montherlant. Kienzle
Civil War: A Narrative, The, Vol. I. Shelby Foote. Magill '59, S
Civil War: A Narrative, The, Vol. II. Shelby Foote. Magill '64, S
Civil War: Red River to Appomattox, The. Shelby Foote. Magill '75
Civilization and Its Discontents. Sigmund Freud. Downs M, FG
Claire Ambler. Booth Tarkington. Keller suppl.
Clandestine Marriage, The.

George Colman the Elder and David Garrick. Drury; Shank; Sobel
Clansman, The. Thomas Dixon. Kaye
Clara Vaughan. Richard Doddridge Blackmore. Keller
Clare Avery. Emily Sarah Holt. Kaye
Clarel. Herman Melville. Gale-M
Clarence. Booth Tarkington. Best '19; Drury; Keller suppl.; Sobel
Clarissa Furiosa. William Edward Norris. Keller
Clarissa, or, The History of a Young Lady. Samuel Richardson. Haydn; Johnson; Johnson-18th; Keller; Magill I, CE, M1&2, MC, MEF
Clark's Field. Robert Herrick. Keller
Clash of Arms, The. John Edward Bloundelle-Burton. Kaye
Classical Poetry of Japan see Manyoshiu, The
Claude's Confession. Emile Zola. Johnson
Claudia. Rose Franken. Best '40; Drury; French
Claudius the God. Robert Graves. Magill I, CE, M1&2, MC, MEF
Claverings, The. Anthony Trollope. Gerould; Keller
Clayhanger Trilogy, The. Arnold Bennett. (See also Hilda Lessways and These Twain.) Haydn; Heiney; Keller; Magill I, CE, M1&2, MC, MEF; Ward
Clea. Lawrence Durrell. Magill '61, MB, S
Clean Kill, A. Michael Gilbert. French
Cleared for Landing. Ann Darr. Magill '79
Clearing in the Woods, A. Arthur Laurents. Best '56; Drury; NCTE
Clélie. Madeleine de Scudéry. Keller
Clemenceau Case, The. Alexander Dumas (son). Johnson
Clemens of the Call. Mark Twain. Gale-T
Clementina. A. E. W. Mason. Kaye
Cleopatra. Henry Rider Haggard. Keller

Clérambard. Marcel Aymé.
Kienzle; Matlaw; Shank
Clevely Sahib. Herbert Hayens.
Kaye
Cliff-Dwellers, The. Henry B.
Fuller. Keller
Cligés. Chrétien de Troyes.
Magill III, CE, M1&2, MC,
MP
Climate of Eden, The. Moss Hart.
Best '52; Chapman '53
Climb the Greased Pole. Vincent
Longhi. Bonin
Climbers, The. Clyde Fitch.
Best '99; Drury; Lovell; Sobel
Climbing into the Roots. Reg
Saner. Magill '77
Clipper of the Clouds. Jules Verne.
Magill SF
Cloak, The. Nikolai V. Gogol.
Haydn
Clock Without Hands. Carson
McCullers. Magill '62, M1, S
Clockmaker, The. Thomas Chand-
ler Haliburton. Keller
Clockwork Man, The. E. V. Odle.
Magill SF
Clockwork Orange, A. Anthony
Burgess. Magill SF
Cloister, The. Emile Verhaeren.
Shipley
Cloister and the Hearth, The.
Charles Reade. Cohen; Good-
man; Haydn; Johnson; Kaye;
Keller; Magill I, CE, M1&2,
MC, MEF
Cloister to Court. Frances M.
Cotton Walker. Kaye
Cloned Lives. Pamela Sargent.
Magill SF
Clope. Robert Pinget. Kienzle
Closed Garden, The. Julien
Green. Heiney; Magill II,
CE, M1&2, MC, MEUF
Cloud Cuckoo Land. Naomi
Mitchinson. Ward
Cloud Forest, The. Peter Mat-
thiessen. Magill IV, '62, M1,
MB, MC, S
Cloud Howe see Scots Quair, A
Cloud of Danger: Current Real
ities of American Foreign
Policy, The. George F.
Kennan. Magill '78
Cloud of Unknowing, The. Un-
known. Magill CAL, CHL
Clouds, The. Aristophanes.
Downs F, FG; Drury; Feder;

Gassner; Hathorn; Haydn; Kel-
ler; Magill I, CE, M1&2, MC,
MD; Reinhold; Shank; Shipley;
Sobel; Wilson
Clown, The. Heinrich Böll.
Magill '66, S
Clown and His Daughter, The.
Halide Edib Adivar. Haydn
Clown on Fire. Aaron Judah.
Magill '68, S
Clutch of Circumstance, The.
Dorothy Senior. Kaye
Clutterbuck. Benn W. Levy.
Best '49; Drury; French
Coast of Bohemia, The. William
Dean Howells. Carrington
Coast of Freedom, The. Adele
Marie Shaw. Kaye
Cobbler, The. Herondas.
Hathorn (a)
Cobbler of Nimes, The. Mary
Imlay Taylor. Kaye
Cocalus. Aristophanes. Hathorn
Cochons d'inde, Les (Guinea
Pigs). Yves Jamiaque. Ki-
enzle
Cock Robin. Elmer Rice. Drury;
Shipley
Cock-a-Doodle Dandy. Sean
O'Casey. Gassner; Matlaw;
Shank; Sprinchorn
Cock-a-Doodle-Doo. Wilson
Barnes. French
Cock-a-Doodle-Doo! Herman Mel-
ville. Gale-M
Cockatoos, The. Patrick White.
Magill '76
Cockpit. Jerzy Kosinski. Magill
'76
Cocktail Party, The. T. S. Eliot.
Anderson; Best '49; Bonin;
Drury; Kienzle; Matlaw; Magill
II, CE, M1&2, MC, MD; NCTE;
Shank; Sobel; Ward
Cocteau: A Biography. Francis
Steegmuller. Magill '71
Code of Hammurabi. Hammurabi.
Downs F, FG; Haydn
Code of Victor Jallot. Edward
Childs Carpenter. Kaye
Codex Argenteus Ulfilas. Keller
Coelebs in Search of a Wife.
Hannah More. Johnson; Keller
Coeur d'Alene. Mary Hallock
Foote. Keller
Coffee-House, The. Carlo Goldoni.
Drury
Coffin for King Charles, A. C. V.

M1&2, MC, MEF
Colloquia peripatetica. John Duncan. Magill CHL
Colloquies of Erasmus, The.
  Desiderius Erasmus. Keller
Colloquy of Monos and Una.
  Edgar Allan Poe. Gale-PP
Colomba. Prosper Mérimée.
  Keller; Magill II, CE, M1&2,
  MC, MEUF
Colombe see Mademoiselle
  Colombe
Colonel Carter of Cartersville.
  Francis Hopkinson Smith.
  Johnson
Colonel Enderby's Wife. Lucas
  Malet. Keller
Colonel Kate. K. L. Montgomery.
  Kaye
Colonel's Children, The. Jules
  Supervielle. Kienzle
Colonel's Daughter, The. Charles
  King. Keller
Colonel's Opera-Cloak. Christine
  Chaplin Brush. Johnson
Colonia Felice, La. Carlo Dossi.
  Magill SF
Colonial Mind, The. Vernon
  Louis Parrington. Keller
  suppl.
Colonials, The. Allen French.
  Kaye
Color of a Great City, The. Theodore Dreiser. Gerber
Color of Darkness. James Purdy.
  Magill IV, MC, Ss
Colossus. D. F. Jones. Magill
  SF
Colossus and Other Poems, The.
  Sylvia Plath. Magill Ss
Combat in the Erogenous Zone.
  Ingrid Bengis. Magill '73
Come Back, Little Sheba. William
  Inge. Best '49; Drury; Lass
  AP; Kienzle; Matlaw; NCTE;
  Shank; Sobel
Come Back Peter. A. P. Dearsley. French
Come Blow Your Horn. Neil
  Simon. Drury; French; NCTE
Come Gentle Spring. Jesse Stuart. Magill '70
Come ladro di notte. Mauro
  Antonio Miglieruolo. Magill SF
Come, Let Us Worship. Godfrey
  Diekmann, O. S. B. Magill
  CAL
Come nasce un soggetto cinema-

tografico (How a Film Script Is
  Born). Cesare Zavattini. Kienzle
Come Out into the Sun. Robert
  Francis. Magill '67, S
Come Rack! Come Rope! Robert
  H. Benson. Kaye
Come Slowly, Eden. Norman
  Rosten. Drury
Comedian, The. Henri Ghéon.
  Shank
Comedians, The. Louis Marie
  Ann Couperus. Keller suppl.
Comedians, The. Graham Greene.
  Magill '67, S
Comedians. Trevor Griffiths.
  Best '76; Magill '77
Comedy of Asses, The see
  Asinaria
Comedy of Errors, The. William
  Shakespeare. (See also adaptation The Boys from Syracuse
  by George Abbott et al.)
  Campbell; Chute; Clark; Gassner; Guerber-SC; Halliday;
  Haydn; Keller; Lamb; McCutchan-SC; McSpadden S;
  Magill II, CE, M1&2, MC,
  MD; Ruoff; Shank; Shipley;
  Sobel
Comedy of Love, The (Love's
  Comedy). Henrik Ibsen.
  Shipley
Comedy of Mucedorus, The. Unknown. Sobel
Comic Strip. George Panetta.
  NCTE
Coming Fury, The. Bruce Catton.
  Magill '62, M1, S
Coming of Age, The. Simone de
  Beauvoir. Magill '73
Coming of Navarre, The. O. V.
  Caine. Kaye
Coming of Rain, The. Richard
  Marius. Magill '70
Coming of the King, The. Joseph
  Hocking. Kaye
Coming of the Preachers, The.
  John Ackworth. Kaye
Coming Race, The. Lord Edward
  Bulwer-Lytton. Johnson; Keller; Magill SF
Command. William McFee.
  Keller suppl.
Command Decision. William
  Wister Haines. Best '47;
  Drury; Lovell
Commemoration Masque. Gerhart

Hauptmann. Matlaw
Comment va le monde, Môssieu?
Il tourne, Môssieu.' (How's
the World, Môssieu? It's
Turning, Môssieu). François
Billetdoux. Kienzle
Commentaries. Pius II. Keller
Commentaries of Ser Pantaleone.
Annie Manning. Kaye
Commentaries on American Law.
James Kent. Keller
Commentaries on The Gallic War.
Gaius Julius Caesar. Haydn;
Keller (Caesar's); Magill III,
M1, MC, MNF
Commentaries on the Laws of Eng-
land. Sir William Blackstone.
Downs M, FG; Haydn; Keller
Commentarii rerum in ecclesia
gestarum see Acts and Monu-
ments of These Latter and
Perilous Days, Touching Mat-
ters of the Church
Commentary on Aristotle's De
anima. Saint Albert the Great.
Magill CAL
Commentary on Galatians. Rag-
nar Bring. Magill CHL
Commentary on the Apostles' Creed,
A. Rufinus of Aquileia. Magill
CAL
Commentary on the Summa theo-
logica of Saint Thomas. Saint
Cajetan. Magill CAL
Commerce of Nations, The. C.
F. Bastable. Keller
Committee-Man of "The Terror, "
A. Thomas Hardy. Pinion
Commodore Bainbridge. James
Barnes. Kaye
Commodore's Daughters, The.
Jonas Lie. Haydn; Keller
Common Lot, The. Robert Her-
rick. Smith
Common Reader, The. Virginia
Woolf. Ward
Common Sense. Thomas Paine.
Downs M, FG; Haydn
Common Story, A. Ivan Alex-
androvich Goncharov. Berry-2
Commonitory, A. Saint Vincent
of Lérins. Magill CAL, CHL
Commonwealth of Oceana. James
Harrington. Ruoff p. 447
Communism and the Conscience
of the West. Fulton J. Sheen.
Magill CAL
Communist Manifesto, The.

Karl Marx and Friedrich En-
gels. Downs M, FG; Haydn
Communist World and Ours, The.
Walter Lippmann. Magill '60,
S
Companions of Jehu, The. Alex-
andre Dumas (father). Kaye
Company. George Furth and
Stephen Sondheim. Best '69;
NCTE
Company of Death, The. Albert
L. Cotton. Kaye
Compass Flower, The. W. S.
Merwin. Magill '78
Compendious History of New Eng-
land, A. Rev. John Gorham
Palfrey. Keller (New England)
Complaint: or, Night Thoughts,
The. Edward Young. Haydn
(Night); Magill IV, MC
Complaints Containing Sundry
Small Poems of the World's
Vanity, The. Edmund Spenser.
Ruoff
Complaisant Lover, The. Graham
Greene. Best '61; Drury;
French; Kienzle; Magill '62, S;
Matlaw
Compleat Angler, The. Izaak
Walton. Haydn; Keller (Com-
plete...); Magill III, M1, MC,
MNF; Ruoff (Angler)
Complete Gentleman, The. Henry
Peacham. Ruoff
Complete Poems. Elizabeth
Bishop. Magill '70
Complete Poems. Marianne
Moore. Magill '68, M1, S
Complete Poems of Cavafy, The.
Constantine P. Cavafy. Magill
'62, S
Complete Ronald Firbank, The.
Arthur Annesley Ronald Firbank.
Magill '62, S
Complete Works of Nathanael
West, The. Nathanael West.
Magill '58, MB, S
Complexe de Philemon, Le. Jean
Bernard Luc. (See adaptation
The Happy Marriage by John
Clements.)
Composition of Four Quartets, The.
Helen Gardner. Magill '79
Comrades see Marauders (Com-
rades)
Comrades. August Strindberg.
Drury; Magill III, CE, M1&2,
MC, MD; Matlaw; Shank; Sobel

Comus. John Milton. Drury; Haydn; Hix; Magill III, CE, M1&2, MC, MD; Ruoff; Shank; Shipley; Sobel

Concept of Mind, The. Gilbert Ryle. Magill WP

Concerning Illustrious Men. Suetonius. Magill IV, MC

Concerning Isabel Carnaby. Ellen Thorneycroft Fowler. Keller

Concerning Rhetoric and Virtue. Alcuin. Magill CAL

Concerning the Revolutions of the Heavenly Spheres see De revolutionibus orbium coelestium

Concert, The. Hermann Bahr. Drury; Sobel

Conciliation with the American Colonies, Speech on see Speech on Conciliation with the Colonies

Concluding Unscientific Postscript. Søren Kierkegaard. Magill CHL, WP

Condemned, The. Stig Dagerman. Matlaw; Shank

Condemned for Mistrustfulness. Tirso de Molina. Haydn

Condemned of Altona, The. Jean-Paul Sartre. Anderson (Séquestrés); Drury; Kienzle; Matlaw

Condition humaine, La see Man's Fate

Conditionally Human. Walter M. Miller, Jr. Magill SF

Conditioned Reflexes: An Investigation on the Physiological Activity of the Cerebral Cortex. Ivan Petrovich Pavlov. Downs M, FG

Conduct Unbecoming. Barry England. Best '70; Drury

Confederacy, The. Sir John Vanbrugh. Sobel

Confessio amantis. John Gower. Haydn

Confession, A. Count Leo Tolstoy. Haydn

Confession of a Fool, The. August Strindberg. Haydn; Keller

Confession of Harry Lorrequer, The. Charles Lever. Keller (Harry)

Confessions. Jean Jacques Rousseau. Armstrong; Haydn;

Keller; Magill III, M1, MC, MNF

Confessions of a Child of the Century. Alfred de Musset. Johnson

Confessions of a Disloyal European. Jan Myrdal. Magill '69, M1, S

Confessions of a Workingman. Emile Souvestre. Johnson

Confessions of an English Opium Eater. Thomas De Quincey. Armstrong; Haydn; Keller; Magill II, CE, M1&2, MC, MNF

Confessions of Felix Krull, Confidence Man, The. Thomas Mann. Magill III, '55, CE, M1&2, MB, MC, MEUF, S

Confessions of Nat Turner, The. William Styron. Magill '68, M1, S

Confessions of Saint Augustine, The. Saint Augustine. Armstrong; Downs; Haydn; Keller; Magill III, CAL, CHL, M1, MC, MNF, WP

Confessions of Zeno. Italo Svevo. Olfson

Confidence. Henry James. Gale-J

Confidence Man, The. Herman Melville. Gale-M; Magill III, CE, M1&2, MAF, MAL4, MC; Olfson

Confidential Clerk, The. T. S. Eliot. Best '53; Chapman '54; Drury; Kienzle; Magill IV, '54, M1, MB, MC, S; Matlaw; Shank; Sobel

Conflict and Crisis: The Presidency of Harry S. Truman, 1945-1948. Robert J. Donovan. Magill '78

Conformist, The. Alberto Moravia. Heiney

Congo, The. Vachel Lindsay. Haydn (a)

Coningsby. Benjamin Disraeli. Johnson; Keller; Magill II, CE, M1&2, MC, MEF

Coniston. Winston S. Churchill. Haydn p. 637; Smith

Conjure Woman, The. Charles Waddell Chesnutt. Magill II, CE, M1&2, MAF, MAL1, MC

Conjurer's House. Stewart E. White. Kaye

Conjurors of the Dead, The.
Aeschylus. Hathorn
Connecticut Yankee in King Arthur's
Court, A. Mark Twain. Gale-
T; Goodman; Kaye (Yankee);
Keller; Magill I, CE, M1&2,
MAF, MAL5, MC, SF; More-
head
Connection, The. Jack Gelber.
Bonin; Lass AP; Kienzle;
Matlaw; Ward
Connoisseur, The. Evan S. Con-
nell, Jr. Magill '75
Conquering Hero, The. Allan
Noble Monkhouse. Matlaw
Conquest of Civilization, The.
James Henry Breasted. Keller
suppl.
Conquest of Everest, The. John
Hunt. Magill '54, S
Conquest of Granada, The. John
Dryden. Gassner; Sobel
Conquest of Plassans see Con-
quête de Plassans, La
Conquest of Rome, The. Matilde
Serao. Johnson
Conquête de Plassans, La. Emile
Zola. Keller (Rougon)
Conquistador. Archibald MacLeish.
Magill III, M1, MC, MP
Conrad in Quest of His Youth.
Leonard Merrick. Keller
suppl.
Conscience. Hector Malot. John-
son
Conscience of the Rich, The. C.
P. Snow. Magill IV, '59, MC,
S
Conscious Lovers, The. Sir
Richard Steele. Drury; Gass-
ner; Haydn; Magill II, CE,
M1&2, MC, MD; Sobel
Consciousness in Concord. Henry
David Thoreau. Magill '59,
M1, S
Conscript, The. Emile Erckmann
and Alexander Chatrian. John-
son; Kaye; Keller
Conservationist, The. Nadine
Gordimer. Magill '76
Considerations on Representative
Government. John Stuart Mill.
Keller (Representative)
Considerations on the Greatness
and Decay of the Romans.
Charles Louis de Secondat
Montesquieu. Keller (Great-
ness)

Considerations on the Principal
Events of the French Revolu-
tion. Madame de Staël.
Magill IV, MC
Consolation of Philosophy, The.
Saint Anicius Manlius Severinus
Boethius. Haydn; Keller;
Magill III, CAL, M1, MC,
MNF, WP
Constable de Bourbon, The. Wil-
liam Harrison Ainsworth.
Kaye
Constable's Tower, The. Char-
lotte Mary Yonge. Kaye
Constant Circle, The. Sara May-
field. Magill '68, S
Constant Nymph, The. Margaret
Kennedy. Haydn; Keller suppl.;
Matlaw; Sobel; Ward
Constant Wife, The. W. Somer-
set Maugham. Best '26; Drury;
French; Keller suppl.; Matlaw;
Shank; Shipley; Sobel; Ward
Constitution of Athens. Aristotle.
Haydn
Constitutional History of England.
Sir Thomas Erskine May, Baron
Farnborough. Keller (England)
Constitutional History of England.
William Stubbs. Keller (Eng-
land)
Consuelo. George Sand. John-
son; Keller; Magill I, CE,
M1&2, MC, MEUF
Consul's File, The. Paul The-
roux. Magill '78
Contarini Fleming. Benjamin
Disraeli. Johnson
Conte del Graal. Chrétien de
Troyes. Haydn
Contemplative Life, The. Juli-
anus Pomerius. Magill CAL
Contemporaries. Jules Lemaître.
Haydn
Contemporary European Thought
and Christian Faith. Albert
Dondeyne. Magill CAL
Contemporary Japanese Literature.
Anthology. Haydn
Contemporary Writers. Virginia
Woolf. Magill '67, M1, S
Contenders, The. John Wain.
Magill '59, S
Contents of the Nasks, The.
Unknown. Keller (Sacred
Books)
Contour in Time. Travis Bogard.
Magill '73

Contra celsum (Against Celsus).
Origen. Magill CAL, CHL
Contractor, The. David Storey.
Best '73; Drury; NCTE
Contrast, The. Royall Tyler.
Drury; Gassner; Lovell; Shank;
Shipley
Contributions to the Theory of
Natural Selection. Alfred Rus-
sel Wallace. Keller (Natural)
Conundrum of the Workshops, The.
Rudyard Kipling. Ward
Convention. Theodore Dreiser.
Gerber
Conversation at Night with a
Despised Man. Friedrich
Dürrenmatt. Kienzle
Conversation of Eiros and Charmion,
The. Edgar Allan Poe. Gale-
PP
Conversations of Ben Jonson with
Drummond. Ben Jonson and
William Drummond. Ruoff
p. 234
Conversations of Goethe with Eck-
ermann and Soret. Johann
Peter Eckermann. Magill IV,
MC
Cool Fire, The. Bob Shanks.
Magill '77
Cooper's Creek. Alan Moorehead.
Magill '65, S
Cooper's Hill. Sir John Denham.
Ruoff p. 108
Coorinna. Erle Wilson. Magill
'54, S
Copa (The Hostess). Attributed
to Vergil. Feder
Copper Beeches, The. Sir Arthur
Conan Doyle. Hardwick SH
Copperhead, The. Harold Fred-
eric. Magill III, CE, M1&2,
MAF, MC
Copperhead, The. Augustus
Thomas. Drury
Coquette. George Abbott and Ann
Preston Bridgers. Best '27;
Drury; Sobel
Coral, The. Georg Kaiser.
Matlaw; Shank
Cord and Crease. James Du
Mille. Johnson
Corinne. Madame de Staël.
Johnson
Coriolanus. William Shakespeare.
Campbell; Chute; Clark; Gassner;
Guerber-ST; Halliday; Haydn;
Keller; Lamb; McCutchan-ST;

McSpadden S; Magill II, CE,
M1&2, MC, MD; Ruoff; Shipley;
Sobel
Corn Is Green, The. Emlyn Wil-
liams. Best '40; Drury; Mat-
law; NCTE; Shank; Shipley
Cornada, La (Death in the Arena).
Alfonso Sastre. Kienzle
Cornelius Chronicles, The.
Michael Moorcock. Magill SF
Cornerstone, The. Zoé Olden-
bourg. Magill IV, '55, M1,
MC, S
Corpus juris civilis. Justinian.
Downs F
Corrida at San Feliu, The. Paul
Scott. Magill '65, S
Corridors of Power. C. P.
Snow. Magill '65, M1, S
Corruption in the Palace of Jus-
tice. Ugo Betti. Drury; Gass-
ner; Kienzle; Matlaw; NCTE
Corsican Brothers, The. Alex-
andre Dumas (father). Johnson;
Magill II, CE, M1&2, MC,
MEUF
Cortegiano, Il see Book of the
Courtier, The
Cosi fan tutte (Everybody's Doing
It or The School for Lovers).
Lorenzo Da Ponte. Shipley
Cosmicomics. Italo Calvino.
Magill SF
Cosmopolitans. W. Somerset
Maugham. Ward
Cosmos. Alexander von Hum-
boldt. Downs M; Haydn (Kos-
mos)
Cossacks, The. Count Leo Tol-
stoy. Haydn; Keller; Magill II,
CE, M1&2, MC, MEUF
Cost of Discipleship, The. Diet-
rich Bonhoeffer. Magill CHL
Cotter's Saturday Night, The.
Robert Burns. Haydn
Council, Reform and Reunion, The.
Hans Küng. Magill CAL
Counsellor-at-Law. Elmer Rice.
Drury; Matlaw; Shank; Shipley;
Sobel
Counsellor's Opinion. Gilbert Wake-
field. French
Count Dracula. Ted Tiller.
(Based on Dracula by Bram
Stoker.) Drury; NCTE
Count Frontenac and New France
Under Louis XIV. Francis
Parkman. Magill IV, MC

Count Julian. Walter Savage
Landor. Sobel
Count Lucanor. Juan Manuel.
Haydn
Count Oederland. Max Frisch.
Kienzle; Matlaw
Count of Monte Cristo, The.
Alexandre Dumas (father).
Cohen; Goodman; Grozier;
Haydn; Johnson; Keller; Lass
EN; Magill I, CE, M1&2,
MC, MEUF; Sobel; Wilson
Count of the Saxon Shore, The.
Alfred John Church. Kaye
Count Robert of Paris. Sir Walter
Scott. Johnson; Kaye; Keller;
McSpadden W
Count Your Blessings. Ronald
Jeans. French
Counterfeiters, The. André Gide.
Haydn; Heiney; Keller suppl.;
Lass EN; Magill I, CE, M1&2,
MC, MEUF; Olfson
Countess Cathleen, The. William
Butler Yeats. Matlaw
Countess de Charny, The. Alex-
andre Dumas (father). Johnson;
Kaye; Magill III, CE, M1&2,
MC, MEUF
Country and the City, The. Ray-
mond Williams. Magill '74
Country Doctor, The. Honoré de
Balzac. Johnson; Keller; Magill
II, CE, M1&2, MC, MEUF
Country Doctor, A. Sarah Orne
Jewett. Johnson; Magill II,
CE, M1&2, MAF, MAL3, MC
Country Girl, A. Lionel Monck-
ton, Paul A. Rubens, James T.
Tanner, Adrian Ross and Percy
Greenbank. Drinkrow
Country Girl, The. Clifford Odets.
Best '50; Drury; Kienzle; Mat-
law; NCTE; Shank
Country House, The. John Gals-
worthy. Keller; Magill III,
CE, M1&2, MC, MEF
Country of Old Men. Paul Olsen.
Magill '67, S
Country of the Blind, The. H. G.
Wells. Ward
Country of the Minotaur. Brewster
Ghiselin. Magill '71
Country of the Pointed Firs, The.
Sarah Orne Jewett. Haydn;
Keller; Magill I, CE, M1&2,
MAF, MAL3, MC; Morehead
Country Scandal, A. Anton Chek-

hov. Drury
Country Wife, The. William
Wycherley. Gassner; Haydn;
Magill II, CE, M1&2, MC,
MD; Shank; Shipley; Sobel
County Chairman, The. George
Ade. Best '99; Shipley
Coup, The. John Updike. Magill
'79
Couples. John Updike. Magill
'69, S
Courage to Be, The. Paul Tillich.
Magill WP
Course on the Positive Philosophy.
Auguste Comte. Downs M;
Magill WP
Court of Lucifer, The. Nathan
Gallizier. Kaye
Court of Pilate, The. Roe R.
Hobbs. Kaye
Court Singer, The. Frank Wede-
kind. Matlaw
Courtesan, The. Pietro Aretino.
Magill III, CE, M1&2, MC, MD
Courtier, The see Book of the
Courtier, The
Courtship of Miles Standish, The.
Henry Wadsworth Longfellow.
Haydn (a); Magill I, CE, M1&2,
MAL4, MC, MP; Smith
Courtship of Susan Bell, The.
Anthony Trollope. Gerould
Cousin Bette. Honoré de Balzac.
Johnson; Keller; Magill I, CE,
M1&2, MC, MEUF
Cousin Henry. Anthony Trollope.
Gerould
Cousin Kate. Hubert Henry
Davies. Drury
Cousin Maria see Mrs. Temper-
ly
Cousin Pons. Honoré de Balzac.
Grozier; Johnson; Keller; Magill
II, CE, M1&2, MC, MEUF
Coventry Plays, The. Unknown.
Keller
Covering End. Henry James.
Gale-J
Cowperwood Novels, The. Theo-
dore Dreiser. (See also The
Financier; The Stoic; The
Titan.) Haydn
Cox and Box. Francis Cowley
Burnand and Arthur Sullivan.
(Based on Box and Cox by John
Addison Morton.) Shipley
Coxcomb, The. Francis Beaumont
and John Fletcher. Magill III,

Cripps the Carrier.   Richard
Doddridge Blackmore.   Keller
Crisis, The.   Winston S. Churchill.
Grozier; Haydn p. 637; Keller;
Magill I, CE, M1&2, MAF,
MC
Crisis, The.   Thomas Paine.
Magill III, M1, MC, MNF
Crisis on the Left: Cold War
Politics and American Liberals,
1947-1954.   Mary Sperling Mc-
Auliffe.   Magill '79
Critias.   Plato.   Feder
Critic, The.   Baltasar Graciǎn.
Haydn
Critic, The.   Richard Brinsley
Sheridan.   Keller; Magill II,
CE, M1&2, MC, MD; Shank;
Shipley
Critical and Miscellaneous Essays
see   Critical, Historical and
Miscellaneous Essays
Critical Essays.   Roland Barthes.
Magill '73
Critical Essays of William Haz-
litt, The.   William Hazlitt.
Magill IV, MC
Critical, Historical and Miscel-
laneous Essays.   Thomas Bab-
ington Macaulay.   Haydn;
Keller (Essays)
Critical Period of American His-
tory, 1783-1789, The.   John
Fiske.   Keller
Critical Point, The.   Irving Howe.
Magill '74
Criticón, El   see   Critic, The
Critique of Judgment.   Immanuel
Kant.   Keller p. 196; Magill
WP
Critique of Practical Reason.
Immanuel Kant.   Haydn; Keller
p. 196; Magill WP
Critique of Pure Reason.   Im-
manuel Kant.   Armstrong;
Haydn; Keller; Magill III, M1,
MC, MNF, WP
Crito.   Plato.   Downs FG; Feder;
Haydn; Magill WP
Crock of Gold, The.   James
Stephens.   Haydn; Heiney;
Lass BN; Magill I, CE, M1&2,
MC, MEF; Olfson; Ward
Crocodile Fever.   Lawrence Earl.
Magill '54, S
Crome Yellow.   Aldous Huxley.
Heiney; Keller suppl.; Magill
I, CE, M1&2, MC, MEF

Cromwell.   Roger Howell, Jr.
Magill '78
Cromwell's Place in History.
Samuel Rawson Gardiner.
Keller
Crooked Man, The.   Sir Arthur
Conan Doyle.   Hardwick SH
Cross of Honor, The.   Mary
Openshaw.   Kaye
Cross of Iron, The.   Willi Hein-
rich.   Magill '57, S
Cross of Pearls, The.   Mrs.
Catherine Mary Bearne.   Kaye
Crossbowman's Story, A.   George
Millar.   Magill '55, S
Crossing, The.   Winston S.
Churchill.   Haydn p. 637
Crossroads.   James McConkey.
Magill '68, S
Crotchet Castle.   Thomas Love
Peacock.   Haydn; Keller; Magill
II, CE, M2, MC, MEF
Crown-Bride, The.   August Strind-
berg.   Matlaw
Crown of Feathers and Other
Stories, A.   Isaac Bashevis
Singer.   Magill '74
Crown of Pine, The.   Alfred John
Church.   Kaye
Crucial Conversations.   May Sar-
ton.   Magill '76
Crucial Decade, The.   Eric G.
Goldman.   Magill '57, S
Crucible, The.   Arthur Miller.
Anderson; Best '52; Bonin;
Chapman '53; Drury; Gassner;
Kienzle; Lass AP; Matlaw;
NCTE; Shank; Sprinchorn
Cruise of the Cachalot, The.
Frank T. Bullen.   Magill I,
CE, M1&2, MC, MEF
Cruise of the "Idlewild, " The.
Theodore Dreiser.   Gerber
Cruise of the Thestis, The.
Harry Collingwood.   Kaye
Crusaders, The.   Alfred John
Church.   Kaye
Crusades, The.   Zoé Oldenbourg.
Magill '67, S
Crushed Yet Conquering.   Deborah
Alcock.   Kaye
Cry of the Peacock, The   see
Ardèle
Cry, the Beloved Country.   Alan
Paton.   (See also adaptation
Lost in the Stars by Maxwell
Anderson and Kurt Weill.)
Magill II, CE, M1&2, MC,

MEUF; Olfson
Crying of Lot 49, The. Thomas
Pynchon. Magill '67, S
Cryptozoic! Brian W. Aldiss.
Magill SF
Crystal Age, A. William Henry
Hudson. Magill SF
Crystal Clear. Falkland L. Cary
and Philip King. French
Crystal World, The. J. G. Bal-
lard. Magill SF
Cuba: Island of Paradox. R.
Hart Phillips. Magill '60, S
Cuckoo in the Nest, A. Ben
Travers. French
Cudjo's Cave. John Townsend
Trowbridge. Johnson; Keller;
Magill II, CE, M1&2, MAF,
MC
Cue for Passion. Elmer Rice.
Drury
Cuirassier of Arran's, A. Claude
Bray. Kaye
Cuisine des anges, La. Albert
Husson. (See adaptation My
Three Angels by Samuel and
Bella Spewack.)
Culex. Attributed to Vergil.
Feder
Cult of Boredom, The see Art
of Being Bored, The
Cultural Contradictions of Capital-
ism, The. Daniel Bell. Magill
'77
Culture and Anarchy. Matthew
Arnold. Haydn; Keller; Magill
IV, MC
Culture Demanded by Modern Life.
E. L. Youmans, editor. Keller
Cunning of the Dove, The. Alfred
Duggan. Magill '61, S
Cuore. Edmondo de Amicis.
Keller
Cup, The. Alfred, Lord Tenny-
son. Sobel
Cup and Saucer. Gerald Savory.
French
Cupid and Psyche. Unknown.
Magill I, CE, M1&2, MC,
MEUF
Cur Deus homo. Saint Anselm
of Canterbury. Magill CAL,
CHL
Curculio. Titus Maccius Plautus.
Feder; Hathorn; Reinhold;
Shipley
Cure, The. William Carlos Wil-
liams. Kienzle

Cure for a Cuckold, A. John
Webster and William Rowley.
Sobel
Cure for Love, The. Walter
Greenwood. French
Curée, La. Emile Zola. Keller
(Rougon)
Curiosities of Literature. Isaac
Disraeli. Keller
Curiosities of Natural History.
Francis Trevelyan Buckland.
Keller
Curious Mishap, A. Carlo Gold-
oni. Drury
Curious Savage, The. John Pat-
rick. Drury; NCTE
Cursor mundi. Unknown. Haydn
Cursus theologicus. John of St.
Thomas. Magill CAL
Curtain Going Up. Gregory John-
ston. Drury
Curtmantle. Christopher Fry.
Kienzle; Matlaw
Custom and Myth. Andrew Lang.
Keller
Custom House, The. Nathaniel
Hawthorne. Gale-H
Custom of the Country, The.
John Fletcher and Philip Mas-
singer. Sobel
Custom of the Country, The.
Edith Wharton. Magill III,
CE, M1&2, MAF, MC
Cyberiad, The. Stanislaw Lem.
Magill SF
Cycle of Cathay, A. W. A. P.
Martin. Keller
Cyclops, The. Euripides. Feder;
Gassner; Hathorn; Magill III,
CE, M1&2, MC, MD; Reinhold;
Shank; Shipley; Sobel
Cymbeline. William Shakespeare.
Campbell; Chute; Clark; Gass-
ner; Guerber-SH; Halliday;
Haydn; Keller; Lamb; Mc-
Cutchan-SC; McSpadden S; Ma-
gill II, CE, M1&2, MC, MD;
Ruoff; Shipley; Sobel
Cymbeline Refinished. George
Bernard Shaw. Hardwick; Mat-
law
Cynara. Harold Marsh Harwood
and Robert Gore-Browne.
(Based on An Imperfect Lover
by R. Gore-Browne.) Best '31
Cynthia's Revels. Ben Jonson.
Shank; Shipley; Sobel
Cypresses Believe in God, The.

José María Gironella. Magill IV, '55, M1, MC, S

Cyrano de Bergerac. Edmond Rostand. Armstrong; Cartmell; Drury; Gassner; Haydn; Heiney; Keller; Magill II, CE, M1&2, MC, MD; Matlaw; NBC 2; NCTE; Shank; Shipley; Sobel; Thomas; Wilson

Cyropaedia. Xenophon. Magill IV, MC

-D-

D. H. Lawrence: A Composite Biography. Edward Nehls, editor. Magill '60, MB, S

D. L. Moody, a Worker in Souls. Gamaliel Bradford. Keller suppl. (Moody)

"Da." Hugh Leonard. Best '77

Daddy Long-Legs. Jean Webster. French; Ward

Daedalus, or, Science and the Future. J. B. S. Haldane. Keller suppl.

Daffodil Fields, The. John Masefield. Ward

Dagon. Fred Chappell. Magill '69, S

Daimon. Gianni Montanari. Magill SF

Daisy Mayme. George Kelly. Best '26; Drury

Daisy Miller. Henry James. Gale-J; Haydn; Johnson; Keller; Magill I, CE, M1&2, MAF, MAL3, MC; Morehead

Dalla Terra alle stelle. Ulisse Grifoni. Magill SF

Damaged Goods. Eugène Brieux. Drury; Haydn; Heiney; Matlaw; Sobel

Damaged Souls. Gamaliel Bradford. Keller suppl.; Magill IV, MC

Damask Cheek, The. John van Druten and Lloyd Morris. Best '42; Drury; NCTE; Shank

Damask Drum, The. Yukio Mishima. Kienzle

Dame Care. Hermann Sudermann. Haydn; Keller; Magill II, CE, M1&2, MC, MEUF

Dame Nature. André Birabeau.

Shipley

Dames at Sea. George Haimsohn, Robin Miller and Jim Wise. NCTE

Damiano. Giulio Carcano. Johnson

Damn Yankees. George Abbott, Douglass Wallop, Richard Adler and Jerry Ross. (Based on The Year the Yankees Lost the Pennant by Douglass Wallop.) NCTE

Damnable Question, The. George Dangerfield. Magill '77

Damnation of Theron Ware, The. Harold Frederic. Haydn; Johnson; Keller; Magill II, CE, M1&2, MAF, MAL2, MC

Damon and Pythias. Richard Edwards. Sobel

Damon's Epitaph see Epitaphium Damonis

Dan Monroe. William O. Stoddard. Kaye

Danaïd Tetralogy see Suppliants, The; Egyptians, The; Danaïdes

Danaïdes. Aeschylus. Hathorn

Dance in the Sun, A. Dan Jacobson. Magill '57, S

Dance of Death, The. Wystan Hugh Auden. Sobel

Dance of Death, The. August Strindberg. Gassner; Heiney; Magill II, CE, M1&2, MC, MD; Matlaw; Shipley; Sobel; Sprinchorn

Dance of Life, The. Havelock Ellis. Haydn; Keller suppl.

Dance the Eagle to Sleep. Marge Piercy. Magill '71

Dance to the Music of Time, A. Anthony Powell. Magill IV, '63, MC, S

Dance to the Music of Time: Second Movement, A. Anthony Powell. Magill IV, MC

Dancer in Darkness, A. David Stacton. Magill '63, S

Dancers at the End of Time. Michael Moorcock. Magill SF

Dancing Men, The. Sir Arthur Conan Doyle. Hardwick SH

Dancing Mistress, The. Lionel Monckton, James T. Tanner, Adrian Ross and Percy Greenbank. Drinkrow

Dancing Mothers. Edgar Selwyn and Edmund Goulding. Best '24

Dancing Years, The. Ivor Novello
and Christopher Hassall. Drink-
row
Dandy Dick. Arthur Wing Pinero.
Drury
Danger Inside. Falkland L. Cary
and Ivan Butler. French
Dangerous Acquaintances. Pierre
Choderlos de Laclos. Magill
III, CE, M1&2, MC, MEUF
Dangerous Corner. J. B. Priest-
ley. Drury; French; Matlaw;
NCTE; Ward
Daniel Deronda. George Eliot.
Halperin; Johnson; Keller;
Magill III, CE, M1&2, MC,
MEF
Daniel Martin. John Fowles.
Magill '78
Daniel Webster. Irving H. Bart-
lett. Magill '79
Daniel Webster. Henry Cabot
Lodge. Keller (Webster)
Daniela. Angel Guimerá. Drury
Dans sa candeur naive. Jacques
Deval. (See adaptation Her
Cardboard Lover by Valerie
Wingate and P. G. Wode-
house.)
Dante. Thomas Bergin. Magill
'66, S
Dante. T. S. Eliot. Magill IV,
MC
Danton. Romain Rolland. Drury;
Shipley
Danton's Death. Georg Buchner.
Gassner; Haydn; Shank; Shipley;
Sobel
Danvers Jewels, The. Mary
Cholmondeley. Keller
Daphne Laureola. James Bridie.
French; Kienzle; Matlaw
Daphnis and Chloë. Attributed to
Longus. Haydn; Keller; Magill
I, CE, M1&2, MC, MEUF
Dark and the Light, The. Elio
Vittorini. Magill '62, S
Dark As the Grave Wherein My
Friend Is Laid. Malcolm
Lowry. Magill '69, S
Dark at the Top of the Stairs,
The. William Inge. Best '57;
Drury; Magill '59, M1, S;
Matlaw; NCTE
Dark Flower, The. John Gals-
worthy. Keller
Dark Forest, The. Hugh Walpole.
Keller

Dark Hours, The. Don Marquis.
Drury
Dark Is Light Enough, The.
Christopher Fry. Best '54;
Kienzle; Magill '54, S; Matlaw
Dark Journey, The. Julien Green.
Heiney; Magill II, CE, M1&2,
MC, MEUF
Dark Labyrinth, The. Lawrence
Durrell. Magill '63, S
Dark Lady, The. Louis Auchin-
closs. Magill '78
Dark Lady of the Sonnets, The.
George Bernard Shaw. Hard-
wick; Matlaw; Ward
Dark Laughter. Sherwood Ander-
son. Keller suppl. ; Magill I,
CE, M1&2, MAF, MC
Dark Night of the Soul, The.
Saint John of the Cross. Ma-
gill CAL, CHL
Dark of the Moon. Howard
Richardson and William Berney.
Drury; Lovell; NCTE; Shank
Dark Tower, The. Alexander
Woollcott and George S. Kauf-
man. Drury
Dark Universe. Daniel F. Gal-
ouye. Magill SF
Dark Victory. George E. Brewer,
Jr. and Bertram Bloch. Drury;
NCTE
Darkening Island. Christopher
Priest. Magill SF
Darkness. Gerhart Hauptmann.
Matlaw
Darkness and Dawn. George A.
England. Magill SF
Darkness and Dawn. Frederick
W. Farrar. Kaye
Darkness at Noon. Sidney Kings-
ley. (Based on the novel by
Arthur Koestler.) Best '50;
Bonin; Drury; Kienzle; NCTE;
Shank
Darkness at Noon. Arthur Koest-
ler. (See also adaptation by
Sidney Kingsley.) Heiney; Lass
EN; Magill I, CE, M1&2, MC,
MEUF; Olfson; Ward
Darkover. Marion Zimmer Brad-
ley. Magill SF
Darling of the Gods, The. David
Belasco and John Luther Long.
Best '99; Drury; Matlaw; Shipley
Darwin and the Darwinian Revolu-
tion. Gertrude Himmelfarb.
Magill '60, S

Das Kapital see Kapital, Das
Date Kurabe Okuni Kabui. Hal-
ford
Dauber. John Masefield. Ward
Daughter of France. Hon. Vic-
toria Mary Sackville-West.
Magill '60, M1, S
Daughter of Heth, A. William
Black. Keller
Daughter of Jorio, The (La figlia
di Iorio). Gabriele D'Annunzio.
Drury; Gassner (Figlia);
Haydn; Keller; Matlaw;
Shipley; Sobel
Daughter of Silence. Morris L.
West. Magill '62, S
Daughter of Slava, The. Jan
Kollár. Haydn
Daughter of the Cathedral, The.
Gerhart Hauptmann. Matlaw
Daughter of the Legend. Jesse
Stuart. Magill '66, S
Daughter of the Manse, A. Sarah
Tytler. Kaye
Daughter of the Middle Border,
A. Hamlin Garland. Keller
suppl.
Daughter of the Regiment, The.
Jean François Alfred Bayard,
Jules H. Vernoy and Gaetano
Donizetti. Shipley
Daughter of the Samurai, A.
Etsu Inagaki Sugomoto. Keller
suppl.
Daughter of the Storage, The.
William Dean Howells. Car-
rington
Daughter to Napoleon. Constance
Wright. Magill '62, S
Daughters of Atreus. Robert
Turney. Best '36
Daughters of Pelias, The see
Peliades
Daughters of the Revolution and
Their Times. Charles C.
Coffin. Kaye
Daumier: Man of His Time.
Oliver W. Larkin. Magill '67,
S
David. D. H. Lawrence. Keller
suppl.
David and Bathsheba. Max Ehr-
mann. Drury
David and Lisa. Eleanor Perry.
(Screenplay; see adaptation by
James Reach.)
David and Lisa. James Reach.
(Based on the book by Theodore

Isaac Rubin and the screenplay
by Eleanor Perry.) Drury
David and Lisa. Theodore Isaac
Rubin. (See adaptations by
James Reach and Eleanor Per-
ry.)
David Balfour. Robert Louis
Stevenson. Haydn; Johnson;
Keller
David Blaize. E. F. Benson.
Keller
David Copperfield. Charles Dick-
ens. Armstrong; Goodman;
Grozier; Hardwick CD; Haydn;
Johnson; Keller; Lass BN; Mc-
Spadden-D; McSpadden-DH; Ma-
gill I, CE, M1&2, MC, MEF;
Wilson
David Elginbrod. George Mac-
donald. Johnson
David Garrick. Thomas William
Robertson. Drury
David Harum. Edward Noyes
Westcott. Haydn; Keller; Magill
I, CE, M1&2, MAF, MC
David Penstephen. Richard Pryce.
Keller
David Swan: A Fantasy. Nathan-
iel Hawthorne. Gale-H
David Whicher: A North American
Story. Attributed to Nathaniel
Hawthorne. Gale-H
Davy. Edgar Pangborn. Magill
SF
Davy Crockett. Frank Hitchcock
Murdoch. Lovell
Dawn. Theodore Dreiser. Ger-
ber
Dawn, a Lost Romance of the
Time of Christ. Irving Bachel-
ler. Keller suppl.
Dawn of Astronomy, The. Sir
J. Norman Lockyer. Keller
Dawn of the XIXth Century in Eng-
land, The. John Ashton.
Keller
Day, The. Giuseppe Parini.
Haydn
Day After Judgment, The. James
Blish. Magill SF
Day After Sunday, The. Hollis
Summers. Magill '69, S
Day by Day. Robert Lowell.
Magill '78
Day I Stopped Dreaming About
Barbara Steele and Other Po-
ems, The. R. H. W. Dillard.
Magill '67, S

Day in Late September, A.
Merle Miller. Magill '64, S
Day in the Death of Joe Egg, A.
Peter Nichols. Best '67;
Drury
Day Is Dark, The. Marie-Claire
Blais. Magill '68, S
Day Lincoln Was Shot, The. Jim
Bishop. Magill '55, M1, S
Day of Absence. Douglas Turner
Ward. Drury
Day of Days, A. Henry James.
Gale-J
Day of Doom, The. Michael
Wigglesworth. Keller
Day of Infamy. Walter Lord.
Magill '58, MB, S
Day of the Leopards. W. K.
Wimsatt. Magill '77
Day of the Lion, The. Giose
Rimanelli. Magill '54, S
Day of the Locust, The. Nathanael
West. Morehead
Day of the Triffids, The. John
Wyndham. Magill SF
Day of Their Wedding, The.
William Dean Howells. Car-
rington
Day Sailing. David R. Slavitt.
Magill '70
Day the Money Stopped, The.
Brendan Gill. Magill '58, S
Day the Perfect Speakers Left,
The. Leonard Nathan. Magill
'70
Day the Whores Came Out to
Play Tennis, The. Arthur
L. Kopit. Kienzle
Daybreak. Arthur Schnitzler.
Keller suppl.
Days and Nights. Konstantin
Simonov. Haydn
Days and Nights of Beebee Fen-
stermaker, The. William
Snyder. Kienzle
Days in the Trees. Marguerite
Duras. Kienzle
Days in the Yellow Leaf. William
Hoffman. Magill '59, S
Day's Mischief, The. Lesley
Storm. French
Days Near Rome. Augustus J.
C. Hare. Keller
Days of Henry Thoreau, The.
Walter Harding. Magill '66, S
Days of Jeanne d'Arc, The.
Mrs. Mary H. Catherwood.
Kaye

Days of the Commune, The.
Bertolt Brecht and Hanns Eis-
ler. Kienzle; Matlaw
Days of the Phoenix. Van Wyck
Brooks. Magill '58, S
Days of the Turbins, The. Mik-
hail Afanas'evich Bulgakov.
Matlaw
Days of Wine and Roses. J. P.
Miller. Drury
Days on a Cloud. Kjeld Abell.
Matlaw
Day's Pleasure and Other Sketches,
A. William Dean Howells.
Carrington
Days Without End. Eugene
O'Neill. Matlaw; Shipley; Sobel
Dazzling Prospect. M. J. Far-
rell and John Perry. French
De Bello Civili see On the Civil
War
De contemptu mundi. Pope Inno-
cent III. Magill CAL
De Corpore. Thomas Hobbes.
Magill WP
De corpore Christi. William of
Ockham. Magill CHL
De Doctrina Christiana. John
Milton. Ruoff
De magistro. Saint Augustine.
Magill CAL
De magnete. William Gilbert.
Haydn
De medicina. Aulus Cornelius
Celsus. Downs F
De monarchia. Dante Alighieri.
Magill CAL, CHL
De motu cordis et sanguinis see
Anatomical Exercise on the
Motion of the Heart and Blood
in Animals
De oratore see On Oratory
De potestate regia et papali.
John of Paris. Magill CAL
De primo principio. John Duns
Scotus. Magill CAL, WP
De principiis (On First Prin-
ciples). Origen. Magill CAL,
CHL, WP
De Profundis. Oscar Wilde.
Haydn, Magill IV MC; Ward
De re metallica. Georgius Agri-
cola. Haydn
De re publica. Marcus Tullius
Cicero. Downs F, FG (Re-
public); Feder
De re rustica see Agriculture
De Regno Christi. Martin Bucer.

ville. Gale-M
Death Dance. Angus Wilson.
Magill '70
Death in Life: Survivors of Hiro-
shima. Robert Jay Lifton.
Magill S
Death in Midsummer and Other
Stories. Yukio Mishima.
Magill '67, S
Death in the Family, A. James
Agee. (See also adaptation
All the Way Home by Tad
Mosel.) Magill IV, '58, M1,
MB, MC, S; Morehead
Death in the Sánchez Family, A.
Oscar Lewis. Magill '70
Death in Venice. Thomas Mann.
Heiney; Keller suppl. ; Magill
II, CE, M1&2, MC, MEUF
Death Kit. Susan Sontag. Magill
'68, S
Death of a Hero. Richard Alding-
ton. Haydn; Magill II, CE,
M1&2, MC, MEF; Ward
Death of a Nobody, The. Jules
Romains. Olfson
Death of a Salesman. Arthur
Miller. Anderson; Best '48;
Bonin; Drury; Gassner; Haydn;
Kienzle; Lass AP; Lovell;
Magill II, CE, M1&2, MC,
MD; Matlaw; NCTE; Shank;
Shipley; Sobel; Sprinchorn;
Ward
Death of Artemio Cruz, The.
Carlos Fuentes. Magill IV,
'65, M1, MC, S
Death of Bessie Smith, The.
Edward Albee. French; Kienzle
Death of Cuchulain, The. Wil-
liam Butler Yeats. Matlaw
Death of Ivan Ilyich, The. Count
Leo Tolstoy. Berry-1; Haydn;
Keller; Magill III, CE, M1&2,
MC, MEUF
Death of Lorca, The. Ian Gibson.
Magill '74
Death of Satan, The. Ronald
Frederick Henry Duncan.
Kienzle
Death of Simon Fuge, The.
Arnold Bennett. Stade p. 39
Death of the Detective, The.
Mark Smith. Magill '77
Death of the Dragon, The.
Sakyo Komatsu. Magill SF
Death of the Earth, The. J.
H. Rosny (the Elder). Magill

SF
Death of the Gods, The. Dmitri
Merejkowski. Magill I, CE,
M1&2, MC, MEUF
Death of the Governor. Leon
Kruczkowski. Anderson
(Smierć)
Death of the Heart, The. Eliza-
beth Bowen. Magill II, CE,
M1&2, MC, MEF; Ward
Death of the King's Canary, The.
Dylan Thomas and John Daven-
port. Magill '78
Death of the Laird's Jock. Sir
Walter Scott. McSpadden W
Death of the Lion, The. Henry
James. Gale-J
Death of Virgil, The. Hermann
Broch. Magill III, CE, M1&2,
MC, MEUF
Death of Wallenstein, The. Johann
Christoph Friedrich von Schil-
ler. Drury; Shank (Wallen-
stein's)
Death Ship, The. B. Traven.
Magill IV, MC
Death, Sleep & the Traveler.
John Hawkes. Magill '75
Death Takes a Holiday. Alberto
Casella. Best '29; Drury;
French; NCTE
Death's Duel. John Donne.
Magill MC; Ruoff
Death's Test Book; or, The Fool's
Tragedy. Thomas Lovell Bed-
does. Sobel
Deathtrap. Ira Levin. Best '77
Deathwatch. Jean Genet. Drury;
Gassner; Kienzle; Matlaw
Deathworld Trilogy, The. Harry
Harrison. Magill SF
Deb Clavel. Mary E. Palgrave.
Kaye
Débâcle, La see Downfall, The
Debenham's Vow. Amelia Ann
Blanford Edwards. Kaye
Debit and Credit. Gustav Frey-
tag. Haydn; Johnson; Keller;
Magill III, CE, M1&2, MC,
MEUF
Debit and Credit. August Strind-
berg. Matlaw
Debonair. Gladys Bronwyn Stern.
Keller suppl.
Deburau. Sacha Guitry. Best
'20; Drury; Shipley
Decade of Decisions: American
Policy Toward the Arab-Israeli

Keller
Delectable Mountains, The.
Struthers Burt. Keller suppl.
Delicate Balance, A. Edward
Albee. Best '66; Bonin; Drury;
Magill '67, M1, S; Matlaw;
NCTE
Deliverance. James Dickey.
Magill '71
Deliverance, The. Ellen Glasgow.
Johnson; Keller
Deliverer, The. Lady (Isabella
Augustus) Gregory. Matlaw
Delmore Schwartz: The Life of
an American Poet. James
Atlas. Magill '78
Delphine. Madame de Staël.
Haydn; Keller; Magill II, CE,
M1&2, MC, MEUF
Delta Wedding. Eudora Welty.
Magill II, CE, M1&2, MAF,
MC; Morehead
Deluge, The. Henning Berger.
Drury
Deluge, The. David Graham Phil-
lips. Keller
Delusions, Etc., of John Berry-
man. John Berryman. Magill
'73
Demes, The. Eupolis. Hathorn
(a)
Demian. Hermann Hesse. Heiney;
Magill '66, S
Demigod, The see Hero, The
Demi-Monde, The (The Outer Edge
of Society). Alexandre Dumas
(son). Drury; Shipley; Sobel
Democracy and Education. John
Dewey. Keller
Democracy and Liberty. William
Edward Hartpole Lecky. Keller
Democracy and the Organization
of Political Parties. M. Ostro-
gorski. Keller
Democracy in America. Alexis
de Tocqueville. Downs M,
FG; Haydn; Keller; Magill
IV, MC
Democracy in Europe. T. Er-
skine. Keller
Democratic Vistas. Walt Whitman.
Downs M; Magill IV, MAL5,
MC
Democritus: Fragments. Demo-
critus of Abdera. Magill WP
Demoiselle of France, A. W. J.
Eccott. Kaye
Demolished Man, The. Alfred

Bester. Magill SF
Demon: An Eastern Tale, The.
Mikhail Yurievich Lermontov.
Magill IV, MC
Demonology and Devil-Lore.
Moncure D. Conway. Keller
Demons, The. Heimito von Dod-
erer. Magill '62, S
Demonstration of Apostolic Teach-
ing, The. Saint Irenaeus.
Magill CAL
De Montfort's Squire. Frederick
Harrison. Kaye
Dennis Duval. William Makepeace
Thackeray. Mudge
Departures. Donald Justice.
Magill '74
Deputy, The. Rolf Hochhuth.
Anderson; Best '63; Drury;
Kienzle; Magill '65, M1, S;
Matlaw; NCTE
Derby Day. Alfred Reynolds and
A. P. Herbert. Drinkrow
Descent into Hell. Charles Wil-
liams. Magill IV, MC
Descent into the Maelström, A.
Edgar Allan Poe. Gale-P, PP
Descent of Man, and Selection in
Relation to Sex, The. Charles
Darwin. Keller; Magill IV, MC
Descent of Woman, The. Elaine
Morgan. Magill '73
Desert Music and Other Poems,
The. William Carlos Williams.
Magill '54, S
Desert of Love, The. François
Mauriac. Heiney
Desert Solitaire. Edward Abbey.
Magill '69, S
Desert Song, The. Sigmund Rom-
berg, Otto Harbach, Oscar
Hammerstein II and Frank
Mandel. Drinkrow
Deserted House, The. Lydia
Chukovskaya. Magill '68, S
Deserted Village, The. Oliver
Goldsmith. Haydn
Design for Living. Noel Coward.
Best '32; Cartmell; Drury;
Matlaw; Ward
Design for Murder. George Dat-
son. Drury
Desire Under the Elms. Eugene
O'Neill. Best '24; Drury;
Gassner; Haydn; Keller suppl.;
Lass AP; Lovell; Magill II,
CE, M1&2, MC, MD; Matlaw;
NCTE; Shank; Shipley; Sobel;

Discourse on the Priesthood.
Saint John Chrysostom. Magill
CAL
Discourse on Universita History.
Jacques Bénigne Bossuet.
Magill CAL
Discourses. Pietro Aretino.
Magill IV, MC
Discourses. Sir Joshua Reynolds.
Haydn; Keller
Discourses Against the Arians.
Saint Athanasius. Magill CAL
Discourses and Manual. Epictetus.
Haydn; Keller (Morals); Magill
WP
Discourses on the First Ten Books
of Titus Livius. Niccolò
Machiavelli. Haydn
Discourses on Two New Sciences.
Galileo Galilei. Haydn
Discourses upon the Existence and
Attributes of God. Stephen
Charnock. Magill CHL
Discoveries of America. Arthur
James Weise. Keller
Discovery of a New World. Joseph
Hall. Ruoff p. 448
Discovery of America, The. John
Fiske. Keller
Discovery of God, The. Henri
de Lubac, S. J. Magill CAL
Discrepancies and Apparitions.
Diane Wakoski. Magill '66,
S
Disdain Met with Disdain. Au-
gustín Moreto y Cavana.
Haydn
Disenchanted, The. Budd Schul-
berg. (See adaptation by
Budd Schulberg and Harvey
Breit.)
Disenchanted, The. Budd Schul-
berg and Harvey Breit. (Based
on the novel by Budd Schulberg.)
Best '58; Chapman '59; Drury;
NCTE
Disenchantment. C. E. Montague.
Keller suppl. ; Ward
Disowned, The. Lord Edward
Bulwer-Lytton. Johnson
Dispatches. Michael Herr. Magill
'78
Dispossessed, The. Ursula K.
Le Guin. Magill SF
Disputation of the Sacrament of
the Eucharist, A. Peter Martyr
Vermigli. Magill CHL
Disquisitiones Arithmeticae. Karl

Friedrich Gauss. Haydn
Disraeli. Louis Napoleon Parker.
Best '09; Drury; Matlaw; Ship-
ley
Disraeli, a Picture of the Victorian
Age. André Maurois. Keller
suppl.
Dissertation on the Epistles of
Phalaris. Richard Bentley.
Keller (Phalaris)
Distaff Side, The. John van
Druten. Best '34; Drury
Distant Mirror: The Calamitous
14th Century, A. Barbara W.
Tuchman. Magill '79
Distant Music, The. H. L.
Davis. Magill '58, S
Distinguished Gathering. James
Parish. French
Distinguished Provincial at Paris,
A. Honoré de Balzac. Johnson
Distracted Preacher, The. Thomas
Hardy. Pinion; Saxelby
Divan, The. Haifix Hafiz. Haydn;
Magill III, M1, MC, MP
Divers Voyages Touching the Dis-
covery of America see Hak-
luyt's Voyages
Diversions of Purley, The. John
Horne. Keller
Diversity of Creatures, A. Rud-
yard Kipling. Keller
Diverting History of John Gilpin,
The. William Cowper. Haydn
(John)
Divided Left: American Radical-
ism, 1900-1975, The. Milton
Cantor. Magill '79
Divided Soul: The Life of Gogol.
Henri Troyat. Magill '74
Divine Comedies. James Merrill.
Magill '77
Divine Comedy, The. Dante
Alighieri. Armstrong; Downs
F, FG; Fleming; Haydn; Keller;
Magill I, CAL, CE, CHL,
M1&2, MC, MP; Sabater
Divine Fire, The. May Sinclair.
Johnson; Keller; Magill II, CE,
M1&2, MC, MEF; Ward
Divine Imperative, The. Emil
Brunner. Magill CHL
Divine Institutes, The. Lucius
Caecilius Firmianus Lactantius.
Magill CAL, CHL
Divine Love and Wisdom. Emanu-
el Swedenborg. Magill III,
M1, MC, MNF

Divine Milieu, The.   Pierre
Teilhard de Chardin, S. J.
Magill CAL, CHL
Divine Names, The.   Dionysius,
the Pseudo-Areopagite.   Magill
CHL
Divine Relativity, The.   Charles
Hartshorne.   Magill CHL
Divine Words.   Ramón María del
Valle-Inclán.   Matlaw
Diving into the Wreck; Poems,
1971-1972.   Adrienne Cecile
Rich.   Magill '74
Divinity School Address, The.
Ralph Waldo Emerson.   Magill
CHL
Divino Afflante Spiritu.   Pope
Pius XII.   Magill CAL
Dmitri Roudin see Rudin
Do Androids Dream of Electric
Sheep?   Philip K. Dick.
Magill SF
Do, Lord, Remember Me.   George
Garrett.   Magill '66, M1, S
Do with Me What You Will.
Joyce Carol Oates.   Magill '74
Do You Know the Milky Way?
Karl Wittlinger.   Kienzle
Dock Brief, The.   John Mortimer.
French; Kienzle; Matlaw
Docteur Lerne, Le.   Maurice
Renard.   Magill SF
Doctor, The.   Ralph Connor.
Keller
Doctor, The.   Robert Southey.
Keller
Dr. Adriaan.   Louis Marie Anne
Couperus.   Keller suppl.
Dr. Adrian.   Deborah Alcock.
Kaye
Doctor and the Devils, The.   Dylan
Thomas.   Kienzle
Dr. Angelus.   James Bridie.
French
Doctor Antonio.   Giovanni Ruffini.
Johnson; Keller
Doctor Birch and His Young
Friends.   William Makepeace
Thackeray.   Mudge
Dr. Bloodmoney, or How We Got
Along After the Bomb.   Philip
K. Dick.   Magill SF
Dr. Breen's Practice.   William
Dean Howells.   Carrington
Doctor Brodie's Report.   Jorge
Luis Borges.   Magill '73
Dr. Bullivant.   Nathaniel Haw-
thorne.   Gale-H

Dr. Claudius.   Francis Marion
Crawford.   Keller
Dr. Dolittle Tales.   Hugh Lofting.
Haydn
Doctor Faustus.   Thomas Mann.
Haydn; Heiney; Magill II, CE,
M1&2, MC, MEUF
Doctor Faustus.   Christopher Mar-
lowe.   Drury; Haydn; Holz-
knecht; Keller; Magill II, CE,
M1&2, MC, MD; NBC 2; Ruoff;
Shank; Shipley; Sobel
Dr. Grimshawe's Secret.   Nathan-
iel Hawthorne.   Gale-H
Dr. Heidegger's Experiment.
Nathaniel Hawthorne.   Gale-H
Doctor in Spite of Himself, The
(The Physician in Spite of Him-
self).   Molière.   Drury;
Magill III, CE, M1&2, MC,
MD; Shank; Shipley; Sobel
Doctor Jekyll and Mr. Hyde.   Lu-
ella Forpaugh and George F.
Fisk.   (Based on the story by
Robert Louis Stevenson.)   Sobel
Dr. Jekyll and Mr. Hyde.   Robert
Louis Stevenson.   (See also
adaptation by Luella Forpaugh
and George F. Fisk.)   Cart-
mell; Goodman; Grozier; Haydn;
Johnson; Keller; Magill I, CE,
M1&2, MC, MEF; Magill SF
(Strange Case of...);   Wilson
Doctor Johns.   Ik Marvel.   John-
son (under Mitchell, Donald G.)
Doctor Knock, or The Triumph of
Medicine (Knock).   Jules Ro-
mains.   Drury; Matlaw; Shank
(Knock); Shipley; Sobel (Knock)
Dr. Latimer.   Clara Louise Burn-
ham.   Keller
Doctor Marigold.   Charles Dick-
ens.   Hardwick CD
Doctor Mirabilis.   James Blish.
Magill SF
Doctor Pascal.   Emile Zola.
Keller (Rougon); Magill III, CE,
M1&2, MC, MEUF
Dr. Sevier.   George W. Cable.
Keller
Doctor Thorne.   Anthony Trol-
lope.   Gerould; Haydn; Keller;
Magill II, CE, M1&2, MC,
MEF
Dr. Wortle's School.   Anthony
Trollope.   Gerould
Doctor Zhivago.   Boris Pasternak.
Grozier; Lass EN; Magill IV,

'59, M1, MB, MC, S
Doctor's Dilemma, The. George
Bernard Shaw. Hardwick;
Haydn; Heiney; Matlaw; Shank;
Shipley; Sobel; Ward
Doctor's Duty, The. Luigi Piran-
dello. Matlaw
Doctor's Legend, The. Thomas
Hardy. Pinion
Doctors of Philosophy. Muriel
Spark. Kienzle
Doctor's Wife, The. Brian Moore.
Magill '77
Doctrine and Discipline of Divorce,
The. John Milton. Ruoff
Dodsworth. Sidney Howard.
(Based on the novel by Sin-
clair Lewis.) Best '33; Drury;
Sobel
Dodsworth. Sinclair Lewis. (See
also adaptation by Sidney
Howard.) Haydn; Heiney;
Magill II, CE, M1&2, MAF,
MC
Does Anyone Else Have Something
Further to Add? R. A. Laf-
ferty. Magill SF
Dog Beneath the Skin; or, Where
Is Francis?, The. Wystan
Hugh Auden and Christopher
Isherwood. Matlaw
Dog in the Manger, The see
Gardener's Dog, The
Dog of Flanders, A. Ouida.
Haydn
Dog of Montargis, The or The
Forest of Bondy. René
Charles Guilbert Pixerécourt.
Shipley; Sobel
Dog Soldiers. Robert Stone.
Magill '75
Dog Who Wouldn't Be, The.
Farley Mowat. Magill '58,
S
Dog Years. Günter Grass.
Magill '66, M1, S
Dogmatics. Emil Brunner.
Magill CHL
Dogs of War, The. Edgar Pick-
ering. Kaye
Dolliver Romance, The. Nathaniel
Hawthorne. Gale-H
Dollmaker, The. Harriette
Simpson Arnow. Magill '54,
S
Doll's House, A. Henrik Ibsen.
Armstrong; Cartmell; Downs M;
Drury; French; Gassner; Haydn;

Heiney; Keller; Magill I, CE,
M1&2, MC, MD; Matlaw;
NBC 2; NCTE; Shank; Shipley;
Sobel; Wilson
Dolly Reforming Herself. Henry
Arthur Jones. Drury
Dolphin; For Lizzie and Harriet;
and History, The. Robert
Lowell. Magill '74
Dolphin of the Sepulchre. Gert-
rude Hollis. Kaye
Dom Casmurro. Joaquim Maria
Machado de Assis. Haydn
Domain of Arnheim, The. Edgar
Allan Poe. Gale-PP
Domains. James Whitehead.
Magill '69, S
Domaren (The Judge). Vilhelm
Moberg. Kienzle
Dombey and Son. Charles Dick-
ens. Hardwick CD; Haydn;
Johnson; Keller; McSpadden-D;
McSpadden-DH; Magill II, CE,
M1&2, MC, MEF
Domestic Relations. Frank
O'Connor. Magill '58, S
Dominique. Eugène Fromentin.
Magill III, CE, M1&2, MC,
MEUF
Don Carlos. Thomas Otway.
Sobel
Don Carlos, Infante of Spain.
Johann Christoph Friedrich von
Schiller. Gassner; Magill II,
CE, M1&2, MC, MD; Shank;
Sobel
Don Fernando; or, Variations on
Some Spanish Themes. W.
Somerset Maugham. Ward
Don Flows Home to the Sea, The.
Mikhail Sholokhov. (See also
series title The Silent Don.)
Magill II, CE, M1&2, MC,
MEUF
Don John. Jean Ingelow. Keller
Don Juan. George Gordon, Lord
Byron. Haydn; Keller; Magill
I, CE, M1&2, MC, MP
Don Juan in Hell (third act of
Man and Superman). George
Bernard Shaw. Shank
Don Juan or The Love of Geom-
etry. Max Frisch. Gassner;
Kienzle
Don Juan or The Stone Guest (Don
Juan or, The Feast with the
Statue). Molière. Gassner
(Dom Juan); Magill III, CE,

M1&2, MC, MD; Sobel
Don Juan Tenorio. José Zorrilla
y Moral. Haydn; Magill II,
CE, M1&2, MC, MD; Shipley
Don Orsino. Francis Marion
Crawford. Keller
Don Quixote de la Mancha. Miguel
de Cervantes Saavedra. (See
also adaptation Wonderful Ad-
ventures of ... by Conrad
Seiler.) Armstrong; Cohen;
Downs M, FG; Goodman;
Grozier; Haydn; Johnson; Kel-
ler; Lass EN; Magill I, CE,
M1&2, MC, MEUF; Sabater;
Wilson
Don Sebastian. John Dryden.
Sobel
Don Segundo Sombra. Ricardo
Güiraldes. Haydn; Magill II,
CE, M1&2, MAF, MC
Don Tarquinio. Baron Corvo.
Kaye (under F. W. Rolfe)
Doña Barbara. Rómulo Gallegos.
Haydn; Magill II, CE, M1&2,
MAF, MC
Doña Clarines. Serafín and
Joaquín Alvarez Quintero.
Drury
Dona Flor and Her Two Husbands.
Jorge Amado. Magill '71
Doña Luz. Juan Valera. Keller
Doña Perfecta. Benito Pérez
Galdós. Haydn; Keller; Magill
III, CE, M1&2, MC, MEUF
Doña Rosita, the Spinster, or
The Language of the Flowers.
Federico García Lorca. Matlaw
Donadieu. Fritz Hochwälder.
Kienzle
Donal Grant. George Macdonald.
Keller
Done and Dared in Old France.
Deborah Alcock. Kaye
Donelson. Herman Melville.
Gale-M
Donnerstag (Thursday). Fritz
Hochwälder. Kienzle
Donovan. Edna Lyall. Johnson;
Keller
Donovan Affair, The. Owen
Davis. Drury
Donovan's Brain. Curt Siodmak.
Magill SF
Don't Drink the Water. Woody
Allen. Drury
Don't Go Near the Water. William
Brinkley. Magill '57, S

Don't Listen Ladies. Stephen
Powys and Guy Bolton. French
Doomed City, The. Augustus
David Crake. Kaye
Doomsday Syndrome, The. John
Maddox. Magill '73
Doors of His Face, The Lamps
of His Mouth, and Other
Stories, The. Roger Zelazny.
Magill SF
Dora. Victorien Sardou. Shipley
Doris Kingsley, Child and Colonist.
Emma Rayner. Kaye
Dorothea Angermann. Gerhart
Hauptmann. Matlaw
Dorothy. Alfred Cellier and B.
C. Stephenson. (Based on The
City Heiress by Aphra Behn.)
Drinkrow
Dorothy Forster. Sir Walter
Besant. Kaye
Dorothy South. George Cary Eg-
gleston. Johnson
Dorothy Vernon of Haddon Hall.
Charles Major. Johnson
Dosia. Henri Gréville. Johnson;
Keller
Dostigaev and the Others. Máxim
Górky. Matlaw; Sobel
Dostoevsky. Nikolai Berdyaev.
Magill IV, MC
Dostoevsky. Anna Dostoevsky.
Magill '77
Dostoevsky. Joseph Frank.
Magill '77
Dostoevsky. David Magarshack.
Magill '64, M1, S
Double, The. Fyodor Mikhailovich
Dostoevskii. Berry-2
Double-Cross in the War of 1939-
1945, The. J. C. Masterman.
Magill '73
Double-Dealer, The. William
Congreve. Magill II, CE,
M1&2, MC, MD; Shipley; Sobel
Double Door. Elizabeth A. Mc-
Fadden. French
Double Helix, The. James D.
Watson. Magill '69, M1, S
Double Honeymoon. Evan S. Con-
nell, Jr. Magill '77
Double Image. Roger MacDougall
and Ted Allan. French
Double Star. Robert A. Heinlein.
Magill SF
Double Take. Ronald Jeans.
French
Double Thread, A. Ellen Thorney-

croft Fowler. Johnson
Double Witness, The. Ben Belitt.
Magill '78
Doubtful Man, The. Juan Ruiz
de Alarcón. Haydn
Doubting Heart, A. Annie Keary.
Keller
Doughgirls, The. Joseph Fields.
Best '42; Drury
Douglas. John Home. Drury;
Shipley
Dour Man, The see Dyskolos
Dover Road, The. A. A. Milne.
Best '21; Drury; French; Sobel
Down There. Joris Karl Huys-
mans. Magill III, M1, MC,
MEUF
Downfall, The. Emile Zola.
Haydn; Johnson; Kaye; Keller
(Rougon); Magill I, CE, M1&2,
MC, MEUF
Downstream. Sigfrid Siwertz.
Haydn
Downward to the Earth. Robert
Silverberg. Magill SF
Dracula. Hamilton Deane and
John L. Balderston. (Based
on the novel by Bram Stoker.)
Drury
Dracula. Bram Stoker. (See
also adaptations Count Dracula
by Ted Tiller and Dracula by
Hamilton Deane and John L.
Balderston.) Haydn; Magill
II, CE, M1&2, MC, MEF
Dragon, The. Yevgeni Lvovich
Shvarts. Matlaw
Dragon and the Raven, The.
George A. Henty. Kaye
Dragon: Fifteen Stories, The.
Evgeny Zamyatin. Magill '67,
S
Dragon in the Sea, The. Frank
Herbert. Magill SF
Dragon Masters, The. Jack
Vance. Magill SF
Dragon of Wessex, The. Percy
Dearmer. Kaye
Dragon Seed. Pearl S. Buck.
Magill I, CE, M1&2, MAF,
MC
Dragonflight. Anne McCaffrey.
Magill SF
Dragon's Wine. Borden Deal.
Magill '61, S
Dramas or Niobus. Aristophanes.
Hathorn
Dramas or The Centaur. Aristo-

phanes. Hathorn
Dramatic Monologues and Lyrics
of Browning. Robert Browning.
Magill IV, MC
Dramatic Poesy. John Dryden.
Sobel
Dramatis Personae. Robert
Browning. Magill IV, MC
Drame d' Adam et d'Eve. Un-
known. Sobel
Drapier Letters, The. Jonathan
Swift. Keller
Dreadful Dragon of Hay Hill, The.
Max Beerbohm. Ward
Dream, The see Rêve, Le
Dream, The. Herondas. Hathorn
(a)
Dream and the Deal, The. Jerre
Mangione. Magill '73
Dream Children. Horace E.
Scudder. Keller
Dream Doctor, The. Henri-René
Lenormand. Drury
Dream Girl. Elmer Rice. Best
'45; Drury; Kienzle; Matlaw;
NCTE
Dream House. Philip King and
Falkland L. Cary. French
Dream Master, The. Roger Zel-
azny. Magill SF
Dream Millennium, The. James
White. Magill SF
Dream of a Common Language:
Poems 1974-1977, The. Adri-
enne Cecile Rich. Magill '79
"Dream of a Ridiculous Man,
The." Fyodor Mikhailovich
Dostoevskii. Magill SF
Dream of Arcadia, The. Van
Wyck Brooks. Magill '59, S
Dream of Kings, A. Davis
Grubb. Magill '55, S
Dream of Kings, A. Harry Mark
Petrakis. Magill '68, M1, S
Dream of Love, A. William
Carlos Williams. Kienzle
Dream of Peter Mann, The.
Bernard Kops. Matlaw; Shank
Dream of Reason: American
Consciousness and Cultural
Achievement from Independence
to the Civil War, The. Clive
Bush. Magill '79
Dream of the Red Chamber.
Tsao Hsueh-chin. Magill III,
'59, CE, M1&2, MB, MC,
MEUF, S; Olfson
Dream of the Rood, The. Un-

known. Haydn
Dream Play, A. August Strind-
berg. Gassner; Heiney; Mat-
law; Shank; Shipley; Sobel;
Sprinchorn
Dream Weaver, The. Antonio
Buero Vallejo. Matlaw
Dreaming of the Bones, The.
William Butler Yeats. Matlaw
Dreamthorpe. Alexander Smith.
Keller
Dreamy Kid, The. Eugene
O'Neill. Matlaw
Dreht euch nicht um (Don't Turn
About). Hans-Joachim Haecker.
Kienzle
Drei Akte (Three Acts). Hans
Günter Michelsen. Kienzle
Dreiser. W. A. Swanberg.
Magill '66, S
Dreiser Looks at Russia. Theo-
dore Dreiser. Gerber
D'ri and I. Irving Bacheller.
Keller
Driftglass. Samuel R. Delany.
Magill SF
Drink. Emile Zola. Johnson;
Magill III, CE, M1&2, MC,
MEUF
Drought, The. J. G. Ballard.
Magill SF
Drovers, The. Louis Esson.
Matlaw
Drowned World, The. J. G.
Ballard. Magill SF
Drowne's Wooden Image. Nathaniel
Hawthorne. Gale-H
Drowning with Others. James
Dickey. Magill '63, S
Druid Circle, The. John van
Druten. Drury
Druidess, The. Florence Gay.
Kaye
Drums. James Boyd. Keller
suppl.; Magill I, CE, M1&2,
MAF, MC
Drums Along the Mohawk. Walter
D. Edmonds. Haydn; Magill
I, CE, M1&2, MAF, MC;
Morehead; Smith
Drums in the Night. Bertolt
Brecht. Matlaw; Sobel
Drums of Father Ned, The.
Sean O'Casey. Magill '61,
S; Matlaw
Drums of War, The. Henry De
Vere Stacpoole. Kaye
Drunkard, or, The Fallen Saved,

The. William H. Smith.
Drury; Lovell; Shipley; Sobel
Druso. Friedrich Freksa. Ma-
gill SF
Dry Salvages, The. T. S. Eliot.
Ward
Dual Autobiography, A. Will and
Ariel Durant. Magill '78
Du Barry. David Belasco. Mat-
law
Dubliners. James Joyce. Haydn;
Ward
Dubrovskii. Alexander Pushkin.
Berry-1
Duc De L'Omelette, The. Edgar
Allan Poe. Gale-PP
Duchess de Langeais, The.
Honoré de Balzac. Keller
Duchess of Hamptonshire, The.
Thomas Hardy. Pinion; Saxelby
Duchess of Malfi, The. John
Webster. Drury; Gassner;
Haydn; Holzknecht; Keller;
Magill I, CE, M1&2, MC, MD;
Ruoff; Shank; Shipley; Sobel
Duchess of Padua, The. Oscar
Wilde. Matlaw
Duchess of San Quentin. Benito
Peréz Galdós. Drury
Duchess of Wrexe; Her Decline
and Death, The. Hugh Walpole.
Keller
Ductor Dubitantium. Jeremy Tay-
lor. Magill CHL
Dudley Castle. C. G. Gardner.
Kaye
Due Preparations for the Plague,
As Well for Soul As Body.
Daniel Defoe. Johnson-18th
Duecentomila e uno (Two Hundred
Thousand and One). Salvato
Cappelli. Kienzle
Duel, The. Alexander Ivanovich
Kuprin. Haydn; Heiney; Keller
Duel of Angels. Jean Giraudoux.
Best '59; Matlaw; NCTE; Shank
Duet for Two Hands. Mary Hay-
ley Bell. French
Duino Elegies. Rainer Maria
Rilke. Magill III, M1, MC,
MP
Duke of Britain, A. Herbert E.
Maxwell. Kaye
Duke of Stockbridge, The. Edward
Bellamy. Johnson
Duke's Children, The. Anthony
Trollope. (See also series title
Parliamentary Novels.) Ger-

Earth. Emile Zola. Magill III, CE, M1&2, MC, MEUF

Earth Abides. George R. Stewart. Magill SF

Earth and Man, The. Arnold Guyoi. Keller

Earth and Stars. Randolph Edmonds. NCTE

Earth Is Ours, The. Vilhelm Moberg. Haydn

Earth-Spirit. Frank Wedekind. Matlaw; Shank; Sprinchorn

Earth Walk. William Meredith. Magill '71

Earthly Delights, Unearthly Adornments: American Writers As Image-Makers. Wright Morris. Magill '79

Earthly Paradise, The. William Morris. Haydn; Keller; Magill IV, MC

Earth's Holocaust. Nathaniel Hawthorne. Gale-H

Earthsea Trilogy, The. Ursula K. Le Guin. Magill SF

Easiest Way, The. Eugene Walter. Best '09; Cartmell; Drury; Lovell; Matlaw; Sobel

East Angels. Constance Fenimore Woolson. Keller

East Is West. Samuel Shipman and John B. Hymer. Drury

East Lynne. Mrs. Henry Wood. Cartmell; Cohen; Drury; Johnson; Keller; Shank; Shipley; Sobel

East of Eden. John Steinbeck. Magill III, CE, M1&2, MAF, MC

East to West. Arnold Toynbee. Magill '59, M1, MB, S

Easter. August Strindberg. Matlaw; Shank

Easter Parade, The. Richard Yates. Magill '77

Eastward Ho! George Chapman, Ben Jonson and John Marston. Haydn; Holzknecht; Magill III, CE, M1&2, MC, MD; Ruoff; Shipley; Sobel

Eastward in Eden. Dorothy Gardner. Best '47; Drury

Easy Money. Aleksandr Ostrovskii. Drury; Shank

Easy Money. Arnold Ridley. French

Eben Holden. Irving Bacheller. Johnson; Keller

Ebony and Ivory. Llewelyn Powys. Magill III, M1, MC, MEF

Ebony Tower, The. John Fowles. Magill '75

Ecce Homo. Sir John Robert Seeley. Keller; Magill CHL

Ecclesiastical History. Eusebius of Caesarea. Magill CHL

Ecclesiastical History. Eusebius Pamphili. Magill CAL

Ecclesiastical History of the English People. Saint Bede. Downs F; Haydn; Keller; Magill CAL, CHL

Ecclesiazusae, The (The Women in Parliament). Aristophanes. Feder; Gassner; Hathorn; Magill III, CE, M1&2, MC, MD; Reinhold; Shipley; Sobel

Echo of Passion, An. George Parsons Lathrop. Keller

Eclectic Readers. William Holmes McGuffey. Downs M

Eclogues. Vergil. Feder; Haydn; Magill IV, MC

Economic Consequences of the Peace, The. John Maynard Keynes. Downs M; Keller suppl.

Economic Interpretation of History. James Edwin Thorold Rogers. Keller

Economics and the Public Purpose. John Kenneth Galbraith. Magill '74

Economists, The. Leonard Silk. Magill '77

Eddas, The. Unknown. Haydn (Poetic Edda); Johnson

Edgar Allan Poe. George E. Woodberry. Keller (Poe)

Edge of Darkness, The. Mary Ellen Chase. Magill '58, M1, S

Edge of Day, The. Laurie Lee. Magill '61, S

Edge of Sadness, The. Edwin O'Connor. Magill '62, M1, S

Edge of the Sea, The. Rachel Carson. Magill '55, MB, S

Edge of the Storm, The. Agustín Yáñez. Magill '64, S

Edge of the Woods, The. Heather Ross Miller. Magill '65, S

Edison: A Biography. Matthew Josephson. Magill '60, MB, S

Edison: The Man Who Made the Future. Ronald W. Clark.

Magill '78
Edison's Conquest of Mars. Gar-
rett P. Serviss. Magill SF
Edith Wharton: A Biography.
R. W. B. Lewis. Magill '76
Edmund Campion. Evelyn Waugh.
Magill I, CAL, CE, M1&2,
MC, MNF
Edonians, The see Lycurgeia
Education. Herbert Spencer.
Keller
Education of Henry Adams, The.
Henry Adams. Haydn; Keller
suppl.; Magill I, CE, M1&2,
MC, MNF; Ward
Education of Mr. Surrage, The.
Allan Noble Monkhouse. Drury
Education of the World, The.
Dr. Frederick Temple. Keller
(Essays and Reviews)
Edward Fane's Rosebud. Nathaniel
Hawthorne. Gale-H
Edward, My Son. Robert Morley
and Noel Langley. Best '48;
Drury; NCTE
Edward Randolph's Portrait.
Nathaniel Hawthorne. Gale-H
Edward the Second. Christopher
Marlowe. Drury; Haydn; Holz-
knecht; Keller; Magill II, CE,
M1&2, MC, MD; NBC 3; Ruoff;
Shank; Shipley; Sobel
Edwardians, The. Ronald Gow.
French
Edwin Mullhouse, the Life and
Death of an American Writer
1943-1954 by Jeffrey Cartwright.
Steven Millhauser. Magill '73
Edwy the Fair. Augustus David
Crake. Kaye
Een Zerver Verliefd. Arthur van
Schendel. Haydn (a)
Effect of Gamma Rays on Man-
in-the-Moon Marigolds, The.
Paul Zindel. Best '69; Bonin;
Drury
Effi Briest. Theodore Fontane.
Haydn; Magill III, CE, M1&2,
MC, MEUF
Egg, The. Félicien Marceau.
Best '61; Kienzle; Shank
Egg and I, The. Betty MacDonald.
(See adaptation by Anne Coulter
Martens.)
Egg and I, The. Anne Coulter
Martens. (Based on the novel
by Betty MacDonald.) Drury
Egmont. Johann Wolfgang von

Goethe. Gassner; Magill II,
CE, M1&2, MC, MD; Shank
Egoist, The. George Meredith.
Grozier; Haydn; Johnson; Keller;
Magill I, CE, M1&2, MC,
MEF; Olfson
Egotism: or, The Bosom Serpent.
Nathaniel Hawthorne. Gale-H
Egypt and Chaldea, the Dawn of
Civilization. Gaston Maspero.
Keller (Dawn)
Egyptian Princess, An. Georg
Moritz Ebers. Kaye; Keller
Egyptians, The. Aeschylus.
Hathorn
Eh? Henry Livings. NCTE
Ehon Taikoki (The Picture Book of
the Taiko). Chikamatsu Yanagi.
Halford
Ehrengard. Isak Dinesen. Olfson
Eight Contemporary Poets. Calvin
Bedient. Magill '75
1876. Gore Vidal. Magill '77
Eighth Day, The. Thornton Wild-
er. Magill '68, M1, S
Eikon Basilike. John Gauden.
Keller
Eikonoklastes. John Milton.
Ruoff
Einer von uns (One of Us).
Michael Mansfeld. Kienzle
Einstein Intersection, The.
Samuel R. Delany. Magill SF
Eirene see Peace, The
Eirenicon, An. Edward B. Pusey.
Magill CHL
Either of One or of No One. Luigi
Pirandello. Matlaw
Either/Or. Søren Kierkegaard.
Magill WP
Ekkehard. Joseph Victor von
Scheffel. Keller
Elder Sister, The. Frank Swin-
nerton. Keller suppl.
Elder Statesman, The. T. S.
Eliot. Drury; Kienzle; Magill
IV, '60, MB, MC, S; Matlaw
Eleanor. Mrs. Humphry Ward.
Keller
Eleanor: The Years Alone.
Joseph P. Lash. Magill '73
Eleanora. Edgar Allan Poe.
Gale-PP
Elective Affinities. Johann Wolf-
gang von Goethe. Johnson;
Keller; Magill III, CE, M1&2,
MC, MEUF
Electra. Aeschylus. Jolliffe

Electra. Euripides. Cartmell; Feder; Gassner; Hathorn; Haydn; Magill I, CE, M1&2, MC, MD; Reinhold; Shank; Sobel

Electra. Jean Giraudoux. Matlaw; Shank; Sprinchorn

Electra. Hugo von Hofmannsthal. Gassner; Heiney; Matlaw

Electra. Benito Peréz Galdós. Drury (Peréz)

Electra. Sophocles. Drury; Feder; Gassner; Hathorn; Haydn; Jolliffe; Reinhold; Shank; Shipley; Sobel

Electric Kool-Aid Acid Test, The. Tom Wolfe. Magill '69, M1, S

Electricity. William Hooker Gillette. Drury

Elegantiae Latinae sermonis. Laurentius Valla. Keller

Elegies. Tibullus. Feder

Elegies of Propertius, The. Sextus Propertius. Feder; Magill IV, MC

Elegy Written in a Country Churchyard. Thomas Gray. Haydn

Elementa Chemiae. Hermann Boerhaave. Haydn

Elementa Physiologiae Corporis Humani. Albrecht von Haller. Haydn

Elementary Treatise of Chemistry see Traité élémentaire de chimie

Elements of Geometry. Euclid. Downs F, FG; Haydn

Elene. Cynewulf. Haydn

Elephant Man, The. Bernard Pomerance. Best '78

Eleusinians, The. Aeschylus. Hathorn

Eleventh Commandment, The. Anton Giulio Barrili. Johnson

Elga. Gerhart Hauptmann. Matlaw

Elgiva, Daughter of the Thegn. Ryles D. Griffiths. Kaye

Eli. Nelly Sachs. Kienzle

Elio oder eine fröhliche Gesellschaft (Elio, or A Merry Party). Otto F. Walter. Kienzle

Elizabeth. Sophie Cottin. Keller

Elizabeth and Essex. Lytton Strachey. Haydn

Elizabeth and Her German Garden.

Countess von Arnim. Keller

Elizabeth Bowen. Victoria Glendinning. Magill '79

Elizabeth of England. Ferdinand Bruckner. Matlaw

Elizabeth the Great. Elizabeth Jenkins. Magill '60, MB, S

Elizabeth the Queen. Maxwell Anderson. Best '30; Drury; Matlaw; NBC 2; NCTE; Shank; Shipley; Sobel

Elizabethans, The. John Moore. French

Elle et lui. George Sand. Keller

Ellen Terry. Roger Manvell. Magill '69, S

Ellen Terry and Bernard Shaw, a Correspondence. Dame Ellen Terry and Christopher St. John, editor. Haydn

Elm-Tree on the Mall, The see Orme du mail, L'

Elmer Gantry. Sinclair Lewis. Magill IV, MC

Eloges and Other Poems. St.-John Perse. Magill IV, '57, MB, MC, S

Elsa. Alexander Lange Kjelland. Johnson

Elsie Venner. Oliver Wendell Holmes. Cohen; Johnson; Keller

Elusive Pimpernel, The. Baroness Orczy. Kaye

Elza Pilóta, vagy a tökéletes társadalom. Mihály Babits. Magill SF

Embedding, The. Ian Watson. Magill SF

Embezzler, The. Louis Auchincloss. Magill '67, S

Emblems. Francis Quarles. Keller

Emerald Isle, The. Arthur Sullivan, Edward German and Basil Hood. Drinkrow

Emergence of Modern America, The. Allan Nevins. Keller suppl.

Emergence of the New South, 1913-1945, The. George Brown Tindall. Magill '68, S

Emerging South, The. Thomas D. Clark. Magill '62, MB, S

Emigrants, The. Johan Bojer. Keller suppl.; Magill I, CE, M1&2, MC, MEUF

Emigrants, The. José Maria

Ferreira de Castro. Magill
'63, S
Emigrants of Ahadarra, The.
William Carleton. Magill III,
CE, M1&2, MC, MEF
Emigré de Brisbane, L' (The
Emigrant from Brisbane).
Georges Schéhadé. Kienzle
Emile. Jean Jacques Rousseau.
Haydn; Keller; Magill III, M1,
MC, MEUF
Emilia Galotti. Gotthold Ephraim
Lessing. Magill III, CE, M1&2,
MC, MD
Emily Dickinson. Thomas H.
Johnson. Magill '55, S
Eminent Authors of the Nineteenth
Century. Georg Brandes.
Haydn; Keller
Eminent Victorians. Lytton
Strachey. Haydn; Keller suppl.;
Magill III, M1, MC, MNF;
Ward
Emma. Jane Austen. Halperin;
Haydn; Johnson; Keller; Magill
I, CE, M1&2, MC, MEF;
Olfson
Emmanuel: The Story of the
Messiah. William Forbes
Cooley. Kaye
Empedocles: Fragments. Empedo-
cles of Acragas. Magill WP
Emperor and Galilean. Henrik
Ibsen. Matlaw; Shipley
Emperor Jones, The. Eugene
O'Neill. Best '20; Cartmell;
Drury; Gassner; Haydn; Heiney;
Keller suppl.; Magill II, CE,
M1&2, MC, MD; Matlaw;
NCTE; Shank; Shipley; Sobel;
Thomas; Ward
Emperor of Haiti. Langston
Hughes. NCTE
Emperor of Ice-Cream, The.
Brian Moore. Magill '66, S
Emperor of the If. Guy Dent.
Magill SF
Emperor's Clothes, The. George
Tabori. Best '52; Drury
Empire Builders, The. Boris
Vian. Kienzle
Empire of Reason: How Europe
Imagined and America Realized
the Enlightenment, The. Henry
Steele Commager. Magill '78
Empress Josephine. Ernest John
Knapton. Magill '65, S
Empty Canvas, The. Alberto

Moravia. Magill '62, S
Empty House, The. Sir Arthur
Conan Doyle. Hardwick SH
En Route. Joris-Karl Huysmans.
Keller; Magill CAL
Enarrations on the Psalms. Saint
Augustine. Magill CAL
Encantadas, The. Herman Mel-
ville. Gale-M
Enchanted see In Chains
Enchanted, The (Intermezzo).
Jean Giraudoux. Best '49;
Drury; Matlaw (Intermezzo);
NCTE; Shank (Intermezzo);
Sprinchorn
Enchanted April, The. Countess
von Arnim. Keller suppl.
Enchanted Cottage, The. Arthur
Wing Pinero. Drury
Enchantment. Enrico Annibale
Butti. Johnson
Enchiridion militis christiani.
Desiderius Erasmus. Magill
CAL, CHL
Enchiridion on Faith, Hope, and
Love, The. Saint Augustine.
Magill CHL
Enchiridion symbolorum et defini-
tionum. Heinrich Joseph Dom-
inicus Denzinger. Magill CAL
Encounter with an Angry God.
Carobeth Laird. Magill '76
Encyclopaedia Britannica, The.
Keller
Encyclopédie, The. Denis Did-
erot. Downs M; Keller
End As a Man. Calder Willing-
ham. NCTE
End of It, The. Mitchell Good-
man. Magill '62, S
End of Obscenity, The. Charles
Rembar. Magill '69, S
End of Summer. S. N. Behrman.
Best '35; Drury; Matlaw; Shank;
Sprinchorn
End of the Affair, The. Graham
Greene. Olfson
End of the Battle, The. Evelyn
Waugh. Magill '62, MB, S
End of the Old Order in Rural
Europe, The. Jerome Blum.
Magill '79
End of the Road, The. John
Barth. Magill IV, MC
End of Time, The. Josef Pieper.
Magill CAL
End Zone. Don DeLillo. Magill
'73

Enderby. Anthony Burgess. Magill '69, S

Endgame. Samuel Beckett. Anderson; Drury; French; Gassner; Kienzle; Matlaw; Shank

Endicott and the Red Cross. Nathaniel Hawthorne. Gale-H

Endymion. Benjamin Disraeli. Johnson; Keller

Endymion. John Keats. Haydn

Endymion. John Lyly. Haydn; Holzknecht; Magill III, CE, M1&2, MC, MD; Ruoff; Sobel

Endymion and Phoebe. Michael Drayton. Ruoff

Enemies. Arkady Leokum. Kienzle

Enemies, a Love Story. Isaac Bashevis Singer. Magill '73

Enemies of Promise. Cyril Connolly. Ward

Enemy, The. Channing Pollock. Best '25; Drury

Enemy Camp, The. Jerome Weidman. Magill '59, S

Enemy of Idleness. William Fulwood. Ruoff p. 252

Enemy of Society, An see Enemy of the People, An

Enemy of the People, An. Henrik Ibsen. Drury; French; Haydn; Heiney; Magill II, CE, M1&2, MC, MD; Matlaw; Shank; Shipley; Sobel

Enemy to the King, An. Robert N. Stephens. Kaye

Enfants terribles, Les. Jean Cocteau. Heiney

Engelbrekt. August Strindberg. Matlaw

Engine Summer. John Crowley. Magill SF

Engineer's Thumb, The. Sir Arthur Conan Doyle. Hardwick SII

England, Its People, Polity and Pursuits. T. H. S. Escott. Keller

England Under the Stuarts. George Macaulay Trevelyan. Magill IV, MC

England Without and Within. Richard Grant White. Keller

England's Heroical Epistles. Michael Drayton. Ruoff p. 121

English and Scottish Popular Ballads. Francis James Child.

Haydn (Ballads); Keller (Ballads)

English Auden: Poems, Essays and Dramatic Writings, 1927-1939, The. Wystan Hugh Auden. Magill '79

English Constitution and Other Essays, The. Walter Bagehot. Keller

English Humorists of the Eighteenth Century, The. William Makepeace Thackeray. Keller

English Notebooks, The. Nathaniel Hawthorne. Keller; Magill IV, MAL2, MC

English Novel, The. Sidney Lanier. Keller

English Secretary, The. Angel Day. Ruoff p. 252

English Traits. Ralph Waldo Emerson. Keller

English Traveller, The. Thomas Heywood. Sobel

English Village Community, The. F. Seebohm. Keller

Enid Starkie. Joanna Richardson. Magill '75

Enlightenment: An Interpretation, The. Peter Gay. Magill '67, S

Enlightenment: An Interpretation, The, Vol. II. Peter Gay. Magill '70

Enneads. Plotinus. Haydn; Magill WP

Ennemi, L' (The Enemy). Julien Green. Kienzle

Enoch Arden. Alfred, Lord Tennyson. Haydn; Magill I, CE, M1&2, MC, MP

Enormous Changes at the Last Minute. Grace Paley. Magill '75

Enormous Room, The. E. E. Cummings. Haydn; Magill I, CE, M1&2, MAF, MC; Morehead

Enough Silliness in Every Wise Man see Even a Wise Man Stumbles

Enough Stupidity in Every Wise Man see Diary of a Scoundrel, The

Enquiry Concerning Human Understanding, An. David Hume. Magill III, M1, MC, MNF

Enquiry Concerning the Principles of Morals, An. David Hume.

Magill WP
Enter a Dragoon. Thomas Hardy.
Pinion
Enter Laughing. Carl Reiner.
(See adaptation by Joseph
Stein.)
Enter Laughing. Joseph Stein.
(Based on the novel by Carl
Reiner.) Drury; NCTE
Enter Madame. Gilda Varesi and
Dolly Byrne. Best '20; Drury
Enter Solly Gold. Bernard Kops.
Matlaw
Entertainer, The. John Osborne.
Anderson; Best '57; Drury;
Gassner; Kienzle; Matlaw;
NCTE; Shank
Entertaining Mr. Sloane. Joe
Orton. Kienzle
Enthusiasm. Ronald Knox. Magill
CAL
Eōthen. Alexander William King-
lake. Keller
Ephesiaca, The see Anthia and
Habrocomus, or The Ephesiaca
Epic of America, The. James
Truslow Adams. Haydn
Epic of Gilgamesh, The. Unknown.
Fleming; Magill III, CE, M1&2,
MC, MP
Epicoene; or The Silent Woman.
Ben Jonson. Drury; Gassner;
Holzknecht; Keller; Ruoff;
Shank; Shipley; Sobel
Epicurean, The. Thomas Moore.
Johnson; Kaye
Epidicus. Titus Maccius Plautus.
Feder; Hathorn; Reinhold;
Shipley
Epigrams, The. John Heywood.
Ruoff p. 206
Epigrams of Martial. Martial.
Downs F; Feder; Haydn;
Magill III, M1, MC, MP
Epigrams of Meleager, The.
Meleager. Magill IV, MC
Epinicia, The. Pindar. Magill
III, M1, MC, MP
Epipsychidion. Percy Bysshe
Shelley. Haydn (a)
Episode of Sparrows, An. Rumer
Godden. Magill '55, M1, S
Episodes Before Thirty. Algernon
Blackwood. Keller suppl.
Epistle of Barnabas, The. Attri-
buted to the Apostle Barnabas.
Magill CHL
Epistle to a Godson. Wystan

Hugh Auden. Magill '73
Epistle to Diognetus, The. Un-
known. Magill CAL, CHL
Epistle to Posterity, An. Mrs.
M. E. W. Sherwood. Keller
Epistle to the Philippians. Saint
Polycarp of Smyrna. Magill
CHL
Epistle to the Romans, The.
Karl Barth. Magill CHL
Epistle XXI: To the Most Clement
Emperor and Most Blessed Au-
gustus. Saint Ambrose. Magill
CAL
Epistles. Joseph Hall. Ruoff p.
253
Epistles. Saint Polycarp of
Smyrna. Magill CAL
Epistles of Horace, The. Horace.
Downs M; Feder; Haydn; Magill
IV, MC
Epistles of Saint Ignatius of Anti-
och, The. Saint Ignatius,
Bishop of Antioch. Magill CAL
Epistolae Ho-Elianae. James
Howell. Ruoff pp. 138, 253
Epistolae obscurorum virorum.
Johannes Crotus Rubeanus and
Ulrich von Hutten. Keller
Epistulae ex Ponto. Ovid. Feder
Epitaph for Dixie, An. Harry S.
Ashmore. Magill '59, S
Epitaph for George Dillon. John
Osborne and Anthony Creighton.
Best '58; Drury; Kienzle; Mat-
law; NCTE
Epitaph of a Small Winner. Joa-
quim Maria Machado de Assis.
Magill II, CE, M1&2, MAF,
MC
Epitaphium Damonis. John Milton.
Ruoff
Epithalamion. Edmund Spenser.
Haydn; Ruoff
Epodes. Horace. Feder
Epp. Axel Jensen. Magill SF
Equality. Edward Bellamy.
Keller (Looking Backward)
Equites see Knights, The
Equus. Peter Shaffer. Best '74;
Drury; Magill '75
Era of Reconstruction, 1865-1877,
The. Kenneth M. Stampp.
Magill '66, S
Erasers, The. Alain Robbe-Gril-
let. Magill '65, S
Erasmus Montanus. Ludvig Hol-
berg. Drury; Haydn; Shank

(Rasmus); Shipley (Rasmus)
Erec and Enide. Chrétien de
Troyes. Magill III, CE, M1&2,
MC, MP
Erewhon. Samuel Butler. Haydn;
Lass BN; Magill I, CE, M1&2,
MC, MEF, SF
Erewhon Revisited. Samuel Butler. Haydn; Magill SF
Erik Dorn. Ben Hecht. Haydn
(a)
Erik XIV. August Strindberg.
Matlaw
Ernest Hemingway. Carlos Baker.
Magill '70
Ernest Hemingway and His World.
Anthony Burgess. Magill '79
Ernest Maltravers. Lord Edward
Bulwer-Lytton. Johnson; Keller
Eroberung der Prinzessin Turandot, Die (The Conquest of
Princess Turandot). Wolfgang
Hildesheimer. Kienzle
Eröffnung des indischen Zeitalters
(The Inauguration of the Indian
Age). Peter Hacks. Kienzle
Esau and Jacob. Joaquim Maria
Machado de Assis. Magill
'66, S
Escapade. Roger MacDougall.
French
Escape, The. Eugène Brieux.
Drury
Escape. John Galsworthy. Best
'27; Drury; Keller suppl.;
Matlaw; Sobel
Escape of Socrates, The. Robert
Pick. Magill '54, S
Esoteric Buddhism. A. P. Sinnett. Keller
Essais. Michel Eyquem de
Montaigne. Downs M; Haydn
(Essays); Keller; Magill III,
M1, MC, MNF
Essay Concerning Human Understanding, An. John Locke.
Armstrong; Haydn; Keller;
Magill III, M1, MC, MNF,
WP
Essay of Dramatic Poesy, An.
John Dryden. Haydn; Magill
IV, MC
Essay on Catholicism, Liberalism, and Socialism. Juan
Francisco Maria de la Saludad
Donoso Cortés. Magill CAL
Essay on Criticism. Alexander
Pope. Haydn; Magill IV, MC

Essay on Human Love. Jean
Guitton. Magill CAL
Essay on Indifference in Matters
of Religion. Félicité Robert
de Lamennais. Magill CAL
Essay on Liberty see On Liberty
Essay on Man. Alexander Pope.
Haydn; Magill IV, MC
Essay on Metaphysics, An. Robin
George Collingwood. Magill
WP
Essay on Nationalism. Carlton
J. H. Hayes. Keller suppl.
(Nationalism)
Essay on the Development of
Christian Doctrine, An. John
Henry Cardinal Newman. Magill CAL
Essay on the Principle of Population, The. Thomas Robert
Malthus. Downs M, FG; Haydn
Essay Towards a New Theory of
Vision, An. George Berkeley.
Magill IV, MC
Essays. Sir Francis Bacon.
Haydn; Magill III, M1, MC,
MNF
Essays and Reviews. Keller
Essays: First and Second Series.
Ralph Waldo Emerson. Downs
M; Haydn; Keller; Magill III,
M1, MAL1, MC, MNF
Essays in Criticism. Matthew
Arnold. Haydn; Keller
Essays in Literary Interpretation.
Hamilton Wright Mabie. Keller
(Essays ... Mabie)
Essays of a Biologist. Julian
Huxley. Magill IV, MC
Essays of Aldous Huxley, The.
Aldous Huxley. Magill IV, MC
Essays of E. B. White. E. B.
White. Magill '78
Essays of Edgar Allan Poe, The.
Edgar Allan Poe. Magill IV,
MAL5, MC
Essays of Elia and Last Essays of
Elia. Charles Lamb. Haydn;
Keller; Magill III, M1, MC,
MNF
Essays of G. K. Chesterton, The.
Gilbert Keith Chesterton.
Magill IV, MC
Essays of Hamilton Wright Mabie.
Hamilton Wright Mabie. Keller
Essays of Henry David Thoreau,
The. Henry David Thoreau.
Magill IV, MAL5, MC

Essays of Max Beerbohm, The.
Max Beerbohm.   Magill IV,
MC
Essays on Heredity.   August
Weismann.   Haydn
Essays on Nature and Culture.
Hamilton Wright Mabie.   Keller
(Essays ... Mabie)
Essays on the Art of Pheidias.
Charles Waldstein.   Keller
(Pheidias)
Essays on the Intellectual Powers
of Man and Essays on the Ac-
tive Powers of the Human
Mind.   Thomas Reid.   Magill
W P
Essence of Christianity, The.
Ludwig Feuerbach.   Magill
CHL
Estate of Memory, An.   Ilona
Karmel.   Magill '70
Esther.   Jean Racine.   Drury
Esther Waters.   George Moore.
Haydn; Johnson; Keller; Magill
I, CE, M1&2, MC, MEF;
Olfson
Estrella Range, The.   Gil Vicente.
Shipley
Eté, L' (Summer).   Romain Wein-
garten.   Kienzle
Eternal City, The.   Hall Caine.
Keller
Eternal Husband, The.   Fyodor
Mikhailovich Dostoevskii.
Berry-2; Haydn; Keller suppl.
Eternal Moment, The.   E. M.
Forster.   Slade p. 227
Eternal Now, The.   Paul Tillich.
Magill '64, M1, S
Eternal Peace; a Philosophical
Proposal.   Immanuel Kant.
Downs M
Ethan Brand: A Chapter from an
Abortive Romance.   Nathaniel
Hawthorne.   Gale-H
Ethan Frome.   Owen Davis.
(Based on the novel by Edith
Wharton.)   Best '35; Drury;
NCTE; Shank; Sobel
Ethan Frome.   Edith Wharton.
(Dtc also adaptation by Owen
Davis.)   Goodman; Haydn;
Heiney; Keller; Lass AN;
Magill I, CE, M1&2, MAF,
MC; Morehead; Smith; Ward
Ethica Nicomachea.   Aristotle.
Armstrong (Nichomachean);
Downs; Feder (Nichomachean);

Haydn (Nicomachean); Magill
W P
Ethical Studies.   Francis Herbert
Bradley.   Magill WP
Ethics.   Dietrich Bonhoeffer.
Magill CHL
Ethics.   Nicolai Hartmann.   Magill
W P
Ethics.   Frank Chapman Sharp.
Magill WP
Ethics.   Benedict de Spinoza.
(See also Intellectual Love of
God, The.)   Haydn; Magill III,
M1, MC, MNF, WP
Ethics and Language.   Charles
Leslie Stevenson.   Magill WP
Etiology of Tuberculosis, The.
Robert Koch.   Downs M
Ettore Fieramosca.   Massimo
Tapparelli Azeglio.   Johnson;
Kaye
Etymologies, The.   Saint Isidore
of Seville.   Magill CAL
Eugene Aram.   Lord Edward Bul-
wer-Lytton.   Johnson; Keller;
Magill II, CE, M1&2, MC,
MEF
Eugene Onegin.   Alexander Push-
kin.   Berry-1; Haydn; Magill
II, CE, M1&2, MC, MP
Eugene Pickering.   Henry James.
Gale-J
Eugénie Grandet.   Honoré de Bal-
zac.   Armstrong; Goodman;
Haydn p. 355; Johnson; Keller;
Lass EN; Magill I, CE, M1&2,
MC, MEUF
Eumenides.   Aeschylus.   Feder
(Oresteia); Hathorn (Oresteia);
Reinhold; Shank; Sobel
Eunuch, The.   Terence.   Feder;
Gassner; Hathorn; Haydn;
Magill II, CE, M1&2, MC,
MD; Reinhold; Shank; Shipley
Euphues and His England.   John
Lyly.   Keller; Magill III, CE,
M1&2, MC, MEF; Ruoff
Euphues' Golden Legacy see
Rosalynde, or Euphues' Golden
Legacy
Euphues, the Anatomy of Wit
John Lyly.   Haydn; Keller;
Magill III, CE, M1&2, MC,
MEF; Ruoff
Eureka.   Edgar Allan Poe.
Gale-PP
Europe.   Henry James.   Gale-J
European Cities at Work.   F. C.

Howe. Keller
European Discovery of America:
The Southern Voyages, 1492-
1616, The. Samuel Eliot Mori-
son. Magill '75
Europeans, The. Henry James.
Gale-J; Keller
Eurydice (Legend of Lovers; Point
of Departure). Jean Anouilh.
Matlaw; Shank
Eustace Diamonds, The. Anthony
Trollope. Gerould
Eutaw. William Gilmore Simms.
Kaye
Euthydemus. Plato. Feder
Euthyphro. Plato. Feder; Magill
W P
Eva Trout. Elizabeth Bowen.
Magill '69, S
Evan Harrington. George Meredith.
Magill II, CE, M1&2, MC,
MEF
Evangeline. Henry Wadsworth
Longfellow. Haydn (a); Hix;
Keller; Magill I, CE, M1&2,
MAL4, MC, MP; Smith; Wilson
Evangelist, The. Alphonse
Daudet. Johnson
Eve future, L'. Count Jean
Marie Mathias Philippe Auguste
Villiers de l'Isle-Adam. Magill
SF
Eve of St. Agnes, The. John
Keats. Haydn; Magill I, CE,
M1&2, MC, MP
Eve of St. Mark, The. Maxwell
Anderson. Best '42; Drury;
NCTE
Evelina. Fanny Burney. Haydn;
Johnson; Keller; Magill II,
CE, M1&2, MC, MEF
Evelyn Inness. George Moore.
Johnson; Keller
Evelyn Nesbit and Stanford White.
Michael Macdonald Mooney.
Magill '77
Even a Wise Man Stumbles.
Aleksandr Ostrovskii. Drury
Evening of the Holiday, The.
Shirley Hazzard. Magill '67,
S
Everlasting Man, The. Gilbert
Keith Chesterton. Magill
CAL
Everlasting Mercy, The. John
Masefield. Ward
Every Man in His Humour. Ben
Jonson. Drury; Haydn;

Holzknecht; Keller; Magill II,
CE, M1&2, MC, MD; Ruoff;
Shank; Shipley; Sobel
Every Man Out of His Humour.
Ben Jonson. Magill II, CE,
M1&2, MC, MD; Ruoff; Shipley
Everybody Loves Opal. John
Patrick. Drury
Everyman. Hugo von Hofmanns-
thal. Gassner (Jedermann);
Matlaw; Shank (Jedermann)
Everyman. Unknown. Cartmell;
Drury; Gassner; Haydn; Magill
II, CE, M1&2, MC, MD; NBC
1, 2, 3; Shank; Shipley; Sobel;
Thomas
Everything in the Garden. Ed-
ward Albee. (Based on the
play by Giles Cooper.) Drury
Everything in the Garden. Giles
Cooper. (See adaptation by
Edward Albee.)
Everything That Rises Must Con-
verge. Flannery O'Connor.
Magill '66, M1, S
Eveshams, The. James B. Pat-
ton. Kaye
Evil Doers of Good, The. Jacinto
Benavente y Martínez. Heiney;
Matlaw
Evolution and Ethics. Thomas
Henry Huxley. Haydn
Evolution and Religion. Henry
Ward Beecher. Magill CHL
Evolution of Modern Germany,
The. W. H. Dawson. Keller
Evolution of Political Thought,
The. C. Northcote Parkinson.
Magill '59, SCL
Exagoge. Ezekiel. Hathorn (a)
Except the Lord. Joyce Cary.
Ward
Exception and the Rule, The.
Bertolt Brecht and Paul Des-
sau. Matlaw
Excursion. Victor Wolfson.
Best '36; Drury; Shank
Excursion, The. William Words-
worth. Haydn; Keller
Executive Privilege: A Constitu-
tional Myth. Raoul Berger.
Magill '75
Exekutionen (The Execution).
Väinö Vilhelm Järner. Kienzle
Exemplary Novels. Miguel de
Cervantes Saavedra. Magill
III, M1, MC, MEUF
Exile and the Kingdom. Albert

Face of Battle, The. John Keegan. Magill '78
Face of Defeat, The. David Pryce-Jones. Magill '74
Face to Face with Napoleon. O. V. Caine. Kaye
Faces, The see Two Faces, The
Facing Death. August Strindberg. Matlaw
Facing the Lions. Tom Wicker. Magill '74
Facts in the Case of M. Valdemar, The. Edgar Allan Poe. Gale-PP
Facts of Life, The. Roger Mac-Dougall. French
Fading Mansions see Romeo and Jeannette
Fadren see Father, The
Faerie Queene, The. Edmund Spenser. Fleming; Haydn; Keller; Magill I, CE, M1&2, MC, MP; Ruoff
Fahrenheit 451. Ray Bradbury. Magill SF
Failure of a Hero, The. Miss Mary Bramston. Kaye
Failures, The. Henri René Lenormand. Haydn; Shipley
Faint Perfume. Zona Gale. Keller suppl.
Fair and Warmer. Avery Hopwood. Shipley
Fair Barbarian. Frances Hodgson Burnett. Keller
Fair God, The. Lew Wallace. Keller
Fair Maid of Perth, The. Sir Walter Scott. Johnson; Keller; McSpadden W; Magill III, CE, M1&2, MC, MEF
Fair Maid of the West, or A Girl Worth Gold, The. Thomas Heywood. Holzknecht (Part I, II); Ruoff
Fair Margaret. Henry Rider Haggard. Kaye
Fair One with the Golden Locks; or, Harlequinade and Davy Jones's Locker. James Robinson Planché. Shipley
Fair Penitent, The. Nicholas Rowe. Shipley
Fair Prisoner, A. Morice Gerard. Kaye
Fair Rosamond. Thomas Miller. Kaye

Fair Sister, The. William Goyen. Magill '64, S
Fairly Good Time, A. Mavis Gallant. Magill Ss
Fairy Gold see Easy Money
Fairy Tale of New York, A. J. P. Donleavy. Kienzle
Fairy Tales. Jacob and Wilhelm Grimm. Haydn
Fairy Tales. Unknown. Keller
Faith and History. Reinhold Niebuhr. Magill CHL
Faith and Knowledge. John Hick. Magill CHL
Faith Gartney's Girlhood. Mrs. A. D. T. Whitney. Keller
Faith Healer, The. William Vaughan Moody. Drury; Gassner; Matlaw
Faith, Hope, and Charity. Saint Augustine. Magill CAL
Faith of a Moralist, The. Alfred Edward Taylor. Magill CHL
Faith of the Christian Church, The. Gustaf Aulén. Magill CHL
Faithful, But Not Famous. Emma Leslie. Kaye
Faithful Shepherdess, The. John Fletcher. Haydn; Holzknecht; Magill III, CE, M1&2, MC, MD; Ruoff
Falconer. John Cheever. Magill '78
Falk. Joseph Conrad. Ward
Falkland. Lord Edward Bulwer-Lytton. Johnson
Falkners of Mississippi: A Memoir, The. Murry C. Falkner. Magill '68, S
Fall, The. Albert Camus. Magill IV, '58, M1, MB, MC, S
Fall Guy, The. George Abbott and James Gleason. Best '24; Drury
Fall of a Sparrow, The. Nigel Balchin. Magill '57, S
Fall of a Titan, The. Igor Gouzenko. Magill '54, S
Fall of Athens, The. Alfred John Church. Kaye
Fall of Paris, The. Alistair Horne. Magill '67, S
Fall of the City, The. Archibald MacLeish. Sobel
Fall of the House of Hapsburg, The. Edward Crankshaw. Magill '64, S

Farce of Master Pierre Patelin, The see Master Pathelin
"Farewell, Farewell, Eugene. " John Vari. French
Farewell Party, The. Milan Kundera. Magill '77
Farewell to Arms, A. Ernest Hemingway. Goodman; Haydn; Heiney; Lass AN; Magill I, CE, M1&2, MAF, MC; Morehead; Smith; Ward
Farfetched Fables. George Bernard Shaw. Hardwick; Matlaw
Farm of Apotonga, The. J. M. Neale. Kaye
Farmer Forsworn, The. Ludwig Anzengruber. Drury
Farmer Takes a Wife, The. Frank B. Elser. Best '34
Farmers' Daughters, The. William Carlos Williams. Magill '62, S
Farmer's Glory. A. G. Street. Ward
Farmer's Wife, The. Eden Phillpotts. French
Farther Adventures of Robinson Crusoe. Daniel Defoe. Johnson-18th
Farthest North. Dr. Fridtjof Nansen. Keller
Fascinating Foundling, The. George Bernard Shaw. Hardwick
Fascinating Mr. Vanderveldt, The. Alfred Sutro. Drury
Fashion. Anna Cora (Ogden) Mowatt Ritchie. Drury; Gassner; Lovell; Shank; Shipley; Sobel
Fashion and Famine. Ann Sophia Stephens. Johnson
Fashionable Follies. Joseph Hutton. Sobel
Fashions for Men. Ferenc Molnár. Drury; Matlaw
Fasti. Ovid. Feder; Haydn
Fat City. Leonard Gardner. Magill '70
Fata Morgana. Ernö Vajda. Drury; Keller suppl.; Sobel
Fatal Boots, The. William Makepeace Thackeray. Mudge
Fatal Dowry, The. Philip Massinger. Holzknecht; Ruoff
Fatal Impact, The. Alan Moorehead. Magill '67, S
Fatal Weakness, The. George Kelly. Best '46; Drury

Fate of Father Sheehy, The. Mrs. James Sadlier. Kaye
Fate of Mansfield Humphreys, The. Richard Grant White. Keller
Fate of Reading, The. Geoffrey H. Hartman. Magill '76
Father, The. R. V. Cassill. Magill '66, S
Father, The. August Strindberg. Cartmell; Drury; Gassner; Haydn; Heiney; Magill II, CE, M1&2, MC, MD; Matlaw; Shank; Shipley; Sobel; Sprinchorn; Thomas
Father and His Fate, A. Ivy Compton-Burnett. Magill '59, S
Father and Son. Edmund Gosse. Ward
Father Giles of Ballymoy. Anthony Trollope. Gerould
Father Goriot see Père Goriot
Father of the Bride. Caroline Francke. (Based on the novel by Edward Streeter.) NCTE
Father of the Bride. Edward Streeter. (See adaptation by Caroline Francke.)
Fathers. Herbert Gold. Magill '68, S
Fathers, The. Allen Tate. Magill IV, '61, M1, MB, MC, S; Morehead
Fathers and Children. Michael Paul Rogin. Magill '76
Fathers and Sons. Ivan Turgenev. Armstrong; Berry-1; Goodman; Grozier; Haydn; Johnson; Keller; Lass EN; Magill I, CE, M1&2, MC, MEUF
Father's Day. Oliver Hailey. NCTE
Fathers of the Revolution. Philip Guedalla. Keller suppl.
Faulkner: A Biography. Joseph Blotner. Magill '75
Faust. Estanislao del Campo. Haydn
Faust. Johann Wolfgang von Goethe. Armstrong (Tragedy); Cartmell; Cohen; Drury; Gassner; Haydn; Keller; Magill I, CE, M1&2, MC, MD; Shank; Shipley; Sobel; Thomas
Faust et Yorick. Jean Tardieu. Kienzle
Fausto and Anna. Carlo Cassola.

Magill '61, S
Faute de l'Abbé Mouret, La
(The Abbé Mouret's Trans-
gression). Emile Zola. John-
son; Keller (Rougon)
Fear. Alexander Afinogenov.
Matlaw; Shipley
Fear. L. Ron Hubbard. Magill
SF
Fear and Misery of the Third
Reich. Bertolt Brecht and
Paul Dessau. Matlaw
Fear Came to Supper. Rosemary
Anne Sisson. French
Fear of Flying. Erica Jong.
Magill '74
Fearful Responsibility, A. Wil-
liam Dean Howells. Carrington
Fearful Void, The. Geoffrey
Moorehouse. Magill '75
Fearless Heart, The see
Carmelites, The
Feast at Solhoug, The. Henrik
Ibsen. Matlaw
Feast of July, The. H. E. Bates.
Magill '54, S
Feast of Lupercal, The. Brian
Moore. Magill '58, S
Feast of Reconciliation, The.
Gerhart Hauptmann. Matlaw
Feast of St. Barnabas, The.
Jesse Hill Ford. Magill '70
Feast of Words: The Triumph
of Edith Wharton, A. Cynthia
Griffin Wolff. Magill '78
Feathertop: A Moralized Legend.
Nathaniel Hawthorne. Gale-H
Federalist, The. Alexander
Hamilton, James Madison, and
John Jay. Downs M; Haydn;
Keller; Magill III, M1, MC,
MNF
Feiffer's People. Jules Feiffer.
Drury
Felix Holt, Radical. George
Eliot. Halperin; Johnson;
Kaye; Keller; Magill III, CE,
M1&2, MC, MEF
Felix O'Day. Francis Hopkinson
Smith. Keller
Fellow-Townsmen. Thomas
Hardy. Pinion; Saxelby
Fellowship of the Ring, The.
J. R. R. Tolkien. Magill
IV, CE, M2, MC
Female Imagination, The. Patricia
Meyer Spacks. Magill '76
Female Man, The. Joanna Russ.

Magill SF
Female of the Species, The.
Rudyard Kipling. Ward
Femme qui dit la vérité, Une (A
Woman Who Speaks the Truth).
André Roussin. Kienzle
Femmes savantes, Les (The
Learned Ladies). Molière.
Drury; Gassner; Keller
(Learned); Shank; Shipley; Sobel
Fen Dogs, The. Stephen Fore-
man. Kaye
Fennel and Rue. William Dean
Howells. Carrington
Fenwick's Career. Mrs. Humphry
Ward. Keller
Ferdinand, Count Fathom. Tobias
George Smollett. Johnson;
Johnson-18th/2
Festival of Our Lord of the Ship,
The. Luigi Pirandello. Mat-
law
Festus. Philip James Bailey.
Keller
Fête. Roger Vailland. Magill
'62, S
Fêtes galantes and Other Poems.
Paul Verlaine. Magill III, M1,
MC, MP
Feu sur la terre, ou le pays sans
chemin, Le (Fire on Earth, or
Land Without a Path). Fran-
çois Mauriac. Kienzle
Feuerwasser (Firewater). Ulrich
Becher. Kienzle
Few Crusted Characters, A.
Thomas Hardy. Pinion; Saxelby
Ficciones. Jorge Luis Borges.
Magill IV, '63, MC, S
Fiddler, The. Herman Melville.
Gale-M
Fiddler of the Reels, The.
Thomas Hardy. Pinion; Saxelby
Fiddler on the Roof. Joseph
Stein, Jerry Bock and Sheldon
Harnick. Best '64; NCTE
Field of Ermine. Jacinto Bena-
vente y Martínez. Matlaw
Field of Vision, The. Wright
Morris. Magill IV, MC, Ss
Fields, The. Conrad Richter.
Magill II, CE, M1&2, MAF,
MC
Fiery Dawn, The. Mary E. Col-
eridge. Kaye
Fiesta in November. Eduardo
Mallea. Magill IV, CE, M2,
MC

Fiestas. Juan Goytisolo. Magill
'61, S
Fifteen Decisive Battles of the
World. Sir E. S. Creasy.
Keller
Fifteen Sermons Preached at the
Rolls Chapel. Joseph Butler.
Magill WP
Fifth Column, The. Ernest Hem-
ingway. Magill '70
Fifth Head of Cerberus, The.
Gene Wolfe. Magill SF
5th of July, The. Lanford Wilson.
Best '77
Fifth Queen, The. Ford Madox
Ford. Kaye; Magill IV, '64,
MC, S
Fifth Season. Sylvia Regan.
Drury
Fifty-Four Forty or Fight. Emer-
son Hough. Kaye
Fifty Mark, The. Dan Sutherland.
French
Fig Tree, The. Aubrey Menen.
Magill '60, S
Fight for the Valley, The. Wil-
liam O. Stoddard. Kaye
Fight Night on a Sweet Saturday.
Mary Lee Settle. Magill '65,
S
Fighting Chance, The. Robert
William Chambers. Keller
Fighting Cock, The. Jean Anouilh.
Drury; Kienzle; Matlaw
Fighting in Cuban Waters. Ed-
ward Stratemeyer. Kaye
Fighting with Fremont. Everett
McNeil. Kaye
Figlia di Iorio, La see
Daughter of Jorio, The
Figure in the Carpet, The.
Henry James. Gale-J
Figure of Fun. Arthur Macrae.
(Based on the comedy by
André Roussin.) French
Figure of Fun. André Roussin.
(See adaptation by Arthur
Macrae.)
Figures in a Landscape. Barry
England. Magill '68, S
Figures of Thought: Speculations
on the Meaning of Poetry &
Other Essays. Howard Nem-
erov. Magill '79
File No. 113. Emile Gaboriau.
Cohen; Grozier; Johnson;
Keller; Magill I, CE, M1&2,
MC, MEUF

File on Stanley Patton Buchta, The.
Irvin Faust. Magill Ss
Filostrato, Il. Giovanni Boccaccio.
Magill IV, CE, M2, MC
Filumena Marturano. Eduardo de
Filippo. Gassner; Kienzle;
Matlaw
Final Circle of Paradise, The.
Arkady and Boris Strugatsky.
Magill SF
Final Entries, 1945: The Diaries
of Joseph Goebbels. Joseph
Goebbels. Magill '79
Final Payments. Mary Gordon.
Magill '79
Final Problem, The. Sir Arthur
Conan Doyle. Hardwick SH
Final Solutions. Frederick Seidel.
Magill '64, S
Financial Expert, The. R. K.
Narayan. Magill Ss
Financier, The. Theodore Dreis-
er. (See also The Cowperwood
Novels.) Gerber; Heiney;
Magill I, CE, M1&2, MAF,
MC
Find Your Way Home. John Hop-
kins. Best '73; Drury
Findings. Wendell Berry. Magill
'70
Fine Furniture. Theodore Dreis-
er. Gerber
Fine Madness, A. Elliot Baker.
Magill '65, S
Finest Stories of Seán O'Faoláin,
The. Seán O'Faoláin. Magill
'58, S
Fingal. James Macpherson.
Keller
Finian's Rainbow. E. Y. Harburg,
Fred Saidy and Burton Lane.
NCTE; Shipley
Finishing Touches. Jean Kerr.
Best '72; Drury
Finn Cycle, The. Unknown.
Magill III, CE, M1&2, MC,
MEF
Finnegans Wake. James Joyce.
Haydn; Heiney; Magill III, M1,
MC, MEF; Ward
Fiorello! Jerome Weidman,
George Abbott, Jerry Bock and
Sheldon Harnick. Best '59;
Bonin; NCTE
Fire and Sword in the Sudan.
Rudolf C. Slatin. Keller
Fire from Heaven. Mary Renault.
Magill '70

Fire in the Lake. Frances
FitzGerald. Magill '73
Fire Next Time, The. James
Baldwin. Magill '64, M1, S
Fire-Raisers, The. Marris
Murray. Magill '54, S
Fire Screen, The. James Mer-
rill. Magill '71
Fire Worship. Nathaniel Haw-
thorne. Gale-H
Firebrand, The. Edwin Justus
Mayer. Best '24; Drury
Firebugs, The see Biedermann
and the Firebugs
Fires on the Plain. Shohei Ooka.
Magill '58, S
Firing Line, The. Robert Wil-
liam Chambers. Keller
Firmament of Time, The. Loren
Eiseley. Magill '61, S
First Americans, The. Thomas
Jefferson Wertenbaker. Keller
suppl.
First and Last Dinner, The.
Attributed to Nathaniel Haw-
thorne. Gale-H
First Apology, The. Saint Justin
Martyr. Magill CAL, CHL
First Blood. David Morrell.
Magill '73
First Blood: The Story of Fort
Sumter. W. A. Swanberg.
Magill '59, S
First Catechetical Instruction,
The. Saint Augustine. Magill
CAL
First Circle, The. Aleksandr
I. Solzhenitsyn. Magill '69,
M1, S
First Countess of Wessex, The.
Thomas Hardy. Pinion; Saxelby
First Day of Friday, The.
Honor Tracy. Magill '64, S
First Epistle of Clement to the
Corinthians, The. Saint
Clement of Rome. Magill CHL
First Fish, The. Frank Tarloff.
French
First Gentleman, The. Norman
Ginsbury. French
First Lady. Katharine Dayton
and George S. Kaufman.
Best '35; Drury; NCTE; Sobel
First Lady of the South. Ishbel
Ross. Magill '59, S
First Legion, The. Emmet G.
Lavery. Shank
First Love. Ivan Turgenev.

Berry-1
First Man, The. Eugene O'Neill.
Matlaw
First Men in the Moon, The.
H. G. Wells. Magill SF; Ward
First Monday in October. Jerome
Lawrence and Robert E. Lee.
Best '78
First Mrs. Fraser, The. St.
John G. Ervine. Best '29;
Drury; Matlaw; Sobel
First on Mars. Rex Gordon.
Magill SF
First Principles. Herbert Spencer.
Magill WP
First Violin, The. Jessie Fother-
gill. Johnson; Keller
First Warning, The. August
Strindberg. Matlaw
First Year, The. Frank Craven.
Best '20; Drury
First, You Cry. Betty Rollin.
Magill '77
Firstborn, The. Christopher Fry.
Kienzle; Matlaw; Shank
Fisher Maiden, The. Bjørnstjerne
Bjørnson. Johnson; Keller;
Magill II, CE, M1&2, MC,
MEUF
Fisherman's Revenge, The. Un-
known. Gassner
Fishermen, The see Dictyulci
Fishes, Birds and Sons of Men.
Jesse Hill Ford. Magill '68, S
Fishmonger's Fiddle. A. E.
Coppard. Keller suppl.
Fiston, Le. Robert Pinget. (See
his adaptation Dead Letter.)
Fit to Print. Alastair M. Dun-
nett. French
Fitz-Boodle Papers. William
Makepeace Thackeray. Mudge
Five Finger Exercise. Peter
Shaffer. Best '59; Drury;
French; Kienzle; Matlaw; NCTE
Five Orange Pips, The. Sir
Arthur Conan Doyle. Hardwick
SH
Five Smooth Stones. Ann Fair-
bairn. Magill '67, S
Five Stages of Grief, The. Linda
Pastan. Magill '79
Five-Star Final. Louis Weitzen-
korn. Best '30; Drury
Five Theological Orations. Saint
Gregory of Nazianzus. Magill
CAL, CHL
Five Women Who Loved Love.

Ibara Saikaku. Magill III, CE, M1&2, MC, MEUF
Fixed Period, The. Anthony Trollope. Gerould
Fixer, The. Bernard Malamud. Magill '67, M1, S
Flame of Fire, A. Joseph Hocking. Kaye
Flame of Life, The. Gabriele D'Annunzio. Keller
Flame Trees of Thika, The. Elspeth Huxley. Magill '60, S
Flare Path. Terence Rattigan. French
Flashpoint. R. F. Delderfield. French
Flatland: A Romance of Many Dimensions. Edwin A. Abbott. Magill SF
Flaubert. Enid Starkie. Magill '68, M1, S
Flea in Her Ear, A. Georges Feydeau. Drury; NCTE
Fleur de cactus. Pierre Barillet and Jean-Pierre Gredy. (See adaptation Cactus Flower by Abe Burrows.)
Fleur-de-camp. A. G. Campbell. Kaye
Flickerbridge. Henry James. Gale-J
Flies, The. Mariano Azuela. Magill IV, MC
Flies, The. Jean-Paul Sartre. Drury; Gassner; Magill IV, MC; Matlaw; NCTE; Shank; Shipley
Flight from the Enchanter, The. Iris Murdoch. Magill '57, S
Flight of Pony Baker, The. William Dean Howells. Carrington
Flight to Arras. Antoine de Saint-Exupéry. Heiney
Flight to the West. Elmer Rice. Best '40; Drury; Shipley
Flint Anchor, The. Sylvia Townsend Warner. Magill '54, S
Floating Opera, The. John Barth. Magill Ss
Flood, The. Ernst Barlach. Matlaw
Flood. Günter Grass. Kienzle
Flood. Robert Penn Warren. Magill '65, S
Floradora. Leslie Stuart, Owen Hall, E. Boyd-Jones and Paul A. Rubens. Drinkrow; Shipley
Florestan Dimension, The.

Gabriel Marcel. Kienzle
Florian Geyer. Gerhart Hauptmann. Matlaw; Shipley
Flounder, The. Günter Grass. Magill '79
Flow My Tears, the Policeman Said. Philip K. Dick. Magill SF
Flower and the Nettle, The. Anne Morrow Lindbergh. Magill '77
Flower Drum Song. C. Y. Lee. (See adaptation by Richard Rodgers et al.)
Flower Drum Song. Richard Rodgers, Oscar Hammerstein II and Joseph Fields. (Based on the novel by C. Y. Lee.) Chapman '59; Drinkrow; NCTE
Flower, Fruit and Thorn Pieces. Jean Paul Richter. Keller (Fruit)
Flower Girls, The. Clemence Dane. Magill '55, S
Flower Herding on Mount Monadnock. Galway Kinnell. Magill '65, S
Flower o' the Corn. Samuel Rutherford Crockett. Kaye
Flower of Destiny, The. William D. Orcutt. Kaye
Flowering Cherry. Robert Bolt. Drury; French; Kienzle
Flowering of New England, The. Van Wyck Brooks. Haydn
Flowering of the Cumberland. Harriette Simpson Arnow. Magill '64, M1, S
Flowering Peach, The. Clifford Odets. (See also adaptation Two by Two by Peter Stone et al.) Best '54; Matlaw; Sprinchorn
Flowers, The. Serafín and Joaquín Alvarez Quintero. Sobel
Flowers for Algernon. Daniel Keyes. (See also adaptation by David Rogers.) Magill SF
Flowers for Algernon. David Rogers. (Based on the novel by Daniel Keyes.) Drury
Flowers of Evil, The. Charles Baudelaire. Haydn; Magill III, M1, MC, MP
Flush. Virginia Woolf. Stade p. 180
Fly Away Peter. A. P. Dearsley. French

Frank Ernest Hill. Magill '58, S

Ford: The Times, The Man, The Company. Allan Nevins. Magill '54, S

Fordham Castle. Henry James. Gale-J

Foregone Conclusion, A. William Dean Howells. Carrington; Keller

Forest, The. Aleksandr Ostrovskii. Drury; Gassner

Forest Folk. James Prior. Kaye

Forest Lovers, The. Maurice Hewlett. Haydn; Johnson; Keller

Forest of the Night. Madison Jones. Magill '61, S

Forest Prince, The. Bryan W. Ward. Kaye

Forest Rose, The. Samuel Woodworth. Lovell

Foresters, Robin Hood and Maid Marian, The. Alfred, Lord Tennyson. Drury

Forever Free. Honoré Willsie Morrow. Keller suppl.

Forever Panting. Peter De Vries. Magill '74

Forever War, The. Joe Haldeman. Magill SF

Forever Young. Jonathan Cott. Magill '79

Forewords and Afterwords. Wystan Hugh Auden. Magill '74

Forgotten Door, The. Frank Cowper. Kaye

Forgotten Writings of Mark Twain, The. Mark Twain. Gale-T

Fork River Space Project, The. Wright Morris. Magill '78

Form, The. N. F. Simpson. French

Form of the Personal, The. John Macmurray. Magill CHL

Forsaken Nook, A. Peretz Hirshbein. Matlaw

Forsyte Saga, The. John Galsworthy. Haydn; Keller suppl.; Magill I, CE, M1&2, MC, MEF; Ward

Fort in the Wilderness, The. Edward Stratemeyer. Kaye

Fortitude. Hugh Walpole. Magill I, CE, M1&2, MC, MEF

Fortress, The. Hugh Walpole. Magill I, CE, M1&2, MC, MEF

Fortunata and Jacinta. Benito Pérez Galdós. Magill II, CE, M1&2, MC, MEUF

Fortune's My Foe. John Edward Bloundelle-Burton. Kaye

Fortunes of Nigel, The. Sir Walter Scott. Johnson; Kaye; McSpadden W; Magill II, CE, M1&2, MC, MEF

Fortunes of Perkin Warbeck, The. Mary Wollstonecraft (Godwin) Shelley. Kaye

Fortunes of Richard Mahony, The. Henry Handel Richardson. Haydn; Magill II, CE, M1&2, MC, MEF; Ward

Forty Carats. Jay Allen. (Based on the play by Pierre Barillet and Jean-Pierre Gredy.) Best '68; Drury

Forty Carats. Pierre Barillet and Jean-Pierre Gredy. (See adaptation by Jay Allen.)

Forty Days of Musa Dagh, The. Franz Werfel. Armstrong; Haydn; Heiney; Magill I, CE, M1&2, MC, MEUF

Forty-Five Guardsmen, The. Alexandre Dumas (father). Johnson; Keller

Forty-One Years in India. Lord Roberts of Kandahar. Keller

42nd Parallel, The. John Dos Passos. (See also U. S. A.) Haydn p. 773; Lass AN

Fo-sho-hing-tsan-king: A Life of Buddha, The. Asvaghosha Bodhisattva. Keller (Sacred Books)

Fossils, The. François de Curel. Drury; Matlaw

Foul Play. Charles Reade. Johnson

Found, Lost, Found. J. B. Priestley. Magill '78

Foundation of Christian Doctrine. Menno Simons. Magill CHL

Foundation Trilogy, The. Isaac Asimov. Magill SF

Foundations of Belief, The. Arthur James Balfour. Keller

Foundations of Freedom, The. John Lilburne. Magill CHL

Founding of New England, The. James Truslow Adams. Keller suppl.

Founding of the German Empire by William I, The. Heinrich von Sybel. Keller

Fountain, The. George Calderon. Drury

Fountain, The. Eugene O'Neill. Matlaw

Fountain of Wisdom, The. Saint John of Damascus. Magill CHL

Fountain Overflows, The. Rebecca West. Magill '57, S

Four Beasts in One. Edgar Allan Poe. Gale-PP

Four Feathers, The. A. E. W. Mason. Keller

Four-Gated City, The. Doris Lessing. Magill '70

Four Georges, The. William Makepeace Thackeray. Keller

Four Horsemen of the Apocalypse, The. Vicente Blasco Ibáñez. Goodman; Grozier; Haydn

Four Horsemen of the Apocalypse, The. Unknown. Keller suppl.

Four Loves, The. Clive Staples Lewis. Magill '61, M1, MB, S

Four Meetings. Henry James. Gale-J

Four Million, The. O. Henry. Keller; Ward

Four PP, The. John Heywood. Holzknecht; Ruoff; Shipley; Sobel

Four Plays for Dancers. William Butler Yeats. Matlaw; Sprinchorn

Four Quartets. T. S. Eliot. Heiney; Magill III, M1, MC, MP, Ward

Four Saints in Three Acts. Gertrude Stein. Heiney; Sobel

Four Winds. Alex Atkinson. French

Fourberies de Scapin, Les (The Cheats of Scapin). Molière. (See also adaptation Scapino by Frank Dunlop and Jim Dale.) Gassner; Shank

Fourmi dans le corps, La (Ant in the Flesh). Jacques Audiberti. Kionzle

Fourposter, The. Jan de Hartog. (See also adaptation I Do! I Do! by Tom Jones and Harvey Schmidt.) Best '51; Bonin; Drury; NCTE

Fourteenth of July, The. Romain Rolland. Drury

Fourth Estate, The. Armando

Palacio Valdés. Keller

Fourth of June, The. David Benedictus. Magill '63, S

Fourth Wall, The. A. A. Milne. French

Fowre Hymnes. Edmund Spenser. Ruoff

Fox and the Camellias, The. Ignazio Silone. Magill '62, S

Fox in the Attic, The. Richard Hughes. Magill '63, S

Foxe's Book of Martyrs see Acts and Monuments of These Latter and Perilous Days, Touching Matters of the Church

Foxfire Book, The. Eliot Wiginton. Magill '73

Fragment in the Manner of Rabelais, The. Laurence Sterne. Johnson-18th/2

Fragments. Ayi Kwei Armah. Magill '71

Fragments from a Writing Desk. No. 1. Herman Melville. Gale-M

Fragments from a Writing Desk. No. 2. Herman Melville. Gale-M

Fragments from the Journal of a Solitary Man. Nathaniel Hawthorne. Gale-H

Framley Parsonage. Anthony Trollope. Gerould; Magill I, CE, M1&2, MC, MEF

France and England in North America. Francis Parkman. Keller

Francesca da Rimini. Gabriele d'Annunzio. Drury; Matlaw; Sobel

Francesca da Rimini. George Henry Boker. Drury; Gassner; Lovell

Francesca da Rimini. Silvio Pellico. Drury

Francis Bacon. Catherine Drinker Bowen. Magill '64, M1, S

Frank der Fünfte (Frank the Fifth). Friedrich Dürrenmatt and Paul Burkhard. Kienzle

Frankenstein. Mary Wollstonecraft (Godwin) Shelley. Armstrong; Cohen; Goodman; Haydn; Johnson; Keller; Magill I, CE, M1&2, MC, MEF, SF

Frankenstein Unbound. Brian W. Aldiss. Magill SF

Franklin D. Roosevelt: Launching

the New Deal. Frank Freidel.
Magill '74
Franny and Zooey. J. D. Salinger.
Magill IV, '62, M1, MB, MC,
S
Fraternity. John Galsworthy.
Keller; Magill II, CE, M1&2,
MC, MEF
Fräulein Else. Arthur Schnitzler.
Keller suppl.
Freaks: Myths and Images of the
Secret Self. Leslie Fiedler.
Magill '79
Free. Theodore Dreiser. Gerber
Free and Other Stories. Theodore
Dreiser. Gerber
Free Fall. William Golding.
Magill IV, '61, M1, MB, MC,
S
Free-Loader, The see Parasite,
The
Free Thought in the Social Sci-
ences. J. A. Hobson. Keller
suppl.
Freedom and the Spirit. Nikolai
Berdyaev. Magill CHL
Freedom Comes to Krähwinkel
see Liberty Comes to Kräh-
winkel
Freedom of the Poet, The.
John Berryman. Magill '77
Freedom of the Will. Jonathan
Edwards. Keller; Magill
CHL, WP
Freedom or Death. Nikos Kazant-
zakis. Magill IV, '57, MC, S
Freedom Road. Howard Fast.
Magill Ss
Freedom Spent. Richard Harris.
Magill '77
Freethinker, The. August Strind-
berg. Matlaw
Freezing Down. Anders Bodelsen.
Magill SF
Freiheit für Clemens (Freedom
for Clement). Tankred Dorst.
Kienzle
Frémont. Allan Nevins. Keller
suppl.
Fremont and Risler. Alphonse
Daudet. Johnson
French and German Socialism in
Modern Times. Richard T.
Ely. Keller
French Humorists, The. Sir
Walter Besant. Keller
French Lieutenant's Woman, The.
John Fowles. Magill '70

French Mistress, The. Robert
Monro. French
French Revolution, The. A.
Aulard. Keller
French Revolution, The. Thomas
Carlyle. Haydn; Keller; Magill
III, M1, MC, MNF
French Traits. William Crary
Brownell. Keller
French Without Tears. Terence
Rattigan. Drury; French; Mat-
law; Sobel
Frescoes for Mr. Rockefeller's
City. Archibald MacLeish.
Haydn (a)
Fresh Fields. Ivor Novello.
French
Freud. Max Schur. Magill '73
Freya of the Seven Isles: A Story
of Shallow Waters. Joseph
Conrad. Ward
Friar Bacon and Friar Bungay.
Robert Greene. Drury; Haydn;
Holzknecht; Magill II, CE,
M1&2, MC, MD; Ruoff; Sobel
Friar of Wittenberg, The. Wil-
liam Stearns Davis. Kaye
Friend Fritz. Enide Erckmann
and Alexandre Chatrian. Keller
Friend in Power, A. Carlos
Baker. Magill '59, S
Friend of Caesar, A. William
Stearns Davis. Kaye
Friend of Kafka, A. Isaac Bashe-
vis Singer. Magill '71
Friend of the People, The. Mary
C. Rowsell. Kaye
Friend Olivia. Amelia Edith Barr.
Kaye; Keller
Friendly Arctic, The. Vilhjalmur
Stefansson. Keller suppl.
Friendly Fire. C. D. B. Bryan.
Magill '77
Friendly Relations. James Liggat.
French
Friends. Arkady Leokum. Ki-
enzle
Friends: A Duet. Elizabeth Stu-
art Phelps. Johnson
Friends and Neighbours. Austin
Steele. French
Friends in Council. Sir Arthur
Helps. Keller
Friends of the Friends, The (The
Way It Came). Henry James.
Gale-J
Friendship. Ouida. Johnson
Friers, The. Aristophanes.

Hathorn
Frithiof's Saga. Esaias Tegnér.
Haydn. Magill II, CE, M1&2,
MC, MP
Frogs, The. Aristophanes.
Downs F, FG; Drury; Feder;
Gassner; Hathorn; Haydn;
Keller; Magill I, CE, M1&2,
MC, MD; Reinhold; Shank;
Shipley; Sobel; Wilson
From Here to Eternity. James
Jones. Morehead; Smith
From Immigrant to Inventor.
Michael Pupin. Keller suppl.
From Morn to Midnight. Georg
Kaiser. Drury; Heiney; Mat-
law; Shank; Shipley; Sobel;
Sprinchorn
From the Danube to the Yalu.
General Mark W. Clark.
Magill '54, M1, MB, S
From the Diary of a Snail. Günter
Grass. Magill '74
From the Earth to the Moon.
Jules Verne. Downs M;
Magill SF
From the Hand of the Hunter.
John Braine. Magill '61, S
From the Insect World see
Insect Comedy, The
From the South Seas. Margaret
Mead. Haydn
From the Terrace. John O'Hara.
Magill '59, M1, S
Front Page, The. Ben Hecht
and Charles MacArthur.
Best '28; Drury; Haydn; Lass
AP; Lovell; Matlaw; NCTE;
Sobel
Frontenacs, The. François
Mauriac. Magill '62, S
Frontier in American History,
The. Frederick Jackson
Turner. Downs M; Haydn (a);
Magill IV, MC
Frost at Midnight. André Obey.
French
Frown of Majesty, The. Albert
Lee. Kaye
Fruit of the Tree, The. Edith
Wharton. Magill III, CE,
M1&2, MAF, MC
Fruitfulness. Emile Zola. John-
son
Fruits of Enlightenment, The.
Count Leo Tolstoy. Drury;
Matlaw
Fugitive, The. Ugo Betti.

Kienzle
Fulfilment. Theodore Dreiser.
Gerber
Fulgens and Lucrece. Henry
Medwall. Holzknecht
Full Fathom Five. John Stewart
Carter. Magill '66, S
Full Moon in March, A. William
Butler Yeats. Gassner
Fumed Oak. Noel Coward.
French
Funa Benkei (Benkei in the Boat).
Kawatake Mokuami. Halford
Funeral, The. Sir Richard
Steele. Magill II, CE, M1&2,
MC, MD; Sobel
Fünfzehn Schnüre Geld (Fifteen
Purses of Money). Günther
Weisenborn. Kienzle
Funny Girl. Isobel Lennart, Bob
Merrill and Jule Styne. NCTE
Funny Thing Happened on the Way
to the Forum, A. Burt Sheve-
love, Larry Gelbart and Stephen
Sondheim. NCTE
Further Fables for Our Time.
James Thurber. Magill '57, S
Fury. Lawrence O'Donnell.
Magill SF
Future Is in Eggs, or It Takes
All Sorts to Make a World,
The. Eugène Ionesco. Matlaw
Future of China After Mao, The.
Ross Terrill. Magill '79
Future of Mankind, The. Karl
Jaspers. Magill '62, S
Future Shock. Alvin Toffler.
Magill '71

-G-

Gabriel Conroy. Bret Harte.
Johnson; Keller
Gabriel Schilling's Flight. Ger-
hart Hauptmann. Matlaw
Gabriel Tolliver. Joel Chandler
Harris. Johnson
Gabriela, Clove and Cinnamon.
Jorge Amado. Magill IV, '63,
M1, MC, S
Gabrielle de Bergerac. Henry
James. Gale-J
Gadfly, The. Mrs. Ethel L.
Voynich. Kaye; Keller
Gage of Red and White, The.

Drury; Matlaw; NCTE; Shank;
Sobel
Gentleman Dancing Master, The.
William Wycherley. Haydn;
Magill III, CE, M1&2, MC,
MD; Sobel
Gentleman from Athens, The.
Emmet G. Lavery. Drury
Gentleman from Indiana, The.
Booth Tarkington. Johnson;
Smith
Gentleman from San Francisco,
The. Ivan Alexeyevich Bunin.
Haydn; Heiney
Gentleman in the Parlour, The.
W. Somerset Maugham. Ward
Gentleman of France, A. Stanley
J. Weyman. Johnson; Kaye;
Keller
Gentleman Player, A. Robert
N. Stephens. Kaye
Gentleman Usher, The. George
Chapman. Magill III, CE,
M1&2, MC, MD; Ruoff; Sobel
Gentlemen Prefer Blonds: The
Illuminating Diary of a Pro-
fessional Lady. Anita Loos.
Drury; Morehead; Ward
Gentry Nest, A. Ivan Turgenev.
Berry-1
Genuine Works of Hippocrates,
The. Hippocrates. Keller
(Hippocrates)
Geographical Pivot of History,
The. Halford Mackinder.
Downs M, FG
Geography. Claudius Ptolemy.
Downs F, FG; Haydn
Geography. Strabo. Downs M;
Haydn; Keller
Geography III. Elizabeth Bishop.
Magill '77
Géométrie, La. René Descartes.
Haydn
George. Emlyn Williams.
Magill '63, S
George a Greene, the Pinner of
Wakefield. Unknown. Holz-
knecht
George and Margaret. George
Savory. French
George Bernard Shaw. Archibald
Henderson. Magill '57, M1,
S
George C. Marshall: Education
of a General. Forrest C.
Pogue. Magill '64, S
George C. Marshall: Ordeal and

Hope, 1939-1942. Forrest C.
Pogue. Magill '67, S
George C. Marshall: Organizer
of Victory, 1943-1945. For-
rest C. Pogue. Magill '74
George Eliot: A Biography.
Gordon S. Haight. Magill '69,
M1, S
George Eliot: The Emergent Self.
Ruby V. Redinger. Magill '76
George M.' Michael Stewart, John
Pascal, Fran Pascal, George
M. Cohan and Mary Cohan.
NCTE
George Meredith and English
Comedy. V. S. Pritchett.
Magill '71
George Silverman's Explanation.
Charles Dickens. Hardwick
CD
George Walker at Suez. Anthony
Trollope. Gerould
George Washington. James
Thomas Flexner. Magill '73
George Washington. Rupert
Hughes. Keller suppl. (Wash-
ington)
George Washington Slept Here.
George S. Kaufman and Moss
Hart. Best '40; Drury
George Washington, the Image and
the Man. William E. Wood-
ward. Keller suppl. (Washing-
ton)
Georgia Scenes. Augustus Bald-
win Longstreet. Magill III,
M1, MAF, MC
Georgian Poetry. Sir Edward
Marsh, editor. Ward
Georgics. Vergil. Feder; Haydn;
Magill IV, MC
Georgina's Reasons. Henry
James. Gale-J
Gerald the Sheriff. C. W.
Whistler. Kaye
Gerfaut. Charles de Bernard.
Johnson
German Army, 1933-1945: Its
Political and Military Failure,
The. Matthew Cooper. Magill
'79
German Lesson, The. Siegfried
Lenz. Magill '73
Germania. Publius Cornelius
Tacitus. Feder; Haydn
Germany. Madame de Staël.
Haydn; Keller
Germany and the Next War.

Friedrich Adam Julius von Bernhardi. Keller Germany 1866-1945. Gordon A. Craig. Magill '79
Germinal. Emile Zola. Haydn; Johnson; Keller (Rougon); Lass EN; Magill II, CE, M1&2, MC, MEUF
Germinie Lacerteux. Edmond and Jules de Goncourt. Lass EN; Magill II, CE, M1&2, MC, MEUF
Geronimo Rex. Barry Hannah. Magill '73
Gertrude of Wyoming. Thomas Campbell. Keller
Gerytades. Aristophanes. Hathorn
Gesang im Feuerofen, Der (The Song in the Fiery Furnace). Carl Zuckmayer. Kienzle
Gesta Romanorum moralizata. Haydn
Get Away Old Man. William Saroyan. Drury
Getting Married. George Bernard Shaw. Hardwick; Matlaw; Shank; Sobel
Getting Out. Marsha W. Norman. Best '78
Gettysburg. Elsie Singmaster. Magill II, CE, M1&2, MAF, MC
Gettysburg Address, The. Abraham Lincoln. Haydn; Hix
Ghetto, The. Herman Heijermans. Drury; Sobel
Ghost at Noon, A. Alberto Moravia. Magill '55, S
Ghost of Doctor Harris, The. Nathaniel Hawthorne. Gale-H
Ghost of Guy Thyrle, The. Edgar Fawcett. Magill SF
Ghost Sonata, The. August Strindberg. Gassner; Matlaw; Shank; Shipley (Spook Sonata); Sprinchorn
Ghost Train, The. Arnold Ridley. French
Ghost Voyage, The. Gontran de Poncins. Magill '54, S
Ghostly Rental, The. Henry James. Gale-J
Ghosts. Henrik Ibsen. Drury; French; Gassner; Haydn; Heiney; Keller; Magill I, CE, M1&2, MC, MD; Matlaw; Shank; Shipley; Sobel
Giant Dwarfs, The. Gisela Elsner. Magill '66, S
Giants in the Earth. Thomas Job. Lovell
Giants in the Earth. O. E. Rölvaag. Haydn; Heiney; Keller suppl.; Lass AN; Magill I, CE, M1&2, MAF, MC; Smith
Giant's Robe, The. F. Anstey. Johnson
Giants: Russia and America, The. Richard J. Barnet. Magill '78
Giboyer's Son. Emile Augier. Drury
Gideon. Paddy Chayefsky. Best '61; Kienzle; Matlaw; NCTE
Gideon's Trumpet. Anthony Lewis. Magill '65, S
Gift, The. Mary Lumsden. French
Gift, The. Vladimir Nabokov. Magill '64, S
Gift from the Sea. Anne Morrow Lindbergh. Magill '55, M1, S
Gift of the Magi, The. O. Henry. Haydn (a); Ward
Gift of Time, A. Garson Kanin. (Based on the book by Lael T. Wertenbaker.) NCTE
Gift of Time, A. Lael T. Wertenbaker. (See adaptation by Garson Kanin.)
Gigi. Vicki Baum. (Based on the novel by Colette.) Kienzle
Gigi. Colette. (See adaptations by Anita Loos, Vicki Baum and Alan Jay Lerner and Frederick Loewe.)
Gigi. Anita Loos. (Based on the novel by Colette.) Best '51;
Gigi. Alan Jay Lerner and Frederick Loewe. (Based on the novel by Colette.) NCTE Drury; French; NCTE
Gijsbreght van Aemstel. Joost van den Vondel. Haydn (a)
Gil Blas de Santillane. Alain René Le Sage. Goodman; Grozier; Haydn; Johnson; Keller; Magill I, CE, M1&2, MC, MEUF
Gilded Age, The. Mark Twain and Charles Dudley Warner. Gale-T; Magill II, CE, M1&2, MAF, MAL5, MC
Giles Goat-Boy. John Barth. Magill '67, M1, S, SF
Gilgamesh see Epic of Gilgamesh
Gimme Shelter. Barrie Keeffe.

Best '78
Gin Game, The. D. L. Coburn.
  Best '77
Ginger Man, The. J. P. Don-
  leavy. Magill '59, S
Ginger Tree, The. Oswald Wynd.
  Magill '78
Gingerbread Lady, The. Neil
  Simon. Best '70; Drury
Ginx's Baby. John Edward Jenkins.
  Keller
Gioconda, La. Gabriele D'Annun-
  zio. Drury; Gassner; Matlaw;
  Shank; Sobel; Thomas
Gioconda Smile, The. Aldous
  Huxley. French; Kienzle
Gion Sairei Shinkoki. Asada Itcho
  and Nakamura Ake. Halford
Giovanni Boccaccio. John Adding-
  ton Symonds. Keller (Boccac-
  cio)
Girl Crazy. George Gershwin,
  Guy Bolton, John McGowan and
  Ira Gershwin. Drinkrow
Girl Friend, The. Con Conrad,
  Gus Kahn, Richard Rodgers,
  Lorenz Hart, R. P. Weston
  and Bert Lee. (Based on
  Kitty's Kisses by P. Bartholo-
  mae and Otto Harbach.)
  Drinkrow
Girl from Andros, The see
  Andria
Girl from Persia, The see
  Persa
Girl from Samos, The (Samia).
  Menander. Feder; Hathorn
  (Samia); Reinhold
Girl in the Carpathians, A. Menie
  Muriel Dowie. Keller
Girl in the Golden Atom, The.
  Ray Cummings. Magill SF
Girl in Winter, A. Philip Larkin.
  Magill '63, S
Girl of the Golden West, The.
  David Belasco. Drury; Lovell;
  Matlaw
Girl on the Via Flaminia, The.
  Alfred Hayes. Best '53
Girl, the Gold Watch, & Every-
  thing, The. John D. Mac-
  Donald. Magill SF
Girl Who Couldn't Quite, The.
  Leo Marks. French
Girl Who Sang with the Beatles
  and Other Stories. Robert
  Hemenway. Magill '71
Girl with Her Hair Cut Short,

The see Shearing of Glycera,
  The
Girl with the Green Eyes, The.
  Clyde Fitch. Drury; Matlaw
Girl Worth Gold, A see Fair
  Maid of the West; or A Girl
  Worth Gold, The
Girls in 509, The. Howard Teich-
  mann. NCTE
Girls of Slender Means, The. Muriel
  Spark. Magill '64, M1, S
Girondin, The. Hilaire Belloc. Kaye
Gitagovinda (The Son of the Divine
  Herdsman). Jayadeva. Gassner
Give Us This Day. Sidney Stewart.
  Magill '58, S
Given Case, The. Henry James.
  Gale-J
Gladiator, The. Robert Mont-
  gomery Bird. Drury; Gassner;
  Lovell
Gladiator. Philip Wylie. Magill
  SF
Gladiator-at-Law. Frederik Pohl
  and Cyril M. Kornbluth. Magill
  SF
Gladiators, The. George John
  White Melville. Kaye
Glamorous Night. Ivor Novello
  and Christopher Hassall.
  Drinkrow
Glance at New York, A. Ben-
  jamin A. Baker. Lovell
Glaspearlgame, The (The Glass
  Bead Game). Hermann Hesse.
  Haydn (a); Heiney; Magill SF
  (Glass)
Glass Bead Game, The see
  Glaspearlgame, The
Glass Key, The. Dashiell Ham-
  mett. Magill I, CE, M1&2,
  MAF, MC
Glass Menagerie, The. Tennessee
  Williams. Anderson; Best '44;
  Bonin; Drury; French; Gassner;
  Haydn; Lass AP; Lovell; Magill
  III, M1, MC, MD; Matlaw;
  NCTE; Shank; Sobel; Sprinchorn
Glass of Water, A. Augustin
  Eugène Scribe. Shipley
Glass Slipper, The. Ferenc Mol-
  nár. Matlaw
Glasse of Time in the First Age,
  The. Thomas Peyton. Keller
Glasses. Henry James. Gale-J
Glaucia: The Greek Slave. Emma
  Leslie. Kaye
Glaucus and Scylla see Scylla's

Metamorphosis Glaucus of Potniae. Aeschylus. Hathorn
Glaucus the Sea God. Aeschylus. Hathorn
Gleanings in Buddha Fields. Lafcadio Hearn. Keller
Glen o' Weeping, The. Marjorie Bowen. Kaye
Glimpse of Reality, The. George Bernard Shaw. Hardwick
Glittering Gate, The. Lord Dunsany. Heiney; Keller; Matlaw; Shipley
Global Reach. Richard J. Barnet and Ronald E. Müller. Magill '76
'Gloria Scott, ' The. Sir Arthur Conan Doyle. Hardwick SH
Glories of Mary. Saint Alphonsus Mary de Liguori. Magill CAL
Glorieuses, Les (Saints in Glory). André Roussin. Kienzle
Glory and the Dream, The. William Manchester. Magill '75
Glory Be! McGlathery see St. Columba and the River
Glory of War, The. Henry A. Hinkson. Kaye
Głos pana. Stanisław Lem. Magill SF
Glosses on Porphyry, The. Peter Abelard. Magill WP
Głupiec i inni (The Fool and the Others). Jerzy Broszkiewicz. Kienzle
Gnat, The see Culex
Gnomes & Occasions. Howard Nemerov. Magill '74
Go Back for Murder. Agatha Christie. French
Go-Between, The. L. P. Hartley. Magill '54, M1, S
Go Down, Moses. William Faulkner. Magill IV, MC
Go East, Young Man. William O. Douglas. Magill '75
Go-Go Years, The. John Brooks. Magill '74
Go Taiheiki Shiraishi Banashi. Kino Jotaro. Halford
Go Tell It on the Mountain. James Baldwin. Magill IV, MC
Goat Song. Franz Werfel. Magill II, CE, M1&2, MC, MD; Matlaw; Shank; Shipley; Sobel
God Against the Gods, A. Allen Drury. Magill '77

God and His Gifts, A. Ivy Compton-Burnett. Magill '65, M1, S
God and Intelligence in Modern Philosophy. Fulton J. Sheen. Magill CAL
God and Kate Murphy. Kieran Tunney and John Synge. Chapman '59
God and the Man. Robert Buchanan. Johnson
God in Christ. Horace Bushnell. Magill CHL
God in Modern Philosophy. James D. Collins. Magill CAL
God, Man, and Devil. Jacob Gordin. Matlaw; Shipley
God of Love, The. Justin Huntley McCarthy. Kaye
God of Vengeance. Sholem Asch. Gassner; Matlaw; Shipley; Sobel
God Save King Alfred. E. Gilliat. Kaye
God Was in Christ. Donald M. Baillie. Magill CHL
God Wills It. William Stearns Davis. Kaye
Goddess and Other Women, The. Joyce Carol Oates. Magill '75
Godolphin. Lord Edward Bulwer-Lytton. Johnson
Godot jg dosao (Godot Has Come). Miodrag Bulatović. Kienzle
Gods Are Athirst, The. Anatole France. Keller; Magill III, CE, M1&2, MC, MEUF
God's Fool. Maarten Maartens. Johnson; Keller
God's Grace and Man's Hope. Daniel Day Williams. Magill CHL
God's Little Acre. Erskine Caldwell. Heiney; Lass AN; Morehead; Smith
God's Oddling. Jesse Stuart. Magill '61, M1, S
Gods of the Lightning. Maxwell Anderson. Matlaw; Shipley; Sobel
Gods of the Mountain, The. Lord Dunsany. Drury; Sobel
God's Providence House. Mrs. G. L. Banks. Kaye
Gods Themselves, The. Isaac Asimov. Magill SF
Godspell. John-Michael Tebelak and Stephen Schwarts. NCTE
Goethe. Richard Friedenthal.

Magill '66, S
Goethe and Schiller. Louise Muhl-
bach. Kaye
Goetz Von Berlichingen. Johann
Wolfgang von Goethe. Gassner;
Shank; Shipley; Sobel
Gog. Andrew Sinclair. Magill
'68, S
Goin' a Buffalo. Ed Bullins.
NCTE
Going Away. Clancy Sigal.
Magill '63, S
Going into Society. Charles
Dickens. Hardwick CD
Goju no To (The Five-Storied
Pagoda). Rohan Koda. Hal-
ford
Gold. Eugene O'Neill. Matlaw
Gold and Iron: Bismarck, Bleich-
röder, and the Building of the
German Empire. Fritz Stern.
Magill '78
Gold Bug, The. Edgar Allan
Poe. Gale-PP; Keller; Magill
II, CE, M1&2, MAF, MAL5,
MC
Golden Apple, The. Lady (Isa-
bella Augusta) Gregory. Chap-
man '54
Golden Apple, The. John La-
touche and Jerome Moross.
Best '53
Golden Apples, The. Eudora
Welty. Magill IV, MC
Golden Ass of Lucius Apuleius,
The. Lucius Apuleius. Feder;
Haydn; Keller; Magill I, CE,
M1&2, MC, MEUF; Olfson
Golden Book of Venice, The.
Mrs. Lawrence Turnbull.
Kaye
Golden Bough, The. Sir James
George Frazer. Downs M;
Haydn; Keller; Magill IV, MC;
Ward
Golden Bowl, The. Henry James.
Gale-J; Haydn; Keller; Magill
II, CE, M1&2, MAF, MAL3,
MC; Olfson; Ward
Golden Boy. Clifford Odets.
Best '37; Drury; Gassner;
Haydn; Magill III, CE, M1&2,
MC, MD; Matlaw; NCTE;
Shank; Sobel; Sprinchorn
Golden Butterfly, The. Sir
Walter Besant and James
Rice. Keller
Golden Chersonese, The. Isabella

Bird Bishop. Keller
Golden Day, The. Lewis Mum-
ford. Keller suppl.
Golden Dog, The. William Kirby.
Keller
Golden Echo, The. David Garnett.
Magill '54, S
Golden Fleece. Franz Grillparzer.
Haydn; Shipley
Golden Fleecing. Lorenzo Semple,
Jr. NCTE
Golden Fruits, The. Nathalie
Sarraute. Magill '65, S
Golden Harp, The. Gerhart
Hauptmann. Matlaw
Golden Hope, The. R. H. Fuller.
Kaye
Golden House, The. Charles Dud-
ley Warner. Johnson
Golden Lion of Granpère, The.
Anthony Trollope. Gerould
Golden Notebook, The. Doris
Lessing. Magill '63, S
Golden Pince-nez, The. Sir
Arthur Conan Doyle. Hardwick
SH
Golden Rain. R. F. Delderfield.
French
Golden Shadows, Flying Hooves.
George B. Schaller. Magill
'74
Golden Sovereign, The. Richard
Church. Magill '58, S
Golden Spur, The. Dawn Powell.
Magill '63, S
Golden Treasury, The. Francis
Turner Palgrave, editor.
Haydn (Palgrave's); Keller
Golden Trust, A. Theo. Douglas.
Kaye
Golden Weather, The. Louis
Rubin. Magill '62, S
Goldmakers' Village, The. Johann
Heinrich Zschokke. Keller
Golem, The. H. Leivick. Gass-
ner; Matlaw; Shipley
Golovlyov Family, The. M. E.
Shchedrin. Haydn
Goncourt Journals, The. Edmond
and Jules de Goncourt. Haydn
(Journals); Magill IV, MC
Gondoliers, The. William
Schwenck Gilbert and Arthur
Sullivan. Drury; Magill II,
CE, M1&2, MC, MD; Shipley;
Sobel
Gone a Hundred Miles. Heather
Ross Miller. Magill '69, S

Gone with the Wind. Margaret
Mitchell. Haydn; Magill III,
M1, MAF, MC; Morehead;
Olfson; Smith
Good Anna, The <u>see</u> Three
Lives
Good Companions, The. J. B.
Priestley. Haydn; Magill I,
CE, M1&2, MC, MEF; Ward
Good Doctor, The. Neil Simon.
Best '73; Drury
Good Earth, The. Pearl S. Buck.
Goodman; Haydn; Lass AN;
Magill I, CE, M1&2, MAF,
MC; Morehead; Smith
Good Gracious Annabelle. Clare
Kummer. Best '09; Drury
Good Hope, The. Herman Heijer-
mans. Drury; Haydn (Op
Hoop); Matlaw; Shank; Ship-
ley; Sobel
Good Light, The. Karl Bjarnhof.
Magill '61, S
Good Man Is Hard to Find, A.
Flannery O'Connor. Magill
'55, M1, S
Good Man's Miracle, A. Nathaniel
Hawthorne. Gale-H
Good Morning, Midnight. Jean
Rhys. Magill '71
Good Morning, Miss Dove. Wil-
liam McCleery. (Based on
the novel by Frances G. Pat-
ton.) Drury
Good Morning, Miss Dove.
Frances G. Patton. (See
adaptation by William Mc-
Cleery.)
Good Natured Man, The. Oliver
Goldsmith. Sobel
Good News Yesterday and Today,
The. Josef Andreas Jung-
mann, S. J. Magill CAL
Good Shepherd, The. C. S.
Forester. Magill '55, M1, S
Good Soldier: A Tale of Passion,
The. Ford Madox Hueffer.
Ward
Good Soldier: Schweik, The.
Jaroslav Hašek. Haydn;
Magill IV, M2, MC
Good Thoughts in Bad Times.
Thomas Fuller. Keller
Good Times/Bad Times. James
Kirkwood. Magill '69, S
Good Woman, A. Louis Brom-
field. Keller suppl.
Good Woman of Setzuan, The.

Bertolt Brecht. Drury; Gass-
ner; Matlaw; Shank; Sprinchorn
Goodbye. William Sansom.
Magill '67, S
Good-Bye Again. Allan Scott and
George Haight. Drury
Goodbye Charlie. George Axelrod.
Drury
Goodbye, Columbus. Philip Roth.
Magill Ss
Goodbye, Mr. Chips. James
Hilton. Haydn; Magill I, CE,
M1&2, MC, MEF
Goodbye, My Fancy. Fay Kanin.
Best '48; Drury
Good-bye Sweetheart. Rhoda
Broughton. Johnson; Keller
Goodbye to a River. John Graves.
Magill '61, S
Goodbye to Uncle Tom. J. C.
Furnas. Magill '57, S
Goodbye, World. Bernard Kops.
Kienzle
Goodnight Mrs. Puffin. Arthur
Lovegrove. French
Goose Hangs High, The. Lewis
Beach. Best '23; Sobel
Gorboduc or Ferrex and Porrex.
Thomas Norton and Thomas
Sackville. Gassner; Haydn;
Holzknecht; Magill II, CE,
M1&2, MC, MD; Ruoff; Shipley;
Sobel
Gordian Knot, The. Charles Wil-
liam Shirley Brooks. Johnson
Gordon Keith. Thomas Nelson
Page. Keller
Gorgeous Borgia, The. Justin
Huntly McCarthy. Kaye
Gorgias. Plato. Feder; Magill
WP
Gospel and the Church, The. Al-
fred Loisy. Magill CHL
Gossip from the Forest. Thomas
Keneally. Magill '77
Gösta Berling's Saga. Selma
Lagerlöf. Haydn; Heiney; Lass
EN
Government in Switzerland. J. M.
Vincent. Keller
Government Inspector, The <u>see</u>
Inspector-General, The
Governments and Parties in Con-
tinental Europe. A. L. Lowell.
Keller
Governor, A Book Named the <u>see</u>
Book Named the Governor, The
Governor's Daughter, The. Norman

Innes. Kaye
Governor's Wife, The. Jacinto
Benavente y Martínez. Drury
Gowrie. George Pain Rainsford
James. Kaye
Grace Abounding to the Chief of
Sinners. John Bunyan. Haydn;
Keller; Magill CHL
Grafting. Luigi Pirandello.
Matlaw
Gramercy Ghost. John Cecil
Holm. Drury
Grammar of Assent, A. John
Henry Cardinal Newman.
Magill CAL, WP
Grammar of Greek Art, A.
Percy Gardner. Keller
Grand Hotel. Vicki Baum. Best
'30; Cartmell; Drury; Magill I,
CE, M1&2, MC, MEUF; Sobel
Grand Inquisitor, The. Fyodor
Mikhailovich Dostoevskii.
Magill CHL
Grand Mademoiselle, The. Fran-
cis Steegmuller. Magill '57,
S
Grand National Night. Dorothy
and Campbell Christie. French
Grand Tour, The. Elmer Rice.
Drury
Grandee, The. Armando Palacio
Valdés. Keller
Grandfather Stories. Samuel
Hopkins Adams. Magill '55, S
Grandfathers, The. Conrad Rich-
ter. Magill '65, S
Grandissimes, The. George W.
Cable. Johnson; Keller; Magill
I, CE, M1&2, MAF, MAL1,
MC
Grandmothers, The. Glenway
Wescott. Haydn; Keller suppl.;
Magill I, CE, M1&2, MAF,
MC; Morehead
Grania. Lady (Isabella Augusta)
Gregory. Matlaw
Grania: The Story of an Island.
Emily Lawless. Keller
Granite. Clemence Dane. French
Granite and Rainbow. Virginia
Woolf. Magill '59, S
Granite Lady. Susan Fromberg
Schaeffer. Magill '75
Grant Moves South. Bruce Cat-
ton. Magill '61, MB, S
Granth, The. Unknown. Haydn
Grapes of Wrath, The. John
Steinbeck. Armstrong;

Haydn; Heiney; Lass AN; Magill
I, CE, M1&2, MAF, MC; More-
head; Olfson; Smith
Grasp of Consciousness, The.
Jean Piaget. Magill '77
Grass Harp, The. Truman Capote.
Kienzle; NCTE; Shank
Grass Roof, The. Younghill Kang.
Haydn
Graustark. George Barr Mc-
Cutcheon. Johnson; Keller
Grave by the Handpost, The.
Thomas Hardy. Pinion
Graves and Goblins. Nathaniel
Hawthorne. Gale-H
Gravity's Rainbow. Thomas Pyn-
chon. Magill '74, SF
Gray Champion, The. Nathaniel
Hawthorne. Gale-H
Gray Fox. Burke Davis. Magill
'57, S
Gray Matters. William Hjorts-
berg. Magill SF
Grayslaer. Charles Fenno Hoff-
man. Johnson
Graziella. Alphonse Marie Louis
de Lamartine. Johnson
Grease. Jim Jacobs and Warren
Casey. NCTE
Great Adventure, The. E. Arnold
Bennett. Drury; Sobel
Great American Band Wagon, The.
Charles Merz. Keller suppl.
Great American Jackpot, The.
Herbert Gold. Magill '70
Great American Novel, The.
Philip Roth. Magill '74
Great Big Doorstep, The. Fran-
ces Goodrich and Albert Hack-
ett. NCTE
Great Captains, The. Henry
Treece. Magill '57, S
Great Carbuncle: A Mystery of
the White Mountains, The.
Nathaniel Hawthorne. Gale-H
Great Catechism, The. Saint
Gregory of Nyssa. Magill
CAL, CHL
Great Catherine. George Bernard
Shaw. Hardwick; Matlaw
Great Christian Doctrine of Orig-
inal Sin Defended, The. Jona-
than Edwards. Magill CHL
Great Condition, The. Henry
James. Gale-J
Great Conspiracy Trial, The.
Jason Epstein. Magill '71
Great Democracies, The. Winston

S. Churchill. Magill '59, MB,
S
Great Diamond Robbery, The.
Edward M. Alfriend and A.
C. Wheeler. Lovell
Great Divide, The. William
Vaughn Moody. Best '99;
Drury; Gassner; Keller; Lovell;
Matlaw; Shipley; Sobel; Thomas
Great Duke of Florence, The.
Philip Massinger. Ruoff
Great Expectations. Charles
Dickens. Hardwick CD; Haydn;
Johnson; Keller; Lass BN;
McSpadden-D; McSpadden-DH;
Magill I, CE, M1&2, MC,
MEF; Olfson
Great Fear: The Anti-Communist
Purge Under Truman and
Eisenhower, The. David
Caute. Magill '79
Great Galeoto, The. José Eche-
garay. Drury; Haydn; Keller;
Magill II, CE, M1&2, MC,
MD; Matlaw; Shank; Shipley;
Sobel; Thomas
Great Gatsby, The. F. Scott
Fitzgerald. Haydn; Heiney;
Keller suppl.; Lass AN; Magill
I, CE, M1&2, MAF, MC;
Morehead; Olfson; Smith; Ward
Great General's Battle, The see
Kokusenya Kassen
Great God Brown, The. Eugene
O'Neill. Best '25; Drury;
Gassner; Keller suppl.; Mat-
law; NCTE; Shank; Shipley;
Sobel; Sprinchorn
Great Good Place, The. Henry
James. Gale-J
Great Heart Gillian. John Oxen-
ham. Kaye
Great Highway, The. August
Strindberg. Matlaw; Sprinchorn
Great Hunger, The. Johan Bojer.
Haydn; Keller suppl.
Great Hunger, The. Cecil Wood-
ham-Smith. Magill '64, M1,
S
Great Learning, The. Attributed
to Tseng Tzu or Tzu Sau.
Magill WP
Great Magician, The. Arranged
by Lawrence Carra. NBC 1,
2
Great Meadow, The. Elizabeth
Madox Roberts. Magill II,
CE, M1&2, MAF, MC; Smith

Great Plains, The. Walter Pres-
cott Webb. Magill IV, MC
Great Proconsul, The. Sidney C.
Grier. Kaye
Great Railway Bazaar, The. Paul
Theroux. Magill '76
Great Republic: A History of the
American People, The. Bernard
Bailyn et al. Magill '78
Great River. Paul Horgan. Ma-
gill '54, M1, MB, S
Great Sebastians, The. Howard
Lindsay and Russel Crouse.
NCTE
Great Shadow, The. Sir Arthur
Conan Doyle. Kaye; Keller
Great Stone Face, The. Nathaniel
Hawthorne. Gale-H
Great Terror, The. Robert Con-
quest. Magill '69, S
Great Testament, The. François
Villon. Magill III, M1, MC,
MP
Great Theatre of the World.
Pedro Calderon de la Barca.
Shank
Great Tradition, The. Katharine
Fullerton Gerould. Keller
Great Valley, The. Mary John-
ston. Magill III, CE, M1&2,
MAF, MC
Great Victorian Collection, The.
Brian Moore. Magill '76
Great War and Modern Memory,
The. Paul Fussell. Magill
'76
Great White Hope, The. Howard
Sackler. Best '68; Bonin;
Drury; Magill '70
Greatest Thing in the World, The.
Henry Drummond. Keller
Greatness and Decline of Rome.
Guglielmo Ferrero. Keller
Greece Under Foreign Domination.
George Finlay. Keller
Greek Anthology, The. Constanti-
nus Cephalas. Feder
Greek Anthology, The. Unknown.
Haydn
Greek Interpreter, The. Sir
Arthur Conan Doyle. Hardwick
SH
Greek Passion, The. Nikos
Kazantzakis. Magill IV, '54,
M1, MC, S
Greek Slave, A. Sidney Jones,
Owen Hall, Harry Greenbank
and Adrian Ross. Drinkrow

Greek Studies. Walter Pater.
Keller
Green Bay Tree, The. Louis
Bromfield. Haydn; Keller
suppl.; Magill I, CE, M1&2,
MAF, MC; Morehead
Green Bay Tree, The. Mordaunt
Shairp. Best '33; Drury;
Matlaw; Sobel
Green Book, The. Maurice Jókai.
Keller
Green Carnation, The. Robert
S. Hichens. Johnson; Keller
Green Cockatoo, The. Arthur
Schnitzler. Gassner; Matlaw;
Shank; Sobel
Green Fields. Peretz Hirsh-
bein. Gassner; Matlaw
Green Goddess, The. William
Archer. Best '20; Cartmell;
Drury; Matlaw; Shipley
Green Grow the Lilacs. Lynn
Riggs. (See also adaptation
Oklahoma by Richard Rodgers
and Oscar Hammerstein.)
Best '30; Drury; Magill III,
CE, M1&2, MC, MD; Matlaw;
NCTE; Shank; Shipley; Sobel
Green Hat, The. Michael Arlen.
Best '25; Keller suppl.; Sobel
Green Helmet, The. William
Butler Yeats. Matlaw
Green Henry see Grüne Hein-
rich, Der
Green House, The. Mario Vargas
Llosa. Magill '70
Green Julia. Paul Ableman.
Best '72; Drury
Green Man, The. Kingsley Amis.
Magill Ss
Green Mansions. William Henry
Hudson. Armstrong; Goodman;
Haydn; Keller; Lass BN; Magill
I, CE, M1&2, MC, MEF;
Ward; Wilson
Green Mare, The. Marcel Aymé.
Magill '57, S
Green Mirror, The. Hugh Wal-
pole. Keller suppl.
Green Mountain Boys, The.
Daniel Pierce Thompson.
Kaye; Magill II, CE, M1&2,
MAF, MC
Green Pastures, The. Marc
Connelly. Best '29; Bonin;
Cartmell; Drury; Haydn; Lass
AP; Lovell; Matlaw; Shank;
Shipley; Sobel; Thomas

Green Pastures and Piccadilly.
William Black. Keller
Greenback Era, The. Irwin Unger.
Magill Ss
Greene's Groatsworth of Wit
Bought with a Million of Re-
pentance. Robert Greene.
Keller (Groats-); Magill IV,
MC; Ruoff
Greengage Summer, The. Rumer
Godden. Magill '59, S
Greening of America, The.
Charles Reich. Magill '71
Greenwillow. B. J. Chute.
Magill '57, S
Greifenstein. Francis Marion
Crawford. Keller
Grettir the Strong. Unknown.
Magill I, CE, M1&2, MC,
MEUF
Greville Fane. Henry James.
Gale-J
Grey Days and Gold. William
Winter. Keller
Grey Granite see Scots Quair,
A
Greybeard. Brian W. Aldiss.
Magill SF
Griffith Gaunt. Charles Reade.
Johnson; Keller
Grihya-Sûtras, Rules of Vedic
Domestic Ceremonies, The.
Keller (Sacred Books)
Gringa, La. Florencio Sánchez.
Magill II, CE, M1&2, MC, MD
Gringoire. Theodore de Banville.
Shipley
Griselda. Gerhart Hauptmann.
Matlaw
Groatsworth of Wit Bought with a
Million of Repentance, A
see Greene's Groatsworth of
Wit Bought with a Million of
Repentance
Grosse Verzicht, Der (The Great
Renunciation). Reinhold
Schneider. Kienzle
Grouch, The see Dyskolos
"Ground Arms!" Bertha Felicie
Sophie (Kinsky) von Suttner.
Keller
Group, The. Mary McCarthy.
Magill '64, M1, S
Group, The. Mercy Warren.
Lovell
Group of Noble Dames, A.
Thomas Hardy. Saxelby
Group Portrait with Lady. Hein-

rich Böll. Magill '74
Grover Cleveland, the Man and
the Statesman. Robert McNutt
McElroy. Keller suppl.
(Cleveland)
Growing into Love. X. J. Ken-
nedy. Magill '70
Growth and Influence of Classical
Greek Poetry, The. R. C.
Jebb. Keller (Classical)
Growth of British Industry and
Commerce, The. William
Cunningham. Keller
Growth of the Idea of God, The.
Shailer Mathews. Magill CHL
Growth of the Soil. Knut Ham-
sun. Haydn; Heiney; Keller
suppl.; Lass EN; Magill I,
CE, M1&2, MC, MEUF
Growth or Decline?: The Church
Today. Emmanuel Cardinal
Suhard. Magill CAL
Grüne Heinrich, Der (Green
Henry). Gottfried Keller.
Haydn (Green); Magill III, CE,
M1&2, MC, MEUF
Gryll Grange. Thomas Love
Peacock. Keller
Guard of Honor. James Gould
Cozzens. Magill III, CE,
M1&2, MAF, MC
Guardian Angel, The. Oliver
Wendell Holmes. Johnson;
Keller
Guardsman, The. Ferenc Mol-
nár. Cartmell; Drury; Keller
suppl.; Matlaw; Sobel
Cuenn. Blanche Willis (Howard)
von Teuffel. Johnson
Guermantes Way, The. Marcel
Proust. (See also series
title Remembrance of Things
Past.) Haydn p. 631; Heiney
Guernica. Fernando Arrabal.
Kienzle
Guerre au XXe Siècle, La. Albert
Robida. Magill SF
Guerrillas. V. S. Naipaul.
Magill '76
Guest and His Going, A. P. H.
Newby. Magill '61, S
Guest Friend, The see Golden
Fleece
Guest in the House. Hagar
Wilde and Dale Eunson. (See
adaptation Dear Evelyn by
Emlyn Williams.)
Guest the One-Eyed. Gunnar

Gunnarsson. Magill III, M1,
MC, MEUF
Guest's Confession. Henry James.
Gale-J
Guggenheims: An American Epic,
The. John H. Davis. Magill
'79
Guide, The. R. K. Narayan.
Magill IV, '59, M1, MC, S
Guide for the Perplexed. Mai-
monides. Haydn; Magill WP
Guide for the Perplexed, A.
E. F. Schumacher. Magill '78
Guilty Party. George Ross and
Campbell Singer. French
Guilty Pleasures. Donald Barthel-
me. Magill '75
Guinea-Pig, The. Warren Chet-
ham-Strode. French
Gulag Archipelago: Parts I-II,
The. Aleksandr I. Solzhenitsyn.
Magill '75
Gulag Archipelago: Two, Parts
III-IV, The. Aleksandr I.
Solzhenitsyn. Magill '76
Gulag Archipelago: Three, Parts
V-VII, 1918-1956, The.
Aleksandr I. Solzhenitsyn.
Magill '78
Gulistān, The. Sa'dī. Haydn;
Keller
Gulliver's Travels. Jonathan
Swift. Armstrong; Downs M,
FG; Goodman; Grozier; Haydn;
Johnson; Johnson-18th; Keller;
Lass BN; Magill I, CE, M1&2,
MC, MEF; Wilson
Gull's Hornbook, The. Thomas
Dekker. Magill IV, MC; Ruoff
Gun-Maker of Moscow, The.
Sylvanus Cobb, Jr. Johnson;
Keller
Gunnar. Jhalmar Jhorth (Hjalmar
Hjorth) Boyesen. Johnson;
Keller
Guns of August, The. Barbara
W. Tuchman. Magill '63, M1,
S
Gustav Adolf. August Strindberg.
Matlaw
Gustav den tredge. Per Hall-
ström. Sobel
Gustav III. August Strindberg.
Matlaw
Gustav Vasa. August Strindberg.
Matlaw; Shank
Guy Domville. Henry James.
Matlaw

Guy Fawkes. William Harrison
Ainsworth. Kaye
Guy Livingstone. George Alfred
Lawrence. Keller; Magill M1
Guy Mannering. Sir Walter Scott.
Haydn; Johnson; Keller; Mc-
Spadden W; Magill II, CE,
M1&2, MC, MEF
Guy of Warwick. Unknown.
Keller; Magill III, CE, M1&2,
MC, MP
Guys and Dolls: A Musical Fable
of Broadway. Jo Swerling,
Abe Burrows and Frank Loes-
ser. Best '50; Drinkrow;
NCTE
Guzmán d'Alfarache. Mateo Ale-
mán. Haydn; Johnson; Keller;
Magill II, CE, M1&2, MC,
MEUF
Guzman, Go Home. Alan Sillitoe.
Magill '70
Gyges and His Ring. Christian
Friedrich Hebbel. Haydn;
Shank
Gypsies Metamorphosed, The.
Ben Jonson. Ruoff
Gypsy. Maxwell Anderson. Best
'28
Gypsy. Gypsy Rose Lee. (See
adaptation by Jule Styne et
al.)
Gypsy. Jule Styne, Stephen
Sondheim and Arthur Laurents.
(Based on the book by Gypsy
Rose Lee.) Chapman '59;
NCTE

-H-

H. G. Wells. Lovat Dickson.
Magill '70
H. G. Wells. Norman and Jeanne
MacKenzie. Magill '74
H. M. S. Pinafore. William
Schwenck Gilbert and Arthur
Sullivan. Drury; Magill I,
CE, M1&2, MC, MD; Shipley;
Sobel (Pinafore)
Habbakkuk Hilding. Tobias
George Smollett. Johnson-
18th/2
Hachi-no-Ki. Seami. Sobel
Hadassah, Queen of Persia.
Agnese Laurie-Walker. Kaye

Hadrian the Seventh. Baron Corvo.
(See also adaptation by Peter
Luke.) Ward
Hadrian VII. Peter Luke. (Based
on the story by Baron Corvo.)
Best '68; Drury; Magill '70
Hadrian's Memoirs. Marguerite
Yourcenar. Magill IV, '54,
M1, MC, S
Haglets, The. Herman Melville.
Gale-M
Hagoromo (The Robe of Feathers).
Seami. Gassner; Sobel
Hail and Farewell. George Moore.
Keller; Ward
Hair. Gerome Ragni, James
Rado and Galt MacDermot.
Anderson; NCTE
Hair of Harold Roux, The.
Thomas Williams. Magill '75
Hairy Ape, The. Eugene O'Neill.
Drury; Gassner; Heiney; Keller
suppl. ; Lovell; Matlaw; NCTE;
Shank; Shipley; Sobel
Hajji Baba of Ispahan. James
Morier. Johnson; Keller;
Magill I, CE, M1&2, MC, MEF
Hakluyt's Voyages. Richard Hak-
luyt. Haydn; Magill I, CE,
M1&2, MC, MNF; Ruoff
Hakon Jarl. Adam Gottlob Oehlen-
schläger. Drury
Halcyon Drift. Brian Stableford.
Magill SF
Half a Loaf. E. Eynon Evans.
French
Half Past Human. T. J. Bass.
Magill SF
Half Sun Half Sleep. May Swen-
son. Magill '68, S
Halfway House. Maurice Hewlett.
Ward
Hall of Fantasy, The. Nathaniel
Hawthorne. Gale-H
Hall of Mirrors, A. Robert
Stone. Magill '68, S
Hamilton. Mary P. Hamlin and
George Arliss. Drury
Hamlet, The. William Faulkner.
Heiney; Magill II, CE, M1&2,
MC
Hamlet in Wittenberg. Gerhart
Hauptmann. Matlaw
Hamlet of Stepney Green, The.
Bernard Kops. Kienzle; Matlaw
Hamlet, Prince of Denmark.
William Shakespeare. Arm-
strong; Baker; Campbell; Cart-

mell; Chute; Clark; Downs M;
Drury; Gassner; Guerber-ST;
Halliday; Haydn; Hix; Keller;
Lamb; McCutchan-ST; Mc-
Spadden S; Magill I, CE,
M1&2, MAF, MC, MD; Ruoff;
Shank; Shipley; Sobel; Thomas;
Wilson
Hammarskjöld.   Brian Urquhart.
Magill '74
Hammer and Anvil.   Friedrich
Spielhagen.   Johnson; Keller
Hamp.   John Wilson.   (Based
on the novel Return to the
Wood by J. L. Hodson.)
Best '66
Hampdenshire Wonder, The.
John Davys Beresford.   Magill
SF
Hampshire Days.   W. H. Hudson.
Magill IV, MC
Han Fei Tzu.   Han Fei.   Magill
WP
Hand, The.   Theodore Dreiser.
Gerber
Hand of Ethelberta, The.
Thomas Hardy.   Saxelby
Hand of Leonore, The.   Hugh
Noel Williams.   Kaye
Hand of the Potter, The.   Theo-
dore Dreiser.   Gerber
Handful of Dust, A.   Evelyn
Waugh.   Magill I, CE, M1&2,
MC, MEF; Stade p. 65
Handley Cross.   Robert Smith
Surtees.   Magill I, CE,
M1&2, MC, MEF
Hands Across the Sea.   Noel
Coward.   French
Hands Around (La Ronde).
Arthur Schnitzler.   Drury
(Ronde); Gassner (Ronde);
Matlaw; Shank (Ronde)
Handy Andy.   Samuel Lover.
Johnson; Keller; Magill II,
CE, M1&2, MC, MEF
Hanger Stout, Awake!   Jack
Mathews.   Magill '68, S
Hangman, The.   Pär Lagerkvist.
Matlaw
Hangman's House.   Donn Byrne.
Magill II, CE, M1&2, MC,
MEF
Hanna Jagert.   Otto Erich
Hartleben.   Drury
Hannah.   Dinah Maria Mulock.
Keller
Hannah Thurston.   Bayard Taylor.

Keller
Hannele's Journey to Heaven (As-
sumption of Hannele).   Gerhart
Hauptman.   Drury (Assumption);
Haydn; Heiney (Assumption);
Matlaw; Shank; Shipley; Sobel
Hans Brinker, or The Silver
Skates.   Mary Mapes Dodge.
Haydn; Johnson
Hans of Iceland.   Victor Hugo.
Johnson
Hans Phaall.   Edgar Allan Poe.
Gale-PP
Hänsel and Gretel.   Adelheid
Wette.   Shipley
Happiest Days of Your Life, The.
John Dighton.   French
Happiest Millionaire, The.   Kyle
Crichton.   Drury; NCTE
Happy Birthday.   Anita Loos.
Drury
Happy Birthday, Wanda June.
Kurt Vonnegut, Jr.   Drury;
NCTE (drama)
Happy Days.   Samuel Beckett.
Drury; Gassner; Kienzle; Mat-
law; Shank
Happy Days.   Walter Greenwood.
French
Happy Days.   Wilfred Massey.
French
Happy End.   Bertolt Brecht, Elisa-
beth Hauptman and Kurt Weill.
Matlaw
Happy Ending.   Douglas Turner
Ward.   Drury
Happy Exiles, The.   Felicity
Shaw.   Magill '57, S
Happy Failure, The.   Herman
Melville.   Gale-M
Happy Families Are All Alike.
Peter Taylor.   Magill '60, M1,
S
Happy-Go-Lucky, The.   Josef von
Eichendorff.   Johnson
Happy Haunting.   James Seay.
Drury
Happy Hypocrite: A Fairy Tale
for Tired Men, The.   Max
Beerbohm.   Ward
Happy Journey to Trenton and
Camden, The.   Thornton
Wilder.   Matlaw
Happy Landings.   Patrick Cargill
and Jack Beale.   French
Happy Marriage, The.   R. V.
Cassill.   Magill '67, S
Happy Marriage, The.   John

Keller
Henderson the Rain King. Saul
Bellow. Magill IV, '60, M1,
MC, S
Henrietta, The. Bronson Howard.
Drury; Lovell; Sobel
Henrietta Temple. Benjamin
Disraeli. Johnson
Henry Adams: 1877-1890. Ernest
Samuels. Magill '59, MB, S
Henry Adams: 1890-1918. Ernest
Samuels. Magill '65, S
Henry Bourland. Albert E. Han-
cock. Kaye
Henry Esmond. William Make-
peace Thackeray. Goodman;
Grozier; Haydn; Hix; Johnson;
Kaye; Keller; Magill I, CE,
M1&2, MC, MEF; Mudge
Henry James. Leon Edel. Magill
'63, S
Henry James: Autobiography.
Henry James. Magill '57
Henry James Letters, Volume I
(1843-1875). Henry James
and Leon Edel, editor.
Magill '75
Henry Knox. North Callahan.
Magill Ss
Henry Masterton. George Payne
Rainsford James. Johnson
Henry of Guise. George Pain
Rainsford James. Kaye
Henry of Navarre. May Wynne.
Kaye
Henry, Prince of Portugal.
Richard Henry Major. Keller
Henry the Eighth. Francis
Hackett. Haydn
Henry VIII. J. J. Scarisbrick.
Magill '69, S
Henry the Eighth. William
Shakespeare. Campbell;
Chute; Clark; Gassner; Guer-
ber-SH; Halliday; Haydn;
Keller; McCutchan-SH; Mc-
Spadden S; Magill II, CE,
M1&2, MC, MD; Ruoff; Ship-
ley (King); Sobel (King)
Henry the Eighth and His Court.
Louise Muhlbach. Johnson
Henry the Fifth. William Shake-
speare. Baker; Campbell;
Chute; Clark; Drury; Gassner;
Guerber-SH; Halliday; Haydn;
Keller; Lamb; McCutchan-SH;
McSpadden S; Magill I, CE,
M1&2, MC, MD; Ruoff;

Shank; Shipley; Sobel; Wilson
Henry IV (Enrico IV). Luigi
Pirandello. Drury; Gassner
(Enrico IV); Heiney; Matlaw;
Shank; Shipley; Sobel; Sprinchorn
Henry the Fourth, Part One.
William Shakespeare. Baker;
Campbell; Chute; Clark; Gass-
ner; Guerber-SH; Halliday;
Haydn; Keller; Lamb; Mc-
Cutchan-SH; McSpadden S;
Magill II, CE, M1&2, MC, MD;
Ruoff; Shank; Shipley; Sobel
Henry the Fourth, Part Two.
William Shakespeare. Baker;
Campbell; Chute; Clark; Gass-
ner; Guerber-SH; Halliday;
Haydn; Keller; Lamb; Mc-
Cutchan-SH; McSpadden S; Ma-
gill II, CE, M1&2, MC, MD;
Ruoff; Shank; Shipley (King);
Sobel (King)
Henry the Sixth, Part One. Wil-
liam Shakespeare. Baker;
Campbell; Chute; Clark; Gass-
ner; Guerber-SH; Halliday;
Haydn; Keller; Lamb (War of
the Roses); McCutchan-SH;
McSpadden S; Magill II, CE,
M1&2, MC, MD; Ruoff; Shipley;
Sobel
Henry the Sixth, Part Two. Wil-
liam Shakespeare. Baker;
Campbell; Chute; Clark; Gass-
ner; Guerber-SH; Halliday;
Haydn; Keller; Lamb (War of
the Roses); McCutchan-SH;
McSpadden S; Magill II, CE,
M1&2, MC, MD; Ruoff; Shipley;
Sobel
Henry the Sixth, Part Three.
William Shakespeare. Baker;
Campbell; Chute; Clark; Gass-
ner; Guerber-SH; Halliday;
Haydn; Keller; Lamb (War of
the Roses); McCutchan-SH;
McSpadden S; Magill II, CE,
M1&2, MC, MD; Ruoff; Shipley;
Sobel
Henry Ward Beecher. Paxton
Hibben. Keller suppl. (Beech-
er)
Henry's Fate & Other Poems,
1967-1972. John Berryman.
Magill '78
Heptameron, The. Marguerite
d'Angoulême, Queen of Navarre.
Haydn

Her Cardboard Lover. Valerie
Wingate and P. G. Wodehouse.
(Based on Dans sa candeur
naive by Jacques Deval.)
Shipley
Her Dearest Foe. Mrs. Alexander.
Keller
Her Master's Voice. Clare Kum-
mer. Best '33; Drury
Her Son's Wife. Dorothy Can-
field Fisher. Keller suppl.
Heracles see Herakles Mad
Heracles at Taenarum. Sophocles.
Hathorn
Heraclidae. Euripides. Hathorn
Heraclitus: Fragments. Hera-
clitus of Ephesus. Magill WP
Herakleiskos. Sophocles. Hathorn
Herakles. Archibald MacLeish.
Magill '68, S
Herakles Mad. Euripides. Feder
(Madness); Gassner (Heracles);
Hathorn (Heracles); Magill III,
CE, M1&2, MC, MD; Rein-
hold (Mad Heracles); Shipley
(Heracles)
Herakles Mad (Hercules furens;
Mad Hercules). Lucius
Annaeus Seneca. Feder;
Hathorn; Reinhold
Herakles Mainomenos see
Herakles Mad
Herald of the West, A. Joseph
A. Altsheler. Kaye
Heralds, The. Aeschylus.
Hathorn
Heralds of Empire. Agnes C.
Laut. Kaye
Herbe rouge, L'. Boris Vian.
Magill SF
Herberge, Die (The Inn). Fritz
Hochwälder. Kienzle
Hercules and His Twelve Labors.
Unknown. Magill I, CE,
M1&2, MC, MEUF
Hercules and the Augean Stables.
Friedrich Dürrenmatt. Kienzle
Hercules Furens see Herakles
Mad
Hercules on Oeta. Lucius
Annaeus Seneca. Feder;
Hathorn; Reinhold
Herdsmen, The. Elizabeth Mar-
shall Thomas. Magill '66, S
Here Abide Monsters. Andre
Norton. Magill SF
Here and Now. David Rogers.
Drury

Here at the New Yorker. Brendan
Gill. Magill '76
Here Come the Clowns. Philip
Barry. Best '38; Drury; Mat-
law; Shank; Shipley
Here We Come Gathering. Philip
King and Anthony Armstrong.
French
Hereditary Genius, Its Laws and
Consequences. Francis Galton.
Haydn; Keller
Heretics. Gilbert Keith Chester-
ton. Keller
Hereward the Wake. Charles
Kingsley. Johnson; Kaye;
Keller; Magill I, CE, M1&2,
MC, MEF
Heritage. Philip Barry. NCTE
Heritage, The. Burton E. Steven-
son. Kaye
Heritage. Anthony West. Magill
'55, S
Heritage and Its History, A.
Ivy Compton-Burnett. Magill
IV, '61, MC, S
Hermann and Dorothea. Johann
Wolfgang von Goethe. Haydn;
Keller
Hermaphrodeity. Alan Friedman.
Magill '73
Hermetic Books. Unknown.
Keller
Hermione. August Strindberg.
Matlaw
Hernani. Victor Hugo. Cart-
mell; Drury; NBC 2; Shank;
Shipley; Sobel; Thomas
Herne's Egg, The. William Butler
Yeats. Matlaw
Hero, The. Gilbert Emery.
Best '21; Drury
Hero, The. Menander. Hathorn
Hero and Leander. Franz Grill-
parzer. Gassner; Shank
Hero and Leander. Christopher
Marlowe. Ruoff; Haydn
Hero of Lucknow, A. Frederick
S. Brereton. Kaye
Hero of Our Time, A. Mikhail
Yurievich Lermontov. Berry-
1; Haydn; Keller; Magill III,
CE, M1&2, MC, MEUF
Hero of Sedan, A. Frederick S.
Brereton. Kaye
Herod. Stephen Phillips. Drury
Herod and Mariamne. Christian
Friedrich Hebbel. Shipley
Herodias. Gustave Flaubert.

Kaye
Herod's Children. Ilse Aichinger.
Magill '64, S
Heroes. Aristophanes. Hathorn
Heroides. Ovid. Feder; Magill
IV, MC
Heroische Komödie (Heroic Come-
dy). Ferdinand Bruckner.
Kienzle
Heron, The. Giorgio Bassani.
Magill '71
Heropaideia, or The Institution
of a Young Nobleman. John
Aleland. Ruoff p. 81
Herovit's World. Barry N. Malz-
berg. Magill SF
Herr Karl, Der. Carl Merz and
Helmut Qualtinger. Kienzle
Herr Paulus. Sir Walter Besant.
Johnson
Herr Puntila and His Servant
Matti. Bertolt Brecht and
Paul Dessau. Kienzle; Matlaw
Herself Surprised. Joyce Cary.
Magill III, CE, M1&2, MC,
MEF; Olfson; Ward
Herzog. Saul Bellow. Magill
'65, M1, S
Hesperides. Robert Herrick.
Haydn; Magill III, M1, MC,
MP
Het Fregatschip Johanna Maria.
Arthur van Schendel. Haydn
(a)
Hey Rub-A-Dub-Dub. Theodore
Dreiser. Gerber
Hiawatha see Song of Hiawatha,
The
Hidalla, or Karl Hetmann, the
Midget-Giant. Frank Wede-
kind. Matlaw
Hidden Persuaders, The. Vance
Packard. Magill '58, M1,
MB, S
Hidden River, The. Ruth and
Augustus Goetz. (Based on
the novel by Storm Jameson.)
Chapman '57
Hidden River, The. Storm
Jameson. (See adaptation
by Ruth and Augustus Goetz.)
Hidden Spring, The. Roberto
Bracco. Drury; Shipley
Hige Yagura (The Tower for
Whiskers). Miyake Tokuro.
Halford
High and Low. John Betjeman.
Magill '68, S

High Button Shoes. Stephen Long-
street, Sammy Cahn and Jule
Styne. (Based on the novel by
Stephen Longstreet.) NCTE
High Crusade, The. Poul Ander-
son. Magill SF
High Life Below Stairs. James
Townley. Drury
High New House, A. Thomas
Williams. Magill '64, S
High Place, The. James Branch
Cabell. Keller suppl.
High Priestess, The. Robert
Grant. Keller
High Road, The. Frederick Lons-
dale. Drury
High Tide at Gettysburg. Glenn
Tucker. Magill '59, S
High Tor. Maxwell Anderson.
Best '36; Bonin; Drury; Mat-
law; Shipley; Sobel
High Valley, The. Kenneth E.
Read. Magill '66, S
High Water. Richard Bissell.
Magill '54, S
High, Wide and Lonesome. Hal
Borland. Magill '57, S
High Wind in America, A see
Innocent Voyage, The
High Wind Rising, A. Elsie Sing-
master. Magill II, CE, M1&2,
MAF, MC
High Windows. Philip Larkin.
Magill '75
Highland Mary. Clayton M.
Legge. Kaye
Highland Widow, The. Sir Walter
Scott. McSpadden W
Hiketides see Suppliants, The
Hikosan Gongen Chikai no Suke-
dachi. Ume no Shiakaze and
Chikamatsu Yasuzo. Halford
Hilda Lessways. Arnold Bennett.
(See also trilogy title The
Clayhanger Trilogy.) Heiney;
Ward
Hildebrandslied. Unknown. Haydn
Hill Country. Ramsay Benson.
Keller suppl.
Hill of Dreams, The. Arthur
Machen. Magill II, CE, M1&2,
MC, MEF
Hill of Venus, The. Nathan Gal-
lizier. Kaye
Hillingdon Hall. Robert Smith
Surtees. Magill II, CE, M1&2,
MC, MEF
Hills of Home. Norman MacLean.

suppl. (American)
History of Animals.   Aristotle.
Downs F, FG
History of Architecture, A.
James Fergusson.   Keller
History of Art, A.   Joseph Pijoan.
Keller suppl.
History of Charles the Bold,
Duke of Burgundy.   John
Foster Kirk.   Keller (Charles)
History of Charles XII.   Voltaire.
Keller (Charles)
History of Civilization in England.
Henry Thomas Buckle.   Haydn;
Keller (Civilization)
History of Civilization in Europe.
François P. G. Guizot.
Keller (Civilization)
History of Colonel Jacque, The.
Daniel Defoe.   Johnson-18th
(Colonel); Magill II, CE, M1&2,
MC, MEF
History of Creation.   Ernst
Heinrich Haeckel.   Keller
(Creation)
History of Criticism and Literary
Taste in Europe, A.   George
Saintsbury.   Haydn
History of David Grieve, The.
Mrs. Humphry Ward.   Keller
(David)
History of Egypt, A.   James
Henry Breasted.   Haydn;
Keller (Egypt)
History of Egypt, A.   William
Matthew Flinders Petrie, Sir
John Pentland Mahaffy, Joseph
Grafton Milne and Stanley
Lane-Poole.   Keller (Egypt)
History of England, The.   John
Lingard.   Magill CAL
History of England, The.   Thomas
Babington Macaulay.   Haydn;
Magill III, M1, MC, MNF
History of England in the Eight-
eenth Century.   William Edward
Hartpole Lecky.   Keller
(England)
History of English Literature.
Hippolyte Adolphe Taine.
Haydn; Keller (English)
History of English Poetry.   Wil-
liam John Courthope.   Keller
(English)
History of English Thought in the
Eighteenth Century.   Sir Leslie
Stephen.   Keller (English)
History of European Morals from

Augustus to Charlemagne.   Wil-
liam Edward Hartpole Lecky.
Haydn; Keller
History of Fiction.   John Dunlop.
Keller
History of Florence, The.   Nic-
colò Machiavelli.   Keller
(Florence)
History of France.   Jules Miche-
let.   Haydn; Keller (France)
History of Frederick II of Prus-
sia.   Thomas Carlyle.   Keller;
Magill IV, MC
History of Freedom and Other Es-
says, The.   John Emerich Ed-
ward Dalberg Acton.   Magill
CAL
History of French Literature.
Henri Van Laun.   Keller
(French)
History of French Society, The.
Edmond and Jules de Goncourt.
Keller (French)
History of Greece, A.   John B.
Bury.   Haydn
History of Greek, Etruscan and
Roman Ancient Pottery.   H. B.
Walters.   Keller (Ancient)
History of Human Marriage, The.
E. A. Westermarck.   Keller
History of Italian Literature.
Francesco de Sanctis.   Haydn
History of King Richard III.
Sir Thomas More.   Magill IV,
MC; Ruoff (Richard)
History of Methodism in the
United States, A.   James M.
Buckley.   Keller (Methodism)
History of Mr. Polly, The.   H.
G. Wells.   Haydn; Heiney;
Magill II, CE, M1&2, MC,
MEF; Ward
History of Music, The.   W. S.
Pratt.   Keller (Music)
History of New York by Diedrich
Knickerbocker, A.   Washington
Irving.   Keller (Knickerbocker);
Magill III, M1, MC, MNF
History of Painting.   Dr. Alfred
Woltmann and Dr. Karl Woer-
mann.   Keller (Painting)
History of Roman Literature, A.
A. C. T. Cruttwell.   Keller
(Roman)
History of Rome.   Victor Duruy.
Keller (Rome)
History of Rome.   Livy.   Downs
F; Haydn

History of Samuel Titmarsh and
the Great Hoggarty Diamond.
William Makepeace Thackeray.
Mudge
History of Sir Richard Calmady,
The. Lucas Malet. Keller
(Sir)
History of Spanish Literature,
The. George Ticknor. Keller
(Spanish)
History of the American Drama
from the Beginning to the
Civil War, A. Arthur Hobson
Quinn. Keller suppl. (Ameri-
can)
History of the American Drama
from the Civil War to the
Present Day, A. Arthur Hob-
son Quinn. Keller suppl.
(American)
History of the American Frontier.
Frederic L. Paxson. Keller
suppl. (American)
History of the Caliph Vathek see
Vathek
History of the Catholic Church in
the United States, A. John
Dawson Gilmary Shea. Magill
CAL
History of the Civil War in Amer-
ica, A. Comte de Paris
Philippe. Keller
History of the Conquest of Mexico.
William Hickling Prescott.
Haydn; Magill III, M1, MC,
MNF
History of the Consulate and the
Empire. Louis Adolphe Thi-
ers. Haydn; Keller (Consulate)
History of the Councils. Karl
Joseph von Hefele. Magill
CAL
History of the Decline and Fall
of the Roman Empire. Edward
Edward Gibbon. Downs M;
Haydn (Decline); Magill III,
M1, MC, MNF
History of the Development of the
Doctrine of the Person of
Christ. Isaac August Dorner.
Magill CHL
History of the English Constitution.
Dr. Rudolf Gneist. Keller
(English)
History of the English Language.
Thomas Raynesford Lounsbury.
Keller (English)
History of the Four Georges, A.

Justin McCarthy. Keller (Four)
History of the Franks. Saint
Gregory of Tours. Magill CAL
History of the French Revolution,
A. H. Morse Stephens. Kel-
ler (French)
History of the German Resistance,
1933-1945, The. Peter Hoff-
mann. Magill '78
History of the Hardcomes, The.
Thomas Hardy. Saxelby
History of the Inductive Sciences.
William Whewell. Keller (In-
ductive)
History of the Inquisition of the
Middle Ages, A. Henry
Charles Lea. Keller (Inquisi-
tion)
History of the Jews see Anti-
quities of the Jews
History of the Kings of England.
Geoffrey of Monmouth. Downs
F; Haydn
History of the Ottoman Empire
and Modern Turkey: Vol. II,
The. Stanford J. and Ezel
Kural Shaw. Magill '78
History of the Peace Conference,
A. H. W. V. Temperley, ed.
Keller suppl. (Peace)
History of the Peloponnesian War.
Thucydides. Downs M; Feder
(Peloponnesian); Haydn; Magill
III, M1, MC, MNF
History of the People of Israel.
Ernest Renan. Keller (Israel)
History of the People of the
United States, A. John Bach
McMaster. Keller (People)
History of the Persian Wars, The.
Herodotus. Downs F, FG;
Feder (Persian); Haydn; Magill
III, M1, MC, MNF
History of the Popes from the
Close of the Middle Ages, The.
Ludwig von Pastor. Magill
CAL
History of the Rebellion and Civil
Wars in England. Edward
Hyde, Earl of Clarendon.
Magill IV, MC
History of the Reformation in
Scotland. John Knox. Magill
CHL
History of the Reformation of the
Church of England. Bishop
Burnet. Keller (Reformation)
History of the Reign of Ferdinand

and Isabella. William Hickling
Prescott. Keller (Reign)
History of the Reign of King
Henry VII. Sir Francis
Bacon. Magill IV, MC; Ruoff
History of the Renaissance in
Italy see Renaissance in
Italy, The
History of the Sky. Tycho Brahe.
Haydn
History of the Standard Oil Com-
pany, The. Ida M. Tarbell.
Keller (Standard)
History of the United Netherlands.
John Lothrop Motley. Keller
(United)
History of the United States from
the Compromise of 1850.
James Ford Rhodes. Keller
(United States)
History of the Variations of the
Protestant Religion. Jacques
Bénigne Bossuet. Haydn
History of the Warfare of Science
with Theology in Christendom,
A. Andrew Dickson White.
Keller (Warfare)
History of the Wars, The. Pro-
copius of Caocarea. Haydn
History of the Westward Move-
ment. Frederick Merk.
Magill '79
History of the World, The. Sir
Walter Raleigh. Haydn; Keller;
Ruoff p. 351
History of Trade Unionism. Sid-
ney and Beatrice Webb. Keller
(Trade)
Histrio-Mastix. William Prynne.
Ruoff p. 342
Hit the Deck. Vincent Youmans.
(Based on Shore Leave by
R. P. Weston and Bert Lee.)
Drinkrow
Hitler. Alan L. C. Bullock.
Magill '65, S
Hitler Among the Germans.
Rudolph Binion. Magill '77
Hitler's Spies: German Military
Intelligence in World War II.
David Kahn. Magill '79
Hitler's War. David Irving.
Magill '78
Hive, The. Camilio José Cela.
Magill IV, MC
Hiyoku no Cho Yume no Yoshi-
wara (Lover's Nightmare in
the Yoshiwara). Fukumori

Kyusuke. Halford
Hizakurige Tokaido Chu (On
Shank's Mare Along the Tok-
aido). Jippensha Ikku. Hal-
ford; Magill III, MC, MEUF
(Hiza-Kurige)
Hobbit. Patricia Gray. (Based
on the novel by J. R. R. Tol-
kein.) Drury
Hobbit, The. J. R. R. Tolkein.
(See adaptation by Patricia
Gray.)
Hobson's Choice. Harold Brig-
house. (See also adaptation
Walking Happy by Roger O.
Hirson et al.) Drury; French;
Sobel; Ward
Hochzeit (Wedding). Elias Can-
etti. Kienzle
Hocus Pocus. Jack Popplewell.
French
Hogan's Goat. William Alfred.
Best '65; Drury; Magill '67, S;
NCTE
Hogarth's Progress. Peter Quen-
nell. Magill '55, S
Hold April. Jesse Stuart. Magill
'63, S
Hole, The. N. F. Simpson.
French
Hole in the Head, A. Arnold
Schulman. Drury
Holiday. Philip Barry. Best '28;
Drury; Lovell; Matlaw; Shipley;
Sobel
Holiday Romance. Charles Dick-
ens. Hardwick CD
Hollow, The. Agatha Christie.
Drury; French
Hollow Crown, The. John Barton.
French
Hollow of the Three Hills, The.
Nathaniel Hawthorne. Gale-H
Hollow Universe, The. George
De Koninck. Magill CAL
Holly Tree, The. Charles Dick-
ens. Hardwick CD
Holmby House. George John
White Melville. Kaye
Holocaust and the Literary Imagin-
ation, The. Lawrence L.
Langer. Magill '76
Holy Experiment, The. Fritz
Hochwälder. Matlaw; Shank
(The Strong Are Lonely)
Holy State and the Profane State,
The. Thomas Fuller. Keller;
Magill IV, MC; Ruoff p. 165

Holy Terrors, The. Jean Cocteau.
Magill III, CE, M1&2, MC,
MEUF
Holy the Firm. Annie Dillard.
Magill '78
Holy Week. Louis Aragon.
Magill '62, S
Homage to Clio. Wystan Hugh
Auden. Magill '61, S
Homage to Mistress Bradstreet.
John Berryman. Magill IV,
'57, MC, S
Home. David Storey. Best '70;
Drury
Home and Beauty. W. Somerset
Maugham. French
Home and the Heart. Rosemary
Anne Sisson. French
Home As Found. James Fenimore
Cooper. Johnson; Walker
Home at Seven. Robert Cedric
Sherriff. Drury; French
Home from the Hill. William
Humphrey. Magill '59, S
Home Influence. Grace Aguilar.
Johnson
Home Is the Hunter. Helen
MacInnes. Drury
Home Is the Sailor. Jorge Amado.
Magill '65, S
Home of the Brave. Arthur
Laurents. Best '45; Drury;
Lass AP; NCTE
Home to Harlem. Claude McKay.
Keller suppl.
Homecoming, The. Harold
Pinter. Best '66; Drury;
Kienzle; Matlaw; NCTE
Homecoming. C. P. Snow.
Magill '57, S
Homecoming Game, The. Howard
Nemerov. (See adaptation Tall
Story by Howard Lindsay and
Russel Crouse.)
Homemade World, A. Hugh Ken-
ner. Magill '76
Homeric Hymns. Homeric
School. Feder; Haydn
Homeward Bound. James Feni-
more Cooper. Johnson;
Walker
Homilies. Aelfric. Magill CAL
Homilies of Saint John Chrysostom.
Saint John Chrysostom. Magill
CAL
Homilies on the Statues. Saint
John Chrysostom. Magill
CHL

Homme seul, Un (A Man Alone).
Armand Gatti. Kienzle
Homo Sum. Georg Moritz Ebers.
Johnson
Homo Viator. Gabriel Marcel.
Magill CAL
Honcho Nijushiko (The Twenty-Four
Examples of Filial Piety).
Chikamatsu Hanji, assisted by
Miyoshi Shoraku and Takeda
Inaba. Halford
Honest Man's Revenge, The see
Atheist's Tragedy, The; or The
Honest Man's Revenge
Honest Whore, Part One, The.
Thomas Dekker. Holzknecht;
Magill III, CE, M1&2, MC,
MD; Ruoff; Shipley; Sobel
Honest Whore, Part Two, The.
Thomas Dekker. Holzknecht;
Magill III, CE, M1&2, MC, MD;
Ruoff; Shipley; Sobel
Honey in the Horn. H. L. Davis.
Magill I, CE, M1&2, MAF, MC
Honeymoon, The. E. Arnold Ben-
nett. Drury
Honeymoon, The. John Tobin.
Drury
Hong Kildong. Huh Kyun. Haydn
Honor. Hermann Sudermann.
Drury
Honourable Laura, The. Thomas
Hardy. Pinion; Saxelby
Hon. Peter Sterling, The. Paul
Leicester Ford. Johnson;
Keller
Honorary Consul, The. Graham
Greene. Magill '74
Honzo Shimoyashiki (Honzo in the
Detached Palace). Akeshiba
Genzo. Halford
Hoopla! Such Is Life! Ernst
Toller. Matlaw; Shipley
Hoosier Chronicle, A. Meredith
Nicholson. Keller
Hoosier Holiday, A. Theodore
Dreiser. Gerber
Hoosier Schoolmaster, The. Ed-
ward Eggleston. Keller; Magill
I, CE, M1&2, MAF, MAL1,
MC
Hop-Frog. Edgar Allan Poe.
Gale-PP
Hop o'My Thumb. Keller (Fairy
Tales)
Hop, Signor! Michel de Gheld-
erode. Matlaw
Hope for a Harvest. Sophie

Hughie. Eugene O'Neill. Kienzle;
Matlaw
Hugo Black and the Judicial Revo-
lution. Gerald T. Dunne.
Magill '78
Huguenot, The. George Pain
Rainsford James. Kaye
Huh Saing Chun. Park Jiwon.
Haydn
Hulda. Fanny Lewald. Johnson
Human Brutes see Bête humaine,
La
Human Comedy, The. William
Saroyan. Haydn; Lass AN;
Magill I, CE, M1&2, MAF,
MC; Morehead
Human Destiny. Pierre Lecomte
du Noüy. Magill CAL
Human Factor, The. Graham
Greene. Magill '79
Human Intercourse. Philip Gilbert
Hamerton. Keller
Human Mind, The. Karl A.
Menninger. Haydn
Human Nature and Conduct. John
Dewey. Magill WP
Human Situation: Lectures at
Santa Barbara, 1959, The.
Aldous Huxley. Magill '78
Humanity of Christ, The. Romano
Guardini. Magill CAL
Humanizing of Knowledge, The.
James Harvey Robinson.
Keller suppl.
Humanoids, The. Jack William-
son. Magill SF
Humboldt. Helmut De Terra.
Magill '55, S
Humboldt's Gift Saul Bellow.
Magill '76
Humphry Clinker. Tobias George
Smollett. Haydn; Johnson;
Johnson-18th/2; Keller; Lass
BN; Magill I, CE, M1&2,
MC, MEF; Olfson
Hunchback, The. James Sheridan
Knowles. Drury; Shipley
Hunchback of Notre Dame, The.
Victor Hugo. Cohen; Goodman;
Haydn (Nôtre); Johnson
(Notre); Kaye (Notre); Keller
(Notre); Lass EN; Magill I,
CE, M1&2, MC, MEUF
Hundred Years Old (The Centen-
arian). Serafín and Joaquín
Alvarez Quintero. Sobel
Hundred Years War: The English
in France, 1337-1453, The.

Desmond Seward. Magill '79
Hung Lou Meng. Tsao Hsueh-
chin. Haydn
Hungarian Nabob, A. Maurice
Jókai. Haydn
Hunger. Knut Hamsun. Haydn;
Magill I, '68, CE, M1&2, MC,
MEUF, S
Hunger and Thirst. Eugène
Ionesco. Anderson (Soif);
Gassner; Kienzle
Hungerfield and Other Poems.
Robinson Jeffers. Magill Ss
Hunted Down. Charles Dickens.
Hardwick CD
Hunter's Sketches, A. Ivan Tur-
genev. Berry-1
Hunting Hypothesis, The. Robert
Ardrey. Magill '77
Huntresses, The. Aeschylus.
Hathorn
Huon de Bordeaux. Unknown.
Magill III, CE, M1&2, MC,
MEUF
Hurrish. Emily Lawless. Keller
Hurry on Down. John Wain.
Ward
Hyacinth Halvey. Lady (Isabella
Augusta) Gregory. Matlaw;
Sobel
Hyaku-nin Isshu. Sedaiye. Haydn
Hyde Park. James Shirley.
Magill III, CE, M1&2, MC,
MD; Ruoff
Hydriotaphia: Urn-Burial. Sir
Thomas Browne. Haydn; Magill
IV, MC
Hymns of Ephraem the Syrian, The.
Ephraem the Syrian. Magill CHL
Hymns of Saint Ambrose, The.
Saint Ambrose. Magill CAL
Hymns of Saint Thomas Aquinas,
The. Saint Thomas Aquinas.
Magill CAL
Hypatia. Charles Kingsley.
Haydn; Johnson; Kaye; Keller;
Magill I, CE, M1&2, MC, MEF
Hyperion. Friedrich Hölderlin.
Haydn (a)
Hyperion. Henry Wadsworth Long-
fellow. Cohen; Johnson
Hyperion, a Fragment. John
Keats. Haydn
Hypndei Chosun Moonhak. Un-
known. Haydn
Hypochondriac, The see Imagin-
ary Invalid, The
Hypsipyle. Euripides. Hathorn

-I-

I Am a Camera. John van Druten.
(See also adaptation Cabaret
by Joe Masteroff et al.)
Best '51; Bonin; Drury; Mat-
law; NCTE
I Am Legend. Richard Matheson.
Magill SF
I Am Mary Dunne. Brian Moore.
Magill '69, S
I Am Thinking of My Darling.
Vincent McHugh. Magill SF
I and My Chimney. Herman Mel-
ville. Gale-M
I and Thou. Martin Buber.
Magill CHL, WP
I Capture the Castle. Dodie
Smith. French
I, Claudius. Robert Graves.
Magill I, CE, M1&2, MC,
MEF
I Do! I Do! Tom Jones and
Harvey Schmidt. (Based on
The Fourposter by Jan de
Hartog.) NCTE
I Don't Need You Any More.
Arthur Miller. Magill '68, S
I Have Been Here Before. J.
B. Priestley. French
I Have Five Daughters. Margaret
Macnamara. (Based on Pride
and Prejudice by Jane Austen.)
French
I Hear America Swinging. Peter
De Vries. Magill '77
I Heard My Sister Speak My
Name. Thomas Savage.
Magill '78
I Killed the Count. Alec Coppel.
French
I Know My Love. S. N. Behrman.
Best '49; Drury
I Know Why the Caged Bird Sings.
Maya Angelou. Magill Ss
I Married an Angel. Richard
Rodgers and Lorenz Hart.
Sobel
I Never Sang for My Father.
Robert Anderson. Best '67;
Drury
I Never Saw Another Butterfly.
Celeste Raspanti.
I Remember! I Remember!
Seán O'Faoláin. Magill '63,
S
I Remember Mama. John van
Druten. (Based on Mama's

Bank Account by Kathryn
Forbes.) Best '44; Drury;
French; Matlaw; NCTE; Shank
I, Robot. Isaac Asimov. Magill
SF
I Speak for Thaddeus Stevens.
Elsie Singmaster. Magill I,
CE, M1&2, MC, MNF
I Spy. John Mortimer. French
I Would Have Saved Them If I
Could. Leonard Michaels.
Magill '76
Ibaraki. Onoe Baiko VI. Halford
Iberians, The. Sophocles.
Hathorn
Ibis. Ovid. Feder
Ice. Anna Kavan. Magill SF
Ice Age, The. Margaret Drabble.
Magill '78
Icebound. Owen Davis. Best '22;
Bonin; Drury; Keller suppl. ;
Matlaw; Shipley; Sobel
Iceland Fisherman, An. Pierre
Loti. Armstrong; Haydn;
Heiney; Keller; Magill I, CE,
M1&2, MC, MEUF
Iceman Cometh, The. Eugene
O'Neill. Anderson; Best '46;
Drury; Gassner; Kienzle; Lass
AP; Matlaw; Shipley; Sobel;
Sprinchorn
Ichi no Tani Futabagunski (The
Chronicle of the Battle of Ichi
no Tani). Namiki Sosuke.
Halford
Ichneutae see Trackers, The
Icon and the Axe, The. James
H. Billington. Magill '67, S
Iconoclasts. James Gibbons
Huneker. Keller
Iconographs. May Swenson.
Magill '71
I'd Rather Be Right. George S.
Kaufman. Drury; Sobel
Idea of a Christian Society, The.
T. S. Eliot. Magill CHL
Idea of a University, The. John
Henry Cardinal Newman.
Haydn; Magill CAL
Idea of Christ in the Gospels,
The. George Santayana.
Magill CHL
Idea of Comedy and the Uses of
the Comic Spirit, The. George
Meredith. Haydn
Idea of the Holy, The. Rudolf
Otto. Magill CHL, WP
Ideal Husband, An. Oscar Wilde.

Drury; Matlaw; Shipley; Sobel
Idealist View of Life, An. Sarve-
palli Radhakrishnan. Magill
WP
Ideas: General Introduction to
Pure Phenomenology. Edmund
Husserl. Magill WP
Ideological Origins of the American
Revolution, The. Bernard
Bailyn. Magill Ss
Ides of March, The. Thornton
Wilder. Heiney; Magill I,
CE, M1&2, MAF, MC; Ward
Idiot, The. Fyodor Mikhailovich
Dostoevskii. Berry-2; Haydn;
Keller; Magill I, CE, M1&2,
MC, MEUF; Olfson
Idiot's Delight. Robert E. Sher-
wood. Best '35; Bonin; Drury;
Lass AP; Matlaw; NCTE;
Shank; Shipley; Sobel
Idiots First. Bernard Malamud.
Magill '64, S
Idle Inn, The. Peretz Hirsch-
bein. Shipley
Idler, The. Samuel Johnson.
Magill IV, MC
Idylls of the King, The. Alfred,
Lord Tennyson. Armstrong;
Haydn; Keller; Magill I, CE,
M1&2, MC, MP, Wilson
Idyls. Theocritus. Feder; Haydn
If. Lord Dunsany. Drury;
Matlaw; Sobel
If a Man Answers. David Rogers.
(Based on the novel by Winifred
Wolfe.) Drury
If a Man Answers. Winifred
Wolfe. (See adaptation by
David Rogers.)
If Booth Had Missed. Arthur
Goodman. Drury
If Five Years Pass. Federico
García Lorca. Matlaw
If I Were King. Justin Huntly
McCarthy. (See also adapta-
tion The Vagabond King by
Rudolf Friml et al.) Best '99;
Cartmell; Drury; Matlaw;
Shipley; Sobel
If My Wings Heal. James For-
syth. Drury
If Not Thus. Luigi Pirandello.
Matlaw
If the Stars Are Gods. Gregory
Benford and Gordon Eklund.
Magill SF
If This Be Error. Rachel Grieve.

French
If This Be Treason. John Haynes
Holmes and Reginald Lawrence.
Drury
If Winter Comes. A. S. M.
Hutchinson. Keller suppl.;
Magill I, CE, M1&2, MC,
MEF
If You Please. André Breton and
Philippe Soupault. Matlaw
Ignatius His Conclave. John
Donne. Magill IV, MC; Ruoff
Ik En Mijn Speelman. Aart van
der Leeuw. Haydn
Ikutama Shinju (Double Suicide at
Ikutama). Chikamatsu Monzae-
mon. Halford
Il faut passer par les nuages
(Passing Through the Clouds).
François Billetdoux. Kienzle
Il pleut dans ma maison (It's
Raining into My House). Paul
Willems. Kienzle
Ile. Eugene O'Neill. Matlaw;
Sobel
Iliad, The. Homer. (See also
adaptation Trojan War by
Derek Bowskill.) Cohen;
Downs F, FG; Feder; Fleming;
Grozier; Haydn; Johnson; Kel-
ler, Magill I, CE, M1&2, MC,
MP; Sabater
I'll Get There. It Better Be
Worth the Trip. John Donovan.
Benedict
I'll Leave It to You. Noel Coward.
Drury; French
Illegalen, Die (The Illegals).
Günther Weisenborn. Kienzle
Illness As Metaphor. Susan Son-
tag. Magill '79
Illusion of Peace: Foreign Policy
in the Nixon Years, The. Tad
Szulc. Magill '79
Illustrated Man, The. Ray Brad-
bury. Magill SF
Illustrious Client, The. Sir
Arthur Conan Doyle. Hardwick
SH
Illustrious Prince, The. E. Phil-
lips Oppenheim. Keller
I'm Expecting to Live Quite Soon.
Paul West. Magill '71
I'm Radcliffe! Fly Me! Liva
Baker. Magill '77
I'm Really Dragged But Nothing
Gets Me Down. Nat Hentoff.
Benedict

I'm Talking About Jerusalem.
Arnold Wesker. Kienzle;
Matlaw
Image-Bearers, The. Sophocles.
Hathorn
Image Breaker see Eikonok-
lastes
Image of America. R. L. Bruck-
berger. Magill '60, S
Images of Truth. Glenway Wes-
cott. Magill '63, S
Imaginary Conversations. Walter
Savage Landor. Haydn; Kel-
ler; Magill III, M1, MC, MNF
Imaginary Interviews. William
Dean Howells. Carrington
Imaginary Invalid, The (Le Malade
imaginaire; The Hypochondriac).
Molière. Drury; French;
Gassner (Malade); Haydn (Mal-
ade); Keller (Malade); Magill
II, CE, M1&2, MC, MD;
Shank; Shipley; Sobel; Wilson
Imaginary Life of the Garbage
Collector Auguste G. Armand
Gatti. Anderson (Vie); Kienzle
Imagination. James Fenimore
Cooper. Walker
Imaginations. William Carlos
Williams. Magill '71
Imaginative Woman, An. Thomas
Hardy. Pinion; Saxelby
Imbecile, The. Luigi Pirandello.
Matlaw
Imitation of Christ, The. Thomas
à Kempis. Haydn; Magill III,
CAL, CHL, M1, MC, MNF
Imitations. Robert Lowell. Magill
Ss
Immanuel Kant, His Life and
Doctrine. F. Paulsen. Keller
(Kant)
Immensee. Theodor Storm.
Haydn; Keller
Immoralist, The. André Gide.
(See also adaptation by Ruth
and Augustus Goetz.) Heiney
Immoralist, The. Ruth and Au-
gustus Goetz. (Based on the
novel by André Gide.) Best '53
Immortal, The. Alphonse Daudet.
Johnson; Keller
Immortal Lady, The. Clifford
Bax. French
Immortal Marriage, The. Gert-
rude Atherton. Keller suppl.
Immortale Dei. Pope Leo XIII.
Magill CAL

Immortals, The. James E. Gunn.
Magill SF
Imogen. Emily Sarah Holt. Kaye
Imoseyama Onna Teikin (An Ex-
ample of Noble Womanhood).
Chikamatsu Hanji. Halford
Imp of the Perverse, The. Edgar
Allan Poe. Gale-PP
Imperative Duty, An. William
Dean Howells. Carrington
Imperfect Lover, An. R. Gore-
Browne. (See adaptation Cynara
by H. M. Harwood and R.
Gore-Browne.)
Imperial Earth. Arthur C. Clarke.
Magill SF
Imperial Experience in Sub-Saharan
Africa Since 1870, The. Henry
S. Wilson. Magill '78
Imperial Lover, An. Mary Imlay
Taylor. Kaye
Imperial Presidency, The. Arthur
Meier Schlesinger, Jr. Magill
'74
Imperial Woman. Pearl S. Buck.
Magill '57, M1, S
Imperialism. Nikolay Lenin.
Haydn
Imperialism and World Politics.
Parker Thomas Moon. Keller
suppl.
Imperialism at Bay: The United
States and the Decolonization
of the British Empire, 1941-
1945. Wm. Roger Louis.
Magill '79
Importance of Being Earnest, The.
Oscar Wilde. Cartmell; Drury;
Gassner; Haydn; Magill II, CE,
M1&2, MC, MD; Matlaw;
NCTE; Shank; Shipley; Sobel
Impossible Years, The. Bob
Fisher and Arthur Marx.
Drury; NCTE
Impressions and Experiences.
William Dean Howells. Car-
rington
Impressions of a Cousin, The.
Henry James. Gale-J
Impressions of London Social
Life. E. S. Nadal. Keller
Improvisation, or The Shepherd's
Chameleon. Eugène Ionesco.
Matlaw
Improvisatore, The. Hans Chris-
tian Andersen. Keller
In a Garden. Philip Barry.
Drury

In a Shallow Grave. James Purdy. Magill '77
In a Summer Season. Elizabeth Taylor. Magill '62, S
In a Wild Sanctuary. William Harrison. Magill '70
In Abraham's Bosom. Paul Green. Best '26; Bonin; Drury; Haydn; Keller suppl.; Matlaw; NCTE; Shipley; Sobel
In Castle and Colony. Emma Rayner. Kaye; Shank
In Celebration. David Storey. Drury
In Chains. Paul E. Hervieu. Drury
In Chancery see Forsyte Saga, The
In Circling Camps. Joseph A. Altsheler. Kaye
In Cold Blood. Truman Capote. Magill '67, M1, S
In Darkest England and the Way Out. William Booth. Keller
In Dewisland. Sabine Baring-Gould. Kaye
In Dubious Battle. John Steinbeck. Magill II, CE, M1&2, MAF, MC
In Fair Granada. Evelyn Everett Green. Kaye
In Freedom's Cause. George A. Henty. Kaye
In Good King Charles's Golden Days. George Bernard Shaw. Hardwick; Matlaw; Shipley
In Hiding. Ronald Fraser. Magill '73
In His Name. E. Everett Hale. Kaye; Keller
In His Steps. Charles M. Sheldon. Magill CHL
In Hostile Red. Joseph A. Altsheler. Kaye
In Kedar's Tents. Henry S. Merriman. Kaye
In Mediterranean Air. Ann Stanford. Magill '78
In Memoriam. Alfred, Lord Tennyson. Haydn; Keller; Magill IV, MC
In My Father's Court. Isaac Bashevis Singer. Magill '67, S
In My Father's House. Ernest J. Gaines. Magill '79
In Old Kentucky. Charles T. Dazey. Drury

In Paradise. Paul Heyse. Johnson
In Parenthesis. David Jones. Magill '63, S
In Perilous Times. Bessie Merchant. Kaye
In Praise of Darkness. Jorge Luis Borges. Magill '75
In Press-Gang Days. Edgar Pickering. Kaye
In Rome. August Strindberg. Matlaw
In Sarsfield's Days. Miss L. McManus. Kaye
In Search of Happiness. Viktor Sergeyevich Rozov. Kienzle
In Search of History: A Personal Adventure. Theodore Harold White. Magill '79
In Spite of All. Edna Lyall. Kaye
In Steel and Leather. Robert H. Forster. Kaye
In Taunton Town. Evelyn Everett Green. Kaye
In the American Grain. William Carlos Williams. Magill IV, MC
In the Blue Pike. Georg Moritz Ebers. Kaye
In the Boom Boom Room. David Rabe. Magill '76
In the Cage. Henry James. Gale-J
In the Camp of Cornwallis. James O. Kaler. Kaye
In the Camp of Cornwallis. Everett T. Tomlinson. Kaye
In the Clearing. Robert Frost. Magill '63, MB, M1, S
In the Clouds. Charles Egbert Craddock. Keller
In the Country of Ourselves. Nat Hentoff. Benedict
In the Days of Adversity. John Edward Bloundelle-Burton. Kaye
In the Days of Anselm. Gertrude Hollis. Kaye
In the Days of McKinley. Margaret Leech. Magill '60, S
In the Days of My Youth. Amelia Ann Blanford Edwards. Johnson
In the Days of Nelson. F. H. Shaw. Kaye
In the Days of Queen Mary. Edward Ebenezer Crake. Kaye

In the Days of Simon Stern.
Arthur A. Cohen.   Magill '74
In the Grip of Life.   Knut Ham-
sun.   Sobel
In the Grip of the Spaniard.
Herbert Hayens.   Kaye
In the Heart of the Country.   Wil-
liam H. Gass.   Magill '69, S
In the Irish Brigade.   George A.
Henty.   Kaye
In the Jungle of the Cities.
Bertolt Brecht.   Matlaw; Shank
In the King's Favor.   Joyce E.
Muddock.   Kaye
In the Matter of J. Robert Oppen-
heimer.   Heinar Kipphardt.
Best '68; Drury; Kienzle; NCTE
In the Midst of Alarms.   Robert
Barr.   Kaye
In the Name of the People.   Adam
Bruno Ulam.   Magill '78
In the Ocean of Night.   Gregory
Benford.   Magill SF
In the Olden Time.   Margaret
Roberts.   Kaye
In the Palace of the King.   Fran-
cis Marion Crawford.   Kaye;
Keller (Palace)
In the Reign of Terror.   George
A. Henty.   Kaye
In the Rose of Time.   Robert
Fitzgerald.   Magill '58, S
In the Shadow of the Glen.   John
Millington Synge.   Gassner;
Matlaw; Sobel
In the Summer House.   Jane
Bowles.   Best '53
In the Time of Greenbloom.
Gabriel Fielding.   Magill '58,
M1, S
In the Valley.   Harold Frederic.
Kaye
In the Wars of the Roses.   Eve-
lyn Everett Green.   Kaye
In the Wilderness.   Sigrid Undset.
Magill II, CE, M1&2, MC,
MEUF
In the Wine Time.   Ed Bullins.
NCTE
In the Year of Jubilee.   George
Gissing.   Keller
In the Year of Waterloo.   O. V.
Caine.   Kaye
In the Year '13.   Fritz Reuter.
Johnson; Keller
In the Zone.   Eugene O'Neill.
(See also series title S. S.
Glencairn.)   Matlaw

In Time of War.   James F. Cobb.
Kaye
In Time to Come.   Howard Koch
and John Huston.   Best '41
In Times of Peril.   George A.
Henty.   Kaye
In Troubled Times.   A. S. C.
Wallis.   Kaye
In White America.   Martin B.
Duberman.   Drury; NCTE
Inadmissible Evidence.   John Os-
borne.   Anderson; Best '65;
Drury; Kienzle; Magill '66, S;
Matlaw; NCTE
Inazuma-Byôshi.   Santô Kyôden.
Magill III, CE, M1&2, MC,
MEUF
Inca of Perusalem, The.   George
Bernard Shaw.   Hardwick
Incantation, The.   Herondas.
Hathorn (a)
Incarnation of the Word of God,
The.   Saint Athanasius.   Magill
CAL, CHL
Incarnations.   Robert Penn War-
ren.   Magill '69, M1, S
Inca's Ransom, The.   Albert Lee.
Kaye
Incense to Idols.   Sylvia Ashton-
Warner.   Magill '61, S
Inchbracken.   Robert Cleland.
Kaye
Incident at Vichy.   Arthur Miller.
Anderson; Best '64; Drury;
Kienzle; Matlaw; NCTE
Incidents of Travel in Central
America, Chiapas and Yucatan.
John Lloyd Stephens.   Keller
(Central)
Incognito.   Petru Dumitriu.   Ma-
gill IV, '65, MC, S
Incoherence of the Incoherence,
The.   Averroës.   Magill WP
Incomplete Enchanter, The.
Lyon Sprague De Camp and
Fletcher Pratt.   Magill SF
Independent Means.   W. Stanley
Houghton.   Drury
Independent People.   Halldór
Laxness.   Magill I, CE, M1&2,
MC, MEUF
India Today.   Frank Moraes.
Magill '61, S
Indian Bible, The.   John Eliot.
Keller
Indian Emperor, The (The Con-
quest of Mexico by the Span-
iards).   John Dryden.   Sobel

Indian Journey. Waldemar Bonsels. Keller suppl.
Indian Princess, The. James Nelson Barker. Lovell
Indian Summer. William Dean Howells. Carrington; Magill II, CE, M1&2, MAF, MAL2, MC
Indiana. George Sand. Johnson; Keller; Magill II, CE, M1&2, MC, MEUF
Indians. Arthur L. Kopit. Best '69; Drury; Magill '70; NCTE
Indipohdi. Gerhart Hauptmann. Matlaw
Indirizzo sconosciuto (Address Unknown). Paolo Levi. Kienzle
Indiscretion in the Life of an Heiress, An. Thomas Hardy. Pinion
Individuality and Immortality. Wilhelm Ostwald. Keller
Indoor Fireworks. Arthur Macrae. French
Industrial Efficiency. Arthur Shadwell. Keller
Industrial System, The. J. A. Hobson. Keller
Inês de Castro. António Ferreira. Magill III, CE, M1&2, MC, MD
Infants of the Spring. Anthony Powell. Magill '78
Infernal Machine, The. Jean Cocteau. Gassner; Magill '65, M1, S; Matlaw; Shank; Sprinchorn
Infidel, The. Mary E. Braddon. Kaye
Infinity of Mirrors, An. Richard Condon. Magill '65, S
Influence of Sea-Power upon History, The. Alfred Thayer Mahan. Downs M, FG; Keller
Informer, The. Liam O'Flaherty. Magill II, CE, M1&2, MC, MEF
Ingannati, Gli ("The Deceived Ones"). Unknown. Gassner
Ingoldsby Legends, The. Thomas Ingoldsby. Keller; Magill IV, MC
Ingomar the Barbarian. Frederich Halm. Sobel
Inherit the Wind. Jerome Lawrence and Robert E. Lee. Best '54; Chapman '55; Drury;

Lass AP; Lovell; NCTE
Inheritance, The. Susan Edmonstone Ferrier. Johnson; Keller
Inheritors, The. Susan Glaspell. Haydn (a)
Inheritors, The. William Golding. Magill IV, '63, MC, S, SF
Initials, The. Baroness Tautphoeus. Johnson
Ink-Stain, The. René Bazin. Johnson
Inkling, The. Fred Chappell. Magill '66, S
Inn Keeper, The. Carlo Goldoni. Haydn
Inner Law, The. Will N. Harben. Keller
Inner Shrine, The. Basil King. Keller
Innocence of Father Brown, The. Gilbert Keith Chesterton Haydn (Father); Heiney
Innocencia. Sylvio Dinarte. Johnson
Innocent, The. Madison Jones. Magill '58, S
Innocent Eréndira and Other Stories. Gabriel García Márquez. Magill '79
Innocent Party, The. John Hawkes. Magill '67, S
Innocent Voyage. Richard Hughes. (English title A High Wind in Jamaica; see also adaptation by Paul Osborn.) Magill II, CE, M1&2, MC, MEF; Ward (High)
Innocent Voyage, The. Paul Osborn. (Based on the novel by Richard Hughes.) Boot '43
Innocents, The. William Archibald. (Based on The Turn of the Screw by Henry James.) Best '49; Drury; NCTE
Innocents Abroad, The. Mark Twain. Gale-T; Haydn; Keller
Inquiry at Lisieux. Marcelle Maurette. French
Inquiry Concerning Political Justice, An. William Godwin. Downs M; Magill IV, MC
Inquiry into Meaning and Truth, An. Bertrand Russell. Magill WP
Inquiry into the Causes and Effects of the Variolae Vaccinae, a Disease Discovered in Some of the Western Counties of England, Particularly Gloucester-

Dance of Death at Ise). Chika-
matsu Tokuzo. Halford
Ishmael. Mary E. Braddon.
Kaye
Islam Inflamed. James Morris.
Magill '58, S
Island, The. Robert Creeley.
Magill '64, S
Island, The. Athol Fugard, John
Kani and Winston Ntshona.
Best '74
Island. Aldous Huxley. Magill
'63, M1, S, SF
Island of Doctor Moreau, The.
H. G. Wells. Magill SF
Island of the Fay, The. Edgar
Allan Poe. Gale-PP
Island Princess, The. John
Fletcher. Holzknecht; Ruoff
Islanders, The. Philip Booth.
Magill '62, S
Islandia. Austin Tappan Wright.
Magill SF
Islands, The. Attributed to
Aristophanes. Hathorn
Islands in the Stream. Ernest
Hemingway. Magill '71
Isle of Man, The see Purple
Island, or The Isle of Man,
The
Isle of the Dead. August Strind-
berg. Matlaw
Ismay's Children. Mrs. May
Hartley. Kaye
Israel Among the Nations. Ana-
tole Leroy-Beaulieu. Keller
Israel Potter. Herman Melville.
Gale-M; Magill III, CE, M1&2,
MAF, MAL4, MC
Israfel; the Life and Times of
Edgar Allan Poe. Hervey
Allen. Keller suppl.
Issue, The. George Morgan.
Kaye
Istar of Babylon. Margaret
Horton Potter. Kaye
Isthmiasts, The. Aeschylus.
Hathorn
Isutzu. Seami. Sobel
It Can't Happen Here. Sinclair
Lewis. (See adaptation by
Sinclair Lewis and John C.
Moffitt.) Magill SF
It Can't Happen Here. Sinclair
Lewis and John C. Moffitt.
(Based on the novel by Sin-
clair Lewis.) Sobel
It Happened in Irkutsk. Aleksei

Nikolaevich Arbuzov. Matlaw
It Is Better Than It Was. Pedro
Calderón de la Barca. Magill
III, CE, M1&2, MC, MD
It Is Never Too Late to Mend.
Charles Reade. Johnson; Kaye
It Is Really Not Serious. Luigi
Pirandello. Matlaw
It Is Worse Than It Was. Pedro
Calderón de la Barca. Magill
III, CE, M1&2, MC, MD
Italian, The. Mrs. Ann Radcliffe.
Magill III, CE, M1&2, MC,
MEF
Italian Journeys. William Dean
Howells. Keller
Italian Republics. Jean Charles
Léonard Simonde de Sismondi.
Keller
Italian Straw Hat, The (The Leg-
horn Hat). Eugene M. Labiche.
Drury; Shank; Shipley
Italy of To-day. Bolton King and
Thomas Okey. Keller
Itching Parrot, The. José Joaquín
Fernández de Lizardi. Haydn;
Magill II, CE, M1&2, MAF,
MC
"It's a Bird It's a Plane It's
Superman." David Newman,
Robert Benton, Charles Strouse
and Lee Adams. Best '65
Ivan de Biron. Sir Arthur Helps.
Kaye
Ivanhoe. Sir Walter Scott. Arm-
strong; Goodman; Grozier;
Haydn; Hix; Johnson; Kaye;
Keller; Lass BN; McSpadden
W; Magill I, CE, M1&2, MC,
MEF; Wilson
Ivanov. Anton Chekhov. Matlaw;
Sobel
Ivory Apes and Peacocks. James
Gibbons Huneker. Haydn
Ivory Door, The. A. A. Milne.
Drury
Ivory Tower, The. Henry James.
Gale-J
Iwona, księzniczka Burgunda
(Yvonne, Princess of Bur-
gundy). Witold Gombrowicz.
Kienzle

-J-

J. B. Archibald MacLeish.
Best '58; Bonin; Chapman '59;
Drury; French; Kienzle; Lass
AP; Lovell; Magill '59, M1,
MB, S; Matlaw; NCTE; Shank
J R. William Gaddis. Magill
'76
Jack. Alphonse Daudet. John-
son; Keller
Jack: A Biography of Jack Lon-
don. Andrew Sinclair.
Magill '78
Jack and His Island. Lucy M.
Thruston. Kaye
Jack Cade. Robert T. Conrad.
Sobel
Jack Gentian. Herman Melville.
Gale-M
Jack Juggler. Unknown. Holzknecht
Jack of Newberry. Thomas
Deloney. Magill II, CE, M1&2,
MC, MEF; Ruoff (Pleasant
History of John Winchcomb)
Jack, or The Submission. Eugène
Ionesco. Kienzle; Matlaw
Jack Sheppard. William Harrison
Ainsworth. Johnson; Magill II,
CE, M1&2, MC, MEF
Jack Tier. James Fenimore
Cooper. Johnson; Walker
Jacob Faithful. Frederick Mar-
ryat. Keller
Jacobowsky and the Colonel.
S. N. Behrman. (Based on
the play by Franz Werfel.)
Best '43
Jacobowsky and the Colonel.
Franz Werfel. (See also
adaptation by S. N. Behrman.)
Drury; Heiney; Matlaw; Shank
Jacob's Dream. Richard Beer-
Hofmann. Matlaw; Shipley
Jacob's Ladder, The. Denise
Levertov. Magill '64, S
Jacob's Room. Virginia Woolf.
Haydn; Keller suppl.; Ward
Jacqueline. Thérèse Bentzon.
Johnson
Jagged Orbit, The. John Brunner.
Magill SF
Jalna. Mazo de la Roche. Keller
suppl.; Magill II, CE, M1&2,
MAF, MC
James Boswell: The Earlier
Years, 1740-1769. Frederick

A. Pottle. Magill '67, M1, S
James Forrestal. Arnold A.
Rogow. Magill '65, S
James Joyce. Richard Ellmann.
Magill '60, S
James Madison: 1809-1812. Ir-
ving Brant. Magill '57, S
James Madison: 1812-1836. Ir-
ving Brant. Magill '62, S
James Russell Lowell. Martin B.
Duberman. Magill '67, S
James the Fourth. Robert Greene.
Holzknecht; Ruoff
Jan Van Elselo. Gilbert and
Marion Coleridge. Kaye
Jan Vedder's Wife. Amelia Edith
Barr. Keller
Jane. S. N. Behrman. Best '51;
Drury; Kienzle
Jane Clegg. St. John G. Ervine.
Best '19; Drury; Keller suppl.;
Matlaw; Shipley; Sobel
Jane Eyre. Charlotte Brontë.
(See also adaptation by Helen
Jerome.) Armstrong; Cohen;
Drury; Goodman; Grozier; Hal-
perin; Haydn; Johnson; Keller;
Lass BN; Magill I, CE, M1&2,
MC, MEF; Wilson
Jane Eyre. Helen Jerome.
(Based on the novel by Char-
lotte Brontë.) French; NCTE
Jane Field. Mary Eleanor (Wil-
kins) Freeman. Johnson
Jane Shore. Joyce E. Muddock.
Kaye
Jane Shore, a Tragedy. Nicholas
Rowe. Drury; Shipley
Jane Steps Out. Kenneth Horne.
French
Janet's Repentance. George Eliot.
Halperin
Janice Meredith. Paul Leicester
Ford. Keller
Janie. Josephine Bentham and
Herschel Williams. Drury
January Thaw. William Roos.
Drury
Janus. Carolyn Green. French;
NCTE
Janus: A Summing Up. Arthur
Koestler. Magill '79
Japan, an Attempt at Interpreta-
tion. Lafcadio Hearn. Keller
Japanese, The. Edwin O.
Reischauer. Magill '78
Japanese Inn. Oliver Statler.
Magill '62, S

Japhet in Search of a Father.
Frederick Marryat. Johnson
Jar, The. Luigi Pirandello.
Matlaw
Jason. Samson Raphaelson.
Best '41; Drury
Jason and the Golden Fleece.
Unknown. Magill I, CE,
M1&2, MC, MEUF
Jason Group, The. Nicholas
Palmer. French
Java Head. Joseph Hergesheimer.
Haydn; Keller suppl.; Magill I,
CE, M1&2, MAF, MC
Jay of Italy, A. Bernard Capes.
Kaye
Jazz-Singer, The. Samson
Raphaelson. Drury
Je ne parle pas français. Kath-
erine Mansfield. Heiney
Jealous Wife, The. George Col-
man the Elder. Sobel
Jealousy. Mikhail Artsybashev.
Sobel
Jealousy. Herondas. Hathorn (a)
Jealousy: Nine Women Out of
Ten see Shadow, The
Jean-Christophe. Romain Rolland.
Goodman; Heiney; Keller; Lass
EN; Magill I, CE, M1&2, MC,
MEUF
Jean Santeuil. Marcel Proust.
Magill '57, M1, S
Jean Teterol's Idea. Victor
Cherbuliez. Keller
Jean Valjean. Victor Hugo.
(See also Les Miserables.)
Armstrong
Jeanne d'Arc. Percy MacKaye.
Drury; Shank
Jeanne d'Arc. Max Mell. Kienzle
Jeb Stuart, the Last Cavalier.
Burke Davis. Magill '58,
M1, S
Jedermann see Everyman
Jefferson. Albert Jay Nock.
Keller suppl.
Jefferson and Hamilton: The
Struggle for Democracy in
America. Claude G. Bowers.
Keller suppl.; Magill IV, MC
Jefferson and the Ordeal of Lib-
erty. Dumas Malone. Magill
'63, M1, S
Jefferson and the Presidency:
Leadership in the Young Re-
public. Robert M. Johnstone,
Jr. Magill '79

Jefferson Davis: American Patri-
ot. Hudson Strode. Magill
'55, MB, S
Jefferson Davis: Confederate
President. Hudson Strode.
Magill '60, MB, S
Jefferson Davis: Private Letters,
1823-1889. Hudson Strode.
Magill '67, S
Jefferson Davis: The Sphinx of
the Confederacy. Clement
Eaton. Magill '78
Jefferson Davis: Tragic Hero.
Hudson Strode. Magill '65, S
Jefferson the President. Dumas
Malone. Magill '71
Jefferson the President: Second
Term, 1805-1809. Dumas
Malone. Magill '75
Jehanne of the Golden Lips.
Francis G. K. Foster. Kaye
Jennie Gerhardt. Theodore Dreis-
er. Gerber; Haydn; Magill I,
CE, M1&2, MAF, MC
Jenny Kissed Me. Jean Kerr.
Drury
Jenusia. René de Obaldia. Ki-
enzle
Jeppe of the Hill, or The Peas-
ant Transformed. Ludvig
Holberg. Drury; Shank
(Transformed)
Jeremiah. Stefan Zweig. Drury
Jeremiah's Christmas. Malcolm
Kay. French
Jeremy. Hugh Walpole. Keller
suppl.
Jeremy and Hamlet. Hugh Wal-
pole. Keller suppl.
Jeremy at Crale. Hugh Walpole.
Keller suppl.
Jeremy's Version. James Purdy.
Magill '71
Jerome: A Poor Man. Mary
Eleanor (Wilkins) Freeman.
Grozier; Keller
Jersey Villas see Sir Dominick
Ferrand
Jerusalem. Selma Lagerlöf.
Keller
Jerusalem Delivered. Torquato
Tasso. Fleming; Haydn; Kel-
ler; Magill I, CAL, CE,
M1&2, MC, MP
Jerusalem, Jerusalem. Konrad
Wünsche. Kienzle
Jerusalem, the City of Herod and
Saladin. Sir Walter Besant

and E. H. Palmer. Keller
Jesse and the Bandit Queen.
David Freeman. Best '75;
Drury
Jesse Stuart. Ruel E. Foster.
Magill '69, S
Jest, The (The Banquet of Jests).
Sem Benelli. Best '19;
Drury; Keller suppl.; Sobel
Jest, Satire, Irony and Deeper
Significance. Christian Dietrich
Grabbe. Shank
Jesters, The. Miguel Zamacoïs.
Drury
Jesuit, The. Jose Marteniaño
de Alençar. Drury
Jesuit Relations and Allied Docu-
ments, The. Reuben Gold
Thwaites, editor. Keller
Jesus and His Times. Henri
Daniel-Rops. Magill CAL
Jesus of Nazareth. S. C. Bradley.
Kaye
Jesus the Lord. Karl Heim.
Magill CHL
Jeu de l'amour et du hasard, Le
(The Game of Love and Chance).
Pierre Carlet de Chamblain
de Marivaux. Gassner; Shank
Jew, The. Joseph Ignatius
Kraszewski. Keller
Jew of Malta, The. Christopher
Marlowe. Haydn; Holzknecht;
Magill I, CE, M1&2, MC, MD;
Ruoff; Shank; Shipley; Sobel
Jewess of Toledo, The. Franz
Grillparzer. Magill III, CE,
M1&2, MC, MD
Jewish War, The. Flavius
Josephus. Haydn
Jewish Widow, The. Georg Kais-
er. Matlaw
Jews of Angevin England, The.
Joseph Jacobs. Keller
Jill Darling. Vivian Ellis, Ed-
ward Horan, Marriott Edgar,
Desmond Carter and Conrad
Carter. Drinkrow
Jimmy Rose. Herman Melville.
Gale-M
Jitta's Atonement. George Ber-
nard Shaw. Hardwick; Matlaw
Joan and Peter. H. G. Wells.
Keller suppl.
Joan of Arc. Edward Lucie-
Smith. Magill '78
Joan of Arc. Albert Bigelow
Paine. Keller suppl.

Joan of Arc. Thomas Wood
Stevens. Drury
Joan of Lorraine. Maxwell Ander-
son. Best '46; Drury; Kienzle;
Matlaw; NCTE; Shipley
Joanna Godden. Sheila Kaye-
Smith. Keller suppl.; Magill II,
CE, M1&2, MC, MEF
Job, Book of, The see Book of
Job, The
Jocelyn. Alphonse Marie Louis
de Lamartine. Keller
Joel Brand. Heinar Kipphardt.
Kienzle
Joel Chandler Harris. Paul M.
Cousins. Magill '69, S
Johan Johan the Husband, Tyb His
Wife, and Sir John the Priest.
John Heywood. Holzknecht;
Ruoff
Johan Ulfstjerna. Tor Hedberg.
Drury
Johannes Kreisler. Rudolf Ber-
nauer and Carl Meinhard.
Shipley
John. Philip Barry. Drury;
Sobel
John Adams. Page Smith. Magill
'63, S
John and Abigail Adams. Family
of Destiny. Bertha Johnson.
Drury
John Brent. Theodore Winthrop.
Keller
John Brown Buccaneer. George
Griffith. Kaye
John Brown's Body. Stephen Vin-
cent Benét. Haydn; Magill I,
CE, M1&2, MC, MP, Shank
John Bull. George Colman the
Younger. Sobel
John Bull and His Island. Max
O'Rell. Keller
John Bull on the Guadalquivir.
Anthony Trollope. Gerould
John Bull's Other Island. George
Bernard Shaw. Hardwick; Mat-
law; Shipley; Sobel; Ward
John Cabot, the Discoverer of
North America, and Sebastian,
His Son. Henry Harrisse.
Keller (Cabot)
John Caldigate. Anthony Trollope.
Gerould
John Deane. William H. G.
Kingston. Kaye
John Delavoy. Henry James.
Gale-J

John Donne: A Life. R. C.
Bald. Magill '71
John Dryden: The Poet, the
Dramatist, the Critic. T. S.
Eliot. Magill IV, MC
John Ferguson. St John G. Er-
vine. Best '09; Drury; Mat-
law; Shipley; Sobel
John Gabriel Borkman. Henrik
Ibsen. Drury; French; Mat-
law; Shipley; Sobel
John Godfrey's Fortunes. Bayard
Taylor. Johnson
John Gow. Daniel Defoe.
Johnson-18th
John Halifax, Gentleman. Dinah
Maria Mulock. Haydn; John-
son; Keller; Magill II, CE,
M1&2, MC, MEF
John Inglefield's Thanksgiving.
Nathaniel Hawthorne. Gale-H
John Inglesant. Joseph Henry
Shorthouse. Haydn; Johnson;
Keller; Magill II, CE, M1&2,
MC, MEF
John John, the Husband; Tyb,
His Wife, and Sir John, the
Priest see Johan Johan. . .
John Keats. Walter Jackson Bate.
Magill Ss
John Keats. Amy Lowell. Keller
suppl.
John Keats. Aileen Ward. Magill
'64, S
John Keats; His Life and Poetry,
His Friends, Critics, and
After-Fame. Sir Sidney Col-
vin. Keller suppl.
John Keats: The Living Year.
Robert Gittings. Magill '54,
S
John L. Lewis: A Biography.
Melvyn Dubofsky and Warren
Van Tine. Magill '78
John Loves Mary. Norman Kras-
na. Best '46; Drury
John March, Southerner. George
W. Cable. Kaye
John Marr. Herman Melville.
Gale-M
John of Gerisau. John Oxenham.
Kaye
John Paul Jones: A Sailor's
Biography. Samuel Eliot
Morison. Magill '60, M1,
MB, S
John Ploughman's Talks. Charles
Haddon Spurgeon. Magill CHL

John Quincy Adams and the Union.
Samuel Flagg Bemis. Magill
'57, MB, S
John Temple. John Durand. Kaye
John the Baptist. Hermann Suder-
mann. Drury
John Ward, Preacher. Margaret
Deland. Keller
John Winchcomb, The Pleasant
History of. In His Younger
Years Called Jack of Newbury
see Pleasant History of John
Winchcomb
Johnny Belinda. Elmer Harris.
French; NCTE
Johnny Johnson. Paul Green and
Kurt Weill. Best '36; Drury;
NCTE; Shank; Sobel
Johnson over Jordan. J. B.
Priestley. Matlaw
Johnsonian Miscellanies. George
Birkbeck Hill. Keller
Joie de vivre, La. Emile Zola.
Keller (Rougon)
Jolly Beggars, The. Robert
Burns. Keller
Jolly Corner, The. Henry James.
Gale-J
Jonah and the Whale. James
Bridie. French
Jonas und der Nerz (Jonas and the
Mink Coat; The White Chairs).
Herbert Meier. Kienzle
Jonathan Wild. Daniel Defoe.
Johnson-18th
Jonathan Wild. Henry Fielding.
Haydn; Johnson; Johnson-18th/2;
Keller; Magill II, CE, M1&2,
MC, MEF
Jones of the 64th. Frederick A.
Brereton. Kaye
Jörn Uhl. Gustav Frenssen.
Keller
Jorrocks' Jaunts and Jollities.
Robert Smith Surtees. Magill
II, CE, M1&2, MC, MEF
Joscelyn Cheshire. Sarah B. Ken-
nedy. Kaye
Joseph and His Brethren. Louis
Napoleon Parker. Drury
Joseph and His Brothers. Thomas
Mann. Haydn; Heiney; Lass EN
Joseph Andrews. Henry Fielding.
Haydn; Johnson; Johnson-18th/2;
Keller; Magill I, CE, M1&2,
MC, MEF; Olfson
Joseph Balsamo. Alexandre Dumas
(father). Johnson

Joseph Conrad. Jocelyn Baines.
Magill '61, M1, MB, S
Joseph Conrad, Life & Letters.
Joseph Conrad and Georges
Jean Aubry, editor. Keller
suppl. (Conrad)
Joseph in Dothan. Joost van
den Vondel. Haydn (a)
Joseph: The Man Closest to
Jesus. Francis L. Filas, S. J.
Magill CAL
Joseph Vance. William De Mor-
gan. Keller; Magill I, CE,
M1&2, MC, MEF; Ward
Josephine de Montmorenci. An-
thony Trollope. Gerould
Joshua Davidson, Christian and
Communist. E. Lynn Linton.
Keller
Joshua Marvel. Benjamin Leo-
pold Farjeon. Johnson
Journal of a Disappointed Man,
The. W. N. P. Barbellion.
Ward
Journal of a Tour to the Hebrides.
James Boswell. Magill IV,
MC
Journal of Edwin Carp, The.
Richard Haydn. Magill '54, S
Journal of Eugène Delacroix,
The. Eugène Delacroix.
Haydn
Journal of Francis Asbury, The.
Francis Asbury. Magill CHL
Journal of George Fox, The.
George Fox. Keller (a);
Magill CHL
Journal of John Wesley, The.
John Wesley. Keller; Magill
CHL
Journal of John Woolman, The.
John Woolman. Keller (a);
Magill CHL
Journal of Julius Rodman, The.
Edgar Allan Poe. Gale-PP
Journal of Marie Bashkirtseff,
The. Marie Bashkirtseff.
Keller (a)
Journal of the Plague Year, A.
Daniel Defoe. Haydn; Johnson-
18th; Magill IV, MC
Journal of Thoreau, The. Henry
David Thoreau. Magill IV,
MAL5, MC
Journal to Eliza. Laurence
Sterne. Magill IV, MC
Journal to Stella. Jonathan Swift.
Magill IV, MC

Journalists, The. Gustav Frey-
tag. Drury; Shipley
Journals: Early Fifties Early Six-
ties. Allen Ginsberg. Magill
'78
Journals of André Gide, The.
André Gide. Haydn; Magill IV,
MC
Journals of Dorothy Wordsworth.
Dorothy Wordsworth. Magill
IV, MC
Journals of George Whitefield.
George Whitefield. Magill CHL
Journals of Henry Melchior Müh-
lenberg, The. Henry Melchior
Mühlenberg. Magill CHL
Journals of Lewis and Clark, The.
Meriwether Lewis and William
Clark. Magill IV, MC
Journey. Robert K. and Suzanne
Massie. Magill '76
Journey, The. Jiro Osaragi.
Magill '61, S
Journey, The. Lillian Smith.
Magill '54, M1, S
Journey for Joedel. Guy Owen.
Magill '71
Journey from This World to the
Next, A. Henry Fielding.
Johnson-18th /2
Journey in Other Worlds, A.
John Jacob Astor. Johnson;
Magill SF
Journey in the Seaboard Slave
States, A. Frederick Law
Olmsted. Keller
Journey into Summer. Edwin
Way Teale. Magill '61, S
Journey Not the Arrival Matters,
The. Leonard Woolf. Magill
'71
Journey of the Fifth Horse. Ron-
ald Ribman. Bonin
Journey of the Mind to God.
Saint Bonaventure. Magill
CHL, WP
Journey to Ixtlan. Carlos Castan-
eda. Magill '73
Journey to Matecumbe, A. Robert
Lewis Taylor. Magill '62, S
Journey to Panama, The. Anthony
Trollope. Gerould
Journey to the Center of the Earth.
Jules Verne. Magill SF
Journey to the End of the Night.
Louis-Ferdinand Céline. Ma-
gill I, CE, M1&2, MC, MEUF
Journey to the Sky. Jamake

Gould Cozzens. Magill '79
Just Think, Giacomino? Luigi
Pirandello. Matlaw
Justice. John Galsworthy.
Cartmell; Drury; Gassner;
Haydn; Heiney; Keller; Magill
I, CE, M1&2, MC, MD;
Matlaw; NBC 2; Shank; Shipley;
Sobel; Sprinchorn; Ward
Justice Crucified: The Story of
Sacco and Vanzetti. Roberta
Strauss Feuerlicht. Magill '78
Justice Oliver Wendell Holmes.
Mark DeWolfe Howe. Magill
'58, MB, S
Justine. Lawrence Durrell.
Magill '58, M1, MB, S

-K-

"K. " Mary Roberts Rinehart.
Keller
Kagami Jishi (The Dancing Lion).
Fukuchi Ochi. Halford
Kagamiyama Kokyo no Nishikie
(The Women's Chushingura).
Yo Yodai. Halford
Kagekiyo. Unknown. Halford
Kagotsurube Sato no Eizame.
Kawatake Shinhichi III. Hal-
ford
Kaitei Gunkan. Shunro Oshikawa.
Magill SF
Kajiwara Heiza Homare no Ishi-
kiri (The Stonecutting Feat of
Kajiwara). Bunkodo and
Hasegawa Senshi. Halford
Kalevala, The. Elias Lönnrot.
Fleming; Haydn; Magill III,
CE, M1&2, MC, MP
Kallocain. Karin Boye. Magill
SF
Kalte Licht, Das (The Cold Light).
Carl Zuckmayer. Kienzle
Kamakura Sandaiki (The Kamakura
Trilogy). Chikamatsu Hanji.
Halford
Kami no Megumi Uago no Tori-
kumi. Takeshiba Kisui. Hal-
ford
Kamongo. Homer W. Smith.
Magill IV, MC
Kanadehon Chushingura (The
Treasury of Loyal Retainers).
Takeda Izumo, Miyoshi Shoraku

and Namiki Senryo. Halford
Kandy-Kolored Tangerine-Flake
Streamline Baby, The. Tom
Wolfe. Magill '66, S
Kanjincho (The Subscription List).
Namike Gohei. Halford
Kapital, Das. Karl Marx. Arm-
strong (Capital); Haydn; Keller
(Capital); Magill III, M1, MC,
MNF
Karavane. Tor Age Bringsvoerd.
Magill SF
Karen Borneman. Hjalmar Berg-
ström. Drury
Karl Heinrich. Wilhelm Meyer-
Förster. (See his adaptation
Old Heidelberg.)
Karl Marx: An Intimate Biography.
Sauk K. Padover. Magill '79
Kassandra. Paul Ernst. Heiney
Kataki (The Enemy). Shimon
Wincelberg. Best '58
Katakiuchi Tengajaya Mura (Re-
venge at Tengajaya). Naka
Kamesuke I and II. Halford
Katchen's Caprices. Anthony
Trollope. Gerould
Kate Fennigate. Booth Tarking-
ton. Magill I, CE, M1&2,
MAF, MC
Katherine. Anya Seton. Magill
'54, M1, S
Kathleen and Frank. Christopher
Isherwood. Magill '73
Kathleen Mavourneen. Randal
McDonnell. Kaye
Katzengold (Cat Gold). Horst
Salomon. Kienzle
Kaution (The Surety). Hans
Lucke. Kienzle
Kazohinia. Sándor Szathmári.
Magill SF
Kean, or Disorder and Genius.
Jean-Paul Sartre. Kienzle
Keep, The. Gwyn Thomas.
French
Keepers of the House, The.
Shirley Ann Grau. Magill '65,
M1, S
Kellys and the O'Kellys; or, Land-
lords and Tenants, The. An-
thony Trollope. Gerould
Kelly's Eye. Henry Livings.
Kienzle
Kempy. J. C. and Elliott Nugent.
Drury
Kenelm Chillingly. Lord Edward
Bulwer-Lytton. Johnson; Keller

Kenilworth. Sir Walter Scott.
Goodman; Grozier; Haydn;
Johnson; Kaye; Keller; McSpad-
den W; Magill I, CE, M1&2,
MC, MEF
Kennedy Square. Francis Hopkin-
son Smith. Keller
Kenneth. Charlotte Mary Yonge.
Kaye
Kenneth Grahame: A Biography.
Peter Green. Magill '60, S
Kensington Squares, The. Robert
Monro. French
Kentons, The. William Dean
Howells. Carrington
Kentuckians, The. John Fox, Jr.
Keller
Kentucky Cardinal, A. James
Lane Allen. Keller
Kept in the Dark. Anthony Trol-
lope. Gerould
Kettle of Fire. H. L. Davis.
Magill '60, S
Key Largo. Maxwell Anderson.
Best '39; Drury; Matlaw; Shipley
Key to the Doctrine of the Euchar-
ist, A. Dom Anscar Vonier,
O. S. B. Magill CAL
Keys of Heaven, The. August
Strindberg. Matlaw
Keys of the Kingdom of Heaven,
The. John Cotton. Magill
CHL
Keywords. Raymond Williams.
Magill '77
Khat. Theodore Dreiser. Gerber
Kichisama Mairu Yukari no Otozure
(Kichi's Strange Homecoming).
Kawatake Mokuami. Halford
Kickleburys on the Rhine, The.
William Makepeace Thackeray.
Mudge
Kidnap. George Waller. Magill
'62, S
Kidnapped. Robert Louis Steven-
son. Grozier; Haydn; Johnson;
Keller; Magill I, CE, M1&2,
MC, MEF; Wilson
Kidnapped Regiment, The. Robert
Leighton. Kaye
Kiichi Hogen Sanryaku no Maki
(Kiichi Hogen's Book of Tac-
tics). Bunkodo and Hasegawa
Senshi. Halford
Kill Two Birds. Philip Levene.
French
Killer, The. Eugène Ionesco.
Drury; Kienzle; Matlaw; Shank

Killer Angels, The. Michael
Shaara. Magill '75
Killer Thing, The. Kate Wilhelm.
Magill SF
Killing Frost, A. Sylvia Wilkin-
son. Magill Ss
Killing of Sister George, The.
Frank Marcus. Best '66;
Drury
Killing Time. Thomas Berger.
Magill '68, S
Kim. Rudyard Kipling. Haydn;
Heiney; Keller; Lass BN; Magill
I, CE, M1&2, MC, MD, MEF;
Olfson; Ward
Kimitake, Hiraoka see Mishima,
Yukio
Kind and Usual Punishment. Jes-
sica Mitford. Magill '74
Kind Lady. Edward Chodorov.
Drury; NCTE; Shipley
Kindling. Charles Kenyon. Drury
Kindly Ones, The. Anthony
Powell. Magill '63, S
Kinflicks. Lisa Alther. Magill
'77
King, The. Pär Lagerkvist.
Matlaw
King Alfred's Viking. C. W.
Whistler. Kaye
King and I, The. Oscar Hammer-
stein II and Richard Rodgers.
(Based on Anna and the King
of Siam by Margaret Landon.)
Drinkrow; NCTE
King and No King, A. Francis
Beaumont and John Fletcher.
Drury; Magill III, CE, M1&2,
MC; Ruoff; Sobel
King and the Duke, The. Francis
Fergusson. Shank
King Arthur and His Knights see
Bulfinch's Mythology
King Coal. Upton Sinclair.
Heiney
King David and His Wives. David
Pinski. Matlaw
King Edward VII. Sir Sidney
Lee. Keller suppl.
King Edward the Seventh. Philip
Magnus. Magill '65, S
King Henry. Ernst von Wilden-
bruch. Drury
King Horn. Unknown. Magill
IV, MC
King Hunger. Leonid N. Andrey-
ev. Sobel
King John. John Bale. Magill

Lady's Not for Burning, The.
Christopher Fry.   Drury;
Heiney; Kienzle; Magill II,
CE, M1&2, MC, MD; Matlaw;
NCTE; Shank; Shipley;
Sprinchorn; Ward
Lafayette: A Biography.   Peter
Buckman.   Magill '78
Lafcadio Hearn.   Elizabeth Steven-
son.   Magill '62, M1, S
L'aiglon see Aiglon, L'
Laird's Legacy, The.   Mary H.
Debenham.   Kaye
Lais, Le.   François Villon.
Magill IV, MC
Lais of Marie de France, The.
Marie de France.   Magill IV,
CE, M2, MC
Laius.   Aeschylus.   Hathorn
(Theban)
Lake Gun, The.   James Fenimore
Cooper.   Walker
Lalla Rookh.   Thomas Moore.
Haydn; Keller; Magill III, CE,
M1&2, MC, MP
Lally of the Brigade.   Miss L.
McManus.   Kaye
Lamb, The.   François Mauriac.
Magill '57, S
Lament for Adonis.   Bion.   Feder
Lament for Bion.   Attributed to
Moschus.   Feder
Lament for the Molly Maguires.
Arthur H. Lewis.   Magill
'65, S
Lamia.   John Keats.   Haydn
L'amorosa Fiammetta see
Amorosa Fiammetta, L'
Lamp Post, The.   Martin Gregor-
Dellin.   Magill '65, S
Lamplighter, The.   Maria Susanna
Cummins.   Johnson; Keller
Lamy of Santa Fe.   Paul Horgan.
Magill '76
Lancelot.   Walker Percy.
Magill '78
Lancelot.   Edwin Arlington Robin-
son.   Haydn (a)
Lanchester Tradition, The.   G.
F. Bradby.   Ward
Land, The.   Hon. Victoria Mary
Sackville-West.   Ward
Land and Labor.   Seebohm
Rowntree.   Keller
Land Beyond the River, A.
Loften Mitchell.   Drury; NCTE
Land Is Bright, The.   George S.

Kaufman and Edna Ferber.
Drury
Land of Cockayne, The.   Matilde
Serao.   Keller
Land of Cokaine, The.   Unknown.
Keller
Land of Cotton, The.   Randolph
Edmonds.   NCTE
Land of Heart's Desire, The.
William Butler Yeats.   Gass-
ner; Keller; Matlaw; Shipley;
Sobel
Land of Many Names.   Joseph
Capek.   Sobel
Land of Poco Tiempo, The.
Charles F. Lummis.   Keller
Land of Promise, The.   W. Somerset
Maugham.   Matlaw
Land That Time Forgot, The.
Edgar Rice Burroughs.   Magill
SF
Land They Fought For, The.
Clifford Dowdey.   Magill '55,
S
Land Without Justice.   Milovan
Djilas.   Magill '59, M1, S
Landleaguers, The.   Anthony
Trollope.   Gerould
Landlord at Lion's Head, The.
William Dean Howells.   Car-
rington; Keller
Landor's Cottage.   Edgar Allan
Poe.   Gale-PP
Landscape.   Harold Pinter.
Anderson
Landscape Painter, A.   Henry
James.   Gale-J
Landschaft mit Figuren (Landscape
with Figures).   Wolfgang Hilde-
sheimer.   Kienzle
Landslide at North Station.   Ugo
Betti.   Matlaw
Language and the Study of Lan-
guage.   William Dwight Whit-
ney.   Keller
Language, Counter-Memory, Prac-
tice: Selected Essays and In-
terviews.   Michel Foucault.
Magill '78
Language, Truth and Logic.   Al-
fred Jules Ayer.   Magill WP
Languages of Pao, The.   Jack
Vance.   Magill SF
Lanseloet.   Unknown.   Haydn p.
473
Lantern, The.   Alois Jirásek.
Drury

Lantern and Candlelight. Thomas Dekker. Ruoff

Lanterns and Lances. James Thurber. Magill '62, S

Laocoön Group, The. Tadeusz Rosewicz. Kienzle

Laodicean, A. Thomas Hardy. Saxelby

Laokoon. Gotthold Epharim Lessing. Keller

Lapsed, Not Lost. Elizabeth R. Charles. Kaye

Lardners, The. Ring Lardner, Jr. Magill '77

Larissaeans, The. Sophocles. Hathorn

Lark, The. Jean Anouilh. Best '55; Chapman '56; Drury; French; Gassner; Kienzle; Matlaw; NCTE; Shank

Lark Rise. Flora Thompson. Ward

L'assommoir see Assommoir, L'

Last Adam, The. James Gould Cozzens. Haydn

Last Analysis, The. Saul Bellow. Magill '66, S

Last and First Men. Olaf Stapledon. Magill SF

Last Angry Man, The. Gerald Green. Magill '58, S

Last Athenian, The. Viktor Rydberg. Haydn; Keller; Magill II, CE, M1&2, MC, MEUF

Last Austrian Who Left Venice, The. Anthony Trollope. Gerould

Last Castle, The. Jack Vance. Magill SF

Last Chronicle of Barset, The. Anthony Trollope. Gerould; Haydn; Magill II, CE, M1&2, MC, MEF

Last Convertible, The. Anton Myrer. Magill '79

Last Day the Dogbushes Bloomed, The. Lee Smith. Magill '69, S

Last Days of Pompeii, The. Lord Edward Bulwer-Lytton. Cohen; Goodman; Grozier; Haydn; Johnson; Keller; Lass BN; Magill I, CE, M1&2, MC, MEF

Last Frontier, The. Howard Fast. Haydn (a)

Last Gentleman, The. Walker Percy. Magill '67, M1, S

Last Hunt, The. Milton Lott. Magill '54, S

Last Hurrah, The. Edwin O'Connor. Magill '57, MB, S

Last Innocence, The. Célia Bertin. Magill '55, S

Last Kaiser, The. Michael Tyler-Whittle. Magill '78

Last Knight, The. August Strindberg. Matlaw

Last Letters from Egypt. Lady Lucie (Austin) Duff-Gordon. Keller (Letters)

Last Man, The. Mary Wollstonecraft (Godwin) Shelley. Magill SF

Last Meeting of the Knights of the White Magnolia, The. Preston Jones. Best '76

Last Mile, The. John Wexley. Best '29; Drury; Sobel

Last Night of Don Juan, The. Edmond Rostand. Drury

Last of Her Race, The. John Edward Bloundelle-Burton. Kaye

Last of Mrs. Cheyney, The. Frederick Lonsdale. Best '25; Drury; Keller suppl.; Sobel

Last of Mrs. Lincoln. James Prideaux. Drury

Last of Summer, The. Kate O'Brien. Magill II, CE, M1&2, MC, MEF

Last of the Barons, The. Lord Edward Bulwer-Lytton. Johnson; Magill I, CE, M1&2, MC, MEF

Last of the Chiefs, The. Joseph A. Altsheler. Kaye

Last of the Crazy People, The. Timothy Findley. Magill '68, S

Last of the DeMullins, The. St. John E. C. Hankin. Drury; Matlaw

Last of the Just, The. André Schwarz-Bart. Magill '61, S

Last of the Mohicans, The. James Fenimore Cooper. (See also Leatherstocking Saga, The.) Cohen; Goodman; Grozier; Haydn p. 416; Hix; Johnson; Keller; Lass AN; Magill I, CE, M1&2, MAF, MAL1, MC; Morehead; Smith; Walker; Wilson

Last of the Red Hot Lovers. Neil

Simon. Best '69; Drury
Last of the Valerii, The. Henry
James. Gale-J
Last of the Vikings, The. Johan
Bojer. Magill II, CE, M1&2,
MC, MEUF
Last of the Wine, The. Mary
Renault. Magill IV, '57, M1,
MB, MC, S
Last Picture Show, The. Larry
McMurtry. Magill Ss
Last Post, The. Ford Madox
Ford. Keller suppl.
Last Puritan, The. George
Santayana. Haydn; Magill I,
CE, M1&2, MAF, MC
Last Starship from Earth, The.
John Boyd. Magill SF
Last Tales. Isak Dinesen.
Magill '58, M1, S
Last Temptation of Christ, The.
Nikos Kazantzakis. Lass EN;
Magill '61, S
Last Things. C. P. Snow.
Magill '71
Last Tycoon, The. F. Scott
Fitzgerald. Magill III, CE,
M1&2, MAF, MC
Last Unicorn, The. Peter S.
Beagle. Magill '69, M1, S
Last Valley, The. A. B. Guthrie,
Jr. Magill '76
Last Words, The. Jack Popplewell.
French
Late Christopher Bean, The.
Sidney Howard. (Based on
Prenez-garde à la peinture
by René Fauchois.) Best '32;
Drury, Matlaw, NCTD, Oobel
Late Christopher Bean, The.
Emlyn Williams. (Based on
Prenez garde à la peinture
by René Fauchois.) French
Late Edwina Black, The. William
Dinner and William Morum.
French
Late George Apley, The. John
P. Marquand. (See also
adaptation by George S. Kauf-
man and John P. Marquand.)
Haydn, Lass AN, Magill I,
CE, M1&2, MAF, MC; More-
head; Olfson
Late George Apley, The. John
P. Marquand and George S.
Kaufman. (Based on the novel
by John P. Marquand.) Best
'44; NCTE

Late Lord Byron, The. Doris
Langley Moore. Magill '62,
MB, S
Late Love. Rosemary Casey.
French
Late Mattia Pascal, The. Luigi
Pirandello. Magill II, CE,
M1&2, MC, MEUF
Late Summer, The. Adalbert
Stifter. Haydn
Laternenfest (Lantern Festival).
Hans Pfeiffer. Kienzle
Lathe of Heaven, The. Ursula
K. Le Guin. Magill SF
Laughable Loves. Milan Kundera.
Magill '75
Laughing Boy. Oliver La Farge.
Haydn; Morehead
Laughter. Henri Bergson. Magill
IV, MC
Laura. Vera Caspary and George
Sklar. (Based on the novel by
Vera Caspary.) Drury; NCTE
Laurette. Marguerite Courtney.
Magill '55, MB, S
Laval. Hubert Cole. Magill '64,
S
Lavender at Dusk. Tom Judd.
French
Lavengro. George Henry Borrow.
Haydn; Johnson; Keller; Magill
I, CE, M1&2, MC, MEF
Lavka snovidenyi. Ilya Varshav-
sky. Magill SF
Law, The. Roger Vailland.
Magill '59, S
Lawrie Todd. John Galt. Johnson
Laws. Marcus Tullius Cicero.
Downs F, FG
Laws. Plato. Downs FG; Feder;
Keller; Magill WP
Laws of Ecclesiastical Polity.
Richard Hooker. Magill CHL
(Treatise on); Haydn; Keller; Ruoff
Laws of Manu, The. Unknown.
Haydn
Lay of Havelok the Dane, The
see Havelok the Dane
Lay of Igor's Campaign, The.
Unknown. Fleming; Haydn;
Magill IV, MC
Lay of the Last Minstrel, The.
Sir Walter Scott. Haydn;
Magill II, CE, M1&2, MC, MP
Lay Sermons, Addresses, and
Reviews. Thomas Henry Hux-
ley. Keller
Lays of Ancient Rome. Thomas

Babington Macaulay. Haydn
Lazarillo de Tormes. Attributed
to Diego Hurtado de Mendoza.
Haydn; Johnson; Magill II, CE,
M1&2, MC, MEUF; Ruoff p.
361
Lazarre. Mrs. Mary H. Cather-
wood. Johnson; Kaye; Keller
Lazarus. André Malraux. Magill
'78
Lazarus. Luigi Pirandello.
Matlaw
Lazarus Laughed. Eugene O'Neill.
Keller suppl.; Matlaw; Shipley;
Sobel
Lazy Tour of Two Idle Apprentices,
The. Charles Dickens. Hard-
wick CD
Lead, Kindly Light. Vincent
Sheean. Haydn p. 574
Leaf Storm. Gabriel García
Márquez. Magill '73
Leah Kleschna. C. M. S. McLel-
lan. Best '99; Drury
Leaping Clear. Irving Feldman.
Magill '77
Learned Ladies, The see
Femmes savantes, Les
Leatherstocking Saga, The. James
Fenimore Cooper. (See also
The Deerslayer, The Last of
the Mohicans, The Pathfinder,
The Pioneers, The Prairie.)
Haydn; Keller; Magill '54, S
Leatherwood God, The. William
Dean Howells. Carrington
Leavenworth Case, The. Anna
Katherine Green. Johnson
Leaves of Grass. Walt Whitman.
Haydn; Keller; Magill III, M1,
MAL5, MC, MP
Leben des Horace A. W. Tabor,
Das (The Life of Horace A.
W. Tabor). Carl Zuckmayer.
Kienzle
Lectures on Art. Hippolyte
Adolphe Taine. Keller (Art)
Lectures on Calvinism. Abraham
Kuyper. Magill CHL
Lectures on Godmanhood. Vladi-
mir Solovyev. Magill CHL
Lectures on Preaching. Phillips
Brooks. Magill CHL
Lectures on Revivals of Religion.
Charles Grandison Finney.
Magill CHL
Lectures on the Philosophy of Life.
Friedrich von Schlegel.

Magill CAL
Lectures on the Principles of Poli-
tical Obligation. Thomas Hill
Green. Haydn
Led Horse Claim, The. Mary
Hallock Foote. Keller
Lee; a Dramatic Poem. Edgar
Lee Masters. Keller suppl.
Lee in the Capitol. Herman Mel-
ville. Gale-M
Left Bank, The. Elmer Rice.
Best '31
Left Hand of Darkness, The.
Ursula K. Le Guin. Magill
SF
Left Hand, Right Hand. Osbert
Sitwell. Ward
Left-Handed Woman, The. Peter
Handke. Magill '79
Legacy. Charles Patterson.
NCTE
Legend of Good Women, The.
Geoffrey Chaucer. Haydn;
Magill III, M1, MC, MP
Legend of Montrose, A. Sir
Walter Scott. Johnson; Kaye;
McSpadden W
Legend of Reading Abbey, A.
Charles MacFarlane. Kaye
Legend of Sleepy Hollow, The.
Washington Irving. Cohen;
Goodman; Grozier; Johnson;
Magill II, CE, M1&2, MAF,
MAL2, MC; Smith
Legend of the Moor's Legacy.
Washington Irving. Magill II,
CE, M1&2, MAF, MC
Legend of the Rhine. William
Makepeace Thackeray. Mudge
Legend of Tyl Ulenspiegel, The.
Charles de Coster. Magill II,
CE, M1&2, MC, MEUF
Legends of Charlemagne see
Bulfinch's Mythology
Legends of King Arthur, The
see Age of Chivalry or The
Legends of King Arthur, The
Leghorn Hat, A see Italian
Straw Hat, The
Legion of Time, The. Jack Wil-
liamson. Magill SF
Legittima difesa (Self Defense).
Paolo Levi. Kienzle
Leighton Court. Henry Kingsley.
Keller
Leila. Lord Edward Bulwer-
Lytton. Johnson; Kaye
Leisure the Basis of Culture.

Twain. Magill '63, M1, S
Letters from the Sandwich Islands.
Mark Twain. Gale-T
Letters from the Underworld.
Fyodor Mikhailovich Dostoevskii.
Magill II, CE, M1&2, MC,
MEUF
Letters Home. William Dean
Howells. Carrington
Letters Home. Sylvia Plath.
Magill '76
Letters of Anton Chekhov. Anton
Chekhov. Magill '74
Letters of Bernard DeVoto. Ber-
nard DeVoto. Magill '76
Letters of C. S. Lewis. Clive
Staples Lewis. Magill '67, S
Letters of Carl Sandburg, The.
Carl Sandburg. Magill '69, S
Letters of Charles Lamb, The.
Charles Lamb. Magill IV,
MC
Letters of Cicero. Marcus Tul-
lius Cicero. Downs F, FG;
Haydn
Letters of E. B. White. E. B.
White. Magill '77
Letters of Elizabeth Barrett
Browning, by Elizabeth Bar-
rett Browning. Frederic G.
Kenyon, editor. Keller (a)
Letters of Emily Dickinson, The.
Emily Dickinson. Magill IV,
'59, M1, MB, MC, S
Letters of F. Scott Fitzgerald,
The. F. Scott Fitzgerald.
Magill IV, '64, M1, MC, S
Letters of Gertrude Bell, selected
and edited by Lady Bell.
Gertrude Lowthian Bell.
Keller suppl.
Letters of Henry James, The.
Henry James and Percy Lub-
bock, editor. Keller suppl.
Letters of James Agee to Father
Flye. James Agee. Magill
'63, S
Letters of James Joyce. James
Joyce. Magill '58, M1, S
Letters of John Keats, The.
John Keats. Haydn; Magill
IV, MC
Letters of Junius, The. "Junius."
Haydn; Keller (a)
Letters of Madame de Sévigné,
The. Madame Marie de
Sévigné. Magill IV, MC
Letters of Oscar Wilde, The.

Oscar Wilde. Magill '63, M1,
MB, S
Letters of Pliny the Younger, The.
Pliny the Younger. Haydn;
Keller; Magill IV, MC
Letters of Robert Browning and
Elizabeth Barrett Browning,
The. Robert Barrett Browning.
Keller
Letters of Robert Frost, The.
Robert Frost. Magill IV, MC
Letters of Robert Frost to Louis
Untermeyer, The. Robert
Frost. Magill '64, M1, S
Letters of Rupert Brooke, The.
Rupert Brooke. Magill '69, S
Letters of Saint Basil, The.
Saint Basil. Magill CAL
Letters of Saint Bernard of Clair-
vaux, The. Saint Bernard.
Magill CAL
Letters of Saint Jerome, The.
Saint Jerome. Magill CAL,
CHL
Letters of Sidney and Beatrice
Webb, The. Vols. 1-3. Sid-
ney and Beatrice Webb. Magill
'79
Letters of Thomas Gray, The.
Thomas Gray. Keller; Magill
IV, MC
Letters of Thomas Wolfe, The.
Thomas Wolfe. Magill IV, '57,
M1, MB, MC, S
Letters of Virginia Woolf, Vol.
I: 1888-1912, The. Virginia
Woolf. Magill '76
Letters of Virginia Woolf, Vol.
II: 1912-1922, The. Virginia
Woolf. Magill '77
Letters of Virginia Woolf, Vol.
III: 1923-1928, The. Virginia
Woolf. Magill '79
Letters of Wallace Stevens. Wal-
lace Stevens. Magill '67, S
Letters of Walpole, The. Horace
Walpole. Haydn; Keller; Magill
III, M1, MC, MNF
Letters of William Cowper, The.
William Cowper. Magill IV,
MC
Letters of William James, The.
William James and Henry
James, editor. Keller suppl.
Letters on Literature and Politics,
1912-1972. Edmund Wilson.
Magill '78
Letters to an Unknown. Prosper

Keller (a)
Life of Charlemagne, The. Ein-
hard. Magill CAL
Life of Charles Dickens, The.
John Forster. Keller (Dickens)
Life of Charlotte Brontë. Mrs.
Elizabeth Cleghorn Gaskell.
Keller (Brontë)
Life of Christ. Giovanni Papini.
Keller suppl. (Christ)
Life of Dylan Thomas, The.
Constantine Fitz Gibbon.
Magill '66, S
Life of Edward II of England.
Bertolt Brecht and Lion Feucht-
wanger. Matlaw
Life of Emily Dickinson, The.
Richard B. Sewall. Magill
'75
Life of Ezra Pound, The. Noel
Stock. Magill '71
Life of Fisher, The. Richard
Hall. Ruoff p. 40
Life of Galileo. Bertolt Brecht
and Hanns Eisler. Matlaw
Life of Goethe, The. George
Henry Lewes. Keller (Goethe)
Life of Ivy Compton-Burnett,
The. Elizabeth Sprigge.
Magill '74
Life of Jack Wilton, The see
Unfortunate Traveller; or,
The Life of Jack Wilton, The
Life of Jesus, The. Ernest
Renan. Armstrong; Haydn;
Keller (Jesus); Magill CHL
Life of Jesus, v. 1 see History
of the People of Israel
Life of Jesus Critically Examined,
The. David Friedrich Strauss.
Magill CHL
Life of John Bright, The. George
Macaulay Trevelyan. Keller
(Bright)
Life of John Milton, The. David
Masson. Keller (Milton)
Life of John Sheppard, The.
Daniel Defoe. Johnson-18th
Life of Lady Mary Wortley
Montagu, The. Robert Hals-
band. Magill '50, S
Life of Laurence Oliphant and
of Alice Oliphant, His Wife,
The. Margaret Wilson Oli-
phant. Keller (Oliphant)
Life of Lenin, The. Louis
Fischer. Magill '65, S
Life of Marcus Tullius Cicero.

William Forsyth. Keller
(Cicero)
Life of More see Lyfe of Sir
Thomas More, Knighte
Life of Napoleon Bonaparte, The.
William Milligan Sloane (1850-
1928). Keller (Napoleon)
Life of Napoleon I, The. J. Hol-
land Rose. Keller (Napoleon)
Life of Nelson, The. Alfred
Thayer Mahan. Keller (Nelson)
Life of Nelson. Robert Southey.
Haydn; Keller; Magill III, M1,
MC, MNF
Life of Our Lord Jesus Christ,
The. Louis Veuillot. Magill
CAL
Life of Raymond Chandler, The.
Frank MacShane. Magill '77
Life of Reason, The. George
Santayana. Haydn; Magill WP
Life of Richard Savage. Samuel
Johnson. Magill IV, MC
Life of Saint Francis of Assisi.
Paul Sabatier. Keller (Francis)
Life of Saint Louis, The. Jean
de Joinville. Haydn (History
of); Magill CAL
Life of St. Martin, The. Sulpicius
Severus. Magill CHL
Life of St. Teresa of Avila, The.
Saint Teresa of Avila. Magill
CHL
Life of Samuel Johnson, LL.D.,
The. James Boswell. Haydn;
Keller (Johnson); Magill III,
M1, MC, MNF
Life of Samuel Johnson, LL.D.,
The. Sir John Hawkins.
Magill '62, S
Life of Sir Ernest Shackleton, The.
Hugh Robert Mill. Keller
suppl.
Life of Sir Walter Scott, The.
John Gibson Lockhart. Haydn;
Keller (Scott)
Life of Sir William Osler, The.
Harvey Cushing. Keller suppl.
(Osler)
Life of the Bee, The. Maurice
Maeterlinck Keller
Life of the Mind in America, The.
Perry Miller. Magill Ss
Life of the Mind: One/Thinking,
Two/Willing, The. Hannah
Arendt. Magill '79
Life of Thomas Carlyle. J. A.
Froude. Keller (Carlyle)

Life of Wesley. Robert Southey.
Haydn
Life of William Shakespeare, A.
Sir Sidney Lee. Keller
(Shakespeare)
Life on the Border. "Texas Jac' "
Crawford. Drury
Life on the Lagoons. Horatio
F. Brown. Keller
Life on the Mississippi. Mark
Twain. Gale-T; Haydn; Keller;
Magill I, CE, M1&2, MAL5,
MC, MNF
Life/Situations: Essays Written
and Spoken. Jean-Paul Sartre.
Magill '78
Life Studies. Robert Lowell.
Magill '60, M1, MB, S
Life with Father. Clarence Day,
Jr. (See also adaptation by
Howard Lindsay and Russel
Crouse.) Haydn; Magill I,
CE, M1&2, MAF, MC
Life with Father. Howard Lindsay
and Russel Crouse. (Based
on the novel by Clarence Day.)
Best '39; Cartmell; Drury;
French; Lass AP; Lovell; Mat-
law; NCTE; Shipley
Life with Mother. Clarence Day.
(See adaptation by Howard
Lindsay and Russel Crouse.)
Life with Mother. Howard Lindsay
and Russel Crouse. (Based
on the book by Clarence Day.)
Best '48; Drury; NCTE
Lifted Veil, The. George Eliot.
Halperin; Magill SF
Ligeia. Edgar Allan Poe.
Gale-P, PP; Magill II, CE,
M1&2, MAF, MAL5, MC
Light Around the Body, The.
Robert Bly. Magill '68, S
Light-House, The. Edgar Allan
Poe. Gale-PP
Light in August. William Faulk-
ner. Haydn; Heiney; Lass
AN; Magill I, CE, M1&2,
MAF, MC; Morehead; Olfson
Light in the Piazza, The. Eliza-
beth Spencer. Magill '61,
M1, S
Light Infantry Ball, The. Hamilton
Basso. Magill '60, S
Light Is Dark Enough, The.
Christopher Fry. Magill '54
Light Man, A. Henry James.
Gale-J

Light o' Love see Game of
Love, The
Light of Asia, The. Sir Edwin
Arnold. Keller
Light That Failed, The. Rudyard
Kipling. Goodman; Johnson;
Keller
Light That Shines in Darkness,
The. Count Leo Tolstoy.
Gassner; Matlaw
Light Up the Sky. Moss Hart.
Best '48; Drury
Lightnin'. Winchell Smith and
Frank Bacon. Cartmell; Drury;
Matlaw; Sobel
Lightning Conductor, The. C. N.
and A. M. Williamson. Keller
Lightning-Rod Man, The. Herman
Melville. Gale-M
Lights and Shadows of Scottish
Life. Christopher North.
Keller
Lights in the Sky Are Stars, The.
Fredric Brown. Magill SF
Like a Bulwark. Marianne Moore.
Magill '57, MB, S
Like Another Helen. Sidney C.
Grier. Kaye
Likely Tale, A. Gerald Savory.
French; Kienzle
Liki, The. Keller (Sacred Books)
Li'l Abner. Norman Panama,
Melvin Frank, Johnny Mercer
and Gene De Paul. NCTE
Lilac Sunbonnet, The. Samuel
Rutherford Crockett. Johnson
Lilies of the Field. William E.
Barrett. (See adaptation by F.
Andrew Leslie.)
Lilies of the Field. F. Andrew
Leslie. (Based on the novel
by William E. Barrett.) Drury
Liliom. Ferenc Molnár. Best
'20; Cartmell; Drury; Haydn;
Heiney; Keller suppl. ; Magill
I, CE, M1&2, MC, MD; Mat-
law; NBC 3; NCTE; Shank;
Shipley; Sobel; Sprinchorn;
Thomas
Lillecrona's Home. Selma Lager-
löf. Keller suppl.
Lily Dafon. William Saroyan.
Kienzle
Lily of France, A. Caroline A.
Mason. Kaye
Lily of the Valley, The. Honoré
de Balzac. Johnson
Lily's Quest: An Apologue, The.

Nathaniel Hawthorne. Gale-H
Limbo. Bernard Wolfe. Magill
SF
Lime Twig, The. John Hawkes.
Magill IV, '62, MC, S
Lin McLean. Owen Wister.
Keller
Lincoln Finds a General. Ken-
neth P. Williams. Magill
'60, MB, S
Lincoln the President. James
G. Randall and Richard N.
Current. Magill '55, MB, S
Linda Condon. Joseph Herge-
sheimer. Keller suppl.
Linda Tressel. Anthony Trollope.
Gerould
Lindbergh. Leonard Mosley.
Magill '77
Lindbergh's Flight. Bertolt
Brecht, Kurt Weill and Paul
Hindemith. Matlaw
Linden Tree, The. J. B.
Priestley. Drury; French
Lindmann. Frederic Raphael.
Magill '65, S
Lines Written a Few Miles above
Tintern Abbey. William
Wordsworth. Haydn (Tintern)
Link, The. August Strindborg.
Magill III, CE, M1&2, MC,
MD
Linnet. Grant Allen. Keller
Lion, The. Aeschylus. Hathorn
Lion and the Jewel, The. Wole
Soyinka. Matlaw
Lion and the Mouse. Charles
Klein. Drury
Lion and the Throne, The.
Catherine Drinker Bowen.
Magill '58, MB, S
Lion in the Garden. James B.
Meriwether and Michael Mill-
gate, eds. Magill '68, S
Lion in Winter, The. James
Goldman. Best '65; Drury;
NCTE
Lion of Flanders, The. Hendrik
Conscience. Kaye; Keller;
Magill III, CE, M1&2, MC,
MEUF
Lion of the North, The. George
A. Henty. Kaye
Lion of Wessex, A. Tom Bevan.
Kaye
Lion-Tamer, or, English As It
Is Eaten, The. Alfred Savoir.
Shipley

Lionel Lincoln. James Fenimore
Cooper. Johnson; Kaye; Walker
Lionizing. Edgar Allan Poe.
Gale-PP
Lion's Brood. Duffield Osborne.
Johnson; Kaye
Lion's Mane, The. Sir Arthur
Conan Doyle. Hardwick SH
Lion's Skin, The. Rafael Sabatini.
Kaye
Lisbon Story, The. Harry Parr
Davies and Harold Purcell.
Drinkrow
List of Assets, A. Yuri Olesha.
Gassner; Matlaw
Listeners, The. James E. Gunn.
Magill SF
Literary and Social Essays.
George William Curtis. Keller
Literary Essays of Virginia
Woolf. Virginia Woolf.
Magill IV, MC
Literary History of the American
Revolution, The. Moses Coit
Tyler. Keller
Literary Landmarks of London.
Laurence Hutton. Keller
Literary Lapses. Stephen Lea-
cock. Keller
Literary Life of Thingum Bob,
Esq., The. Edgar Allan Poe.
Gale-PP
Literary Movement in France
During the Nineteenth Century.
Georges Pellissier. Keller
Literary Women. Ellen Moers.
Magill '77
Literature. Hermann Grimm.
Keller
Literature and Dogma. Matthew
Arnold. Magill CHI,
Literature and Life. William
Dean Howells. Carrington
Little Accident. Floyd Dell and
Thomas Mitchell. Best '28
Little Annie's Ramble. Nathaniel
Hawthorne. Gale-H
Little Barefoot. Berthold Auer-
bach. Keller
Little Big Man. Thomas Berger.
Magill '65, S
Little Bit of Fluff, A. Walter
W. Ellis. French
Little Book of Eternal Wisdom,
The. Blessed Henry Suso,
O. P. Magill CAL
Little Carthaginian, The see
Poenulus, The

Little Clay Cart, The. Attributed
to Shudraka. Gassner; Haydn;
Magill III, CE, M1&2, MC,
MD; Shank; Shipley; Sobel
Little Daffydowndilly. Nathaniel
Hawthorne. Gale-H
Little Demon, The. Feodor
Sologub. Haydn
Little Dinner at Timmins's. Wil-
liam Makepeace Thackeray.
Mudge
Little Door, The. A. C. Thomas.
French
Little Dorrit. Charles Dickens.
Hardwick CD; Haydn; Johnson;
Keller; McSpadden-D, DH;
Magill II, CE, M1&2, MC,
MEF
Little Eyolf. Henrik Ibsen.
Matlaw; Shipley
Little Fadette. George Sand.
Keller
Little Flowers of Saint Francis,
The. Unknown. Magill CAL,
CHL
Little Foxes, The. Lillian Hell-
man. Best '38; Drury; Haydn
(a); Lass AP; Lovell; Magill
III, CE, M1&2, MC, MD;
Matlaw; NCTE; Shank; Shipley;
Sobel; Sprinchorn
Little French Girl, The. Anne
Douglas Sedgwick. Keller
suppl.
Little Fuzzy. H. Beam Piper.
Magill SF
Little Gidding. T. S. Eliot.
Ward
Little Girls, The. Elizabeth
Bowen. Magill '64, S
Little Ham. Langston Hughes.
NCTE
Little Hotel, The. Christina
Stead. Magill '76
Little Hut, The. André Roussin.
Kienzle; Magill '54, S
Little Jarvis. Molly Elliot Sea-
well. Kaye
Little Journey, A. Rachel
Crothers. Drury
Little Karoo, The. Pauline
Smith. Magill '60, S
Little Ladyship. Ian Hay.
French
Little Lambs Eat Ivy. Noel
Langley. French
Little Learning, A. Evelyn
Waugh. Magill '65, S

Little Lord Fauntleroy. Frances
Hodgson Burnett. Haydn; John-
son; Sobel
Little Man, The. John Galsworthy.
Sobel
Little Mary Sunshine. Rick Beso-
yan. NCTE
Little Me. Neil Simon, Carolyn
Leigh and Cy Coleman. NCTE
Little Minister, The. Sir James
M. Barrie. Best '94; Good-
man; Grozier; Haydn; Johnson;
Keller; Magill I, CE, M1&2,
MC, MEF; Matlaw; Shipley;
Sobel
Little Moorland Princess, A. E.
Marlitt. Johnson
Little Murders. Jules Feiffer.
Drury
Little Night Music, A. Hugh
Wheeler and Stephen Sondheim.
Best '72
Little Orphan of the Family of
Tchao, The. Attributed to Chi
Chun-hsiang. Gassner
Little Parish Church, The. Al-
phonse Daudet. Johnson
Little People of the Snow, The.
William Cullen Bryant. Hix
Little Plays of St. Francis.
Laurence Housman. Matlaw
Little Prince, The. Antoine de
Saint-Exupéry. Olfson
Little Red Riding-Hood. Unknown.
Keller (Fairy Tales)
Little Rivers. Rev. Henry Van
Dyke. Keller
Little Savage, The. Frederick
Marryat. Johnson
Little Smoke. William O. Stod-
dard. Kaye
Little Union Scout, A. Joel
Chandler Harris. Kaye
Little Women. Louisa May Alcott.
(See also adaptation by Marion
de Forest.) Goodman; Grozier;
Haydn; Johnson; Keller; Magill
I, CE, M1&2, MAF, MAL1,
MC; Morehead
Little Women. Marion de Forest.
(Based on the novel by Louisa
May Alcott.) French; Sobel
Liturgical Piety. Louis Bouyer.
Magill CAL
Liturgy and Personality. Dietrich
Von Hildebrand. Magill CAL
Live Corpse, The see Living
Corpse, The

Lonely Way, The. Arthur Schnitz-
ler. Drury; Heiney; Keller;
Matlaw; Sobel
Lonesome Traveler and Other
Stories, The. John William
Corrington. Magill '69, S
Long Afternoon of Earth, The.
Brian W. Aldiss. Magill SF
Long and Happy Life, A. Rey-
nolds Price. Magill IV, '63,
M1, MC, S
Long Christmas Dinner, The.
Thornton Wilder. Matlaw
Long Day's Journey into Night.
Eugene O'Neill. Anderson;
Best '56; Bonin; Chapman '57;
Drury; Kienzle; Lass AP;
Lovell; Magill '57, M1, MB,
MC, S; Matlaw; NCTE; Shank;
Sobel
Long Echo, The. Lesley Storm.
French
Long Journey, The. Johannes
V. Jensen. Haydn; Keller
suppl.; Magill II, CE, M1&2,
MC, MEUF
Long-Legged House, The. Wen-
dell Berry. Magill Ss
Long Loud Silence, The. Wilson
Tucker. Magill SF
Long March, The. William
Styron. Magill Ss
Long Night, The. Andrew Lytle.
Magill II, CE, M1&2, MAF,
MC
Long Roll, The. Mary Johnston.
Kaye; Keller
Long Ships, The. Frans Gunner
Bengtsson. Magill '54, S
Long Street, The. Donald David-
son. Magill '62, MB, S
Long Sunset, The. Robert Cedric
Sherriff. French
Long Tomorrow, The. Leigh
Drackett. Magill SF
Long Voyage, The. Jorge Sem-
prun. Magill '65, S
Long Voyage Home, The. Eugene
O'Neill. (See also series title
S. S. Glencairn.) Matlaw
Long Will. Florence Converse.
Kaye
Longer Rules, The. Saint Basil.
Magill CHL
Longest Day: June 6, 1944, The.
Cornelius Ryan. Magill '60,
M1, S
Longest Journey, The. E. M.

Forster. Heiney; Magill III,
CE, M1&2, MC, MEF; Stade
p. 241; Ward
Longstaff's Marriage. Henry
James. Gale-J
Longtime Californ'. Victor G.
Nee and Bret de Bary Nee.
Magill '74
Look at the Harlequins! Vladimir
Nabokov. Magill '75
Look Back in Anger. John Os-
borne. Anderson; Best '57;
Drury; Kienzle; Magill IV, '58,
M1, MB, MC, S; Matlaw;
NCTE; Shank; Sprinchorn; Ward
Look Homeward, Angel. Ketti
Frings. (Based on the novel
by Thomas Wolfe.) Best '57;
Bonin; Drury; NCTE
Look Homeward, Angel. Thomas
Wolfe. (See also adaptation
by Ketti Frings.) Haydn;
Heiney; Lass AN; Magill I, CE,
M1&2, MAF, MC; Morehead;
Olfson; Smith
Looking Backward. Edward Bell-
amy. Downs M; Goodman;
Haydn; Johnson; Keller; Lass
AN; Magill I, CE, M1&2, MAF,
MAL1, MC, SF
Looking Up at Leaves. Barbara
Howes. Magill '67, S
Lookout Cartridge. Joseph Mc-
Elroy. Magill '76
Loot. Joe Orton. Kienzle
Lopotkin Inheritance, The. Vas-
silli Gregorovich Smirnov.
French
Lord, The. Romano Guardini.
Magill CAL
Lord Arthur Savile's Crime.
Constance Cox. (Based on the
short story by Oscar Wilde.)
French
Lord Arthur Savile's Crime.
Oscar Wilde. (See adaptation
by Constance Cox.)
Lord Beaupre. Henry James.
Gale-J
Lord Byron's Wife. Malcolm
Elwin. Magill '64, S
Lord Grizzly. Frederick Feikema
Manfred. Magill '54, S
Lord Jim. Joseph Conrad.
Goodman; Grozier; Haydn;
Heiney; Keller; Lass BN; Ma-
gill I, CE, M1&2, MC, MEF;
Stade p. 149; Ward

LYNDON 166

Lyndon Johnson and the American
Dream. Doris Kearns. Magill
'77
Lynggaard & Co. Hjalmar Berg-
ström. Drury
Lyric Poetry of Byron, The.
George Gordon, Lord Byron.
Magill IV, MC
Lyric Poetry of Lowell, The.
James Russell Lowell. Magill
IV, MAL4, MC
Lyric Poetry of Milton, The.
John Milton. Magill IV, MC
Lyric Poetry of Spenser, The.
Edmund Spenser. Magill IV,
MC
Lyrical and Critical Essays.
Albert Camus. Magill '69, S
Lyrical Ballads. William Words-
worth. Keller
Lyrical Ballads. William Words-
worth and Samuel Taylor
Coleridge. Haydn
Lyrics. Alcaeus. Feder
Lyrics. Anacreon. Feder
Lyrics. Catullus. Feder
Lyrics. Sappho. Feder
Lysis. Plato. Feder
Lysistrata. Aristophanes. Cart-
mell; Downs F, FG; Drury;
Feder; Gassner; Hathorn;
Haydn; Magill II, CE, M1&2,
MC, MD; Reinhold; Shank;
Shipley; Sobel; Thomas
Lytton Strachey. Michael Holroyd.
Magill '69, S

-M-

Mabinogion, The. Unknown.
Haydn; Magill III, CE, M1&2,
MC, MEF
Macaulay: The Shaping of the
Historian. John Clive.
Magill '74
Macbeth. William Shakespeare.
Baker; Campbell; Cartmell;
Chute; Clark; Drury; Gassner;
Guerber-ST; Halliday; Haydn;
Hix; Keller; Lamb; McCutchan-
ST; McSpadden S; Magill I,
CE, M1&2, MC, MD; NBC 3;
Ruoff; Shank; Shipley; Sobel;
Wilson
Macdermots of Ballycloran, The.

Anthony Trollope. Gerould
McEwen of the Shining Slave Mak-
ers (The Shining Slave Makers).
Theodore Dreiser. Gerber
McFingal. John Trumbull. Kel-
ler
Machinal. Sophie Treadwell.
Best '28; Matlaw; Sobel
Machine Stops, The. E. M.
Forster. Magill SF
Machine-Wreckers, The. Ernst
Toller. Drury; Heiney; Mat-
law; Shipley
Macht der drei, Die. Hans
Dominik. Magill SF
Mackerel Plaza, The. Peter De
Vries. Magill '59, S
Macleod of Dare. William Black.
Johnson
Macroscope. Piers Anthony.
Magill SF
McTeague. Frank Norris. Haydn;
Magill I, CE, M1&2, MAF,
MAL4, MC; Morehead; Smith
Mad Heracles see Herakles Mad
Madam Cassia. Unknown. Gass-
ner
Madam Tic-Tac. Falkland L.
Cary and Philip Weathers.
French
Madam, Will You Walk. Sidney
Howard. Chapman '54
Madame Bovary. Gustave Flau-
bert. Armstrong; Goodman;
Grozier; Haydn; Johnson; Keller;
Lass EN; Magill I, CE, M1&2,
MC, MEUF; Wilson
Madame Butterfly. David Belasco
and John Luther Long. Lovell;
Matlaw; Shipley
Madame Chrysanthème. Pierre
Loti. Johnson; Keller
Madame De --. Jean Anouilh.
French
Madame De Maintenon. J. Cotter
Morison. Keller (Maintenon)
Madame de Mauves. Henry
James. Gale-J
Madame Louise. Vernon Sylvaine.
French
Madame Pepita. Gregorio Mar-
tinez-Sierra. Drury
Madame Roland. Ida M. Tarbell.
Keller (Roland)
Madame Sand. Philip Moeller.
Drury
Madame Sans-Gêne. Edmond
Lepelletier. Johnson

Madame Sans-Gêne. Victorien
Sardou and Emile Moreau.
Drury; Haydn; Shipley; Sobel
Madame Theresa. Emile Erck-
mann and Alexander Chatrian.
Kaye
Madame X. Alexandre Bisson.
Sobel
Madamscourt. H. May Poynter.
Kaye
Madder Music. Peter De Vries.
Magill '78
Madeleine. Jules Sandeau.
Johnson
Mademoiselle Colombe. Jean
Anouilh. Drury; Kienzle;
Matlaw (Colombe); Shank
Mademoiselle de Maupin. Théo-
phile Gautier. Armstrong;
Goodman; Haydn; Johnson;
Lass EN; Magill I, CE,
M1&2, MC, MEUF
Mademoiselle Ixe. Lance Fal-
coner. Keller
Mademoiselle Mori. Mary
Roberts. Kaye
Madman or Saint. José Eche-
garay. Drury
Madonna of the Future, The.
Henry James. Gale-J
Madonna's Child. Alfred Austin.
Keller
Madras House, The. Harley
Granville-Barker. Drury;
Keller; Magill III, CE, M1&2,
MC, MD; Matlaw; Shipley;
Sobel; Ward
Madwoman of Chaillot, The.
Jean Giraudoux. Best '40,
Drury; Gassner; Magill III,
M1, MC, MD; Matlaw;
NCTE; Shank; Shipley;
Sprinchorn
Maeviad, The. William Gifford.
Keller (Baviad)
Magada, The. W. M. Ardagh.
Kaye
Magda. Hermann Sudermann.
Drury; Haydn; Keller; Matlaw;
Shipley; Sobel
Magdeburg Centuries, The.
Matthias Flacius (and others).
Magill CHL
Maggie: A Girl of the Streets.
Stephen Crane. Magill I,
CE, M1&2, MAF, MAL1, MC
Magic. Gilbert Keith Chesterton.
Shipley

Magic and the Loss, The. Julian
Funt. Best '53
Magic Barrel, The. Bernard
Malamud. Magill Ss
Magic Mountain, The. Thomas
Mann. Haydn; Heiney; Keller
suppl.; Lass EN; Magill I,
CE, M1&2, MC, MEUF; Olfson
Magic Skin, The. Honoré de Bal-
zac. Johnson
Magic Striptease, The. George
Garrett. Magill '74
Magistrate, The. Arthur Wing
Pinero. Drury; Shank
Magna Carta. Downs F
Magnalia Christi Americana.
Cotton Mather. Keller; Magill
III, CHL, M1, MC, MNF
Magnificent Ambersons, The.
Booth Tarkington. Morehead;
Smith
Magnificent Cuckold, The. Fer-
nand Crommelynck. Matlaw;
Shipley
Magnificent Obsession, The.
Lloyd C. Douglas. Magill I,
M1, MAF, MC
Magnificent Yankee, The. Emmet
G. Lavery. Best '45; Drury;
NCTE
Magnus Garbe. Gerhart Haupt-
mann. Matlaw
Magus, The. John Fowles.
Magill Ss
Mahabharata, The. Unknown.
Fleming; Haydn; Keller; Magill
III, CE, M1&2; MC, MP
Mahagonny. Bertolt Brecht and
Kurt Weill. Matlaw
Maias, The. José Maria Eça de
Queiroz. Magill '66, S
Maid Margaret of Galloway.
Samuel Rutherford Crockett.
Kaye
Maid of Belleville, The. Charles
Paul de Kock. Johnson
Maid of Brittany, A. May
Wynne. Kaye
Maid of Honour, The. Philip
Massinger. Holzknecht; Magill
III, M1, MC, MD, Ruoff
Maid of London Bridge, The.
Somerville Gibney. Kaye
Maid of Maiden Lane, The.
Amelia Edith Barr. Kaye
Maid of Old New York, The.
Amelia Edith Barr. Kaye
Maid of Orleans, The. Johann

Christoph Friedrich von Schiller. Sobel
Maid of Salem Towne, A. Mrs. Lucy Madison. Kaye
Maid of Sker, The. Richard Doddridge Blackmore. Keller
Maid of the Malverns, A. T. H. Porter. Kaye
Maid of the Mountains, The. Harold Fraser-Simson, James W. Tate, Frederick Lonsdale, Harry Graham, F. Clifford Harris and Valentine. Drinkrow
Maiden Song see Partheneion
Maidens of Bischofsberg, The. Gerhart Hauptmann. Matlaw
Maidens of Trachis. Sophocles. Reinhold
Maids, The. Jean Genet. Drury; Gassner; Kienzle; Matlaw
Maids of Paradise, The. Robert William Chambers. Kaye
Maid's Tragedy, The. Francis Beaumont and John Fletcher. Drury; Haydn; Holzknecht; Keller; Magill II, CE, M1&2, MC, MD; Ruoff; Shipley; Sobel
Mail Boat, The. Alexander Randolph. Magill '54, S
Main Currents in American Thought. Vernon Louis Parrington. Haydn; Magill IV, MC
Main Currents in Nineteenth Century Literature. Georg Brandes. Haydn; Keller
Main Street. Nathaniel Hawthorne. Gale-H
Main Street. Sinclair Lewis. Haydn; Heiney; Keller suppl. ; Magill I, CE, M1&2, MAF, MC; Morehead; Olfson; Smith
Main-Travelled Roads. Hamlin Garland. Magill III, M1, MAF, MAL2, MC
Maine Woods, The. Henry David Thoreau. Keller
Mainly on the Air. Max Beerbohm. Ward
Majesty. Louis Marie Anne Couperus. Keller
Majitele klíčů (The Key Owners). Milan Kundera. Kienzle
Major Barbara. George Bernard Shaw. Drury; Gassner; Hardwick; Haydn; Magill III, M1, MC, MD; Matlaw; NCTE; Shank; Shipley; Sobel; Sprinchorn; Ward

Major Gentian and Colonel J. Bunkum. Herman Melville. Gale-M
Majority of One, A. Leonard Spigelgass. Drury; NCTE
Make Room! Make Room! Harry Harrison. Magill SF
Makepeace Experiment, The. Abram Tertz. Magill '66, S
Making of a Marchioness, The. Frances Hodgson Burnett. Keller
Making of Adolf Hitler: The Birth and Rise of Nazism, The. Eugene Davidson. Magill '78
Making of an American, The. Jacob A. Riis. Haydn; Keller
Making of an Assassin, The. George McMillan. Magill '77
Making of Charles Dickens, The. Christopher Hibbert. Magill '68, S
Making of Christopher Ferringham, The. Beulah M. Dix. Kaye
Making of Europe, The. Christopher Dawson. Magill CAL
Making of the President, 1960, The. Theodore Harold White. Magill '62, MB, S
Making of the President, 1964, The. Theodore Harold White. Magill '66, S
Making of the President, 1968, The. Theodore Harold White. Magill '70
Making of the President, 1972, The. Theodore Harold White. Magill '74
Makropoulos Secret, The. Karel Capek. Drury; Matlaw; Shipley
Malachi's Cove. Anthony Trollope. Gerould
Malade imaginaire, Le see Imaginary Invalid, The
Malady of Youth, The see Sickness of Youth
Mal-aimés, Les (The Unloved). François Mauriac. Kienzle
Malatesta. Henry de Montherlant. Kienzle; Matlaw
Malavoglia, The. Giovanni Verga. Johnson
Malay Archipelago, The. Alfred Russel Wallace. Keller
Malcolm. Edward Albee. (Based on the book by James Purdy.) Drury

Malcolm. James Purdy. (See
also adaptation by Edward Al-
bee.) Magill IV, '60, MC, S
Malcolm Lowry. Douglas Day.
Magill '74
Malcontent, The. John Marston.
Gassner; Holzknecht; Magill
III, CE, M1&2, MC, MD;
Ruoff
Male Animal, The. James Thur-
ber and Elliott Nugent. Best
'39; Drury; Lass AP; Lovell;
NCTE; Shank
Malefactors, The. Caroline Gor-
don. Magill Ss
Malevil. Robert Merle. Magill
SF
Maltaverne. François Mauriac.
Magill '71
Maltese Falcon, The. Dashiell
Hammett. Magill I, CE,
M1&2, MAF, MC
Malvaloca. Serafín and Joaquín
Alvarez Quintero. Drury;
Matlaw; Sobel
Mama's Bank Account. Kathryn
Forbes. (See adaptation I
Remember Mama by John van
Druten.)
Mame. Jerome Lawrence,
Robert E. Lee and Jerry
Herman. (Based on their play
Auntie Mame.) NCTE
Mamillia, a Mirror or Looking-
glass for the Ladies of Eng-
land. Robert Greene. Ruoff
p. 176
Mamma's Affair. Rachel Barton
Butler. Best '19
Man, The. Mel Dinelli. Drury
Man a Machine. Julien Offray
de La Mettrie. Magill WP
Man About the House, A. John
Perry. (Based on the book
by Francis Brett Young.)
French
Man About the House, A. Francis
Brett Young. (See adaptation
by John Perry.)
Man Against the Sky, The. Edwin
Arlington Robinson. Magill
III, M1, MC, MP
Man Alive! John Dighton. French
Man and Boy. Terence Rattigan.
Drury
Man and Masses. Ernst Toller.
Drury; Haydn; Heiney; Matlaw;
Shank; Shipley; Sobel; Sprinchorn

Man and Nature. George Perkins
Marsh. Keller
Man and Superman. George Ber-
nard Shaw. (See also his Don
Juan in Hell.) Drury; Gassner;
Hardwick; Haydn; Heiney; Kel-
ler; Magill III, M1, MC, MD;
Matlaw; NCTE; Shank; Shipley;
Sobel; Sprinchorn; Ward
Man and the Masses see Man
and Masses
Man and the State. Jacques
Maritain. Magill CAL
Man and Two Women, A. Doris
Lessing. Magill '64, S
Man and Wife. William Wilkie
Collins. Johnson
Man at Arms, The. George P.
R. James. Kaye
Man, Beast, and Virtue. Luigi
Pirandello. Matlaw; Shipley
Man Called Intrepid, A. William
S. Stevenson. Magill '77
Man Called Peter, A. John Mc-
Greevey. (Based on the novel
by Catherine Marshall.) Drury
Man Called Peter, A. Catherine
Marshall. (See adaptation by
John McGreevey.)
Man Could Stand Up, A. Ford
Madox Ford. Keller suppl.
Man-Eater of Malgudi, The. R.
K. Narayan. Magill '62, M1,
S
Man for All Seasons, A. Robert
Bolt. Best '61; Drury; French;
Kienzle; Matlaw; NCTE
Man from Glengarry, The. Ralph
Connor. Keller
Man from Home, The. Booth
Tarkington and II. L. Wilson.
Best '99; Drury
Man from Toronto, The. Douglas
Murray. French
Man Hater, The see Misanthrope,
The
Man in Half-Moon Street, The.
Barré Lyndon. Drury
Man in Motion. Michael Mew-
shaw. Magill '71
Man in the Glass Booth, The.
Robert Shaw. Best '68; Drury;
NCTE
Man in the Gray Flannel Suit,
The. Sloan Wilson. Magill
'55, M1, S
Man in the High Castle, The.
Philip K. Dick. Magill SF

Man in the Moon, The.   Francis
Godwin.   Ruoff p. 446
Man Is Strong.   Corrado Alvaro.
Heiney
Man Just Ahead of You, The.
Robert M. Coates.   Magill
'65, S
Man Like Me, A.   Henry Marshall.
French
Man of Adamant: An Apologue,
The.   Nathaniel Hawthorne.
Gale-H
Man of Destiny, The.   George
Bernard Shaw.   Hardwick;
Matlaw; Sobel
Man of Feeling, The.   Henry
Mackenzie.   Haydn; Johnson;
Keller; Magill II, CE, M1&2,
MC, MEF
Man of La Mancha.   Dale Was-
serman, Mitch Leigh and Joe
Darion.   (Based on Don Quixote
by Cervantes.)   Best '65;
NCTE
Man of Mode, The.   Sir George
Etherege.   Gassner; Haydn;
Magill II, CE, M1&2, MC,
MD; Shank; Shipley; Sobel
Man of Property, The.   John
Galsworthy.   Goodman; Lass
BN
Man of the Crowd, The.   Edgar
Allan Poe.   Gale-PP
Man of the Hour, The.   Octave
Thanet.   Keller
Man of the People, A.   Emile
Erckmann and Alexander
Chatrian.   Kaye
Man on the Box, The.   Harold
MacGrath.   Keller
Man Outside, The.   Wolfgang
Borchert.   Kienzle; Matlaw;
Shank
Man Plus.   Frederik Pohl.
Magill SF
Man That Was Used Up, The.
Edgar Allan Poe.   Gale-PP
Man Versus the State, The.
Herbert Spencer.   Downs M
Man Who Came to Dinner, The.
George S. Kaufman and Moss
Hart.   Best '39; Drury;
Matlaw; NCTE; Sobel
Man Who Conquered Death.
Franz Werfel.   Keller suppl.
Man Who Cried I Am, The.
John A. Williams.   Magill
Ss

Man Who Died, The.   D. H. Law-
rence.   Ward
Man Who Died Twice, The.   Ed-
win Arlington Robinson.   Haydn
(a)
Man Who Folded Himself, The.
David Gerrold.   Magill SF
Man Who Kept His Money in a
Box, The.   Anthony Trollope.
Gerould
Man Who Laughs, The.   Victor
Hugo.   Goodman; Johnson
Man Who Loved Children, The.
Christina Stead.   Magill '66, S
Man Who Married a Dumb Wife,
The.   Anatole France.   Drury;
Shipley
Man Who Never Was, The.
Ewen Montagu.   Magill '54,
M1, S
Man Who Shook Hands, The.
Diane Wakoski.   Magill '79
Man Who Was Dead, The see
Living Corpse, The
Man Who Was Thursday, The.
Gilbert Keith Chesterton.
Heiney; Magill II, CE, M1&2,
MC, MEF
Man with a Bull-Tongue Plow.
Jesse Stuart.   Magill III, M1,
MC, MP
Man with a Flower in His Mouth,
The.   Luigi Pirandello.   Mat-
law
Man with a Load of Mischief,
The.   Ashley Dukes.   Drury;
French; Shipley; Sobel
Man with the Broken Ear, The.
Edmond About.   Johnson;
Magill SF
Man with the Golden Arm, The.
Jack Kirkland.   Drury
Man with the Twisted Lip, The.
Sir Arthur Conan Doyle.
Hardwick SII
Man Without a Country, The.
Edward Everett Hale.   Cohen;
Haydn; Magill I, CE, M1&2,
MAF, MAL1, MC; Olfson
Man Without a Soul, The.   Pär
Lagerkvist.   Drury; Matlaw;
Shank
Man Without Qualities: Volume
II, The.   Robert Musil.   Ma-
gill '54, S
Manchild in the Promised Land.
Claude Brown.   Magill '66,
M1, S

Mandalay. Rudyard Kipling.
Ward
Mandarins, The. Simone de
Beauvoir. Magill '57, M1, S
Mandate for Change, 1953-1956.
Dwight D. Eisenhower. Magill
'64, M1, S
Mandelbaum Gate, The. Muriel
Spark. Magill '66, S
Mandragola, La (The Mandrake).
Niccolò Machiavelli. Gassner;
Shipley
Manette Salomon. Edmond and
Jules de Goncourt. Magill III,
CE, M1&2, MC, MEUF
Manfred. George Gordon, Lord
Byron. Haydn; Magill II, CE,
M1&2, MC, MP; Sobel
Manhattan Transfer. John Dos
Passos. Heiney; Magill I,
CE, M1&2, MAF, MC
Mani. Patrick Leigh Fermor.
Magill '61, S
Manière forte, La. (In the Strong
Manner). Jacques Deval.
Kienzle
Manjiro. Hisakazu Kaneko. Magill
'57, S
Manly-Hearted Woman, The.
Frederick Feikema Manfred.
Magill '77
Mannequin d'osier, Le. Anatole
France. Keller (Histoire)
Manner Is Ordinary, The. John
LaFarge, S.J. Magill CAL
Mannerhouse. Thomas Wolfe.
Shank
Manon Lescaut. Abbé Prévost.
Haydn; Johnson; Keller; Magill
I, CE, M1&2, MC, MEUF;
Olfson
Manor, The. Isaac Bashevis
Singer. Magill '68, S
Manor of Northstead, The. Wil-
liam Douglas Home. French
Man's a Man. Bertolt Brecht.
Matlaw
Man's Fate. André Malraux.
(See also adaptation by Thierry
Maulnier.) Haydn; Heiney;
Lass EN; Magill I, CE, M1&2,
MC, MEUF; Olfson
Man's Fate. Thierry Maulnier.
(Based on the novel by André
Malraux.) Kienzle
Man's Foes, A. Euphans H.
Strain. Kaye
Man's House, A. John Drinkwater.

Drury; French
Mansfield Park. Jane Austen.
Halperin; Johnson; Magill I,
CE, M1&2, MC, MEF
Mansion, The. William Faulkner.
Magill IV, '60, MB, MC, S
Mantello, Il (The Overcoat). Dino
Buzzati. Kienzle
Mantle of the Emperor, The.
Robert Lynd and Ladbroke
Black. Kaye
Manu. Unknown. Keller (Sacred
Books)
Manual for Manuel, A. Julio
Cortázar. Magill '79
Manual of Egyptian Archaeology.
Gaston Maspero. Keller
(Egyptian)
MS. Found in a Bottle. Edgar
Allan Poe. Gale-P, PP
Manxman, The. Hall Caine.
Keller
Many Loves of Dobie Gillis, The.
William Davidson. (Based on
the novel by Max Shulman.)
Drury
Many Loves of Dobie Gillis, The.
Max Shulman. (See adaptation
by William Davidson.)
Manyoshiu, The. Unknown. Haydn
Mao ch'eng chi. Lao She. Magill
SF
Mao's China: A History of the
People's Republic. Maurice
Meisner. Magill '78
Marat/Sade see Persecution and
Assassination of Jean-Paul
Marat as Performed by the In-
mates of the Asylum of Charen-
ton under the Direction of the
Marquis de Sade, The
Marathon: The Pursuit of the
Presidency, 1972-1976. Jules
Witcover. Magill '78
Marauders (Comrades). August
Strindberg. Matlaw
Mårbacka. Selma Lagerlöf.
Keller suppl.
Marble Faun, The. Nathaniel
Hawthorne. Gale-H; Goodman;
Grozier; Johnson; Keller; Magill
I, CE, M1&2, MAF, MAL2,
MC
Marcel Proust. Roger Shattuck.
Magill '75
Marcella. Mrs. Humphry Ward.
Keller
Marching Against the Iroquois.

Everett T. Tomlinson. Kaye
Marching On. James Boyd.
Keller suppl.; Magill I, CE,
M1&2, MAF, MC
Marching on Niagara. Edward
Stratemeyer. Kaye
Marching Song. John Howard
Lawson. Sobel
Marching Song. John Whiting.
French; Kienzle
Marchioness of Stonehenge, The.
Thomas Hardy. Pinion; Saxelby
Marco Millions. Eugene O'Neill.
Matlaw; Shank; Sobel
Marco Visconti. Thommaso
Grossi. Johnson; Kaye
Marcus and Faustina. Frederic
Carrel. Kaye
Marcus, the Young Centurion.
George Manville Fenn. Kaye
Mardi. Herman Melville. Gale-
M; Magill II, CE, M1&2,
MAF, MAL4, MC
Margaret Ballentine. Frank
Templeton. Kaye
Margaret Fleming. James A.
Herne. Drury; Lovell; Matlaw;
Sobel
Margaret Fuller: From Trans-
cendentalism to Revolution.
Paula Blanchard. Magill '79
Margaret Ogilvy. Sir James M.
Barrie. Keller
Margarethe. Elisabetta Juncker.
Johnson
Margherita Pusterla. Cesare
Cantù. Johnson
Margin for Error. Clare Boothe.
Best '39; Drury
Marguerite de Roberval. Thomas
G. Marquis. Kaye
Marguerite de Valois. Alexandre
Dumas (father). Johnson; Kaye
Maria Chapdelaine. Louis Hémon.
Keller suppl.; Magill II, CE,
M1&2, MAF, MC
Maria Magdalena. Christian
Friedrich Hebbel. Drury;
Magill II, CE, M1&2, MC,
MD; Shank; Shipley
Maria Marten see Murder in
the Old Red Barn, The
Maria Stuart. Johann Christoph
Friedrich von Schiller.
Drury; Gassner (Mary); NBC 2;
Shank; Sobel
Mariana Pineda. Federico Gar-
cía Lorca. Matlaw

Marianela. Benito Pérez Galdós.
Johnson
Marianne. Pierre Carlet de
Chamblain de Marivaux.
Magill III, CE, M1&2, MC,
MEUF
Marianne Thornton. E. M. For-
ster. Magill '57, S
Marie Antoinette and Her Son.
Louise Muhlbach. Johnson;
Kaye
Marie Grubbe, a Lady of the
Seventeenth Century. Jens
Peter Jacobsen. Haydn
Marion DeLorme. Victor Hugo.
Sobel
Marion Fay. Anthony Trollope.
Gerould
Marius. Marcel Pagnol. Shipley
Marius the Epicurean. Walter
Pater. Haydn; Johnson; Kaye;
Keller; Magill II, CE, M1&2,
MC, MEF
Marjorie Daw. Thomas Bailey
Aldrich. Keller
Marjorie Morningstar. Herman
Wouk. Magill '55, M1, S
Mark of the Cross, The. Edgar
Swan. Kaye
Mark Twain: An American
Prophet. Maxwell Geismar.
Magill '71
Mark Twain in Three Moods.
Mark Twain. Gale-T
Mark Twain of the Enterprise.
Mark Twain. Gale-T
Mark Twain's Autobiography.
Albert Bigelow Paine. Keller
suppl.
Mark Twain's Margins on Thack-
eray's "Swift." Mark Twain.
Gale-T
Mark Twain's San Francisco.
Mark Twain. Gale-T
Mark Twain's Travels with Mr.
Brown. Mark Twain. Gale-T
Market Harborough. George J.
Whyte-Melville. Magill II,
CE, M1&2, MC, MEF
Markets of Paris; or, Fat and
Thin, The see Ventre de
Paris, Le
Markings. Dag Hammarskjold.
Magill '65, M1, S
Marko the King's Son. Unknown.
Haydn
Marlborough's Duchess. Louis
Kronenberger. Magill '59, S

Marmion. Sir Walter Scott. Haydn; Magill II, CE, M1&2, MC, MP

Marquis de Grandvin, The. Herman Melville. Gale-M

Marquis de Grandvin: At the Hostelry. Herman Melville. Gale-M

Marquis de Grandvin: Naples in the Time of Bomba. Herman Melville. Gale-M

Marquis de Montcalm, Le. Thomas Chapais. Keller (Montcalm)

Marquis of Keith, The. Frank Wedekind. Matlaw; Shank

Marquise Went Out at Five, The. Claude Mauriac. Magill '63, S

Marriage à la Mode. John Dryden. Gassner; Haydn; Magill III, CE, M1&2, MC, MD; Sobel

Marriage Customs in Many Lands. Rev. H. N. Hutchinson. Keller

Marriage - for One. Theodore Dreiser. Gerber

Marriage-Go-Round, The. Leslie Stevens. Chapman '59; Drury; Kienzle

Marriage of Figaro, The. Pierre A. Caron de Beaumarchais. Drury; Gassner; Haydn; Keller; Magill II, CE, M1&2, MC, MD; Shank; Shipley; Sobel

Marriage of Heaven and Hell, The. William Blake. Haydn

Marriage of Loti. Pierre Loti. Keller

Marriage of Mister Mississippi, The. Friedrich Dürrenmatt. Kienzle; Matlaw; Shank

Marriage of Olympe, The. Emile Augier. Drury

Marriage of William Ashe, The. Mrs. Humphry Ward. Keller

Marriages, The. Henry James. Gale-J

Marriages and Infidelities. Joyce Carol Oates. Magill '73

Married. Theodore Dreiser. Gerber

Marry Me. John Updike. Magill '77

Marrying of Ann Leete. Harley Granville-Barker. Drury; Sobel

Marse Chan. Thomas Nelson

Page. Magill II, CE, M1&2, MAF, MC

Marta of the Lowlands. Angel Guimerá. Drury; Haydn

Martereau. Nathalie Sarraute. Magill '60, S

Martha and Mary. Johannes Anker-Larsen. Keller suppl.

Martian, The. George Du Maurier. Keller

Martian Chronicles, The. Ray Bradbury. Magill SF

Martian Odyssey and Other Science Fiction Tales, A. Stanley G. Weinbaum. Magill SF

Martian Time Slip. Philip K. Dick. Magill SF

Martians, Go Home. Fredric Brown. Magill SF

Martin Chuzzlewit. Charles Dickens. Hardwick CD; Haydn; Johnson; McSpadden-D; Magill II, CE, M1&2, MC, MEF

Martin Eden. Jack London. Haydn (a); Morehead

Martín Fierro. Jose Hernández. Haydn

Martine. Jean-Jacques Bernard. Drury

Martyrdom of Ali, The. Unknown. Haydn

Martyrdom of Peter O'Hey, The. Slawomir Mrożek. Kienzle

Martyrdom of Saint Polycarp, The. Saint Polycarp of Smyrna. Magill CAL

Martyred, The. Richard E. Kim. Magill '65, M1, S

Marvellous History of St. Bernard, The. Henri Ghéon. Shank

Marvelous Adventures of Baron von Munchausen see Baron Munchausen's Narrative

Mary. Vladimir Nabokov. Magill '71

Mary Barton. Mrs. Elizabeth Cleghorn Gaskell. Keller; Magill IV, MC

Mary Broome. Allan Noble Monkhouse. Drury

Mary Goes First. Henry Arthur Jones. Drury

Mary Gresley. Anthony Trollope. Gerould

Mary Magdalene. Maurice Maeterlinck. Matlaw

Mary Magdalene. Unknown. Sobel

Mary, Mary. Jean Kerr. Best
'60; Drury; Kienzle; NCTE
Mary, Mary, Quite Contrary.
St. John G. Ervine. Drury
Mary of Scotland. Maxwell
Anderson. Best '33; Drury;
Matlaw; NCTE; Shank; Shipley;
Sobel
Mary Queen of Scots. Lady An-
tonia Fraser. Magill '70
Mary Rose. Sir James M.
Barrie. Best '20; French;
Keller suppl.; Matlaw; Sobel
Mary Stuart see Maria Stuart
Mary Stuart. John Drinkwater.
Drury; Sobel
Mary the Third. Rachel Crothers.
Best '22; Drury
Mary Wollstonecraft. Eleanor
Flexner. Magill '73
Marya. Isaac Emmanuelovich
Babel. Matlaw
M*A*S*H*. Richard Hooker.
(See adaptation by Tim Kelly.)
M*A*S*H*. Tim Kelly. (Based
on the book by Richard Hook-
er.) Drury
Mask and the Face, The. Luigi
Chiarelli. Matlaw; Shipley;
Sobel
Mason-Bees, The. Jean Henri
Casimir Fabre. Keller
Masque of Kings, The. Maxwell
Anderson. Matlaw; Sobel
Masque of the Inner Temple and
Gray's Inn, The. Francis
Beaumont. Ruoff p. 33
Masque of the Red Death, The.
Edgar Allan Poe. Gale-P,
PP
Masquerade. Mikhail Yurievich
Lermontov. Shipley
Masquerader, The. Katherine
Cecil Thurston. Keller
Mass for the Dead, A. William
Gibson. Magill '69, S
Mass of the Roman Rite, The.
Josef Andreas Jungmann,
S.J. Magill CAL
Massacre at Montségur. Zoé
Oldenbourg. Magill '63, S
Massemensch see Man and
Masses
Masses and Man see Man and
Masses
Master, The. Hermann Bahr.
Drury
Master, The. Israel Zangwill.

Keller
Master and Man see Germinal
Master Builder, The. Henrik
Ibsen. Drury; Gassner; Haydn;
Magill II, CE, M1&2, MC,
MD; Matlaw; Shank; Shipley;
Sobel
Master Christian, The. Marie
Corelli. Keller
Master Crook. Bruce Walker.
French
Master Eustace. Henry James.
Gale-J
Master Humphrey's Clock.
Charles Dickens. Hardwick
CD
Master John Horseleigh, Knight.
Thomas Hardy. Pinion
Master of Ballantrae, The.
Robert Louis Stevenson.
Grozier; Haydn; Johnson;
Keller; Magill I, CE, M1&2,
MC, MEF
Master of Go, The. Yasunari
Kawabata. Magill '73
Master of Palmyra, The. Adolf
Wilbrandt. Drury
Master of Santiago, The. Henry
de Montherlant. Kienzle; Mat-
law; Shank
Master of the Ceremonies, The.
George Manville Fenn. Johnson
Master of the Strong Hearts.
Elbridge S. Brooks. Kaye
Master of the World, The. Jules
Verne. Magill SF
Master Olof. August Strindberg.
Matlaw
Master Pathelin. Unknown.
Drury (Farce of ...); Haydn;
Shipley (Master Pierre P.);
Sobel (Pathelin)
Masterman Ready. Frederick
Marryat. Keller
Masters, The. C. P. Snow.
Magill IV, MC; Ward
Masters of Deceit. J. Edgar
Hoover. Magill '59, M1, S
Masters of the World. Mary A.
M. Hoppus. Kaye
Mastro-Don Gesualdo. Giovanni
Verga. Haydn; Magill III,
CE, M1&2, MC, MEUF
Matchmaker, The. Thornton Wilder.
(See also adaptation Hello, Dolly!
by Michael Stewart and Jerry
Herman.) Best '55; Chapman
'56; Drury; French; Kienzle;

Matlaw; NCTE; Shank
Mate in Three. L. du Garde
Peach. French
Mater. Percy MacKaye. Drury
Mater et Magistra. Pope John
XXIII. Magill CAL
Materia medica. Pedacius Dios-
corides. Downs F
Maternity. Eugène Brieux.
Matlaw; Sobel
Mathematical Principles of Natural
Philosophy see Philosophiae
naturalis principia mathematica
Mathematische Schriften. Gott-
fried Wilhelm von Leibniz.
Haydn
Mating of Lydia, The. Mrs.
Humphry Ward. Keller
Matriarch, The. Gladys Bronwyn
Stern. Keller suppl.
Matriarkatet. Tage Eskestad.
Magill SF
Matrimony. William Edward
Norris. Keller
Matter and Memory. Henri Berg-
son. Magill IV, MC
Maud-Evelyn. Henry James.
Gale-J
Mauprat. George Sand. Johnson
Maureen's Fairing. Jane Barlow.
Keller
Maurice. E. M. Forster.
Stade p. 258
Maurice Tiernay. Charles Lever.
Kaye
Mauve Decade, The. Thomas
Beer. Haydn; Keller suppl.
Mawkin of the Flow, The.
Ernest Hamilton. Kaye
Max. Lord David Cecil. Magill
'66, S
Max Havelaar. Multatuli.
Haydn; Johnson (under a
Dekker, E. D.); Magill III,
CE, M1&2, MC, MEUF
Max Jamison. Wilfrid Sheed.
Magill '71
Max Perkins: Editor of Genius.
A. Scott Berg. Magill '79
Maximina. Armando Palacio
Valdés. Keller
Maximo, The. François, Duc
de La Rochefoucauld. Haydn;
Keller; Magill III, M1, MC,
MNF
May-Pole of Merry Mount, The.
Nathaniel Hawthorne. Gale-H
May We Borrow Your Husband?

Graham Greene. Magill '68, S
Maya. Simon Gantillon. Sobel
Mayerling Affair, The. R. F.
Delderfield. French
Mayor of Casterbridge, The.
Thomas Hardy. Haydn; John-
son; Lass BN; Magill I, CE,
M1&2, MC, MEF; Saxelby
Mayor of Troy, The. Sir Arthur
Thomas Quiller-Couch. Kaye
Mayor of Zalamea, The. Pedro
Calderón de la Barca. Drury;
Gassner; Haydn; Magill II, CE,
M1&2, MC, MD; Shank; Shipley
Maz doskonaly (The Blameless
Man). Jerzy Zawieyski.
Kienzle
Mazarin Stone, The. Sir Arthur
Conan Doyle. Hardwick SH
Maze, The. Eileen Simpson.
Magill '76
Maze Maker, The. Michael Ay-
tron. Magill '68, S
Me and Molly. Gertrude Berg.
Best '47; Drury
Me and My Girl. L. Arthur
Rose, Douglas Furber and
Noel Gay. Drinkrow; French;
Shipley
"Me, Candido!" Walt Anderson.
NCTE
Me, Cassie. Anita MacRae
Feagles. Benedict
Meaning of God in Human Experi-
ence, The. William Ernest
Hocking. Magill CHL
Meaning of Man, The. Jean
Mouroux. Magill CAL
Meaning of Revelation, The. H.
Richard Niebuhr. Magill CHL
Meaning of Truth, The. William
James. Magill WP
Meanwhile. H. G. Wells. Keller
suppl.
Measure for Measure. William
Shakespeare. Campbell; Chute;
Clark; Gassner; Guerber; Hal-
liday; Haydn; Keller; Lamb;
McCutchan-SC; McSpadden S;
Magill II, CE, M1&2, MC,
MD; Ruoff; Shank; Shipley;
Sobel
Measure My Love. Helga Sand-
burg. Magill '60, S
Measure of Man, The. Joseph
Wood Krutch. Magill Ss
Measures Taken, The. Bertolt
Brecht and Hanns Eisler.

Matlaw
Mécanique céleste. Pierre Simon
Laplace. Downs M; Haydn;
Keller (Mechanism)
Mechanical Operation of the Spirit,
The. Jonathan Swift. Johnson-
18th
Mechanics. Aristotle. Downs F,
FG
Mechanism of the Heavens, The
see Mécanique céleste
Medea see Golden Fleece
Medea. Jean Anouilh. Kienzle
Medea. Euripides. Armstrong;
Downs F, FG; Drury; Feder;
Gassner; Hathorn; Haydn;
Jolliffe; Keller; Magill I, CE,
M1&2, MC, MD; Reinhold;
Shank; Shipley; Sobel; Thomas;
Wilson
Medea. Franz Grillparzer.
Drury
Medea. Robinson Jeffers.
Drury; Kienzle; NCTE; Shank
Medea. Lucius Annaeus Seneca.
Feder; Hathorn; Reinhold
Mediator Dei. Pope Pius XII.
Magill CAL
Medical Nemesis. Ivan D. Illich.
Magill '77
Medici, The. G. F. Young.
Haydn
Medieval Foundation of England,
The. Sir Arthur Bryant.
Magill '68, S
Meditations. Marcus Aurelius.
Haydn; Keller; Magill III, CE,
M1&2, MC, MNF, WP
Meditations of the Lover. Han
Yong-woon. Haydn
Meditations on First Philosophy.
René Descartes. Armstrong;
Magill WP
Meditations on the Life of Christ.
Unknown Franciscan Monk and
Saint Bonaventure. Magill
CAL
Mediterranean and the Mediter-
ranean World in the Age of
Philip II, The. Fernand
Braudel. Magill '76
Medium, The. Gian-Carlo Men-
otti. Lovell
Meek Heritage. Frans Eemil
Sillanpää. Haydn; Magill II,
CE, M1&2, MC, MEUF
Meet a Body. Frank Launder
and Sydney Gilliat. French

Meet Me in St. Louis. Sally Ben-
son. (See adaptations by Chris-
topher Sergel and Perry Clark.)
Meet Me in Saint Louis. Perry
Clark. (Based on the novel by
Sally Benson.) NCTE
Meet Me in St. Louis. Chris-
topher Sergel. (Based on the
novel by Sally Benson.) Drury
Meeting at Potsdam. Charles L.
Mee, Jr. Magill '76
Meeting of Love and Knowledge,
The. Martin Cyril D'Arcy,
S. J. Magill CAL
Meeting of the Ways, The. J.
Dowling Baxter. Kaye
Megumi no Kenka see Kami no
Megumi Uago no Torikumi
Mehalah. Sabine Baring-Gould.
Keller
Mei. Herman Gorter. Haydn
Meiboku Sendai Hagi (The Dis-
puted Succession). Naka Kame-
suke. Halford
Meigetsu Hachiman Matsuri (The
Full Moon on the Hachiman
Festival). Kawatake Mokuami
and adapted by Ikeda Daigo.
Halford
Meilants, Florant Constant Albert
see Hensen, Herwig
Mein Kampf (My Battle). Adolf
Hitler. Downs M, FG
Mekura Nagaya Ume Ja Kagatobi
(The Wicked Masseur and the
Fire Department). Kawatake
Mokuami. Halford
Melancholy Hussar of the German
Legion, The. Thomas Hardy.
Pinion; Saxelby
Melanctha see Three Lives
Melanippe Captive. Euripides.
Hathorn
Melanippe the Wise. Euripides.
Hathorn
Melbourne. Lord David Cecil.
Magill '54, MB, S
Meleager. Sophocles. Hathorn
Mellons: The Chronicle of Amer-
ica's Richest Family, The.
David E, Koskoff. Magill '79
Mellonta Tauta. Edgar Allan Poe.
Gale-PP
Melmoth the Wanderer. Charles
Robert Maturin. Johnson;
Magill II, CE, M1&2, MC,
MEF
Melocotón in almibar (Peaches in

ing. Magill IV, MC
Men at Arms see trilogy title
Sword of Honour
Men Die. H. L. Humes. Magill
'60, S
Men in Shadow. Mary Hayley
Bell. French
Men in White. Sidney Kingsley.
Best '33; Bonin; Drury; Matlaw;
Shipley; Sobel
Men Like Gods. H. G. Wells.
Magill SF
Men of Good Will. Jules Romains.
Heiney
Men of Harlech, The. William
Greener. Kaye
Men of the Moss Hags, The.
Samuel Rutherford Crockett.
Kaye
Men of the Old Stone Age. Henry
Fairfield Osborn. Keller
Men to Match My Mountains.
Irving Stone. Magill '57, S
Men Without Women. Ernest
Hemingway. Keller suppl.
Menaechmi, The (The Twin
Menaechmi). Titus Maccius
Platus. Cartmell; Drury
(Twins); Feder (Twin Menaech-
mi); Gassner; Hathorn; Haydn;
Keller; Magill III, CE, M1&2,
MC, MD; Reinhold; Shank;
Shipley; Sobel; Thomas
Menaphon. Robert Greene. Ruoff
p. 177
Meng Tzu. Mencius. Magill WP
Meno. Plato. Feder; Magill WP
Menotah. Ernest G. Henham.
Kaye
Men's Wives. William Makepeace
Thackeray. Mudge
Menschen im Hotel see Grand
Hotel
Menschenfresser, Die (The Man
Eaters). Herbert Asmodi.
Kienzle
Menteur, Le. Pierre Corneille.
Magill III, CE, M1&2, MC,
MD
Meraviglie del duemila, Le.
Emilio Salgari. Magill SF
Mercadet the Promoter. Honoré
de Balzac. Shipley
Mercator (The Merchant). Titus
Maccius Plautus. Feder (Mer-
chant); Hathorn; Reinhold;
Shipley (Merchant)
Mercedes of Castile. James

Fenimore Cooper. Johnson;
Kaye; Walker
Merchant, The see Mercator
Merchant of Venice, The. Wil-
liam Shakespeare. Baker;
Campbell; Cartmell; Chute;
Clark; Drury; Gassner; Guer-
ber-SC; Halliday; Haydn; Hix;
Keller; Lamb; McCutchan-SC;
McSpadden S; Magill I, CE,
M1&2, MC, MD; Ruoff; Shank;
Shipley; Sobel
Merchant of Yonkers. Thornton
Wilder. Shank
Merchantmen, The. Aristophanes.
Hathorn
Mercier and Camier. Samuel
Beckett. Magill '76
Merciful Disguises. Mona Van
Duyn. Magill '74
Mercy of God, The. Jean Cau.
Magill '64, S
Mercy of God, The. Theodore
Dreiser. Gerber
Mère Bauche, La. Anthony Trol-
lope. Gerould
Mere Interlude, A. Thomas
Hardy. Pinion
Meridian. Alice Walker. Magill
'77
Meriwether Lewis: A Biography.
Richard Dillon. Magill '66, S
Merlin. Edwin Arlington Robinson.
Haydn (a)
Mermaid Madonna, The. Stratis
Myrivilis. Magill '60, S
Mermaids, The. Eva Boros.
Magill '57, S
Merope. Voltaire. Shipley;
Sobel
Merrily We Roll Along. George
S. Kaufman and Moss Hart.
Best '34
Merry Beggars, The see Jovial
Crew, A
Merry Christmas of the Old Woman
Who Lived in a Shoe, The.
George Melville Baker. Lovell
Merry Death, A. Nikolai Nikolae-
vich Yevreinov. Matlaw; Sobel
Merry Devil of Edmonton, The.
Attributed to Michael Drayton.
Holzknecht; Ruoff; Sobel
Merry England. Edward German
and Basil Hood. Drinkrow
Merry Heart, A. H. May Poyn-
ter. Kaye
Merry Monarch. Hesketh Pearson.

Middle Classes, The. Honoré de Balzac. Johnson

Middle of the Night. Paddy Chayefsky. Drury; NCTE

Middle Watch, The. Ian Hay and Stephen King-Hall. French

Middle Years, The. Henry James. Gale-J

Middlemarch. George Eliot. Halperin; Haydn; Johnson; Keller; Magill I, CE, M1&2, MC, MEF; Olfson

Middletown. Robert S. and Helen M. Lynd. Haydn

Midnight Cowboy. James Leo Herlihy. Magill '66, S

Midnight Oil. V. S. Pritchett. Magill '73

Midnight Revel, The. Henri Meilhac and Ludovic Halévy. Shipley

Midpoint and Other Poems. John Updike. Magill '70

Midshipman Farragut. James Barnes. Kaye

Midsummer Night's Dream, A. William Shakespeare. Campbell; Chute; Clark; Drury; Gassner; Guerber-SC; Halliday; Haydn; Keller; Lamb; McCutchan-SC; McSpadden S; Magill II, CE, M1&2, MC, MD; NBC 1, 2; Ruoff; Shank; Shipley; Sobel; Wilson

Midway. Mitsuo Fuchida and Masatake Okumiya. Magill '55, S

Midwich Cuckoos, The. John Wyndham. Magill SF

Migawari Zazen (The Substitute). Okamoto Shiko. Halford

Mightiest Machine, The. John W. Campbell, Jr. Magill SF

Mighty and Their Fall, The. Ivy Compton-Burnett. Magill IV, '63, MB, MC, S

Mighty Stonewall. Frank E. Vandiver. Magill '58, S

Mikado, The. William Schwenck Gilbert and Arthur Sullivan. Drury; Magill I, CE, M1&2, MC, MD; Shipley; Sobel

Milczenie (The Silence). Roman Brandstaetter. Kienzle

Miles gloriosus see Braggart Soldier, The

Miles Wallingford. James Fenimore Cooper. Johnson;

Walker

Milestones. E. Arnold Bennett and Edward Knoblock. Drury; Matlaw; Shipley; Ward

Military Philosophers. Anthony Powell. Magill '70

Milk Train Doesn't Stop Here Anymore, The. Tennessee Williams. Best '62; Drury; Kienzle

Mill on the Floss, The. George Eliot. Goodman; Halperin; Haydn; Johnson; Keller; Magill I, CE, M1&2, MC, MEF; Wilson

Mill on the Po, The. Riccardo Bacchelli. Magill II, CE, M1&2, MC, MEUF

Millennium of Europe, The. Oscar Halecki. Magill CAL

Millie Goes a Miss. Dennis Noble. Drury

Millionaire, The. Mikhail Artsybashev. Keller

Millionaire Baby, The. Anna Katharine Green. Keller

Millionairess, The. George Bernard Shaw. Hardwick; Matlaw

Millions of Strange Shadows. Anthony Hecht. Magill '78

Milton and the English Revolution. Christopher Hill. Magill '79

Mind and Heart of Love, The. Martin Cyril D'Arcy, S. J. Magill CAL

Mind and Its Place in Nature, The. Charlie Dunbar Broad. Magill WP

Mind and the World Order. Clarence Irving Lewis. Magill WP

Mind in the Making, The. James Harvey Robinson. Keller suppl.

Mind of Primitive Man, The. Franz Boas. Haydn; Magill IV, M

Mind Parasites, The. Colin Wilson. Magill '68, S, SF

Mind-Reader, The. Richard Wilbur. Magill '77

Mind, Self, and Society. George Herbert Mead. Magill WP

Mindbridge. Joe Haldeman. Magill SF

Mind's Road to God, The. Saint Bonaventure. Magill CAL

Mindswap. Robert Sheckley. Magill SF

Minick. George S. Kaufman and
Edna Ferber. Best '24; Drury
Minimata. W. Eugene Smith
and Aileen M. Smith. Magill
'76
Minister's Black Veil, The.
Nathaniel Hawthorne. Gale-H
Minister's Charge, The. William
Dean Howells. Carrington
Minister's Wooing, The. Harriet
Beecher Stowe. Johnson;
Keller
Ministry of Fear, The. Graham
Greene. Magill II, CE, M1&2,
MC, MEF
Minna von Barnhelm. Gotthold
Ephraim Lessing. Drury;
Haydn; Magill II, CE, M1&2,
MC, MD; Shank; Shipley;
Sobel
Minnie's Boys. Arthur Marx,
Robert Fisher, Hal Hackady
and Larry Grossman. NCTE
Minor, The. Denis K. Fonvizin.
Gassner; Shipley
Minor Law-Books, The. Unknown.
Keller (Sacred Books)
Minute Boys of Long Island, The.
James O. Kaler. Kaye
Mirabell: Books of Number.
James Merrill. Magill '79
Miracle, The. Karl Vollmoeller.
Sobel
Miracle at Verdun, The. Hans
Chlumberg. Drury; Matlaw;
Shipley; Sobel
Miracle Worker, The. William
Gibson. Bonin; Drury;
French; NCTE
Mirgorod. Nikolai V. Gogol.
Berry-2
Mirifici Logarithmorum Canonis
Descriptio. John Napier.
Haydn
Mirror for Magistrates, The.
George Ferrers, Richard
Niccols, William Baldwin, and
Thomas Sackville. Haydn;
Keller; Ruoff
Mirror for Observers, A. Edgar
Pangborn. Magill SF
Mirror for Witches, A. Esther
Forbes. Keller suppl.; Magill
II, CE, M1&2, MAF, MC
Mirrors & Windows: Poems.
Howard Nemerov. Magill '59,
S
Mirth and Mayhem. Peter

Walker. Drury
Misacmos see Harington, Sir
John
Misalliance. George Bernard
Shaw. Hardwick; Matlaw;
Shank
Misanthrope, The. Molière.
Cartmell; Drury; Gassner;
Haydn; Magill I, CE, M1&2,
MC, MD; Shank; Shipley; Sobel
Misanthropy and Repentance.
August Friedrich Ferdinand
von Kotzebue. (Played in Eng-
lish as The Stranger.) Shipley
Miscellanies. Abraham Cowley.
Magill III, M1, MC, MP
Mischief of Being Clever, The
see Misfortune of Being
Clever, The
Miser, The (L'avare). Molière.
Drury; French; Gassner; Keller
(Avare, L'); Magill II, CE,
M1&2, MC, MD; Shank; Sobel
Misérables, Les. Victor Hugo.
(See also Jean Valjean.)
Cohen; Downs M; Goodman;
Grozier; Haydn; Johnson; Kaye;
Keller; Lass EN; Magill I,
CE, M1&2, MC, MEUF; Wilson
Miseries of Enforced Marriage,
The. George Wilkins. Holz-
knecht; Ruoff
Misfortune, A. Anton Chekhov.
Keller suppl. (Party)
Misfortune of Being Clever, The.
Alexander Griboyedov. Drury;
Haydn
Misfortunes of Arthur, The.
Thomas Hughes. Gassner
Misfortunes of Fred Pickering,
The see Adventures of Fred
Pickering, The
Mishima: A Biography. John
Nathan. Magill '75
Miss Bellard's Inspiration. Wil-
liam Dean Howells. Carrington
Miss Brown. Vernon Lee. Keller
Miss Gunton of Poughkeepsie.
Henry James. Gale-J
Miss Herbert. Christina Stead.
Magill '77
Miss Hook of Holland. Paul A.
Rubens and Austen Hurgon.
Drinkrow
Miss Julie. August Strindberg.
Gassner; Haydn; Heiney; Keller;
Magill II, CE, M1&2, MC, MD;
Matlaw; Shank; Shipley; Sobel;

Sprinchorn
Miss Leonora When Last Seen.
Peter Taylor. Magill '65,
M1, S
Miss Lonelyhearts. Nathanael
West. Haydn; Magill III, CE,
M1&2, MAF, MC
Miss Lulu Bett. Zona Gale.
Bonin; Drury; Keller suppl.;
Shipley
Miss Mabel. Robert Cedric Sher-
riff. French
Miss Mackenzie. Anthony Trol-
lope. Gerould
Miss Ophelia Gledd. Anthony
Trollope. Gerould
Miss Pell Is Missing. Leonard
Gershe. Drury; French
Miss Ravenel's Conversion.
John William De Forest.
Keller; Magill II, CE, M1&2,
MAF, MC
Miss Sarah Jack of Spanish Town,
Jamaica. Anthony Trollope.
Gerould
Miss Thompson. W. Somerset
Maugham. (See also adaptation
Rain by John Colton and
Clemence Randolph.) Haydn
Missing Persons and Other Es-
says. Heinrich Böll. Magill
'78
Missing Three-Quarter, The.
Sir Arthur Conan Doyle.
Hardwick SH; Kienzle
Mission of Gravity. Hal Clement.
Magill SF
Missolonghi Manuscript, The.
Frederic Prokosch. Magill
'69, S
Mist over the Mistletoe. Dan
Sutherland. French
Mr. and Mrs. North. Owen
Davis. (Based on The Norths
Meet Murder by Frances and
Richard Lockridge.) Best '40;
Drury
Mister Angel. Harry Segall.
NCTE
Mr. Arcularis. Conrad Aiken.
(Drama based on his short
story.) Kienzle
Mr. Barry's Etchings. Walter
Bullock and Daniel Archer.
Drury
Mr. Baruch. Margaret L. Coit.
Magill '58, S
Mr. Blandings Builds His Dream

House. Eric Hodgin. (See
adaptation by Reginald Law-
rence.)
Mr. Blandings Builds His Dream
House. Reginald Lawrence.
(Based on the novel by Eric
Hodgin.) Drury
Mr. Bolfry. James Bridie.
French; Ward
Mr. Bridge. Evan S. Connell,
Jr. Magill '70
Mr. Britling Sees It Through.
H. G. Wells. Heiney; Keller;
Magill I, CE, M1&2, MC, MEF
Mr. Bullivant and His Lambs.
Ivy Compton-Burnett. Magill
IV, MC
Mr. Cinders. Vivian Ellis,
Richard Myers, Clifford Grey
and Greatrex Newman. Drink-
row
Mr. Clemens and Mark Twain.
Justin Kaplan. Magill '67, S
Mr. Crewe's Career. Winston S.
Churchill. Haydn p. 637;
Keller
Mr. Dooley. Finley Peter Dunne.
Haydn; Keller
Mr. Facey Romford's Hounds.
Robert Smith Surtees. Magill
II, CE, M1&2, MC, MEF
Mr. Fortune's Maggot. Keller
suppl.
Mr. Gallion's School. Jesse
Stuart. Magill '68, S
Mr. Gilfil's Love-Story. George
Eliot. Halperin
Mr. Gillie. James Bridie.
French
Mr. Higginbotham's Catastrophe.
Nathaniel Hawthorne. Gale-H
Mr. Hobbs' Vacation. F. Andrew
Leslie. (Based on the novel
by Edward Streeter.) Drury
Mr. Hobbs' Vacation. Edward
Streeter. (See adaptation by
F. Andrew Leslie.)
Mr. Isaacs. Francis Marion
Crawford. Johnson; Keller
Mister Johnson. Joyce Cary.
Ward
Mister Johnson. Norman Rosten.
Chapman '56
Mr. Midshipman Easy. Frederick
Marryat. Grozier; Haydn;
Johnson; Keller; Magill I, CE,
M1&2, MC, MEF
Mr. Pickwick. Stanley Young.

Chapman '53
Mr. Pim Passes By.   A. A.
Milne.   Drury; French; Haydn;
Keller suppl.; Matlaw; Shipley;
Sobel
Mr. Pitt.   Zona Gale.   Drury
Mr. Poirier's Son-in-Law.   Emile
Augier and Jules Sandeau.
(Based on Sac et parchemins
by Sandeau.)   Drury (Son-in-
law); Keller (Gendre); Shipley;
Sobel
Mister Roberts.   Thomas Heggen
and Joshua Logan.   Best '47;
Bonin; Drury; Magill I, CE,
M1&2, MAF, MC; NCTE;
Shipley; Sobel
Mr. Salt.   Will Payne.   Kaye
Mr. Sammler's Planet.   Saul
Bellow.   Magill '71
Mr. Scarborough's Family.
Anthony Trollope.   Gerould
Mr. Sleeman Is Coming.   Hjalmar
Bergman.   Matlaw
Mr. Sponge's Sporting Tour.
Robert Smith Surtees.   Magill
II, CE, M1&2, MC, MEF
Mr. Waddington of Wyck.   May
Sinclair.   Keller suppl.
Mr. Weston's Good Wine.   T.
F. Powys.   Magill II, CE,
M1&2, MC, MEF; Ward
Mistletoe Bough, The.   Anthony
Trollope.   Gerould
Mistress Dorothy Marvin.   John
Collis Snaith.   Kaye
Mistress Nell.   George Cochrane
Hazelton.   Drury
Mistress of the Inn, The.   Carlo
Goldoni.   Cartmell; Drury;
Gassner; Magill II, CE, M1&2,
MC, MD; Shank; Shipley; Sobel
Mistress to an Age.   J. Chris-
topher Herold.   Magill '59,
MB, S
Misunderstanding, The.   Albert
Camus.   Matlaw
Mit brennender Sorge.   Pope
Pius XI.   Magill CAL
Mithridate.   Jean Baptiste Racine.
Drury; Gassner; Keller, Magill
III, CE, M1&2, MC, MD;
Sobel
Mixed Marriage.   St. John Ervine.
Matlaw; Sobel
Mixture As Before, The.   W.
Somerset Maugham.   Ward
Mo Tzu.   Mo Ti.   Magill WP

Mob, The.   John Galsworthy.
Sobel
Moby Dick.   Herman Melville.
(See also adaptation Moby
Dick--Rehearsed by Orson
Welles.)   Armstrong; Gale-M;
Goodman; Grozier; Haydn; John-
son; Keller; Lass AN; Magill I,
CE, M1&2, MAF, MAL4, MC;
Morehead; Smith; Wilson
Moby Dick-Rehearsed.   Orson
Welles.   (Based on the novel by
Herman Melville.)   Drury
Mock Astrologer, The.   Pedro
Calderón de la Barca.   Magill
III, CE, M1&2, MC, MD
Modern and Classical Essays.
F. W. H. Myers.   Keller
(Essays)
Modern Chinese Literature.   Un-
known.   Haydn
Modern Chivalry.   Hugh Henry
Brackenridge.   Magill II, CE,
M1&2, MAF, MC
Modern Comedy, A.   John Gals-
worthy.   (Trilogy title; see also
The White Monkey; The Silver
Spoon; Swan Song.)   Heiney;
Magill I, CE, M1&2, MC,
MEF
Modern Democracies.   James
Bryce.   Keller suppl.
Modern European Thought: Con-
tinuity and Change in Ideas,
1660-1950.   Franklin L. Baum-
er.   Magill '78
Modern Instance, A.   William
Dean Howells.   Carrington;
Johnson; Keller; Magill II, CE,
M1&2, MAF, MC; Smith
Modern Love.   George Meredith.
Haydn
Modern Midas, A.   Maurice Jókai.
Magill II, CE, M1&2, MC,
MEUF
Modern Painters.   John Ruskin.
Haydn; Keller
Modern Régime, The.   Hippolyte
Adolphe Taine.   Keller
Modern Utopia, A.   H. G. Wells.
Magill SF
Modern Warning, The.   Henry
James.   Gale-J
Modest Proposal for Preventing
the Children of Poor People
from Being a Burden to Their
Parents or the County and for
Making Them Beneficial to the

Public, A. Jonathan Swift. Haydn
Modeste Mignon. Honoré de Balzac. Johnson; Keller
Modori-Bashi (Modori Bridge). Unknown. Halford
Moksha: Writings on Psychedelics and the Visionary Experience (1931-1963). Aldous Huxley. Magill '79
Molière. Philip Moeller. Drury
Molière, His Life and His Works. Brander Matthews. Keller
Molinos the Quietist. John Bigelow. Keller
Moll Cutpurse see Roaring Girl; Or Moll Cutpurse, The
Moll Flanders. Daniel Defoe. Armstrong; Goodman; Haydn; Johnson-18th; Magill I, CE, M1&2, MC, MEF
Mollusc, The. Hubert Henry Davies. Drury
Molonne. Axel Strindberg. Kienzle
Moment of True Feeling, A. Peter Handke. Magill '78
Momiji-Gari (The Maple-Viewing Party). Kawatake Mokuami. Halford
Momo. Emile Ajar. Magill '79
Mon cher Papa. Calude-Anne Lopez. Magill '67, S
Mon Faust. Paul Valéry. Kienzle
Monadology. Gottfried Wilhelm von Leibniz. Magill WP
Monarch of Mincing Lane, The. William Black. Johnson
Monastery, The. Sir Walter Scott. Johnson; Kaye; McSpadden W
Monastic Order in England, The. Dom David Knowles, O. S. B. Magill CAL
Monday Conversations. Charles Augustin Sainte-Beuve. Magill IV, MC
Monde est nôtre, Ce. Francis Carsac. Magill SF
Mondo d'acqua, Il (The World of Water). Aldo Nicolaj. Kienzle
Money see Argent, L'
Money. Lord Edward Bulwer-Lytton. Drury (Lytton)
Money-Makers, The. Henry Francis Keenan. Johnson
Money: Whence It Came, Where

It Went. John Kenneth Galbraith. Magill '76
Monikins, The. James Fenimore Cooper. Johnson; Walker
Monk, The. Matthew Gregory Lewis. Haydn; Johnson; Keller; Magill II, CE, M1&2, MC, MEF
Monk of Fife, A. Andrew Lang. Johnson; Kaye
Monkey. Wu Ch'eng-en. Magill III, CE, M1&2, MC, MEUF
Monkey Business. Glyn Partos. French
Monna Vanna. Maurice Maeterlinck. Drury; Heiney; Keller; Matlaw; Shipley; Sobel
Monologion. Saint Anselm of Canterbury. Magill CHL, WP
Monroe Doctrine and American Expansionism, 1843-1849, The. Frederick Merk. Magill '67, S
Monsieur Beaucaire. Booth Tarkington. Cartmell; Keller; Magill I, CE, M1&2, MAF, MC
M. Bergeret à Paris. Anatole France. Keller (Histoire)
Monsieur Bob'le. Georges Schéhadé. Kienzle
Monsieur de Camors. Octave Feuillet. Johnson
Monsieur de Paris. Mary C. Rowsell. Kaye
Monsieur D'Olive. George Chapman. Magill III, CE, M1&2, MC, MD; Ruoff
Monsieur du Miroir. Nathaniel Hawthorne. Gale-H
Monsieur Lecoq. Emile Gaboriau. Johnson; Magill II, CE, M1&2, MC, MEUF
Monsieur Masure. Robin Maugham. (See adaptation Odd Man In by Claude Magnier.)
Monsieur Poirier's Son-in-Law see Mr. Poirier's Son-in-Law
Monsignor Ronald Knox. Evelyn Waugh. Magill '61, M1, S
Mont-Oriol. Guy de Maupassant. Johnson; Magill I, CE, M1&2, MC, MEUF
Mont-Saint-Michel and Chartres. Henry Adams. Keller suppl. ; Magill IV, MC
Montgomery Clift: A Biography. Patricia Bosworth. Magill '79
Month in the Country, A. Ivan Turgenev. Drury; Gassner;

Magill II, CE, M1&2, MC,
MD; Shank; Shipley; Sobel
Month of Sundays, A.   Gerald
Savory.   French; Kienzle
Month of Sundays, A.   John
Updike.   Magill '76
Montserrat.   Emmanuel Robles.
Drury; Kienzle
Monuments of Nineveh.   Austen
Henry Layard.   Keller (Nineveh)
Moods.   Louisa May Alcott.
Johnson
Moods, Cadenced and Declaimed.
Theodore Dreiser.   Gerber
Moon and Sixpence, The.   W.
Somerset Maugham.   Haydn;
Heiney; Keller suppl.; Magill
I, CE, M1&2, MC, MEF;
Ward
Moon Calf.   Floyd Dell.   Keller
suppl.
Moon for the Misbegotten, A.
Eugene O'Neill.   Best '56;
Chapman '57; Drury; Kienzle;
Matlaw; NCTE
Moon Hoax, The.   Richard Adams
Locke.   Keller
Moon in the Yellow River, The.
Denis Johnston.   Matlaw; Sobel
Moon Is a Harsh Mistress, The.
Robert A. Heinlein.   Magill
SF
Moon Is Blue, The.   Frederick
Hugh Herbert.   Drury
Moon Is Down, The.   John Stein-
beck.   Best '41
Moon Is Hell, The.   John W.
Campbell, Jr.   Magill SF
Moon of the Caribbees, The.
Eugene O'Neill.   (See also
series title S. S. Glencairn.)
Matlaw
Moon on a Rainbow Shawl.
Errol John.   French
Moon Pool, The.   Abraham Mer-
ritt.   Magill SF
Moonbirds.   Marcel Aymé.
Kienzle
Moonchildren.   Michael Weller.
Best '71; Drury
Moonstone, The.   Willkie Collins
Goodman; Grozier; Haydn;
Johnson; Keller; Magill I,
CE, M1&2, MC, MEF
Moor Born.   Dan Totheroh.
Drury
Mora Montravers.   Henry James.
Gale-J

Moral.   Ludwig Thoma.   Drury;
Sobel
Moral Essays.   Lucius Annaeus
Seneca.   Downs M; Haydn;
Keller (Morals)
Moral Man in Immoral Society.
Reinhold Niebuhr.   Haydn (a)
Moral Philosophy.   Jacques Mari-
tain.   Magill CAL
Moral Tales.   Maria Edgeworth.
Keller
Morals of Epictetus, The   see
Discourses and Manual
More.   Max Beerbohm.   Ward
More Stately Mansions.   Eugene
O'Neill.   Drury; Kienzle; Mat-
law
More Than Human.   Theodore
Sturgeon.   Magill SF
More the Merrier, The.   Ronald
Millar.   French
Morella.   Edgar Allan Poe.   Gale-
PP
Moretum.   Attributed to Vergil.
Feder
Morgan's Men.   John P. True.
Kaye
Morgesons, The.   Elizabeth Drew
(Barstow) Stoddard.   Johnson;
Keller
Moritz Tassow.   Peter Hacks.
Kienzle
Mormon Prophet, The.   Lily
Dougall.   Kaye
Morning and the Evening, The.
Joan Williams.   Magill '62, S
Morning in Antibes.   John Knowles.
Magill '63, S
Morning Noon and Night.   James
Gould Cozzens.   Magill '69, S
Morning on the Wissahiccon.
Edgar Allan Poe.   Gale-PP
Morning's at Seven.   Paul Osborn.
Best '39; Drury
Morocco, Its People and Places.
Edmondo de Amicis.   Keller
Mortal Antipathy, A.   Oliver
Wendell Holmes.   Johnson;
Keller
Mortal Friends.   James Carroll.
Magill '79
Morte d'Arthur, Le.   Sir Thomas
Malory.   Haydn; Keller; Magill
I, CE, M1&2, MC, MEF
Morte d'Urban.   J. F. Powers.
Magill '63, M1, S
Mortgage on the Brain, The.
Vincent Harper.   Magill SF

Morton House.   Christian Reid.
Johnson
Mosby's Memoirs and Other Stories.
Saul Bellow.   Magill '69, S
Moscow.   Frederick J. Whishaw.
Kaye
Moscow.   Theodor Plievier.
Magill '54, S
Moses.   Ivan Franko.   Haydn
Moshe Dayan.   Moshe Dayan.
Magill '77
Mosquitoes, Malaria and Man:
A History of the Hostilities
Since 1880.   Gordon Harrison.
Magill '79
Moss on the North Side.   Sylvia
Wilkinson.   Magill '67, S
Mosses from an Old Manse.
Nathaniel Hawthorne.   Keller
Most Excellent Comedie of Alex-
ander, Campaspe, and Dio-
genes see Campaspe
Most Extraordinary Case, A.
Henry James.   Gale-J
Most Famous Loba, The.   Nellie
K. Blisset.   Kaye
Most Happy Fella, The.   Frank
Loesser.   (Based on They
Knew What They Wanted by
Sidney Howard.)   Chapman '56;
NCTE
Most Likely to Succeed.   John
Dos Passos.   Magill '54, S
Mostellaria (The Haunted House).
Titus Maccius Plautus.   Feder
(Haunted); Gassner; Hathorn;
Reinhold; Shank; Shipley
(Haunted)
Mote in God's Eye, The.   Larry
Niven and Jerry Pournelle.
Magill SF
Mother, The.   Bertolt Brecht and
Hanns Eisler.   Matlaw
Mother, The.   Grazia Deledda.
Haydn; Heiney; Keller suppl. ;
Magill II, CE, M1&2, MC,
MEUF
Mother, The.   Máxim Górky.
Goodman; Keller; Magill III,
CE, M1&2, MC, MEUF
Mother.   Kathleen Norris.   Keller
Mother and Son.   Ivy Compton-
Burnett.   Magill IV, '55, M1,
MB, MC, S
Mother Courage and Her Children.
Bertolt Brecht and Paul Des-
sau.   Anderson; Best '62;
Drury; Gassner; Matlaw; NCTE;

Shank; Sprinchorn
Mother Earth.   Max Halbe.   Drury
Mother Goose's Melodies.   Un-
known.   Keller
Mother Hubberd's Tale.   Edmund
Spenser.   Magill IV, MC; Ruoff
Mother-in-Law, The   see   Hecyra
Mother Night.   Kurt Vonnegut, Jr.
Magill Ss
Motherlove.   August Strindberg.
Matlaw
Mother's Breast and the Father's
House, The.   Reed Whittemore.
Magill '75
Mother's Kisses, A.   Bruce Jay
Friedman.   Magill '65, S
Mother's Recompense, The.   Grace
Aguilar.   Johnson
Mother's Recompense, The.   Edith
Wharton.   Keller suppl.
Moths.   Ouida.   Keller
Motives of Proteus.   José Enrique
Rodó.   Haydn
Mouchoir, Le.   James Fenimore
Cooper.   Walker
Mountain Air.   Ronald Wilkinson.
French
Mountain Giants, The.   Luigi
Pirandello.   Matlaw
Mountain Wreath, The.   Petar
Petrovich Nyegosh.   Haydn
Mountaineering in the Sierra Nev-
ada.   Clarence King.   Keller
Mountains of California, The.
John Muir.   Haydn; Keller
Mountebanks, The.   Alfred Cellier
and W. S. Gilbert.   Drinkrow
Mountolive.   Lawrence Durrell.
Magill '60, MB, S
Mourning Becomes Electra.   Eu-
gene O'Neill.   Best '31; Drury;
Gassner; Haydn; Heiney; Lass
AP; Magill II, CE, M1&2, MC,
MD; Matlaw; Shank; Shipley;
Sobel; Sprinchorn; Ward
Mourning Bride, The.   William
Congreve.   Keller; Shipley;
Sobel
Mouse That Roared, The.   Leonard
Wibberley.   Drury; NCTE
Mousetrap, The.   Agatha Christie.
Drury; Kienzle
Mousetrap and Other Plays, The.
Agatha Christie.   Magill '79
Mousmé, The (The Maids of
Japan).   Lionel Monckton,
Howard Talbot, Alexander M.
Thompson, Robert Courtneidge,

Arthur Wimperis and Percy
Greenbank. Drinkrow
Moveable Feast, A. Ernest Hem-
ingway. Magill IV, '65, M1,
MC, S
Moviegoer, The. Walker Percy.
Magill '62, M1, S
Moving On. Larry McMurtry.
Magill Ss
Moving Target, The. W. S.
Merwin. Magill '64, S
Mrs. Brumby. Anthony Trollope.
Gerould
Mrs. Bullfrog. Nathaniel Haw-
thorne. Gale-H
Mrs. Bumpstead-Leigh. Harry
James Smith. Best '09;
Drury
Mrs. Caudle's Curtain Lectures.
Douglas Jerrold. Keller
Mrs. Dalloway. Virginia Woolf.
Haydn; Heiney; Keller suppl.;
Lass BN; Magill I, CE, M1&2,
MC, MEF; Olfson; Stade p.
193; Ward
Mrs. Dane's Defence. Henry
Arthur Jones. Drury; Magill
II, CE, M1&2, MC, MD;
Matlaw; Sobel
Mrs. Dot. W. Somerset Maugham.
Matlaw
Mrs. Farrell. William Dean
Howells. Carrington
Mrs. General Talboys. Anthony
Trollope. Gerould
Mrs. Gibbons' Boys. William
Glickman and Joseph Stein.
French
Mrs. Lirriper's Legacy. Charles
Dickens. Hardwick CD
Mrs. Lirriper's Lodgings.
Charles Dickens. Hardwick
CD
Mrs. McThing. Mary Coyle Chase.
Best '51; Drury; NCTE
Mrs. Martin's Man. St. John
G. Ervine. Keller
Mrs. Medwin. Henry James.
Gale-J
Mrs. Mike. Nancy and Benedict
Freedman. (Dee adaptation by
William Roos.)
Mrs. Mike. William Roos.
(Based on the book by Nancy
and Benedict Freedman.)
Drury
Mrs. Moonlight. Benn W. Levy.
Drury

Mrs. Partridge Presents. Mary
Kennedy and Ruth Hawthorne.
Best '24; Drury
Mrs. Temperly (Cousin Maria).
Henry James. Gale-J
Mrs. Wallop. Peter De Vries.
Magill '71
Mrs. Warren's Profession.
George Bernard Shaw. Hard-
wick; Haydn; Heiney; Matlaw;
Shipley; Sobel; Ward
Mrs. Wiggs of the Cabbage Patch.
Alice Caldwell Hegan. Keller
Mrs. Willie. Alan Melville.
French
Mucedorus. Unknown. Holz-
knecht; Ruoff
Much Abused Letter, A. George
Tyrrell. Magill CHL
Much Ado About Nothing. William
Shakespeare. Campbell; Chute;
Clark; Drury; Gassner; Guer-
ber-SC; Halliday; Haydn; Keller;
Lamb; McCutchan-SC; McSpad-
den S; Magill II, CE, M1&2,
MC, MD; NBC 3; Ruoff; Shank;
Shipley; Sobel
Mudraraksasa (The Signet Ring of
Rakshasa). Visakhadatta.
Gassner
Mugby Junction. Charles Dickens.
Hardwick CD
Mulata, The. Miguel Angel As-
turias. Magill '68, S
Mulatto. Langston Hughes. NCTE
Müller von Sanssouci, Der (The
Miller of Sanssouci). Peter
Hacks. Kienzle
Mulligan Guard Ball, The Ed-
ward Harrigan. Lovell
Mumbo Jumbo. Ishmael Reed.
Magill '73
Munchausen. Baron Munchausen.
Haydn
Murder at Midnight. Peter Hoar.
French
Murder at the Vicarage. Moie
Charles and Barbara Toy.
(Based on the novel by Agatha
Christie.) French
Murder at the Vicarage. Agatha
Christie. (See adaptation by
Moie Charles and Barbara Toy.)
Murder Delayed. Duncan Green-
wood. French
Murder Happens. Arnold Ridley.
French
Murder Has Been Arranged, A.

MURDER 188

Emlyn Williams. Drury; French
Murder in Motley. Ingram D'Abbes
and Fenn Sherie. French
Murder in the Cathedral. T. S.
Eliot. Drury; Gassner; Heiney;
Magill II, CE, M1&2, MC,
MD; Matlaw; NCTE; Shank;
Shipley; Sobel; Sprinchorn; Ward
Murder in the Old Red Barn, The.
Montague Slater. Shipley
Murder Is a Matter of Opinion.
Ronald Dawson and Joseph
Cochran. Drury
Murder Isn't Cricket. Philip
Weathers. French
Murder on Arrival. George Bat-
son. French
Murder on the Nile. Agatha
Christie. French
Murder Out of Tune. Falkland
L. Cary. French
Murder Party. Falkland L. Cary.
French
Murder Without Crime. J. Lee
Thompson. French
Murders in the Rue Morgue.
Edgar Allan Poe. Cohen;
Gale-P, PP; Smith; Wilson
Murió hace quince años (He Died
Fifteen Years Ago). José
Giménez-Arnau. Kienzle
Museum Pieces. William Plomer.
Magill '54, S
Museums and Women and Other
Stories. John Updike. Magill
'73
Musgrave Ritual, The. Sir Arthur
Conan Doyle. Hardwick SH
Music at Night. J. B. Priestley.
French
Music-Cure, The. George Bernard
Shaw. Hardwick; Kienzle
Music Man, The. Meredith Will-
son. NCTE
Music Master, The. Charles
Klein. Drury
Music School, The. John Updike.
Magill '67, S
Mussolini's Roman Empire.
Denis Mack Smith. Magill '77
Mustapha. Fulke Greville. Sobel
Musume Dojoji (The Maiden at
the Dojo Temple). Halford
Mutability Cantos, The. Edmund
Spenser. Ruoff
Mutable Many, The. Robert Barr.
Keller
Mute Ones, The see Kophoi

Mutineers of the Bounty, The.
Lady Diana (Jolliffe) Belcher.
Keller
Mutiny on the Bounty. Charles
Nordhoff and James Norman
Hall. Haydn; Lass AN; Magill
I, CE, M1&2, MAF, MC
My Antonia. Willa Cather.
Haydn; Heiney; Keller suppl.;
Lass AN; Magill I, CE, M1&2,
MAF, MC; Morehead; Smith;
Ward
My Arctic Journal. Josephine
(Diebitsch) Peary. Keller
My Aunt Margaret's Mirror. Sir
Walter Scott. McSpadden W
My Autobiography. Charles Chap-
lin. Magill '65, S
My Bones Being Wiser. Vassar
Miller. Magill Ss
My Brother's Keeper. Stanislaus
Joyce. Magill '59, S
My Childhood. Máxim Górky.
Keller
My Fair Lady. Alan Jay Lerner
and Frederick Loewe. (Based
on Pygmalion by George Ber-
nard Shaw.) Best '55; Drink-
row; Kienzle; Magill '57, M1,
MB, S; Matlaw; NCTE; Sobel;
Ward
My Father's House. Philip B.
Kunhardt, Jr. Magill Ss
My Father's Son. Frank O'Con-
nor. Magill '70
My Flesh, My Blood. Bill
Naughton. French
My Friend Bingham. Henry
James. Gale-J
My Friend from Limousin. Jean
Giraudoux. (See also his adap-
tation Siegfried.) Heiney
My Garden of Memory. Kate
Douglas Wiggin. Keller suppl.
My Heart and My Flesh. Eliza-
beth Madox Roberts. Keller
suppl.
My Heart's in the Highlands.
William Saroyan. Drury; Mat-
law; NCTE; Shank; Shipley;
Sobel; Sprinchorn
My Kinsman, Major Molineux.
Nathaniel Hawthorne. Gale-H
My Lady Laughter. Dwight Tilton.
Kaye
My Lady Molly. Sidney Jones,
G. H. Jessop, Percy Greenbank
and Charles H. Taylor.

Drinkrow
My Lady of Intrigue. Humfrey
Jordan. Kaye
My Lady of the North. George
Randall Parrish. Kaye
My Lady Pokahontas. John
Esten Cooke. Kaye
My Lady Suffolk. Evelyn Read.
Magill '64, S
My Lady's Kiss. Norman Innes.
Kaye
My Lai 4. Seymour M. Hersh.
Magill '71
My Land Has a Voice. Jesse
Stuart. Magill '67, S
My Life and Hard Times. James
Thurber. Magill III, M1,
MC, MNF
My Life As a Man. Philip Roth.
Magill '75
My Life As an Explorer. Sven
Hedin. Keller suppl.
My Life for My Sheep. Alfred
Duggan. Magill '55, S
My Life in Court. Louis Nizer.
(See adaptation A Case of
Libel by Henry Denker.)
My Mother and I. E. G. Stern.
Keller suppl.
My Mother, My Father and Me.
Lillian Hellman. Drury
My Mother Said. A. P. Dearsley.
French
My Novel. Lord Edward Bulwer-
Lytton. Johnson; Keller
My Official Wife. Colonel Richard
Henry Savage. Keller
My Past and Thoughts. Alexander
Ivanovich Herzen. Haydn (a)
My Petition for More Space.
John Hersey. Magill '75
My Place. Elaine Dundy. French
My Schools and Schoolmasters.
Hugh Miller. Keller
My Several Worlds. Pearl S.
Buck. Magill '54, M1, S
My Sister Eileen. Joseph Fields
and Jerome Chodorov. (See
also adaptation Wonderful Town
by Joseph Fields et al.)
Best '40; Drury; NCTE
My Studio Neighbors. William
Hamilton Gibson. Keller
My Study Fire. Hamilton Wright
Mabie. Keller (Essays . . .
Mabie)
My Study Windows. James Rus-
sell Lowell. Keller

My Sword for Patrick Sarfield.
Randal McDonnell. Kaye
My Sword's My Fortune. Herbert
Hayens. Kaye
My Three Angels. Samuel and
Bella Spewack. (Based on La
cuisine des anges by Albert
Husson.) Best '52; Chapman
'53; Drury; French; NCTE
My Visit to Niagara. Nathaniel
Hawthorne. Gale-H
My Wife's Family. Fred Duprez.
French
Mycenaean Age, The. Dr. Chres-
tos Tsountas and J. Irving
Manatt. Keller
Myrrha. Count Vittorio Alfieri.
Shipley
Mysians, The. Aeschylus.
Hathorn
Mysteries of Christianity, The.
Matthias Jooeph Scheeben
Magill CAL
Mysteries of Marseilles, The.
Emile Zola. Kaye
Mysteries of Paris, The. Eugène
Sue. Cohen; Grozier; Johnson;
Magill I, CE, M1&2, MC,
MEUF
Mysteries of Udolpho, The. Mrs.
Ann Radcliffe. Haydn; Johnson;
Keller; Magill I, CE, M1&2,
MC, MEF
Mysterious Island, The. Jules
Verne. Magill III, CE, M1&2,
MC, MEUF
Mysterious Monsieur Dupont, The.
Frederick Arthur. Kaye
Mysterious Universe, The. Sir
James Jeans. Haydn
Mystery and Manners. Flannery
O'Connor. Magill Ss
Mystery at Blackwater. Dan
Sutherland. (Based on the
novel The Woman in White by
Wilkie Collins.) French
Mystery at Greenfingers. J. B.
Priestley. French
Mystery-Bouffe. W. Somerset
Maugham. Sprinchorn
Mystery Douffe. Vladimir Maya-
kovsky. Matlaw
Mystery of Being, The. Gabriel
Marcel. Magill CAL, WP
Mystery of Edwin Drood, The.
Charles Dickens. Hardwick
CD; Haydn (Edwin); Johnson;
McSpadden-D; Magill II, CE,

M1&2, MC, MEF
Mystery of Marie Rogêt, The.
Edgar Allan Poe. Gale-PP
Mystical Body of Christ, The.
Pope Pius XII. Magill CAL
Mystical Element of Religion,
The. Baron Friedrich John
von Hügel. Magill CAL
Mystical Theology, The. Diony-
sius the Pseudo-Areopagite.
Magill CAL
Mystification. Edgar Allan Poe.
Gale-PP
Myth of Sisyphus, The. Albert
Camus. Magill IV, MC

-N-

N-Town Plays, The. Unknown.
Gassner
Nabob, The. Alphonse Daudet.
Johnson; Keller
Nabokov: His Life in Part.
Andrew Field. Magill '78
Nabou. Günther Krupkat. Magill
SF
Nacht mit Gästen (Night with
Guests). Peter Weiss. Ki-
enzle
Nachtzug (Night Train). Herbert
Reinecker. Kienzle
Naissance des dieux, La.
Charles Henneberg. Magill
SF
Naked (To Clothe the Naked).
Luigi Pirandello. Drury;
Matlaw (To Clothe); Shank;
Shipley; Sobel; Sprinchorn
Naked and the Dead, The. Norman
Mailer. Haydn; Lass AN;
Magill Ss; Morehead
Naked Ape, The. Desmond Mor-
ris. Magill '69, M1, S
Naked Sun, The. Isaac Asimov.
Magill SF
Naked to Mine Enemies. Charles
W. Ferguson. Magill '59, S
Naked Year, The. Boris Pilnyak.
Haydn (a); Heiney; Magill II,
CE, M1&2, MC, MEUF
Nameless Nobleman, A. Jane
Goodwin Austin. Johnson
Names: A Memoir, The. N.
Scott Momaday. Magill '78
Names and Faces of Heroes, The.

Reynolds Price. Magill '64, S
Names of Power, The. Jerzy
Broszkiewicz. Anderson (Imi-
ona)
Nana. Emile Zola. Goodman;
Haydn; Johnson; Keller (Rougon);
Lass EN; Magill I, CE, M1&2,
MC, MEUF
Nancy. Rhoda Broughton. John-
son
Nanga Parbat. Karl M. Herrlig-
koffer. Magill '54, S
Nanine. Voltaire. Sobel
Napoleon. Emil Ludwig. Keller
suppl.
Napoleon and Blucher. Louise
Muhlbach. Kaye
Napoleon Bonaparte. Vincent
Cronin. Magill '73
Napoleon of Notting Hill, The.
Gilbert Keith Chesterton.
Magill II, CE, M1&2, MC,
MEF
Napoleon Symphony. Anthony
Burgess. Magill '77
Narcissus. William Boyd Car-
penter. Kaye
Narrative and Critical History of
America, The. Justin Winsor.
Keller
Narrative of Arthur Gordon Pym,
The. Edgar Allan Poe. Gale-
PP; Johnson; Magill I, CE,
M1&2, MAF, MAL5, MC, SF
Narrative of John Sheppard.
Daniel Defoe. Johnson-18th
Narrative of the Life of David
Crockett, A. David Crockett.
Magill II, CE, M1&2, MC,
MNF
Narrative of the Proceedings in
France, A. Daniel Defoe.
Johnson-18th
Narratives of Exploration and Ad-
venture. John Charles Fré-
mont. Magill '57, S
Narukami. Ichikawa Danjuro I.
Halford
Nasty Swans, The. Arkady and
Boris Strugatsky. Magill SF
Nathalia. Frederick J. Whishaw.
Kaye
Nathan Burke. Mary S. Watts.
Keller
Nathan Hale. Clyde Fitch. Drury
Nathan the Wise. Gotthold Eph-
raim Lessing. Cartmell; Drury;
Gassner; Haydn; Keller; Magill

191   NATION

III, CE, M1&2, MC, MD;
Shank; Shipley; Sobel; Thomas
Nation of Strangers, A. Vance
Packard. Magill '73
National Church, The. Henry
B. Wilson. Keller (Essays
and Reviews)
National Health, The. Peter
Nichols. Best '74; Drury
National Velvet. Enid Bagnold.
Drury
Nationalism: A Religion. Carlton
J. H. Hayes. Magill CAL
Native Son. Paul Green and
Richard Wright. (Based on
the novel by Richard Wright.)
Best '40; Haydn; Lovell
Native Son. Richard Wright.
(See also adaptation by Paul
Green and Richard Wright.)
Magill I, CE, M1&2, MAF,
MC; Morehead; Smith
Natsu Matsuri Naniwa Kagami
(The Summer Festival). Takeda
Koizumo, Miyoshi Shoraku and
Namiki Senryu. Halford
Natural Affection. William Inge.
Drury
Natural and the Supernatural, The.
John Wood Oman. Magill CHL
Natural History. Comte Georges
Louis Leclerc de Buffon.
Haydn (Histoire); Keller
Natural History. Pliny the Elder.
Downs F, FG; Feder; Haydn;
Keller
Natural History and Antiquities
of Selborne, The. Gilbert
White. Haydn; Keller
Natural Religion and Christian
Theology. Charles E. Raven.
Magill CHL
Natural Theology. William Paley.
Magill CHL
Nature. Ralph Waldo Emerson.
Armstrong
Nature and Destiny of Man, The.
Reinhold Niebuhr. Haydn
p. 521; Magill CHL, WP
Nature and Elements of Poetry,
The. Edmund Clarence Sted-
man. Keller
Nature and Mind. Frederick
James E. Woodbridge. Magill
WP
Nature, Man and God. William
Temple. Magill CHL
Nature, Mind, and Death. Curt

John Ducasse. Magill WP
Nature of Faith, The. Gerhard
Ebeling. Magill CHL
Nature of Passion, The. R.
Prawer Jhabvala. Magill '58,
S
Nature of Sleep. Nathaniel Haw-
thorne. Gale-H
Nature of the Atonement, The.
John McLeod Campbell. Magill
CHL
Nature of Thought, The. Brand
Blanshard. Magill WP
Nature of Truth, The. Harold
Henry Joachim. Magill WP
Natyasastra. Attributed to Bhar-
ata. Gassner
Naughty Marietta. Victor Herbert
and Rida Johnson Young.
Drinkrow; Lovell
Nauplius the Fire-Kindler. Sopho-
cles. Hathorn
Nauplius' Voyage. Sophocles.
Hathorn
Nausea. Jean-Paul Sartre.
Lass EN; Magill II, CE, M1&2,
MC, MEUF
Nautch Girl, The. Edward Solo-
mon, George Dance and Frank
Desprez. Drinkrow
Naval Treaty, The. Sir Arthur
Conan Doyle. Hardwick SH
Nave, La. Tomas Salvador.
Magill SF
Navigateurs de l'infini, Les. J.
H. Rosny (the Elder). Magill
SF
Nazarene, The. Sholem Asch.
Haydn; Magill I, CE, M1&2,
MAF, MC
Neaera. John W. Graham. Kaye
Near the Ocean. Robert Lowell.
Magill '67, M1, S
Near the Tsar, Near Death.
Frederick J. Whishaw. Kaye
Nebuly Coat, The. J. Meade
Falkner. Ward
Necessities of Life; Poems, 1962-
1965. Adrienne Cecile Rich.
Magill '67, S
Necessity of Reforming the Church,
The. John Calvin. Magill
CHL
Nectar in a Sieve. Kamala
Markandaya. Magill '55, S
Ned McCobb's Daughter. Sidney
Howard. Drury; Keller suppl.;
Matlaw; Shipley; Sobel

Needle. Hal Clement. Magill SF
Neighbor Jackwood. John Town-
send Trowbridge. Johnson;
Keller
Neighbors, The. Fredrika Brem-
er. Johnson; Keller
Nekrassov. Jean-Paul Sartre.
Kienzle
Nemesis of Faith, The. James
Anthony Froude. Keller
Nephelai see Clouds, The
Nephew, The. James Purdy.
Magill '61, M1, S
Nero. Ernst Eckstein. Kaye;
Keller
Nerves. Lester Del Rey. Magill
SF
Nest, The. Paul Geraldy and
Grace George. Best '21
Nest of Gentlefolk, A. Ivan Tur-
genev. Haydn
Nest of Royalists, A. Esme
Stuart. Kaye
Nest of Simple Folk, A. Seán
O'Faoláin. Magill II, CE,
M1&2, MC, MEF
Net, The. Rex Beach. Keller
Net of the Truth Faith, The.
Peter Chelčiký. Haydn
Net-Pullers, The see Dictyulci
Netty Sargent's Copyhold. Thomas
Hardy. Saxelby
Never Bet the Devil Your Head.
Edgar Allan Poe. Gale-PP
Never Call Retreat. Bruce Catton.
Magill '66, S
Never, Never, - Never, Never.
Anthony Trollope. Gerould
Never Too Late. Arthur Summer
Long. Drury; NCTE
Nevis Mountain Dew. Steve
Carter. Best '78
New Adam and Eve, The. Nathaniel
Hawthorne. Gale-H
New Age Now Begins, A. Page
Smith. Magill '77
New & Collected Poems, 1917-
1976. Archibald MacLeish.
Magill '77
New and Selected Poems. David
Wagoner. Magill '70
New & Selected Things Taking
Place. May Swenson. Magill
'79
New Atlantis. Sir Francis Bacon.
Haydn; Magill III, CE, M1&2,
MC, MNF; Ruoff
New Class, The. Milovan Djilas.

Magill '58, S
New Colony, The. Luigi Piran-
dello. Matlaw
New Criticism, The. John Crowe
Ransom. Magill IV, MC
New Critique of Theoretical
Thought, A. Herman Dooye-
weerd. Magill CHL
New Decalogue of Science, The.
Albert Edward Wiggam. Keller
suppl.
New Drama, A. Manuel Tamayo
y Baus. Drury; Haydn
New England Maid, A. Eliza F.
Pollard. Kaye
New England Primer, The. Un-
known. Keller
New England Village, The. Attri-
buted to Nathaniel Hawthorne.
Gale-H
New England Winter, A. Henry
James. Gale-J
New English Bible, The. Oxford/
Cambridge University Presses.
Magill '62, S
New Essays: Observations, Divine
and Moral. John Robinson.
Keller
New Essays on the Human Under-
standing. Gottfried Wilhelm
von Leibniz. Magill WP
New Faces of 1952. John Murray
Anderson and Others. Lovell
New-Found-Land. Tom Stoppard.
Magill '78
New Freedom; a Call for the
Emancipation of the Generous
Energies of a People, The.
Woodrow Wilson. Downs M;
Keller
New Golden Land, The. Hugh
Honour. Magill '77
New Grub Street, The. George
Gissing. Haydn; Keller; Magill
I, CE, M1&2, MC, MEF
New Héloïse, The. Jean Jacques
Rousseau. Haydn; Johnson;
Magill II, CE, M1&2, MC,
MEUF
New History of India, A. Stanley
Wolpert. Magill '78
New Leaf Mills. William Dean
Howells. Carrington
New Life, A. Bernard Malamud.
Magill '62, S
New Life of Anton Chekhov, A.
Ronald Hingley. Magill '77
New Lives. Dorothy Rabinowitz.

Magill '77
New Machiavelli, The. H. G.
Wells. Keller; Ward
New Men, The. C. P. Snow.
Magill '55, MB, S
New Mencken Letters, The. Carl
Bode, editor. Magill '78
New Moon, The. Sigmund Rom-
berg, Oscar Hammerstein II,
Frank Mandel and Laurence
Schwab. Drinkrow
New Morality, The. Harold Chapin.
Drury
New Poems. Eugenio Montale.
Magill '77
New Poems. Pablo Neruda.
Magill '73
New Poems. Kenneth Rexroth.
Magill '75
New Poems: 1965-1969. A. D.
Hope. Magill '71
New Race, A. Golo Raimund.
Johnson
New Reformation. Paul Goodman.
Magill '71
New Republic, The. William
Hurrell Mallock. Keller
New Science, The. Giovanni Bat-
tista Vico. Downs M; Magill
CAL, WP
New South Creed, The. Paul M.
Gaston. Magill '71
New System of Chemical Philos-
ophy. John Dalton. Downs M;
Haydn
New Tenant, The. Eugène
Ionesco. Kienzle
New View of Society, or, Essays
on the Formation of the Human
Character, A. Robert Owens.
Downs M
New Viewpoints in American His-
tory. Arthur Meier Schlesinger.
Keller suppl.
New Voyage Round the World, by
a Course Never Sailed Before,
A. Daniel Defoe. Johnson-
18th
New Way to Pay Old Debts, A.
Philip Massinger. Drury;
Gassner; Haydn; Holzknecht;
Keller; Magill II, CE, M1&2,
MC, MD; Ruoff; Shipley; Sobel
New Ways in Psychoanalysis.
Karen Horney. Haydn (a)
New World, The. Isaiah Bowman.
Keller suppl.
New World, The. Winston S.

Churchill. Magill '57, MB, S
New Worlds for Old. H. G.
Wells. Keller
New York Idea, The. Langdon
Mitchell. Drury; Lovell; Mat-
law; Shipley
New York Jew. Alfred Kazin.
Magill '79
Newcomes, The. William Make-
peace Thackeray. Haydn;
Johnson; Keller; Magill I, CE,
M1&2, MC, MEF; Mudge
Newer Alchemy, The. Lord
Ernest Rutherford. Haydn
Newly-Married Couple, The.
Bjørnstjerne Bjørnson. Drury;
Matlaw
Newport. George Parsons Lath-
rop. Keller
News from Nowhere. William
Morris. Magill SF
Next. Terrence McNally. Best
'68; Drury
Next Age of Man, The. Albert
Edward Wiggam. Keller suppl.
Next Chapter, The. André
Maurois. Magill SF
Next Time, The. Henry James.
Gale-J
Next Time I'll Sing to You.
James Saunders. Best '63;
Kienzle
Next 200 Years, The. Herman
Kahn, William Brown and Leon
Martel. Magill '77
Nez Perce Indians and the Opening
of the Northwest, The. Alvin
M. Josephy, Jr. Magill '66, S
Niagara Revisited. William Dean
Howells. Carrington
Nibelungen Ring, The. Richard
Wagner. Armstrong
Nibelungenlied, The. Unknown.
Fleming; Haydn; Keller; Magill
I, CE, M1&2, MC, MEUF
Nice People. Rachel Crothers.
Best '20; Drury
Nicholas and Alexandra. Robert
K. Massie. Magill '68, M1,
S
Nicholas Nickleby. Charles Dick-
ens. Hardwick CD; Haydn;
Johnson; McSpadden-D; McSpad-
den-DH (episode); Magill II,
CE, M1&2, MC, MEF
Nicholas I: Emperor and Autocrat
of All the Russias. W. Bruce
Lincoln. Magill '79

Nichomachean Ethics see Ethica Nicomachea

Nick of the Woods. Robert Montgomery Bird. Johnson; Keller; Magill II, CE, M1&2, MAF, MC

Nickel Miseries. Ivan Gold. Magill Ss

Nickel Mountain. John Gardner. Magill '74

Nicole. Owen Johnson. Kaye

Niels Ebbesen. Kaj Munk. Drury; Matlaw

Niels Lyhne. Jens Peter Jacobsen. Magill II, CE, M1&2, MC, MEUF

Nigger, The. Edward Sheldon. Drury; Matlaw; Sobel

Nigger Heaven. Carl Van Vechten. Keller suppl.

Nigger Jeff. Theodore Dreiser. Gerber

Nigger of the Narcissus, The. Joseph Conrad. Haydn; Heiney; Magill II, CE, M1&2, MC, MEF; Stade p. 142; Ward

Night and Day. Virginia Woolf. Stade p. 186

Night and Morning. Lord Edward Bulwer-Lytton. Johnson

Night at an Inn, A. Lord Dunsany. Matlaw; Sobel

Night at Sea, A. Margaret Lane. Magill '66, S

Night Comes to the Cumberlands. Harry M. Caudill. Magill '64, S

Night Flight. Antoine de Saint-Exupéry. Heiney; Magill III, CE, M1&2, MC, MEUF

Night in the Luxembourg, A. Remy de Gourmont. Haydn; Magill I, CE, M1&2, MC, MEUF

Night Life. Sidney Kingsley. Drury

Night Light. Donald Justice. Magill '68, S

Night Must Fall. Emlyn Williams. Drury; Matlaw; NCTE; Sobel

Night of January Sixteenth. Ayn Rand. Drury

Night of the Hunter, The. Davis Grubb. Magill '54, M1, S

Night of the Iguana, The. Tennessee Williams. Anderson; Best '61; Bonin; Drury; Kienzle; Magill '63, M1, S; Matlaw; NCTE

Night of Time, The. René Fülöp-Miller. Magill '55, S

Night Off, A. Augustin Daly. Drury

Night Out, A. Harold Pinter. French

Night over Taos. Maxwell Anderson. Sobel

Night Rider. Robert Penn Warren. Magill IV, MC

Night-Side. Joyce Carol Oates. Magill '78

Night Sketches Beneath an Umbrella. Nathaniel Hawthorne. Gale-H

Night Thoreau Spent in Jail, The. Jerome Lawrence and Robert E. Lee. Drury; NCTE

Night Thoughts see Complaint; or, Night Thoughts, The

Night to Remember, A. Walter Lord. Magill '55, S

Night Visitor and Other Stories, The. B. Traven. Magill '67, S

Night Watch. Lucille Fletcher. Drury

Nightmare. J. Anthony Lukas. Magill '77

Nightmare Abbey. Thomas Love Peacock. Haydn; Magill I, CE, M1&2, MC, MEF; Olfson

Nightmares of Eminent Persons. Bertrand Russell. Magill '55, S

Nights and Days. James Merrill. Magill '67, S

Night's Lodging, The see Lower Depths, The

Nights of Cabiria, The. Federico Fellini. (See adaptation Sweet Charity by Neil Simon et al.)

Nights of Wrath (Nights of Anger). Armand Salacrou. Kienzle; Shipley

Nightwalker and Other Poems. Thomas Kinsella. Magill '69, S

Nightwings. Robert Silverberg. Magill SF

Nijinsky. Richard Buckle. Magill '73

Nina Balatka. Anthony Trollope. Gerould

Nine Coaches Waiting. Guy Bolton. (Based on the novel by Mary Stewart.) Drury

Nine Coaches Waiting. Mary
Stewart. (See adaptation by
Guy Bolton.)
Nine Days, The. T. B. Morris.
French
Nine Hours to Rama. Stanley
Wolpert. Magill '63, S
900 Days, The. Harrison E.
Salisbury. Magill '70
Nine Rivers from Jordan. Denis
Johnston. Magill '55, S
1918: The Last Act. Barrie
Pitt. Magill '64, S
1985. Anthony Burgess. Magill
'79
Nineteen Eighty-Four. George
Orwell. (See also adaptation
by Wilton E. Hall and William
A. Miles.) Heiney; Lass BN;
Magill II, CE, M1&2, MC,
MEF, SF; Olfson; Ward
1984. Robert Owens and Wilton
E. Hall, Jr., and William A.
Miles. (Based on the novel
by George Orwell.) Drury;
NCTE
1945: Year Zero. John Lukacs.
Magill '79
1919. John Dos Passos. (See
also trilogy title U S A.)
Haydn p. 773
1977: The Year of the Hangman.
John S. Pancake. Magill '78
95 Poems. E. E. Cummings.
Magill '59, MB, S
Ninety-Three. Victor Hugo.
Johnson; Kaye; Keller
Ninety-Two in the Shade. Thomas
McGuane. Kienzle; Magill '74
Nineveh and Its Remains. Austen
Henry Layard. Keller
Ninth Wave, The. Eugene Bur-
dick. Magill '57, S
Niobe. Aeschylus. Hathorn
Niobe. Sophocles. Hathorn
Niourk. Stefan Wul. Magill SF
Nipper, The see In Chains
Nippur. John Punnett Peters.
Keller
Nitty Gritty, The. Frank Bonham.
Benedict
Njál Saga, The. Unknown. Haydn
Nju. Ossip Dymov. Shipley
No Blade of Grass. John Chris-
topher. Magill SF
No Concern of Mine. Jeremy
Kingston. French
No Crime in the Streets. Reginald

Rose. Drury
No Cross, No Crown. Deborah
Alcock. Kaye
No Exit. Jean-Paul Sartre.
Drury; Gassner; Heiney; Mat-
law; NCTE; Shank; Shipley;
Sprinchorn
No Laughing Matter. Angus Wil-
son. Magill '68, S
No Love Lost. William Dean
Howells. Carrington
No Man's Son. Henry de Monther-
lant. Matlaw
No More Ladies. Albert Ells-
worth Thomas. Best '33
No More Parades. Ford Madox
Ford. Keller suppl.
No More Peace. Ernst Toller.
Drury; Sobel
No Mother to Guide Her. Lillian
Mortimer. Lovell
No Name. Wilkie Collins. John-
son; Magill I, CE, M1&2, MC,
MEF
No Name in the Street. James
Baldwin. Magill '73
No, No, Nanette. Otto Harbach,
Frank Mandel, Irving Caesar
and Vincent Youmans. NCTE;
Drink row
No One Knows How see One
Does Not Know How
No Place to Be Somebody.
Charles Gordone. Best '68;
Bonin; Drury; NCTE
No Surrender. George A. Henty.
Kaye
No Thoroughfare. Charles Dick-
ens. Hardwick CD
No Time for Comedy. S. N.
Behrman. Best '38; Drury;
Matlaw; Shank; Shipley; Sobel
No Time for Sergeants. Mac
Hyman. (See also adaptation
by Ira Levin.) Magill '54, S
No Time for Sergeants. Ira
Levin. (Based on the novel by
Mac Hyman.) Best '55; Chap-
man '56; Drury; NCTE
No Trifling with Love. Alfred de
Musset. Magill II, CE, M1&2,
MC, MD
Noa Noa. Paul Gauguin. Haydn
Noah. André Obey. Drury;
French; Matlaw; NCTE; Shank
Noah ist tot (Noah Is Dead).
Daniel Christoff. Kienzle
Noah's Ark. Hugh of St. Victor.

Magill CAL
Noank's Log. William O. Stod-
dard. Kaye
Noble Bachelor, The. Sir Arthur
Conan Doyle. Hardwick SH
Noble Jilt, The. Anthony Trol-
lope. Gerould
Nobody Knows My Name. James
Baldwin. Magill '62, MB, S
Nobody's Story. Charles Dickens.
Hardwick CD
Noctes Atticae. Aulus Gellius.
Haydn
Nocturne. Frank Swinnerton.
Keller suppl.; Magill I, CE,
M1&2, MC, MEF
Noel Coward in Two Keys. Noel
Coward. Best '73; Drury
Noemi. Sabine Baring-Gould.
Kaye; Keller
Noh Plays of Japan. Haydn
Noites marcianas, As. Fausto
Cunha. Magill SF
Nommé Judas, Un (A Man Named
Judas). Claude André Puget
and Pierre Bost. Kienzle
Nomoi see Laws
Non Sum Qualis Eram Bonae sub
Regno Cynarae. Ernest Down-
son. Haydn
Nona Vincent. Henry James.
Gale-J
None So Blind. Armitage Owen.
French
Nonsense Novels. Stephen Lea-
cock. Haydn
Noon Has No Shadows. Patricia
Joudry. French
Noon: Twenty-Second Century.
Arkady and Boris Strugatsky.
Magill SF
Norah Moriarty. Amos Reade.
Kaye
Norman. Frank Harvey. French
Norman Conquests, The. Alan
Ayckbourn. Best '75; Drury
Norman Thomas. W. A. Swan-
berg. Magill '77
Norstrilia. Cordwainer Smith.
Magill SF
North Pole, The. Rear Admiral
Robert E. Peary. Keller
North Toward Home. Willie
Morris. Magill '68, S
North-West Passage, The.
Roald Amundsen. Keller
Northanger Abbey. Jane Austen.
Halperin; Haydn; Johnson;

Magill II, CE, M1&2, MC,
MEF
Northern Lass, The. Richard
Brome. Magill III, CE, M1&2,
MC, MD; Ruoff
Northrop Frye on Culture and Lit-
erature. H. Northrop Frye.
Magill '79
Norths Meet Murder, The. Fran-
ces and Richard Lockridge.
(See adaptation Mr. and Mrs.
North by Owen Davis.)
Northward Hoe. John Webster
and Thomas Dekker. Sobel
Northwest Passage. Kenneth
Roberts. Haydn; Magill IV,
MC; Morehead
Norwood. Henry Ward Beecher.
Johnson
Norwood Builder, The. Sir
Arthur Conan Doyle. Hardwick
SH
Nosce Teipsum: This Oracle Ex-
pounded in Two Elegies. Sir
John Davies. Ruoff p. 100
Nostromo. Joseph Conrad.
Haydn; Keller; Magill II, CE,
M1&2, MC, MEF; Stade p. 152;
Ward
Not Angels Quite. Nathan Haskell
Dole. Johnson
Not by Bread Alone. Vladimir
Dudintsev. Magill '58, S
Not for Children. Elmer Rice.
Drury
Not for Publication. Nadine
Gordimer. Magill '66, S
Not Honour More. Joyce Cary.
Magill '55, S
Not If I Know It. Anthony Trol-
lope. Gerould
Not in the Book. Arthur Watkyn.
French
Not Peace But a Sword. Vincent
Sheean. Haydn p. 574
Not This Pig. Philip Levine.
Magill '69, S
Not Wanted. Anton Chekhov.
Keller suppl. (Party)
Notebook 1967-68. Robert Lowell.
Magill '70
Notebooks: 1935-1942. Albert
Camus. Magill '64, S
Notebooks: 1942-1951. Albert
Camus. Magill '66, S
Notebooks of Leonardo da Vinci,
The. Leonardo da Vinci.
Haydn; Magill IV, MC

Notebooks of Samuel Butler, The.
Samuel Butler. Haydn
Notes from a Bottle Found on
the Beach at Carmel. Evan
S. Connell, Jr. Magill IV,
'64, MC, S
Notes from a Dead House. Fyodor
Mikhailovich Dostoevskii.
Berry-2
Notes on Central America. Eph-
raim George Squier. Keller
(Central)
Notes on the State of Virginia.
Thomas Jefferson. Magill
III, M1, MC, MNF
Nothing But the Truth. James
Montgomery. Drury; French
Nothing Ever Breaks Except the
Heart. Kay Boyle. Magill
'67, S
Nothing Like the Sun. Anthony
Burgess. Magill '65, S
Nothing New Under the Sun.
Riccardo Bacchelli. Magill
'55, S
Notorious Mrs. Ebbsmith, The.
Arthur Wing Pinero. Matlaw
Notre Dame de Paris see
Hunchback of Notre Dame, The
Nouveaux Lundis. Charles Augus-
tin Sainte-Beuve. Keller
Nova. Samuel R. Delany.
Magill SF
Nova Express. William S. Bur-
roughs. Magill SF
Novel, a Novella and Four
Stories, A. Andrew Lytle.
Magill '59, S
November Night. Adelaide Champ-
neys. Keller suppl.
Novice, The. Mikhail Yuievich
Lermontov. Magill IV, MC
Novum Organum. Sir Francis
Bacon. Armstrong; Haydn;
Keller; Magill WP
Now and Then: Poems 1976-1978.
Robert Penn Warren. Magill
'79
Now Playing at Canterbury.
Vance Bourjaily. Magill '77
Nowhere But Light: Poems 1964-
1969. Ben Belitt. Magill '71
Nubes see Clouds, The
Nude with Violin. Noel Coward.
Drury; French; Kienzle; Matlaw
Numa Roumestan. Alphonse
Daudet. Johnson; Keller
No. 44, the Mysterious Stranger.

Mark Twain. Gale-T; Keller
suppl. (Mysterious)
No. XIII. The Story of the Lost
Vestal. Emma Marshall. Kaye
Numbered, The. Elias Canetti.
Kienzle
Nun singen sie wieder (They Sing
Again). Max Frisch. Kienzle
Nunquam. Lawrence Durrell.
Magill '71, SF
Nun's Story, The. Kathryn Hulme.
Magill '57, M1, S
Nurses, The. Aeschylus. Hathorn
Nut Factory. Jay Christopher.
Drury
Nymphidia, the Court of Fairy.
Michael Drayton. Ruoff

-O-

O Genteel Lady. Esther Forbes.
Keller suppl.
O Lovely England. Walter De la
Mare. Magill '57, S
O Mistress Mine. Terence Ratti-
gan. Best '45; Drury
O Natsu Kyoran. Onoe Baiko VI.
Halford
O Pioneers! Willa Cather.
Haydn; Magill I, CE, M1&2,
MAF, MC
O Shepherd, Speak. Upton Sin-
clair. Heiney
O. T. Hans Christian Andersen.
Johnson
O Taste and See. Denise Lever-
tov. Magill '65, S
O the Chimneys. Nelly Sachs.
Magill '68, S
O to Be a Dragon. Marianne
Moore. Magill '60, M1, MB,
S
Oak Openings, The. James Feni-
more Cooper. Johnson; Walker
Obedience to Authority. Stanley
Milgram. Magill '75
Oblomov. Ivan Alexandrovich
Goncharov. Berry-2; Haydn;
Keller; Lass EN; Magill II,
CE, M1&2, MC, MEUF
Oblong Box, The. Edgar Allan
Poe. Gale-PP
Obscenities. Michael Casey.
Magill '73
Observations in the Art of English

Poesy.   Thomas Campion.
Ruoff p. 93
Observations on Popular Antiquities.
John Brand.   Keller
Occurrences of the Times; or,
The Transactions of Four Days.
Unknown.   Lovell
Oceana.   James Anthony Froude.
Keller
O'Conors of Castle Conor, The.
Anthony Trollope.   Gerould
Octavia.   Attributed to Lucius
Annaeus Seneca.   Feder; Ha-
thorn; Reinhold; Shipley
Octavius.   Minucius Felix.   Magill
CAL, CHL
October Country, The.   Ray
Bradbury.   Magill SF
October Light.   John Gardner.
Magill '77
October the First Is Too Late.
Fred Hoyle.   Magill SF
Octopus, The.   Frank Norris.
Haydn; Keller; Lass AN;
Smith
Octoroon, The.   Boucicault.
Drury; Lovell; NBC 2; Shipley;
Sobel
Odd Couple, The.   Neil Simon.
Best '64; Drury; NCTE
Odd John: A Story Between Jest
and Earnest.   Olaf Stapledon.
Magill SF
Odd Man In.   Claude Magnier.
(Based on Monsieur Masure
by Robin Maugham.)   French
Odd Number, The.   Guy de Mau-
passant.   Keller
Odd Woman, The.   Gail Godwin.
Magill '75
Ode on Intimations of Immortality
from Recollections of Early
Childhood.   William Words-
worth.   Haydn
Ode to Aphrodite.   Sappho.
Magill III, M1, MC, MP
Odes.   Horace.   Downs M;
Feder; Haydn
Odes.   John Keats.   Haydn
Odes.   Pindar.   Downs F; Haydn
Odo.   Edwin Harris.   Kaye
Odysseus Akanthoplex.   Sophocles.
Hathorn
Odysseus' Madness.   Sophocles.
Hathorn
Odyssey, The.   Homer.   Arm-
strong; Cohen; Downs F, FG;
Feder; Fleming; Grozier;

Haydn; Keller; Magill I, CE,
M1&2, MC, MP; Sabater; Wil-
son
Odyssey: A Modern Sequel, The.
Nikos Kazantzakis.   Magill Ss
Odyssey of a Friend.   Whittaker
Chambers.   Magill '71
Oedipus.   Aeschylus.   Hathorn
Oedipus.   Lucius Annaeus Seneca.
Feder; Hathorn; Reinhold
Oedipus at Colonus.   Sophocles.
Downs M, FG; Feder; Gassner;
Hathorn; Haydn; Jolliffe; Keller;
Magill II, CE, M1&2, MC, MD;
Reinhold; Shank; Shipley; Sobel
Oedipus rex see Oedipus tyrannus
Oedipus the King see Oedipus
tyrannus
Oedipus tyrannus (Oedipus the
King).   Sophocles.   Cartmell;
Downs M, FG; Drury; Feder;
Gassner; Hathorn; Haydn; Jol-
liffe; Keller; Magill I, CE,
M1&2, MC, MD; Reinhold;
Shank; Shipley; Sobel
Oeil du Purgatoire, L'.   Jacques
Spitz.   Magill SF
Oeuvre, L'.   Emile Zola.   Keller
(Rougon)
Oeuvres.   Louis Pasteur.   Haydn
Of Being Numerous.   George Op-
pen.   Magill '69, S
Of Civil Government: The Second
Treatise.   John Locke.   Magill
WP
Of Conscience, Its Power and
Cases.   William Ames.   Magill
CHL
Of Crimes and Punishments.
Cesare Bonesana Beccaria.
Downs M
Of Education.   John Milton.
Haydn; Keller (Tractate); Ruoff
(Education)
Of Human Bondage.   W. Somerset
Maugham.   Grozier; Haydn;
Heiney; Keller suppl. ; Lass
BN; Magill I, CE, M1&2, MC,
MEF; Olfson; Ward
Of Learned Ignorance.   Nicholas
of Cusa (Nicholas Cusanus).
Magill CAL, CHL, WP
Of Mice and Men.   John Steinbeck.
(novel and drama) Best '37;
Bonin; Drury; Heiney; Lass AP;
Lovell; Magill I, CE, M1&2,
MAF, MC; Matlaw; Morehead;
NCTE; Olfson; Shank; Sobel

Shipley; Sobel
Old House, The.   Feodor Sologub.
  Haydn; Keller
Old Ladies, The.   Rodney Ackland.
  Drury
Old Ladies, The.   Hugh Walpole.
  Keller suppl.
Old Lady Says "No, " The.   Denis
  Johnston.   Gassner; Matlaw
Old Lady Shows Her Medals, The.
  Sir James M. Barrie.   Sobel
"Old Lady 31. "   Rachel Crothers.
  Drury
Old Ma'amselle's Secret, The.
  E. Marlitt.   Johnson
Old Maid, The.   Zoë Akins.
  (Based on the novelette by
  Edith Wharton.)   Best '34;
  Bonin; Shipley; Sobel
Old Maid, The.   Edith Wharton.
  (See also Old New York of
  which this is novelette # 2).
  Drury; Magill I, CE, M1&2,
  MAF, MC; Shipley
Old Man and the Sea, The.
  Ernest Hemingway.   Lass AN;
  Magill II, CE, M1&2, MAF,
  MC; Olfson; Smith
Old Man's Love, An.   Anthony
  Trollope.   Gerould
Old Manse, The.   Nathaniel
  Hawthorne.   Gale-H
Old Margaret.   Henry Kingsley.
  Kaye
Old Men at the Zoo, The.   Angus
  Wilson.   Magill '62, S
Old Mortality.   Katherine Anne
  Porter.   Magill II, CE, M1&2,
  MAF, MC, MEF
Old Mortality.   Sir Walter Scott.
  Johnson; Kaye; McSpadden W;
  Magill I, CE, M1&2, MC
Old Mrs. Chundle.   Thomas
  Hardy.   Pinion
Old Myddleton's Money.   Mary
  Cecil Hay.   Johnson
Old Neighborhood, The.   Theodore
  Dreiser.   Gerber
Old New York.   Edith Wharton.
  (See also Old Maid, novelette
  # 2 of the above title.)   Keller
  suppl.
Old News.   Nathaniel Hawthorne.
  Gale-H
Old One and the Wind: Poems,
  The.   Clarice Short.   Magill
  '74
Old Possum's Book of Practical

Cats.   T. S. Eliot.   Ward
Old Red and Other Stories.
  Caroline Gordon.   Magill '64,
  S
Old Regime in Canada, The.
  Francis Parkman.   Magill IV,
  MC
Old Rogaum and His Theresa
  (Butcher Rogaum's Door).
  Theodore Dreiser.   Gerber
Old St. Paul's.   William Harrison
  Ainsworth.   Kaye; Keller;
  Magill II, CE, M1&2, MC,
  MEF
Old Sir Douglas.   Hon. Mrs.
  Norton.   Keller
Old Soak, The.   Don Marquis.
  Best '22; Drury
Old Soldiers Never Die.   Wolf
  Mankowitz.   Magill '57, S
Old Story of My Farming Days.
  Fritz Reuter.   Keller
Old Things, The   see   Spoils of
  Poynton, The
Old Ticonderoga: A Picture of
  the Past.   Nathaniel Hawthorne.
  Gale-H
Old Times.   Harold Pinter.
  Best '71; Drury
Old Wives' Tale, The.   Arnold
  Bennett.   Grozier; Haydn;
  Heiney; Keller; Lass BN; Ma-
  gill I, CE, M1&2, MC, MD,
  MEF; Olfson; Ward
Old Wives' Tale, The.   George
  Peele.   Haydn; Holzknecht;
  Magill II, CE, M1&2, MC;
  Ruoff; Shipley; Sobel
Old Woman, the Wife, and the
  Archer, The.   Donald Keene,
  editor.   Magill '62, S
Old Woman's Tale, An.   Nathaniel
  Hawthorne.   Gale-H
Oldest Living Graduate, The.
  Preston Jones.   Best '76
Oldtown Folks.   Harriet Beecher
  Stowe.   Johnson; Keller; Magill
  II, CE, M1&2, MAF, MC
Oliver!   Lionel Bart.   NCTE
Oliver Cromwell.   John Drink-
  water.   Drury; French; NBC 2
Oliver Cromwell's Letters and
  Speeches.   Oliver Cromwell.
  Keller (a); Magill CHL
Oliver Twist.   Charles Dickens.
  Cohen; Goodman; Grozier;
  Hardwick CD; Haydn; Johnson;
  Keller; McSpadden-D; McSpad-

On the Causes of Plants. Theo-
phrastus. Downs F, FG
On the Christian Faith. Saint
Ambrose. Magill CAL
On the Civil War. Lucan.
Feder
On the Conservation of Force.
Hermann Helmholtz. Downs
M; Haydn (Conservation)
On the Divine Names. Dionysius
the Pseudo-Areopagite. Magill
CAL
On the Division of Nature. Eri-
gena Johannes Scotus. Magill
WP
On the Duties of the Clergy.
Saint Ambrose. Magill CAL,
CHL
On the Education of a Gentleman.
Pier Paolo Vergerio. Magill
CAL
On the Emperor's Service. Emma
Leslie. Kaye
On the Equilibrium of Hetero-
geneous Substances. Josiah
Willard Gibbs. Downs M
On the Errors of the Trinity.
Michael Servetus. Magill
CHL
On the Eternal in Man. Max
Scheler. Magill CHL
On the Eve. Ivan Turgenev.
Berry-1; Haydn; Keller
On the Face of the Waters. Mrs.
Flora A. Steel. Johnson;
Kaye
On the First Principle see
De primo principio
On the Freedom of the Will see
Freedom of the Will
On the Frontier. Wystan Hugh
Auden and Christopher Isher-
wood. Sobel
On the Genesis of the Species.
St. George Jackson Mivart.
Magill CAL
On the Harmfulness of Tobacco.
Anton Chekhov. Matlaw
On the Heavens. Aristotle.
Downs F, FG
On the Heights. Berthold Auer-
bach. Johnson; Keller
On the Highway. Anton Chekhov.
Matlaw
On the History of Plants. Theo-
phrastus. Downs F, FG
On the Holy Trinity (De Trinitate).
Saint Anicius Manlius Severinus

Boethius. Magill CAL, CHL
On the Improvement of the Under-
standing. Benedict de Spinoza.
Haydn
On the Interpretation of Scripture.
Benjamin Jowett. Keller (Es-
says and Reviews)
On the Knees of the Gods. Mrs.
Anna B. Dodd. Kaye
On the Law of War and Peace.
Hugo Grotius. Downs M; Ma-
gill IV, MC
On the Loadstone, Magnetic
Bodies, and On the Great Mag-
net the Earth. William Gilbert.
Downs M
On the Morning of Christ's Nativ-
ity. John Milton. Ruoff
On the Mosaic Cosmogony. C.
W. Goodwin. Keller (Essays
and Reviews)
On the Natural Faculties. Galen.
Downs F, FG; Haydn
On the Nature of Things (De re-
rum natura). Titus Lucretius
Carus. Downs M, FG; Feder;
Haydn; Magill III, M1, MC,
MNF, WP (De rerum)
On the Necessity of Loving God.
Saint Bernard. Magill CAL
On the Old Kearsarge. Cyrus T.
Brady. Kaye
On the Origin of Species. Charles
Darwin. Armstrong (Origin);
Downs M, FG; Haydn; Keller
(Origin); Magill III, CE, M1&2,
MC, MNF
On the Power of God. Saint
Thomas Aquinas. Magill CAL
On the Red Staircase. Mary Im-
lay Taylor. Kaye
On the Reduction of the Arts to
Theology. Saint Bonaventure.
Magill WP
On the Reply of the Haruspices.
Marcus Tullius Cicero. Keller
(Haruspices)
On the Resurrection of the Dead.
Athenagoras. Magill CAL
On the Road. Jack Kerouac.
Magill '58, M1, S; Morehead
On the Rocks. George Bernard
Shaw. Hardwick; Matlaw;
Sobel
On the Soul. Saint Thomas
Aquinas. Magill CAL
On the Soul. Aristotle. Magill
WP

On the Sphere and Cylinder.
Archimedes. Downs F, FG
On the Steps of Humility and
Pride. Saint Bernard. Magill
CAL
On the Structure of the Human
Body (De humani corporis
fabrica). Andreas Vesalius.
Downs M, FG; Haydn (De hu-
mani)
On the Study of the Evidences of
Christianity. Baden Powell.
Keller (Essays and Reviews)
On the Sublime. Attributed to
Longinus. Haydn; Magill IV,
MC
On the Theology of Death. Karl
Rahner. Magill CAL
On the Trail of Ancient Man.
Roy Chapman Andrews. Keller
suppl.
On the Trinity (De Trinitate).
Saint Augustine. Magill CAL,
CHL
On the Trinity. Saint Hilary of
Poitiers. Magill CHL
On the Unity of the Catholic
Church. Saint Cyprian of
Carthage. Magill CAL, CHL
On the Virtues in General. Saint
Thomas Aquinas. Magill CAL
On the Western Circuit. Thomas
Hardy. Pinion; Saxelby
On to Pekin. Edward Stratemeyer.
Kaye
On Translating Homer. Matthew
Arnold. Haydn
On Trial. Elmer Rice. Best
'09; Drury; Matlaw; Shipley
On War. Karl von Clausewitz.
Downs M
Once Aboard the Lugger. R. F.
Delderfield. French
Once and Future King, The.
Terence Hanbury White. (See
also adaptation Camelot by
Alan Jay Lerner and Frederick
Loewe.) Magill IV, '59, MB,
MC, S
Once Bitten-Twice Shy. Armitage
Owen. French
Once for the Last Bandit. Samuel
Hazo. Magill '73
Once in a Lifetime. Moss Hart
and George S. Kaufman. Best
'30; Drury; Matlaw; Shank;
Shipley
Once Is Enough. Frederick Lons-

dale. Drury
Once to Sinai. H. F. M. Pres-
cott. Magill '59, S
Once upon a Mattress. Jay
Thompson, Marshall Barer,
Dean Fuller and Mary Rodgers.
(Based on "The Princess and
the Pea" by Hans Christian
Andersen.) NCTE
Ondine. Jean Giraudoux. Chap-
man '54; Drury; Magill '54, S;
Matlaw; NCTE; Shank; Shipley;
Sprinchorn
One Autumn Evening. Friedrich
Dürrenmatt. Kienzle
One Crowded Hour. Sidney C.
Grier. Kaye
One Day. Wright Morris. Magill
'66, S
One Day in the Life of Ivan Deni-
sovich. Aleksandr I. Solzhenit-
syn. Magill '64, M1, S
One Does Not Know How. Luigi
Pirandello. Drury (No One ...);
Matlaw; Shipley
One Fat Englishman. Kingsley
Amis. Magill '65, S
One, Few, Too Many. Count
Vittorio Alfieri. Shipley
One Flew over the Cuckoo's Nest.
Ken Kesey. Drury; Magill '63,
M1, S
One Hundred Years of Solitude.
Gabriel García Márquez.
Magill '71
One in a Thousand. George P.
R. James. Kaye
One in Twenty. Bryan Magee.
Magill '67, S
One Kind of Freedom: The Eco-
nomic Consequences of Eman-
cipation. Roger L. Ransom
and Richard Sutch. Magill '78
One Man's Life. Herbert Quick.
Keller suppl.
One More Spring. Robert Nathan.
Haydn (a)
One of Cleopatra's Nights. Théo-
phile Gautier. Keller
One of the Red Shirts. Herbert
Hayens. Kaye
One Queen Triumphant. Frank
Mathew. Kaye
One Summer. Blanche Willis
(Howard) von Teuffel. Keller
One Sunday Afternoon. James
Hagan. Best '32
"... one-third of a nation... "

Arthur Arent. Lass AP;
Lovell; Matlaw; Sobel
1003. Fritz Hochwälder. Kienzle
One to Count Cadence. James
Crumley. Magill '70
One Way Pendulum. N. F. Simp-
son. Drury; French; Kienzle;
Matlaw
One Wild Oat. Vernon Sylvaine.
French
One Woman's Life. Robert Her-
rick. Keller
One World. Wendell L. Willkie.
Haydn
One World at a Time. Richard
Stockton. Bonin
O'Neill. Arthur and Barbara
Gelb. Magill '63, MB, S
O'Neill: Son and Artist. Louis
Sheaffer. Magill '74
Onesimus: Memoirs of a Dis-
ciple of St. Paul. Keller
Onion Field, The. Joseph Wam-
baugh. Magill '74
Onions in the Stew. William
Dalzell. (Based on the story
by Betty MacDonald.) Drury
Onions in the Stew. Betty Mac-
Donald. (See adaptation by
William Dalzell.)
Onkel, Onkel. Günter Grass.
Kienzle
Only a Girl. Wilhelmine von
Hillern. Keller
Only Child, An. Frank O'Connor.
Magill '62, S
Only in America. Harry Golden.
(See also adaptation by Jerome
Lawrence and Robert E. Lee.)
Magill '59, M1, S
Only in America. Jerome Law-
rence and Robert E. Lee.
(Based on the book by Harry
Golden.) Drury; NCTE
Only Jealousy of Emer, The.
William Butler Yeats. Matlaw
Only Ten Minutes to Buffalo.
Günter Grass. Kienzle
Ontario Steamboat, An. Nathaniel
Hawthorne. Gale-H
Open Country. Maurice Hewlett.
Ward
Open-Eyed Conspiracy, An.
William Dean Howells. Car-
rington
Open Letter to the Christian Nobil-
ity of the German Nation, An.
Martin Luther. Downs FG, M;

Magill CHL
Open Letters to the Intimate The-
atre. August Strindberg. Mat-
law
Open to Murder. Peter Gent.
French
Open Verdict. Falkland L. Cary
and Philip Weathers. French
Openings. Wendell Berry. Magill
'69, S
Opera omnia. Albertus Magnus.
Haydn
Operators, The. Frank Gibney.
Magill '61, S
Opfer Helena, Das (Helena the
Victim). Wolfgang Hildesheim-
er. Kienzle
Ophiuchi Hotline, The. John
Varley. Magill SF
Opticks. Sir Isaac Newton.
Haydn
Optimistic Tragedy, The. Vse-
volod Vishnevski. Matlaw;
Sprinchorn
Optimist's Daughter, The. Eudora
Welty. Magill '73
Opus majus. Roger Bacon.
Downs; Haydn; Keller; Magill
CAL
Opus oxoniense. John Duns
Scotus. Haydn; Magill CAL
Opus Posthumous. Wallace
Stevens. Magill '58, S
Orange and Green. George A.
Henty. Kaye
Oraşele Inecate. Felix Aderca.
Magill SF
Oration and Panegyric Addressed
to Origen, The. Saint Gregory
Thaumaturgus. Magill CAL
Oration on the Dignity of Man.
Giovanni Pico della Mirandola.
Magill IV, CAL, MC
Orator. Marcus Tullius Cicero.
Feder
Orators, The. Wystan Hugh
Auden. Ward
Orbitsville. Bob Shaw. Magill
SF
Orchard Keeper, The. Cormac
McCarthy. Magill '66, S
Orchard Walls, The. R. F.
Delderfield. French
Orchards of Polovchansk, The.
Leonid Maximovich Leonov.
Matlaw
Orchestra; or A Poem ... of
Dancing. Sir John Davies.

ORPHEUS 206

Orpheus. Jean Cocteau. Gass-
ner; Matlaw; Shank; Sprinchorn
Orpheus and Eurydice. Unknown.
Magill I, CE, M1&2, MC,
MEUF
Orpheus C. Kerr Papers, The.
Robert Henry Newell. Keller
Orpheus Descending. Tennessee
Williams. Best '56; Chapman
'57; Drury; Kienzle; Magill '59,
S; Matlaw
Orrain. Sidney K. Levett Yeats.
Kaye
Orsinian Tales. Ursula K. Le
Guin. Magill '77
Orthodoxy. Gilbert Keith Chester-
ton. Keller; Magill CAL
Osborne's Revenge. Henry James.
Gale-J
Oshi no Fusuma Koi no Mutsugoto.
Unknown. Halford
Osman. Ivan Gundulic. Haydn
Oszlopos Simeon (Simeon the
Stylite). Irme Sarkadi. Ki-
enzle
Othello. William Shakespeare.
Campbell; Chute; Clark; Drury;
Gassner; Guerber-ST; Halliday;
Haydn; Keller; Lamb; Mc-
Cutchan-ST; McSpadden S;
Magill I, CE, M1&2, MC,
MD; NBC 2; Ruoff; Shank;
Shipley; Sobel; Wilson
Other Danger, The. Maurice
Donnay. Drury
Other Days, Other Eyes. Bob
Shaw. Magill SF
Other House, The. Henry James.
Gale-J
Other Kingdom. E. M. Forster.
Stade p. 223
Other Men's Daughters. Richard
Stern. Magill '74
Other One, The. Colette.
Magill III, CE, M1&2, MC,
MEUF
Other Room, The. Herbert
Zbigniew. Kienzle
Other Side, The. Alfred Kubin.
Magill SF
Other Son, The. Luigi Pirandello.
Matlaw
Other Voices, Other Rooms.
Truman Capote. Morehead
Otherwise Engaged. Simon Gray.
Best '76
Our American Cousin. Tom
Taylor. Shipley; Sobel

Our Betters. W. Somerset
Maugham. Drury; Matlaw;
Shipley; Sobel; Ward
Our Calling. Einar Billing.
Magill CHL
Our Daily Bread. Clara (Viebig)
Cohn. Keller
Our Experience of God. H. D.
Lewis. Magill CHL
Our Hearts Were Young and Gay.
Jean Kerr. (Based on the book
by Cornelia Otis Skinner and
Emily Kimbrough.) NCTE
Our Hearts Were Young and Gay.
Cornelia Otis Skinner and
Emily Kimbrough. (See adap-
tation by Jean Kerr.)
Our Inner Conflicts. Karen
Horney. Haydn (a)
Our Knowledge of the External
World. Bertrand Russell.
Magill WP
Our Lady of Deliverance. John
Oxenham. Kaye
Our Lan'. Theodore Ward.
NCTE
Our Man in Havana. Graham
Greene. Magill '59, S
Our Miss Brooks. Christopher
Sergel. Drury
Our Miss Gibbs. Ivan Caryll,
Lionel Monckton, 'Cryptos, '
James T. Tanner, Adrian
Ross and Percy Greenbank.
Drinkrow
Our Mutual Friend. Charles
Dickens. Grozier; Hardwick
CD; Haydn; Johnson; Keller;
McSpadden-D; Magill II, CE,
M1&2, MC, MEF
Our New Alaska. Charles Hal-
lock. Keller
Our New Home. Nathaniel Haw-
thorne. Keller
Our Nuclear Future. Edward
Teller and Albert L. Latter.
Magill '59, S
Our Samoan Adventure. Fanny
and Robert Louis Stevenson.
Magill '55, S
Our Social Heritage. Graham
Wallas. Keller suppl.
Our Theatres in the Nineties.
George Bernard Shaw. Matlaw
Our Times. Mark Sullivan.
Keller suppl.
Our Town. Thornton Wilder.
Best '37; Bonin; Drury; French;

Gassner; Haydn; Heiney; Lass
AP; Lovell; Magill I, CE,
M1&2, MC, MD; Matlaw;
NCTE; Shank; Shipley; Sobel;
Sprinchorn; Ward
Our Village. Mary Russell Mit-
ford. Keller; Magill II, CE,
M1&2, MC, MEF
Ours Is a Nice House. John
Clevedon. French
Ourselves to Know. John O'Hara.
Magill '61, S
Out at Sea. Slawomir Mrożek.
Kienzle
Out of Bounds. Arthur Watkyn.
French
Out of Chaos. Louis J. Halle.
Magill '78
Out of My Life and Thought.
Albert Schweitzer. Magill
IV, MC
Out of the Silent Planet. Clive
Staples Lewis. Magill SF
Out There. Adrien Stoutenburg.
Benedict
Out with Garibaldi. George A.
Henty. Kaye
Outcasts, The. Stephen Becker.
Magill '68, S
Outcasts of Poker Flat, The.
Bret Harte. Smith
Outcry, The. Henry James.
Gale-J
Outer Dark. Cormac McCarthy.
Magill '69, S
Outer Edge of Society, The see
Demi-Monde, The
Outlaw, The. August Strindberg.
Matlaw
Outline of History. H. G. Wells.
Haydn; Keller suppl. (History)
Outline of Literature, The.
John Drinkwater, editor.
Keller suppl. (Literature)
Outline of Psycho-Analysis, An.
Sigmund Freud. Armstrong
Outline of Science, The. Sir
John Arthur Thomson, editor.
Keller suppl.
Outlines of Pyrrhonism. Sextus
Empiricus. Magill WP
Outlines of the History of Greek
Philosophy. Dr. Eduard
Zeller. Keller (Greek)
Outrageous Fortune. Rose Frank-
en. Best '43; Drury
Outsider, The. Colin Wilson.
Magill '57, S

Outsiders, The. S. E. Hinton.
Benedict
Outward Bound. Sutton Vane.
Best '23; Cartmell; Drury;
French; Keller suppl. ; Matlaw;
NCTE; Sobel
Outward Room, The. Millen
Brand. (See adaptation The
World We Make by Sidney
Kingsley.)
Oval Portrait, The. Edgar Allan
Poe. Gale-PP
Over Twenty-One. Ruth Gordon.
Best '43; Drury
Overcoat, The. Nikolai V. Gogol.
Berry-2; Magill II, CE, M1&2,
MC, MEUF
Overruled. George Bernard Shaw.
Hardwick; Matlaw
Overthrow of Allende and the
Politics of Chile, 1964-1976,
The. Paul E. Sigmund.
Magill '78
Overture. William Bolitho.
Best '30
Owen Wingrave. Henry James.
Gale-J
Owl and the Nightingale, The.
Attributed to Nicholas de
Guildford. Haydn
Owl and the Pussycat, The. Bill
Manhoff. Drury; NCTE
Ox-Bow Incident, The. Walter
Van Tilburg Clark. Haydn;
Lass AN; Magill I, CE, M1&2,
MAF, MC; Morehead
Oxcart, The. René Marqués.
NCTE
Oxford 'Essays and Reviews' see
Essays and Reviews
Oxford History of Music, The.
W. H. Hadow. Keller
Oxford Reformers of 1498, The.
Frederic Seebohm. Keller
Oxygen och Aromasia. Claës
Lundin. Magill SF
Oysters of Locmariaquer, The.
Eleanor Clark. Magill Ss

-P-

P. G. T. Beauregard. T. Harry
Williams. Magill '55, MB, S
P. S. 193. David Rayfiel. Best
'62

P. S.				208

P. S. Wilkinson. C. D. B.
Bryan. Magill Ss
Pablos de Segovia, the Spanish
Sharper. Francisco de Que-
vedo. Haydn
Pabo the Priest. Sabine Baring-
Gould. Kaye
Pacem in Terris. Pope John
XXIII. Magill CAL
Pacific Overtures. John Weidman,
Stephen Sondheim and Hugh
Wheeler. Best '75
Pacific War: World War II and
the Japanese, 1931-1945, The.
Saburō Ienaga. Magill '79
Pagan and Christian Rome. Ro-
dolfo Lanciani. Keller
Page d'amour, Une. Emile
Zola. Johnson; Keller (Rougon)
Page of the Duke of Savoy, The.
Alexandre Dumas (father).
Johnson; Kaye
Pahlavi Texts. Unknown. Keller
(Sacred Books)
Paint Your Wagon. Alan Jay
Lerner and Frederick Loewe.
NCTE
Painted Bird, The. Jerzy Kosin-
ski. Magill '66, S
Painter of Signs, The. R. K.
Narayan. Magill '77
Pair of Blue Eyes, A. Thomas
Hardy. Saxelby
Pair of Drawers, A (The Under-
pants). Carl Sternheim.
Gassner; Matlaw
Pair of Patient Lovers, A. Wil-
liam Dean Howells. Carring-
ton
Pajama Game, The. George
Abbott, Richard Adler, Jerry
Ross, and Richard Bissell.
(Based on 7½ Cents by
Richard Bissell.) Chapman '54
Pal Joey. John O'Hara, Lorenz
Hart and Richard Rodgers.
NCTE
Palace, The. Claude Simon.
Magill '64, S
Palace of Danger, The. Mabel
Wagnalls. Kaye
Palace of Eternal Youth, The.
Hung Shen. Gassner
Palace of Pleasure, The. Wil-
liam Painter. Keller
Pale Fire. Vladimir Nabokov.
Magill IV, '63, MB, MC, S
Pale Horse, Pale Rider. Kath-

erine Anne Porter. Magill IV,
MC; Morehead
Palladis Tamia. Francis Meres.
Ruoff p. 93
Pallieter. Felix Timmermans.
Haydn (a)
Palm-Wine Drinkard, The. Amos
Tutuola. Magill IV, MC
Palmerin de Oliva. Unknown.
Keller
Palmerin of England. Unknown.
Keller
Pamela. Samuel Richardson.
Haydn; Johnson; Johnson-18th;
Keller; Magill I, CE, M1&2,
MC, MEF; Olfson
Pampelmousse. André Birabeau.
Shipley
Pan Tadeusz. Adam Mickiewicz.
Haydn
Panama. Arthur Bullard. Keller
Panarion. Saint Epiphanius of
Salamis. Magill CHL
Pandects, The. Justinian. Keller
Pandora. Henry James. Gale-J
Pandora's Box. Frank Wedekind.
Matlaw; Shank; Sprinchorn
Pandosto, the Triumph of Time.
Robert Greene. Ruoff
Panegyric. Isocrates. Haydn
Panic. Archibald MacLeish.
Sobel
Panjandrum, The. Anthony Trol-
lope. Gerould
Pansie: A Fragment. Nathaniel
Hawthorne. Gale-H
Pantagleize. Michel de Ghelderode.
Matlaw; NCTE; Shank
Paolo and Francesca. Stephen
Phillips. Drury; Keller; Mat-
law; Shipley; Sobel
Paolo Paoli. Arthur Adamov.
Kienzle; Matlaw
Papa Bouchard. Molly Elliot Sea-
well. Johnson
Papa Hemingway. A. E. Hotch-
ner. Magill '67, M1, S
Papa Is All. Patterson Greene.
Drury
Papá Juan; or, The Centenarian.
Serafín and Joaquín Alvarez
Quintero. Drury
Paper Chain, The. Falkland L.
Cary and Ivan Butler. French
Paper Horse, A. Robert Watson.
Magill '63, S
Papers, The. Henry James.
Gale-J

Papers of Benjamin Franklin,
The. Benjamin Franklin.
Magill '60, S
Papillon. Henri Charrière.
Magill '71
Parables of the Kingdom, The.
Charles Harold Dodd. Magill
CHL
Paracelsus. Robert Browning.
Haydn
Parachutistes, Les (The Para-
troopers). Jean Cau. Kienzle
Paraclesis, The. Desiderius
Erasmus. Magill CAL
Parade's End. Ford Madox Ford.
Magill II, CE, M1&2, MC,
MEF; Ward
Paradise Lost. John Milton.
Armstrong; Fleming; Haydn;
Keller; Magill I, CE, CHL,
M1&2, MC, MP; Ruoff; Sabater
Paradise Lost: The Decline of
the Auto-Industrial Age. Emma
Rothschild. Magill '74
Paradise of Bachelors and the
Tartarus of Maids, The.
Herman Melville. Gale-M
Paradise Reclaimed. Halldór
Laxness. Magill '63, S
Paradise Regained. John Milton.
Haydn; Keller; Magill III,
M1, MC, MP; Ruoff
Paradox Men, The. Charles L.
Harness. Magill SF
Paradyse of Daynty Devises, The.
M. Edwardes, et al. Keller
Parallel Lives. Plutarch.
Downs F, FG; Haydn; Keller
(a); Magill III, M1, MC, MNF
Paramilitary Politics in Weimar
Germany. James M. Diehl.
Magill '79
Parasite, The. Ivan Turgenev.
Gassner
Pardon, The. Jules Le Maître.
Drury
Pardon wird nicht gegeben (Pardon
Will Not Be Granted). Herbert
Asmodi. Kienzle
Pardoner and the Friar, The.
John Heywood. Holzknecht;
Ruoff
Pariah. August Strindberg.
Matlaw
Paris at Bay. Herbert Hayens.
Kaye
Paris Bound. Philip Barry.
Best '27; Drury; Matlaw; Sobel

Paris in America. Edouard René
Lefebvre. Keller
Paris Sketch Book. William Make-
peace Thackeray. Mudge
Parish Life in Mediaeval England.
Francis Neil Aidan Cardinal
Gasquet. Magill CAL
Parisians, The. Lord Edward
Bulwer-Lytton. Johnson
Parisienne, La (Woman of Paris).
Henri Becque. Matlaw; Shank;
Shipley
Parliament of Fowls, The.
Geoffrey Chaucer. Magill III,
M1, MC, MP
Parliamentary Novels. Anthony
Trollope. Keller
Parliamentary Reform. Walter
Bagehot. Keller
Parlor Story. William McCleery.
Drury
Parmenides. Plato. Feder;
Magill WP
Parnassus Corner. W. S. Tryon.
Magill '64, S
Parnassus Plays, The. Unknown.
Holzknecht (Pilgrimage to Par-
nassus; Return from Parnassus,
Parts I, II); Ruoff; Sobel
Parnassus Trilogy see Parnas-
sus Plays, The
Parnell. Mrs. Elsie T. Schauf-
fler. Drury
Parson's Daughter of Oxney Colne,
The. Anthony Trollope.
Gerould
Part of the Truth: An Autobiog-
raphy. Granville Hicks. Ma-
gill '66, S
Partheneion. Alcman. Feder
Parthenon, The. Herman Mel-
ville. Gale-M
Particular Place, A. Dabney
Stuart. Magill '70
Parting and a Meeting, A. Wil-
liam Dean Howells. Carrington
Partisans. Peter Matthiessen.
Magill Ss
Partners, The. Louis Auchin-
closs. Magill '75
Party, The. Jane Arden. French
Party, and Other Stories, The.
Anton Chekhov. Keller suppl.
Party for Christmas, A. N. C.
Hunter. French
Parzival. Wolfram von Eschen-
bach. Haydn; Magill II, M1,
MC, MP

Passage to Ararat. Michael J.
Arlen. Magill '76
Passage to India, A. E. M.
Forster. (See also adaptation
by Santha Rama Rau.) Haydn;
Heiney; Keller suppl.; Lass
BN; Magill I, CE, M1&2,
MC, MEF; Olfson; Stade p.
264; Ward
Passage to India, A. Santha
Rama Rau. (Based on the
novel by E. M. Forster.)
French; NCTE
Passages from a Relinquished
Work. Nathaniel Hawthorne.
Gale-H
Passe Rose. Arthur Sherburne
Hardy. Kaye
Passing of the Third Floor Back,
The. Jerome K. Jerome.
Cartmell; Drury; French;
Matlaw
Passing of the Torch, The. Paul
Hervieu. Drury (Trail ...);
Matlaw
Passion Flower, The. Jacinto
Benavente y Martínez. Drury;
Haydn; Heiney; Keller suppl.;
Magill III, CE, M1&2, MC,
MD; Matlaw; Shank; Shipley;
Sobel
Passion of Josef D., The. Paddy
Chayefsky. Best '63; Drury
Passion Play, The. Unknown.
Shipley (end section)
Passion, Poison, and Petrifaction,
or The Fatal Gazogene.
George Bernard Shaw. Hard-
wick; Ward
Passionate Pilgrim, A. Henry
James. Gale-J
Passions and Other Stories.
Isaac Bashevis Singer.
Magill '76
Passions of the Soul, The. René
Descartes. Magill IV, MC
Past and Present. Thomas
Carlyle. Haydn; Keller
Past Masters, The. Harold
Macmillan. Magill '77
Past Through Tomorrow, The.
Robert A. Heinlein. Magill
SF
Paste. Henry James. Gale-J
Pastel City, The. Mike John
Harrison. Magill SF
Pasteur. Sacha Guitry. Drury;
Sobel

Paston Letters, The. Paston
Family. Keller; Magill IV,
MC
Pastor Fido, Il (The Faithful
Shepherd). Giovanni Battista
Guarini. Gassner; Keller;
Shipley
Pastor Hall. Ernst Toller.
Drury
Pastoral Care. Saint Gregory the
Great. Magill CAL, CHL
Pastoral Loves of Daphnis and
Chloe, The. George Moore.
Ward
Pastorale oder die Zeit für Kakao
(Pastoral or Time for Cocoa).
Wolfgang Hildesheimer. Kienzle
Pastors and Masters. Ivy Comp-
ton-Burnett. Magill IV, MC
Patagonia, The. Henry James.
Gale-J
Patchwork Quilt, The. Felicity
Douglas. French
Patélin see Master Pathelin
Paterson. William Carlos Wil-
liams. Magill III, M1, MC,
MP
Paterson Five. William Carlos
Williams. Magill '59, S
Path Between the Seas: The
Creation of the Panama Canal,
1870-1914, The. David Mc-
Cullough. Magill '78
Path of Duty, The. Henry James.
Gale-J
Path to Rome, The. Hilaire
Belloc. Magill III, CAL, M1,
MC, MNF; Ward
Pathélin see Master Pathelin
Pathfinder, The. James Fenimore
Cooper. (See also Leather-
stocking Saga, The.) Haydn
p. 416; Johnson; Magill I, CE,
M1&2, MAF, MAL1, MC;
Walker
Pathfinders of the Revolution, The.
William E. Griffis. Kaye
Pathos of Power. Kenneth B.
Clark. Magill '75
Patience. William Schwenck Gil-
bert and Arthur Sullivan. Drury;
Magill II, CE, M1&2, MC, MD;
NBC 2; Shipley; Sobel
Patient, The. Agatha Christie.
French
Patients Are People Like Us:
The Experiences of Half a
Century in Neuropsychiatry.

Henri Baruk. Magill '79
Patricia at the Inn. John Collis
Snaith. Kaye
Patrician, The. John Galsworthy.
Magill III, CE, M1&2, MC,
MEF
Patrick Henry. Richard R. Bee-
man. Magill '75
Patrie.' Victorien Sardou. Drury
Patrins. Louise Imogen Guiney.
Keller
Patriot, The. Antonio Fogazzaro.
Keller; Magill II, CE, M1&2,
MC, MEUF
Patriot and Tory. Edward S.
Ellis. Kaye
Patriot for Me, A. John Osborne.
Kienzle
Patriotic Gore. Edmund Wilson.
Magill '63, MB, S
Patriots, The. Cyrus T. Brady.
Kaye
Patriots, The. Sidney Kingsley.
Best '42; Bonin; Drury; NCTE;
Sobel
Patriots and Liberators: Revolu-
tion in the Netherlands, 1780-
1813. Simon Schama. Magill
'78
Patronage. Maria Edgeworth.
Keller
Patsy, The. Barry Conners.
Drury
Patterns. Rod Serling. Lovell
Patterns of Culture. Ruth Bene-
dict. Haydn
Patty. Katherine Sarah Mac-
quoid. Keller
Paul Among the Jews. Franz
Werfel. Drury
Paul and Virginia. Bernardin
de Saint-Pierre. Goodman;
Grozier; Haydn; Johnson (under
de); Keller
Paul Bronckhorst. Christoph
Bernhard Levin Schücking.
Johnson
Paul Bunyan. James Stevens.
Magill I, CE, M1&2, MAF,
MC
Paul Clifford. Lord Edward
Bulwer-Lytton. Johnson;
Keller
Paul Kauver; or Anarchy. Steele
Mackaye. Drury
Paul Kelver. Jerome K. Jerome.
Johnson
Paul Lange and Tora Parsberg.

Bjørnstjerne Bjørnson. Matlaw
Pausanias the Spartan. Lord Ed-
ward Bulwer-Lytton. Johnson;
Kaye
Pavane. Keith Roberts. Magill
SF
Pawn in the Game, A. William
H. Fitchett. Kaye
Pax see Peace, The
Pax Britannica. James Morris.
Magill '69, S
Pay-Off, The. Barbara S. Har-
per. French
Payment Deferred. Jeffrey Dell.
French
Peace, The. Aristophanes.
Feder; Gassner; Hathorn; Ma-
gill III, CE, M1&2, MC, MD;
Reinhold; Shank; Shipley; Sobel
Peace in Our Time. Noel
Coward. Drury
Peace of Soul. Fulton J. Sheen.
Magill CAL
Peacemakers, The. Richard B.
Morris. Magill '66, S
Peacock Pie. Walter de la Mare.
Ward
Peacock Spring, The. Rumer
Godden. Magill '77
"Peanuts." Charles M. Schulz.
(Comic strip; see adaptation
You're a Good Man Charlie
Brown by Clark Gesner.)
Pearce Amerson's Will. Richard
Malcolm Johnston. Johnson
Pearl. Unknown. Haydn; Keller
Pearl of Orr's Island, The. Har-
riet Beecher Stowe. Keller
Peasants, The. Ladislas Rey-
mont. Haydn; Keller suppl.;
Magill I, CE, M1&2, MC,
MEUF
Peau de chagrin, La. Honoré de
Balzac. Keller
Peck's Bad Boy. George W. Peck.
Haydn
Pedagogics of the Kindergarten.
Friedrich Froebel. Keller
Peder Victorious. O. E. Röl-
vaag. Magill II, CE, M1&2,
MAF, MC
Pedestrian in the Air, The.
Eugène Ionesco. Kienzle; Mat-
law
Pedro Martínez. Oscar Lewis.
Magill '65, S
Pedro Páramo. Juan Rulfo.
Magill IV, '60, M1, MB, MC, S

PEDRO

212

Pedro Sánchez. José María de
Pereda. Magill III, CE, M1&2,
MC, MEUF
Peer Gynt. Henrik Ibsen. Arm-
strong; Cartmell; Drury; Gass-
ner; Haydn; Heiney; Keller;
Magill I, CE, M1&2, MC,
MD; Matlaw; NBC 3; NCTE;
Shank; Shipley; Sobel; Thomas;
Wilson
Peg O' My Heart. J. Hartley
Manners. Drury; Lovell; Mat-
law; Sobel
Peg Woffington. Charles Reade.
Grozier; Johnson; Keller;
Magill I, CE, M1&2, MC,
MEF
Peking and Moscow. Klaus
Mehnert. Magill '64, S
Peleus. Sophocles. Hathorn
Pelham. Lord Edward Bulwer-
Lytton. Johnson; Keller
Peliades. Euripides. Hathorn
Pelican, The. August Strindberg.
Matlaw
Pelle the Conqueror. Martin
Andersen Nexö. Haydn; Kel-
ler; Lass EN; Magill III, CE,
M1&2, MC, MEUF
Pélléas and Mélisande. Maurice
Maeterlinck. Cartmell; Drury;
Heiney; Magill II, CE, M1&2,
MC, MD; Matlaw; NBC 3;
Shank; Sobel; Thomas; Ward
Pellucidar. Edgar Rice Bur-
roughs. Magill SF
Pen Portraits and Reviews.
George Bernard Shaw. Ward
Peñas arriba. José María de
Pereda. Magill III, CE,
M1&2, MC, MEUF
Pendennis. William Makepeace
Thackeray. Grozier; Haydn;
Johnson; Keller; Magill I, CE,
M1&2, MC, MEF; Mudge;
Olfson
Penguin Island. Anatole France.
Haydn; Heiney; Keller; Lass
EN; Magill I, CE, M1&2, MC,
MEUF
Pennies from Heaven. Naomi
Waters. French
Penny for a Song, A. John
Whiting. Kienzle; Shank
Penrod. Booth Tarkington.
Haydn; Keller
Penruddock of the White Lambs.
Samuel H. Church. Kaye

Pensées. Blaise Pascal. Haydn;
Keller; Magill III, CHL, M1,
MC, MNF, WP
Pensées philosophiques. Denis
Diderot. Keller
Pensées sur l'interprétation de la
nature see Thoughts on the
Interpretation of Nature
Penseroso, Il see Allegro, L'
Pension Beaurepas, The. Henry
James. Gale-J
Penthesilea. Heinrich von Kleist.
Gassner; Shank
Pentimento. Lillian Hellman.
Magill '74
Peony Pavilion, The. T'ang
Hsien-tsu. Gassner
People, The. Jules Michelet.
Haydn
People Like Us. Frank Vosper.
French
People: No Different Flesh, The.
Zenna Henderson. Magill SF
People of Juvik, The. Olav
Duun. Haydn; Magill II, CE,
M1&2, MC, MEUF
People of the Abyss. Jack Lon-
don. Haydn (a)
People of the Book. David Stac-
ton. Magill '66, S
People of the Lake: Mankind and
Its Beginnings. Richard E.
Leakey and Roger Lewin. Ma-
gill '79
People Shapers, The. Vance
Packard. Magill '78
People, Yes, The. Carl Sand-
burg. Haydn; Magill III, M1,
MC, MP
People's Lawyer, The. Dr.
Joseph Stevens Jones. Sobel
Pepacton. John Burroughs.
Keller
Pepita Jimenez. Juan Valera.
Haydn; Keller; Magill II, CE,
M1&2, MC, MEUF
Pepys's Diary. Samuel Pepys.
Keller
Perception. Henry Habberley
Price. Magill WP
Père Goriot (Father Goriot; Old
Goriot). Honoré de Balzac.
Goodman; Haydn (Old); Johnson;
Keller; Lass EN; Magill I, CE,
M1&2, MC, MEUF (Father);
Wilson
Peregrine Pickle. Tobias George
Smollett. Haydn; Johnson;

Johnson-18th/2; Magill I, CE,
M1&2, MC, MEF
Perelandra.   Clive Staples Lewis.
Magill SF
Perennial Bachelor, The.   Anne
Parrish.   Keller suppl.
Perfect Alibi, The.   A. A.
Milne.   Drury
Perfect Idiot, The.   Eunice and
Grant Atkinson.   Drury
Perfect Woman, The.   Wallace
Geoffrey and Basil Mitchell.
French
Peribáñez and the Commander of
Ocaña.   Lope Félix de Vega
Carpio.   Haydn; Shank
Pericles and Aspasia.   Walter
Savage Landor.   Kaye
Pericles on 31st Street.   Harry
Mark Petrakis.   Magill Ss
Pericles, Prince of Tyre.   Wil-
liam Shakespeare.   Campbell;
Clark; Gassner; Guerber-ST;
Halliday; Haydn; Keller; Lamb;
McCutchan-SC; McSpadden S;
Magill II, CE, M1&2, MC,
MD; Ruoff; Shipley; Sobel
Perikeiromene see Shearing of
Glycera, The
Peril of the Sword, The.   A. F.
P. Harcourt.   Kaye
Perils of Certain English Pris-
oners, The.   Charles Dickens.
Hardwick CD
Period of Adjustment.   Tennessee
Williams.   Best '60; Drury;
Kienzle; NCTE
Perjury: The Hiss-Chambers
Case.   Allen Weinstein.   Magill
'79
Perkin Warbeck.   John Ford.
Holzknecht; Keller; Ruoff;
Shipley
Permanent Errors.   Reynolds
Price.   Magill '71
Perrhaebians, The.   Aeschylus.
Hathorn
Persa (The Girl from Persia)
Titus Maccius Plautus.   Feder
(Girl); Hathorn; Reinhold;
Shipley (Persian)
Persai see Persians, The
Persecution and Assassination of
Jean-Paul Marat as Performed
by the Inmates of the Asylum
of Charenton under the Direction
of the Marquis de Sade, The.
Peter Weiss.   Anderson

(Marat); Best '65; Drury; Ki-
enzle; Magill Ss; Matlaw (Marat);
NCTE
Persian Letters.   Charles Louis
de Secondat Montesquieu.
Haydn; Keller (Lettres); Magill
III, M1, MC, MNF
Persians, The.   Aeschylus.
Feder; Gassner; Hathorn; Haydn;
Magill II, CE, M1&2, MC,
MD; Reinhold; Shank; Shipley;
Sobel
Person and Place of Jesus Christ,
The.   Peter Taylor Forsyth.
Magill CHL
Personae.   Ezra Pound.   Magill
IV, MC
Personal Anthology, A.   Jorge
Luis Borges.   Magill '67, S
Personal Appearance.   Lawrence
Riley.   Drury
Personal History.   Vincent Sheean.
Haydn
Personal Memoirs of U. S.
Grant.   Ulysses Simpson Grant.
Keller (Grant)
Personal Realism.   James Bis-
sett Pratt.   Magill WP
Personal Recollection from Early
Life to Old Age of Mary Som-
erville.   Martha Somerville.
Keller (Somerville)
Personal Recollections of Joan of
Arc.   Mark Twain.   Gale-T;
Haydn; Keller
Personalism.   Borden Parker
Bowne.   Magill CHL
Personnage combattant, Le (The
Struggling Individual).   Jean
Vauthier.   Kienzle
Persuasion.   Jane Austen.   Hal-
perin; Johnson; Magill I, M1,
MC, MEF
Peruvian Traditions.   Ricardo
Palma.   Haydn
Pervigilium veneris.   Unknown.
Feder
Pesti emberek (People of Buda-
pest).   Lajos Mesterházi.
Kienzle
Peter Abelard.   Helen Waddell.
Ward
Peter Brauer.   Gerhart Haupt-
mann.   Matlaw
Peter Goldthwaite's Treasure.
Nathaniel Hawthorne.   Gale-H
Peter Ibbetson.   George Du
Maurier.   Goodman; Haydn;

Johnson; Keller; Magill I, CE, M1&2, MC, MEF
Peter Pan Bag, The. Lee Kingman. Benedict
Peter Pan, or The Boy Who Would Not Grow Up. Sir James M. Barrie. Cartmell; Drury; Haydn; Keller; Magill II, CE, M1&2, MC, MD; Matlaw; NBC 2; NCTE (musical); Shipley; Sobel; Sprinchorn; Ward
Peter Schlemihl. Adelbert von Chamisso. Haydn; Johnson; Keller
Peter Simple. Frederick Marryat. Magill II, CE, M1&2, MC, MEF
Peter Whiffle. Carl Van Vechten. Magill I, CE, M1&2, MAF, MC
Petite Molière, La (Madame Molière). Jean Anouilh. Kienzle
Petite ville, La. Louis Baptiste Picard. (See adaptation The Merry Widow by Victor Leon and Franz Lehar.)
Petrified Forest, The. Robert E. Sherwood. Best '34; Cartmell; Drury; Lovell; Matlaw; NCTE; Shank; Sobel; Sprinchorn
Petticoat Fever. Mark Reed. Drury
Petticoat Government. Baroness Orczy. Kaye
Petty Demon, The. Feodor Sologub. Magill '63, S
Peveril of the Peak. Sir Walter Scott. Johnson; Kaye; McSpadden W
Pferd, Das (The Horse). Julius Hay. Kienzle
Phaeacians, The. Sophocles. Hathorn
Phaedo. Plato. Downs FG; Feder; Haydn; Magill WP
Phaèdra. Jean Baptiste Racine. Cartmell; Drury; Gassner; Haydn; Magill I, CE, M1&2, MC, MD; Shank; Sobel; Thomas
Phaedra. Lucius Annaeus Seneca. Feder; Hathorn; Reinhold
Phaedrus. Plato. Feder; Magill WP
Phantasms. Roberto Bracco. Drury; Sobel
Phantom Gold. Theodore Dreiser.

Gerber
Phantom Lady, The. Pedro Calderón de la Barca. Gassner; Shank
Pharais. Fiona Macleod. Johnson
Pharaoh and the Priest, The. A. Glovatski. Kaye
Pharsalia see On the Civil War
Phases of Thought and Criticism. Brother Azarias. Keller
Phèdre see Phaèdra
Phenomenology of Spirit, The. Georg Wilhelm Friedrich Hegel. Haydn (... of Mind); Magill CHL
Phenomenon of Man, The. Pierre Teilhard de Chardin, S. J. Magill IV, '60, CAL, M1, MC, S
Philadelphia, Here I Come! Brian Friel. Best '65; Drury; NCTE
Philadelphia Story, The. Philip Barry. Best '38; Drury; Matlaw; NCTE; Sobel
Philanderer, The. George Bernard Shaw. Hardwick; Matlaw
Philanthropist, The. Christopher Hampton. Best '70; Drury; NCTE
Philaster, or Love Lies A-Bleeding. Francis Beaumont and John Fletcher. Drury; Haydn; Holzknecht; Keller; Magill II, CE, M1&2, MC, MD; Ruoff; Sobel
Philebus. Plato. Feder; Magill WP
Philip and His Wife. Margaret Deland. Keller
Philip Augustus. George P. R. James. Kaye
Philip Van Artevelde. Sir Henry Taylor. Keller
Philip Winwood. Robert N. Stephens. Kaye
Philippics, The. Demosthenes. Downs F; Haydn; Magill III, M1, MC, MNF
Philistines, The. Arlo Bates. Keller
Phillip Hotz's Fury. Max Frisch. Kienzle
Philobiblon. Richard Aungerville (known as Richard de Bury). Keller
Philoctetes. Aeschylus. Hathorn

Philoctetes. Euripides. Hathorn
Philoctetes. Sophocles. Drury;
Feder; Gassner; Hathorn;
Magill III, CE, M1&2, MC,
MD; Reinhold; Shank; Shipley;
Sobel
Philoctetes at Troy. Sophocles.
Hathorn
Philosopher and Theology, The.
Etienne Gilson. Magill CAL
Philosopher at Large: An In-
tellectual Autobiography.
Mortimer J. Adler. Magill
'78
Philosopher or Dog? Joaquim
Maria Machado de Assís.
Magill IV, '54, MC, S
Philosopher's Stone, The. Johannes
Anker-Larsen. Keller suppl.
Philosopher's Stone, The. Pär
Lagerkvist. Matlaw
Philosopher's Stone, The. Colin
Wilson. Magill SF
Philosophiae Naturalis Principia
Mathematica (Mathematical
Principles of Natural Philos-
ophy). Sir Isaac Newton.
Downs FG; Haydn; Keller (Prin-
cipia); Magill III, M1, MC,
MNF
Philosophical Bases of Theism,
The. George Dawes Hicks.
Magill CHL
Philosophical Dictionary. Voltaire.
Downs M, FG; Haydn
Philosophical Essays. Marcus
Tullius Cicero. Downs F,
FG; Haydn
Philosophical Fragments. Søren
Kierkegaard. Magill WP
Philosophical Investigations.
Ludwig Wittgenstein. Magill
WP
Philosophical Studies. George
Edward Moore. Magill WP
Philosophical Theology. Frederick
Robert Tennant. Magill CHL
Philosophical Treatises and Moral
Reflections of Seneca. Lucius
Annaeus Seneca. Magill IV,
MC
Philosophie Zoologique. Jean
Baptiste de Monet de Lamarck.
Haydn
Philosophy and Logical Syntax.
Rudolf Carnap. Magill WP
Philosophy and Psycho-Analysis.
John Wisdom. Magill WP

Philosophy of Art. Hippolyte
Adolphe Taine. Magill III,
M1, MC, MNF
Philosophy of Confucius. Con-
fucius. Armstrong
Philosophy of Democratic Govern-
ment. Yves René Marie Simon.
Magill CAL
Philosophy of History, The.
Georg Wilhelm Friedrich Hegel.
Haydn; Magill WP
Philosophy of Physical Realism,
The. Roy Wood Sellars.
Magill WP
Philosophy of Religion, A. Edgar
Sheffield Brightman. Magill
CHL
Philosophy of Religion, The.
Harald Höffding. Magill CHL
Philosophy of Right, The. Georg
Wilhelm Friedrich Hegel.
Downs M
Philosophy of Symbolic Forms,
The. Ernst Cassirer. Magill
WP
Philosophy of the Unconscious,
The. Eduard von Hartmann.
Magill WP
Phineas Finn. Anthony Trollope.
(See also series title Parlia-
mentary Novels.) Gerould;
Keller; Magill III, CE, M1&2,
MC, MEF
Phineas Redux. Anthony Trollope.
(See also series title Parlia-
mentary Novels.) Gerould;
Keller; Magill III, CE, M1&2,
MC, MEF
Phineus. Aeschylus. Hathorn
Phoenician Women, The. Aristo-
phanes. Hathorn
Phoenician Women, The. Euri-
pides. Feder; Gassner; Hathorn;
Magill III, CE, M1&2, MC,
MD; Reinhold; Shipley
Phoenician Women, The. Lucius
Annaeus Seneca. Feder; Ha-
thorn; Reinhold
Phoenix. Sophocles. Hathorn
Phoenix and the Turtle, The.
William Shakespeare. Ruoff
Phoenix Too Frequent, A. Chris-
topher Fry. Drury; Heiney;
Kienzle; Matlaw
Phoinissai see Phoenician
Women, The
Phormio. Terence. Drury;
Feder; Gassner; Hathorn; Haydn;

PHOTO   216

Magill II, CE, M1&2, MC,
MD; Reinhold; Shank; Shipley;
Sobel
Photo Finish.   Peter Ustinov.
Drury; Kienzle
Photograph, The.   Ramón José
Sender.   Kienzle
Phroso.   Anthony Hope.   Keller
Physical Basis of Life, The.
Thomas Henry Huxley.
Magill III, M1, MC, MNF
Physicists.   Friedrich Dürren-
matt.   Best '64; Drury;
French; Kienzle; Matlaw;
NCTE; Sprinchorn
Physics.   Aristotle.   Downs F,
FG; Haydn; Magill WP
Physics and Politics.   Walter
Bagehot.   Haydn
Physiognomy: Fragmentary
Studies.   Johann Caspar
Lavater.   Keller
Physiologus.   Unknown.   Keller
Piazza, The.   Herman Melville.
Gale-M
Picciola.   Joseph Xavier Saintine.
Johnson
Pickett's Charge.   George R.
Stewart.   Magill '60, M1, S
Pick-up Girl.   Elsa Shelley.
Best '43; Kienzle
Pickwick Papers.   Charles Dick-
ens.   Goodman; Grozier; Hard-
wick CD; Haydn; Johnson; Kel-
ler; Lass BN; Magill I, CE,
M1&2, MC, MEF
Picnic.   William Inge.   Best
'52; Bonin; Chapman '53; Drury;
Kienzle; Lovell; Matlaw; NCTE;
Shank
Picnic at Sakkara, The.   P. H.
Newby.   Magill '55, S
Picnic on Paradise.   Joanna
Russ.   Magill SF
Picnic on the Battlefield.   Fer-
nando Arrabal.   Kienzle
Picture of Dorian Gray, The.
Oscar Wilde.   Armstrong;
Goodman; Haydn; Johnson;
Lass BN; Magill I, CE, M1&2,
MC, MEF
Pictures from an Institution.
Randall Jarrell.   Magill '54, S
Pictures from Brueghel.   William
Carlos Williams.   Magill '63,
MB, S
Pictures in the Hallway.   Paul
Shyre.   (Adapted from the

autobiography of Sean O'Casey.)
Drury
Pictures of Fidelman.   Bernard
Malamud.   Magill '70
Pictures of Travel.   Heinrich
Heine.   Keller
Pieces of Life.   Mark Schorer.
Magill '78
Pied Piper of Hamelin, The.
Robert Browning.   Haydn; Hix
Pierre.   Herman Melville.   Gale-
M; Magill II, CE, M1&2, MAF,
MAL4, MC
Pierre and Jean.   Guy de Maupas-
sant.   Armstrong; Haydn; John-
son
Piers Plowman see Vision of
William Concerning Piers the
Plowman, The
Pierwszy dzień wolności (The
First Day of Freedom).   Leon
Kruczkowski.   Kienzle
Pig in a Poke.   Mabel and Denis
Constanduros.   French
Pigeon, The.   John Galsworthy.
Drury; Matlaw; Shipley; Sobel
Pigeon Feathers.   John Updike.
Magill '63, S
Pigeons and People.   George M.
Cohan.   Best '32
Pigman, The.   Paul Zindel.
Benedict
Pigs.   Anne Morrison and Patter-
son McNutt.   Drury
Pilgrim, The.   Arthur H. Lewis.
Kaye
Pilgrim at Tinker Creek.   Annie
Dillard.   Magill '75
Pilgrim Hawk, The.   Glenway
Wescott.   Magill IV, '68, MC, S
Pilgrimage.   Dorothy M. Richard-
son.   Magill III, M1, MC,
MEF
Pilgrimage of Anacharsis the
Younger, The.   Abbé Barthél-
emy.   Keller
Pilgrimage of Charlemagne, The.
Unknown.   Magill III, CE,
M1&2, MC, MP
Pilgrimage: The Book of the
People.   Zenna Henderson.
Magill SF
Pilgrimage to Parnassus, The.
Unknown.   Holzknecht; Ruoff
(Parnassus Plays)
Pilgrim's Progress, The.   John
Bunyan.   Armstrong; Cohen;
Downs M, FG; Goodman;

Poetry of Coleridge, The. Samuel
Taylor Coleridge. Magill IV,
MC
Poetry of Collins, The. William
Collins. Magill IV, MC
Poetry of Corbière, The. Tris-
tan Corbière. Magill IV, MC
Poetry of Cowper, The. William
Cowper. Magill IV, MC
Poetry of Crashaw, The. Richard
Crashaw. Magill IV, MC
Poetry of Cummings, The. E.
E. Cummings. Heiney; Magill
IV, MC
Poetry of Daniel, The. Samuel
Daniel. Magill IV, MC
Poetry of Dante Gabriel Rossetti,
The. Dante Gabriel Rossetti.
Magill III, M1, MC, MP
Poetry of Dickey, The. James
Dickey. Magill IV, MC
Poetry of Donne, The. John
Donne. Magill III, M1, MC,
MP
Poetry of Dowson, The. Ernest
Christopher Dowson. Magill
IV, MC
Poetry of Drayton, The. Michael
Drayton. Magill III, M1, MC,
MP
Poetry of Dryden, The. John
Dryden. Magill IV, MC
Poetry of Du Bellay, The.
Joachim Du Bellay. Magill
IV, MC
Poetry of Dylan Thomas. Dylan
Thomas. Heiney
Poetry of E. A. Robinson.
Edgar Arlington Robinson.
Heiney
Poetry of Eberhart, The. Richard
Eberhart. Magill IV, MC
Poetry of Edith Sitwell, The.
Edith Sitwell. Magill IV, MC
Poetry of Eichendorff, The.
Josef von Eichendorff. Magill
IV, MC
Poetry of Elinor Wylie, The.
Elinor Wylie. Magill IV, MC
Poetry of Emerson, The. Ralph
Waldo Emerson. Magill IV,
MAL1, MC
Poetry of Emily Brontë, The.
Emily Brontë. Magill IV, MC
Poetry of Emily Dickinson, The.
Emily Dickinson. Magill III,
M1, MAL1, MC, MP
Poetry of Esenin, The. Sergei

Esenin. Magill IV, MC
Poetry of Ezra Pound. Ezra
Pound. Heiney
Poetry of Flecker, The. James
Elroy Flecker. Magill IV, MC
Poetry of Freneau, The. Philip
Freneau. Magill III, M1, MC,
MP
Poetry of Frost, The. Robert
Frost. Heiney; Magill III, M1,
MC, MP
Poetry of Gabriela Mistral, The.
Gabriela Mistral. Magill IV,
MC
Poetry of Garrett, The. George
Garrett. Magill IV, MC
Poetry of Gascoigne, The. George
Gascoigne. Magill IV, MC
Poetry of Gautier, The. Théo-
phile Gautier. Magill IV, MC
Poetry of Goldsmith, The. Oliver
Goldsmith. Magill IV, MC
Poetry of Graves, The. Robert
Graves. Magill IV, MC
Poetry of Gray, The. Thomas
Gray. Magill III, M1, MC,
MP
Poetry of H. D., The. Hilda
Doolittle. Magill IV, MC
Poetry of Hall, The. Donald
Hall. Magill IV, MC
Poetry of Hardy, The. Thomas
Hardy. Magill IV, MC
Poetry of Henley, The. William
Ernest Henley. Magill IV,
MC
Poetry of Hérédia, The. José
María de Hérédia. Magill IV,
MC
Poetry of Hodgson, The. Ralph
Hodgson. Magill IV, MC
Poetry of Hofmannsthal, The.
Hugo von Hofmannsthal. Ma-
gill IV, MC
Poetry of Hölderlin, The. Fried-
rich Hölderlin. Magill IV, MC
Poetry of Hopkins, The. Gerard
Manley Hopkins. Magill III,
M1, MC, MP
Poetry of Horace, The. Horace.
Magill III, M1, MC, MP
Poetry of Hugo, The. Victor
Hugo. Magill IV, MC
Poetry of James Stephens. James
Stephens. Heiney
Poetry of Jarrell, The. Randall
Jarrell. Magill IV, MC
Poetry of Jeffers, The. Robinson

Jeffers. Magill IV, MC
Poetry of Jiménez, The. Juan
Ramón Jiménez. Magill IV,
MC
Poetry of John Masefield. John
Masefield. Heiney
Poetry of Johnson, The. Samuel
Johnson. Magill IV, MC
Poetry of Jonson, The. Ben
Jonson. Magill IV, MC
Poetry of Kipling, The. Rudyard
Kipling. Magill IV, MC
Poetry of Laforgue, The. Jules
Laforgue. Magill IV, MC
Poetry of Lamartine, The. Al-
phonse Marie Louis de Lam-
artine. Magill IV, MC
Poetry of Landor, The. Walter
Savage Landor. Magill IV,
MC
Poetry of Lanier, The. Sidney
Lanier. Magill III, M1, MC,
MP
Poetry of Larkin, The. Philip
Larkin. Magill IV, MC
Poetry of Lawrence, The. D.
H. Lawrence. Magill IV,
MC
Poetry of Leopardi, The. Gia-
como Leopardi. Magill IV,
MC
Poetry of Lewis, The. Cecil
Day Lewis. Magill III, M1,
MC, MP
Poetry of Lindsay, The. Vachel
Lindsay. Magill III, M1, MC,
MP
Poetry of Lovelace, The. Richard
Lovelace. Magill III, M1,
MC, MP
Poetry of Machado, The. An-
tonio Machado. Magill IV,
MC
Poetry of MacLeish, The. Archi-
bald MacLeish. Heiney; Magill
IV, MC
Poetry of MacNeice, The. Louis
MacNeice. Heiney; Magill IV,
MC
Poetry of Mallarmé, The.
Stéphane Mallarmé. Magill
III, M1, MC, MP
Poetry of Marianne Moore, The.
Marianne Moore. Magill IV,
MC
Poetry of Marot, The. Clément
Marot. Magill IV, MC
Poetry of Marvell, The. Andrew

Marvell. Magill III, M1, MC,
MP
Poetry of Mayakovsky, The.
Vladimir Mayakovsky. Heiney;
Magill IV, MC
Poetry of Melville, The. Herman
Melville. Magill IV, MAL4,
MC
Poetry of Meredith, The. George
Meredith. Magill IV, MC
Poetry of Michelangelo, The.
Michelangelo Buonarroti.
Magill IV, MC
Poetry of Mörike, The. Eduard
Mörike. Magill IV, MC
Poetry of Moschus, The. Mosch-
us. Magill IV, MC
Poetry of Musset, The. Alfred
de Musset. Magill IV, MC
Poetry of Nekrasov, The. Nikolai
Nekrasov. Magill IV, MC
Poetry of Neruda, The. Pablo
Neruda. Magill IV, MC
Poetry of Nerval, The. Gérard
de Nerval. Magill IV, MC
Poetry of Nicholas Breton, The.
Nicholas Breton. Magill IV,
MC
Poetry of Owen, The. Wilfred
Owen. Magill IV, MC
Poetry of Pasternak, The. Boris
Pasternak. Magill IV, MC
Poetry of Paz, The. Octavio
Paz. Magill IV, MC
Poetry of Péguy, The. Charles
Péguy. Magill IV, MC
Poetry of Prior, The. Matthew
Prior. Magill IV, MC
Poetry of Rainer Maria Rilke.
Rainer Maria Rilke. Heiney
Poetry of Raleigh, The. Sir
Walter Raleigh. Magill IV,
MC
Poetry of Richard Dehmel.
Richard Dehmel. Heiney
Poetry of Robert Bridges. Robert
Bridges. Heiney
Poetry of Robert Lowell, The.
Robert Lowell, Jr. Magill
IV, MC
Poetry of Roethke, The. Theo-
dore Roethke. Magill IV, MC
Poetry of Ronsard, The. Pierre
de Ronsard. Magill III, M1,
MC, MP
Poetry of Shapiro, The. Karl
Shapiro. Magill IV, MC
Poetry of Sidney, The. Sir

Philip Sidney. Magill IV, MC
Poetry of Skelton, The. John
Skelton. Magill IV, MC
Poetry of Smart, The. Christopher Smart. Magill IV, MC
Poetry of Sor Juana Inés de la Cruz, The. Sor Juana Inés de la Cruz. Haydn; Magill IV, MC
Poetry of Spender, The. Stephen Spender. Heiney; Magill III, M1, MC, MP
Poetry of Stefan George, The. Stefan George. Heiney; Magill III, M1, MC, MP
Poetry of Stephen Vincent Benét, The. Stephen Vincent Benét. Magill IV, MC
Poetry of Stevens, The. Wallace Stevens. Heiney; Magill IV, MC
Poetry of Suckling, The. Sir John Suckling. Magill IV, MC
Poetry of Swift, The. Jonathan Swift. Magill IV, MC
Poetry of T. S. Eliot. T. S. Eliot. Heiney
Poetry of Tate, The. Allen Tate. Magill IV, MC
Poetry of Tennyson, The. A. Dwight Culler. Magill '78
Poetry of Theocritus, The. Theocritus. Magill III, M1, MC, MP
Poetry of Thompson, The. Francis Thompson. Magill IV, MC
Poetry of Thoreau, The. Henry David Thoreau. Magill IV, MC
Poetry of Traherne, The. Thomas Traherne. Magill IV, MC
Poetry of Valéry, The. Paul Valéry. Heiney; Magill IV, MC
Poetry of Vaughan, The. Henry Vaughan. Magill IV, MC
Poetry of Vigny, The. Alfred de Vigny. Magill IV, MC
Poetry of Waller, The. Edmund Waller. Magill IV, MC
Poetry of Warren, The. Robert Penn Warren. Magill IV, MC
Poetry of Whittier, The. John Greenleaf Whittier. Magill IV, MAL5, MC
Poetry of Wilbur, The. Richard

Wilbur. Magill IV, MC
Poetry of Wilde, The. Oscar Wilde. Magill IV, MC
Poetry of Williams, The. William Carlos Williams. Magill IV, MC
Poetry of Wither, The. George Wither. Magill IV, MC
Poetry of Wordsworth, The. William Wordsworth. Magill IV, MC
Poetry of Wyatt and Surrey, The. Sir Thomas Wyatt and Henry Howard, Earl of Surrey. Magill IV, MC
Poetry of Yeats, The. William Butler Yeats. Magill III, M1, MC, MP
Poets in a Landscape. Gilbert Highet. Magill '58, S
Poets of America, The. Edmund Clarence Stedman. Keller
Point Counter Point. Aldous Huxley. Haydn; Heiney; Lass BN; Magill I, CE, M1&2, MC, MEF; Olfson; Ward
Point of Departure see Eurydice
Point of No Return. John P. Marquand. (See also adaptation by Paul Osborn.) Grozier
Point of No Return. Paul Osborn. (Based on the novel by John P. Marquand.) Best '51; Drury
Point of View, The. Henry James. Gale-J
Points of My Compass, The. E. B. White. Magill '63, S
Poison Belt, The. Arthur Conan Doyle. Magill SF
Poison Pen. Richard Llewellyn. French
Poisson noir, Le (The Black Fish). Armand Gatti. Kienzle
Police, The. Slawomir Mrożek. Kienzle; Matlaw
Policraticus. John of Salisbury. Magill CAL, CHL
Policy for Murder. Jack Popplewell. French
Polish Jew, The (The Bells). Emile Erckmann and Alexandre Chatrian. Shipley
Political and Social History of the United States, The. Arthur Meier Schlesinger. Keller suppl.
Political Debates ... in the Celebrated Campaign of 1858, in

Illinois.   Abraham Lincoln and
Stephen A. Douglas.   Downs M
Political Education, A.   Harry
McPherson.   Magill '73
Political Romance, A (The His-
tory of a Good Warm Watch-
Coat).   Laurence Sterne.
Johnson-18th/2
Political Theory: The Foundations
of Twentieth-Century Political
Thought.   Arnold Brecht.   Ma-
gill Ss
Political Tinker, The.   Ludvig
Holberg.   Drury
Political Writings.   Saint Robert
Cardinal Bellarmine.   Magill
CAL
Politician, The.   Antonio Fogaz-
zaro.   Keller
Politics.   Aristotle.   Downs;
Haydn; Magill WP
Politics of Lying, The.   David
Wise.   Magill '74
Politicus.   Plato.   Feder
Pollinators of Eden, The.   John
Boyd.   Magill SF
Polonaise.   Piers Paul Read.
Magill '77
Polychrome Bible, The.   Paul
Haupt, editor.   Keller (Bible)
Polyeucte.   Pierre Corneille.
Drury; Gassner; Magill III,
CE, M1&2, MC, MD; Shank
Polygots, The.   William Ger-
hardi.   Keller suppl.
Poly-Olbion.   Michael Drayton.
Keller; Ruoff
Pomander Walk.   Louis Napoleon
Parker.   Drury
Pomme, pomme, pomme.
Jacques Audiberti.   Kienzle
Pomp of the Lavilettes, The.
Sir Gilbert Parker.   Kaye
Pomponia.   Mrs. J. B. Webb.
Kaye
Ponder Heart, The.   Joseph
Fields and Jerome Chodorov.
(Based on the story by Eudora
Welty.)   Best '55; Chapman
'56; Drury; NCTE
Ponder Heart, The.   Eudora
Welty.   (See also adaptation
by Joseph Fields and Jerome
Chodorov.)   Magill IV, '54,
M1, MC, S
Ponedel'nik nachinaetsia v sub-
botu.   Arkady and Boris
Strugatsky.   Magill SF

Ponteach; or The Savages of
America.   Major Robert
Rogers.   Lovell
Pontoosuce.   Herman Melville.
Gale-M
Pools Paradise.   Philip King.
French
Pools Paradise.   Armitage Owen.
French
Poor Bitos, or The Masked Din-
ner.   Jean Anouilh.   Best '64;
Drury; French; Kienzle; Mat-
law; NCTE
Poor Folk see Poor People
Poor Heinrich.   Gerhart Haupt-
mann.   Matlaw
Poor Man's Pudding and Rich
Man's Crumbs.   Herman Mel-
ville.   Gale-M
Poor Nut, The.   J. C. Nugent.
Drury
Poor of New York, The.   Dion
Boucicault.   Shank
Poor People.   Fyodor Mikhailo-
vich Dostoevskii.   Berry-2
(Poor Folk); Haydn (Poor
Folk); Magill II, M1, MC,
MEUF
Poor Relation's Story, The.
Charles Dickens.   Hardwick
CD
Poor Richard.   Henry James.
Gale-J
Poor Richard.   Jean Kerr.
Drury
Poor Sons of a Day.   Allan Mc-
Aulay.   Kaye
Poor White.   Sherwood Anderson.
Keller suppl. ; Magill I, CE,
M1&2, MAF, MC
Poorhouse Fair, The.   John Up-
dike.   Magill IV, '60, MB,
MC, S, SF
Popular Tales from the Norse.
Peter Christian Asbjørnsen.
Keller
Porgy.   Dorothy and DuBose
Heyward.   Best '27; Drury;
Haydn; Keller suppl.; Lass
AP; Magill I, CE, M1&2,
MAF, MC; Matlaw; Morehead;
Shipley; Sobel
Porgy and Bess.   George Gersh-
win, Ira Gershwin and DuBose
Heyward.   Lovell
Port-Royal.   Henry de Monther-
lant.   Anderson; Gassner;
Kienzle; Matlaw

Portion of Labor, A. Mary
Eleanor (Wilkins) Freeman.
Keller
Portnoy's Complaint. Philip Roth.
Magill '70
Portrait in Brownstone. Louis
Auchincloss. Magill '63, S
Portrait of a Lady, The. Henry
James. Gale-J; Goodman;
Grozier; Haydn; Johnson;
Keller; Lass AN; Magill I,
CE, M1&2, MAF, MAL3,
MC; Morehead
Portrait of a Marriage. Nigel
Nicolson. Magill '74
Portrait of Max. S. N. Behr-
man. Magill '61, MB, S
Portrait of Murder. Robert
Bloomfield. French
Portrait of the Artist As a Young
Dog. Dylan Thomas. Magill
IV, MC
Portrait of the Artist As a Young
Man, A. James Joyce.
Haydn; Heiney; Keller suppl.;
Lass BN; Magill I, CE, M1&2,
MC, MEF; Olfson; Ward
Positive Philosophy. Auguste
Comte. Haydn
Possessed, The. Albert Camus.
Kienzle
Possessed, The. Fyodor Mik-
hailovich Dostoevskii. Berry-
2 (The Devils); Haydn; Magill
I, CE, M1&2, MC, MEUF
Possession. Louis Bromfield.
Keller suppl.
Post Office, The. Rabindranath
Tagore. Matlaw
Posthumous Papers of the Pick-
wick Club, The see Pick-
wick Papers
Postman, The. Roger Martin du
Gard. Magill '55, S
Postman Always Rings Twice,
The. James M. Cain.
Magill IV, MC; Morehead
Pot-Bouille. Emile Zola.
Keller (Rougon)
Pot of Gold, The (Aulularia).
Titus Maccius Plautus. Drury;
Feder; Gassner (Aulularia);
Hathorn (Aulularia); Haydn;
Keller (Aulularia); Magill II,
CE, M1&2, MC, MD; Rein-
hold; Shank; Shipley; Sobel
(Aulularia)
Potiphar Papers. George Wil-

liam Curtis. Keller
Potting Shed, The. Graham
Greene. Best '56; Chapman
'57; Drury; French; Magill '58,
S; Matlaw; NCTE; Shank
Poverty, a Study in Town Life.
Seebohm Rowntree. Keller
Poverty Is No Crime. Aleksandr
Ostrovskii. Drury
Powdered Eggs. Charles Sim-
mons. Magill '65, S
Power. Lion Feuchtwanger.
Keller suppl.; Magill I, CE,
M1&2, MC, MEUF
Power and the Glory, The. Denis
Cannan and Pierre Bost.
(Based on the novel by Graham
Greene.) NCTE
Power and the Glory, The.
Graham Greene. (See also
adaptation by Denis Cannan and
Pierre Bost.) Lass BN;
Magill II, CE, M1&2, MC,
MEF
Power Broker: Robert Moses and
the Fall of New York, The.
Robert A. Caro. Magill '75
Power of a Lie, The. Johan
Bojer. Haydn
Power of Darkness, The. Count
Leo Tolstoy. Cartmell; Drury;
Gassner; Haydn; Magill III,
CE, M1&2, MC, MD; Matlaw;
Shank; Shipley; Sobel; Thomas
Power of Words, The. Edgar
Allan Poe. Gale-PP
Power Politics. Margaret At-
wood. Magill '74
Power Shift. Kirkpatrick Sale.
Magill '76
Power Without Glory. Michael
Clayton Hutton. French
Practical Christianity. Rufus
Matthew Jones. Magill CHL
Practice of the Presence of God,
The. Brother Lawrence.
Magill CHL
Pragmatism. William James.
Haydn (a); Keller; Magill III,
M1, MC, MNF, WP
Prairie, The. James Fenimore
Cooper. (See also The Leath-
erstocking Saga.) Haydn p.
416; Johnson; Magill I, CE,
M1&2, MAF, MC; Walker
Praise of Folly, The. Desiderius
Erasmus. Downs M; Haydn;
Magill III, CAL, CHL, M1,

MC, MNF
Prayer. George Arthur Buttrick.
Magill CHL
Prayer Book, The see Book of
Common Prayer, The
Prayer for Katerina Horovitzova,
A. Arnost Lustig. Magill
'74
Prayer for My Daughter. Thomas
Babe. Best '77
Precaution. James Fenimore
Cooper. Johnson; Walker
Preces Privatae. Lancelot
Andrewes. Magill CHL
Précieuses ridicules, Les (The
Precious Damsels; The Affected
Ladies; The Romantic Ladies).
Molière. Gassner; Haydn; Keller;
Magill II, CE, M1&2, MC, MD
(Romantic); Shipley; Sobel
Precious Bane. Mary Webb.
Haydn; Keller suppl. ; Magill
I, CE, M1&2, MC, MEF
Precipice, The. Ivan Alexandro-
vich Goncharov. Berry-2
Predicament, A. Edgar Allan
Poe. Gale-PP
Preface to a Life. Zona Gale.
Keller suppl.
Preface to Morals, A. Walter
Lippmann. Haydn
Preface to Shakespeare. Samuel
Johnson. Magill IV, MC
Preferences. Richard Howard.
Magill '75
Prehistoric Europe. James
Geikie. Keller
Prejudices: Six Series. H. L.
Mencken. Magill III, M1,
MC, MNF
Prelude. Katherine Mansfield.
Heiney; Ward
Prelude, A. Edmund Wilson.
Magill '68, S
Prelude, The. William Words-
worth. Haydn; Keller; Magill
III, M1, MC, MP
Premature Burial, The. Edgar
Allan Poe. Gale-PP
Prenez garde à la peinture.
René Fauchois. (See adapta-
tions The Late Christopher
Bean by Emelyn Williams and
Sidney Howard.)
Presence of Grace, The. J. F.
Powers. Magill '57, S
Presences: Seven Dramatic
Pieces. Peter Taylor.

Magill '74
Present at the Creation. Dean
Acheson. Magill '71
Present Laughter. Noel Coward.
Drury; French
Presentation Piece. Marilyn
Hacker. Magill '75
President, The. R. V. Cassill.
Magill '65, S
President Is Born, A. Fannie
Hurst. Keller suppl.
Presidential Lottery. James A.
Michener. Magill '70
President's Scouts, The. Herbert
Hayens. Kaye
Press Cuttings. George Bernard
Shaw. Hardwick
Pretenders, The see Suppositi,
I
Pretenders, The. Henrik Ibsen.
Drury; Matlaw; Sobel
Pretty Lady, The. Arnold Ben-
nett. Stade p. 30
Preuve par quatre, La (Two and
Two Make Four). Nicola Man-
zari. Kienzle
Priapea. Attributed to Vergil.
Feder
Price, The. Arthur Miller.
Best '67; Drury; Kienzle;
Magill '69, S; Matlaw
Price of Fame. Wilfred Massey.
French
Price of Glory: Verdun, 1916,
The. Alastair Horne. Magill
'64, S
Price Who Was a Thief, The.
Theodore Dreiser. Gerber
Pricksongs and Descants. Robert
Coover. Magill '70
Pride and Prejudice. Jane Aus-
ten. (See also adaptation by
Helen Jerome and I Have Five
Daughters by Margaret Mac-
namara.) Armstrong; Goodman;
Grozier; Halperin; Haydn;
Johnson; Keller; Lass BN;
Magill I, CE, M1&2, MC,
MEF; Wilson
Pride and Prejudice. Helen
Jerome. (Based on the novel
by Jane Austen.) Best '35;
French; NCTE; Sobel
Priest to the Temple, A. George
Herbert. Magill CHL
Priestess of Isis, The. Edouard
Schure. Kaye
Příliš štědry večer (And All That

on Christmas Eve). Vratislav
Blažek. Kienzle
Primacy or World Order: Amer-
ican Foreign Policy Since the
Cold War. Stanley Hoffmann.
Magill '79
Prime Minister, The. Anthony
Trollope. (See also series
title Parliamentary Novels.)
Gerould; Keller
Prime of Miss Jean Brodie, The.
Muriel Spark. Drury; Magill
'63, M1, S
Primitive Culture. Sir Edward
Burnett Tylor. Haydn; Keller
(Early History of Mankind)
Primitive Man. Louis Figuier.
Keller
Primitive Religion. Robert H.
Lowie. Keller suppl.
Prince, The. Niccolò Machia-
velli. Armstrong; Downs M,
FG; Haydn; Keller; Magill
III, CAL, M1, MC, MNF, WP
Prince and the Pauper, The.
Mark Twain. Gale-T; Good-
man; Keller; Magill II, CE,
M1&2, MAF, MAL5, MC
Prince d'Aurec, The. Henri
Lavedan. Drury; Matlaw
Prince Eugen of Savoy. Nicholas
Henderson. Magill '66, S
Prince of Homburg, The. Hein-
rich von Kleist. Drury;
Magill III, CE, M1&2, MC,
MD; Shank; Shipley (Prince
Friedrich)
Prince of India, The. Lew Wal-
lace. Kaye; Keller
Prince of Our Disorder, A.
John E. Mack. Magill '77
Prince of Parthia, The. Thomas
Godfrey. Drury; Lovell
Prince Otto. Robert Louis Steven-
son. Johnson
Prince Rupert the Buccaneer.
Charles J. C. Hyne. Kaye
Prince Who Learned Everything
Out of Books, The. Jacinto
Benavente y Martínez. Matlaw
Prince Zilah. Jules Claretie.
Johnson
Prince's Messenger, The. Albert
Lee. Kaye
Prince's Valet, The. J. Barnet.
Kaye
Princess, The. Alfred, Lord
Tennyson. Haydn; Keller;

Magill IV, MC
Princess Aline, The. Richard
Harding Davis. Keller
Princess and the Pea, The.
Hans Christian Andersen.
(See adaptation Once upon a
Mattress by Jay Thompson et
al.)
Princess Casamassima, The.
Henry James. Gale-J; Keller;
Magill IV, M1, MAL3, MC
Princess Far-Away, The. Ed-
mond Rostand. Drury
Princess Ida. William Schwenck
Gilbert and Arthur Sullivan.
Shipley; Sobel
Princess of Clèves, The. Madame
Marie de Lafayette. Haydn;
Magill II, CE, M1&2, MC,
MEUF; Olfson
Princess of Kensington, A. Ed-
ward German and Basil Hood.
Drinkrow
Princess of Mars, A. Edgar
Rice Burroughs. Magill SF
Princess of Thule, A. William
Black. Johnson
Principal Doctrines and Letter to
Menoeceus. Epicurus. Magill
WP
Principal Navigations, Voyages,
and Discoveries of the English
Nation Made by Sea or over
Land, The see Hakluyt's
Voyages
Principia Ethica. George Edward
Moore. Magill WP
Principle of Individuality and
Value, The. Bernard Bosan-
quet. Magill WP
Principles of Geology, Being an
Attempt to Explain the Former
Changes of the Earth's Surface,
by Reference to Causes Now in
Operation. Sir Charles Lyell.
Downs M
Principles of Human Knowledge,
The see Treatise Concerning
the Principles of Human Knowl-
edge, A
Principles of Literary Criticism.
I. A. Richards. Magill IV,
MC
Principles of Political Economy.
John Stuart Mill. Keller (Poli-
tical); Magill IV, MC
Principles of Political Economy
and Taxation. David Ricardo.

Gale-J
Professor of Desire, The.   Philip
Roth.   Magill '78
Professor Taranne.   Arthur
Adamov.   Gassner; Matlaw
Professor's House, The.   Willa
Cather.   Haydn (Cather);
Keller suppl.; Magill II, CE,
M1&2, MAF, MC
Professor's Love Story, The.
Sir James M. Barrie.   Keller
Profiles in Courage.   John F.
Kennedy.   Magill '57, M1, S
Progress and Poverty.   Henry
George.   Downs M; Haydn;
Keller
Progress and Religion.   Chris-
topher Dawson.   Magill CAL
Prolegomena to Ethics.   Thomas
Hill Green.   Magill WP
Prologue to Glory.   E. P.
Conkle.   Best '37; Drury;
NCTE; Sobel
Promessi sposi, I see Be-
trothed, The
Prometheia see Prometheus
Bound; Prometheus Unbound;
Prometheus the Fire-Bringer
Prometheus.   Aeschylus.   Cart-
mell; Thomas
Prometheus Bound.   Aeschylus.
Downs; Drury; Feder; Gassner;
Hathorn (Prometheia); Haydn;
Keller; Magill I, CE, M1&2,
MC, MD; Reinhold; Shipley;
Sobel
Prometheus; or, Biology and the
Advancement of Man.   H. S.
Jennings.   Keller suppl.
Prometheus the Fire-Bringer.
Aeschylus.   Hathorn (Prome-
theia)
Prometheus the Fire-Kindler.
Aeschylus.   Hathorn
Prometheus: The Life of Balzac.
André Maurois.   Magill '67,
S
Prometheus Unbound.   Aeschylus.
Hathorn (Prometheia)
Prometheus Unbound.   Percy
Bysshe Shelley.   Haydn; Kel-
ler; Magill I, CE, M1&2, MC,
MP; Sobel
Promise, The.   Aleksei Nikolae-
vich Arbuzov.   Matlaw
Promise of American Life, The.
Herbert Croly.   Keller
Promised Land, The.   Henrik

Pontoppidan.   Magill II, CE,
M1&2, MC, MEUF
Promised Land, The.   Mary An-
tin.   Keller
Promised Land, The.   Ladislas
Reymont.   Keller suppl.
Promises.   Robert Penn Warren.
Magill '58, MB, S
Promises, Promises.   Neil
Simon, Hal David and Burt
Bacharach.   (Based on The
Apartment by Billy Wilder and
I. A. L. Diamond.)   NCTE
Promos and Cassandra.   George
Whetstone.   Ruoff
Promotion, The.   John M. Dean.
Kaye
Proof of the Poison, The...!
Falkland L. Cary and Philip
Weathers.   French
Proof of the Pudding, The.
Meredith Nicholson.   Keller
Prophet, The.   Sholem Asch.
Magill '55, S
Prophet, The.   Kahil Gibran.
Haydn; Magill IV, MC
Prophetic Pictures, The.   Nathan-
iel Hawthorne.   Gale-H
Proposal, The.   Anton Chekhov.
Matlaw
Proposed Roads to Freedom.
Bertrand Russell.   Keller
suppl.
Prose Edda, The.   Snorri Sturlu-
son.   Haydn
Proserpine and Ceres.   Unknown.
Magill I, CE, M1&2, MC,
MEUF
Proslogion.   Saint Anselm of
Canterbury.   Magill CAL, CHL
Prosopopoia see Mother Hub-
berd's Tale, or Prosopopoia
Prospects Are Pleasing, The.
Honor Tracy.   Magill '59, S
Protagoras.   Plato.   Feder; Ma-
gill WP
Protestant, The.   Anna Eliza
Bray.   Kaye
Proteus.   Aeschylus.   Hathorn
(Oresteia)
Prothalamion.   Edmund Spenser.
Haydn; Ruoff
Proud Tower, The.   Barbara W.
Tuchman.   Magill '66, M1, S
Proust Screenplay, The.   Harold
Pinter.   Magill '78
Proust: The Early Years.
George D. Painter.   Magill

'60, MB, S
Proust: The Later Years.
George D. Painter. Magill
'66, S
Proverbial Philosophy. Martin
Farquhar Tupper. Keller
Provincial Lady, A. Ivan Tur-
genev. French
Provincial Letters. Blaise Pascal.
Haydn
Provincial Society. James Tru-
slow Adams. Keller suppl.
Provok'd Husband, The. Sir
John Vanbrugh. Shipley; Sobel
Provok'd Wife, The. Sir John
Vanbrugh. Shank; Shipley;
Sobel
Prozess der Jeanne d'Arc zu
Rouen 1431, Der (The Trial
of Jeanne d'Arc at Rouen in
1431). Bertolt Brecht and B.
Besson. Kienzle
Prue and I. George William Cur-
tis. Keller
Prunella. Laurence Housman
and Harley Granville-Barker.
Drury; Matlaw; Shipley
Prusias. Ernst Eckstein. Kaye
P. 's Correspondence. Nathaniel
Hawthorne. Gale-H
Pseudolus. Titus Maccius
Plautus. Feder; Hathorn;
Reinhold; Shipley
Psyche. Walter S. Cramp. Kaye
Psychopathic God: Adolf Hitler,
The. Robert G. L. Waite.
Magill '78
Psychopathology of Everyday Life.
Sigmund Freud. Keller
Public Eye, The. Peter Shaffer.
Drury; French; Kienzle
Public Finance. C. F. Bastable.
Keller
Public Image, The. Muriel Spark.
Magill '69, S
Public Mind, The. Norman
Angell. Keller suppl.
Public Opinion. Walter Lippmann
Keller suppl.
Public Prosecutor, The. Fritz
Hochwälder. French; Kienzle
Publikumsbeschimpfung (An Insult
to the Public). Peter Handke.
Kienzle
Pucelle d'Orléans, Lu. Voltaire.
Haydn (t: Pucelle, The)
Puck of Pook's Hill. Rudyard
Kipling. Keller

Pudd'nhead Wilson. Mark Twain.
Gale-T; Grozier; Haydn p. 430
Pulitzer. W. A. Swanberg.
Magill '68, M1, S
Pullman Car Hiawatha. Thornton
Wilder. Matlaw
Pump House Gang, The. Tom
Wolfe. Magill '69, M1, S
Pupil, The. Henry James. Gale-
J
Puppet Masters, The. Robert A.
Heinlein. Magill SF
Puppet Show, The. Aleksandr
Aleksandrovich Blok. Matlaw
Purchas, His Pilgrims. Samuel
Purchas. Haydn; Keller
Purchase Price, The. Emerson
Hough. Kaye
Pure and the Impure, The.
Colette. Magill '68, M1, S
Pure As the Driven Snow; or A
Working Girl's Secret. Paul
Loomis. Drury
Purgatory. William Butler Yeats.
Gassner; Matlaw
Puritan Carpenter, The. Julia
Randall. Magill '66, S
Puritan in Holland, England and
America, The. Douglas Camp-
bell. Keller
Puritan; or, The Widow of Watling
Street, The. "W. S. " Sobel
Puritan Village. Sumner Chilton
Powell. Magill Ss
Puritan Way of Death, The.
David E. Stannard. Magill
'78
Purlie Victorious. Ossie Davis.
NCTE
Purloined Letter, The. Edgar
Allan Poe. Gale-P, PP
Purple Cloud, The. M. P.
Shiel. Magill SF
Purple Dust. Sean O'Casey.
Gassner; Magill III, CE, M1&2,
MC, MD; Matlaw; Shank;
Sprinchorn
Purple Island, or The Isle of
Man, The. Phineas Fletcher.
Keller; Ruoff p. 160
Purple Land, The. W. H. Hud-
son. Haydn; Magill I, CE,
M1&2, MC, MEF
Purple Love. Morice Gerard.
Kaye
Purple Mask, The. Paul Armont
and J. Manoussi. Drury
Pushcart Prize, III: Best of the

Small Presses, The.   Bill
Henderson, editor.   Magill '79
Puss in Boots.   Unknown.   Keller
(Fairy Tales)
Put Yourself in His Place.
Charles Reade.   Johnson;
Keller
Puzzleheaded Girl, The.   Chris-
tina Stead.   Magill '68, S
Pygmalion.   Georg Kaiser.
Matlaw
Pygmalion.   George Bernard
Shaw.   (See also adaptation
My Fair Lady by Alan Jay
Lerner and Frederick Loewe.)
Drury; Hardwick; Haydn; Magill
III, M1, MC, MD; Matlaw;
NCTE; Shank; Shipley; Sobel;
Sprinchorn
Pygmalion and Galatea.   William
Schwenck Gilbert.   Drury
Pyramid, The.   William Golding.
Magill '68, S

-Q-

Quabbin.   Francis H. Underwood.
Keller
Quadragesimo Anno.   Pope Pius
XI.   Magill CAL
Quadrille.   Noel Coward.   Kienzle
Quaker Girl, The.   Lionel Monck-
ton, James T. Tanner, Adrian
Ross and Percy Greenbank.
Drinkrow
Quality of Mercy, The.   William
Dean Howells.   Carrington
Quality Street.   Sir James M.
Barrie.   Drury; French;
Magill I, CE, M1&2, MC,
MD; NCTE; Sobel; Ward
Quando le Radici.   Lino Aldani.
Magill SF
Quare Fellow, The.   Brendan
Behan.   Drury; Kienzle;
Magill '58, S; Matlaw
Quarry, The.   Richard Eberhart.
Magill '65, S
Quarup.   Antonio Callado.
Magill Ss
Quatre vérités, Les.   Marcel
Aymé.   Kienzle
Queechy.   Elizabeth Wetherell.
Keller
Queed.   Henry Sydnor Harrison.

Keller
Queen After Death.   Henry de
Montherlant.   Gassner; Matlaw;
Sprinchorn
Queen Alexandra.   Georgina Bat-
tiscombe.   Magill '70
Queen and the Rebels, The.   Ugo
Betti.   French; Kienzle; Mat-
law; Shank; Sprinchorn
Queen and the Welshman, The.
Rosemary Anne Sisson.
French
Queen Mary.   James Pope-Hen-
nessy.   Magill '61, MB, S
Queen Mary.   Alfred, Lord Ten-
nyson.   Sobel
Queen of France.   André Caste-
lot.   Magill '58, S
Queen of Nine Days, A.   Edith
C. Kenyon.   Kaye
Queen of Spades, The.   Alexander
Pushkin.   Berry-1
Queen Victoria.   Lytton Strachey.
Haydn; Keller suppl. (Victoria);
Magill IV, MC
Queen Victoria.   Cecil Woodham-
Smith.   Magill '73
Queen Victoria: Born to Succeed.
Elizabeth, Countess of Long-
ford.   Magill '66, S
Queens and the Hive, The.   Edith
Sitwell.   Magill '63, M1, MB,
S
Queen's Fillet, The.   Patrick A.
Sheehan.   Kaye
Queen's Hostage, The.   Harriet
T. Comstock.   Kaye
Queen's Husband, The.   Robert
E. Sherwood.   Drury; NCTE
Queen's Man, The.   Eleanor C.
Price.   Kaye
Queen's Maries, The.   George
John White Melville.   Kaye
Queen's Necklace, The.   Alex-
andre Dumas (father).   John-
son; Kaye; Magill II, CE,
M1&2, MC, MEUF
Queen's Necklace, The.   Frances
Mossiker.   Magill '62, S
Queen's Tragedy, The.   Robert
H. Benson.   Kaye
Queer Fellow, The.   Gyula Illyés.
Kienzle
Quentin Durward.   Sir Walter
Scott.   Haydn; Johnson; Kaye;
Keller; McSpadden W; Magill I,
CE, M1&2, MC, MEF
Querolus (The Complainer).   Un-

known. Gassner; Hathorn; Shipley (end section)
Quest, The see Struggle for Life, The
Quest for Being, The. Sidney Hook. Magill '62, S
Quest for Certainty, The. John Dewey. Haydn (Dewey); Magill WP
Quest of Glory, The. Marjorie Bowen. Kaye
Quest of the Four, The. Joseph A. Altsheler. Kaye
Quest of the Historical Jesus, The. Albert Schweitzer. Magill CHL
Questionable Shapes. William Dean Howells. Carrington
Questions of King Milinda, The. Unknown. Keller (Sacred Books)
Questions of Precedence. François Mauriac. Magill '60, M1, S
Questions of Travel. Elizabeth Bishop. Magill '66, S
Queue and Sword see Sword and Queue
Quiberon Touch, The. Cyrus T. Brady. Kaye
Quick or the Dead?, The. Amélie Rives. Johnson; Keller
Quiet American, The. Graham Greene. Magill '57, M1, S
Quiet Don, The see Silent Don, The
Quiet Enemy, The. Cecil Dawkins. Magill '64, S
Quiet Night. Dorothy Blewett. French
Quiet Wedding. Esther McCracken. French
Quiet Week-end. Esther McCracken. French
Quincy Adams Sawyer. Charles Felton Pidgin. Keller
Quintessence of Ibsenism, The. George Bernard Shaw. Milllaw
Quintus Claudius. Ernst Eckstein. Kaye; Keller
Quinzinzinzili. Régis Messac. Magill SF
Quip for an Upstart Courtier, A. Robert Greene. Ruoff p. 178
Quo Vadis. Henryk Sienkiewicz. Goodman; Grozier; Haydn; Johnson; Kaye; Keller; Magill

I, CE, M1&2, MC, MEUF
Quoat-Quoat. Jacques Audiberti. Anderson; Kienzle; Sprinchorn
Qur'ân, The. Keller (Sacred Books)

-R-

R. E. Lee. Douglas Southall Freeman. Haydn; Magill III, M1, MC, MNF
RN: The Memoirs of Richard Nixon. Richard M. Nixon. Magill '79
R. U. R.: Rossum's Universal Robots. Karel Capek. Best '22; Cartmell; Drury; Haydn; Heiney; Keller suppl.; Magill II, CE, M1&2, MC, MD, SF; Matlaw; NCTE; Shank; Shipley; Sprinchorn; Thomas; Ward
Rab and His Friends. John Brown. Haydn; Keller
Rabbit Race, The. Martin Walser. Kienzle
Rabbit, Run. John Updike. Magill IV, '61, MB, MC, S
Rachel Ray. Anthony Trollope. Gerould
Rack, The. A. E. Ellis. Magill '60, S
Rack, The. J. B. Priestley. Kienzle
Racket, The. Bartlett Cormack. Best '27; Drury
Raditzer. Peter Matthiessen. Magill '62, S
Raffaelle (Raphael). Vitaliano Brancati. Kienzle
Raft of the Medusa, The. Georg Kaiser. Shank
Rage of Edmund Burke: Portrait of an Ambivalent Conservative, The. Isaac Kramnick. Magill '70
Ragged Dick. Horatio Alger, Jr. Downs M
Ragged Lady. William Dean Howells. Carrington
Ragged Trousered Philanthropists, The. Robert Tressell. Ward
Ragtime. E. L. Doctorow. Magill '76
Raider, The. Jesse Hill Ford. Magill '77

Raiders, The. Samuel Ruther-
ford Crockett. Keller
Rain. John Colton and Clemence
Randolph. (Based on "Miss
Thompson" by W. Somerset
Maugham.) Best '22; Cart-
mell; Drury; French; Keller
suppl.; Shipley; Sobel
Rain. W. Somerset Maugham.
Heiney; Ward
Rain from Heaven. S. N. Behr-
man. Drury; Matlaw; Shipley
Rainbird, The. Sara Lidman.
Magill '63, S
Rainbow, The. D. H. Lawrence.
Keller suppl.; Magill I, CE,
M1&2, MC, MEF; Ward
Rainbow Grocery, The. William
Dickey. Magill '79
Rainbow on the Road. Esther
Forbes. Magill '54, S
Rainmaker, The. N. Richard
Nash. Drury; French; Kienzle
Raintree County. Ross Lock-
ridge, Jr. Magill II, CE,
M1&2, MAF, MC
Raise High the Roof Beam, Car-
penters. J. D. Salinger.
Magill '64, M1, S
Raisin in the Sun, A. Lorraine
Hansberry. Best '58; Bonin;
Chapman '59; Drury; Lass AP;
Lovell; Magill '60, M1, S;
Matlaw; NCTE
Rakehells of Heaven, The. John
Boyd. Magill SF
Rakóssy. Cecilia Holland. Magill
'67, S
Rally 'Round the Flag, Boys!
David Rogers. (Based on the
novel by Max Shulman.) Drury
Rally 'Round the Flag, Boys!
Max Shulman. (See adaptation
by David Rogers.)
Ralph 124C 41+. Hugo Gerns-
back. Magill SF
Ralph Roister Doister. Nicholas
Udall. Drury; Gassner; Haydn;
Holzknecht; Keller; Magill II,
CE, M1&2, MC, MD; Ruoff;
Shank; Shipley; Sobel
Ralph the Heir. Anthony Trol-
lope. Gerould
Rama's Later History. Bhavab-
huti. Gassner
Ramayana, The. Aubrey Menen.
Magill '54, S
Ramayana, The. Unknown.

Fleming; Haydn
Ramayana, The. Valmiki. Ma-
gill III, CE, M1&2, MC, MP
Rambler, The. Samuel Johnson.
Magill IV, MC
Rambles and Studies in Greece.
Sir John Pentland Mahaffy.
Keller
Rameau's Nephew. Denis Diderot.
Magill III, M1, MC, MEUF
Rammon. Herman Melville.
Gale-M
Ramona. Helen Hunt Jackson.
Goodman; Grozier; Haydn;
Johnson; Keller
Ramshackle Inn. George Batson.
NCTE
Rancho the Clown see Yukari
no Murasaki Zukin
Random Harvest. Moie Charles
and Barbara Toy. (Based on
the novel by James Hilton.)
French
Random Harvest. James Hilton.
(See adaptation by Moie Charles
and Barbara Toy.)
Random Shaft, A. Jude Mac-
Millar. Kaye
Ranke: The Meaning of History.
Leonard Krieger. Magill '78
Ransom. Cyril Hume and Richard
Maibaum. Drury
Ransom of Hector, The. Aeschy-
lus. Hathorn
Rape of Lucrece, The. Thomas
Heywood. Shipley
Rape of Lucrece, The. William
Shakespeare. Campbell; Clark;
Halliday; Haydn; Magill II, CE,
M1&2, MC, MP; Ruoff
Rape of the Belt, The. Benn W.
Levy. Drury; French
Rape of the Fair Country, The.
Alexander Cordell. Magill '60,
S
Rape of the Lock, The. Alex-
ander Pope. Haydn; Magill I,
CE, M1&2, MC, MP
Rape of the Locks, The see
Shearing of Glycera, The
Rape upon Rape. Henry Fielding.
(See adaptation Lock Up Your
Daughters by Bernard Miles
et al.)
Rappaccini's Daughter. Nathaniel
Hawthorne. Gale-H
Rashomon. Fay and Michael
Kanin. Drury; NCTE

Rasmus Montanus see Erasmus
Montanus
Rasselas. Samuel Johnson.
Haydn; Johnson; Johnson-
18th/2; Magill I, CE, M1&2,
MC, MEF
Ratner's Star. Don DeLillo.
Magill '77
Rats, The. Agatha Christie.
French
Rats, The. Gerhart Hauptmann.
Gassner; Matlaw; Sprinchorn
Rattle of a Simple Man. Charles
Dyer. Best '62; Drury;
French; Kienzle; NCTE
Raven and the Redbird, The.
Raven Hail. NCTE
Ravensdale. Robert Thynne.
Kaye
Ravenshoe. Henry Kingsley.
Johnson; Keller; Magill II,
CE, M1&2, MC, MEF
Raw and the Cooked, The. Claude
Lévi-Strauss. Magill '70
Raw Youth, A. Fyodor Mikhailo-
vich Dostoevskii. Berry-2
(Adolescent); Haydn
Reaching Judgment at Nuremberg.
Bradley F. Smith. Magill '78
Reading a Poem. William Make-
peace Thackeray. Mudge
Ready and Easy Way to Establish
a Free Commonwealth, The.
John Milton. Ruoff
Ready-Money Mortiboy. Sir Walter
Besant and James Rice. John-
son
Real Folks. Mrs. A. D. T.
Whitney. Keller
Real Inspector Hound. Tom Stop-
pard. Drury
Real Life of Sebastian Knight,
The. Vladimir Nabokov.
Magill IV, '60, MC, S
Real Losses, Imaginary Gains.
Wright Morris. Magill '77
Real Majority, The. Richard M.
Scammon. Magill '71
Real Right Things, The. Henry
James. Gale-J
Real Thing, The. Henry James.
Gale-J
Real World, The. Robert Her-
rick. Keller
Reality of Faith, The. Friedrich
Gogarten. Magill CHL
Realms of Being. George Santa-
yana. Magill WP

Realms of Gold, The. Margaret
Drabble. Magill '76
Reason and Existenz. Karl Jas-
pers. Magill WP
Reason Why, The. Cecil Wood-
ham-Smith. Magill '54, S
Reasonableness of Christianity,
The. John Locke. Magill
CHL
Rebecca. Daphne Du Maurier.
French; Haydn; Magill I, CE,
M1&2, MC, MEF
Rebecca and Rowena. William
Makepeace Thackeray. Mudge
Rebecca of Sunnybrook Farm.
Kate Douglas Wiggin. Haydn;
Keller
Rebel, The. Albert Camus.
Magill '54, S, WP
Rebel Generation, The. Johanna
van Ammers-Küller. Magill
III, CE, M1&2, MC, MEUF
Rebel Maid, The. Montague Phil-
lips, Alexander M. Thompson
and Gerald Dodson. Drinkrow
Rebel Without a Cause. Nicholas
Ray. (See adaptation by Clark
F. Sergel.)
Rebel Without a Cause. Clark F.
Sergel. (Based on the novel
by Nicholas Ray.) Drury
Rebel Women. Thomas Babe.
Best '75; Drury
Rebellion in the Backlands.
Euclydes da Cunha. Haydn
Re-Birth. John Wyndham. Magill
SF
Rebound. Donald Ogden Stewart.
Best '29; Drury
Recent Research in Bible Lands:
Its Progress and Results.
Hermann V. Hilprecht. Keller
(Bible)
Recessional. Rudyard Kipling.
Hix; Ward
Reclining Figure. Harry Kurnitz.
Chapman '55
Recognitions, The. William Gad-
dis. Magill SL
Recollections and Letters of Gen-
eral Robert E. Lee. Captain
Robert E. Lee. Keller (Lee)
Recollections, by John, Viscount
Morley. Viscount John Morley.
Keller suppl.
Recollections of Geoffry Hamlyn.
Henry Kingsley. Johnson
Reconstruction in Philosophy.

John Dewey. Keller suppl.
Records of a Girlhood. Frances
Anne Kemble. Keller
Records of Later Life. Frances
Anne Kemble. Keller
Recovery of Confidence, The.
John W. Gardner. Magill '71
Recruiting Officer, The. George
Farquhar. Magill II, CE,
M1&2, MC, MD; Sobel
Rector of Justin, The. Louis
Auchincloss. Magill '65, M1,
S
Red and the Black, The. Stendhal.
Armstrong; Goodman; Grozier;
Haydn; Johnson; Lass EN;
Magill I, CE, M1&2, MC,
MEUF; Wilson
Red and White. Emily Sarah
Holt. Kaye
Red As a Rose Is She. Rhoda
Broughton. Keller
Red Badge of Courage, The.
Stephen Crane. Goodman;
Grozier; Haydn; Keller; Lass
AN; Magill I, CE, M1&2,
MAF, MAL1: MC; Morehead;
Smith; Wilson
Red Bridal, A. William Westall.
Kaye
Red Caps at Lyons, The. Her-
bert Hayens. Kaye
Red Cavalry. Isaac Emmanuelo-
vich Babel. Haydn
Red Chief, The. Everett T.
Tomlinson. Kaye
Red Circle, The. Sir Arthur
Conan Doyle. Hardwick SH
Red Cock, The. Gerhart Haupt-
mann. Matlaw
Red Cock Flies to Heaven, The.
Miodrag Dulatović. Magill '63,
S
Red Cockade, The. Stanley J.
Weyman. Keller
Red Dawn see Struggle for
Life, The
Red Fleur-de-lys, The. May
Wynne. Kaye
Red Fort, The. James Leasor.
Magill '58, S
Red-Headed League, The. Sir
Arthur Conan Doyle. Hardwick
SH
Red House Mystery, The. A.
A. Milne. (See adaptation by
Ruth Sergel.)
Red House Mystery, The. Ruth

Sergel. (Based on the novel
by A. A. Milne.) Drury
Red Laugh, The. Leonid N.
Andreyev. Haydn; Heiney;
Keller
Red Lily, The. Anatole France.
Armstrong; Johnson; Keller
Red Magic. Michel de Ghelder-
ode. Matlaw
Red Mill, The. Ferenc Molnár.
Matlaw; Shipley
Red Neighbor, The. W. J. Ec-
cott. Kaye
Red Orm, The. Frans Gunnar
Bengtsson. Haydn
Red Patriot, The. William O.
Stoddard. Kaye
Red Peppers. Noel Coward.
French
Red Pony, The. John Steinbeck.
Heiney
Red Pottage. Mary Cholmondeley.
Johnson
Red Robe, The. Eugène Brieux.
Drury; Heiney; Keller; Matlaw;
Shipley; Sobel
Red Rock. Thomas Nelson Page.
Kaye; Keller
Red Room, The. August Strind-
berg. Magill III, CE, M1&2,
MC, MEUF
Red Roses for Me. Sean O'Casey.
Drury; Gassner; Matlaw; NCTE
Red Rover, The. James Fenimore
Cooper. Johnson; Keller; Ma-
gill I, CE, M1&2, MAF, MC;
Walker
Red Saint, The. Warwick Deep-
ing. Kaye
Red Sky at Morning. Richard
Bradford. Magill '69, S
Red Sky at Morning. Margaret
Kennedy. Keller suppl.
Red White and Green. Herbert
Hayens. Kaye
Red Wolves and Black Bears.
Edward Hoagland. Magill '77
Redburn. Herman Melville.
Gale-M; Magill II, CE, M1&2,
MAF, MAL4, MC
Redemption see Living Corpse,
The
Redgauntlet. Sir Walter Scott.
Johnson; Keller; McSpadden W
Reds of the Midi, The. Felix
Gras. Johnson; Kaye; Keller
Redskins, The. James Fenimore
Cooper. Johnson; Magill III,

a Budding Grove; The Guer-
mantes Way; Cities of the Plain;
The Captive; The Sweet Cheat
Gone; Time Regained.) Haydn;
Heiney; Keller suppl. ; Magill
I, CE, M1&2, MC, MEUF;
Ward
Remembrance Rock. Carl Sand-
burg. Magill II, CE, M1&2,
MAF, MC
Reminiscences. Douglas Mac-
Arthur. Magill '65, M1, S
Renaissance, The. Walter Pater.
Haydn; Magill IV, MC
Renaissance in Italy, The. John
Addington Symonds. Haydn
(History of); Keller
Rendezvous at Senlis (Dinner
with the Family). Jean
Anouilh. Drury; French;
McGraw
Rendezvous with Rama. Arthur
C. Clarke. Magill SF
René. François René de Chateau-
briand. Johnson; Keller
Renee. Henry Curties. Kaye
Renée Mauperin. Edmond and
Jules de Goncourt. Johnson
(under de); Magill II, CE,
M1&2, MC, MEUF
Report of the President's Com-
mission on the Assassination
of President John F. Kennedy.
J. Lee Rankin, Earl Warren
and Others. Magill '65, M1,
S
Report on Herrnburg. Bertolt
Brecht and Paul Dessau.
Matlaw
Report on Probability, A. Brian
W. Aldiss. Magill SF
Report to Greco. Nikos Kazant-
zakis. Magill '66, M1, S
Representations. Steven Marcus.
Magill '77
Representative Men. Ralph Waldo
Emerson. Magill IV, MAL1,
MC
Reprieve, The. Jean-Paul Sartre.
(See also the trilogy title Roads
to Freedom.) Heiney
Republic, The. Plato. (See
also Allegory of the Cave,
The.) Downs FG; Feder;
Haydn; Keller; Magill III, M1,
MC, MNF, WP
Republic of the Southern Cross,
The. Valery Bryusov.

Magill SF
Republican Letters. Mark Twain.
Gale-T
Requiem for a Dream. Hubert
Selby, Jr. Magill '79
Requiem for a Nun. William
Faulkner. (See also adaptation
by Ruth Ford.) Drury; More-
head; Shank
Requiem for a Nun. Ruth Ford.
(Based on the novel by William
Faulkner.) Best '58; Kienzle
Rerum Novarum. Pope Leo XIII.
Magill CAL
Reruns. Jonathan Baumbach.
Magill '75
Rescue, The. Joseph Conrad.
Keller suppl.
Rescue the Dead. David Ignatow.
Magill '69, S
Research Magnificent, The. H.
G. Wells. Keller
Researches into the Early History
of Mankind. Sir Edward Bur-
nett Tylor. Keller (Early)
Resident Patient, The. Sir Arthur
Conan Doyle. Hardwick SH
Resignation in Protest. Edward
Weisband and Thomas M.
Franck. Magill '76
Resistance: European Resistance
to Nazism, 1940-1945. M. R.
D. Foot. Magill '78
Resistance, Rebellion, and Death.
Albert Camus. Magill '62, S
Resistance to Civil Government.
Henry David Thoreau. Downs
FG, M
Resistible Rise of Arturo Ui, The.
Bertolt Brecht. Kienzle; Mat-
law
Resounding Tinkle, A. N. F.
Simpson. French; Matlaw;
Shank
Respectful Prostitute, The.
Jean-Paul Sartre. Kienzle
Responses. Richard Wilbur.
Magill '77
Responsibilities of the Novelist,
The. Frank Norris. Magill
IV, MC
Rest Harrow. Maurice Hewlett.
Ward
Rest Is Done with Mirrors, The.
Carolyn See. Magill '71
Restless Heart, The. Jean
Anouilh. Matlaw
Restlessness of Shanti Andia,

Storm. French
Roar Lion Roar. Irvin Faust.
Magill '66, S
Roar of the Greasepaint - The
Smell of the Crowd, The.
Leslie Bricusse and Anthony
Newley. NCTE
Roaring Girl; or Moll Cutpurse,
The. Thomas Middleton and
Thomas Dekker. Holzknecht;
Ruoff. Sobel
Rob Roy. Sir Walter Scott.
Johnson; Kaye; McSpadden W;
Magill I, CE, M1&2, MC,
MEF
Robber Count, The. Julius
Wolff. Keller
Robber of the Rhine, The. Leitch
Ritchie. Johnson
Robbers, The. Johann Christoph
Friedrich von Schiller. Gass-
ner; Shipley; Sobel
Robbery Under Arms. Rolf
Boldrewood. Keller
Robe, The. Lloyd C. Douglas.
(See also adaptation by John
McGreevey.) Haydn
Robe, The. John McGreevey.
(Based on the novel by Lloyd
C. Douglas.) Drury; NCTE
Robe mauve de Valentine, La
(Valentine's Mauve Dress).
Françoise Sagan. Kienzle
Robe of Feathers, The see
Hagoromo
Robert Bruce and the Community
of the Realm of Scotland. G.
W. S. Barrow. Magill '66, S
Robert Cavalier. William D.
Orcutt. Kaye
Robert Drury's Journal. Daniel
Defoe. Johnson-18th
Robert E. Lee. John Drink-
water. Drury; French; Sobel
Robert Elsmere. Mrs. Humphry
Ward. Keller
Robert Emmet. Stephen Gwynn.
Kaye
Robert Falconer. George Mac-
donald. Keller
Robert Frank. Sigurd Ibsen.
Sobel
Robert Frost. Elizabeth Shepley
Sergeant. Magill '61, S
Robert Frost: The Work of Know-
ing. Richard Poirier. Magill
'78
Robert Fulton. John S. Morgan.

Magill '78
Robert Helmont. Alphonse Daudet.
Kaye
Robin Hood's Adventures. Un-
known. Cohen; Haydn; Magill
II, CE, M1&2, MC, MEF
Robinson Crusoe. Daniel Defoe.
Cohen; Downs M; Grozier;
Haydn; Johnson; Johnson-18th;
Keller; Lass BN; Magill I, CE,
M1&2, MC, MEF; Olfson; Wil-
son
Rochelle; or Virtue Rewarded.
David R. Slavitt. Magill '68,
S
Rock, The. Mary P. Hamlin.
Drury
Rock of Chickamauga, The.
Joseph A. Altsheler. Kaye
Rock of Chickamauga, The.
Charles King. Kaye
Rock of the Lion, The. Molly
Elliot Seawell. Kaye
Rock Pool, The. Cyril Connolly.
Magill '68, S
Rock-a-Bye, Sailor! Philip King
and Falkland L. Cary. French
Rocket to the Moon. Clifford
Odets. Best '38; Drury; Mat-
law
Roderick Hudson. Henry James.
Gale-J; Haydn (a); Magill IV,
CE, M1&2, MAL3, MC
Roderick Random. Tobias George
Smollett. Haydn; Johnson;
Johnson-18th/2; Keller; Magill
I, CE, M1&2, MC, MEF
Rodogune. Pierre Corneille.
Gassner
Roethke: Collected Poems.
Theodore Roethke. Magill '67,
M1, S
Roger Bloomer. John Howard
Lawson. Shank
Roger Malvin's Burial. Nathaniel
Hawthorne. Gale-H
Roger the Ranger. Eliza F. Pol-
lard. Kaye
Roger the Sixth. Joseph Carole.
French
Rogue, The. William Edward
Norris. Johnson
Rogue Herries. Hugh Walpole.
Magill I, CE, M1&2, MC,
MEF
Rogue Moon. Algis Budrys.
Magill SF
Rogue of Seville see Trickster

of Seville and His Guest of
Stone
Rogue Queen.   Lyon Sprague De
Camp.   Magill SF
Rogues' Trial, The.   Ariano
Suassuna.   Kienzle
Roland Barthes.   Roland Barthes.
Magill '78
Roland Blake.   Silas Weir Mitchell.
Kaye
Roland, Song of see Song of
Roland
Roll, Jordan, Roll.   Eugene D.
Genovese.   Magill '75
Rollo.   Marcel Achard.   French
Romagnola.   Luigi Squarzina.
Kienzle
Roman Actor, The.   Philip Mas-
singer.   Magill III, CE, M1&2,
MC, MD; Ruoff
Roman de Brut.   Robert Wace.
Keller (Brut)
Roman Poets, The.   W. Y.
Sellar.   Keller
Roman Singer, A.   Francis
Marion Crawford.   Johnson;
Keller
Roman Wall.   Winifred Bryher.
Magill '54, S
Romance.   Edward Sheldon.
Best '09; Drury; Matlaw
Romance of a Mummy, The.
Théophile Gautier.   Keller
Romance of a Poor Young Man,
The.   Octave Feuillet.   John-
son; Keller; Sobel
Romance of a Schoolmaster, The.
Edmondo de Amicis.   John-
son (under de); Magill II,
CE, M1&2, MC, MEUF
Romance of Arlington House, A.
Sarah A. Reed.   Kaye
Romance of Certain Old Clothes,
The.   Henry James.   Gale-J
Romance of Dollard, The.
Mrs. Mary H. Catherwood.
Kaye; Keller
Romance of Fra Lippo Lippi,
The.   A. J. Anderson.   Kaye
Romance of Leonardo da Vinci,
The.   Dmitri Merejkowski.
Magill II, CE, M1&2, MC,
MEUF
Romance of the Charter Oak.
William Seton.   Kaye
Romance of the Forest, The.
Mrs. Ann Radcliffe.   Johnson;
Magill II, CE, M1&2, MC,

MEF
Romance of the Fountain, The.
Eugene Lee Hamilton.   Kaye
Romance of the Lute, The.   Kao
Tse-ch'eng.   Gassner
Romance of the Rose, The.
Guillaume de Lorris and Jean
de Meun.   Haydn; Keller
Romance of the Three Kingdoms.
Lo Kuan-chung.   Magill III,
CE, M1&2, MC, MEUF
Romance of the Tuileries, A.
Francis Gribble.   Kaye
Romance of Two Worlds, A.
Marie Corelli.   Johnson
Romance of Youth, A.   François
Coppée.   Johnson
Romancero, The.   Unknown.
Haydn
Romances of the East.   Count
Joseph Arthur de Gobineau.
Keller
Romanesques, Les see Roman-
cers, The
Romanoff and Juliet.   Peter Us-
tinov.   Drury; Kienzle; Matlaw;
NCTE
Romantic Adventures of a Milk-
maid, The.   Thomas Hardy.
Pinion
Romantic Age, The.   A. A.
Milne.   Drury
Romantic Comedians, The.   Ellen
Glasgow.   Keller suppl.; Magill
I, CE, M1&2, MAF, MC
Romantic Egoists, The.   Louis
Auchincloss.   Magill '54, S
Romantic Revolution in America,
The.   Vernon Louis Parrington.
Keller suppl.
Romantic Young Lady, The.
Gregorio Martínez-Sierra.
Drury; Haydn; Sobel
Romany Rye, The.   George Henry
Borrow.   Keller (Lavengro);
Magill I, CE, M1&2, MC,
MEF
Rome Haul.   Walter D. Edmonds.
Magill I, CE, M1&2, MAF,
MC
Rome n'est plus dans Rome (Rome
Is No Longer in Rome).   Gab-
riel Marcel.   Kienzle
Romeo and Jeannette (Fading Man-
sions).   Jean Anouilh.   Drury;
Kienzle
Romeo and Juliet.   William Shake-
speare.   (See also adaptation

West Side Story by Arthur
Laurents et al.) Campbell;
Cartmell; Chute; Clark; Drury;
Gassner; Guerber-ST; Halliday;
Haydn; Keller; Lamb; Mc-
Cutchan-ST; McSpadden S;
Magill I, CE, M1&2, MC,
MD; NBC 3; Ruoff; Shank;
Shipley; Sobel; Wilson
Romola. George Eliot. Good-
man; Grozier; Halperin; Haydn;
Johnson; Kaye; Keller; Magill
I, CE, M1&2, MC, MEF
Romulus the Great. Friedrich
Dürrenmatt. Gassner; Kienzle;
Matlaw
Ronde, La see Hands Around
Roof of Tiger Lilies, A. Donald
Hall. Magill '65, S
Rookery Nook. Ben Travers.
French
Room, The. Harold Pinter.
French
Room at the Top. John Braine.
Magill IV, '58, M1, MB,
MC, S; Ward
Room for One More. William
Davidson. (Based on the novel
by Anna Perrott Rose Wright.)
Drury; NCTE
Room for One More. Anna Per-
rott Rose Wright. (See adap-
tation by William Davidson.)
Room of One's Own, A. Virginia
Woolf. Stade p. 180
Room Service. John Murray and
Allen Boretz. Drury
Room with a View, A. E. M.
Forster. Heiney; Magill III,
CE, M1&2, MC, MEF; Stade
p. 246; Ward
Roomful of Roses, A. Edith
Sommer. Drury; NCTE
Roosevelt and Churchill, 1939-
1941. Joseph P. Lash.
Magill '77
Roosevelt Family of Sagamore
Hill, The. Hermann Hage-
dorn. Magill '54, S
Roosevelt Leadership, 1933-1945,
The. Edgar Eugene Robin-
son. Magill '55, S
Roosevelt: The Lion and the Fox.
James MacGregor Burns.
Magill '57, S
Roosevelt: The Soldier of Free-
dom. James MacGregor
Burns. Magill '71

Root-Cutters, The. Sophocles.
Hathorn
Roots. Alex Haley. Magill '77
Roots. Arnold Wesker. Ander-
son; Kienzle; Matlaw; Shank
Roots of American Communism,
The. Theodore Draper.
Magill '58, S
Roots of Heaven, The. Romain
Gary. Magill '59, M1, S
Rope, The see Rudens
Rope (Rope's End). Patrick Ham-
ilton. Drury; French; NCTE
Rope, The. Eugene O'Neill.
Matlaw
Rope Dancers, The. Morton
Wishengrad. Best '57; NCTE;
Shank
Rory O'More. Samuel Lover.
Keller; Magill II, CE, M1&2,
MC, MEF
Rosalynde, or Euphues' Golden
Legacy. Thomas Lodge.
Ruoff
Rosary, The. Florence L. Bar-
clay. Keller
Rose, The. Charles L. Harness.
Magill SF
Rose-Agathe (Theodolinde). Henry
James. Gale-J
Rose and Ninette. Alphonse Dau-
det. Johnson
Rose and the Cross, The. Alek-
sandr Aleksandrovich Blok.
Matlaw; Shipley
Rose and the Ring, The. William
Makepeace Thackeray. Keller;
Mudge
Rose Bernd. Gerhart Hauptmann.
Matlaw; Sobel
Rose Farmer, The. Herman
Melville. Gale-M
Rose Marie. Herbert Stothart
and Rudolf Friml, Otto Harbach
and Oscar Hammerstein II.
Drinkrow
Rose Mervyn. Ann Beale. Kaye
Rose of Persia, The. Arthur
Sullivan and Basil Hood.
Drinkrow
Rose of the Garden. Katharine
Tynan. Kaye
Rose of the Rancho, The. David
Belasco and R. W. Tully.
Drury
Rose of the World, The. Agnes
and Edgerton Castle. Keller
Rose-Spinner, The. Mary Deane.

Kaye
Rose Tattoo, The. Tennessee
Williams. Best '50; Bonin;
Kienzle; Matlaw; NCTE
Rose Without a Thorn, The.
Clifford Bax. French
Rosemary. Louis Napoleon
Parker and Murray Carson.
Drury
Rosencrantz and Guildenstern Are
Dead. Tom Stoppard. Best
'67; Drury; Kienzle; Magill
'68, M1, S; Matlaw; NCTE
Rosmersholm. Henrik Ibsen.
French; Keller; Magill II,
CE, M1&2, MC, MD; Mat-
law; Shank; Shipley; Sobel
Ross. Terence Rattigan. Mat-
law; NCTE
Ross and Tom. John Leggett.
Magill '75
Rossiters, The. Kenneth Hyde.
French
Rossum's Universal Robots see
R. U. R.: Rossum's Univer-
sal Robots
Rothschilds, The. Frederic Mor-
ton. (See also adaptation by
Sherman Yellen et al.) Magill
'63, M1, S
Rothschilds, The. Sherman
Yellen, Sheldon Harnick and
Jerry Bock. (Based on the
book by Frederic Morton.)
NCTE
Rotters, The. H. F. Maltby.
French
Rough Hewn. Dorothy Canfield
Fisher. Keller suppl.
Roughing It. Mark Twain.
Gale-T; Keller; Magill I, CE,
M1&2, MAL5; MC, MNF
Rougon-Macquart, The. Emile
Zola. Haydn; Keller
Round of Visits, A. Henry
James. Gale-J
Roundabout Papers, The. Wil-
liam Makepeace Thackeray.
Keller
Roundheads and the Peakheads,
The. Bertolt Brecht and
Hanns Eisler. Matlaw
Rounding the Horn. David R.
Slavitt. Magill '79
Rousseau and Revolution. Will
and Ariel Durant. Magill '68,
S
Rout of the Foreigner, The.

Gulielma Zollinger. Kaye
"Rover, The. " Joseph Conrad.
Keller suppl.
Rowley Poems, The. Thomas
Chatterton. Haydn
Roxana. Daniel Defoe. Haydn;
Johnson-18th; Magill II, CE,
M1&2, MC, MEF
Roxy. Edward Eggleston. Kaye
Roy. Agnes Giberne. Kaye
Royal Family, The. George S.
Kaufman and Edna Ferber.
Best '27; Drury; Matlaw; NCTE;
Sobel
Royal Flash. George McDonald
Fraser. Magill '71
Royal Gambit. Hermann Gres-
sieker. Drury
Royal Hunt of the Sun, The.
Peter Shaffer. Best '65;
Drury; Kienzle; Magill '66, S;
NCTE
Royal Pawn of Venice, The.
Mrs. Lawrence Turnbull.
Kaye
Royal Road to Romance, The.
Richard Halliburton. Keller
suppl.
Royal Sister, The. Frank Mathew.
Kaye
Royo County. Robert Roper.
Magill '74
Royston Gower. Thomas Miller.
Kaye
Ruan. Winifred Bryher. Magill
'61, S
Rubáiyát of Omar Khayyám, The.
Edward FitzGerald. Haydn;
Magill III, M1, MC, MP
Rubáiyát of Omar Khayyám, The.
Unknown. Keller
Rückkehr von Elba (Return from
Elba). Daniel Christoff.
Kienzle
Rudder Grange. Frank R. Stock-
ton. Keller
Ruddigore. William Schwenck
Gilbert and Arthur Sullivan.
Shipley
Rudens (The Rope). Titus Mac-
cius Plautus. Feder (Rope);
Gassner; Hathorn; Reinhold;
Shipley (Rope)
Rudin. Ivan Turgenev. Berry-1;
Haydn; Keller (Dmitri Roudin)
Rudolph of Rosenfeldt. John W.
Spear. Kaye
Rugged Path, The. Robert E.

The Texts of Confucianism.
Unknown. Keller (Sacred Books)
Sacred Books of China, The.
The Texts of Tâoism. Un-
known. Keller (Sacred Books)
Sacred Books of the East, The.
Max Müller, editor. Haydn;
Keller
Sacred Flame, The. W. Somer-
set Maugham. French; Mat-
law; Sobel
Sacred Fount, The. Henry James.
Gale-J; Magill IV, MAL3, MC
Sacred Laws of the Aryas, The.
Unknown. Keller (Sacred
Books)
Sacred Wood: Essays on Poetry
and Criticism, The. T. S.
Eliot. Magill IV, MC
Sacrifice. Rabindranath Tagore.
Matlaw
Sad Fortunes of the Rev. Amos
Barton, The. George Eliot.
Halperin
Sad Shepherd; or, A Tale of
Robin Hood, The. Ben Jon-
son. Sobel
Saddharm-pundarīka; or, The
Lotus of the True Law.
Keller (Sacred Books)
Sadness. Donald Barthelme.
Magill '73
Sagan om den stora datamaskine.
Olof Johannesson. Magill SF
Saikaku Gonin Onna (Saikaku's
Five Women). Ibara Saikaku.
Halford
Sailing into the Unknown: Yeats,
Pound, and Eliot. M. L.
Rosenthal. Magill '79
Sailor, The. John Collis Snaith.
Keller suppl.
"Sailor Beware!" Philip King
and Falkland L. Cary. French
Sailor, Sense of Humour, and
Other Stories, The. V. S.
Pritchett. Magill '57, S
Sailors of Cattaro. Friedrich
Wolf. Sobol
Saint, The. Antonio Fogazzaro.
Haydn; Johnson; Keller; Magill
II, CE, M1&2, MC, MEUF
St. Bartholomew's Eve. George
A. Henty. Kaye
Saint Bartholomew's Night.
Philippe Erlanger. Magill
'63, S
Saint Caedmon. Unknown.

Keller (Caedmon)
St. Columba and the River
(Glory Be! McGlathery).
Theodore Dreiser. Gerber
Saint Francis. Nikos Kazantzakis.
Magill '63, M1, S
St. Francis of Assisi. Gilbert
Keith Chesterton. Magill CAL
Saint Francis of Assisi. Johannes
Jörgensen. Magill CAL
Saint Francis Xavier. James
Brodrick, S. J. Magill CAL
Saint Genest (The True St. Gene-
sius). Jean Rotrou. Gassner
St. Helena. Robert Cedric Sher-
riff and Jeanne de Casalis.
Best '36; Drury
St. Ives. Robert Louis Steven-
son. Johnson
Saint Jack. Paul Theroux. Ma-
gill '74
Saint Joan. George Bernard Shaw.
Drury; Gassner; Hardwick;
Haydn; Heiney; Keller suppl.;
Magill III, M1, MC, MD; Mat-
law; NCTE; Shank; Shipley;
Sobel; Sprinchorn; Ward
Saint Joan of the Stockyards.
Bertolt Brecht. Matlaw
St. Leger. Richard Burleigh
Kimball. Johnson
Saint of Bleecker Street, The.
Gian-Carlo Menotti. Chapman
'55
St. Peter's Complaint. Robert
Southwell. Ruoff p. 402
St. Peter's Umbrella. Kálmán
Mikszáth. Magill III, CE,
M1&2, MC, MEUF
St. Ronan's Well. Sir Walter
Scott. Johnson; McSpadden W;
Magill III, CE, M1&2, MC,
MEF
Sainte-Beuve. Sir Harold Nicol-
son. Magill '58, S
Saints and Sinners. Henry Arthur
Jones. Matlaw
Saint's Day. John Whiting.
Kienzle; Shank
Saints' Everlasting Rest, The.
Richard Baxter. Magill CHL
Saison au Congo, Une (A Season
in the Congo). Aimé Césaire.
Kienzle
Sakuntala. Kalidasa. Drury;
Gassner (Shakuntala); Haydn;
Magill II, CE, M1&2, MC,
MD; Shank; Shipley (Shakuntala);

Sobel; Thomas

Sal Si Puedes. Peter Matthiessen. Magill '71

Salad see Moretum

Salad Days. Julian Slade and Dorothy Reynolds. Drinkrow

Salammbô. Gustave Flaubert. Haydn; Johnson; Kaye; Keller; Magill I, CE, M1&2, MC, MEUF; Olfson

Salar the Salmon. Henry Williamson. Magill IV, MC

Salathiel. George Croly. Johnson

Salem Chapel. Margaret Wilson Oliphant. Johnson

Salem Possessed. Paul Boyer and Stephen Nissenbaum. Magill '75

Salerno. Hugh Pond. Magill '63, S

Sally. Jerome Kern, Victor Herbert, Guy Bolton and Clifford Grey. Drinkrow

Salomé. Oscar Wilde. Haydn; Matlaw; Shipley; Sobel

Salvation. Peter Link and C. C. Courtney. Best '69

Salvation Nell. Edward Sheldon. Keller; Matlaw; Sobel

Salvation, 1944-1946. Charles de Gaulle. Magill '61, M1, S

Salve see Hail and Farewell

Salzburg Great Theatre of the World, The. Hugo von Hofmannsthal. Matlaw

Sam Ego's House. William Saroyan. Drury

Same Time, Next Year. Bernard Slade. Best '74; Drury

Samia see Girl from Samos, The

Samson Agonistes. John Milton. Haydn; Magill III, CE, M1&2, MC, MD; Ruoff; Shipley

Samson the Athlete see Samson Agonistes

Samuel Beckett. Deirdre Bair. Magill '79

Samuel Brohl and Company. Victor Cherbuliez. Johnson; Keller

Samuel Gompers and Organized Labor in America. Harold C. Livesay. Magill '79

Samuel Johnson. Joseph Krutch Wood. Haydn (a)

Samuel Johnson: A Biography.

John Wain. Magill '76

Samuel Sewall and the World He Lived In. N. H. Chamberlain. Keller (Sewall)

Samuel Taylor Coleridge. James Dyke Campbell. Keller (Coleridge)

San Kuo Chih. Lo Kuan-chung. Haydn

San Toy. Sidney Jones, Edward Morton, Harry Greenbank and Adrian Ross. Drinkrow

Sanatorium Under the Sign of the Hourglass. Bruno Schulz. Magill '79

Sanctuary. Theodore Dreiser. Gerber

Sanctuary. William Faulkner. Armstrong; Haydn; Heiney; Magill I, CE, M1&2, MAF, MC; Morehead; Olfson

Sand Pebbles, The. Richard McKenna. Magill '64, M1, S

Sandford and Merton. Thomas Day. Keller; Magill II, CE, M1&2, MC, MEF

Sanditon. Jane Austen. Halperin

"Sandman, The." Ernst Theodor Amadeus Hoffmann. Magill SF

Sandoval: A Romance of Bad Manners. Thomas Beer. Keller suppl.

Sandra Belloni. George Meredith. Keller

Sands of Dunkirk, The. Richard Collier. Magill '62, S

Sandy. Alice Hegan Rice. Keller

Sanine. Mikhail Artsybashev. Haydn; Heiney; Magill III, CE, M1&2, MC, MEUF

Sannin Kichiza Kuruwa no Hatsugai (Three Men Called Kichiza). Kawatake Mokuami. Halford

Sanreizan Hiroku. Ryo Hanmura. Magill SF

Santa Claus. E. E. Cummings. Kienzle

Santa Cruz. Max Frisch. Kienzle

Santaroga Barrier, The. Frank Herbert. Magill SF

Sapphira and the Slave Girl. Willa Cather. Haydn (a)

Sappho. Alphonse Daudet. Goodman; Haydn; Johnson; Magill I, CE, M1&2, MC

Sappho. Lawrence Durrell.

Kienzle
Sappho. Franz Grillparzer.
Drury; Gassner; Magill III,
CE, M1&2, MC, MD, MEUF
Saragossa. Benito Pérez Galdós.
Johnson; Keller; Magill II,
CE, M1&2, MC, MEUF
Sarah Bernhardt and Her World.
Joanna Richardson. Magill
'78
Sarchedon. George John White
Melville. Kaye
Sard Harker. John Masefield.
Keller suppl.
Sartor Resartus. Thomas Car-
lyle. Haydn; Keller; Magill
III, M1, MC, MNF
Sartoris. William Faulkner.
Haydn (Faulkner); Magill IV,
MC
Sashka Jigouleff. Leonid N.
Andreyev. Keller suppl.
Satana dei Miracoli. Ugo Mala-
guti. Magill SF
Satanstoe. James Fenimore
Cooper. Johnson; Magill III,
CE, M1&2, MAF, MC;
Walker
Satapatha-Brahmana, The. Un-
known. Keller (Sacred Books)
Satin Slipper, The. Paul Claudel.
Gassner; Matlaw; Sprinchorn
Satires. Nicholas Boileau-
Despréaux. Magill IV, MC
Satires. Horace. Downs M;
Feder; Haydn
Satires. Juvenal. Downs F;
Feder; Haydn; Magill III, M1,
MC, MP
Satires. Lucian of Samosata.
Magill IV, MC
Satires. Persius. Feder
Satires I-V. John Donne.
Ruoff p. 371
Satiromastix. Thomas Dekker.
Keller; Magill III, CE, M1&2,
MC, MD; Ruoff; Shipley; Sobel
Satsunuma Akayu no Tsumari
kawatake Mokuami. Halford
Saturday Night. Jacinto Bena-
vente y Martínez. Haydn;
Matlaw; Shipley
Saturday Night and Sunday Morning.
Alan Sillitoe. Magill '60, M1,
S
Saturday Night at the Crown.
Walter Greenwood. French
Saturday's Children. Maxwell

Anderson. Best '26; Drury;
Keller suppl.; Matlaw; Shipley
Satyricon, The. Gaius Petronius.
Feder; Haydn; Magill II, CE,
M1&2, MC, MEUF
Saul. Count Vittorio Alfieri.
Drury; Haydn; Shipley
Saul of Tarsus. Elizabeth Miller.
Kaye
Saurus. Eden Phillpotts. Magill
SF
Savage God, The. A. Alvarez.
Magill '73
Savage Mind, The. Claude Lévi-
Strauss. Magill Ss
Savage State, The. Georges
Conchon. Magill '66, S
Save Every Lamb. Jesse Stuart.
Magill '65, S
Saved. Edward Bond. Anderson;
Kienzle
Savez-vous planter les choux?
(Do You Know How to Plant
Cabbages?). Marcel Achard.
Kienzle
Saving Grace, The. C. Haddon
Chambers. Drury
'Savonarola' Brown. Max Beer-
bohm. Ward
Saxby. Emma Leslie. Kaye
Scale of Perfection, The. Walter
Hilton. Magill CHL
Scandal in Bohemia, A. Sir
Arthur Conan Doyle. Hardwick
SH
Scandalous Affair of Mr. Kettle
and Mrs. Moon, The. J. B.
Priestley. French; Kienzle
Scapino. Frank Dunlop and Jim
Dale. (Based on Les Four-
beries de Scapin by Molière.)
Drury
Scarecrow, The. Percy MacKaye.
Drury; Lovell; Matlaw; Shank;
Shipley; Sobel
Scarlet Cloak, The. Aubrey De
Haven. Kaye
Scarlet Coat, The. Clinton Ross.
Kaye
Scarlet Letter, The. Nathaniel
Hawthorne. Armstrong; Gale-
H; Goodman; Grozier; Haydn;
Johnson; Keller; Lass AN;
Magill I, CE, M1&2, MAF,
MAL2, MC; Morehead; Smith;
Wilson
Scarlet Pimpernel, The. Baroness
Orczy. Ward

Magill II, CE, M1&2, MC,
MEF
Scottish History of James IV, The
see James the Fourth
Scott's Last Expedition. Captain
Robert Falcon Scott. Keller;
Magill IV, MC
Scottsboro. Dan T. Carter.
Magill '70
Scoundrel Time. Lillian Hellman.
Magill '77
Scourge of God, The. John Ed-
ward Bloundelle-Burton. Kaye
Scourge of Simony, The see
Parnassus Plays, The
Scourge of Villainy, The. John
Marston. Ruoff p. 371
Scouring of the White Horse,
The. Thomas Hughes. Keller
Scout Toward Aldie, The. Herman
Melville. Gale-M
Scouting for a King. Ernest
Protheroe. Kaye
Scouting for Buller. Herbert
Hayens. Kaye
Scouting for Light Horse Harry.
John P. True. Kaye
Scouting for Washington. John P.
True. Kaye
Scrap of Paper, A. Victorien
Sardou. Drury; Matlaw; Shank;
Shipley
Scrapegrace Dick. Frances M.
Peard. Kaye
Scratch. Archibald MacLeish.
(Based on The Devil and Daniel
Webster by Stephen Vincent
Benét.) Drury
Screens, The (Les paravents).
Jean Genet. Anderson (Para-
vents); Best '71; Drury;
Gassner; Kienzle; Matlaw
Screwtape Letters, The. Clive
Staples Lewis. (See also
adaptation Dear Wormwood by
James Forsyth.) Magill CHL;
Ward
Scripture-Doctrine of the Trinity,
The. Samuel Clarke. Magill
CHL
Scrolls from the Dead Sea, The.
Edmund Wilson. Magill '55,
S
Scuba Duba. Bruce Jay Fried-
man. Best '67; Drury
Scylla's Metamorphosis. Thomas
Lodge. Ruoff
Scyrians, The. Euripides.

Hathorn
Scyrians, The. Sophocles.
Hathorn
Scythian Women, The. Sophocles.
Hathorn
Sea and Sardinia. D. H. Law-
rence. Ward
Sea and the Jungle, The. H. M.
Tomlinson. Magill III, CE,
M1&2, MC, MNF
Sea Devils, The. John Edward
Bloundelle-Burton. Kaye
Sea Dreamer, The. Gérard Jean-
Aubry. Magill '58, S
Sea Fights and Shipwrecks. Han-
son W. Baldwin. Magill '55,
S
Sea Gull, The see Seagull, The
Sea Horse, The. Edward J.
Moore. Best '73; Drury
Sea Lions, The. James Fenimore
Cooper. Johnson; Walker
Sea of Grass, The. Conrad Rich-
ter. Haydn; Magill I, CE,
M1&2, MAF, MC; Morehead
Sea Wolf, The. Jack London.
Grozier; Haydn (a); Heiney;
Johnson; Keller; Magill I, CE,
M1&2, MAF, MC; Smith
Seagull, The. Anton Chekhov.
Drury; French; Gassner (Sea
Gull); Haydn; Magill II, CE,
M1&2, MC, MD; Matlaw; NCTE;
Shank; Shipley; Sobel
Seamarks. St.-John Perse.
Magill IV, '59, MB, MC, S
Sean. Eileen O'Casey. Magill
'73
Séance and Other Stories, The.
Isaac Bashevis Singer. Magill
'69, S
Séances historiques de Genève.
Henry B. Wilson. Keller
(Essays and Reviews)
Search, The. C. P. Snow.
Magill '60, MB, S
Search for Captain Slocum, The.
Walter Magnes Teller. Magill
'57, S
Searchers, The. Alan LeMay.
Magill '54, S
Searching for the Ox. Louis
Simpson. Magill '77
Searching Satyrs, The see
Trackers, The
Searching Wind, The. Lillian
Hellman. Best '43
Seascape. Edward Albee. Best

'74; Drury; Magill '76
Season in Hell, A. Percy Knauth.
Magill '76
Season in Hell, A. Arthur Rim-
baud. Magill III, CE, M1&2,
MC, MP
Season in the Sun. Wolcott
Gibbs. Best '50; Drury
Seasonable Thoughts on the State
of Religion in New England.
Charles Chauncy. Magill CHL
Seasons, The. Aristophanes.
Hathorn
Seasons, The. James Thomson
(1700-1748). Haydn; Magill
IV, MC
Seat-Grabbers, The. Aristophanes.
Hathorn
Seat of Wisdom, The. Louis
Bouyer. Magill CAL
Seats of the Mighty, The. Sir
Gilbert Parker. Kaye; Keller
Sébastien. Henri Troyat.
Kienzle
Second Apology, The. Saint Jus-
tin Martyr. Magill CAL,
CHL
Second Blooming, The. W. L.
George. Keller
Second Chance. Louis Auchin-
closs. Magill '71
Second Choice, The. Theodore
Dreiser. Gerber
Second Empire, The. Philip
Guedalla. Keller suppl.
Second Flowering, A. Malcolm
Cowley. Magill '74
Second Generation. Howard
Fast. Magill '79
Second Man, The. S. N. Behr-
man. Drury; Matlaw; NCTE;
Sobel
Second Mrs. Tanqueray, The.
Arthur Wing Pinero. Cart-
mell; Drury; French; Haydn;
Keller; Magill II, CE, M1&2,
MC, MD; Matlaw; NBC 3;
Shank; Shipley; Sobel; Wilson
Second Shepherds' Play, The.
Unknown. Haydn; Magill II,
CE, M1&2, MC, MD; Shank;
Shipley (Shepherd's Play,
end section)
Second Skin. John Hawkes.
Magill '65, S
Second Stain, The. Sir Arthur
Conan Doyle. Hardwick SH
Second Threshold. Philip Barry.

Best '50; Drury; NCTE
Second to None. James Grant.
Kaye
Second Tree from the Corner,
The. E. B. White. Magill
'54, S
Second War of the Worlds, The.
Arkady and Boris Strugatsky.
Magill SF
Second World War, The. Winston
S. Churchill. Magill III, M1,
MC, MNF
Secret, The. Alba de Céspedes.
Magill '59, S
Secret Affairs of Mildred Wild,
The. Paul Zindel. Drury
Secret Agent, The. Joseph Con-
rad. Magill III, CE, M1&2,
MC, MEF; Stade p. 155; Ward
Secret Conversations of Henry
Kissinger, The. Matti Golan.
Magill '77
Secret Diary of Harold L. Ickes:
Volume II, The. Harold L.
Ickes. Magill '54, S
Secret of Heaven, The. Pär
Lagerkvist. Matlaw
Secret of Luca, The. Ignazio
Silone. Magill '59, S
Secret of the Guild, The. August
Strindberg. Matlaw
Secret Service. William Hooker
Gillette. Best '94; Drury;
Lovell; NBC 3; Shank; Shipley
Secret Sharer, The. Joseph Con-
rad. Heiney; Olfson; Ward
Secret Vengeance for Secret Insult.
Pedron Calderón de la Barca.
Gassner
Secret Woman, The. Eden Phill-
potts. Keller
Secrets of Polar Travel, The.
Rear Admiral Robert E. Peary.
Keller suppl.
Secular Song see Carmen Saecu-
lare
Seduction and Betrayal: Women
and Literature. Elizabeth Hard-
wick. Magill '75
Seduttore, Il (The Seducer). Diego
Fabbri. Kienzle
See How They Run. Philip King.
Drury; French
Seed, The. Pierre Gascar.
Magill '60, S
Seed and the Sower, The. Laur-
ens Van Der Post. Magill '64,
S

Seed Beneath the Snow, The.
Ignazio Silone. Heiney;
Magill '66, M1, S
Seed of Light. Edmund Cooper.
Magill SF
Seedling Stars, The. James
Blish. Magill SF
Seeds of Contemplation. Thomas
Merton. Magill CAL
Seeds of Tomorrow. Mikhail
Sholokhov. Heiney
Seedtime on the Cumberland.
Harriette Simpson Arnow.
Magill '61, S
Seelenwanderung (Transmigration
of Souls). Karl Wittlinger.
Kienzle
Seen and the Unseen at Stratford-
on-Avon, The. William Dean
Howells. Carrington
Segaki. David Stacton. Magill
'60, S
Segregation. Robert Penn War-
ren. Magill '57, S
Seidman and Son. Elick Moll.
NCTE
Seize the Day. Saul Bellow.
Magill Ss
Sejanus. Ben Jonson. Haydn;
Holzknecht; Magill III, CE,
M1&2, MC, MD; Ruoff
Sejanus His Fall see Sejanus
Select Party, A. Nathaniel Haw-
thorne. Gale-H
Selected and Collected Poems.
Bill Knott. Magill '78
Selected Letters. Baron Fried-
rich John von Hügel. Magill
CHL
Selected Letters of Conrad Aiken.
Conrad Aiken. Magill '79
Selected Letters of Dylan Thomas.
Dylan Thomas. Magill '67, S
Selected Letters of James Joyce.
James Joyce. Magill '76
Selected Letters of John O'Hara.
John O'Hara. Magill '79
Selected Letters of Malcolm
Lowry. Malcolm Lowry.
Magill '66, S
Selected Letters of Robert Frost.
Robert Frost. Magill '65,
M1, S
Selected Poems. A. R. Am-
mons. Magill '68, S
Selected Poems. Margaret At-
wood. Magill '79
Selected Poems. Joseph Brodsky.

Magill '75
Selected Poems. Austin Clarke.
Magill '77
Selected Poems. Rubén Darío.
Heiney; Magill '66, S
Selected Poems. Randall Jarrell.
Magill '55, S
Selected Poems. Robert Lowell.
Magill '77
Selected Poems. John Masefield.
Magill '79
Selected Poems. Thomas Merton.
Magill '68, S
Selected Poems. John Crowe
Ransom. Heiney; Magill III,
M1, MC, MP, Ss
Selected Poems. Louis Simpson.
Magill '66, S
Selected Poems. Robert Watson.
Magill '75
Selected Poems: New and Old
1923-1966. Robert Penn War-
ren. Magill '67, S
Selected Poems: 1944-1970.
Gwendolyn Brooks. Magill Ss
Selected Poems: 1928-1958.
Stanley Kunitz. Magill Ss
Selected Poems, 1923-1975.
Robert Penn Warren. Magill
'78
Selected Poems 1923-1967. Jorge
Luis Borges. Magill '73
Selected Stories. Nadine Gordi-
mer. Magill '77
Selected Stories. V. S. Pritchett.
Magill '79
Selected Tales. Nikolai Leskov.
Magill '62, S
Selected Writings on the Spiritual
Life. Saint Peter Damian.
Magill CHL
Self Analysis. Karen Horney.
Haydn (a)
Self Condemned. Wyndham Lewis.
Magill '55, S
Self-Help. Samuel Smiles.
Keller
Self Tormons, The. Herondas.
Hathorn (a)
Self-Portrait in a Convex Mirror.
John Ashbery. Magill '76
Self-Tormentor, The. Terence.
Feder; Hathorn; Haydn; Magill
III, CE, M1&2, MC, MD;
Reinhold; Shank; Shipley
Semi-Detached. David Turner.
Kienzle
Seminole: A Drama of the Florida

adaptation Pajama Game by
George Abbott, et al.)
Seven Books of History Against
the Pagans. Paulus Orosius.
Magill CAL, CHL
Seven Champions of Christen-
dom, The. Richard Johnson.
Keller
Seven Deadly Sins of the Petty
Bourgeois, The. Bertolt
Brecht and Kurt Weill. Mat-
law
Seven Epistles of Ignatius, The.
Saint Ignatius, Bishop of
Antioch. Magill CHL
Seven Gothic Tales. Isak Dine-
sen. Magill III, M1, MC,
MEUF
Seven Islands, The. Jon Godden.
Magill '57, S
Seven Keys to Baldpate. George
M. Cohan. Best '09; Drury;
Matlaw; NCTE; Shipley; Sobel
Seven Knights, The. Marion
Fox. Kaye
Seven Lamps of Architecture,
The. John Ruskin. Haydn;
Keller
Seven Men. Max Beerbohm.
Ward
Seven Men Among the Penguins.
Mario Marret. Magill '55, S
Seven-Per-Cent Solution, The.
Nicholas Meyer. Magill '75
Seven Pillars of Wisdom. T. E.
Lawrence. Haydn; Magill III,
M1, MC, MNF; Ward
Seven Plays. Bertolt Brecht.
Magill '62, MB, S
Seven Poor Travellers, The.
Charles Dickens. Hardwick
CD
Seven Short Plays. Lady (Isabella
Augusta) Gregory. Magill III,
M1, MC, MD
Seven Storey Mountain, The.
Thomas Merton. Magill CAL
Seven Vagabonds, The. Nathaniel
Hawthorne. Gale III
Seven Who Fled, The. Frederic
Prokosch. Magill II, CE,
M1&2, MAF, MC
Seven Who Were Hanged, The.
Leonid N. Andreyev. Haydn;
Heiney; Keller; Magill II,
CE, M1&2, MC, MEUF
Seven Year Itch, The. George
Axelrod. Chapman '53;

Drury; NCTE
Seven Years in Tibet. Heinrich
Harrer. Magill '54, S
Sevenoaks. Josiah Gilbert Hol-
land. Johnson
Seventeen. Hugh Stange. Sobel
Seventeen. Booth Tarkington.
Drury (drama); Keller; Magill
I, CE, M1&2, MAF, MC; NCTE
1776. Peter Stone and Sherman
Edwards. Best '68; NCTE
1776 and All That. Leonard Wib-
berley. Drury
Seventh Heaven. Austin Strong.
Drury
77 Dream Songs. John Berryman.
Magill '65, S
73 Poems. E. E. Cummings.
Magill '64, S
Severa. Eva Hartner. Johnson
Severed Head, A. Iris Murdoch.
Drury; Magill '62, S
Sexe et le néant, Le (Sex and
Nothingness). Thierry Maul-
nier. Kienzle
Sexual Behavior in the Human
Male. Dr. Alfred C. Kinsey,
Dr. Wardell B. Pomeroy and
Dr. Clyde E. Martin. Haydn
Sexual Politics. Kate Millett.
Magill '71
Sforza. William Waldorf Astor.
Johnson
Sganarelle. Molière. French
Shabby-Genteel Story, A. Wil-
liam Makepeace Thackeray.
Johnson; Mudge
Shade-Seller: New and Selected
Poems, The. Josephine Jacob-
sen. Magill '75
Shadow, The (Jealousy: Nine
Women Out of Ten). Theodore
Dreiser. Gerber
Shadow, The. Yevgeni Lvovich
Shvarts. Matlaw
Shadow - A Parable. Edgar Allan
Poe. Gale-PP
Shadow and Act. Ralph Ellison
Magill '64, S
Shadow and Substance. Paul Vin-
cent Carroll. Best '37; Drury;
French; Gassner; Heiney; Mat-
law; NCTE; Shank; Shipley;
Sobel
Shadow Box, The. Michael Cris-
tofer. Best '76; Magill '78
Shadow in the Sun. Maurice Mc-
Loughlin. French

SHADOW   254

Shadow Knows, The. David Mad-
  den. Magill '71
Shadow Line, The. Joseph Con-
  rad. Keller suppl.; Stade
  p. 160
Shadow of a Dream, The. Wil-
  liam Dean Howells. Carring-
  ton
Shadow of a Gunman, The. Sean
  O'Casey. Drury; French;
  Gassner; Matlaw; NCTE; Shank
Shadow of Dante, A. Maria
  Francesca Rossetti. Keller
  (Dante)
Shadow of Doubt, The. Norman
  King. French
Shadow of Heroes see Stone
  and Star
Shadow of Night, The. George
  Chapman. Magill IV, MC;
  Ruoff
Shadow of the Eagle. Ronald
  Cockram. French
Shadow of the Sword, The.
  Robert Buchanan. Kaye
Shadow of the Winter Palace,
  The. Edward Crankshaw.
  Magill '77
Shadow Witness, The. Falkland
  L. Cary and Philip Weathers.
  French
Shadows in the Sun. Chad Oliver.
  Magill SF
Shadows on the Grass. Isak
  Dinesen. Magill '62, M1, S
Shadows on the Rock. Willa
  Cather. Magill I, CE,
  M1&2, MAF, MC
Shah-Nameh. Firdusi. Fleming;
  Haydn
Shaker Bridal, The. Nathaniel
  Hawthorne. Gale-II
Shakes Versus Shav. George
  Bernard Shaw. Hardwick;
  Matlaw
Shakespeare and Company.
  Sylvia Beach. Magill '60, S
Shakespeare dringend gesucht
  (Shakespeare Wanted Urgently).
  Heinar Kipphardt. Kienzle
Shakespeare's Sonnets see
  Sonnets of Shakespeare, The
Shakuntala see Sakuntala
Shallow Soil. Knut Hamsun.
  Keller
Shamela. Henry Fielding.
  Johnson-18th/2
Shan Van Vocht, The. James

  Murphy. Kaye
Shanghai Gesture, The. John
  Colton. Drury
Shannons of Broadway, The.
  James Gleason. Drury
Shape of Things to Come, The.
  H. G. Wells. Magill SF
Shattered Peace. Daniel H. Yer-
  gin. Magill '78
Shaughraun, The. Dion Bouci-
  cault. Cartmell; Shipley; Sobel
She. Henry Rider Haggard.
  Johnson; Keller; Magill I, CE,
  M1&2, MC, MEF, SF
She Loved a Sailor. Amelia
  Edith Barr. Kaye
She Loves Me. Howard Lindsay.
  Drury
She Loves Me. Joe Masteroff,
  Jerry Bock and Sheldon Harnick.
  Best '62
She Stoops to Conquer. Oliver
  Goldsmith. Cartmell; Drury;
  Gassner; Haydn; Keller; Magill
  I, CE, M1&2, MC, MD; NBC
  2; Shank; Shipley; Sobel;
  Thomas; Wilson
She That Hesitates. Harris Dick-
  son. Haydn; Kaye
She Who Was Shorn see Shear-
  ing of Glycera, The
She-Wolf, The. Maxime Formont.
  Kaye
She-Wolves of Machecoul, The.
  Alexandre Dumas (father).
  Kaye
She Would Be a Soldier. Morde-
  cai Manuel Noah. Lovell
Shearing of Glycera, The (Peri-
  keiromene). Menander. Feder
  (Perikeiromene); Hathorn
  (Perikeiromene); Reinhold
Sheep Look Up, The. John Brun-
  ner. Magill SF
Sheep Well, The. Lope Félix de
  Vega Carpio. Drury; Haydn;
  Magill II, CE, M1&2, MC,
  MD; Shank
SheLa. Aubrey Menen. Magill
  '63, S
Shelburne Essays. Paul Elmer
  More. Keller; Magill IV, MC
Shelley, His Life and Work,
  1792-1820. Walter Edwin
  Peck. Keller suppl.
Sheltered Life, The. Ellen Glas-
  gow. Magill I, CE, M1&2,
  MAF, MC

Shenandoah. Bronson Howard.
Drury; Keller; Shipley; Sobel
Shepheardes Calendar, The.
Edmund Spenser. Haydn;
Magill IV, MC
Shepherd, The. Hermas.
Magill CAL, CHL
Shepherds, The. Sophocles.
Hathorn
Shepherd's Calendar, The see
Shepheardes Calendar, The
Shepherd's Life: Impressions of
the South Wiltshire Downs, A.
William Henry Hudson. Ward
Shepherds of the Night. Jorge
Amado. Magill '67, S
Sheppey. W. Somerset Maugham.
Matlaw
Sherlock Holmes. Sir Arthur
Conan Doyle. Hardwick SH
(Adventures of . . .); Haydn;
Keller
Sherlock Holmes. William Hooker
Gillette. Cartmell; Drury
Sherwood. Alfred Noyes. Drury
Shewing-Up of Blanco Posnet:
A Sermon in Crude Melo-
drama, The. George Bernard
Shaw. Hardwick; Matlaw; Ward
Shibaraku (Wait a Moment).
Ichikawa Danjuro I. Halford
Shield of Achilles, The. Wystan
Hugh Auden. Magill '55, MB,
S
Shifting Heart, The. Richard
Beynon. French
Shih, The. Unknown. Keller
(Sacred Books)
Shih Ching, The. Confucius.
Magill III, M1, MC, MP
Shijo-Yuchip. Choi Nam-Sun,
editor. Haydn
Shimban Utazaemon (The Strolling
Minstrel's Song Book).
Chikamatsu Hanji. Halford
Shin Usuyuki Monogatari (The
Tale of Usuyuki). Takeda
Koizumo. Halford
Shining Hour, The. Keith Winter.
Best '33; Drury; Sobel
Shining Slave Makers, The see
McEwen of the Shining Slave
Makers
Shinju Tenno Amijima (The Love
Suicide at Amijima). Chika-
matsu Monzaemon. Gassner
(Love); Halford
Shinkei Kasane ga Fuchi (The

Music Mistress' Ghost). Un-
known. Halford
Shinobiyoru Koi wa Kusemono
(The Witch Princess). Un-
known. Halford
Shinrei Yaguchi no Watashi.
Hiraga Gennai. Halford
Shinsarayashiki Tsuki no Amagasa
(O Tsuta's Death). Kawatake
Mokuami. Halford
Ship, The. St. John G. Ervine.
Drury
Ship of Fools. Katherine Anne
Porter. Magill IV, '63, M1,
MC, S; Morehead
Ship Who Sang, The. Anne Mc-
Caffrey. Magill SF
Ships That Pass in the Night.
Beatrice Harraden. Keller
Shira, The. William C. Mac-
Kenzie. Kaye
Shirley. Charlotte Brontë.
Halperin; Haydn; Johnson; Kel-
ler; Magill III, CE, M1&2,
MC, MEF
Shockwave Rider, The. John
Brunner. Magill SF
Shoemakers, The (Szewcy).
Stanisław Ignacy Witkiewicz.
Anderson (Szewcy)
Shoemaker's Holiday, The (The
Gentle Craft). Thomas Dek-
ker. Cartmell; Drury; Gass-
ner; Haydn; Holzknecht; Keller;
Magill II, CE, M1&2, MC,
MD; Ruoff; Shank; Shipley;
Sobel
Shoemaker's Prodigious Wife, The.
Federico García Lorca. Drury
(García); Gassner; Heiney; Mat-
law; Shank; Sprinchorn
Shoes of Gold. Hamilton Drum-
mond. Kaye
Shoes of the Fisherman, The.
Morris L. West. Magill '64,
M1, S
Shogun. James Clavell. Magill
'76
Shoguns Daughter, The. Herbert
Ames Bennet. Kaye
Shojo (The Baboon). Unknown.
Halford
Shooting Star, A. Wallace Steg-
ner. Magill '62, S
Shop Girl, The. Ivan Caryll,
Adrian Ross, Lionel Monckton
and H. J. W. Dam. Drinkrow
Shore Acres. James A. Herne.

Drury; Shipley; Sobel
Shore Leave. R. P. Weston
and Bert Lee. (See adapta-
tion Hit the Deck by Vincent
Youmans.)
Short and Clear Exposition of
the Christian Faith, A. Ul-
rich Zwingli. Magill CHL
Short Eyes. Miguel Piñero.
Best '73; Drury; NCTE
Short Fiction of Arthur C. Clarke,
The. Arthur C. Clarke.
Magill SF
Short Fiction of Avram Davidson,
The. Avram Davidson.
Magill SF
Short Fiction of Dmitri Bilenkin,
The. Dmitri Bilenkin. Magill
SF
Short Fiction of Edmond Hamil-
ton, The. Edmond Hamilton.
Magill SF
Short Fiction of Fitz-James
O'Brien, The. Fitz-James
O'Brien. Magill SF
Short Fiction of Frederik Pohl,
The. Frederik Pohl. Magill
SF
Short Fiction of Fredric Brown,
The. Fredric Brown. Magill
SF
Short Fiction of Fritz Leiber,
Jr. , The. Fritz Leiber, Jr.
Magill SF
Short Fiction of Gennadiy
Samoilovich Gor, The.
Gennadiy Samoilovich Gor.
Magill SF
Short Fiction of H. G. Wells,
The. H. G. Wells. Magill
SF
Short Fiction of H. P. Love-
craft, The. H. P. Lovecraft.
Magill SF
Short Fiction of Harlan Ellison,
The. Harlan Ellison. Magill
SF
Short Fiction of Herman Mel-
ville, The. Herman Melville.
Magill SF
Short Fiction of J. G. Ballard,
The. J. G. Ballard. Magill
SF
Short Fiction of James Tiptree,
Jr. , The. James Tiptree,
Jr. Magill SF
Short Fiction of John W. Camp-
bell, Jr. , The. John W.

Campbell, Jr. Magill SF
Short Fiction of Jorge Luis
Borges, The. Jorge Luis
Borges. Magill SF
Short Fiction of Judith Merril,
The. Judith Merril. Magill
SF
Short Fiction of Kirill Bulychev,
The. Kirill Bulychev. Magill
SF
Short Fiction of Larry Niven, The.
Larry Niven. Magill SF
Short Fiction of Murray Leinster,
The. Murray Leinster. Ma-
gill SF
Short Fiction of Nathaniel Haw-
thorne, The. Nathaniel Haw-
thorne. Magill SF
Short Fiction of Ray Bradbury,
The. Ray Bradbury. Magill
SF
Short Fiction of Robert Sheckley,
The. Robert Sheckley. Magill
SF
Short Fiction of Rudyard Kipling,
The. Rudyard Kipling. Magill
SF
Short Fiction of Theodore Stur-
geon, The. Theodore Sturgeon.
Magill SF
Short Fiction of Thomas M. Disch,
The. Thomas M. Disch.
Magill SF
Short Fiction of William Tenn,
The. William Tenn. Magill
SF
Short Friday and Other Stories.
Isaac Bashevis Singer. Magill
'65, S
Short Happy Life of Francis Ma-
comber, The. Ernest Heming-
way. Heiney
Short History of French Litera-
ture, A. George Saintsbury.
Keller (French)
Short History of the English Peo-
ple. John Richard Green.
Haydn; Keller
Short Letter, Long Farewell.
Peter Handke. Magill '75
Short Novels of Thomas Wolfe,
The. Thomas Wolfe. Magill
Ss
Short Sixes. Henry Cuyler Bun-
ner. Haydn (a)
Short Stories of A. E. Coppard,
The. A. E. Coppard. Magill
IV, MC

Short Stories of D. H. Law-
rence, The. D. H. Law-
rence. Magill IV, MC
Short Stories of E. M. Forster,
The. E. M. Forster.
Magill IV, MC
Short Stories of Ernest Heming-
way, The. Ernest Hemingway.
Magill IV, MC
Short Stories of Eudora Welty,
The. Eudora Welty. Magill
IV, MC
Short Stories of Flannery O'Con-
nor, The. Flannery O'Con-
nor. Magill IV, MC
Short Stories of John Cheever,
The. John Cheever. Magill
IV, MC
Short Stories of John Updike,
The. John Updike. Magill
IV, MC
Short Stories of Katherine Mans-
field. Katherine Mansfield.
Magill III, M1, MC, MEF
Short Stories of O. Henry. O.
Henry. Magill III, M1,
MAF, MC
Short Stories of Peter Taylor,
The. Peter Taylor. Magill
IV, MC
Short Stories of Saki, The. Saki.
Magill IV, MC
Short Studies in Literature.
Hamilton Wright Mabie.
Keller (Essays ... Mabie)
Short Studies on Great Subjects.
James Anthony Froude.
Keller
Shorter Rules, The. Saint Basil.
Magill CHL
Shoscombe Old Place. Sir Arthur
Conan Doyle. Hardwick SH
Shosha. Isaac Bashevis Singer.
Magill '79
Shot in Question, The. Michael
Gilbert. French
Shot in the Dark, A. Marcel
Achard. Drury; Morehead
Shot into Infinity, The. Otto
Willi Gail. Magill SF
Shoutsushi Asagao Nikki (The
Diary of Morning Glory).
Chikamatsu Tokuso. Halford
Show Boat. Edna Ferber.
(See also adaptation by Oscar
Hammerstein II and Jerome
Kern.) Haydn; Keller suppl. ;
Morehead

Show Boat. Oscar Hammerstein
II and Jerome Kern. (Based
on the novel by Edna Ferber.)
Drinkrow; NCTE; Shipley
Show-Off, The. George Kelly.
Best '23; Drury; Keller suppl. ;
Matlaw; NCTE; Shank; Shipley;
Sobel
Show Shop, The. James Forbes.
Drury
Shred of Evidence, A. Robert
Cedric Sherriff. Drury; French
Shrike, The. Joseph Kramm.
Best '51; Bonin; Drury; NCTE
Shropshire Lad, A. A. E. Hous-
man. Haydn; Magill III, M1,
MC, MP
Shrovetide in Old New Orleans.
Ishmael Reed. Magill '79
Shuh, The. Unknown. Keller
(Sacred Books)
Shui Hu Chuan see All Men Are
Brothers
Shut In. Evelyn Everett Green.
Kaye
Shuttle, The. Frances Hodgson
Burnett. Keller
Sibyl, The. Pär Lagerkvist.
Magill '59, S
Sic et non. Peter Abelard.
Magill CAL
Sicilian Carousel. Lawrence Dur-
rell. Magill '78
Sicilian Limes. Luigi Pirandello.
Matlaw
Sicilian Vespers, The. Cassimir
Delavigne. Keller
Sick Fox, The. Paul Brodeur.
Magill '64, S
Sickles the Incredible. W. A.
Swanberg. Magill '57, S
Sickness of Youth. Ferdinand
Bruckner. Shipley
Sickness unto Death, The. Søren
Kierkegaard. Magill III, M1,
MC, MNF
Sie werden sterben, sire (You
Will Die, Sire). Leopold
Ahlsen. Kienzle
Siege at Peking, The. Peter
Fleming. Magill '60, S
Siege of Leed's Castle. Edwin
Harris. Kaye
Siege of London, The. Henry
James. Gale-J
Siege of Norwich Castle, The.
M. M. Blake. Kaye
Siege of Rhodes, The. Sir Wil-

liam Davenant. Magill III,
CE, M1&2, MC, MD
Siegfried. Jean Giraudoux. (Based
on his novel My Friend from
Limousin.) Matlaw; Shank;
Shipley
Sights from a Steeple. Nathaniel
Hawthorne. Gale-H
Sign in Sidney Brustein's Window,
The. Lorraine Hansberry.
Drury; Magill Ss
Sign of Four, The. Sir Arthur
Conan Doyle. Hardwick SH;
Magill II, CE, M1&2, MC,
MEF
Sign of Triumph, The. Sheppard
Stevens. Kaye
Signals from the Safety Coffin.
John Engels. Magill '76
Signor Io, Il. Salvatore Farina.
Keller
Signora Morli, One and Two.
Luigi Pirandello. Matlaw
Signpost to Murder. Monte Doyle.
French
Signs and Seasons. John Bur-
roughs. Keller
Signs, Language and Behavior.
Charles W. Morris. Magill
WP
Sigurd the Bastard. Bjørnstjerne
Bjørnson. Matlaw
Silanus the Christian. Edwin A.
Abbott. Kaye
Silas Marner. George Eliot.
Halperin; Haydn; Hix; Johnson;
Keller; Magill I, CE, M1&2,
MC, MEF; Olfson; Wilson
Silence - A Fable. Edgar Allan
Poe. Gale-PP
Silence in the Snowy Fields.
Robert Bly. Magill '63, S
Silence of Dean Maitland, The.
Maxwell Gray. Johnson;
Keller
Silence of Desire, A. Kamala
Markandaya. Magill '61, S
Silent Don, The. Mikhail Sholok-
hov. (Series title; see also
And Quiet Flows the Don and
The Don Flows Home to the
Sea.) Haydn
Silent Night, Lonely Night.
Robert Anderson. Drury
Silent Spring. Rachel Carson.
Magill '63, M1, S
Silent Storms. Ernest Poole.
Keller suppl.

Silent Woman, The. Ben Jonson.
Magill III, CE, M1&2, MC,
MD
Silken Eyes. Françoise Sagan.
Magill '78
Silmarillion, The. J. R. R.
Tolkien. Magill '78
Silver Blaze. Sir Arthur Conan
Doyle. Hardwick SH
Silver Box, The. John Gals-
worthy. Drury; Matlaw; Sobel;
Ward
Silver Cord, The. Sidney Howard.
Best '26; Drury; Keller suppl. ;
Lovell; Matlaw; NCTE; Shank;
Sobel
Silver King, The. Henry Arthur
Jones. Drury; NBC 1
Silver Maple, The. Marion Keith.
Kaye
Silver Skates, The see Hans
Brinker, or, The Silver Skates
Silver Soldier, The. Charles
Campbell Gairdner. French
Silver Spoon, The. John Gals-
worthy. (See also trilogy title
A Modern Comedy.) Heiney;
Keller suppl.
Silver Tassie, The. Sean O'Casey.
Gassner; Matlaw; Shank; Shipley
Silver Wedding. Michael Clayton
Hutton. French
Silver Whistle, The. Robert E.
McEnroe. Best '48; Drury;
NCTE
Sim-Chung-Chun. Unknown.
Haydn
Simon and Laura. Alan Melville.
French
Simon de Montfort. Edwin Harris.
Kaye
Simon Wheeler, Detective. Mark
Twain. Gale-T
Simoom. August Strindberg.
Matlaw
Simple Honorable Man, A. Con-
rad Richter. Magill IV, '63,
M1, MC, S
Simple Justice. Richard Kluger.
Magill '77
Simple Life, The. Charles Wag-
ner. Keller
Simple Story, A. Mrs. Elizabeth
(Simpson) Inchbald. Keller
Simple Takes a Wife. Langston
Hughes. (See his adaptation
Simply Heavenly.)
Simpleton, A. Charles Reade.

259 SIMPLETON

Johnson
Simpleton of the Unexpected Isles,
The. George Bernard Shaw.
Hardwick; Matlaw; Sprinchorn
Simplicissimus the Vagabond.
H. J. C. von Grimmelshausen.
Haydn; Magill II, CE, M1&2,
M1, MC, MEUF
Simply Heavenly. Langston
Hughes. (Based on his Simple
Takes a Wife.) NCTE
Sin of Joost Avelingh, The.
Maarten Maartens. Keller
Sincerely, Willis Wayde. John
P. Marquand. Magill '55,
M1, S
Sincerity and Authenticity. Lionel
Trilling. Magill '73
Sinclair Lewis. Mark Schorer.
Magill '62, MB, S
Sindbad the Sailor. Unknown.
Cohen
Sing to Me Through the Open
Windows. Arthur L. Kopit.
Kienzle
Singapore: The Japanese Version.
Colonel Masanobe Tsuji.
Magill '62, S
Singin' and Swingin' and Gettin'
Merry like Christmas. Maya
Angelou. Magill '77
Single Man, A. Hubert Henry
Davies. Drury
Single Pebble, A. John Hersey.
Magill '57, S
Singular Life, A. Elizabeth
Stuart Phelps. Keller
Singularities. John Simon.
Magill '77
Sinister Barrier. Eric Frank
Russell. Magill SF
Sinister Street. Compton Mac-
kenzie. Keller; Ward
Sinister Twilight, A. Noel
Barber. Magill '69, S
Sintram. Friedrich de La Motte-
Fouqué. Johnson
Sir Bengt's Wife. August Strind-
berg. Matlaw
Sir Charles Danvers. Mary
Cholmondeley. Keller (Dan-
vers)
Sir Charles Grandison. Samuel
Richardson. Haydn; Johnson;
Johnson-18th; Keller; Magill
III, CE, M1&2, MC, MEF
Sir Dominick Ferrand (Jersey
Villas). Henry James.

Gale-J
Sir Edmund Orme. Henry James.
Gale-J
Sir Gawain and the Green Knight.
Unknown. Magill II, CE, M1&2,
MC, MP; Haydn
Sir George Tressady. Mrs.
Humphry Ward. Keller
Sir Harry Hotspur of Humbleth-
waite. Anthony Trollope.
Gerould
Sir John van Olden Barnavelt.
John Fletcher and Philip Mas-
singer. Ruoff (Barnavelt);
Magill III, CE, M1&2, MC,
MD
Sir Launcelot Greaves. Tobias
George Smollett. Johnson;
Johnson-18th/2
Sir Nigel. Sir Arthur Conan
Doyle. Kaye; Keller
Sir Patrick Spens. Unknown.
Haydn
Sir Raoul. J. M. Ludlow. Kaye
Sir Roger de Coverley Papers,
The. Joseph Addison. Magill
III, M1, MC, MNF
Sir Thomas More, The Book of
see Book of Sir Thomas More,
The
Sir Walter Raleigh. A. L. Rowse.
Magill '63, S
Sir William. David Stacton.
Magill '64, S
Sirens of Titan, The. Kurt Vonne-
gut, Jr. Magill SF
Sirius: A Fantasy of Love and
Discord. Olaf Stapledon.
Magill SF
Sissie. John A. Williams.
Magill Ss
Sister Beatrice. Maurice Maeter-
linck. Shank
Sister Carrie. Theodore Dreiser.
Gerber; Haydn; Heiney; Lass
AN; Magill I, CE, M1&2, MAF,
MC; Morehead; Olfson
Sister Philomène. Edmond and
Jules de Goncourt. Magill III,
CE, M1&2, MC, MEUF
Sister to Evangeline, A. Charles
G. Roberts. Johnson; Kaye
Sister Years..., The. Nathaniel
Hawthorne. Gale-H
Sit Down a Minute, Adrian. Jevan
Brandon-Thomas. French
Six Books of the Republic, The.
Jean Bodin. Haydn; Magill CAL

SIX   260

Six Characters in Search of an
Author. Luigi Pirandello.
Cartmell; Drury; Heiney; Keller
suppl.; Magill III, CE, M1&2,
MC, MD; Matlaw; Shank; Ship-
ley; Sobel; Sprinchorn; Thomas
Six Cylinder Love. William Anthony
McGuire. Best '21
Six Napoleons, The. Sir Arthur
Conan Doyle. Hardwick SH
Six Notorious Street-Robbers,
The. Daniel Defoe. Johnson-
18th
Six of Calais, The. George
Bernard Shaw. Hardwick
Six of the Best. John and Jackie
Waterhouse. French
6 Rms Riv Vu. Bob Randall.
Best '72; Drury
Sketch Book, The. Washington
Irving. Haydn
Sketch of an Historical Picture
of the Progress of the Human
Mind. Jean Antoine Nicolas
Caritat Condorcet. Downs M;
Haydn
Sketches from Memory. Nathaniel
Hawthorne. Gale-H
Skin Game, The. John Galsworthy.
Best '20; Drury; Keller suppl.;
Matlaw; Sobel; Ward
Skin of Our Teeth, The. Thornton
Wilder. Best '42; Bonin;
Drury; French; Gassner; Haydn
p. 557; Heiney; Lass AP; Ma-
gill III, CE, M1&2, MC, MD;
Matlaw; NCTE; Shank; Shipley;
Sobel; Sprinchorn; Ward
Skipper Next to God. Jan de
Hartog. Best '47; Drury
Sky Pilot, The. Ralph Connor.
Johnson
Skylark, The. Ralph Hodgson.
Magill '61, S
Skylark. Samson Raphaelson.
Best '39; Drury
Skylark Series, The. Edward
E. Smith. Magill SF
Sky's the Limit. Arnold Helsby.
French
Skyward. Richard Evelyn Byrd.
Keller suppl.
Slammer. Ben Greer. Magill
'76
Slan. Alfred Elton Van Vogt.
Magill SF
Slapstick. Kurt Vonnegut.
Magill '77

Slaughterhouse-Five. Kurt Vonne-
gut, Jr. Magill '70, SF
Slave, The. Isaac Bashevis Sing-
er. Magill '63, S
Slave, The. LeRoi Jones. Drury
Slave of Truth, The. Miles Mal-
leson. (Based on the comedy
by Molière.) French
Slave of Truth, The. Molière.
(See adaptation by Miles Malle-
son.)
Slaves of Sabinus, Jew and Gen-
tile, The. Charlotte Mary
Yonge. Kaye
Sleep of Baby Filbertson, The.
James Leo Herlihy. Magill Ss
Sleep of Prisoners, A. Chris-
topher Fry. Kienzle; NCTE;
Shank
Sleepers Joining Hands. Robert
Bly. Magill '74
Sleeping Beauty. Unknown. Kel-
ler (Fairy Tales)
Sleeping Clergyman, A. James
Bridie. Drury; French; Mat-
law; Sobel
Sleeping in the Woods. David
Wagoner. Magill '75
Sleeping Prince, The. Terence
Rattigan. French; Kienzle
Sleepwalkers, The. Hermann
Broch. Magill II, CE, M1&2,
MC, MEUF
Sleepwalkers, The. Arthur Koest-
ler. Magill '60, S
Sleuth. Anthony Shaffer. Best
'70; Drury
Slight Accident, A. James
Saunders. Kienzle
Slight Ache, A. Harold Pinter.
French
Slipknot, The. Titus Maccius
Plautus. Magill III, CE, M1&2,
MC, MD
Slow Dance on the Killing Ground.
William Hanley. Best '64;
Drury; NCTE
Slub (The Wedding). Witold Gom-
browicz. Kienzle
Sly Fox. Larry Gelbart. (Based
on Volpone by Ben Jonson.)
Best '76
Small Craft Warnings. Tennessee
Williams. Best '71; Drury
Small Hotel. Rex Frost. French
Small House at Allington, The.
Anthony Trollope. Gerould;
Johnson; Magill II, CE, M1&2,

MC, MEF
Small Souls. Louis Marie Ann
Couperus. Magill III, CE,
M1&2, MC, MEUF
Small Town Tyrant (Professor
Unrat). Heinrich Mann.
Heiney
Small War on Murray Hill.
Robert E. Sherwood. Chapman
'57; Drury
Smallest of All. Sister Mary
Francis. Drury
Smith. W. Somerset Maugham.
Drury
Smith Brunt. Waldron K. Post.
Kaye
Smoke. Ivan Turgenev. Berry-1;
Haydn; Johnson; Magill I, CE,
M1&2, MC, MEUF
Smoke Bellew. Jack London.
Keller
Smug Citizens, The. Máxim
Górky. Matlaw; Shank
Snake Pit, The. Sigrid Undset.
Magill II, CE, M1&2, MC,
MEUF
Sneaky People. Thomas Berger.
Magill '76
Snob, Der (The Snob). Carl
Sternheim. Gassner (Pair of
Drawers); Matlaw; Shank
Snow-Bound. John Greenleaf
Whittier. Haydn; Hix; Magill
I, CE, M1&2, MAL5, MC,
MP; Smith
Snow Country. Yasunari Kawabata.
Magill '70
Snow-Image: A Childish Miracle,
The. Nathaniel Hawthorne.
Gale-H
Snow in Midsummer. Kuan Han-
ch'ing. Gassner
Snow Leopard, The. Peter
Matthiessen. Magill '79
Snow White. Donald Barthelme.
Magill '68, S
Snowflakes. Nathaniel Hawthorne.
Gale-H
Snows of Kilimanjaro, The.
Ernest Hemingway. Heiney
So Big. Edna Ferber. Keller
suppl.; Magill IV, MC
So Human an Animal. René
Dubos. Magill Ss
"So Many Children." Gerald
Savory. French
So Red the Rose. Laurence Stal-
lings, Maxwell Anderson and

Edwin Justin Mayer. Lovell
So Red the Rose. Stark Young.
Magill I, CE, M1&2, MAF,
MC
Social Contract, The. Robert
Ardrey. Magill '71
Social Contract, The. Jean
Jacques Rousseau. Armstrong;
Downs M, FG; Haydn; Keller;
Magill WP
Social Equality. William Hurrell
Mallock. Keller
Social Life in Greece from Homer
to Menander. Sir John Pentland
Mahaffy. Keller
Social Life in Old Virginia Before
the War. Thomas Nelson Page.
Keller
Social Life of the Chinese. Justus
Doolittle. Keller
Social Origins of Dictatorship and
Democracy. Barrington
Moore, Jr. Magill '67, S
Social Problem, The. C. A. Ell-
wood. Keller
Social Silhouettes. Edgar Faw-
cett. Keller
Social Teaching of the Christian
Churches, The. Ernst
Troeltsch. Magill CHL
Socialism. Michael Harrington.
Magill '73
Socialism. O. D. Skelton. Keller
Society. Thomas William Robert-
son. Drury
Society and Solitude. Ralph Waldo
Emerson. Magill IV, MAL1,
MC
Sociology As an Art Form.
Robert A. Nisbet. Magill '77
Sodom and Gomorrah. Jean
Giraudoux. Matlaw; Shank
Sogamoyoo Tateshino Goshozome.
Kawatake Mokuami. Halford
Sogni muoiono all'alba, I (Dreams
Die at Dawn). Indro Montan-
elli. Kienzle
Sohrab and Rustum. Matthew
Arnold. Haydn; Hix; Keller;
Magill III, CE, M1&2, MC,
MP
Soil, The see Terre, La
Soirée des proverbes, La (An
Evening of Proverbs). Georges
Schéhadé. Kienzle
Soirées de Saint-Pétersbourg, Les.
Joseph Marie de Maistre.
Magill CAL

SOLARIS   262

Solaris. Stanislaw Lem. Magill
  SF
Soldier. General Matthew B.
  Ridgway. Magill '57, S
Soldier and the Woman, The.
  Elaine Morgan. French
Soldier of Manhattan, A. Joseph
  A. Altsheler. Kaye
Soldier of Virginia, A. Burton
  E. Stevenson. Kaye
Soldier Rigdale. Beulah M. Dix.
  Kaye
Soldier Tanaka. Georg Kaiser.
  Matlaw
Soldier with the Arabs, A. Sir
  John Bagot Glubb. Magill '59,
  S
Soldiers. Rolf Hochhuth. Kienzle;
  Matlaw
Soldiers and Civilians. Marcus
  Cunliffe. Magill '69, S
Soldier's Art, The. Anthony
  Powell. Magill '69, S
Soldier's Fortune, The. Thomas
  Otway. Magill III, CE, M1&2,
  MC, MD
Soldiers of Fortune. Richard
  Harding Davis. Haydn (a);
  Johnson; Keller
Soldier's Pay. William Faulkner.
  Haydn (a)
Soldier's Wife. Rose Franken.
  Best '44; Drury
Solid Gold Cadillac, The. Howard
  Teichmann and George S. Kauf-
  man. Chapman '54; Drury;
  NCTE
Soliloquy on the Earnest Money
  of the Soul. Hugh of St. Vic-
  tor. Magill CHL
Solitary Cyclist, The. Sir Arthur
  Conan Doyle. Hardwick SH
Solitary Singer, The. Gay Wilson
  Allen. Magill '55, MB, S
Solitudes, The. Luis de Góngora
  y Argote. Haydn
Solntse zakhodit v Donomage.
  Ilya Varshavsky. Magill SF
Solstice, The. Karel Capek.
  Drury
Solution, The. Henry James.
  Gale-J
Sombrero Fallout. Richard
  Brautigan. Magill '78
Some Inner Fury. Kamala
  Markandaya. Magill '57, S
Some Like It Hot. Robert
  Thoeren. (See adaptation

Sugar by Peter Stone et al.)
Some Like It Hot. Billy Wilder
  and I. A. L. Diamond. (See
  adaptation Sugar by Peter Stone
  et al.)
Some People. Sir Harold Nicol-
  son. Magill IV, MC
Some Thoughts Concerning Educa-
  tion. John Locke. Keller
  (Thoughts)
Some Words with a Mummy.
  Edgar Allan Poe. Gale-PP
Somebody's Darling. Larry Mc-
  Murtry. Magill '79
Somebody's Luggage. Charles
  Dickens. Hardwick CD
Someday, Maybe. William Staf-
  ford. Magill '74
Someone Just Like You. Sol
  Yurick. Magill '73
Someone Waiting. Emlyn Wil-
  liams. Drury
Something About a Soldier. Mark
  Harris. Magill '58, S
Something Happened. Joseph
  Heller. Magill '75
Sometimes a Great Notion. Ken
  Kesey. Magill '65, S
Somewhere Is Such a Kingdom.
  Geoffrey Hill. Magill '77
Son Avenger, The. Sigrid Undset.
  Magill II, CE, M1&2, MC,
  MEUF
Son excellence Eugène Rougon.
  Emile Zola. Kaye (His Excel-
  lency); Keller (Rougon)
Son-in-law of M. Poirier, The
  see Mr. Poirier's Son-in-Law
Son of a Tory, The. Clinton
  Scollard. Kaye
Son of Dust. H. F. M. Prescott.
  Magill '57, S
Son of Fortune, The. Gabór
  Drégely. (See adaptation A
  Tailor-Made Man by Harry
  James Smith.)
Son of Issachar, A. Elbridge S.
  Brooks. Kaye
Son of Man, The. Emil Ludwig.
  Keller suppl.
Son of Royal Langbrith, The.
  William Dean Howells. Car-
  rington
Son of the Divine Herdsman, The
  see Gitagovinda
Son of the Emperor, A. Newton
  V. Stewart. Kaye
Son of the Middle Border, A.

Hamlin Garland.   Haydn; Keller
suppl.; Magill IV, MC
Son of the Morning.   Joyce Carol
Oates.   Magill '79
Son of the Revolution, A.   El-
bridge S. Brooks.   Kaye
Sonezaki Shinjû (Double Suicide
at Sonezaki).   Chikamatsu
Monzaemon.   Halford; Magill
III, CE, M1&2, MC, MD
Song of Bernadette, The.   Jean
and Walter Kerr.   (Based on
the novel by Franz Werfel.)
Drury; NCTE
Song of Bernadette, The.   Franz
Werfel.   (See also adaptation
by Jean and Walter Kerr.)
Magill I, CE, M1&2, MC,
MEUF
Song of Hiawatha, The.   Henry
Wadsworth Longfellow.   Haydn
(a; Hiawatha); Keller (Hiawatha);
Magill I, CE, M1&2, MAL4,
MC, MP; Smith; Wilson
Song of Myself (from Leaves of
Grass).   Walt Whitman.   Smith
Song of Roland, The.   Unknown.
Fleming; Haydn; Keller (Chan-
son); Magill I, CE, M1&2,
MC, MEUF
Song of Solomon.   Toni Morrison.
Magill '78
Song of Songs, The.   Hermann
Sudermann.   Keller; Magill I,
CE, M1&2, MC, MEUF
Song of the Lark, The.   Willa
Cather.   Keller; Magill II,
CE, M1&2, MAF, MC
Song of the World.   Jean Giono.
Magill II, CE, M1&2, MC,
MEUF
Songs and Sonnets.   John Donne.
Haydn (a)
Songs Before Sunrise.   Algernon
Charles Swinburne.   Haydn (a)
Songs for Eve.   Archibald Mac-
Leish.   Magill '54, MB, S
Songs of Innocence and of Exper-
ience.   William Blake.   Haydn;
Magill CHL
Songs of Kabir.   Kabir.   Haydn
Songs of Life and Hope.   Rubén
Darío.   Haydn
Sonia.   Henri Gréville.   Keller
Sonnets from the Portuguese.
Elizabeth Barrett Browning.
Haydn; Magill III, M1, MC, MP
Sonnets of Shakespeare, The.

William Shakespeare.   Camp-
bell; Clark; Halliday; Haydn;
Magill IV, MC; Ruoff (Shake-
speare's)
Sonnets to Orpheus.   Rainer Maria
Rilke.   Magill IV, MC
Sons and Lovers.   D. H. Law-
rence.   Goodman; Haydn; Heiney;
Keller suppl.; Lass BN; Magill
I, CE, M1&2, MC, MEF; Ward
Sons of Darkness, Sons of Light.
John A. Williams.   Magill '70
Sons of Heracles, The   see
Heraclidae
Sons of the Morning.   Eden Phill-
potts.   Johnson
Sons of Victory.   O. V. Caine.
Kaye
Son's Veto, The.   Thomas Hardy.
Pinion; Saxelby
Sophie.   Philip Moeller.   Drury
Sophist.   Plato.   Feder; Magill
W P
Sorcerer, The.   William Schwenk
Gilbert and Arthur Sullivan.
Shipley
Sorceress of Rome, The.   Nathan
Gallizier.   Kaye
Sorcière, La.   Victorien Sardou.
Sobel
Sorgen und die Macht, Die (The
Care of Office).   Peter Hacks.
Kienzle
Sorrell and Son.   Warwick Deeping.
Keller suppl.
Sorrow Beyond Dreams, A.   Peter
Handke.   Magill '76
Sorrows of Han, The.   Ma Chih-
yuan.   Gassner; Thomas
Sorrows of Werther, The   see
Sorrows of Young Werther, The
Sorrows of Young Werther, The.
Johann Wolfgang von Goethe.
Cohen; Haydn; Johnson; Magill
I, CE, M1&2, MC, MEUF;
Olfson
Sot-Weed Factor, The.   John
Barth   Magill IV, '61, M1,
MC, S
Sotileza.   José María de Pereda.
Magill II, CE, M1&2, MC,
MEUF
Sotoba Komachi (Komachi and the
Gravestone).   Kwanami Kiyot-
sugo.   Gassner
Soul Enchanted, The.   Romain
Rolland.   Keller suppl.
Soul of a Serf, The.   J. Brecken-

ridge Ellis. Kaye
Soul of an Immigrant, The. Con-
stantine M. Panunzio. Keller
suppl.
Soul of the Far East, The. Per-
cival Lowell. Keller
Soul of Wood and Other Stories.
Jakov Lind. Magill '66, S
Soul on Ice. Eldridge Cleaver.
Magill '68, M1, S
Souls Divided. Matilde Serao.
Haydn
Souls on Fire. Elie Wiesel.
Magill '73
Sound and the Fury, The. William
Faulkner. Haydn (Faulkner);
Heiney; Lass AN; Magill I,
CE, M1&2, MAF, MC; More-
head; Smith
Sound of Murder, The. William
Fairchild. French
Sound of Music, The. Howard
Lindsay, Russel Crouse, Oscar
Hammerstein II and Richard
Rodgers. (Based on The Trapp
Family Singers by Maria Au-
gusta Trapp.) Drinkrow; NCTE
Sound of the Mountain, The.
Yasunari Kawabata. Magill
'71
Sound of Waves, The. Yukio
Mishima. Magill IV, '57,
MC, S
Source of Human Good, The.
Henry Nelson Wieman. Magill
CHL
South. Julien Green. Gassner;
Kienzle
South Pacific. Oscar Hammer-
stein II, Joshua Logan and
Richard Rodgers. (Based on
Tales of the South Pacific by
James Michener.) Bonin;
Drinkrow; Kienzle; Matlaw;
NCTE
South Sea Bubble. Noel Coward.
French
South; the Story of Shackleton's
Last Expedition, 1914-1917.
Sir Ernest Henry Shackleton.
Keller suppl.
South Wind. Norman Douglas.
Haydn; Keller suppl. ; Lass BN;
Magill II, CE, M1&2, MC,
MEF; Ward
Southern Heritage, The. James
McBride Dabbs. Magill Ss
Sovereign Power, The. Violet A.

Simpson. Kaye
Soviet Russia in China. Chiang
Kai-shek. Magill '58, M1, S
Sozdan dla buzi. Henrich Altov.
Magill SF
Space Lords. Cordwainer Smith.
Magill SF
Space Merchants, The. Frederik
Pohl and Cyril M. Kornbluth.
Magill SF
Space, Time and Deity. Samuel
Alexander. Magill WP
Spandau. Albert Speer. Magill
'77
Spañelska zapalka (The Safety
Match). Marie and Alfred
Radok. Kienzle
Spaniards in Peru; or, The Death
of Rolla, The. August Fried-
rich Ferdinand von Kotzebue.
Shipley
Spanish Civil War, The. Hugh
Thomas. Magill '62, MB, S
Spanish Conquest in America, The.
Sir Arthur Helps. Keller
Spanish Friar, The. John Dryden.
Magill III, CE, M1&2, MC, MD
Spanish Gipsy, The. Thomas
Middleton and William Rowley.
Magill III, CE, M1&2, MC,
MD; Ruoff
Spanish Tragedy, The. Thomas
Kyd. Drury; Haydn; Holzknecht;
Magill II, CE, M1&2, MC, MD;
Ruoff; Shipley; Sobel
Spanish Vistas. George Parsons
Lathrop. Keller
Speak, Memory. Vladimir Nabo-
kov. Magill '68, M1, S
Speaking of Murder. Audrey and
William Roos. French
Special Envoy to Churchill and
Stalin, 1941-1946. W. Averell
Harriman and Elie Abel. Ma-
gill '76
Special Type, The. Henry James.
Gale-J
Specimen Days. Walt Whitman.
Magill IV, MAL5, MC
Speckled Band, The. Sir Arthur
Conan Doyle. Hardwick SH
Spectacles, The. Edgar Allan
Poe. Gale-PP
Spectator, The. Joseph Addison
and Richard Steele. Haydn
Spectator Bird, The. Wallace
Stegner. Magill '77
Spectators, The see Isthmiasts,

The
Spectral Boy, The. Donald Peter-
sen. Magill '66, S
Spectral Emanations: New and
Selected Poems. John Hol-
lander. Magill '79
Speculations About Jakob. Uwe
Johnson. Magill IV, '64, MC,
S
Speech on Conciliation with the
Colonies. Edmund Burke.
Haydn; Keller (Conciliation)
Speed the Plough. Thomas Mor-
ton. Keller
Speedboat. Renata Adler. Magill
'77
Spencer Holst Stories. Spencer
Holst. Magill '77
Sphaera mundi. Joannes de Sacro
Bosco. Haydn
Sphekes see Wasps, The
Sphinx, The. Aeschylus. Hathorn
Sphinx, The. Edgar Allan Poe.
Gale-PP
Spider and the Fly, The. John
Heywood. Ruoff
Spider King, The. Lawrence
Schoonover. Magill '54, S
Spider's House, The. Paul
Bowles. Magill '55, S
Spider's Web. Agatha Christie.
Drury; French
Spinoza. Berthold Auerbach.
Kaye
Spinoza of Market Street, The.
Isaac Bashevis Singer. Magill
'62, M1, S
Spinster. Sylvia Ashton-Warner.
Magill '60, S
Spinster of This Parish. William
Babington Maxwell. Keller
suppl.
Spiral Staircase, The. Mel
Dinelli. (See adaptation by
F. Andrew Leslie.)
Spiral Staircase, The. F. Andrew
Leslie. (Based on the novel
by Mel Dinelli.) Drury
Spire, The. William Golding.
Magill '65, S
Spirit of Catholicism, The.
Karl Adam. Magill CAL
Spirit of Mediaeval Philosophy,
The. Etienne Gilson. Magill
CAL, WP
Spirit of Saint Francis of Sales,
The. Jean Pierre Camus.
Magill CAL

Spirit of the Laws, The. Charles
Louis de Secondat Montesquieu.
Downs M; Haydn; Keller; Magill
IV, MC
Spirit of the Service. Edith E.
Woods. Kaye
Spiritual Espousals, The. John
of Ruysbroeck. Magill CAL
Spiritual Exercises. Saint Ignatius
Loyola. Magill CAL
Spiritual Friendship. Saint Aelred.
Magill CAL
Spiritual Song Between the Soul
and the Husband. Saint Juan
de la Cruz. Haydn
Splendid Impostor, A. Frederick
J. Whishaw. Kaye
Splendid Knight, The. Henry A.
Hinkson. Kaye
Splendid Outcasts, The. Rosemary
Ann Sisson. French
Splendid Spur, The. Sir Arthur
Thomas Quiller-Couch. John-
son; Keller
Splendor in the Grass. William
Inge. Drury
Spoilers, The. Rex Beach.
Keller; Magill I, CE, M1&2,
MAF, MC
Spoils of Poynton, The (The Old
Things). Henry James; Gale-
J; Haydn (a); Magill III, CE,
M1&2, MAF, MAL3, MC
Spook Sonata, The see Ghost
Sonata, The
Spoon River Anthology. Charles
Aidman. (Based on the poems
of Edgar Lee Masters.) Drury
Spoon River Anthology. Edgar
Lee Masters. (See also adap-
tation by Charles Aidman.)
Haydn; Magill III, M1, MC,
MP
Sportsman's Sketches. Ivan Tur-
genev. Haydn
Spotted Dog, The. Anthony Trol-
lope. Gerould
Spreading Fires. John Knowles.
Magill '75
Spreading the News. Lady (Isa-
bella Augusta) Gregory.
Heiney; Matlaw; Shipley
Spring Cleaning. Frederick Lons-
dale. Drury
Spring Dance. Philip Barry.
Drury
Spring Freshets. Ivan Turgenev.
Berry-1

Spring of Childhood, The see
Critic, The
Spring of the Thief.   John Logan.
Magill '64, S
Spring Snow.   Yukio Mishima.
Magill '73
Springhaven.   Richard Doddridge
Blackmore.   Kaye
Spring's Awakening see Awaken-
ing of Spring, The
Springtime for Henry.   Benn W.
Levy.   Drury; French; Shipley;
Sobel
Spy, The.   James Fenimore
Cooper.   Haydn; Johnson;
Magill I, CE, M1&2, MAF,
MAL1, MC; Walker
Spy, The.   Charles Gilson.   Kaye
Spy in the House of Love, A.
Anaïs Nin.   Magill '54, S
Squabbles of Chioggia, The.
Carlo Goldoni.   Drury; Gass-
ner (Baruffe)
Square, The.   Marguerite Duras.
Kienzle
Square Root of Wonderful, The.
Carson McCullers.   Drury;
Kienzle
Squares of the City, The.   John
Brunner.   Magill SF
Squaring the Circle.   Valentine
Petrovich Katayev.   Drury;
Matlaw; Shipley; Sobel
Squaw Man, The.   Edwin M.
Royle.   Best '99; Drury
Squire Petrick's Lady.   Thomas
Hardy.   Pinion; Saxelby
Stage Door.   George S. Kaufman
and Edna Ferber.   Best '36;
Drury; Matlaw; NCTE; Sobel
Stainless Steel Rat Novels, The.
Harry Harrison.   Magill SF
Staircase.   Charles Dyer.   Best
'67; Drury; Kienzle
Stalag 17.   Donald Bevan and
Edmund Trzcinski.   Drury;
NCTE
Stalin Embattled, 1943-1948.
William O. McCagg, Jr.
Magill '79
Stalin: The Man and His Era.
Adam Bruno Ulam.   Magill
'74
Stalky & Co.   Rudyard Kipling.
Haydn
Stand on Zanzibar.   John Brunner.
Magill SF
Stand Up, Friend, with Me.

Edward Field.   Magill '64, S
Standish of Standish.   Jane Good-
win Austin.   Keller
Stanzas upon the Death of His
Father.   Jorge Manrique.
Haydn
Staple of News, The.   Ben Jonson.
Holzknecht; Ruoff; Shank
Star.   Charlemagne Ischir Defon-
tenay.   Magill SF
Star Chamber, The.   William
Harrison Ainsworth.   Kaye
Star Maker.   Olaf Stapledon.
Magill SF
Star Man's Son 2250 A. D.   Andre
Norton.   Magill SF
Star of Love, The.   Florence M.
Kingsley.   Kaye
Star of Seville, The.   Unknown.
Haydn; Magill III, CE, M1&2,
MC, MD; Shank
Star of Seville, The.   Lope Félix
de Vega Carpio.   Drury; Shipley
Star Rover.   Jack London.   Magill
SF
Star-Spangled Girl, The.   Neil
Simon.   Drury; NCTE
Star-Wagon, The.   Maxwell Ander-
son.   Best '37
Stardust.   Walter Kerr.   Drury
Starlight: The Great Short Fic-
tion of Alfred Bester.   Alfred
Bester.   Magill SF
Stars My Destination, The.   Alfred
Bester.   Magill SF
Starship Troopers.   Robert A.
Heinlein.   Magill SF
Start in Life, A.   Honoré de Bal-
zac.   Johnson
Starvecrow Farm.   Stanley J.
Weyman.   Kaye
State and Revolution, The.   Niko-
lay Lenin.   Downs M, FG;
Haydn
State Fair.   Luella McMahon and
Christopher Sergel.   (Based on
the novel by Phil Stong.)
Drury
State Fair.   Phil Stong.   (See also
adaptation by Luella McMahon
and Christopher Sergel.)   Ma-
gill I, CE, M1&2, MAF, MC
State in Catholic Thought, The.
Heinrich Rommen.   Magill
CAL
State of Siege.   Albert Camus.
Kienzle; Matlaw; Shank
State of the Union.   Howard Lind-

Summons of the Trumpet: U. S. -
Vietnam in Perspective. Dave
Richard Palmer. Magill '79
Sump'n Like Wings. Lynn Riggs.
Drury
Sumurun. Friedrich Freksa.
Shipley
Sun Also Rises, The. Ernest
Hemingway. Haydn; Heiney;
Keller suppl.; Lass AN; Magill
I, CE, M1&2, MAF, MC;
Morehead; Smith
Sun of Saratoga, The. Joseph
A. Altsheler. Kaye
Sun-Up. Lula Vollmer. Best
'23; Sobel
Sunday at Home. Nathaniel Haw-
thorne. Gale-H
Sunday in New York. Norman
Krasna. Kienzle; NCTE
Sunflower Splendor. Wu-chi Liu
and Irving Yucheng Lo, editors.
Magill '77
Sunken Bell, The. Gerhart Haupt-
mann. Drury; Heiney; Keller;
Magill III, CE, M1&2, MC,
MD; Matlaw; Shank; Shipley;
Sobel
Sunlight Dialogues, The. John
Gardner. Magill '73
Sunny Morning, A. Serafín and
Joaquín Alvarez Quintero.
Shipley
Sunrise at Campobello. Dore
Schary. Best '57; Bonin;
Drury; Lovell; Matlaw; NCTE
Sunset. Isaac Emmanuelovich
Babel. Matlaw
Sunset Song see Scots Quair, A
Sunshine Boys, The. Neil Simon.
Best '72; Drury; NCTE
Suo Otoshi (Dropping the Robe).
Fukuchi Ochi. Halford
Supership. Noël Mostert.
Magill '75
Superstition and Force. Henry
Charles Lea. Keller
Superstitious Man's Story, The.
Thomas Hardy. Gale-H
Suppliant Women, The see
Suppliants, The
Suppliants, The. Aeschylus.
Feder; Gassner (Suppliant
Maidens); Hathorn (Danaïd);
Haydn; Magill II, CE, M1&2,
MC, MD; Reinhold (Suppliant
Women); Shipley; Sobel
Suppliants, The. Euripides.

Feder; Gassner (Suppliant Wom-
en); Hathorn; Magill III, CE,
M1&2, MC, MD; Reinhold;
Shipley
Supplices see Suppliants, The
Support of the Family, The. Al-
phonse Daudet. Johnson
Supposes see Suppositi, I
Supposes. George Gascoigne.
Holzknecht; Ruoff
Suppositi, I. Lodovico Ariosto.
Drury (Supposes); Magill III,
CE, M1&2, MC, MD; Shipley
(Supposes)
Suppressed Desires. Susan Glas-
pell. Haydn (a); Matlaw
Surface of Earth, The. Reynolds
Price. Magill '76
Surfacing. Margaret Atwood.
Magill '74
Surge of War, The. Norman
Innes. Kaye
Surgeon of His Honor, The.
Pedro Calderón de la Barca.
Shank
Surgeon's Daughter, The. Sir
Walter Scott. Kaye; McSpadden
W
Surgeon's Stories, The. Zakarias
Topelius. Keller
Surry of Eagle's-Nest. John Esten
Cooke. Magill III, CE, M1&2,
MAF, MC
Survey of International Affairs, 1920-
1923, 1924, 1925. Arnold Joseph
Toynbee, editor. Keller suppl.
Survival of the Bark Canoe, The.
John J. McPhee. Magill '76
Survivor, The. Terrence Des
Pres. Magill '77
Survivors, The. Peter Viertel
and Irwin Shaw. Drury
Susan and God. Rachel Crothers.
Best '37; Drury
Susannah and the Elders. James
Bridie. Drury
Suspect. Edward Percy and
Reginald Denham. French
Succor. Rudyard Kipling. Ward
Sussex Vampire, The. Sir Arthur
Conan Doyle. Hardwick SH
Swaggering Soldier, The see
Braggart Soldier, The
Swallow Barn. John P. Kennedy.
Magill II, CE, M1&2, MAF,
MC
Swamp Fox. Robert Duncan Bass.
Magill Ss

Swan, The.   Ferenc Molnár.
Best '23; Drury; Keller suppl. ;
Matlaw; NCTE; Shank; Sobel
Swan Song.   John Galsworthy.
(See also trilogy title A Modern
Comedy.) Heiney; Keller suppl.
Swann's Way.   Marcel Proust.
(See also series title Remem-
brance of Things Past.) Good-
man; Haydn p. 630; Heiney;
Lass EN
Swanwhite.   August Strindberg.
Drury; Matlaw
Swedenhielms, The.   Hjalmar
Bergman.   Matlaw; Shank
Sweeney Agonistes.   T. S. Eliot.
Matlaw
Sweeney Todd.   George Dibdin
Pitt.   Shipley
Sweeney Todd, the Demon Barber
of Fleet Street.   Christopher
Bond.   (See adaptation by
Hugh Wheeler.)
Sweeney Todd, the Demon Barber
of Fleet Street.   Hugh Wheeler.
(Based on the version by Chris-
topher Bond.) Best '78
Sweet Bird of Youth.   Tennessee
Williams.   Best '58; Chapman
'59; Drury; Kienzle; Magill
'60, MB, S; Matlaw; NCTE
Sweet Charity.   Neil Simon, Dorothy
Fields and Cy Coleman.   (Based
on The Nights of Cabiria by
Federico Fellini.) NCTE
Sweet Cheat Gone, The.   Marcel
Proust.   (See also series title
Remembrance of Things Past.)
Haydn p. 631; Heiney
Sweet Lavender.   Arthur Wing
Pinero.   Drury; Shipley
Sweet Nell of Old Drury.   Paul
Kester.   Drury; Sobel
Sweet Thursday.   John Steinbeck.
Magill '54, S
Sweetheart of M. Briseux, The.
Henry James.   Gale-J
Swiss Family Robinson, The.
Johann Rudolf Wyss.   Haydn;
Johnson; Keller; Magill I,
CE, M1&2, MC, MEUF
Sword and Assegai.   Anna Howarth.
Kaye
Sword and Queue.   Karl Ferdinand
Gutzkow.   Drury
Sword and the Cowl, The.   Edgar
Swan.   Kaye
Sword Decides, The.   Majorie

Bowen.   Kaye
Sword of Freedom, The.   Charles
Gilson.   Kaye
Sword of Gideon, The.   John Ed-
ward Bloundelle-Burton.   Kaye
Sword of God, The.   René Hardy.
Magill '54, S
Sword of Honour (trilogy title of
Men at Arms, Officers and
Gentlemen, and Unconditional
Surrender).   Evelyn Waugh.
Stade p. 79
Sword of Justice, The.   Sheppard
Stevens.   Kaye
Sword of Rhiannon, The.   Leigh
Brackett.   Magill SF
Sword of the Lord, The.   Joseph
Hocking.   Kaye
Sword of the Old Frontier, A.
George Randall Parrish.   Kaye
Sword of Wealth, The.   H. E.
Thomas.   Kaye
Sybil.   Benjamin Disraeli.   Johnson
Sylph Etherege.   Nathaniel Haw-
thorne.   Gale-H
Sylvia Plath: The Woman and the
Work.   Edward Butscher, edi-
tor.   Magill '78
Symbolism.   Johann Adam Möhler.
Magill CAL
Symbolist Movement in Literature,
The.   Arthur Symons.   Keller
Symposium.   Plato.   Downs FG;
Feder; Haydn; Magill WP
Symzonia.   "Captain Adam Sea-
born. " Magill SF
Syndic, The.   Cyril M. Kornbluth.
Magill SF
Synnöve Solbakken.   Bjørnstjerne
Bjørnson.   Haydn; Keller
Syntagma Philosophicum.   Pierre
Gassendi.   Magill WP
Synthetic Man, The.   Theodore
Sturgeon.   Magill SF
System of Dr. Tarr and Prof.
Fether, The.   Edgar Allan
Poe.   Gale-PP
System of Doctrines.   Samuel
Hopkins.   Magill CHL
System of Logic, A.   John Stuart
Mill.   Magill WP
Systema Naturae (System of Na-
ture).   Carl Linnaeus.   Downs
M; Haydn
Systematic Theology.   Charles
Hodge.   Magill CHL
Systematic Theology.   Augustus
Hopkins Strong.   Magill CHL

Systematic Theology.   Paul Tillich.
Magill CHL, WP
Syzygy.   Michael G.   Coney.
Magill SF

-T-

T. E. Lawrence.   Desmond
Stewart.   Magill '78
Ta fast malen.' (Catch the Moth.').
Väinö Vilhelm Järner.   Kienzle
Tabitha.   Arnold Ridley and
Mary Cathcart Borer.   French
Table Talk.   William Hazlitt.
Haydn; Keller
Table Talk.   John Selden.   Haydn
Taft Story, The.   William Smith
White.   Magill Ss
Tailor-Made Man, A.   Harry
James Smith.   (Based on The
Son of Fortune by Gábor
Drégely.)   Shipley (under
Drégely)
Takasago.   Seami.   Gassner
Take a Giant Step.   Louis Peter-
son.   Best '53; NCTE
Take a Girl Like You.   Kingsley
Amis.   Magill '62, S
Take Her She's Mine.   Phoebe
and Henry Ephron.   Drury;
NCTE
Take Me Along.   Joseph Stein,
Robert Russell and Bob Mer-
rill.   (Based on Ah, Wilder-
ness.' by Eugene O'Neill.)
NCTE
Take the A Train.   Michael
Blankfort.   Magill '79
Taken by Assault.   Morley
Roberts.   Kaye
Takeover, The.   Muriel Spark.
Magill '77
Taking of Miss Janie, The.   Ed
Bullins.   Best '74; Drury
Taking of the Bastille.   Alex-
andre Dumas (father).   John
son; Kaye
Taková láska (Such Love).   Pavel
Kohout.   Kienzle
Tale for Midnight, A.   Frederic
Prokosch.   Magill '55, S
Tale for the Mirror.   Hortense
Calisher.   Magill '63, S
Tale of a Traveling Bag, The
see   Vidularia

Tale of a Tub, A.   Jonathan Swift.
Haydn; Johnson-18th; Keller;
Magill IV, MC
Tale of Genji, The.   Lady Mura-
saki Shikibu.   Haydn; Magill II,
CE, M1&2, MC, MEUF; Olfson
Tale of Jerusalem, A.   Edgar
Allan Poe.   Gale-PP
Tale of Possessors, Self-Dispos-
sessed, A.   Eugene O'Neill.
Matlaw
Tale of the Ragged Mountains, A.
Edgar Allan Poe.   Gale-PP
Tale of the Wolf, The (The Wolf).
Ferenc Molnár.   Drury
Tale of Two Cities, A.   Charles
Dickens.   Goodman; Grozier;
Hardwick CD; Haydn; Hix; John-
son; Kaye; Keller; Lass BN;
McSpadden-D; Magill I, CE,
M1&2, MC, MEF; Wilson
Tales.   LeRoi Jones.   Magill Ss
Tales for Fifteen.   James Feni-
more Cooper.   Walker
Tales from Shakespeare.   Charles
and Mary Lamb.   Haydn; Keller
Tales of a Traveller.   Washington
Irving.   Keller
Tales of Ensign Stal, The.   Johan
Ludvig Runeberg.   Haydn
Tales of Ise.   Arihara no Nari-
hira.   Magill III, M1, MC,
MEUF
Tales of Nasr-ed-Din, The.   Un-
known.   Haydn (Nasr-ed-Din...)
Tales of Soldiers and Civilians.
Ambrose Bierce.   Magill III,
M1, MAF, MAL1, MC
Tales of the Army Surgeon.
Zakarias Topelius.   Haydn
Tales of the South Pacific.   James
Michener.   (See adaptation South
Pacific by Oscar Hammerstein
II et al.)
Tales of Uncle Remus.   Joel
Chandler Harris.   Haydn
(Uncle); Keller (Uncle); Magill
III, M1, MAF, MAL2, MC
Talifer.   Edwin Arlington Robin-
son.   Haydn (a)
Talisman, The.   Sir Walter Scott.
Haydn; Johnson; Kaye; McSpad-
den W; Magill II, CE, M1&2,
MC, MEF; Wilson
Talks to Teachers on Psychology.
William James.   Keller
Tall Story.   Howard Lindsay and
Russel Crouse.   (Based on

The Homecoming Game by
Howard Nemerov.) Drury
Talmud. Unknown. Downs F;
Haydn
Tam O'Shanter. Robert Burns.
Haydn
Tamar. Robinson Jeffers.
Haydn (a); Heiney; Magill I,
CE, M1&2, MC, MP
Tambourines to Glory. Langston
Hughes. NCTE
Tamburlaine the Great. Chris-
topher Marlowe. Cartmell;
Drury; Haydn; Holzknecht (Part
I); Magill I, CE, M1&2, MC,
MD; NBC 1; Ruoff; Shipley;
Sobel; Thomas
Taming of the Shrew, The. Wil-
liam Shakespeare. Campbell;
Chute; Clark; Drury; Gassner;
Guerber-SC; Halliday; Haydn;
Keller; Lamb; McCutchan-SC;
McSpadden S; Magill II, CE,
M1&2, MC, MD; Ruoff; Shank;
Shipley; Sobel; Wilson
Tancred. Benjamin Disraeli.
Johnson
Tanglewood Tales, for Girls and
Boys: Being a Second Wonder-
Book. Nathaniel Hawthorne.
Gale-H
Tango. Slawomir Mrożek.
Anderson; Kienzle; Matlaw
Tante. Anne Douglas Sedgwick.
Keller
Tao Te Ching. Lao Tze. Haydn;
Magill WP
Tapestried Chamber, The. Sir
Walter Scott. McSpadden W
Taps for Private Tussie. Jesse
Stuart. Magill I, '70, CE,
M1&2, MAF, MC
Tar Baby, The. Joel Chandler
Harris. Smith
Taras Bulba. Nikolai V. Gogol.
Haydn; Kaye; Keller; Magill
I, CE, M1&2, MC, MEUF
Tarelkin's Death. Alexander
Sukhovo-Kobylin. Gassner
(Krechinsky's)
Tarka the Otter. Henry William-
son. Magill IV, MC
Tarnish. Gilbert Emery. Best
'23; Drury
Tarr. Wyndham Lewis. Magill
III, CE, M1&2, MC, MEF
Tarry Thou Till I Come. George
Croly. Kaye

Tartarin of Tarascon. Alphonse
Daudet. Haydn; Johnson; Kel-
ler; Magill I, CE, M1&2, MC,
MEUF
Tartuffe. Molière. Armstrong;
Cartmell; Cohen; Drury; French;
Gassner; Haydn; Keller; Magill
I, CE, M1&2, MC, MD; NBC
3; Shank; Shipley; Sobel; Thomas
Tarzan of the Apes. Edgar Rice
Burroughs. Magill SF
Task, The. William Cowper.
Haydn; Keller; Magill III, M1,
MC, MP
Taste of Honey, A. Shelagh De-
laney. Best '60; French; Ki-
enzle; Matlaw; Shank
Tatenberg II. Armand Gatti.
Kienzle
Tatler, The. Richard Steele and
Joseph Addison. Keller
Tau Zero. Poul Anderson. Ma-
gill SF
Tchin-Tchin. François Billetdoux.
(See also adaptation by Sidney
Michaels.) Kienzle
Tchin-Tchin. Sidney Michaels.
(Based on the play by François
Billetdoux.) Best '62
Tea and Sympathy. Robert Ander-
son. Best '53; Chapman '54;
Drury; Lass AP; Magill '54,
MB, S; Matlaw; NCTE
Teach Me How to Cry. Patricia
Joudry. Drury
Teacher of Literature, The.
Anton Chekhov. Keller suppl.
(Party)
Teaching As a Subversive Activity.
Neil Postman and Charles
Weingartner. Magill '70
Teahouse of the August Moon,
The. John Patrick. (Based
on the novel by Vern Sneider;
see also adaptation Lovely
Ladies, Kind Gentlemen by
John Patrick et al.) Best '53;
Bonin; Chapman '54; Drury;
Kienzle; Lovell; Magill '54,
M1, MB, S; Matlaw; NCTE;
Shank; Shipley
Teahouse of the August Moon.
Vern Sneider. (See adaptation
by John Patrick.)
Technics and Civilization. Lewis
Mumford. Haydn
Technique of the Drama. Gustav
Freytag. Keller

Teitelbaum's Window. Wallace
Markfield. Magill '71
Telegraph Girl, The. Anthony
Trollope. Gerould
Telemachus Clay. Salvato Cap-
pelli. Kienzle
Telemessians, The. Aristophanes.
Hathorn
Telepheia. Sophocles. Hathorn
Telephone Poles. John Updike.
Magill '64, S
Telephus see Telepheia
Telescope, The. Robert Cedric
Sherriff. French
Tell Freedom. Peter Abrahams.
Magill '54, S
Tell Me a Riddle. Tillie Olsen.
Magill '62, S
Tell Me, Tell Me. Marianne
Moore. Magill '67, M1, S
Tell Me That You Love Me, Junie
Moon. Marjorie Kellogg.
Drury; Magill '69, S
Tell-Tale Heart, The. Edgar
Allan Poe. Gale-P, PP
Tell Tale Murder. Philip
Weathers. French
Temper of Our Time, The. Eric
Hoffer. Magill '67, S
Tempest, The. William Shake-
speare. Baker; Campbell;
Chute; Clark; Drury; Gassner;
Guerber-SC; Halliday; Haydn;
Keller; Lamb; McCutchan-SC;
McSpadden S; Magill I, CE,
M1&2, MC, MD; Ruoff; Shank,
Shipley; Sobel; Thomas; Wilson
Temple, The. George Herbert.
Haydn; Magill III, M1, MC,
MP
Temple Beau, The. Henry Field-
ing. Magill II, CE, M1&2,
MC, MD
Temple House. Elizabeth Drew
(Barstow) Stoddard. Keller
Temple of Dawn, The. Yukio
Mishima. Magill '74
Temple of the Golden Pavilion,
The. Yukio Mishima. Magill
'60, S
Temple of the Past, The. Stefan
Wul. Magill SF
Tempo. Nikolai Fyodorovich
Pogodin. Matlaw
Temporary Kings. Anthony Powell.
Magill '74
Temptation of Jack Orkney, The.
Doris Lessing. Magill '73

Temptation of Saint Anthony, The.
Gustave Flaubert. Haydn;
Magill III, CE, M1&2, MC,
MEUF
Ten Days That Shook the World.
John Reed. Ward
Ten Little Indians. Agatha Chris-
tie. Drury; Kienzle; NCTE
Ten Little Niggers. Agatha Chris-
tie. French
Ten Nights in a Barroom. Timo-
thy Shay Arthur. Johnson
Ten North Frederick. John
O'Hara. Magill '55, S; Smith
Ten Thousand a Year. Samuel C.
Warren. Johnson; Keller
Ten Thousand Things, The. Maria
Dermoût. Magill '59, S
Ten Years' Digging in Egypt.
William Matthew Flinders
Petrie. Keller
Tenant of Wildfell Hall, The.
Anne Brontë. Halperin; John-
son; Magill I, CE, M1&2, MC,
MEF
Tenants of Moonbloom, The. Ed-
ward Lewis Wallant. Magill
IV, '64, MC, S
Tendencies of Religious Thought
in England, 1688-1750. Mark
Pattison. Keller (Essays and
Reviews)
Tender Buttons. Gertrude Stein.
Heiney
Tender Is the Night. F. Scott
Fitzgerald. Heiney; Magill II,
CE, M1&2, MAF, MC; More-
head; Olfson
Tender Trap, The. Max Shulman
and Robert Paul Smith. Chap-
man '55; French
Tengajaya Mura see Katakiuchi
Tengajaya Mura
Tenno Amijima see Shinju Tenno
Amijima
Tenor, The. Frank Wedekind.
Sobel
Tent Life in Siberia. George
Kennan. Keller
Tenth Man, The. Paddy Chayef-
sky. Best '59; Drury; Kienzle;
Lass AP; Matlaw; NCTE
'Tention! George Manville Fenn.
Kaye
Tenure of Kings and Magistrates,
The. John Milton. Ruoff
Terezín Requiem, The. Josef
Bor. Magill '64, S

Terms of Endearment. Larry
McMurtry. Magill '76
Termush, Atlanterhavskysten.
Sven Holm. Magill SF
Terra Nostra. Carlos Fuentes.
Magill '77
Terre, La (The Land). Emile
Zola. Johnson (Land); Keller
(Rougon)
Terrible Beauty, A. Arthur J.
Roth. Magill '59, S
Terrible Czar, The. Count
Alexei Tolstoy. Kaye
Terrible Temptation, A. Charles
Reade. Johnson
Terror. Anton Chekhov. Keller
suppl. (Party)
Teseide, La. Giovanni Boccaccio.
Magill IV, CE, M2, MC
Tess of the d'Urbervilles. Thomas
Hardy. Goodman; Grozier;
Haydn; Johnson; Keller; Magill
I, CE, M1&2, MC, MEF;
Saxelby
Testament of Beauty, The. Robert
Bridges. Haydn; Ward
Tetralogy of the Atrides, The.
Gerhart Hauptmann. Heiney
Tevya and His Daughter. Arnold
Perl. Drury
Texas Nightingale, The. Zoë
Akins. Shipley
Texas Steer, A. Randolph Carter.
Drury
Texas Trilogy, A. Preston
Jones. Magill '77
Thackeray: The Age of Wisdom,
1847-1863. Gordon N. Ray.
Magill '59, MB
Thackeray: The Uses of Adver-
sity. Gordon N. Ray. Magill
'55, MB, S
Thaddeus of Warsaw. Jane Porter.
Haydn; Johnson; Kaye; Keller;
Magill I, CE, M1&2, MC,
MEF
Thaddeus Stevens: Scourge of
the South. Fawn M. Brodie.
Magill Ss
Thaïs. Anatole France. Kaye;
Keller; Olfson
Thanatopsis. William Cullen
Bryant. Haydn
Thank You, Fog. Wystan Hugh
Auden. Magill '75
That Championship Season. Jason
Miller. Best '71; Drury;
Magill '73

That Hideous Strength. Clive
Staples Lewis. Magill SF
That Lass o'Lowrie's. Frances
Hodgson Burnett. Johnson
That Man Heine. Lewis Browne.
Keller suppl.
That Thou Art. Selection from
The Upanishads. Armstrong
That Uncertain Feeling. Kingsley
Amis. Magill IV, MC
That Was Then, This Is Now.
S. E. Hinton. Benedict
Theaetetus. Plato. Feder; Magill
WP
Theater Essays of Arthur Miller,
The. Arthur Miller. Magill
'79
Theatre of the Soul, The. Nikolai
Nikolaevich Yevreinov. Matlaw;
Sobel
Thebais, The. Publius Papinius
Statius. Feder (Thebaid);
Magill III, M1, MC, MP
Theban Tetralogy see Laius;
Oedipus; Seven Against Thebes,
The; Sphinx, The
Their Silver Wedding Journey.
William Dean Howells. Car-
rington
Their Wedding Journey. William
Dean Howells. Carrington
them. Joyce Carol Oates.
Magill '70
Theodicy. Gottfried Wilhelm von
Leibniz. Magill WP
Theodolinde see Rose-Agathe
Theodore Roosevelt and His Time.
Joseph Bucklin Bishop. Keller
suppl. (Roosevelt)
Theodore Roosevelt: The Forma-
tive Years. Carlton Putnam.
Magill '59, S
Theodore Roosevelt's Letters to
His Children. Joseph Bucklin
Bishop, editor. Keller suppl.
(Letters)
Theogony. Hesiod. Feder; Haydn
Theologica germanica. Unknown.
Magill CHL
Theological and Literary Essays.
Richard Holt Hutton. Keller
Theology and Sanity. Francis
Joseph Sheed. Magill CAL
Theology As an Empirical Science.
Douglas Clyde Macintosh.
Magill CHL
Theology for the Social Gospel, A.
Walter Rauschenbusch.

Smith. Keller
Three Gables, The. Sir Arthur
Conan Doyle. Hardwick SH
Three Garridebs, The. Sir
Arthur Conan Doyle. Hard-
wick SH
Three Greek Children. Alfred
John Church. Kaye
Three Hearts and Three Lions.
Poul Anderson. Magill SF
Three Kingdoms. Storm Jameson.
Keller suppl.
Three Lectures on Aesthetic.
Bernard Bosanquet. Magill
WP
Three Lives. Gertrude Stein.
Heiney
Three Men in a Boat. Jerome
K. Jerome. Magill II, CE,
M1&2, MC, MEF
Three Men on a Horse. John
Cecil Holm and George Abbott.
Drury; Lass AP; Sobel
Three Miss Kings, The. Ada
Cambridge. Johnson
Three Musketeers, The. Alex-
andre Dumas (father). (See
also adaptation by Rudolf
Friml et al.) Goodman;
Grozier; Haydn; Johnson; Kaye;
Keller; Magill I, CE, M1&2,
MC, MEUF; Wilson
Three Musketeers, The. Rudolf
Friml, Anthony McGuire and
Clifford Grey. (Based on the
novel by Alexandre Dumas.)
Three Penny Day, The see
Trinummus
Three Plays. Harold Pinter.
Magill '63, S
Three Saints and a Sinner. Louise
Hall Tharp. Magill '57, S
Three Sisters, The. Anton Chek-
hov. Cartmell; Drury; Gass-
ner; Haydn; Magill II, CE,
M1&2, MC, MD; Matlaw; NBC
3; NCTE; Shank; Shipley; Sobel
Three Soldiers. John Dos Passos.
Magill I, CE, M1&2, MAF,
MC
Three Stigmata of Palmer Eld-
ritch, The. Philip K. Dick.
Magill SF
Three Strangers, The. Thomas
Hardy. Pinion; Saxelby
Three Students, The. Sir Arthur
Conan Doyle. Hardwick SH
Three Sundays in a Week. Edgar

Allan Poe. Gale-PP
334. Thomas M. Disch. Magill
SF
Three Thousand Years Among the
Microbes. Mark Twain. Gale-
T
Three Tickets to Adventure.
Gerald Durrell. Magill '55, S
Three Tours of Dr. Syntax, The.
William Combe. Keller (Dr.)
Three Travelers. Marie-Claire
Blais. Magill '68, S
Three Voyages of Captain Cook
Around the World, The. James
Cook. Haydn; Keller (Voyages)
Three Ways, The. Saint Bona-
venture. Magill CAL
Three Wise Fools. Austin Strong.
Drury
Three Years of Arctic Service.
Adolphus W. Greely. Keller
Threefold Destiny: A Fairy Leg-
end, The. Nathaniel Haw-
thorne. Gale-II
Threepenny Opera, The. Bertolt
Brecht and Kurt Weill. (Based
on The Beggar's Opera by John
Gay.) Best '75; Gassner; Mat-
law; NCTE; Sprinchorn
Three's a Family. Phoebe and
Henry Ephron. Drury
Three's Company. Alfred Duggan.
Magill '59, S
Threescore and Ten. Walter Al-
len. Magill '60, S
Thrice Captive. Arthur G. F.
Griffiths. Kaye
Through Night to Light. Fried-
rich Spielhagen. Keller
Through Russian Snows. George
A. Henty. Kaye
Through Streets Broad and Nar-
row. Gabriel Fielding. Magill
'61, S
Through Swamp and Glade. Kirk
Monroe. Kaye
Through the Dark Continent. Sir
Henry Morton Stanley. Keller
Through the Eye of the Needle.
William Dean Howells. Car-
rington
Through the Looking Glass. Lewis
Carroll. Magill II, CE, M1&2,
MC, MEF, SF; Olfson
Through the Sikh War. George A.
Henty. Kaye
Thunder on the Left. Christopher
Morley. Keller suppl.

Thunder Rock. Robert Ardrey.
Drury; NCTE
Thunderbolt, The. Arthur Wing
Pinero. Drury; Matlaw
Thunderstorm, The (The Storm).
Aleksandr Ostrovskii. Gass-
ner; Sobel
Thurber Carnival, A. James
Thurber. Best '59; Drury;
NCTE
Thurso's Landing. Robinson
Jeffers. Heiney
Thus Spake Zarathustra. Fried-
rich Wilhelm Nietzsche.
Keller; Magill III, M1, MC,
MNF, WP
Thy Tears Might Cease. Michael
Farrell. Magill '65, S
Thyestes. Lucius Annaeus Seneca.
Feder; Hathorn; Magill II, CE,
M1&2, MC, MD; Reinhold;
Shipley
Tiao Ch'an (Sable Cicada; Têng
I T'ing; Lu Pu Hsi Tiao
Ch'an). Unknown. Sobel
Ticket-of-Leave Man, The. Tom
Taylor. Shank; Shipley
Tides of Barnegat, The. Francis
Hopkinson Smith. Keller
Tidings Brought to Mary, The.
Paul Claudel. Drury; Gass-
ner; Heiney; Matlaw; Shank;
Shipley; Sprinchorn
Tiger, The. Murray Schisgal.
Kienzle
Tiger and the Horse, The. Robert
Bolt. French; Kienzle
Tiger at the Gates. Christopher
Fry. (Based on the play by
Jean Giraudoux.) Drury
Tiger at the Gates (The Trojan
War Will Not Take Place).
Jean Giraudoux. (See also
adaptation by Christopher Fry.)
Best '55; Chapman '56; Gass-
ner; Heiney; Magill IV, '55,
M1, MB, MC, S; Matlaw;
NCTE; Shank; Sprinchorn
Tiger of Mysore, The. George
A. Henty. Kaye
Tiger of the Snows. Tenzing
Norgay. Magill '55, S
Till Eulenspiegel. Unknown.
Haydn; Keller
Till We Have Faces. Clive
Staples Lewis. Magill '58,
M1, S
Tilly of Bloomsbury. Ian Hay.

French
Timaeus. Plato. Downs FG;
Feder; Haydn; Magill WP
Timar's Two Worlds. Maurice
Jókai. Johnson
Timber, or Discoveries Made upon
Men and Matter As They Have
Flowed Out of His Daily Read-
ings. Ben Jonson. Ruoff
Timbuctoo the Mysterious. Felix
Dubois. Keller
Time and a Place, A. William
Humphrey. Magill '69, S
Time and Again. Jack Finney.
Magill '71, SF
Time and Chance. Elbert Hub-
bard. Kaye
Time and Eternity. Walter T.
Stace. Magill CHL
Time and Free Will. Henri Berg-
son. Haydn; Magill WP
Time and Place. Bryan Woolley.
Magill '78
Time and the Conways. J. B.
Priestley. Drury; French;
Matlaw; Shank
Time in Rome, A. Elizabeth
Bowen. Magill '61, S
Time Is a Dream. Henri-René
Lenormand. Drury; Matlaw;
Shank; Shipley
Time Limit! Henry Denker and
Ralph Berkey. Chapman '56;
NCTE
Time Machine, The. H. G.
Wells. Heiney; Lass BN; Ma-
gill I, CE, M1&2, MC, MEF,
SF; Ward
Time of Changes, A. Robert
Silverberg. Magill SF
Time of Friendship, The. Paul
Bowles. Magill '68, S
Time of Illusion, The. Jonathan
Schell. Magill '77
Time of Man, The. Elizabeth
Madox Roberts. Haydn; Keller
suppl. ; Magill I, CE, M1&2,
MAF, MC; Morehead
Time of the Cuckoo. Arthur
Laurents. Best '52; Chapman
'53; Drury
Time of Your Life, The. William
Saroyan. Best '39; Bonin;
Drury; Haydn; Lass AP; Lovell;
Matlaw; NCTE; Shank; Shipley;
Sobel
Time Out for Ginger. Ronald
Alexander. Drury

Time Regained (The Past Recaptured). Marcel Proust. (See also series title Remembrance of Things Past.) Haydn p. 631; Heiney

Time Remembered. Jean Anouilh. Best '57; Drury; NCTE; Shank

Time to Die, A. Tom Wicker. Magill '76

Time to Hear and Answer: Essays for the Bicentennial Season, A. Taylor Littleton, editor. Magill '78

Time to Speak. Sylvia Rayman. French

Time's Betrayal. Herman Melville. Gale-M

Time's Portraiture.... Nathaniel Hawthorne. Gale-H

Timoleon. Herman Melville. Gale-M

Timon of Athens. William Shakespeare. Campbell; Chute; Clark; Gassner; Guerber-ST; Halliday; Haydn; Keller; Lamb; McCutchan-ST; McSpadden S; Magill II, CE, M1&2, MC, MD; Ruoff; Shipley; Sobel

Tin Can, The. William Jay Smith. Magill '67, S

Tin Drum, The. Günter Grass. Magill IV, '64, MC, S

Tin Wedding. Margaret Leech. Keller suppl.

Tinker, The. Laurence Dobie and Robert Sloman. French

Tinker's Wedding, The. John Millington Synge. Gassner; Matlaw; Sobel

Tinted Venus, The. F. Anstey. Johnson

Tiny Alice. Edward Albee. Best '64; Drury; Kienzle; NCTE

'Tis Pity She's a Whore. John Ford. Gassner; Haydn; Holzknecht; Magill II, CE, M1&2, MC, MD; Ruoff; Shipley; Sobel

Titan, The. Theodore Dreiser. (See also his The Cowperwood Novels.) Gerber; Heiney; Magill I, CE, M1&2, MAF, MC

Titan. Jean Paul Richter. Johnson

Titans, The. André Maurois. Magill '59, S

Titus Andronicus. William Shakespeare. Campbell; Chute; Clark; Gassner; Guerber-ST; Halliday; Haydn; Keller; McCutchan-ST; McSpadden S; Magill II, CE, M1&2, MC, MD; Ruoff; Shipley; Sobel

To a Blossoming Pear Tree. James Wright. Magill '78

To an Early Grave. Wallace Markfield. Magill '65, S

To Appomattox. Burke Davis. Magill '60, S

To Be a Pilgrim. Joyce Cary. Magill III, CE, M1&2, MC, MEF; Ward

To Be Young, Gifted, and Black. Lorraine Hansberry. Drury

To Criticize the Critic. T. S. Eliot. Magill '67, S

To Damascus, Part I. August Strindberg. Matlaw; Shank; Sprinchorn

To Damascus, Part II. August Strindberg. Matlaw; Sprinchorn

To Damascus, Part III. August Strindberg. Matlaw; Sprinchorn

To Die see Dying

To Find Oneself. Luigi Pirandello. Matlaw

To Have and to Hold. Mary Johnston. Johnson; Keller; Smith

To Herat and Cabul. George A. Henty. Kaye

To Jerusalem and Back. Saul Bellow. Magill '77

To Kill a Mockingbird. Harper Lee. (See also adaptation by Christopher Sergel.) Magill '61, M1, MB, S

To Kill a Mockingbird. Christopher Sergel. (Based on the novel by Harper Lee.) Drury

To Leave Before Dawn. Julien Green. Magill '68, S

To Let see Forsyte Saga, The

To Live in Peace. Giovacchino Forzano. French

To Major John Gentian, Dean of the Burgundy Club. Herman Melville. Gale-M

To Mix with Time. May Swenson. Magill '64, S

To Please His Wife. Thomas Hardy. Pinion; Saxelby

To Teach, To Love. Jesse Stuart. Magill '71

To the Ladies! George S. Kaufman and Marc Connelly. Drury

To the Lighthouse.   Virginia
Woolf.   Haydn; Keller suppl. ;
Magill I, CE, M1&2, MC,
MEF; Stade p. 195; Ward
Toads and Diamonds.   Unknown.
Keller (Fairy Tales)
Tobacco Road.   Erskine Caldwell.
(See also adaptation by Jack
Kirkland.)   Haydn; Heiney;
Magill I, CE, M1&2, MAF,
MC; Morehead; Smith
Tobacco Road.   Jack Kirkland.
(Based on the novel by Erskine
Caldwell.)   Cartmell; Drury;
Lass AP; Lovell; Matlaw;
Shipley; Sobel
Tobias and the Angel.   James
Bridie.   Drury; French; Mat-
law; NCTE; Ward
Tod einer Puppe, Der (A Doll's
Death).   Ferdinand Bruckner.
Kienzle
Together.   Robert Herrick.
Keller
Toilers of the Sea, The.   Victor
Hugo.   Grozier; Johnson;
Keller; Magill II, CE, M1&2,
MC, MEUF
Toilet, The.   Leroi Jones.
Best '64
Toki wa Ima Kikkyo no Hataage
(The Standard of Revolt).
Tsuruya Namboku IV.   Halford
Told by an Idiot.   Rose Macaulay.
Ward
Tolkien: A Biography.   Humphrey
Carpenter.   Magill '78
Toll-Gatherer's Day: A Sketch
of Transitory Life, The.
Nathaniel Hawthorne.   Gale-H
Tolstoy.   Henri Troyat.   Magill
'69, M1, S
Tolstoy's Letters.   Vols. 1-2.
Count Leo Tolstoy.   Magill
'79
Tom Barber.   Forrest Reid.
Magill '55, S
Tom Brown's School Days.
Thomas Hughes.   Grozier;
Haydn; Johnson; Keller; Magill
II, CE, M1&2, MC, MEF
Tom Burke of Ours.   Charles
Lever.   Johnson; Kaye;
Keller; Magill II, CE, M1&2,
MC, MEF
Tom Cringle's Log.   Michael
Scott.   Johnson; Keller; Magill
I, CE, M1&2, MC, MEF

Tom Deadlight.   Herman Melville.
Gale-M
Tom Grogan.   Francis Hopkinson
Smith.   Keller
Tom Jones.   Henry Fielding.   (See
also adaptation by David Rogers
and Edward German, et al.)
Armstrong; Goodman; Grozier;
Haydn; Johnson; Johnson-18th/2;
Keller; Lass BN; Magill I, CE,
M1&2, MC, MEF; Wilson
Tom Jones.   Edward German,
Alexander M. Thompson, Robert
Courtneidge and Charles H.
Taylor.   (Based on the novel
by Henry Fielding.)   Drinkrow
Tom Jones.   David Rogers.
(Based on the novel by Henry
Fielding.)   Drury
Tom Paine.   Paul Foster.   NCTE
Tom Sawyer.   Mark Twain.
Armstrong (Adventures); Gale-
T; Haydn; Lass AN; Magill I,
CE, M1&2, MAF, MAL5, MC;
Morehead (Adventures); Olfson
(Adventures); Smith (Adventures);
Wilson
Tom Sawyer Abroad.   Mark Twain.
Gale-T
Tom Sawyer, Detective.   Mark
Twain.   Gale-T
Tom Swift Novels, The.   "Victor
Appleton. "   Magill SF
Tom Thumb the Great.   Henry
Fielding.   Magill II, CE, M1&2,
MC, MD; Shipley (Tragedy...);
Sobel
Tom Tiddler's Ground.   Charles
Dickens.   Hardwick CD
Tome.   Saint Leo the Great.
Magill CAL, CHL
Tommy.   Howard Lindsay and
Bertrand Robinson.   Drury
Tommy and Grizel.   Sir James
M. Barrie.   Keller
Tomorrow and Tomorrow.   Philip
Barry.   Best '30; Drury; Shipley
Tomorrow and Yesterday.   Hein-
rich Böll.   Magill '58, S
Tomorrow the Dawn.   Henry de
Montherlant.   Matlaw
Tomorrow the World.   James
Gow and Arnaud d'Usseau.
Best '42; Drury
Tone of Time, The.   Henry
James.   Gale-J
Tong-Moon-Sun.   Haydn
Tonight at 8:30.   Noel Coward.

TONIGHT

Matlaw; Shipley; Sobel
Tonight in Samarkand. Jacques
Deval. Kienzle
Tonight We Improvise. Luigi
Pirandello. Drury; Matlaw;
Shipley; Sprinchorn
Tono-Bungay. H. G. Wells.
Armstrong; Haydn; Heiney;
Keller; Lass BN; Magill I,
CE, M1&2, MC, MEF; Ward
Tons of Money. Will Evans and
Valentine. French
Tony Draws a Horse. Lesley
Storm. French
Tony Kytes, the Arch-Deceiver.
Thomas Hardy. Saxelby
Too True to Be Good. George
Bernard Shaw. Hardwick;
Matlaw; Sobel
Top of the Ladder. Tyrone
Guthrie. French
Topaze. Marcel Pagnol. Shipley;
Sobel
Torch-Bearers, The. George
Kelly. Drury; French; NCTE;
Sobel
Toreador, The. Ivan Caryll,
Lionel Monckton, James T.
Tanner, Harry Nicholls, Adrian
Ross and Percy Greenbank.
Drinkrow
Toribeyama Shinju (Double Suicide
at Toribeyama). Kido Oka-
moto. Halford
Toro! Toro! Toro! William
Hjortsberg. Magill '75
Torquato Tasso. Johann Wolfgang
von Goethe. Gassner
Torrents of Spring. Ivan Tur-
genev. Haydn
Tortesa, the Usurer. Nathaniel
P. Willis. Sobel
Tory Lover, The. Sarah Orne
Jewett. Keller
Tosca, La. Victorien Sardou.
Shipley; Sobel
Tottel's Miscellany. Richard
Tottel. Haydn; Ruoff p. 300;
Keller
Touch. Thom Gunn. Magill
'69, S
Touch of Fear, The. Dorothy
and Campbell Christie. French
Touch of the Poet, A. Eugene
O'Neill. Anderson; Best '58;
Chapman '59; Drury; Kienzle;
Magill '58, M1, MB, S;
Matlaw; NCTE

Touchstone, The. Charles Major.
Kaye
Tous contre tous (All Against All).
Arthur Adamov. Kienzle
Tovarich. Jacques Deval. Best
'36; Drury; NCTE
Toward Freedom. Jawaharlal
Nehru. Haydn
Toward the Final Solution: A His-
tory of European Racism.
George L. Mosse. Magill '79
Towards Zero. Agatha Christie.
Drury; French
Tower, The. Hugo von Hofmanns-
thal. Matlaw
Tower Beyond Tragedy, The.
Robinson Jeffers. Kienzle;
Shank
Tower of Glass. Robert Silver-
berg. Magill SF
Tower of London, The. William
Harrison Ainsworth. Cohen;
Johnson; Kaye; Magill I, CE,
M1&2, MC, MEF
Tower of Nesle, The. Alexandre
Dumas (father). Shipley
Towers of Trebizond, The. Rose
Macaulay. Magill '58, S
Town, The. William Faulkner.
Magill III, '58, CE, M1&2,
MAF, MD, MC, S
Town, The. Conrad Richter.
Magill II, CE, M1&2, MAF,
MC
Town That Would Have a Pageant,
The. L. du Garde Peach.
French
Towneley Plays, The see Wake-
field Plays, The
Toxophilus. Roger Ascham.
Ruoff p. 17
Toy Cart, The see Little Clay
Cart, The
Toys in the Attic. Lillian Hell-
man. Best '59; Bonin; Drury;
Kienzle; Magill '61, M1, S;
Matlaw; NCTE
Trachiniae (Women of Trachis).
Sophocles. (See also adaptation
Women of Trachis by Ezra
Pound.) Feder (Women); Gass-
ner; Hathorn; Magill III, CE,
M1&2, MC, MD (Women);
Shank; Shipley
Trachinian Women, The see
Trachiniae
Track of the Cat, The. Walter
Van Tilburg Clark. Magill II,

CE, M1&2, MAF, MC
Track to Bralgu, The. B. Wongar.
Magill '79
Trackers, The. Sophocles.
Feder (Ichneutai); Hathorn
(Ichneutae); Reinhold
Tract Concerning the First Prin-
ciple, The see De primo
principio
Tractate on Education see Of
Education
Tractatus logico-philosophicus.
Ludwig Wittgenstein. Magill WP
Tractatus Theologico-Politicus.
Benedict de Spinoza. Haydn
Tracts for the Times. Unknown.
Keller
Trader Horn. Alfred Aloysius
Horn. Keller suppl.
Tradition of Eighteen Hundred and
Four, A. Thomas Hardy.
Pinion; Saxelby
Trafalgar. Benito Perez Galdós.
Kaye; Keller
Tragedian in Spite of Himself, A.
Anton Chekhov. Matlaw
Tragedies. Lucius Annaeus
Seneca. Downs M; Haydn
Tragedy of Error, A. Henry
James. Gale-J
Tragedy of Faust, The see Faust
Tragedy of Locrine, The. Un-
known. Sobel
Tragedy of Love, The. Gunnar
Heiberg. Drury
Tragedy of Nan, The. John
Masefield. Drury; Matlaw;
Shipley; Sobel
Tragedy of Superstition, The.
James Nelson Barker. Drury;
Lovell
Tragedy of the Dacres, The.
Edward Ebenezer Crake.
Kaye
Tragedy of Tragedies, or, The
Life and Death of Tom Thumb
the Great see Tom Thumb
the Great
Tragedy of Two Ambitions, A.
Thomas Hardy. Pinion; Saxelby
Tragedy of Waste, The. Stuart
Chase. Keller suppl.
Tragic America. Theodore
Dreiser. Gerber
Tragic Comedians, The. George
Meredith. Kaye
Tragic Idyll, A. Paul Bourget.
Keller

Tragic Muse, The. Henry James.
Gale-J; Magill IV, CE, M2,
MAL3, MC
Tragic Sense of Life in Men and
in Peoples, The. Miguel de
Unamuno y Jugo. Haydn; Magill
IV, MC
Trail of the Fox, The. David
Irving. Magill '78
Trail of the Lonesome Pine, The.
John Fox, Jr. Haydn
Trail of the Sword, The. Sir
Gilbert Parker. Kaye
Trail of the Torch, The see
Passing of the Torch, The
Train of Powder, A. Rebecca
West. Magill '55, S
Train Whistle Guitar. Albert
Murray. Magill '75
Training in Christianity. Søren
Kierkegaard. Magill CHL
Traité de la lumière. Christiaan
Huygens. Haydn
Traité du libre arbitre. Yves
René Marie Simon. Magill
CAL
Traité élémentaire de chimie
(Elementary Treatise of Chem-
istry). Antoine Laurent La-
voisier. Downs M; Haydn
Traitor, The. Thomas Dixon.
Kaye
Traitor, The. James Shirley.
Magill III, CE, M1&2, MC,
MD; Ruoff
Traitor, The. Herman Wouk.
Drury
Traitor or Loyalist. Henry K.
Webster. Kaye
Traitor's Escape, A. James O.
Kaler. Kaye
Tramp Abroad, A. Mark Twain.
Gale-T
Transatlantic Blues. Wilfrid
Sheed. Magill '79
Transatlantic Patterns: Cultural
Comparisons of England with
America. Martin Green.
Magill '78
Transformation in Christ. Dietrich
Von Hildebrand. Magill CAL
Transformation of Southern Poli-
tics, The. Jack Bass and
Walter DeVries. Magill '77
Transgressor, The. Julien
Green. Magill '58, S
Transient and Permanent in Chris-
tianity, The. Theodore Parker.

Magill CHL
Translations and Adaptations of the
Aeneid. Keller (Aeneid)
Translations of Homer. Alexander
Pope. Haydn
Transparent Things. Vladimir
Nabokov. Magill '73
Transposed Heads, The. Thomas
Mann. Heiney
Trap, The. Dan Jacobson. Magill
'55, S
Trapp Family Singers, The.
Maria August Trapp. (See
adaptation The Sound of Music
by Howard Lindsay et al.)
Travel Diary of a Philosopher,
The. Count Hermann Keyser-
ling. Keller suppl.
Traveler at Forty, A. Theodore
Dreiser. Gerber
Travelers. Ruth Prawer Jhabvala.
Magill '74
Traveling Through the Dark.
William Stafford. Magill Ss
Traveller from Altruria, A.
William Dean Howells. Car-
rington
Traveller Without Luggage. Jean
Anouilh. Drury; French;
Matlaw
Travellers, The. Jean Stubbs.
Magill '64, S
Traveller's Joy. Arthur Macrae.
French
Travelling Companions. Henry
James. Gale-J
Travels and Adventures of Baron
Munchausen, The see
Baron Munchausen's Narrative
Travels in Arabia Deserta.
Charles M. Doughty. Haydn
(Arabia); Magill III, M1, MC,
MNF; Ward (Arabia)
Travels in France. Arthur
Young. Keller
Travels of Jaimie McPheeters,
The. Robert Lewis Taylor.
Magill '59, M1, S
Travels of Marco Polo, Marco
Polo. Downs F, FG; Haydn;
Keller; Magill I, CE, M1&2,
MC, MNF
Travels of Sir John Mandeville,
The. Unknown. Haydn; Keller
Travels to the Interior Districts
of Africa. Mungo Park.
Magill IV, MC
Travels with a Donkey. Robert

Louis Stevenson. Keller; Ma-
gill I, CE, M1&2, MC, MNF
Travels with Charley. John Stein-
beck. Magill '63, M1, S
Travels with My Aunt. Graham
Greene. Magill '71
Travesties. Tom Stoppard. Best
'75; Drury; Magill '76
Travesty. John Hawkes. Magill
'77
Tread the Dark: New Poems.
David Ignatow. Magill '79
Treasure, The. David Pinski.
Drury; Matlaw; Shipley
Treasure Hunt. M. J. Farrell
and John Perry. French
Treasure Island. Robert Louis
Stevenson. Armstrong; Grozier;
Haydn; Johnson; Lass BN; Ma-
gill I, CE, M1&2, MC, MEF;
Olfson; Wilson
Treasure of the Humble, The.
Maurice Maeterlinck. Keller
Treatise Concerning Religious Af-
fections, A. Jonathan Edwards.
Magill CHL
Treatise Concerning the Principles
of Human Knowledge, A.
George Berkeley. Haydn
(Principles); Magill WP
Treatise Concerning the Pursuit
of Learning. Hugh of St. Vic-
tor. Magill CAL
Treatise Concerning the Search
After Truth. Nicholas Male-
branche. Magill CHL
Treatise of Excommunication.
Thomas Erastus. Magill CHL
Treatise of Human Nature, A
(Book I). David Hume. Haydn;
Magill WP
Treatise of Moral Philosophy,
Containing the Sayings of the
Wise, A. William Baldwin.
Ruoff p. 27
Treatise of Reformation Without
Tarrying for Any. Robert
Browne. Magill CHL
Treatise on Ceramic Industries.
Emile Bourry. Keller
Treatise on Christian Liberty, A.
Martin Luther. Magill CHL
Treatise on Conic Sections. Apol-
lonius of Perga. Haydn
Treatise on Electricity and Mag-
netism. James Clerk-Maxwell.
Haydn
Treatise on Human Nature see

Treatise of Human Nature
Treatise on Laws. Francisco
Suarez, S. J. Magill CAL
Treatise on Painting. Leonardo
da Vinci. Keller
Treatise on the Church. John
Huss. Magill CHL
Treatise on the Fermentation
Known as Lactic. Louis
Pasteur. Downs M
Treatise on the Four Gospels.
Joachim of Fiore. Magill
CHL
Treatise on the Holy Spirit. Saint
Basil. Magill CAL
Treatise on the Laws and Customs
of England. Henry of Bracton.
Magill CAL
Treatise on the Mysteries. Saint
Hilary of Poitiers. Magill
CAL
Treatise on the Passion. Sir
Thomas More. Magill CAL
Treatise on the Promises. Saint
Dionysius of Alexandria.
Magill CAL
Treatise on Tolerance. Voltaire.
Haydn
Treatises of Cicero, The. Mar-
cus Tullius Cicero. Magill
IV, MC
Treatises on Marriage. Tertul-
lian. Magill CAL
Treblinka. Jean-Francois Steiner.
Magill '68, S
Trébol florido, El (Flowering
Clover). Rafael Alberti.
Kienzle
Tree Grows in Brooklyn, A.
Betty Smith. Haydn; Magill I,
CE, M1&2, MAF, MC
Tree of Heaven, The. May Sin-
clair. Keller suppl.
Tree of Knowledge, The. Henry
James. Gale-J
Tree of Man, The. Patrick
White. Magill IV, '55, M1,
MC, S
Tree of the Folkungs, The.
Verner von Heidenstam.
Magill II, CE, M1&2, MC,
MEUF
Tree on Fire, A. Alan Sillitoe.
Magill '69, S
Trees, The. Conrad Richter.
Magill II, CE, M1&2, MAF,
MC
Trelawney of the Wells. Arthur

Wing Pinero. Best '94; Cart-
mell; Drury; French; Haydn;
Matlaw; Sobel
Trembling of a Leaf, The. W.
Somerset Maugham. Ward
Tremendous Adventures of Major
Gahagan. William Makepeace
Thackeray. Mudge
Trial, The. André Gide and Jean-
Louis Barrault. (Based on the
novel by Franz Kafka.) Shank
Trial, The. Franz Kafka. (See
also adaptation by André Gide.)
Haydn; Heiney; Lass EN; Magill
I, CE, M1&2, MC, MEUF;
Olfson
Trial and Error. Kenneth Horne.
French
Trial by Jury. William Schwenck
Gilbert and Arthur Sullivan.
Magill II, CE, M1&2, MC,
MD; Shipley; Sobel
Trial of a Judge. Stephen Spend-
er. Matlaw
Trial of Jesus, The. John Mase-
field. Drury
Trial of Lucullus, The. Bertolt
Brecht. Matlaw
Trial of Mary Dugan, The.
Bayard Veiller. Drury; French;
Sobel
Trial of the Catonsville Nine, The.
Daniel Berrigan, S. J. Best
'70; Drury; NCTE
Trialogus. John Wycliffe. Magill
CHL
Trials of Brother Jero, The.
Wole Soyinka. Matlaw
Tribe That Lost Its Head, The.
Nicholas Monsarrat. Magill
'57, S
Tribute. Bernard Slade. Best
'77
Trick to Catch the Old One, A.
Thomas Middleton. Holz-
knecht; Keller; Magill II, CE,
M1&2, MC, MD; Ruoff; Shipley
Trickster, The. Titus Maccius
Plautus. Magill III, CE,
M1&2, MC, MD
Trickster of Seville and His Guest
of Stone. Tirso de Molina.
Shank
Trifle from Life, A. Anton
Chekhov. Keller suppl. (Party)
Trifles. Susan Glaspell. Matlaw
Trifles and Tomfooleries. George
Bernard Shaw. Ward

Trilby. George Du Maurier. (See also adaptation by Paul M. Potter.). Goodman; Grozier; Haydn; Johnson; Keller; Magill I, CE, M1&2, MC, MEF
Trilby. Paul M. Potter. (Based on the novel by George Du Maurier.) Sobel
Trilogy of Desire see Cowperwood Novels, The
Trinity. Leon Uris. Magill '77
Trinummus (The Three Penny Day). Titus Maccius Plautus. Feder (Three); Hathorn; Reinhold; Shipley (Three)
Trip Abroad, A see Voyage of Monsieur Perrichon, The
Trip to Chinatown, A. Charles H. Hoyt. Lovell; Shipley
Trip to Scarborough, A. Richard Brinsley Sheridan. Sobel
Tripitaka: The Pali Canon of Buddhism. Haydn
Tripitakas. Siddhartha Gautama. Downs F
Triple Crown, The. Rose Schuster. Kaye
Tristan and Isolde. Gottfried von Strassburg. Haydn; Magill III, CE, M1&2, MC, MP
Tristan and Isolt. John Masefield. Keller suppl. ; Sobel
Tristia. Ovid. Feder
Tristram. Edwin Arlington Robinson. Haydn (a); Keller suppl. ; Magill I, CE, M1&2, MC, MP
Tristram and Iseult. Matthew Arnold. Haydn
Tristram of Lyonesse. Algernon Charles Swinburne. Haydn
Tristram Shandy. Laurence Sterne. Haydn; Johnson; Johnson-18th/2; Keller; Lass BN; Magill I, CE, M1&2, MC, MEF; Olfson
Tristram the Jester. Ernst Hardt. Drury
Triton. Samuel R. Delany. Magill SF
Triumph in the West. Sir Arthur Bryant. Magill '60, MB, S
Triumph of Death, The. Gabriele D'Annunzio. Heiney; Johnson; Magill II, CE, M1&2, MC, MEUF
Triumph of the Egg, The. Sherwood Anderson. Keller suppl.

Triumph of the Novel, The. Albert J. Guerard. Magill '77
Triumph or Tragedy: Reflections on Vietnam. Richard N. Goodwin. Magill '67, S
Triumphant Democracy. Andrew Carnegie. Keller
Troades see Trojan Women, The
Troilus and Cressida. William Shakespeare. Campbell; Chute; Clark; Gassner; Guerber-ST; Halliday; Haydn; Keller; Lamb; McCutchan-SC; McSpadden S; Magill II, M1, MC, MD; Ruoff; Shipley; Sobel
Troilus and Criseyde. Geoffrey Chaucer. Armstrong; Haydn; Keller; Magill I, CE, M1&2, MC, MP
Trois Contes. Gustave Flaubert. Haydn
Trojan War. Derek Bowskill. (Based on The Iliad by Homer.) Drury
Trojan War Will Not Take Place, The see Tiger at the Gates
Trojan Women, The. Euripides. Cartmell; Downs F, FG; Drury; Feder; Gassner; Hathorn; Haydn; Magill III, CE, M1&2, MC, MD; NBC 2; Reinhold; Shank; Shipley
Trojan Women, The. Lucius Annaeus Seneca. Feder; Hathorn; Reinhold
Tropic of Capricorn. Henry Miller. Heiney; Magill IV, MC
Tropical Africa. Henry Drummond. Keller
Troubadours and Trouvères. Harriet Waters Preston. Keller
Trouble with Reason, The see Woe from Wit
Troubled Sleep see Roads to Freedom
Troy and Its Remains. Dr. Heinrich Schliemann. Keller
Truculentus. Titus Maccius Plautus. Feder; Hathorn; Reinhold; Shipley
True Adventures of Huckleberry Finn. John Seeyle. Magill '70
True Christianity. Johann Arndt. Magill CHL
True Grit. Charles Portis. Magill '69, M1, S
True Heart. Frederick Breton.

Kaye
True History, The. Lucian of
Samosata. Downs M; Magill
III, CE, M1&2, MC, MEUF
True Humanism. Jacques Mari-
tain. Magill CHL
True Intellectual System of the
Universe, The. Ralph Cud-
worth. Magill CHL
True Man and Traitor. Matthias
M. Bodkin. Kaye
True Relation of Such Occur-
rences and Accidents of Note
as Hath Hapned in Virginia
Since the First Planting of
That Colony, A. Capt. John
Smith. Haydn; Keller
True to the Old Flag. George
A. Henty. Kaye
True unto Death. Eliza F. Pol-
lard. Kaye
Trumpet-Major, The. Thomas
Hardy. Saxelby
Trumps. George William Curtis.
Johnson
Trustee from the Toolroom.
Nevil Shute. Magill '61, S
Trusting and the Maimed, The.
James Plunkett. Magill '55,
S
Truth, The. Clyde Fitch.
Drury; Keller; Matlaw; Shipley
Truth About Blayds, The. A. A.
Milne. Drury; Keller suppl.;
Matlaw; Shipley
Truth and Justice. Anton Hansen
Tammsaare. Haydn
Truth of the Christian Religion,
The. Hugo Grotius. Magill
CHL
Truth Suspected. Juan Ruiz de
Alarcón y Mendoza. Magill
III, CE, M1&2, MC, MD;
Shank; Shipley
Tryst at an Ancient Earthwork,
A. Thomas Hardy. Pinion
Tsuchigumo (The Ground Spider).
Kawatake Mokuami. Halford
Tsuchiya Chikara. Watanabe
Katei. Halford
Tsumoru Koi no Seki no To (The
Love Story at the Snow-Covered
Barrier). Unknown. Halford
Tsuyu Kosode Mukashi Hachijo
(The Old Story About the Wet
Wadded Silk Coat). Kawatake
Mokuami. Halford
Tube of Plenty. Erik Barnouw.

Magill '76
Tunc. Lawrence Durrell. Magill
'69, S, SF
Tuned Out. Maia Wojciechowska.
Benedict
Tunnel, The. Bernhard Keller-
mann. Magill SF
Tunnel of Love, The. Peter De
Vries. (See also adaptation by
Joseph Fields and Peter De
Vries.) Magill '54, S
Tunnel of Love, The. Joseph
Fields and Peter De Vries.
(Based on the novel by Peter
De Vries.) NCTE
Tunnel Sottomarino, Il. Luigi
Motta. Magill SF
Tunnel Through the Deeps, The.
Harry Harrison. Magill SF
Tunning of Elynoure Rummynge,
The. John Skelton. Haydn
Turandot, Princess of China.
Carlo Gozzi. Gassner; Shipley
Turbulent Town, A. E. N.
Hoare. Kaye
Turcaret. Alain René Le Sage.
Magill III, CE, M1&2, MC,
MD; Shipley
Turkish Bath, The. Anthony Trol-
lope. Gerould
Turmoil. Booth Tarkington.
Keller
Turn of the Century, The. Mark
Sullivan. Keller suppl. (Our
Times)
Turn of the Screw, The. Henry
James. (See also adaptation
The Innocents by William Archi-
bald.) Gale-J; Haydn; Keller;
Lass AN; Magill II, CE, M1&2,
MAF, MAL3, MC; Olfson
Turn of the Tide, The. Sir
Arthur Bryant. Magill '58,
MB, S
Turnstile, The. A. E. W. Mason.
Keller
Turtle Diary. Russell Hoban.
Magill '77
Turtle Island. Gary Snyder.
Magill '75
Tutor, The see Private Tutor,
The
Twelfth Night. William Shake-
speare. (See also adaptation
Your Own Thing by Donald
Driver et al.) Campbell;
Chute; Clark; Drury; Gassner;
Guerber-SC; Halliday; Haydn;

Keller; Lamb; McCutchan-SC;
McSpadden S; Magill II, CE,
M1&2, MC, MD; Ruoff; Shank;
Shipley; Sobel; Wilson
Twelve, The. Aleksandr Alek-
sandrovich Blok. Haydn
Twelve Angry Men. Reginald
Rose. (Teleplay; see adapta-
tion by Sherman L. Sergel.)
Twelve Angry Men. Sherman
L. Sergel. (Based on the
teleplay by Reginald Rose.)
Drury; Kienzle
Twelve Men. Theodore Dreiser.
Gerber
Twelve Pictures, The. Edith
Simon. Magill '55, S
Twelve-Pound Look, The. Sir
James M. Barrie. Matlaw;
Sobel
Twelve Thousand. Bruno Frank.
Shipley
Twenties, The. Edmund Wilson.
Magill '76
Twenty-Five Years. Edward
Grey, First Viscount of Fal-
lodon. Keller suppl.
Twenty Letters to a Friend.
Svetlana Alliluyeva. Magill
'68, M1, S
Twenty-Six Men and a Girl.
Máxim Górky. Heiney
Twenty Thousand Leagues Under
the Sea. Jules Verne.
Cohen; Grozier, Haydn; John-
son; Lass EN; Magill I, CE,
M1&2, MC, MEUF, SF;
Wilson
Twenty Years After. Alexandre
Dumas (father). Johnson;
Kaye; Keller; Magill II, CE,
M1&2, MC, MEUF
Twenty Years at Hull-House.
Jane Addams. Keller
Twenty Years of Congress:
From Lincoln to Garfield.
James G. Blaine. Keller
Twice-Told Tales. Nathaniel
Hawthorne. Keller
Twilight. Elsa Porges Bernstein.
Drury
Twilight Crane. Junji Konoshita.
Kienzle
Twilight in Italy. D. H. Law-
rence. Magill IV, MC
Twilight of Capitalism, The.
Michael Harrington. Magill
'77

Twilight of the Old Order, 1774-
1778. Claude Manceron.
Magill '78
Twin Menaechmi, The see
Menaechmi, The
Two Admirals, The. James
Fenimore Cooper. Johnson;
Walker
Two Adolescents. Alberto Mora-
via. Lass EN
Two Angry Women of Abingdon,
The Pleasant History of see
Pleasant History of Two Angry
Women of Abingdon, The
Two Bacchides, The see Bac-
chides
Two Baronesses, The. Hans
Christian Andersen. Johnson
Two Blind Mice. Samuel Spewack.
Best '48; Drury
Two by Two. Peter Stone, Martin
Charnin and Richard Rodgers.
(Based on The Flowering Peach
by Clifford Odets.) NCTE
Two Chiefs of Dunboy, The.
James Anthony Froude. Keller
Two Cities, The. Otto of Freis-
ing. Magill CAL
Two Citizens. James Wright.
Magill '74
Two Deaths of Quincas Wateryell,
The. Jorge Amado. Magill
'66, S
Two Dianas, The. Alexandre
Dumas (father). Johnson; Kaye
Two Discourses on Universal His-
tory. Anne Robert Jacques
Turgot. Magill CAL
Two Drovers, The. Sir Walter
Scott. McSpadden W
Two-Edged Sword, The. John L.
McKenzie, S. J. Magill CAL
Two Essays on Analytical Psychol-
ogy. Carl G. Jung. Magill
IV, MC
Two Executioners, The. Fernando
Arrabal. Kienzle
Two Faces, The (The Faces).
Henry James. Gale J
Two Faces of Murder, The.
George Batson. French
Two for the Seesaw. William
Gibson. Drury; French; Ki-
enzle; NCTE
Two Generals, The. Anthony
Trollope. Gerould
Two Gentlemen of Verona. Wil-
liam Shakespeare. Campbell;

Chute; Clark; Gassner; Guer-
ber-SC; Halliday; Haydn; Kel-
ler; Lamb; McCutchan-SC;
McSpadden S; Magill II, CE,
M1&2, MC, MD; Ruoff; Ship-
ley; Sobel
Two-Handed Sword, The.   Frank
Ormerod.   Kaye
Two Heroines of Plumplington,
The.   Anthony Trollope.
Gerould
Two Hundred Were Chosen.   E.
P. Conkle.   Drury
Two Lamentable Tragedies.
Robert Yarington.   Ruoff p.
114
Two Living and One Dead.   Sigurd
Christiansen.   Haydn
Two Loves of Heaven   see   Love
After Death
Two Men.   Elizabeth Drew (Bar-
stow) Stoddard.   Keller
Two Mr. Wetherbys, The.   St.
John E. C. Hankin.   Drury
Two Mrs. Carrolls, The.   Martin
Vale.   Drury; French
Two Noble Kinsmen, The.   Wil-
liam Shakespeare and John
Fletcher.   Campbell; Clark;
Drury; Gassner; Halliday;
Haydn; Holzknecht; Keller;
Magill II, CE, M1&2, MC,
MD; Ruoff; Shipley; Sobel
Two on a Tower.   Thomas Hardy.
Saxelby
Two on an Island.   Elmer Rice.
Drury
Two Orphans, The.   Adolphe P.
d'Ennery and Eugène Cormon.
Drury; Shipley; Sobel
Two-Part Inventions.   Richard
Howard.   Magill '75
Two Planets.   Kurd Lasswitz.
Magill SF
Two Shepherds, The.   Gregorio
Martinez-Sierra.   Drury
Two Sides of an Island.   Martin
Halpern.   Magill '64, S
Two Sources of Morality and
Religion, The.   Henri Berg-
son.   Magill CHL, WP
Two Stars for Comfort.   John
Mortimer.   French; Kienzle
Two Tales.   Shmuel Yosef Agnon.
Magill '67, S
Two Temples, The.   Herman
Melville.   Gale-M
Two Theaters, The (Dwa teatry).

Jerzy Szaniawski.   Anderson
(Dwa)
2001: A Space Odyssey.   Arthur
C. Clarke.   Magill SF
2018 A. D. or The King Kong
Blues.   Sam J. Lundwall.
Magill SF
Two Thousand Years Ago.   Alfred
John Church.   Kaye
2 x 2 = 5.   Gustav Johannes
Wied.   Drury
Two Towers, The.   J. R. R.
Tolkien.   Magill IV, CE, M2,
MC
Two Treatises ... Immortality of
Reasonable Souls.   Sir Kenelm
Digby.   Ruoff p. 110
Two Treatises of Government.
John Locke.   Downs M, FG;
Haydn
Two Under the Indian Sun.   Jon
and Rumer Godden.   Magill
'67, S
Two Virtues, The.   Alfred Sutro.
Drury
Two Weeks in Another Town.
Irvin Shaw.   Magill '61, S
Two Women.   Alberto Moravia.
Magill IV, '59, M1, MC, S
Two Years Ago.   Charles Kings-
ley.   Johnson
Two Years Before the Mast.
Richard Henry Dana, Jr.
Haydn; Keller; Magill I, CE,
M1&2, MAL1, MC, MNF; Wil-
son
Tympanists, The.   Sophocles.
Hathorn
Typee.   Herman Melville.   Gale-
M; Johnson; Keller; Magill I,
CE, M1&2, MAF, MAL4, MC
Typewriter in the Sky.   L. Ron
Hubbard.   Magill SF
Typhoon.   Joseph Conrad.   Haydn;
Heiney
Typhoon (The Wages of Sin).
Theodore Dreiser.   Gerber
Typhus.   Anton Chekhov.   Keller
suppl. (Party)
Typists, The.   Murray Schisgal.
Kienzle
Tyranny of Tears, The.   C.
Haddon Chambers.   Drury
Tyrants Destroyed.   Vladimir
Nabokov.   Magill '76
Tyro.   Sophocles.   Hathorn

-U-

U. S. A.   John Dos Passos.
(Trilogy title; see also The
42nd Parallel; 1919; The Big
Money; adaptation by John
Dos Passos and Paul Shyre.)
Cartmell; Haydn; Heiney; Ma-
gill I, CE, M1&2, MAF, MC:
Morehead; Smith
U. S. A.   John Dos Passos and
Paul Shyre. (Based on the
trilogy by John Dos Passos.)
Drury
Uarda.   Georg Moritz Ebers.
.. Johnson; Kaye; Keller
Über den Gartenzaun (Across the
Garden Fence).   Konrad
Wünsche.   Kienzle
Überlebensgross Herr Krott (Mr.
Krott, Larger Than Life).
Martin Walser.   Kienzle
Ubik.   Philip K. Dick.   Magill SF
Ubu Roi (King Ubu).   Alfred
Jarry.   Gassner; Matlaw (King);
Sprinchorn
Ugly American, The.   Eugene
Burdick and William J. Led-
erer.   (See adaptation by
Bernard Lubar.)
Ugly American, The.   Bernard
Lubar.   (Based on the novel
by Eugene Burdick and William
J. Lederer.)   Drury
Ugly Duchess, The.   Lion Feucht-
wanger.   Keller suppl. ; Magill
I, CE, M1&2, MC, MEUF
Uhr schlägt Eins, Die (The Clock
Strikes One).   Carl Zuckmayer.
Kienzle
Uhren, Die (The Clocks).   Wolf-
gang Hildesheimer.   Kienzle
Ukiyozuka Hiyoku no Inazuma.
Tsuruya Namboku IV.   Halford
Ulenspiegel.   Ashley Duke.   Drury
Ultima Thule   see   Fortunes of
Richard Mahony, The
Ulysses   James Joyce.   (See
also adaptation Bloomsday by
Allan McClelland.)   Armstrong;
Haydn; Heiney; Magill I, CE,
M1&2, MC, MEF; Ward
Ulysses.   Stephen Phillips.
Drury
Unbearable Bassington, The.
Saki.   Magill I, CE, M1&2,
MC, MEF

Unbelehrbare, Der (The Unteach-
able).   Konrad Wünsche.   Ki-
enzle
Uncertain Greatness: Henry Kis-
singer and American Foreign
Policy.   Roger Morris.   Magill
'78
Uncertain Joy.   Charlotte Hastings.
French
Unchastened Woman, The.   Louis
K. Anspacher.   Best '09; Drury
Unclassed, The.   George Gissing.
Keller
Uncle.   Julia Markus.   Magill '79
Uncle Harry.   Thomas Job.   Best
'41; Drury; French; NCTE
Uncle of Europe.   Gordon Brook-
Shepherd.   Magill '77
Uncle Remus   see   Tales of Uncle
Remus
Uncle Silas.   Joseph Sheridan Le
Fanu.   Magill II, CE, M1&2,
MC, MEF
Uncle Tom's Cabin.   George L.
Aiken.   Gassner; Lovell; Ship-
ley; Sobel
Uncle Tom's Cabin.   Harriet
Beecher Stowe.   Cartmell;
Downs M, FG; Drury; Goodman;
Grozier; Haydn; Johnson; Kaye;
Keller; Lass AN; Magill I, CE,
M1&2, MAF, MAL5, MC; More-
head; Shank; Smith; Wilson
Uncle Vanya.   Anton Chekhov.
Drury; Gassner; Magill II, CE,
M1&2, MC, MD; Matlaw; Shank;
Shipley; Sobel
Uncle Willie.   Julie Berns and
Irving Elman.   NCTE
Uncompleted Past, The.   Martin
B. Duberman.   Magill '70
Unconditional Surrender   see
trilogy title Sword of Honour
Under Fire.   Henri Barbusse.
Heiney; Magill I, CE, M1&2,
MC, MEUF
Under Milk Wood: A Play for
Voices   Dylan Thomas   Best
'57; Drury; Kienzle; Magill IV,
'54, M1, MB, MC, S; Matlaw;
NCTE; Shank; Ward
Under Pontius Pilate.   William
Schuyler.   Kaye
Under the Dome of St. Paul's.
Emma Marshall.   Kaye
Under the Foeman's Flag.   Robert
Leighton.   Kaye
Under the Gaslight.   Augustin

Best '34; Drury; Matlaw; NBC
1; Shipley; Sobel
Valley Forge.   Alden W. Quinby.
Kaye
Valley of Bones, The.   Anthony
Powell. Magill '65, S
Valley of Darkness: The Japanese
People and World War Two.
Thomas R. H. Havens. Magill
'79
Valley of Decision, The.   Edith
Wharton. Keller
Valley of Fear, The.   Sir Arthur
Conan Doyle. Hardwick SH
Van Bibber and Others.   Richard
Harding Davis. Keller
Vandemark's Folly.   Herbert
Quick. Keller suppl.
Vanessa. Hugh Walpole. Magill
I, CE, M1&2, MC, MEF
Vanguard, The. Arnold Bennett.
Keller suppl.
Vanished Cities. Herman and
Georg Schreiber. Magill '58,
S
Vanishing Smuggler, The.   Stephen
Chalmers. Kaye
Vanity Fair. Constance Cox.
(Based on the novel by William
Makepeace Thackeray.) French
Vanity Fair. William Makepeace
Thackeray. (See also adapta-
tion by Constance Cox.) Arm-
strong; Goodman; Grozier;
Haydn; Hix; Johnson; Keller;
Lass BN; Magill I, CE,
M1&2, MC, MEF; Mudge;
Wilson
Varieties of Religious Experience,
The. William James. Magill
CHL
Variety of Things, A.   Max
Beerbohm. Ward
Variety Photoplays.   Edward Field.
Magill '68, S
Vasco. Georges Schehadé.
Anderson (Histoire); Kienzle;
Sprinchorn
Vasconcelos. William Gilmore
Simms. Kaye
Vathek. William Beckford.
Haydn; Johnson; Keller; Magill
II, CE, M1&2, MC, MEF
Vatican Swindle, The. André
Gide. Heiney; Keller suppl.
Vechno zhivye (Those Who Live
Forever). Viktor Sergeyevich
Rozov. Kienzle

Vedânta-Sûtras, The.   Unknown.
Keller (Sacred Books)
Vedas, The. Unknown.   Haydn
Vedic Hymns. Unknown.   Keller
(Sacred Books)
Veiled Lodger, The.   Sir Arthur
Conan Doyle. Hardwick SH
Vein of Iron. Ellen Glasgow.
Haydn
Veland. Gerhart Hauptmann.
Matlaw
Velvet Glove, The. Henry James.
Gale-J
Velvet Glove, The. Henry S.
Merriman. Kaye
Velvet Horn, The. Andrew Lytle.
Magill IV, '58, MB, MC, S
Vendée, La. Anthony Trollope.
Gerould; Kaye
Venetia. Benjamin Disraeli.
Johnson
Venetian Glass Nephew, The.
Elinor Wylie. Keller suppl. ;
Magill II, CE, M1&2, MAF,
MC
Venetian Red. P. M. Pasinetti.
Magill '61, S
Venexiana, La. Unknown.   Gass-
ner
Venice Preserved; or A Plot Dis-
covered. Thomas Otway.
Drury; Gassner; Haydn; Magill
II, CE, M1&2, MC, MD; Ship-
ley; Sobel
Ventre de Paris, Le.   Emile
Zola. Keller (Rougon)
Ventriloquist, The. Robert Huff.
Magill '78
Venus and Adonis. William
Shakespeare. Campbell; Clark;
Halliday; Haydn; Magill I, CE,
M1&2, MC, MP; Ruoff
Venus Observed. Christopher
Fry. Best '51; Drury; Kienzle;
Matlaw; NCTE; Shank
Venus Plus X. Theodore Stur-
geon. Magill SF
Vera; or, The Nihilists. Oscar
Wilde. Matlaw
Vera Vorontsoff. Sonya Kovalev-
sky. Keller
Veranilda. George Gissing. Kaye
Verdi. George Martin. Magill
'64, S
Verdict. Agatha Christie.
French
Veronica Playfair. Maud W.
Goodwin. Kaye

Verspätung, Die (The Delay).
Wolfgang Hildesheimer.
Kienzle
Very Private Life, A. Michael
Frayn. Magill '69, S
Very Special Baby, A. Robert
Alan Aurthur. Best '56;
NCTE
Vespae see Wasps, The
Vestiges of Creation see Vestiges
of the Natural History of Crea-
tion
Vestiges of the Natural History
of Creation. Robert Chambers.
Haydn
Via Crucis. Francis Marion
Crawford. Keller
Viaducts of Seine-et-Oise, The.
Marguerite Duras. Kienzle
Vibrations. George A. Woods.
Benedict
Vicar of Bullhampton, The.
Anthony Trollope. Gerould;
Magill II, CE, M1&2, MC,
MEF
Vicar of Wakefield, The. Oliver
Goldsmith. Armstrong; Cohen;
Goodman; Grozier; Haydn;
Hix; Johnson; Johnson-18th/2;
Keller; Lass BN; Magill I,
CE, M1&2, MC, MEF; Wilson
Vice Versa. F. Anstey. Johnson
Viceroy Sarah. Norman Gins-
bury. French
Vicomte de Dragelonne, The.
Alexandre Dumas (father).
Johnson; Kaye; Keller; Magill
I, CE, M1&2, MC, MEUF
Victim, The. Saul Bellow.
Magill IV, MC
Victims of Duty. Eugène Ionesco.
Kienzle; Matlaw
Victims of the Devil's Triangle.
David Sawn. Drury
Victor, The (Victory). Theodore
Dreiser. Gerber
Victor of Salamis, A. William
Stearns Davis. Kaye
Victor; ou, les enfants au pouvoir
(Victor; or, The Children Take
Power). Roger Vitrac. Gass-
ner
Victoria Regina. Laurence Hous-
man. Best '35; Drury; Mat-
law; Sobel
Victorian Poets, The. Edmund
Clarence Stedman. Keller
Victors, The (Men Without

Shadows). Jean-Paul Sartre.
Kienzle
Victory. Joseph Conrad. Arm-
strong; Haydn; Heiney; Keller;
Magill I, CE, M1&2, MC,
MEF; Ward
Victory. Oliver Warner. Magill
'59, MB, S
Victory in the Pacific, 1945.
Samuel Eliot Morison. Magill
'61, M1, S
Vida, La. Oscar Lewis. Magill
'67, S
Vidularia. Plautus. Feder;
Hathorn
Vie de Bohème, La. Théodore
Barrière and Henri Murger.
(Based on Scènes de la vie
de Bohème by Henri Murger.)
Shipley
Viet Rock. Megan Terry. NCTE
View from Highway 1, The.
Michael J. Arlen. Magill '77
View from Pompey's Head, The.
Hamilton Basso. Magill '54, S
View from the Bridge, A. Arthur
Miller. Best '55; Chapman '56;
Drury; Kienzle; Magill '55, M1,
MB, S; Matlaw; NCTE; Shank;
Sprinchorn
View from the UN. U Thant.
Magill '79
View of the Evidences of Chris-
tianity, A, William Paley.
Magill WP
View of Victorian Literature, A.
Geoffrey Tillotson. Magill '79
Vigil, The. Ladislaus Fodor.
French
Vigil of Venus, The see Per-
vigilium veneris
Vikings at Helgeland, The. Hen-
rik Ibsen. Matlaw
Vile Bodies. Evelyn Waugh.
Magill II, CE, M1&2, MC,
MEF; Stade p. 60
Village, The. Ivan Alexeyevich
Bunin. Heiney; Magill II, CE,
M1&2, MC, MEUF
Village, The. George Crabbe.
Haydn; Magill III, M1, MC,
MP
Village Labourer, The. J. L.
and Barbara Hammond. Keller
Village of Stepanchikogo, The.
Fyodor Mikhailovich Dostoevskii.
Berry-2
Village on the Cliff, The. Anne

-W-

'74; Drury
Wages of Sin, The see Typhoon
Wages of Sin, The. Lucas Malet.
  Keller
Wait Until Dark. Frederick Knott.
  Drury
Waiting for Gillian. Ronald Millar.
  French
Waiting for Godot. Samuel Beck-
  ett. Anderson; Best '55; Drury;
  Gassner; Kienzle; Magill III,
  '57, CE, M1&2, MB, MC,
  MD, S; Matlaw; NCTE; Shank;
  Sprinchorn; Ward
Waiting for Lefty. Clifford Odets.
  Drury; Haydn; Lovell; Matlaw;
  Shipley; Sobel; Sprinchorn
Waiting for the Verdict. Rebecca
  Harding Davis. Johnson
Waiting in the Wings. Noel
  Coward. Drury; French
Waiting Supper, The. Thomas
  Hardy. Pinion
Wakefield. Nathaniel Hawthorne.
  Gale-H
Wakefield Plays, The. Unknown.
  Gassner
Walden. Henry David Thoreau.
  Haydn; Keller; Magill II, CE,
  M1&2, MAL5, MC, MNF
Walden Two. B. F. Skinner.
  Magill SF
Walk Egypt. Vinnie Williams.
  Magill '61, S
Walking Happy. Roger O. Hirson,
  Ketti Frings, Sammy Cahn and
  James Van Heusen. (Based on
  Hobson's Choice by Harold
  Brighouse.) NCTE
Walking to Sleep. Richard Wilbur.
  Magill '70
Wall, The. John Hersey. (See
  adaptation by Millard Lampell.)
Wall, The. Millard Lampell.
  (Based on the novel by John
  Hersey.) Kienzle
Wall-Street; or, Ten Minutes Be-
  fore Three. Richard W. Mead.
  Lovell
Wallenstein. Johann Christoph
  Friedrich von Schiller. Gass-
  ner; Keller; Magill II, CE,
  M1&2, MC, MD; Shipley; Sobel
Walls of Jericho, The. Alfred
  Sutro. Drury
Walnut Door, The. John Hersey.
  Magill '78
Walter Hines Page: The South-

erner As American, 1855-1918.
  John Milton Cooper, Jr. Magill '78
Waltz of the Dogs, The. Leonid
  N. Andreyev. Keller suppl.;
  Shipley
Waltz of the Toreadors, The.
  Jean Anouilh. Best '56; Chap-
  man '57; French; Kienzle;
  Magill '58, S; Matlaw; Shank;
  Sprinchorn
Wanda. Ouida. Keller
Wanderer, The. Henri Alain-
  Fournier. Magill I, CE, M1&2,
  MC, MEUF; Olfson
Wanderer, The. Fritz Leiber, Jr.
  Magill SF
Wanderer and King. O. V.
  Caine. Kaye
Wandering Jew, The. Moncure
  D. Conway. Keller
Wandering Jew, The. Eugène
  Sue. Goodman; Haydn; John-
  son; Keller; Magill I, CE,
  M1&2, MC, MEUF
Wandering Scholar from Paradise,
  The. Hans Sachs. Magill III,
  CE, M1&2, MC, MD
Wandering Scholars, The. Helen
  Waddell. Ward
Wanderings of Oisin, The. Wil-
  liam Butler Yeats. Haydn (a)
Waning of the Middle Ages, The.
  Johan Huizinga. Magill IV,
  MC
Wanna Go Home, Baby? see
  Sweeney Agonistes
Wanting Seed, The. Anthony
  Burgess. Magill SF
Wanton, The. Frances Harrod.
  Kaye
Wapshot Chronicle, The. John
  Cheever. Magill IV, '58, M1,
  MB, MC, S; Morehead
Wapshot Scandal, The. John
  Cheever. Magill IV, '64, M1,
  MC, S; Morehead
War. Mikhail Artsybashev.
  Drury
War Against the Jews, 1933-1945,
  The. Lucy S. Dawidowicz.
  Magill '76
War and Peace. Count Leo Tol-
  stoy. Berry-1; Haydn; John-
  son; Kaye; Keller; Lass EN;
  Magill I, CE, M1&2, MC,
  MEUF; Olfson
War Between the Tates, The.
  Alison Lurie. Magill '75

War for the Union, The, Vol. I.
Allan Nevins. Magill '60,
MB, S
War for the Union, The, Vol. II.
Allan Nevins. Magill '61,
MB, S
War in Algeria, The. Jules Roy.
Magill '62, S
War in the Air, The. H. G.
Wells. Magill SF; Ward
War Lover, The. John Hersey.
Magill '60, M1, S
War of Catiline, The. Sallust.
Downs F; Haydn
War of the Wing-Men. Poul
Anderson. Magill SF
War of the Worlds, The. H.
G. Wells. Goodman; Grozier;
Magill I, CE, M1&2, MC,
MEF, SF; Ward
War of Women, The. Alexandre
Dumas (father). Kaye
War Path: Hitler's Germany in
the Years 1933-1939, The.
David Irving. Magill '79
War That Hitler Won: The Most
Infamous Propaganda Campaign
in History, The. Robert
Edwin Herzstein. Magill '79
War with Mexico, The. Justin
H. Smith. Keller suppl.
War with the Newts. Karel
Capek. Magill SF
Ward of King Canute, The.
Ottilia Adelina Liljencrantz.
Kaye
Ward of the King, A. Katherine
Sarah Macquoid. Kaye
Warden, The. Anthony Trollope.
Gerould; Haydn; Johnson; Ma-
gill I, CE, M1&2, MC, MEF;
Olfson
Warna ou le poids de la neige
(Warna or The Weight of
Snow). Paul Willems. Kienzle
Warnings. Eugene O'Neill.
Matlaw
Warren Hastings. Lion Feucht-
wanger. Drury
Warrior's Barrow, The. Henrik
Ibsen. Matlaw
Wartime. Milovan Djilas.
Magill '78
Warwick the Kingmaker. Paul
Murray Kendall. Magill '58,
S
Washing of the Spears, The.
Donald R. Morris. Magill

'66, S
Washington. Constance McLaugh-
lin Green. Magill Ss
Washington in 1868. Mark Twain.
Gale-T
Washington Journal: A Diary of
the Events of 1973-1974.
Elizabeth Drew. Magill '76
Washington Square. Henry
James. (See also adaptation
The Heiress by Ruth and Au-
gustus Goetz.) Gale-J; Magill
III, CE, M1&2, MAF, MAL3,
MC; Olfson; Wilson
Washington: The Indispensable
Man. James Thomas Flexner.
Magill '75
Washington's Young Aids. Everett
T. Tomlinson. Kaye
Wasps, The. Aristophanes.
Feder; Gassner; Hathorn; Magill
III, CE, M1&2, MC, MD;
Reinhold; Shank; Shipley
Waste. Harley Granville-Barker.
Matlaw
Waste Land, The. T. S. Eliot.
Haydn (Eliot); Heiney; Magill
III, M1, MC, MP; Ward
Waste Makers, The. Vance
Packard. Magill '61, M1, S
Watch and Ward. Henry James.
Gale-J
Watch It, Sailor! Philip King
and Falkland L. Cary. French
Watch on the Rhine. Lillian
Hellman. Best '40; Bonin;
Drury; Haydn (a); Lovell
Watch That Ends the Night, The.
Hugh MacLennan. Magill '60,
S
Watches of the Night, The.
Harry M. Caudill. Magill '77
Water Babies, The. Charles
Kingsley. Haydn; Johnson
Water Engine and Mr. Happiness,
The. David Mamet. Magill
'79
Water Witch, The. James Feni-
more Cooper. Johnson; Walker
Watergate and the Constitution.
Philip B. Kurland. Magill '79
Waterlily Fire. Muriel Rukeyser.
Magill '63, S
Waterloo. Emile Erckmann and
Alexander Chatrian. Kaye
Waterloo: Day of Battle. David
Howarth. Magill '69, S
Watermelon Wine: The Spirit of

topher Morley. Keller suppl.
Where the Cross Is Made. Eugene
O'Neill. Matlaw
Where the Light Falls. Chard
Powers Smith. Magill '66, S
Where the Red Volleys Poured.
C. W. Dahlinger. Kaye
Where There's a Will. . . . R. F.
Delderfield. French
Where's Charley? George Abbott
and Frank Loesser. (Based
on Charley's Aunt by Brandon
Thomas.) NCTE
Which Shall It Be? Mrs. Alex-
ander. Johnson
Which Was It? Mark Twain.
Gale-T
While Parents Sleep. Anthony
Kimmins. French
While Paris Laughed. Leonard
Merrick. Keller suppl.
While the Sun Shines. Terence
Rattigan. French; Matlaw
Whip and Spur. George E.
Waring. Keller
Whirligigs. O. Henry. Keller
Whispering Land, The. Gerald
Durrell. Magill '63, S
Whistle. James Jones. Magill
'79
Whistling in the Dark. Laurence
Gross and Edward Childs Car-
penter. Drury
White Aprons. Maud W. Good-
win. Kaye; Keller
White Carnation, The. Robert
Cedric Sherriff. French
White Cockade, The. Charles
Gilson. Kaye
White Cockade, The. Lady (Isa-
bella Augustus) Gregory.
Matlaw
White Company, The. Sir Arthur
Conan Doyle. Grozier; Haydn;
Johnson; Kaye; Keller; Magill
I, CE, M1&2, MC, MEF
White Conquerors of Mexico, The.
Kirk Monroe. Kaye
White Desert. Maxwell Anderson.
Matlaw
White Devil, The. John Webster.
Gassner; Haydn; Holzknecht;
Keller; Magill III, CE, M1&2,
MC, MD; Ruoff; Shank; Shipley
White Fang. Jack London. Ward
White Gauntlet, The. Percy J.
Brebner. Kaye
White-Headed Boy, The. Lennox

Robinson. Drury
White Hoods, The. Anna Eliza
Bray. Kaye
White Horse Inn. Hans Müller,
Ralph Benatzky and Robert
Stolz. Shipley
White House Murder Case, The.
Jules Feiffer. Best '69; Drury;
NCTE
White-Jacket. Herman Melville.
Gale-M; Magill II, CE, M1&2,
MAF, MAL4, MC
White Liars. Peter Shaffer.
Drury
White Lies. Charles Reade.
Johnson
White Man's Indian: Images of
the American Indian from
Columbus to the Present, The.
Robert F. Berkhofer, Jr.
Magill '79
White Monkey, The. John Gals-
worthy. (See also trilogy title
A Modern Comedy.) Heiney;
Keller suppl.
White Nile, The. Alan Moorehead.
Magill '62, M1, MB, S
White Old Maid, The. Nathaniel
Hawthorne. Gale-H
White Queen, The. Russell M.
Garnier. Kaye
White Rocks, The. Edouard Rod.
Keller
White Saviour, The. Gerhart
Hauptmann. Drury; Matlaw
White Sheep of the Family, The.
L. du Garde Peach and Ian
Hay. French
White Shield, The. Caroline A.
Mason. Kaye
White Snake, The. Unknown.
Gassner
White Steed, The. Paul Vincent
Carroll. Best '38; Drury;
French; Matlaw; Shipley
White Terror and the Red, The.
Abraham Cahan. Kaye
White Wings. Philip Barry.
Shipley; Sobel
Whitefriars. Emma Robinson.
Kaye
Whiteheaded Boy, The. Lennox
Robinson. Matlaw; NBC 2;
Sobel
Whiteoaks. Mazo de la Roche.
French
Whites and the Blues, The. Alex-
andre Dumas (father). Kaye

French
Wild Duck, The. Henrik Ibsen.
  Drury; Gassner; Haydn; Heiney;
  Keller; Magill I, CE, M1&2,
  MC, MD; Matlaw; Shank;
  Shipley; Sobel
Wild Geese. Martha Ostenso.
  Keller suppl.
Wild-Goose Chase, The. John
  Fletcher. Ruoff; Holzknecht
Wild Horses. Ben Travers.
  French
Wild Irish Girl, The. Lady
  Sydney (Owenson) Morgan.
  Keller
"Wild Old Wicked Men, The" and
  Other Poems. Archibald Mac-
  Leish. Magill '69, M1, S
Wild Palms, The. William
  Faulkner. Magill IV, MC
Wild Wales. George Henry Bor-
  row. Magill IV, MC
Wilderness of Ladies. Eleanor
  Ross Taylor. Magill '61, S
Wilderness Road, The. Joseph
  A. Altsheler. Kaye
Wilhelm Meister. Johann Wolf-
  gang von Goethe. Goodman
Wilhelm Meister's Apprenticeship.
  Johann Wolfgang von Goethe.
  Haydn; Johnson; Keller; Magill
  II, CE, M1&2, MC, MEUF
Wilhelm Meister's Travels.
  Johann Wolfgang von Goethe.
  Magill II, CE, M1&2, MC,
  MEUF
Wilhelm Tell see William Tell
Wilhelm von Humboldt: A Biog-
  raphy, Vol. I: 1767-1808.
  Paul Robinson Sweet. Magill
  '79
Will Any Gentleman? Vernon
  Sylvaine. French
Will Shakespeare. Clemence Dane.
  Drury; French; Sobel
Will Success Spoil Rock Hunter?
  George Axelrod. Drury
Will to Believe, The William
  James. Haydn (a); Magill WP
Will You Please Be Quiet,
  Please? Raymond Carver.
  Magill '77
Will You Walk into My Parlor?
  Theodore Dreiser. Gerber
William Blackwood and His Sons.
  Margaret Wilson Oliphant.
  Keller (Blackwood)
William Butler Yeats. Harold

Bloom. Magill '71
William Carlos Williams: The
  Knack of Survival in America.
  Robert Coles. Magill '76
William Caxton: A Biography.
  George D. Painter. Magill '78
William Ewart Gladstone. Viscount
  John Morley. Keller (Glad-
  stone)
William Faulkner. Cleanth
  Brooks. Magill '64, M1, S
William Faulkner: The Journey
  to Self-Discovery. H. Edward
  Richardson. Magill '70
William Faulkner: Toward Yok-
  napatawpha and Beyond.
  Cleanth Brooks. Magill '79
William James: A Biography.
  Gay Wilson Allen. Magill '68,
  S
William Lloyd Garrison. Wendell
  Phillips Garrison and Francis
  Jackson Garrison. Keller
  (Garrison)
William Morris. Philip Hender-
  son. Magill '68, S
William Morris: Romantic to
  Revolutionary. E. P. Thomp-
  son. Magill '78
William of Ockham: Selections.
  William of Ockham. Magill
  WP
William Penn. Catherine Owens
  Peare. Magill '58, S
William Tell. Johann Christoph
  Friedrich von Schiller. Cart-
  mell; Cohen; Drury (Wilhelm);
  Haydn; Keller; Magill I, CE,
  M1&2, MC, MD; NBC 3; Shank;
  Shipley; Sobel; Thomas
William the Conqueror. David C.
  Douglas. Magill '65, S
William Wilson. Edgar Allan Poe.
  Gale-P, PP
Willy Reilly. William Carleton.
  Johnson
Wilson: Confusions and Crises,
  1915 1916. Arthur S. Link.
  Magill '66, S
Wind and the Rain, The. Thomas
  Burke. Keller suppl.
Wind and the Rain, The. Merton
  Hodge. Drury
Wind from Nowhere, The. J. G.
  Ballard. Magill SF
Wind in the Branches of Sassafras.
  René de Obaldia. Kienzle
Wind in the Willows, The. Ken-

neth Grahame. Haydn; Magill
II, CE, M1&2, MC, MEF;
Ward
Wind, Sand and Stars. Antoine
de Saint-Exupéry. Heiney;
Magill IV, MC; Olfson
Wind Will Not Subside, The.
David Milton and Nancy Dall
Milton. Magill '77
Windfall. Michael Gilbert. French
Window in Thrums, A. Sir
James M. Barrie. Johnson;
Keller
Window on Russia, A. Edmund
Wilson. Magill '73
Windsor Castle. William Harrison
Ainsworth. Magill I, CE,
M1&2, MC, MEF
Wine of Astonishment, The.
Rachel MacKenzie. Magill
'75
Wine, Water and Song. Gilbert
Keith Chesterton. Ward
Winesburg, Ohio. Sherwood
Anderson. Haydn; Heiney;
Keller suppl.; Lass AN; Magill
I, CE, M1&2, MAF, MC;
Morehead; Smith
Wing and Wing. James Fenimore
Cooper. Johnson; Walker
Winged Victory. Moss Hart.
Best '43
Wingless Victory, The. Maxwell
Anderson. Drury; Matlaw;
NCTE
Wings. Arthur L. Kopit. Best
'78
Wings of the Dove. Guy Bolton.
(Based on the novel by Henry
James.) Drury
Wings of the Dove, The. Henry
James. (See also adaptations
by Christopher Taylor and
Guy Bolton.) Gale-J; Haydn;
Keller; Magill II, CE, M1&2,
MAF, MAL3, MC; Ward
Wings of the Dove, The. Chris-
topher Taylor. (Based on the
novel by Henry James.) French
Wings of Youth. Elizabeth Jordan.
Keller suppl.
Wings over Europe. Robert M.
B. Nichols and Maurice Browne.
Best '28; Drury; Matlaw;
Shipley; Sobel
Winner Names the Age, The.
Lillian Smith. Magill '79
Winners, The. Julio Cortázar.

Magill '66, S
Winnie-the-Pooh. A. A. Milne.
Haydn
Winning His Spurs. George A.
Henty. Kaye
Winning of Barbara Worth, The.
Harold Bell Wright. Haydn;
Keller
Winning of the West, The. Theo-
dore Roosevelt. Keller
Winslow Boy, The. Terence Rat-
tigan. Best '47; Drury; French;
Matlaw; NCTE; Shank; Shipley;
Ward
Winston S. Churchill: The Prophet
of Truth, Vol. V: 1922-1939.
Martin Gilbert, editor. Magill
'78
Winter Ballad. Gerhart Haupt-
mann. Matlaw
Winter in the Air. Sylvia Town-
send Warner. Magill '57, S
Winter in the Blood. James
Welch. Magill '75
Winter in the Hills, A. John
Wain. Magill '71
Winter Journey. Clifford Odets.
French
Winter News. John Haines.
Magill '67, S
Winter of Old Age, The see
Critic, The
Winter of Our Discontent, The.
John Steinbeck. Magill '62, S
Winter Quarters. Alfred Duggan.
Magill '57, S
Winter Soldiers. Dan James.
Best '42
Winter Solstice. Gerald Warner
Brace. Magill '61, S
Winter Sunshine. G. A. Thomas.
French
Winter Trees. Sylvia Plath.
Magill '73
Winters and the Palmleys, The.
Thomas Hardy. Saxelby
Winter's Tale, The. William
Shakespeare. Campbell; Chute;
Clark; Gassner; Guerber-SC;
Halliday; Haydn; Keller; Lamb;
McCutchan-SC; McSpadden S;
Magill II, CE, M1&2, MC,
MD; Ruoff; Shank; Shipley; Sobel
Winterschlacht (Winter Battle).
Johannes R. (Robert) Becher.
Kienzle
Winterset. Maxwell Anderson.
Best '35; Bonin; Drury; Haydn;

Lass AP; Lovell; Magill I,
CE, M1&2, MC, MD; Matlaw;
NBC 3; NCTE; Shank; Shipley;
Sobel; Sprinchorn
Wintersmoon.   Hugh Walpole.
Keller suppl.
Winterspelt.   Alfred Andersch.
Magill '79
Winthrop Covenant, The.   Louis
Auchincloss.   Magill '77
Wisdom of God, The.   Sergius
Bulgakov.   Magill CHL
Wisdom of the Sands, The.
Antoine de Saint-Exupéry.
Magill IV, MC
Wisdom Tooth, The.   Marc Con-
nelly.   Best '25; Drury
Wise Blood.   Flannery O'Connor.
Magill IV, MC
Wish You Were Here.   Arthur
Kober, Joshua Logan and
Harold Rome.   Chapman '53
Wishing Well.   E. Eynon Evans.
French
Wisteria Lodge.   Sir Arthur
Conan Doyle.   Hardwick SH
Wisteria Trees, The.   Joshua
Logan.   (Based on The Cherry
Orchard by Anton Chekhov.)
Best '49; Drury; Matlaw;
NCTE
Wit Works Woe   see   Woe from
Wit
Witch, The   Hans Wiers-Jens-
sen.   Drury
Witch of Edmonton, The.   Thomas
Dekker, John Ford and Wil-
liam Rowley.   Holzknecht;
Ruoff
Witch Queen of Khem, The.
Eno Fitzgerald.   Kaye
Witches of Karres, The.   James
H. Schmitz.   Magill SF
Witching Hour, The.   Augustus
Thomas.   Best '99; Cartmell;
Drury; Keller; Lovell; Mat-
law; Shipley; Sobel
Witch's Ride.   Gerhart Haupt-
mann.   Matlaw
With Buller in Natal.   George
A. Henty.   Kaye
With Cochrane the Dauntless.
George A. Henty.   Kaye
With Fire and Sword.   Henryk
Sienkiewicz.   Haydn; Kaye;
Keller; Magill II, CE, M1&2,
MC, MEUF
"With Folded Hands. "   Jack

Williamson.   Magill SF
With Frederick the Great.   George
A. Henty.   Kaye
With Ignorance.   C. K. Williams.
Magill '78
With Lafayette at Yorktown.
James O. Kaler.   Kaye
With Lawrence in Arabia.   Lowell
Thomas.   Keller suppl.
With Lee in Virginia.   George A.
Henty.   Kaye
With Love from Gracie.   Grace
Hegger Lewis.   Magill '57, S
With Moore at Corunna.   George
A. Henty.   Kaye
With Musqueteer and Redskin.
W. M. Graydon.   Kaye
With Perry on Lake Erie.   James
O. Kaler.   Kaye
With Porter in the Essex.   James
O. Kaler.   Kaye
With Roberts to Pretoria.   George
A. Henty.   Kaye
With Rogers' Rangers.   George W.
Browne.   Kaye
With Shield and Assegai.   Fred-
erick A. Brereton.   Kaye
With Shuddering Fall.   Joyce
Carol Oates.   Magill '65, S
With the Allies to Pekin.   George
A. Henty.   Kaye
With the British Legion.   George
A. Henty.   Kaye
With the Flag in the Channel.
James Barnes.   Kaye
With the Procession.   Henry B.
Fuller.   Keller
With Vacant Possession.   Wilfred
Massey.   French
With Warren at Bunker Hill.
James O. Kaler.   Kaye
With Wellington to Waterloo.
Harold Avery.   Kaye
With Wolfe in Canada.   George A.
Henty.   Kaye
With Wolseley to Kumasi.   Fred-
erick A. Brereton.   Kaye
Withered Arm, The.   Thomas
Hardy.   Pinion; Saxelby
Within a Budding Grove.   Marcel
Proust.   (See also series title
Remembrance of Things Past.)
Haydn p. 631; Heiney
Within the Gates.   Sean O'Casey.
Gassner; Magill III, CE, M1&2,
MC, MD; Matlaw; Sobel
Within the Law.   Bayard Veiller.
Drury

Women, The. Clare Boothe.
Best '36; Drury; NCTE; Sobel
Women and Thomas Harrow.
John P. Marquand. Magill
'59, S
Women Are Like That. Tom Judd.
French
Women at Point Sur, The. Robin-
son Jeffers. Heiney
Women at the Thesmophoria, The
see Thesmophoriazusae
Women Beware Women. Thomas
Middleton. Magill III, CE,
M1&2, MC, MD; Ruoff
Women Celebrating the Thesmo-
phoria see Thesmophoriazusae
Women in Asclepius' Temple.
Herondas. Hathorn (a)
Women in Love. D. H. Lawrence.
Heiney; Magill IV, MC; Ward
Women in Parliament, The see
Ecclesiazusae
Women in the Assembly, The
see Ecclesiazusae
Women in the Nineteenth Century.
Margaret Fuller Ossoli. Keller
Women of Salamis, The. Aeschy-
lus. Hathorn
Women of the Shadows. Ann
Cornelisen. Magill '77
Women of Trachis, The see
Trachiniae
Women of Trachis. Ezra Pound.
(Based on Trachiniae by
Sophocles.) Kienzle
Won by the Sword. George A.
Henty. Kaye
Wonder-Book for Girls and Boys,
A. Nathaniel Hawthorne.
Gale-H
Wonder Working Magician, The.
Pedro Calderón de la Barca.
Haydn; Keller (Wonderful);
Shipley
Wonderful Adventures of Don
Quixote. Conrad Seiler.
(Based on Don Quixote by Cer-
vantes.) French
Wonderful Adventures of Nils,
The. Selma Lagerlöf. Keller
Wonderful Adventures of Phra
the Phoenician, The see
Strange Adventures of Phra
the Phoenician, The
Wonderful Lamp see Aladdin,
or the Wonderful Lamp
Wonderful Magician, The see
Wonder Working Magician, The

Wonderful Town. Joseph Fields,
Jerome Chodorov, Betty Com-
den, Adolph Green and Leonard
Bernstein. (Based on My Sister
Eileen by Joseph Fields and
Jerome Chodorov.) Best '52;
Chapman '53; NCTE
Wonderful Year, The. Thomas
Dekker. Ruoff
Wonderful Year, The. William
John Locke. Keller
Wondrous Tale of Alroy, The.
Benjamin Disraeli. Johnson
Wood Demon, The. Anton Chek-
hov. Matlaw
Woodcutter's House, The see
Barley Fields, The
Wooden Dish, The. Edmund Mor-
ris. French
Wooden Shepherdess, The.
Richard Hughes. Magill '74
Woodland Queen, A. Claude
André Theuriet. Johnson
Woodlanders, The. Thomas
Hardy. Haydn; Magill II, CE,
M1&2, MC, MEF; Saxelby
Woodman, The. George P. R.
James. Kaye
Woodrow Wilson. Arthur Wal-
worth. Magill '59, S
Woodrow Wilson and World Settle-
ment. Ray Stannard Baker.
Keller suppl. (Wilson)
Woodrow Wilson; Life and Letters.
Ray Stannard Baker. Keller
suppl. (Wilson)
Woodrow Wilson: The Years of
Preparation. John M. Mulder.
Magill '79
Woodstock. Sir Walter Scott.
Johnson; Kaye; Keller; McSpad-
den W; Magill II, CE, M1&2,
MC, MEF
Wooing O't, The. Mrs. Alex-
ander. Johnson
Word, The. Kaj Munk. Matlaw;
Shank
Word Child, A. Iris Murdoch.
Magill '76
Word for World Is Forest, The.
Ursula K. Le Guin. Magill
SF
Word of the Campaign of Igor see
Lay of Igor's Campaign, The
Words, The. Jean-Paul Sartre.
Magill '65, M1, S
Words for Dr. Y: Uncollected
Poems with Three Stories.

Anne Sexton. Magill '79
Words upon the Window-Pane, The.
William Butler Yeats. Matlaw;
Sprinchorn
Work see Oeuvre, L'
Work Ethic in Industrial America,
1850-1920, The. Daniel T.
Rodgers. Magill '79
Work Suspended. Evelyn Waugh.
Stade p. 68
Workers, The. Walter A. Wyckoff.
Keller
Workhouse Donkey, The. John
Arden. Kienzle
Workhouse Ward, The. Lady
(Isabella Augusta) Gregory.
Heiney; Matlaw; Sobel
Working. Studs Terkel. Magill
'76
Working It Out. Sara Ruddick
and Pamela Daniels, editors.
Magill '78
Works. Aristotle. Keller (a)
Works and Days. Hesiod.
Downs F; Feder; Haydn;
Magill III, M1, MC, MP
Works of Jonathan Edwards.
Jonathan Edwards. Magill
III, M1, MC, MNF
Works of Lyman Beecher, The.
Lyman Beecher. Magill CHL
Works of Max Beerbohm, The.
Max Beerbohm. Ward
World According to Garp, The.
John Irving. Magill '79
World After the Peace Confer-
ence, The. Arnold Joseph
Toynbee. Keller suppl.
World and His Wife, The see
Great Galeoto, The
World and the Individual, The.
Josiah Royce. Magill WP
World As Will and Idea, The.
Arthur Schopenhauer. Arm-
strong; Haydn; Keller; Magill
III, CE, M1&2, MC, MNF,
WP
World Below, The. S. Fowler
Wright. Magill SF
World Destroyed, A. Martin J.
Sherwin. Magill '76
World Enough and Time. Robert
Penn Warren. Magill II, CE,
M1&2, MAF, MC
World Is Round, The. Armand
Salacrou. Matlaw; Shank
World of Apples, The. John
Cheever. Magill '74

World of Carl Sandburg, The.
Carl Sandburg. Drury
World of Chance, The. William
Dean Howells. Carrington
World of John McNulty, The.
John McNulty. Magill '58, S
World of Light, A. May Sarton.
Magill '77
World of Love, A. Elizabeth
Bowen. Magill '55, S
World of Null-A, The. Alfred
Elton Van Vogt. Magill SF
World of Our Fathers. Irving
Howe. Magill '77
World of Profit, A. Louis Auch-
incloss. Magill '69, M1, S
World of Silence, The. Max
Picard. Magill CAL
World of Strangers, A. Nadine
Gordimer. Magill '59, S
World of the Thibaults, The.
Roger Martin du Gard. Heiney;
Magill I, CE, M1&2, MC,
MEUF
World of William Clissold, The.
H. G. Wells. Keller suppl.
World of Wonders. Robertson
Davies. Magill '77
World Runs on Wheels, The see
All Fools
World Soul. Mikhail Emtsev and
Eremei Parnov. Magill SF
World the Slaveholders Made, The.
Eugene D. Genovese. Magill
'71
World We Live In, The see
Insect Comedy, The
World We Live In, The. Lincoln
Barnett. Drury; Magill '55, S
World We Make, The. Sidney
Kingsley. (Based on The Out-
ward Room by Millen Brand.)
Best '39
World Well Lost, The see All
for Love
World Within the Word, The.
William H. Gass. Magill '79
World Without Borders. Lester
R. Brown. Magill '73
World's Desire, The. Henry
Rider Haggard. Kaye
World's Desire, The. Andrew
Lang. Kaye
World's End. Upton Sinclair.
Heiney
World's Great Religions, The.
The Editors of Life. Magill
'58, M1, S

World's Illusion, The. Jacob Wassermann. Haydn; Keller suppl.; Lass EN; Magill I, CE, M1&2, MC, MEUF; Olfson
Worlds of the Imperium. Keith Laumer. Magill SF
Worm in Horseradish, A. Esther Kaufman. NCTE
Worm of Consciousness and Other Essays, The. Nicola Chiaromonte. Magill '77
Worm's Eye View. R. F. Delderfield. French
Worship. Evelyn Underhill. Magill CHL
Worthies of England, The. Thomas Fuller. Haydn
Would-Be Gentleman, The see Bourgeois Gentleman, The
Woyzeck. Georg Büchner. Gassner; Magill II, CE, M1&2, MC, MD; Shank; Shipley
Wreath for Udomo, A. Peter Abrahams. Magill '57, S
Wreck of the Golden Mary, The. Charles Dickens. Hardwick CD
Wreck of the Grosvenor, The. William Clark Russell. Johnson; Keller; Magill I, CE, M1&2, MC, MEF
Wreck of the Thresher and Other Poems, The. William Meredith. Magill '65, S
Wrecker, The. Robert Louis Stevenson. Keller
Wreckers, The. Saul Bellow. Kienzle
Wrinkles. Charles Simmons. Magill '79
Write Me a Murder. Frederick Knott. French
Writer's Diary, A. Virginia Woolf. Magill '54, MB, S
Writings of Saint Patrick, The. Saint Patrick. Magill CAL
Written for a Lady. Leo Marks. French
Wrong Side of the Park, The. John Mortimer. French
Wulnoth the Wanderer. H. E. Inman. Kaye
Wuthering Heights. Emily Brontë. Armstrong; Cohen; Drury; Goodman; Grozier; Halperin; Haydn; Johnson; Keller; Lass BN; Magill I, CE, M1&2, MC, MEF; Wilson

Wyandotte. James Fenimore Cooper. Johnson; Walker
Wycliffite Bible. John Wycliffe. Downs F

-X-

Xantriai. Aeschylus. Hathorn
X-ing a Paragrab. Edgar Allan Poe. Gale-PP
Xipéhuz, Les. J. H. Rosny (the Elder). Magill SF

-Y-

Yadonashi Danhichi Shiguregasa (The Fishmonger Danhichi). Namiki Shozo. Halford
Yama: The Pit. Alexander Ivanovich Kuprin. Heiney
Yamada-no-Kakashi see Shoutsushi Asagao Nikki
Yankee at the Court of King Arthur see Connecticut Yankee in King Arthur's Court, A
Yanone (The Arrowhead). Ichikawa Danjuro II. Halford
Yard of Sun, A. Christopher Fry. Magill '71
Yarn of Old Harbor Town, The. William Clark Russell. Kaye
Yasuna. Unknown. Halford
Year of My Rebirth, The. Jesse Stuart. Magill '57, M1, MB, S
Year of the Dragon, The. Frank Chin. NCTE
Year of the Quiet Sun, The. Wilson Tucker. Magill SF
Year of the Whale, The. Victor B. Scheffer. Magill '70
Year One, The. John Edward Bloundelle-Burton. Kaye
Yearling, The. Marjorie Kinnan Rawlings. Haydn; Magill I, CE, M1&2, MAF, MC
Years, The. Virginia Woolf. Haydn; Magill III, CE, M1&2, MC, MEF
Years Ago. Ruth Gordon. Best '46; Drury; NCTE

Years with Ross, The. James
Thurber. Magill '60, M1, S
Yegor Bulitchev and Others.
Máxim Górky. Haydn (a);
Matlaw; Shank (Egor); Sobel
Yellow Danger, The. M. P.
Shiel. Magill SF
Yellow Face, The. Sir Arthur
Conan Doyle. Hardwick SH
Yellow Frigate, The. James
Grant. Kaye
Yellow Jack. Sidney Howard.
Drury; Matlaw; Shank; Shipley;
Sobel
Yellow Jacket, The. George
Cochrane Hazelton and Harry
Benrimo. Cartmell; Drury;
Shipley; Sobel
Yellow Sands. Eden and Adelaide
Phillpotts. French
Yellow Shield, The. William
Johnston. Kaye
Yemassee, The. William Gilmore
Simms. Johnson; Kaye; Keller;
Magill II, CE, M1&2, MAF,
MC
Yeomen of the Guard, The. Wil-
liam Schwenck Gilbert and
Arthur Sullivan. Shipley; Sobel
Yerma. Federico García Lorca.
Gassner; Heiney; Matlaw;
Shank
Yes and No. Kenneth Horne.
French
Yes Is for a Very Young Man.
Gertrude Stein. Matlaw; Shank
Yes, My Darling Daughter. Mark
Reed. Best '36; Drury; French
Yesterday. Maria Dermoût.
Magill '60, S
Yesterday, To-Day and Forever.
Edward Henry Bickersteth.
Keller
Yesterdays with Authors. James
T. Fields. Keller
Yet Again. Max Beerbohm.
Ward
Yevtushenko Poems. Yevgeny
Yevtushenko. Magill '67, S
Yî, The. Unknown. Keller
(Sacred Books)
Yoikoshin (The Eve of the Koshin
Festival). Chikamatsu Monzae-
mon. Halford
Yoke and the Arrows, The. Her-
bert Lionel Matthews. Magill
'58, S
Yolando, Maid of Burgundy.

Charles Major. Kaye
Yone Santo. Edward H. House.
Keller
Yonnondio: From the Thirties.
Tillie Olsen. Magill '75
York Plays, The. Unknown.
Gassner
Yorkshire Tragedy, A. Unknown.
Gassner; Holzknecht; Ruoff;
Sobel
Yoshitsune Sembonzakura (The
Thousand Cherry Trees).
Takeda Izumo, Miyoshi Shoraku
and Namiki Senryu. Halford
Yotsuya Kaidan (The Ghost of Yot-
suya). Namboku Tsuruya.
Halford
You and I. Philip Barry. Best
'22; Drury
You Can't Go Home Again.
Thomas Wolfe. Haydn p. 440;
Heiney; Magill I, CE, M1&2,
MAF, MC; Smith
You Can't Take It with You.
George S. Kaufman and Moss
Hart. Best '36; Bonin; Cart-
mell; Drury; Lovell; Lass AP;
Matlaw; NCTE; Shank; Shipley;
Sobel; Sprinchorn
You, Emperors, and Others.
Robert Penn Warren. Magill
'61, S
You Know I Can't Hear You When
the Water's Running. Robert
Anderson. Best '66; Drury
You Know Me Al. Ring Lardner.
Magill III, CE, M1&2, MAF,
MC
You Might As Well Live. John
Keats. Magill '71
You Must Know Everything. Isaac
Emmanuelovich Babel. Magill
'70
You Never Can Tell. George
Bernard Shaw. Drury; Hard-
wick; Haydn; Matlaw; NCTE;
Shank; Shipley; Sobel; Ward
You Shall Know Them. Vercors.
Magill SF
You Too Can Have a Body. Fred
Robinson. French
You Touched Me! Tennessee Wil-
liams and Donald Windham.
Drury; Shank
You Were Born on a Rotten Day.
Christopher Sergel. Drury
Youchi Soga Kariba no Akebono
(The Soga Brothers' Revenge).

Kawatake Mokuami. Halford
Youma. Lafcadio Hearn. Johnson; Magill II, CE, M1&2,
MAF, MC
Young and the Fair, The. N.
Richard Nash. Drury
Young Blockaders, The. Everett
T. Tomlinson. Kaye
Young Buglers, The. George A.
Henty. Kaye
Young Carthaginian, The. George
A. Henty. Kaye
Young Colonists, The. George
A. Henty. Kaye
Young Duke, The. Benjamin Disraeli. Johnson
Young Elizabeth, The. Jennette
Dowling and Francis Letton.
French
Young Goodman Brown. Nathaniel
Hawthorne. Gale-H
Young Hamilton: A Biography,
The. James Thomas Flexner.
Magill '79
Young Hopeful, The see Minor,
The
Young Idea, The. Noel Coward.
Drury
Young Lions, The. Irwin Shaw.
Haydn (a)
Young Lonigan: A Boyhood in
Chicago Streets. James
Thomas Farrell. (See also
his Studs Lonigan: A Trilogy.)
Haydn; Lass AN
Young Macedonian in the Army
of Alexander, A. Alfred John
Church. Kaye
Young Man Married, A. Sidney
C. Grier. Kaye
Young Manhood of Studs Lonigan,
The. James Thomas Farrell.
Morehead
Young Mrs. Winthrop. Bronson
Howard. Drury
Young Pioneers, The. Evelyn
Everett Green. Kaye
Young Provincial, The. Attributed
to Nathaniel Hawthorne. Gale-
H
Young Sam Johnson. James L.
Clifford. Magill '55, MB, S
Young Volunteer in Cuba, A.
Edward Stratemeyer. Kaye
Young Wives' Tale. Ronald
Jeans. French
Young Woodley. John van Druten.
Best '25; Drury; Keller suppl.;

Sobel
Younger Generation, The. W.
Stanley Houghton. Drury
Youngest, The. Philip Barry.
Best '24; Drury
"Your Isadora." Francis Steegmuller. Magill '75
Your Own Thing. Donald Driver,
Hal Hester, Danny Apolinar.
(Based on Twelfth Night by William Shakespeare.) Best '67;
NCTE
Your Uncle Dudley. Howard
Lindsay and Bertrand Robinson.
Drury
You're a Good Man Charlie Brown.
Clark Gesner. (Based on the
comic strip "Peanuts" by
Charles M. Schulz.) Best '66;
NCTE
Youth. Max Halbe. Drury
Youth: A Narrative Story.
Joseph Conrad. Helney; Ward
Youths, The see Lycurgeia
Yowa Nasaki Ukinano Yokogushi.
Segawa Joko III. Halford
Yukari no Murasaki Zukin (The
Purple Headcloth). Unknown.
Halford
Yuki Kurete Iriya no Azemichi.
Kawatake Mokuami. Halford
Yukiko. MacDonald Harris.
Magill '78
Yvain. Chrétien de Troyes.
Magill III, CE, M1&2, MC,
MP

-Z-

Zachary Phips. Edwin Lassetter
Bynner. Kaye
Zadig. Voltaire. Cohen; Johnson;
Magill III, CE, M1&2, MC,
MEUF
Zahradní slavnost (The Garden
Party). Václav Havel. Kienzle
Zaïre. Voltaire. Drury; Gassner; Magill III, CE, M1&2,
MC, MD; Shipley
Zanoni. Lord Edward Bulwer-
Lytton. Johnson; Kaye
Zapata and the Mexican Revolution.
John Womack, Jr. Magill '70
Zarco, El. Ignacio Manuel Altamirano. Magill III, CE,

M1&2, MAF, MC
Zecea Lume, A.   Vladimir Colin.
Magill SF
Zeit der Schuldlosen (Days of
the Guiltless).   Siegfried Lenz.
Kienzle
Zeluco.   John Moore.   Johnson
Zen Buddhism.   Daisetz T.
Suzuki.   Magill WP
Zen Catholicism.   Dom Aelred
Graham, O. S. B.   Magill CAL
Zend Avesta.   Zoroaster.
Haydn; Keller (Sacred Books)
Zincali, The.   George Henry
Borrow.   Keller; Magill IV,
MC
Zohar, The.   Simeon ben Yohai.
Haydn
Zolotaya kareta (The Golden
Carriage).   Leonid Maximo-
vich Leonov.   Kienzle
Zone Null.   Herbert W.   Franke.
Magill SF
Zoo ou l'assassin philanthrope
(Zoo or The Philanthropic
Murderer).   Vercors.   Kienzle
Zoo Story, The.   Edward Albee.
Drury; French; Kienzle; Lass
AP; Matlaw
Zorba.   Joseph Stein, Fred Ebb
and John Kander.   (Based on

Zorba the Greek by Nikos
Kazantzakis.)   NCTE
Zorba the Greek.   Nikos Kazant-
zakis.   (See also adaptation
Zorba by Joseph Stein et al.)
Magill IV, MC
Zoroaster.   Francis Marion
Crawford.   Kaye
Zuleika Dobson.   Max Beerbohm.
Haydn; Magill II, CE, M1&2,
MC, MEF; Olfson
Zum Frühstück zwei Männer (Two
Men for Breakfast).   Karl
Wittlinger.   Kienzle
Zur zeit der Distelblüte (When
the Thistles Bloom).   Her-
mann Moers.   Kienzle
Zury; the Meanest Man in Spring
County.   Joseph Kirkland.
Keller
Zwei Rechts, zwei Links (Two
Right, Two Left).   Karl Witt-
linger.   Kienzle
Zwie Family, The.   David Pinski.
Matlaw
Zwiesprache, Die (The Dialogue).
Fritz Kortner.   Kienzle
Zwillingsbruder, Der (The Twin
Brother; Life After Death).
Joachim Maass.   Kienzle

AUTHOR INDEX

315

ADAMS   316

Adams, Henry
  Education of Henry Adams, The
  Mont-Saint-Michel and Chartres
Adams, Henry H.
  Harry Hopkins: A Biography
Adams, James Truslow
  Epic of America, The
  Founding of New England, The
  Provincial Society
  Revolutionary New England,
    1691-1776
Adams, John
  Adams Papers, The
  Defense of the Constitutions of
    Government of the United
    States of America, A
Adams, Lee et al.
  Applause
  "It's a Bird   It's a Plane   It's
    Superman"
Adams, Lee, Michael Stewart and
    Charles Strouse
  Bye Bye Birdie
Adams, Richard
  Plague Dogs, The
  Watership Down
Adams, Robert M.
  Bad Mouth: Fugitive Papers on
    the Dark Side
Adams, Samuel Hopkins
  Grandfather Stories
Adamson, Joy
  Born Free
Addams, Jane
  Twenty Years at Hull-House
Addison, Joseph
  Cato
  Sir Roger de Coverley Papers,
    The
Addison, Joseph and Richard Steele
  Spectator, The
  Tatler, The
Ade, George
  County Chairman, The.
Aderca, Felix
  Oraşele Înecate.
Adivar, Hâlide Edib
  Clown and His Daughter, The
Adler, Mortimer J.
  Philosopher at Large: An In-
    tellectual Autobiography
Adler, Renata
  Speedboat
Adler, Richard et al.
  Damn Yankees
  Pajama Game, The
Aelfric
  Homilies

Aelred, Saint
  Spiritual Friendship
Aeneas Sylvius   see   Pius II
Aeschylus
  Aetnaeans, The
  Agamemnon
  Award of Armor, The
  Bone-Gatherers, The
  Builders of the Bridal Chamber,
    The
  Carians, The
  Choephori (Libation Bearers)
  Conjurors of the Dead, The
  Cretan Women, The
  Danaïdes
  Dictyulci
  Egyptians, The
  Electra
  Eleusinians, The
  Eumenides
  Glaucus of Potniae
  Glaucus the Sea God
  Heralds, The
  House of Atreus, The
  Huntresses, The
  Isthmiasts, The
  Laius
  Lemnians, The
  Lion, The
  Lycurgeia
  Mysians, The
  Niobe
  Nurses, The
  Oedipus
  Oresteia (See also Agamemnon;
    Choephori; Eumenides; Prote-
    us.)
  Perrhaebians, The
  Persians, The
  Philoctetes
  Phineus
  Prometheus
  Prometheus Bound
  Prometheus the Fire-Bringer
  Prometheus the Fire-Kindler
  Prometheus Unbound
  Proteus
  Ransom of Hector, The
  Seven Against Thebes
  Sphinx, The
  Suppliants, The
  Thracian Women, The
  Women of Salamis, The
  Xantriai
Aesop
  Aesop's Fables
Afinogenov, Alexander
  Fear

ARBUZOV

Arbuzov, Aleksei Nikolaevich
  It Happened in Irkutsk
  Promise, The
Archer, Daniel and Walter Bullock
  Mr. Barry's Etchings
Archer, William
  Green Goddess, The
Archibald, William
  Innocents, The
Archimedes
  On the Sphere and Cylinder
Ardagh, W. M.
  Knightly Years, The
  Magada, The
Arden, Jane
  Party, The
Arden, John
  Armstrong's Last Goodnight
  Live Like Pigs
  Serjeant Musgrave's Dance
  Workhouse Donkey, The
Arden, John and Margaretta
    D'Arcy.
  Ars Longa, Vita Brevis
Ardrey, Robert
  Hunting Hypothesis, The
  Social Contract, The
  Stone and Star
  Thunder Rock
Arendt, Hannah
  Life of the Mind: One/Think-
    ing, Two/Willing, The
  On Revolution
Arent, Arthur
  "... one-third of a nation... "
Aretino, Pietro
  Courtesan, The
  Discourses
  Letters
Arihara no Narihira
  Tales of Ise
Ariosto, Lodovico
  Lena, La (The Bawd Lena)
  Orlando Furioso
  Suppositi, I
Aristides
  Apology of Aristides, The
Aristocles see Plato
Aristophanes
  Acharnians, The
  Aeolosicon
  Anagyrus
  Babylonians, The
  Banqueters, The
  Birds, The (Aves)
  Clouds, The
  Cocalus
  Dramas or Niobus

Dramas or The Centaur
Ecclesiazusae, The (The Women
  in Parliament)
Farmers, The
Friers, The
Frogs, The
Gerytades
Heroes
Islands, The (Attributed to)
Knights, The
Lemnian Women, The
Lysistrata
Merchantmen, The
Peace, The
Phoenician Women, The
Plutus
Seasons, The
Seat-Grabbers, The
Storks, The
Telemessians, The
Thesmophoriazusae, The (The
  Women at the Festival)
Wasps, The
Aristotle
  Constitution of Athens
  Ethica Nicomachea
  History of Animals
  Mechanics
  Metaphysics
  Meteorologics
  On the Heavens
  On the Soul
  Organon
  Physics
  Poetics
  Politics
  Rhetoric
  Works
Arlen, Michael
  Green Hat, The
  These Charming People
Arlen, Michael J.
  American Verdict, An
  Passage to Ararat
  View from Highway 1, The
Arliss, George and Mary P.
  Hamlin
  Hamilton
Armah, Ayi Kwei
  Beautiful Ones Are Not Yet
    Born, The
  Fragments
Arminius, Jacobus
  Declaration of Sentiments, The
Armont, Paul and J. Manoussi
  Purple Mask, The
Armstrong, Anthony and Philip
  King

Mulata, The
Señor Presidente, El
Athanasius, Saint
  Discourses Against the Arians
  Incarnation of the Word of
    God, The
  Life of Antony, The
Athenagoras
  Apology of Athenagoras, The
  On the Resurrection of the Dead
  Plea for the Christians, The
Atherton, Gertrude
  Black Oxen
  Immortal Marriage, The
  Julia France and Her Times
Atkinson, Alex
  Four Winds
Atkinson, Eunice and Grant
  Perfect Idiot, The
Atkinson, Grant see Atkinson,
  Eunice and Grant
Atkinson, Thomas Dinham
  Cambridge Described and Illus-
    trated
Atlas, James
  Delmore Schwartz: The Life
    of an American Poet
Atlas, Leopold
  Wednesday's Child
Atwood, Margaret
  Animals in That Country, The
  Lady Oracle
  Power Politics
  Selected Poems
  Surfacing
Aubrey, John
  Brief Lives
Aubry, Georges Jean, editor,
  and Joseph Conrad
  Joseph Conrad, Life & Letters
Auchincloss, Louis
  Dark Lady, The
  Embezzler, The
  House of Five Talents, The
  Partners, The
  Portrait in Brownstone
  Rector of Justin, The
  Romantic Egoists, The
  Second Chance
  Winthrop Covenant, The
  World of Profit, A
Auden, Wystan Hugh
  About the House
  Age of Anxiety, The
  City without Walls and Other
    Poems
  Dance of Death, The
  Dyer's Hand and Other Essays,

  The
  English Auden: Poems, Essays
    and Dramatic Writings, 1927-
    1939, The
  Epistle to a Godson
  Forewords and Afterwords
  Homage to Clio
  Orators, The
  Poetry of Auden, The
  Shield of Achilles, The
  Thank You, Fog
Auden, Wystan Hugh and Chris-
  topher Isherwood
  Ascent of F6, The
  Dog Beneath the Skin; or,
    Where Is Francis?, The
  On the Frontier
Audiberti, Jacques
  Bête noire, La (The Black
    Beast)
  Black Feast, The
  Fourmi dans le corps, La (Ant
    in the Flesh)
  Logeuse, La (The Landlady)
  Pomme, pomme, pomme
  Quoat-Quoat
Audubon, John James
  Birds of America
Aue, Hartmann von see Hart-
  maan von Aue
Auerbach, Berthold
  Little Barefoot
  On the Heights
  Spinoza
Auerbach, Jerold S.
  Unequal Justice
Augier, Emile
  Giboyer's Son
  House of Fourchambault, The
  Marriage of Olympe, The
Augier, Emile and Jules Sandeau
  Mr. Poirier's Son-in-Law
Augustine, Saint
  City of God
  Confessions of Saint Augustine,
    The
  De magistro
  Disertations on the Psalms
  Enchiridion on Faith, Hope,
    and Love, The
  Faith, Hope, and Charity
  First Catechetical Instruction,
    The
  On the Trinity (De Trinitate)
Aulard, A.
  French Revolution, The
Aulén, Gustaf
  Christus Victor

Blouet, Paul see O'Rell, Max
Bloundelle-Burton, John Edward
  Across the Salt Seas
  Clash of Arms, The
  Fortune's My Foe
  In the Days of Adversity
  King's Mignon, The
  Knighthood's Flower
  Last of Her Race, The
  Scourge of God, The
  Sea Devils, The
  Servants of Sin
  Sword of Gideon, The
  Year One, The
Bloy, Léon
  Woman Who Was Poor, The
Blum, Jerome
  End of the Old Order in Rural
    Europe, The
Blum, John Morton
  V Was for Victory
Blunden, Edmund Charles
  Poetry of Blunden, The
  Undertones of War
Bly, Robert
  Light Around the Body, The
  Silence in the Snowy Fields
  Sleepers Joining Hands
Blythe, James
  Bid for Loyalty, A
  King's Guerdon, The
Blythe, Ronald
  Akenfield
Boas, Franz
  Mind of Primitive Man, The
Bocage, Louis Colin du see
  Verneuil, Louis
Boccaccio, Giovanni
  Amorosa Fiammetta, L'
  Decameron, The (Selections)
  Filostrato, Il
  Teseide, La
Bock, Jerry et al.
  Fiorello!
Bock, Jerry, Sheldon Harnick
  and Jerome Coopersmith
  Apple Tree, The
Bock, Jerry, Joe Masteroff and
  Sheldon Harnick
  She Loves Me
Bock, Jerry, Joseph Stein and
  Sheldon Harnick
  Fiddler on the Roof
Bock, Jerry, Sherman Yellen and
  Sheldon Harnick
  Rothschilds, The
Bode, Carl, editor
  New Mencken Letters, The

Bodelsen, Anders
  Freezing Down
Bodhisattva, Asvaghosha
  Fo-sho-hing-tsan-king: A Life
    of Buddha, The
Bodin, Jean
  Method for the Easy Comprehen-
    sion of History
  Six Books of the Republic, The
    (The Six Books on the State)
Bodkin, Matthias M.
  True Man and Traitor
Boehme, Jakob
  Way to Christ, The
Boerhaave, Hermann
  Elementa Chemiae
Boethius, Saint Anicius Manlius
  Severinus
  Consolation of Philosophy, The
  On the Holy Trinity (De Trini-
    tate)
Bogan, Louise
  Blue Estuaries, The
  What the Woman Lived
Bogard, Travis
  Contour in Time
Bohn, Henry George
  Bohn's Libraries
Bohr, Niels
  Atomic Theory and the Descrip-
    tion of Nature
Boiardo, Matteo Maria
  Orlando Innamorato
Boileau-Despréaux, Nicolas
  Art of Poetry, The
  Dialogues des Héros de Roman
  Satires
Boissier, Gaston
  Cicero and His Friends
Bojer, Johan
  Emigrants, The
  Great Hunger, The
  Last of the Vikings, The
  Life
  Power of a Lie, The
Bok, Edward
  Americanization of Edward Bok,
    The
Boker, George Henry
  Francesca da Rimini
Bokser, Ben Zion
  Judaism: Profile of a Faith
Boland, Bridget
  Return, The
Boldrewood, Rolf
  Robbery Under Arms
Bolitho, William
  Overture

Boruff, John
  Loud Red Patrick, The
Bosanquet, Bernard
  Principle of Individuality and
    Value, The
  Three Lectures on Aesthetic
Bossuet, Jacques Bénigne
  Discourse on Universita His-
    tory
  History of the Variations of
    the Protestant Religion
Bost, Pierre and Denis Cannan
  Power and the Glory, The
Bost, Pierre and Claude André
    Puget
  Nommé Judas, Un (A Man
    Named Judas)
Boswell, James
  Boswell for the Defence, 1769-
    1774
  Boswell in Search of a Wife,
    1766-1769
  Boswell: Laird of Auchinleck,
    1778-1782
  Boswell on the Grand Tour
  Boswell: The Ominous Years
  Boswell's London Journal:
    1762-1763
  Journal of a Tour to the
    Hebrides
  Life of Samuel Johnson, LL. D.,
    The
Bosworth, Patricia
  Montgomery Clift: A Biography
Boucicault, Dion
  Arrah-na-Pogue
  Colleen Bawn, or The Brides
    of Garryowen, The
  London Assurance
  Octoroon, The
  Poor of New York, The
  Shaughraun, The
  Streets of London, The
Boucicault, Dion, Charles Burke
    and Joseph Jefferson
  Rip Van Winkle
Boulle, Pierre
  Bridge over the River Kwai,
    The
  Planet of the Apes
Bourdet, Edouard
  Captive, The
Bourget, Paul
  Disciple, The
  Tragic Idyll, A
Bourjaily, Vance
  Now Playing at Canterbury
  Violated, The

Bourne, George
  Wheelwright's Shop, The
Bourrienne, Louis Antoine Fauve-
    let de
  Memoirs of Napoleon Bonaparte
Bourry, Emile
  Treatise on Ceramic Industries
Bouyer, Louis
  Christian Humanism
  Liturgical Piety
  Seat of Wisdom, The
Bowen, Catherine Drinker
  Francis Bacon
  Lion and the Throne, The
Bowen, Elizabeth
  Death of the Heart, The
  Eva Trout
  Heat of the Day, The
  Hotel, The
  House in Paris, The
  Little Girls, The
  Time in Rome, A
  World of Love, A
Bowen, John
  After the Rain
Bowen, Marjorie
  Glen o' Weeping, The
  Knight of Spain, A
  Quest of Glory, The
  Sword Decides, The
Bowers, Claude G.
  Jefferson and Hamilton: The
    Struggle for Democracy in
    America
Bowker, Alfred
  Armadin
Bowles, Jane
  Collected Works of Jane
    Bowles, The
  In the Summer House
Bowles, Paul
  Spider's House, The
  Time of Friendship, The
Bowles, Samuel
  Across the Continent
Bowman, Isaiah
  New World, The
Bunnu, Boruch Talkel
  Personalism
Bowskill, Derek
  Trojan War
Boyd, James
  Drums
  Marching On
Boyd, John
  Last Starship from Earth, The
  Pollinators of Eden, The
  Rakehells of Heaven, The

Boyd-Jones, E. et al.
Floradora
Boye, Karin
Kallocain
Boyer, Paul and Stephen Nissen-
baum
Salem Possessed
Boyesen, Jhalmar Jhorth (Hjalmar
Hjorth)
Gunnar
Boyle, Kay
Nothing Ever Breaks Except
the Heart
Boyle, Robert
Sceptical Chymist, The
Bracco, Roberto
Hidden Spring, The
Phantasms
Brace, Gerald Warner
Winter Solstice
Brackenridge, Hugh Henry
Modern Chivalry
Brackett, Leigh
Long Tomorrow, The
Sword of Rhiannon, The
Bradbury, Ray
Fahrenheit 451
Illustrated Man, The
Martian Chronicles, The
October Country, The
Short Fiction of Ray Bradbury,
The
Bradby, G. F.
Lanchester Tradition, The
Braddon, Mary E.
Infidel, The
Ishmael
Bradford, Gamaliel
American Portraits, 1875-1900
Bare Souls
D. L. Moody, a Worker in
Souls
Damaged Souls
Bradford, Richard
Red Sky at Morning
Bradford, William
Of Plimouth Plantation
Bradley, Rev. Edward see
Bede, Cuthbert
Bradley, Francis Herbert
Appearance and Reality
Ethical Studies
Bradley, Marion Zimmer
Darkover
Bradley, S. C.
Jesus of Nazareth
Brady, Cyrus T.
On the Old Kearsarge

Patriots, The
Quiberon Touch, The
Brahe, Tycho
History of the Sky
Braine, John
From the Hand of the Hunter
Life at the Top
Room at the Top
Brainerd, David
Diary of David Brainerd, The
Braly, Malcolm
False Starts
Bramston, Miss Mary
Banner of St. George, The
Failure of a Hero, The
For Faith and Fatherland
Story of a Cat and a Cake, The
Brancati, Vitaliano
Raffaelle (Raphael)
Brand, John
Observations on Popular Antiq-
uities
Brand, Millen
Outward Room, The
Brandes, Georg
Eminent Authors of the Nine-
teenth Century
Main Currents in Nineteenth
Century Literature
Brandon-Thomas, Jevan
Sit Down a Minute, Adrian
Brandstaetter, Roman
Ludzie z martirej winnicy
(The People of the Dead
Vineyard)
Milczenie (The Silence)
Branner, Hans Christian
Judge, The
Brant, Irving
James Madison: 1809-1812
James Madison: 1812-1836
Braudel, Fernand
Mediterranean and the Mediter-
ranean World in the Age of
Philip II, The
Braun, Gunter see Braun,
Johanna and Gunter
Braun, Johanna and Gunter
Unheimliche Erscheinungsformen
auf Omega XI
Brautigan, Richard
Brautigan's
Hawkline Monster, The
Sombrero Fallout
Bray, Anna Eliza
Adopted, The
Protestant, The
White Hoods, The

Bricusse, Leslie and Anthony
    Newley
    Roar of the Greasepaint - The
        Smell of the Crowd, The
    Stop the World - I Want to Get
        Off
Bridges, Ann P. and George
    Abbott
    Coquette
Bridges, Robert
    Poetry of Robert Bridges
    Testament of Beauty, The
Bridgman, Percy Williams
    Logic of Modern Physics, The
Bridie, James
    Anatomist, The
    Daphne Laureola
    Dr. Angelus
    Jonah and the Whale
    Mr. Bolfry
    Mr. Gillie
    Sleeping Clergyman, A
    Susannah and the Elders
    Tobias and the Angel
Brieux, Eugène
    Blanchette
    Damaged Goods
    Escape, The
    False Gods
    Maternity
    Red Robe, The
    Three Daughters of M. Dupont,
        The
Brighouse, Harold
    Hobson's Choice
Brightman, Edgar Sheffield
    Philosophy of Religion, A
Bring, Ragnar
    Commentary on Galatians
Bringsvoerd, Tor Åge
    Karavane
Brinkley, William
    Don't Go Near the Water
Broad, Charlie Dunbar
    Mind and Its Place in Nature,
        The
Broadhurst, George H.
    What Happened to Jones
Broch, Hermann
    Death of Virgil, The
    Sleepwalkers, The
Brod, Max
    Amerika
    Schloss, Das (The Castle)
Brodeur, Paul
    Sick Fox, The
Brodie, Fawn M.
    Devil Drives, The

Thaddeus Stevens: Scourge of
    the South
Brodrick, James, S. J.
    Origin of the Jesuits, The
    Saint Francis Xavier
Brodsky, Joseph
    Selected Poems
Brome, Richard
    City Wit, or, The Woman
        Wears the Breeches, The
    Jovial Crew, A
    Northern Lass, The
Bromfield, Louis
    Early Autumn
    Good Woman, A
    Green Bay Tree, The
    Possession
Brontë, Anne
    Agnes Grey
    Tenant of Wildfell Hall, The
Brontë, Charlotte
    Jane Eyre
    Professor, The
    Shirley
    Villette
Brontë, Emily
    Poetry of Emily Brontë, The
    Wuthering Heights
Brook-Shepherd, Gordon
    Uncle of Europe
Brooke, Eleanore and Jean Kerr
    King of Hearts
Brooke, Henry
    Fool of Quality, The
Brooke, Lord see Greville,
    Fulke
Brooke, Rupert
    Letters of Rupert Brooke, The
    Poetry of Brooke, The
Brooks, Charles William Shirley
    Gordian Knot, The
Brooks, Cleanth
    William Faulkner
    William Faulkner: Toward
        Yoknapatawpha and Beyond
Brooks, Elbridge S.
    Master of the Strong Hearts
    Son of Issachar, A
    Son of the Revolution, A
Brooks, Gwendolyn
    Selected Poems: 1944-1970
Brooks, John
    Go-Go Years, The
Brooks, Phillips
    Lectures on Preaching
Brooks, Van Wyck
    America's Coming-of-Age
    Days of the Phoenix

Ours Is a Nice House
Clifford, James L.
Young Sam Johnson
Clifton, Lucille
Generations
Ordinary Woman, An
Clifton, Mark
They'd Rather Be Right
Climacus, Saint John
Ladder of Divine Ascent, The
Clive, John
Macaulay: The Shaping of the Historian
Clodd, Edward
Story of Creation, The
Coates, Robert M.
Man Just Ahead of You, The
Cobb, James F.
In Time of War
Cobb, Sylvanus, Jr.
Gun-Maker of Moscow, The
Cobbe, Frances Power
Studies New and Old in Ethical and Social Subjects
Cobbett, William
Rural Rides
Coburn, D. L.
Gin Game, The
Cochran, Joseph and Ronald Dawson
Murder Is a Matter of Opinion
Cockram, Ronald
Shadow of the Eagle
Cockton, Henry
Valentine Vox, the Ventriloquist
Cocteau, Jean
Bacchus
Eagle Has Two Heads, The
Enfants terribles, Les
Holy Terrors, The
Infernal Machine, The
Intimate Relations
Knights of the Round Table, The
Orpheus
Plays of Cocteau, The
Coffee, Lenore see Cowen, Lenore Coffee
Coffin, Charles C.
Daughters of the Revolution and Their Times
Coghill, Nevill et al.
Canterbury Tales
Cohan, George M.
Pigeons and People
Seven Keys to Baldpate
Cohan, George M. et al.
George M!
Cohan, Mary et al.
George M!
Cohen, Arthur A.
In the Days of Simon Stern
Cohn, Clara (Viebig)
Our Daily Bread
Coit, Margaret L.
Mr. Baruch
Coke, Peter
Breath of Spring
Fool's Paradise
Cole, Hubert
Laval
Coleman, Cy, Neil Simon and Dorothy Fields
Sweet Charity
Coleman, Cy, Neil Simon and Carolyn Leigh
Little Me
Coleridge, Gilbert and Marion
Jan Van Elselo
Coleridge, Marion and Gilbert see Coleridge, Gilbert and Marion
Coleridge, Mary E.
Fiery Dawn, The
Coleridge, Samuel Taylor
Aids to Reflection
Biographia Literaria
Christabel
Kubla Khan
Poetry of Coleridge, The
Rime of the Ancient Mariner, The
Coleridge, Samuel Taylor and William Wordsworth
Lyrical Ballads
Coles, Robert
William Carlos Williams: The Knack of Survival in America
Colette
Chéri
Gigi
Other One, The
Pure and the Impure, The
Colette, Sidonie Gabrielle Claudine see Colette
Colin, Vladimir
Zecea Lume, A
Colinvaux, Paul
Why Big Fierce Animals Are Rare: An Ecologist's Perspective
Collier, Richard
Sands of Dunkirk, The
Collingwood, Harry
Cruise of the Thetis, The
Collingwood, Robin George

Arcadians, The
Mousmé, The (The Maids of
    Japan)
Tom Jones
Courtney, C. C. and Peter Link
    Salvation
Courtney, Marguerite
    Laurette
Cousins, Paul M.
    Joel Chandler Harris
Cousteau, Jacques-Yves
    Living Sea, The
Coward, Noel
    Astonished Heart, The
    Bitter Sweet
    Blithe Spirit
    Cavalcade
    Design for Living
    Fallen Angels
    Family Album
    Fumed Oak
    Hands Across the Sea
    Hay Fever
    I'll Leave It to You
    Noel Coward in Two Keys
    Nude with Violin
    Peace in Our Time
    Present Laughter
    Private Lives
    Quadrille
    Red Peppers
    Relative Values
    South Sea Bubble
    Still Life
    This Happy Breed
    Tonight at 8:30
    Vortex, The
    Waiting in the Wings
    Ways and Means
    We Were Dancing
    Young Idea, The
Cowen, Lenore Coffee and William
    J.
    Family Portrait
Cowen, William J. see Cowen,
    Lenore Coffee and William
    J.
Cowley, Abraham
    Miscellanies
Cowley, Mrs. Hannah
    Belle's Stratagem, The
Cowley, Malcolm
    - And I Worked at the Writer's
    Trade: Chapters of Literary
    History, 1918-1978
    Blue Juniata
    Second Flowering, A
Cowper, B. H., trans.

Apocryphal Gospels, and Other
    Documents Relating to the
    History of Christ
Cowper, Edith E.
    Viva Christina
Cowper, Frank
    Caedwalla
    Captain of the Wight, The
    Forgotten Door, The
Cowper, William
    Diverting History of John Gil-
    pin, The
    Letters of William Cowper,
    The
    Poetry of Cowper, The
    Task, The
Cox, Constance
    Lord Arthur Savile's Crime
    Vanity Fair
Coxe, Louis S. and Robert Chap-
    man
    Billy Budd
Cozzens, James Gould
    By Love Possessed
    Guard of Honor
    Just and the Unjust, The
    Just Representations: A James
    Gould Cozzens Reader
    Last Adam, The
    Morning Noon and Night
Crabbe, George
    Borough: A Poem in Twenty-
    Four Letters, The
    Village, The
Craddock, Charles Egbert
    His Vanished Star
    In the Clouds
Craft, Robert
    Stravinsky
Craig, Gordon A.
    Germany 1866-1945
Crake, Augustus David
    Aemilius
    Brian Fitz Count
    Camp on the Severn, The
    Doomed City, The
    Edwy the Fair
Crake, Edward Ebenezer
    In the Days of Queen Mary
    Tragedy of the Dacres, The
Cramp, Walter S.
    Psyche
Crane, Hart
    Bridge, The
Crane, Stephen
    Maggie: A Girl of the Streets
    Red Badge of Courage, The
Crankshaw, Edward

359   CRUTTWELL

Cruttwell, A. C. T.
History of Roman Literature, A
"Cryptos" et al.
Our Miss Gibbs
Csokor, Franz Theodor
Caesars Witwe (Caesar's Widow)
Cudworth, Ralph
True Intellectual System of the
Universe, The
Culler, A. Dwight
Poetry of Tennyson, The
Cullmann, Oscar
Christ and Time
Culver, Roland
River Breeze, A
Cumberland, Richard
Brothers, The
West Indian, The
Cummings, E. E.
Anthropos, or the Future of
Art
Enormous Room, The
him
95 Poems
Poems: 1923-1954
Poetry of Cummings, The
Santa Claus
73 Poems
Cummings, Ray
Girl in the Golden Atom, The
Cummins, Maria Susanna
Lamplighter, The
Cunha, Euclydes da
Rebellion in the Backlands
Cunha, Fausto
Noites marcianas, As
Cunliffe, Marcus
Soldiers and Civilians
Cunningham, Alice
Love Story of Giraldus, The
Cunningham, William
Growth of British Industry and
Commerce, The
Curel, François de
Beat of the Wing, The
False Saint, A
Fossils, The
Current, Richard N. and James
G. Randall
Lincoln the President
Curties, Henry
Renee
Curtis, George William
Literary and Social Essays
Potiphar Papers
Prue and I
Trumps
Curzon, Hon. Robert

Visits to the Monasteries of the
Levant
Cushing, Harvey
Life of Sir William Osler, The
Custer, Elizabeth B.
Boots and Saddles: or Life in
Dakota with General Custer
Cuvier, Georges
Règne animal, Le
Cynewulf
Elene
Cyprian of Carthage, Saint
On the Unity of the Catholic
Church
Cyril, Saint, Bishop of Jerusalem
Cathechetical Lectures, The

-D-

D'Abbes, Ingram and Fenn Sherie
Murder in Motley
Dabbs, James McBride
Southern Heritage, The
Dagerman, Stig
Condemned, The
Dahl, Roald
Kiss, Kiss
Dahlinger, C. W.
Where the Red Volleys Poured
Dahn, Felix
Struggle for Rome, A
Daigo, Ikeda, adaptor, and Kawa-
take Mokuami
Meigetsu Hachiman Matsuri
(The Full Moon on the Hachi-
man Festival)
Dale, J. S. of
Crime of Henry Vane, The
King Noanett
Dale, Jim and Frank Dunlop
Scapino (Based on Les Four-
beries de Scapin by Molière)
Dallas, Eneas Sweetland
Gay Science, The
Dalton, John
New System of Chemical Philos-
ophy
Daly, Augustin
Horizon
Night Off, A
Under the Gaslight
Dalzell, William
Onions in the Stew
Dam, H. J. W. et al.
Shop Girl, The

Deland, Margaret
  Awakening of Helena Richie,
    The
  Iron Woman, The
  John Ward, Preacher
  Philip and His Wife
Delaney, Shelagh
  Taste of Honey, A
Delany, Samuel R.
  Babel-17
  Dhalgren
  Driftglass
  Einstein Intersection, The
  Nova
  Triton
De La Roche, Mazo
  Jalna
Delavigne, Cassimir
  Sicilian Vespers, The
Delderfield, R. F.
  Flashpoint
  Golden Rain
  Mayerling Affair, The
  Once Aboard the Lugger
  Orchard Walls, The
  Where There's a Will...
  Worm's Eye View
Deledda, Grazia
  Mother, The (The Woman and
    the Priest)
DeLillo, Don
  End Zone
  Players
  Ratner's Star
  Running Dog
Dell, Floyd
  Moon Calf
Dell, Floyd and Thomas Mitchell
  Little Accident
Dell, Jeffrey
  Payment Deferred
Deloney, Thomas
  Gentle Craft, The
  Jack of Newberry
  Thomas of Reading
Delord, Taxile and J. J. Grand-
    ville
  Another World
Del Rey, Lester
  Nerves
Demetrius of Tarsus
  On Style
De Mille, James
  Cord and Creese
DeMille, William C.
  Strongheart
Democritus of Abdera
  Democritus: Fragments

De Morgan, William
  Alice-for-Short
  Joseph Vance
Demosthenes
  Philippics, The
Denham, Reginald and Edward
    Percy
  Ladies in Retirement
  Suspect
Denhan, Sir John
  Cooper's Hill
Denker, Henry
  Case of Libel, A
  Far Country, A
Denker, Henry and Ralph Berkey
  Time Limit!
d'Ennery, Adolphe P. and Eugène
    Cormon
  Two Orphans, The
Dennis, Nigel
  August for the People
  Cards of Identity
Dennis, Patrick
  Auntie Mame
Dent, Guy
  Emperor of the If
Denti di Pirajno, Alberto
  Ippolita
Denzinger, Heinrich Joseph Dom-
    inicus
  Enchiridion symbolorum et
    definitionum
De Paul, Gene et al.
  Li'l Abner
De Quincey, Thomas
  Avenger, The
  Confessions of an English Opium
    Eater
Dermoût, Maria
  Ten Thousand Things, The
  Yesterday
De Santillana, Giorgio
  Crime of Galileo, The
Descartes, René
  Discourse on Method
  Géométrie, La
  Meditations on First Philosophy
  Passions of the Soul, The
Des Pres, Terrence
  Survivor, The
Desprez, Frank, Edward Solomon
    and George Dance
  Nautch Girl, The
Dessau, Paul and Bertolt Brecht
  Exception and the Rule, The
  Fear and Misery of the Third
    Reich
  Herr Puntila and His Servant

Captain Jinks of the Horse
Marines
City, The
Climbers, The
Girl with the Green Eyes, The
Nathan Hale
Stubbornness of Geraldine, The
Truth, The
Fitchett, William H.
Pawn in the Game, A
Fitzgerald, Mrs. E. A. see
Dowie, Menie Muriel
FitzGerald, Edward
Rubáiyát of Omar Khayyám,
The
Fitzgerald, Eno
Witch Queen of Khem, The
Fitzgerald, F. Scott
Afternoon of an Author
Beautiful and Damned, The
Great Gatsby, The
Last Tycoon, The
Letters of F. Scott Fitzgerald,
The
Tender Is the Night
This Side of Paradise
FitzGerald, Frances
Fire in the Lake
Fitzgerald, Robert
In the Rose of Time
Fitz Gibbon, Constantine
Devil He Did
Life of Dylan Thomas, The
When the Kissing Had to Stop
Fitzhugh, Percy K.
Galleon Treasure, The
Flaccus, Quintus Horatius see
Horace
Flacius, Matthias (and others)
Magdeburg Centuries, The
Flammarion, Camille
Lumen
Omega: The Last Days of the
World
Flaubert, Gustave
Bouvard and Pécuchet
Herodias
Madame Bovary
Salammbô
Sentimental Education, A
Temptation of Saint Anthony,
The
Trois Contes
Flavin, Martin
Broken Dishes
Children of the Moon
Criminal Code, The
Flecker, James Elroy

Hassan: The Story of Hassan
of Bagdad. . .
Poetry of Flecker, The
Fleming, Peter
Siege at Peking, The
Fletcher, John see also Beau-
mont, Francis and John
Fletcher; Shakespeare, Wil-
liam and John Fletcher
Bonduca
Chances, The
Faithful Shepherdess, The
Island Princess, The
Rule a Wife and Have a Wife
Wild-Goose Chase, The
Woman's Prize, The
Fletcher, John and Ben Jonson
Bloody Brother; or, Rollo, Duke
of Normandy, The
Fletcher, John and Philip Mas-
singer
Beggars' Bush, The
Custom of the Country, The
Sir John van Olden Barnavelt
Fletcher, Lucille
Night Watch
Fletcher, Phineas
Purple Island, or The Isle of
Man, The
Flexner, Eleanor
Mary Wollstonecraft
Flexner, James Thomas
George Washington
Washington: The Indispensable
Man
Young Hamilton: A Biography,
The
Fodor, Ladislaus
Vigil, The
Fodor, László see Fodor, Ladis-
laus
Fogazzaro, Antonio
Patriot, The
Politician, The
Saint, The
Fontaine, Jean de La see La
Fontaine, Jean de
Fontane, Theodore
Effi Briest
Fontenelle, Bernard Le Bovier de
Dialogues of the Dead
Fonvizin, Denis K.
Minor, The
Foot, M. R. D.
Resistance: European Resist-
ance to Nazism, 1940-1945
Foote, Mary Hallock
Coeur d'Alene

Freeman, Douglas Southall
R. E. Lee
Freeman, Mary Eleanor (Wilkins)
Heart's Highway, The
Jane Field
Jerome: A Poor Man
Portion of Labor, A
Freeman, Stan, John Patrick and
Franklin Underwood
Lovely Ladies, Kind Gentlemen
Freidel, Frank
Franklin D. Roosevelt: Launch-
ing the New Deal
Freksa, Friedrich
Druso
Sumurun
Frémont, John Charles
Narratives of Exploration and
Adventure
French, Miss Alice see Thanet,
Octave
French, Allen
Colonials, The
Freneau, Philip
Poetry of Freneau, The
Frenssen, Gustav
Jörn Uhl
Klaus Hinrich Baas
Freud, Sigmund
Civilization and Its Discontents
General Introduction to Psycho-
analysis, A
Interpretation of Dreams, The
Outline of Psycho-Analysis, An
Psychopathology of Everyday
Life
Freud, Sigmund and Josef Breuer
Studies on Hysteria
Freytag, Gustav
Debit and Credit
Journalists, The
Lost Manuscript, The
Technique of the Drama
Friebus, Florida and Eva Le
Galliene
Alice in Wonderland
Friedenthal, Richard
Goethe
Friedman, Alan
Hermaphrodeity
Friedman, Bruce Jay
Dick, The
Mother's Kisses, A
Scuba Duba
Steambath
Stern
Friedman, Myra
Buried Alive: The Biography

of Janis Joplin
Friel, Brian
Lovers
Loves of Cass McGuire, The
Philadelphia, Here I Come!
Friend, Theodore
Between Two Empires
Friml, Rudolf et al.
Rose Marie
Friml, Rudolf, Brian Hooker and
W. H. Post
Vagabond King, The
Friml, Rudolf, Anthony McGuire
and Clifford Grey
Three Musketeers, The
Frings, Ketti
Look Homeward, Angel
Walking Happy
Frisby, Terence
Subtopians, The
Frisch, Max
Als der Krieg zu ende War
(When the War Was Over)
Andorra
Biedermann and the Firebugs
Biography
Chinese Wall, The
Count Oederland
Don Juan or The Love of
Geometry
Nun singen sie wieder (They
Sing Again)
Phillip Hotz's Fury
Santa Cruz
Froebel, Friedrich
Pedagogics of the Kindergarten
Froissart, Jean
Chronicles of Froissart
Fromentin, Eugène
Dominique
Frost, Elinor see Frost, Robert
and Elinor
Frost, Rex
Small Hotel
Frost, Robert
In the Clearing
Letters of Robert Frost, The
Letters of Robert Frost to
Louis Untermeyer, The
Poetry of Frost, The
Selected Letters of Robert
Frost
Frost, Robert and Elinor
Family Letters of Robert and
Elinor Frost, The
Froude, James Anthony
Caesar: A Sketch
Life of Thomas Carlyle

Taras Bulba
Gohei, Namike
Kanjincho (The Subscription List)
Golan, Matti
Secret Conversations of Henry
Kissinger, The
Gold, Herbert
Fathers
Great American Jackpot, The
Therefore Be Bold
Gold, Ivan
Nickel Miseries
Goldberg, Dick
Family Business
Golden, Harry
Only in America
Goldenweiser, Alexander A.
Early Civilization
Golding, William
Brass Butterfly, The
Free Fall
Inheritors, The
Lord of the Flies
Pyramid, The
Spire, The
Goldman, Eric G.
Crucial Decade, The
Goldman, James
Lion in Winter, The
Goldman, James and William
Blood, Sweat and Stanley Poole
Goldman, James and Stephen
Sondheim
Follies
Goldman, William see Goldman,
James and William
Goldoni, Carlo
Beneficent Bear, The
Coffee-House, The
Curious Mishap, A
Fan, The
Inn Keeper, The
Mistress of the Inn, The
Servant of Two Masters, The
Squabbles of Chioggia, The
(The Chioggian Brawls)
Goldsmith, Clifford
What a Life
Goldsmith, Oliver
Citizen of the World, The
Deserted Village, The
Good Natured Man, The
Poetry of Goldsmith, The
She Stoops to Conquer
Vicar of Wakefield, The
Gombrowicz, Witold
Iwona, ksiezniczka Burgunda
(Yvonne, Princess of Bur-

gundy)
Slub (The Wedding)
Goncharov, Ivan Alexandrovich
Common Story, A
Oblomov
Precipice, The
Goncourt, Edmond and Jules de
Charles Demailly
Germinie Lacerteux
Goncourt Journals, The
History of French Society, The
Manette Salomon
Renée Mauperin
Sister Philomène
Goncourt, Jules de see Goncourt,
Edmond and Jules de
Góngora y Argote, Luis de
Solitudes, The
Gonse, Louis
Art of Japan, The
Goodhart, William
Generation
Goodman, Arthur
If Booth Had Missed
Goodman, George
Wheeler Dealers, The
Goodman, Mitchell
End of It, The
Goodman, Paul
New Reformation
Goodrich, Arthur and Rose A.
Palmer
Caponsacchi
Goodrich, Frances and Albert
Hackett
Diary of Anne Frank, The
Great Big Doorstep, The
Goodwin, C. W.
On the Mosaic Cosmogony
Goodwin, Maud W.
Veronica Playfair
White Aprons
Goodwin, Richard N.
Triumph or Tragedy: Reflec-
tions on Vietnam
Gor, Gennadiy Samoilovich
Short Fiction of Gennadiy
Samoilovich Gor, The
Gordimer, Nadine
Conservationist, The
Not for Publication
Selected Stories
World of Strangers, A
Gordin, Jacob
God, Man, and Devil
Gordon, Caroline
Aleck Maury, Sportsman
Malefactors, The

Old Red and Other Stories
Gordon, Mary
Final Payments
Gordon, Rex
First on Mars
Gordon, Ruth
Over Twenty-One
Years Ago
Gordon, Suzanne
Lonely in America
Gordone, Charles
No Place to Be Somebody
Gore, Charles
Christ and Society
Gore-Browne, Robert and Harold
Marsh Harwood
Cynara
Górky, Máxim
Artamonov Business, The
Autobiography
Dostigaev and the Others
Foma Gordyeeff
Lower Depths, The
Mother, The
My Childhood
Orloff and His Wife
Smug Citizens, The
Submerged
Twenty-Six Men and a Girl
Yegor Bulitchev and Others
Gorter, Herman
Mei
Gosse, Edmund
Father and Son
Gosselin, Louis Léon Théodore
see Le Nôtre, G.
Cosson, Stephen
Schoole of Abuse
Gottfried von Strassburg
Tristan and Isolde
Goulding, Edmund and Edgar Selwyn
Dancing Mothers
Gourmont, Remy de
Night in the Luxembourg, A
Gouzenko, Igor
Fall of a Titan, The
Gow, James and Arnaud d'Usseau
Deep Are the Roots
Tomorrow the World
Gow, Ronald
Edwardians, The
Gow, Ronald and Walter Greenwood
Love on the Dole
Gower, John
Confessio amantis

Goyen, William
Fair Sister, The
Goytisolo, Juan
Fiestas
Gozzi, Carlo
Love for Three Oranges, The
Turandot, Princess of China
Grabbe, Christian Dietrich
Jest, Satire, Irony and Deeper
Significance
Gracián, Baltasar
Critic, The
Graffigny, Henri de and Georges
Le Faure
Aventures extraordinaires d'un
savant russe
Graham, Dom Aelred, O. S. B.
Zen Catholicism
Graham, Harry et al.
Maid of the Mountains, The
Graham, John W.
Neaera
Grahame, Kenneth
Wind in the Willows, The
Grammaticus, Saxo
Chronicles of Denmark, The
Grand, Madame Sarah
Heavenly Twins, The
Grandville, J. J. and Taxile Delord
Autre monde, Un
Grant, James
Adventures of an Aide-de-Camp,
The
Bothwell
Captain of the Guard, The
Harry Ogilvie
Lucy Arden
Second to None
Yellow Frigate, The
Grant, Robert
Average Man, The
High Priestess, The
Reflections of a Married Man
Unleavened Bread
Grant, Ulysses Simpson
Personal Memoirs of U. S.
Grant
Granville-Barker, Harley
Madras House, The
Marrying of Ann Leete
Voysey Inheritance, The
Waste
Granville-Barker, Harley and
Laurence Housman
Prunella
Gras, Felix
Reds of the Midi, The

San Toy
Greenbank, Harry, Sidney Jones
    and Owen Hall
  Geisha, The
Greenbank, Percy et al.
  Cingalee, The
  Country Girl, A
  Dancing Mistress, The
  Messenger Boy, The
  Mousmé, The (The Maids of
    Japan)
  My Lady Molly
  Our Miss Gibbs
  Quaker Girl, The
  Street Singer, The
  Toreador, The
Greenbank, Percy, Ivan Caryll
    and Seymour Hicks
  Earl and the Girl, The
Greene, Graham
  Brighton Rock
  Burnt-Out Case, A
  Comedians, The
  Complaisant Lover, The
  End of the Affair, The
  Heart of the Matter, The
  Honorary Consul, The
  Human Factor, The
  Living Room, The
  Lord Rochester's Monkey
  May We Borrow Your Husband?
  Ministry of Fear, The
  Our Man in Havana
  Potting Shed, The
  Power and the Glory, The
  Quiet American, The
  Sense of Reality, A
  Travels with My Aunt
Greene, Patterson
  Papa Is All
Greene, Robert
  Friar Bacon and Friar Bungay
  George a Greene, the Pinner
    of Wakefield
  Greene's Groatsworth of Wit
    Bought with a Million of
    Repentance
  James the Fourth
  Mamillia, a Mirror or Look-
    ing-glass for the Ladies of
    England
  Menaphon
  Pandosto, the Triumph of Time
  Quip for an Upstart Courtier,
    A
Greene, Sarah Pratt McLean
  Cape Cod Folks
Greene, Will

Riot Act, The
Greener, William
  Men of Harlech, The
Greenwood, Duncan
  Cat Among the Pigeons
  Murder Delayed
  Strike Happy
Greenwood, Walter
  Cure for Love, The
  Happy Days
  Saturday Night at the Crown
Greenwood, Walter and Ronald
    Gow
  Love on the Dole
Greer, Ben
  Slammer
Greg, Percy
  Across the Zodiac: The Story
    of a Wrecked Record
Gregg, Hubert
  We Have Company
Gregor-Dellin, Martin
  Lamp Post, The
Gregory, Horace
  Collected Poems
Gregory, Lady (Isabella Augusta)
  Deliverer, The
  Gaol Gate, The
  Golden Apple, The
  Grania
  Hyacinth Halvey
  Rising of the Moon, The
  Seven Short Plays
  Spreading the News
  White Cockade, The
  Workhouse Ward, The
Gregory of Nazianzus, Saint
  Five Theological Orations
Gregory of Nyssa, Saint
  Great Catechism, The
  Lord's Prayer, The
Gregory of Tours, Saint
  History of the Franks
Gregory Thaumaturgus, Saint
  Oration and Panegyric Ad-
    dressed to Origen, The
Gregory the Great, Saint
  Dialogues, The
  Pastoral Care
Grenfell, Wilfred Thomason
  Labrador Doctor, A
Gressieker, Hermann
  Royal Gambit
Greville, Fulke
  Alaham
  Mustapha
Gréville, Henri
  Dosia

George Washington Slept Here
Man Who Came to Dinner,
  The
Merrily We Roll Along
Once in a Lifetime
You Can't Take It with You
Hart, Moss, Ira Gershwin and
  Kurt Weill
Lady in the Dark
Harte, Bret
Gabriel Conroy
Luck of Roaring Camp and Oth-
  er Sketches, The
Outcasts of Poker Flat, The
Harte, Francis Bret see Harte,
  Bret
Hartleben, Otto Erich
Hanna Jagert
Hartley, L. P.
Go-Between, The
Hartley, Mrs. May
Ismay's Children
Hartman, Geoffrey H.
Fate of Reading, The
Hartmann, Eduard von
Philosophy of the Unconscious,
  The
Hartmann, Nicolai
Ethics
Hartmann von Aue
Arme Heinrich, Der
Hartner, Eva
Severa
Hartog, Jan de
Fourposter, The
Inspector, The
Skipper Next to God
Hartshorne, Charles
Divine Relativity, The
Harvey, Frank
Norman
Harvey, William
Anatomical Exercise on the
  Motion of the Heart and
  Blood in Animals (De motu
  cordis et sanguinis)
Harwood, Harold Marsh and
  Robert Gore-Browne
Cynara
Hašek, Jaroslav
Good Soldier: Schweik, The
Haslip, Joan
Catherine the Great
Hassall, Christopher
Rupert Brooke
Hassall, Christopher and Ivor
  Novello
Dancing Years, The

Glamorous Night
King's Rhapsody
Hastings, Charlotte
Bonaventure
Uncertain Joy
Hauff, Wilhelm
Cold Heart of Peter Munk, The
Iron Heart, The
Haupt, Paul, editor
Polychrome Bible, The
Hauptmann, Elisabeth, Bertolt
  Brecht and Kurt Weill
Happy End
Hauptmann, Gerhart
Agamemnon's Death
And Pippa Dances!
Atlantis
Atrides-Tetralogy, The
Beaver Coat, The
Before Dawn (Before Sunrise)
Black Mask, The
Bow of Odysseus, The
Charlemagne's Hostage
Colleague Crampton
Commemoration Masque
Darkness
Daughter of the Cathedral, The
Dorothea Angermann
Elga
Feast of Reconciliation, The
Florian Geyer
Fool in Christ, The
Gabriel Schilling's Flight
Golden Harp, The
Griselda
Hamlet in Wittenberg
Hannele's Journey to Heaven
Indipohdi
Iphigenia in Aulis
Iphigenia in Delphi
Lonely Lives
Magnus Garbe
Maidens of Bischofsberg, The
Michael Kramer
Peter Brauer
Poor Heinrich
Rats, The
Red Cock, The
Rose Bernd
Schluck and Jau
Sunken Bell, The
Tetralogy of the Atrides, The
Veland
Weavers, The
White Saviour, The
Winter Ballad
Witch's Ride
Hausrath, Adolph D.

Hayes, Carlton J. H.
  Essay on Nationalism
  Nationalism: A Religion
Hayes, Henry
  Story of Margaret Kent, The
Hayes, Isaac Israel
  Arctic Boat Journey, An
Hayes, Joseph
  Desperate Hours, The
Hazel, Robert
  American Elegies
  Poems: 1951-1961
Hazelton, George Cochrane
  Mistress Nell
Hazelton, George Cochrane and
  Harry Benrimo
  Yellow Jacket, The
Hazlitt, William
  Critical Essays of William
    Hazlitt, The
  Familiar Essays of William
    Hazlitt, The
  Liber Amoris
  Plain Speaker, The
  Table Talk
Hazo, Samuel
  Once for the Last Bandit
Hazzard, Shirley
  Bay of Noon, The
  Evening of the Holiday, The
Hearn, Lafcadio
  Chita
  Gleanings in Buddha Fields
  Japan, an Attempt at Inter-
    pretation
  Youma
Hebbel, Christian Friedrich
  Agnes Bernauer
  Gyges and His Ring
  Herod and Mariamne
  Judith
  Maria Magdalena
Hecht, Anthony
  Hard Hours, The
  Millions of Strange Shadows
Hecht, Ben
  Milk Run
Hecht, Ben and Charles Mac-
  Arthur
  Front Page, The
Hector, Annie (French) see
  Alexander, Mrs.
Hedberg, Tor
  Johan Ulfstjerna
Hedin, Sven
  My Life As an Explorer
Hefele, Karl Joseph von
  History of the Councils

Hegan, Alice Caldwell
  Mrs. Wiggs of the Cabbage
    Patch
Hegel, Georg Wilhelm Friedrich
  Early Theological Writings
  Logic
  Phenomenology of Spirit, The
  Philosophy of History, The
  Philosophy of Right, The
Heggen, Thomas
  Mister Roberts
Heggen, Thomas and Joshua Logan
  Mister Roberts
Heiberg, Gunnar
  Aunt Urikke
  Balcony, The
  Tragedy of Love, The
Heidegger, Martin
  Being and Time
Heidenstam, Verner von
  Birth of God, The
  Tree of the Folkungs, The
Heijermans, Herman
  Ghetto, The
  Good Hope, The
  Jesus the Lord
Heimert, Alan E.
  Religion and the American Mind
Heine, Heinrich
  Book of Songs
  Harzreise, Die
  Pictures of Travel
Heinlein, Robert A.
  Beyond This Horizon
  Citizen of the Galaxy
  Double Star
  Moon Is a Harsh Mistress, The
  Past Through Tomorrow, The
  Puppet Masters, The
  Starship Troopers
  Stranger in a Strange Land
Heinrich, Willi
  Cross of Iron, The
Heliodorus of Emesa in Syria
  Aethiopica
Heller, Joseph
  Catch-22
  Something Happened
  We Bombed in New Haven
Hellman, Lillian
  Another Part of the Forest
  Autumn Garden, The
  Children's Hour, The
  Collected Plays, The
  Little Foxes, The
  My Mother, My Father and Me
  Pentimento
  Scoundrel Time

Searching Wind, The
Toys in the Attic
Unfinished Woman, An
Watch on the Rhine
Hellman, Lillian et al.
Candide
Helmholtz, Hermann
On the Conservation of Force
Héloïse and Abélard
Letters
Helps, Sir Arthur
Friends in Council
Ivan de Biron
Spanish Conquest in America,
The
Helsby, Arnold
Camel's Back, The
Sky's the Limit
Hemenway, Robert
Girl Who Sang with the Beatles
and Other Stories
Hemingway, Ernest
Farewell to Arms, A
Fifth Column, The
For Whom the Bell Tolls
Islands in the Stream
Men Without Women
Moveable Feast, A
Old Man and the Sea, The
Short Happy Life of Francis
Macomber, The
Short Stories of Ernest Hem-
ingway, The
Snows of Kilimanjaro, The
Sun Also Rises, The
Hemingway, Mary Welsh
How It Was
Hemmer, Jarl
Fool of Faith, A
Hémon, Louis
Maria Chapdelaine
Henderson, Archibald
George Bernard Shaw
Henderson, Bill, editor
Pushcart Prize, III: Best
of the Small Presses, The
Henderson, Nicholas
Prince Eugen of Savoy
Henderson, Philip
William Morris
Henderson, Zenna
People: No Different Flesh,
The
Pilgrimage: The Book of the
People
Hendrick, Burton J.
Life and Letters of Walter H.
Page, The

Henham, Ernest G.
Menotah
Henley, William Ernest
Poetry of Henley, The
Henneberg, Charles
Naissance des dieux, La
Henry, O.
Cabbages and Kings
Four Million, The
Gift of the Magi, The
Short Stories of O. Henry
Whirligigs
Henry of Bracton
Treatise on the Laws and Cus-
toms of England
Hensen, Herwig
Andere Jehanne, De (The Other
Joan)
Hentoff, Nat
I'm Really Dragged But Nothing
Gets Me Down
In the Country of Ourselves
Henty, George A.
At the Point of the Bayonet
Bonnie Prince Charlie
Both Sides of the Border
Bravest of the Brave, The
By Conduct and Courage
By England's Aid
By Right of Conquest
By Sheer Pluck
Cat of Bubastes
Dragon and the Raven, The
For the Temple
Held Fast for England
In Freedom's Cause
In the Irish Brigade
In the Reign of Terror
In Times of Peril
Lion of the North, The
No Surrender
Orange and Green
Out with Garibaldi
St. Bartholomew's Eve
Through Russian Snows
Through the Sikh War
Tiger of Mysore, The
To Herat and Cabul
True to the Old Flag
Under Wellington's Command
When London Burned
Winning His Spurs
With Buller in Natal
With Cochrane the Dauntless
With Frederick the Great
With Lee in Virginia
With Moore at Corunna
With Roberts to Pretoria

With the Allies to Pekin
With the British Legion
With Wolfe in Canada
Wolf the Saxon
Won by the Sword
Young Buglers, The
Young Carthaginian, The
Young Colonists, The
Hepburn, Ronald W.
   Christianity and Paradox
Heraclitus of Ephesus
   Heraclitus: Fragments
Herbert, A. P. and Vivian
   Ellis
   Bless the Bride
Herbert, A. P. and Alfred Rey-
   nolds
   Derby Day
Herbert, Edward, Lord of Cher-
   bury
   Autobiography of Edward,
   Lord Herbert of Cherbury,
   The
   De Religione Laici
   De Veritate
Herbert, Frank
   Children of Dune
   Dragon in the Sea, The
   Dune
   Dune Messiah
   Santaroga Barrier, The
Herbert, Frederick Hugh
   For Love or Money
   Kiss and Tell
   Moon Is Blue, The
Herbert, George
   Priest to the Temple, A
   Temple, The
Herbert, Victor et al.
   Sally
Herbert, Victor and Rida Johnson
   Young
   Naughty Marietta
Herck, Paul van
   Caroline, O Caroline
Hérédia, José María de
   Poetry of Heredia, The
Hergesheimer, Joseph
   Java Head
   Linda Condon
   Three Black Pennys, The
Herlihy, James Leo
   All Fall Down
   Midnight Cowboy
   Sleep of Baby Filbertson, The
   Stop, You're Killing Me
   Story That Ends with a Scream
   and Eight Others, A

Herlihy, James Leo and William
   Noble
   Blue Denim
Herm, Gerhard
   Celts: The People Who Came
   Out of the Darkness, The
Herman, Jerry, Jerome Lawrence
   and Robert E. Lee
   Mame
Herman, Jerry and Michael Stewart
   Hello, Dolly!
Herman, Nicholas   see   Lawrence,
   Brother
Hermas
   Shepherd, The
Hernández, José
   Gaucho: Martín Fierro, The
   Martín Fierro
Herndon, William Henry
   Abraham Lincoln, the True
   Story of a Great Life
Herne, James A.
   Hearts of Oak
   Margaret Fleming
   Shore Acres
Herodas   see   Herondas
Herodotus
   History of the Persian Wars,
   The
Herold, J. Christopher
   Mistress to an Age
Herondas
   Cobbler, The
   Dream, The
   Incantation, The
   Jealousy
   Pimp, The
   Schoolmaster, The
   Self-Lovers, The
   Women in Asclepius' Temple
Herr, Michael
   Dispatches
Herrick, Robert
   Clark's Field
   Common Lot, The
   Hesperides
   Memoirs of an American Citizen,
   The
   One Woman's Life
   Real World, The
Herrligkoffer, Karl M.
   Nanga Parbat
Hersey, John
   Algiers Motel Incident, The
   Bell for Adano, A
   Child Buyer, The
   Hiroshima
   My Petition for More Space

Down There
En Route
Hyde, Kenneth
Rossiters, The
Hygeberth
Beowulf
Hyman, Mac
No Time for Sergeants
Hymer, John B. and Samuel Ship-
man
East Is West
Hyne, Charles J. C.
Prince Rupert the Buccaneer

-I-

Ibáñez, Vicente Blasco
Cabin, The
Four Horsemen of the Apocalypse,
The
Ibsen, Henrik
Brand
Catiline
Comedy of Love, The (Love's
Comedy)
Doll's House, A
Emperor and Galilean
Enemy of the People, An
Feast at Solhoug, The
Ghosts
Hedda Gabler
John Gabriel Borkman
Lady from the Sea, The
Lady Inger of Østråt
Little Eyolf
Love's Comedy
Master Builder, The
Olaf Liljekrans
Peer Gynt
Pillars of Society, The
Pretenders, The
Rosmersholm
Vikings at Helgeland, The
Warrior's Barrow, The
When We Dead Awaken
Wild Duck, The
Ibsen, Sigurd
Robert Frank
Icaza, Jorge
Huasipungo
Ickes, Harold L.
Secret Diary of Harold L.
Ickes: Volume II, The
Ienaga, Saburō
Pacific War: World War II

and the Japanese, 1931-1945,
The
Ignatius, Saint, Bishop of Antioch
Epistles of Saint Ignatius of An-
tioch, The
Seven Epistles of Ignatius, The
Ignatow, David
Rescue the Dead
Tread the Dark: New Poems
Ikku, Jippensha
Hizakurige Tokaido Chu (On
Shank's Mare Along the Tok-
aido)
Illich, Evan D.
Medical Nemesis
Illyés, Gyula
Queer Fellow, The
Inaba, Takeda and Miyoshi Shoraku,
assistants to Chikamatsu Hanji
Honcho Nijushiko (The Twenty-
Four Examples of Filial Piety)
Inchbald, Mrs. Elizabeth (Simpson)
Simple Story, A
Inge, William
Bus Stop
Come Back, Little Sheba
Dark at the Top of the Stairs,
The
Loss of Roses, A
Natural Affection
Picnic
Splendor in the Grass
Inge, William Ralph
Christian Mysticism
Ingelow, Jean
Don John
Off the Skelligs
Ingoldsby, Thomas
Ingoldsby Legends, The
Inman, H. E.
Wulnoth the Wanderer
Innes, Norman
Governor's Daughter, The
My Lady's Kiss
Surge of War, The
Innocent III, Pope
De contemptu mundi
De sacro altaris mysterio
Ionesco, Eugene
Amédée or How to Get Rid of It
Bald Soprano, The
Chairs, The
Exit the King
Future Is in Eggs, or It Takes
All Sorts to Make a World,
The
Hunger and Thirst
Improvisation, or The Shepherd's

Herdsman)
Jean-Aubry, Gérard
Sea Dreamer, The
Jean de Meun and Guillaume de
Lorris
Romance of the Rose, The
Jeans, A.
Stronger Wings, The
Jeans, Sir James
Mysterious Universe, The
Jeans, Ronald
Count Your Blessings
Double Take
Young Wives' Tale
Jebb, R. C.
Growth and Influence of Clas-
sical Greek Poetry, The
Jefferies, Richard
Amateur Poacher, The
Jeffers, Robinson
Cawdor
Cretan Woman, The
Hungerfield and Other Poems
Medea
Poetry of Jeffers, The
Roan Stallion
Tamar
Thurso's Landing
Tower Beyond Tragedy, The
Women at Point Sur, The
Jefferson, Joseph
Autobiography of Joseph Jeffer-
son, The
Jefferson, Joseph, Charles Burke,
and Dion Boucicault
Rip Van Winkle
Jefferson, Thomas
Declaration of Independence,
The
Notes on the State of Virginia
Summary View of the Rights of
British America, A
Thoughts on Democracy
Jellicoe, Ann
Knack, The
Jenkins, Elizabeth
Elizabeth the Great
|||||||||| ||||||| |||||||||
Ginx's Baby
Jenkins, Roy
Asquith
Jenner, Edward
Inquiry into the Causes and Ef-
fects of the Variolae Vaccinae,
a Disease Discovered in Some
of the Western Counties of
England, Particularly Glou-
cestershire, and Known by

the Name of the Cow Pox, An
Jennings, Gertrude
Olympian, The
Jennings, H. S.
Prometheus; or, Biology and the
Advancement of Man
Jensen, Axel
Epp
Jensen, Johannes V.
Long Journey, The
Jerome, Saint
De viris illustribus
Letters of Saint Jerome, The
Jerome, Helen
Charlotte Corday
Jane Eyre
Pride and Prejudice
Jerome, Jerome K.
Passing of the Third Floor Back,
The
Paul Kelver
Three Men in a Boat
Jerrold, Douglas
Chronicles of Clovernook, The
Mrs. Caudle's Curtain Lectures
Jessop, G. H. et al.
My Lady Molly
Jevons, William Stanley
Methods of Social Reform
Jewett, Sarah Orne
Country Doctor, A
Country of the Pointed Firs, The
Deephaven
Tory Lover, The
Jewu, Choi et al.
Chuntokyo Kyochi
Jhabvala, Ruth Prawer
Amrita
Heat and Dust
Nature of Passion, The
Travelers
Jiménez, Juan Ramón
Platero and I
Poetry of Jiménez, The
Jirásek, Alois
Lantern, The
Jisuke, Sakurada
Daihoiin Chobei Shoin Manaita
Jiwon, Turk
Hugh Saing Chun
Joachim, Harold Henry
Nature of Truth, The
Joachim of Fiore
Treatise on the Four Gospels
Joannes Scotus, Erigena
On the Division of Nature
Job, Thomas
Barchester Towers

Duke's Vengeance, The
Kaye-Smith, Sheila
Joanna Godden
Kazantzakis, Nikos
Freedom or Death
Greek Passion, The
Last Temptation of Christ,
The
Odyssey: A Modern Sequel,
The
Report to Greco
Saint Francis
Zorba the Greek
Kazin, Alfred
New York Jew
Keane, Mary Nesta (Skrine) see
Farrell, M. J.
Kearney, Patrick
American Tragedy, An
Kearns, Doris
Lyndon Johnson and the Amer-
ican Dream
Keary, Annie
Castle Daly
Doubting Heart, A
Keats, John
Endymion
Eve of St. Agnes, The
Hyperion, a Fragment
Insolent Chariots, The
Isabella or The Pot of Basil
Lamia
Letters of John Keats, The
Odes
You Might As Well Live
Keble, John
Christian Year, The
Keeffe, Barrie
Gimme Shelter
Keegan, John
Face of Battle, The
Keenan, Henry Francis
Money-Makers, The
Keene, Donald, editor
Old Woman, the Wife, and
the Archer, The
Keightley, Samuel R.
Cavaliers, The
Keith, Marion
Silver Maple, The
Keller, Gottfried
Grüne Heinrich, Der (Green
Henry)
Kellermann, Bernhard
Tunnel, The
Kellogg, Marjorie
Tell Me That You Love Me,
Junie Moon

Kelly, George
Behold the Bridegroom
Craig's Wife
Daisy Mayme
Deep Mrs. Sykes, The
Fatal Weakness, The
Show-Off, The
Torch-Bearers, The
Kelly, Laurence
Lermontov: Tragedy in the
Caucasus
Kelly, Tim
Lizzie Borden of Fall River
M*A*S*H*
Merry Murders at Montmarie
Kemal, Yashar
Memed, My Hawk
They Burn the Thistles
Undying Grass, The
Kemble, Frances Anne
Records of a Girlhood
Records of Later Life
Kempis, Thomas à see Thomas
à Kempis
Kendall, Paul Murray
Warwick the Kingmaker
Keneally, Thomas
Gossip from the Forest
Kennan, George
Tent Life in Siberia
Kennan, George F.
Cloud of Danger: Current Real-
ities of American Foreign
Policy, The
Decision to Intervene, The
Memoirs: 1925-1950
Memoirs: 1950-1963
Russia and the West Under Lenin
and Stalin
Russia Leaves the War, Volume
I
Russia, the Atom and the West
Kennedy, Charles Rann
Servant in the House, The
Kennedy, Eugene
Himself! The Life and Times
of Mayor Richard J. Daley
Kennedy, John F.
Profiles in Courage
Kennedy, John P.
Horseshoe Robinson
Swallow Barn
Kennedy, Margaret
Act of God
Constant Nymph, The
Red Sky at Morning
Kennedy, Mary and Ruth Hawthorne
Mrs. Partridge Presents

Kennedy, Sarah B.
Cicely
Joscelyn Cheshire
Kennedy, X. J.
Growing into Love
Kenner, Hugh
Bucky
Homemade World, A
Joyce's Voices
Kenny, Mrs. Stacpoole
Love Is Life
Kent, James
Commentaries on American
Law
Kenyon, Charles
Kindling
Kenyon, Edith C.
Adventures of Timothy, The
Queen of Nine Days, A
Kenyon, Frederic G., editor
Letters of Elizabeth Barrett
Browning, by Elizabeth Bar-
rett Browning
Kenyon, O.
Amor Victor
Kepler, Johannes
Astronomia Nova (The New
Astronomy)
Harmony of the World
Ker, David
Wizard King, The
Kerker, Gustav and Hugh Morton
Belle of New York
Kern, Jerome et al.
Sally
Kern, Jerome and Oscar Ham-
merstein II
Show Boat
Kerouac, Jack
On the Road
Kerr, Jean
Finishing Touches
Jenny Kissed Me
Mary, Mary
Our Hearts Were Young and
Gay
Poor Richard
Kerr, Jean and Hugh Morton
King of Hearts
Kerr, Jean and Walter
Song of Bernadette, The
Kerr, Walter see also Kerr,
Jean and Walter
Stardust
Kesey, Ken
One Flew over the Cuckoo's
Nest
Sometimes a Great Notion

Kesselring, Joseph
Arsenic and Old Lace
Kester, Paul
Sweet Nell of Old Drury
Key, Ellen
Woman Movement, The
Keyes, Daniel
Flowers for Algernon
Keynes, John Maynard
Economic Consequences of the
Peace, The
Revision of the Treaty, A
Keyserling, Count Hermann
Travel Diary of a Philosopher,
The
Kielland, Alexander L.
Three Couples
Kierkegaard, Søren
Attack on Christendom
Christian Discourses
Concluding Unscientific Postscript
Either/Or
Philosophical Fragments
Sickness unto Death, The
Training in Christianity
Kilty, Jerome
Dear Liar
Kim, Richard E.
Martyred, The
Kimball, Richard Burleigh
St. Leger
Kimbrough, Emily and Cornelia
Otis Skinner
Our Hearts Were Young and Gay
Kimmins, Anthony
Amorous Prawn, The
While Parents Sleep
King, Basil
Inner Shrine, The
King, Bolton and Thomas Okey
Italy of To-day
King, Charles
Colonel's Daughter, The
General's Double, The
Rock of Chickamauga, The
King, Clarence
Mountaineering in the Sierra
Nevada
King, Norman
Shadow of Doubt, The
King, Philip
"How Are You, Johnnie?"
On Monday Next
Pools Paradise
See How They Run
Serious Charge
Without the Prince
King, Philip and Anthony Armstrong

Inazuma-Byôshi
Kyun, Huh
Hong Kildong
Kyusuke, Fukumori
  Hiyoku no Cho Yume no
  Yoshiwara (Lover's Night-
  mare in the Yoshiwara)

-L-

Labiche, Eugene M.
  Italian Straw Hat, The (The
  Leghorn Hat)
  Voyage of Monsieur Perrichon,
  The (Perrichon's Trip)
Laboulaye, Edouard
  Abdallah
La Bruyère, Jean de
  Caractères, ou moeurs de ce
  siècle
Laclos, Pierre Choderlos de
  Dangerous Acquaintances
Lacouture, Jean
  André Malraux
Lactantius, Lucius Caecilius
  Firmianus
  Divine Institutes, The
Laertius, Diogenes
  Lives of the Philosophers
La Farge, John
  Artist's Letters from Japan,
  An
La Farge, Oliver
  Laughing Boy
LaFargo, John, S. J.
  Manner Is Ordinary, The
Lafayette, Madame Marie de
  Princess of Clèves, The
Lafferty, R. A.
  Does Anyone Else Have Some-
  thing Further to Add?
La Fontaine, Jean de
  Fables
Laforgue, Jules
  Poetry of Laforgue, The
Lagerkvist, Pär
  Barabbas
  Difficult Hour, The
  Hangman, The
  He Who Lived His Life Over
  Again
  King, The
  Man Without a Soul, The
  Philosopher's Stone, The
  Secret of Heaven, The

Sibyl, The
Lagerlöf, Selma
  Gösta Berling's Saga
  Lillecrona's Home
  Mårbacka
  Story of Gösta Berling
  Wonderful Adventures of Nils,
  The
  Laird, Carobeth
  Encounter with an Angry God
Laird, Jenny and John Fernald
  "And No Birds Sing"
Lall, Anand
  House at Adampur, The
Lamarck, Jean Baptiste de Monet
  de
  Philosophie Zoologique
Lamartine, Alphonse Marie Louis
  de
  Graziella
  Jocelyn
  Poetry of Lamartine, The
Lamb, Charles
  Essays of Elia and Last Essays
  of Elia
  Letters of Charles Lamb, The
Lamb, Charles and Mary
  Tales from Shakespeare
Lamb, Mary see Lamb, Charles
  and Mary
Lamennais, Félicité Robert de
  Affaires de Rome (Roman Af-
  fairs)
  Essay on Indifference in Matters
  of Religion
La Mettrie, Julien Offray de
  Man a Machine
Lamont, Miss see Jourdain,
  Eleanor
La Motte-Fouqué, Friedrich de
  Aslauga's Knight
  Sintram
  Undine
Lampodusa, Giuseppe di
  Leopard, The
Lampell, Millard
  Wall, The
Lanciani, Rodolfo
  Ancient Rome in the Light of
  Recent Discoveries
  Pagan and Christian Rome
Landon, Margaret
  Anna and the King of Siam
Landor, Walter Savage
  Count Julian
  Imaginary Conversations
  Pericles and Aspasia
  Poetry of Landor, The

Where the Cross Is Made
Wife for a Life
Ong, Walter J., S.J.
    American Catholic Crossroads
Ooka, Shohei
    Fires on the Plain
Openshaw, Mary
    Cross of Honor, The
Oppen, George
    Of Being Numerous
Oppenheim, E. Phillips
    Illustrious Prince, The
Orcutt, William D.
    Flower of Destiny, The
    Robert Cavalier
Orczy, Baroness
    Elusive Pimpernel, The
    Petticoat Government
    Scarlet Pimpernel, The
O'Rell, Max
    John Bull and His Island
Origen
    Contra Celsum (Against Cel-
        sus)
    De principiis (On First Prin-
        ciples)
Ormerod, Frank
    Two-Handed Sword, The
Orosius, Paulus
    Seven Books of History Against
        the Pagans
Orr, Mary
    All About Eve
Ortega y Gasset, José
    Revolt of the Masses, The
Orton, James
    Andes and the Amazon, or
        Across the Continent of
        South America, The
Orton, Joe
    Entertaining Mr. Sloane
    Loot
    What the Butler Saw
Orwell, George
    Animal Farm
    Nineteen Eighty-Four
Osaragi, Jiro
    Homecoming
Osborn, Francis
    Advice to a Son
Osborn, Henry Fairfield
    Men of the Old Stone Age
    Origin and Evolution of Life,
        The
Osborn, Paul
    Bell for Adano, A
    Innocent Voyage, The
    Morning's at Seven

On Borrowed Time
Point of No Return
Vinegar Tree, The
Osborne, Duffield
    Lion's Brood, The
Osborne, John
    Entertainer, The
    Epitaph for George Dillon
    Inadmissible Evidence
    Look Back in Anger
    Luther
    Patriot for Me, A
Osborne, John and Anthony Creigh-
    ton
    Epitaph for George Dillon
Oshikawa, Shunro
    Kaitei Gunkan
Ossendowski, Ferdinand
    Beasts, Men and Gods
Ossoli, Margaret Fuller
    Women in the Nineteenth Century
Ostenso, Martha
    Wild Geese
Ostrogorski, M.
    Democracy and the Organization
        of Political Parties
Ostrovskii, Aleksandr
    Diary of a Scoundrel, The (Enough
        Stupidity in Every Wise Man)
    Easy Money
    Even a Wise Man Stumbles
    Forest, The
    Poverty Is No Crime
    Thunderstorm, The (The Storm)
    Wolves and Sheep
Ostwald, Wilhelm
    Individuality and Immortality
Othmill, Lord (Jack of the Mill)
    see Howitt, William
Otloh of St. Emmeram
    Book of Proverbs
Otto, Rudolf
    Idea of the Holy, The
Otto of Freising
    Two Cities, The
Otway, Thomas
    Don Carlos
    Orphan, The
    Soldier's Fortune, The
    Venice Preserved; or A Plot
        Discovered
Ouida
    Bimbi: Stories for Children
    Dog of Flanders, A
    Friendship
    Moths
    Under Two Flags
    Wanda

Ovid
  Amores
  Ars amatoria
  Epistulae ex Ponto
  Fasti
  Heroides
  Ibis
  Metamorphoses, The
  Remedia amoris
  Tristia
Owen, Armitage
  None So Blind
  Once Bitten-Twice Shy
  Pools Paradise
Owen, Guy
  Journey for Joedel
Owen, John
  Discourse Concerning the
    Holy Spirit
Owen, Wilfred
  Poetry of Owen, The
Owens, Robert
  New View of Society, or, Es-
    says on the Formation of
    the Human Character, A
Owens, Robert and Wilton E.
    Hall, Jr., and William A.
    Miles
  1984
Oxenford, John
  Well Spent Day, A
Oxenham, John
  Coil of Carne, The
  Great Heart Gillian
  John of Gerisau
  Our Lady of Deliverance
  Under the Iron Flail
Oxford/Cambridge University
    Presses
  New English Bible, The
Ozick, Cynthia
  Bloodshed and Three Novellas

                 -P-

Packard, Vance
  Hidden Persuaders, The
  Nation of Strangers, A
  People Shapers, The
  Status Seekers, The
  Waste Makers, The
Padover, Saul K.
  Karl Marx: An Intimate Biog-
    raphy
Page, Thomas Nelson

  Gordon Keith
  Marse Chan
  Red Rock
  Social Life in Old Virginia Be-
    fore the War
Paget, Violet see Lee, Vernon
Pagnol, Marcel
  Judas
  Marius
  Topaze
Pailleron, Edouard
  Art of Being Bored, The
Paine, Albert Bigelow
  Joan of Arc
  Mark Twain's Autobiography
Paine, Thomas
  Age of Reason, The
  American Crisis, The
  Common Sense
  Crisis, The
Painter, George D.
  Chateaubriand: A Biography,
    Vol. I (1768-93): The Longed-
    For Tempests
  Proust: The Early Years
  Proust: The Later Years
  William Caxton: A Biography
Painter, William
  Palace of Pleasure, The
Palacio Valdés, Armando
  Fourth Estate, The
  Grandee, The
  Maximina
Paley, Grace
  Enormous Changes at the Last
    Minute
Paley, William
  Natural Theology
  View of the Evidences of Chris-
    tianity, A
Palfrey, Rev. John Gorham
  Compendious History of New
    England, A
Palgrave, Francis Turner,
    editor
  Golden Treasury, The
Palgrave, Mary E.
  Deb Clavel
Palgrave, William Gifford
  Central and Eastern Arabia
Palinurus see Connolly, Cyril
Palma, Ricardo
  Peruvian Traditions
Palmer, A. Smythe
  Babylonian Influence on the Bible
    and Popular Beliefs
Palmer, David Richard
  Summons of the Trumpet: U.S. -

Peck's Bad Boy
Peck, Walter Edwin
  Shelley, His Life and Work,
    1792-1820
Peele, George
  Arraignment of Paris, The
  Battle of Alcazar, The (attri-
    buted to)
  Old Wives' Tale, The
Péguy, Charles
  Basic Verities
  Poetry of Péguy, The
Peirce, Charles Sanders
  Collected Papers
Pellico, Silvio
  Francesca da Rimini
Pellissier, Georges
  Literary Movement in France
    during the Nineteenth Cen-
    tury
Peltier
  Acts of the Apostles
Pemberton, Max
  Footsteps of a Throne, The
  Garden of Swords, The
  Virgin Fortress, The
Penycate, Jack
  Ordeal by Marriage
Peple, Edward Henry
  Semiramis
Pepys, Samuel
  Diary
Percy, Edward and Reginald
    Denham
  Ladies in Retirement
  Suspect
Percy, Walker
  Lancelot
  Last Gentleman, The
  Love in the Ruins
  Message in the Bottle, The
  Moviegoer, The
Pereda, José María de
  Ascent to the Heights
  Pedro Sánchez
  Peñas arriba
  Sotileza
Pereda, Gaildós, Benito
  Abuelo, El (The Grandfather)
  Angel Guerra
  Doña Perfecta
  Duchess of San Quentin
  Electra
  Fortunata and Jacinta
  Leon Roche
  Marianela
  Saragossa
  Trafalgar

Perl, Arnold
  Tevya and His Daughter
Perlmann, O. see Dymov, Ossip
Perrot, Georges and Charles
    Chipiez
  History of Art in Ancient Egypt,
    A
Perry, Eleanor
  David and Lisa
Perry, John
  Man About the House, A
Perry, John and M. J. Farrell
  Dazzling Prospect
  Treasure Hunt
Perry, Ralph Barton
  General Theory of Value
Perse, St.-John
  Anabasis
  Chronique
  Eloges and Other Poems
  Sea marks
Persius
  Satires
Persse, Isabella Augusta see
    Gregory, Lady (Isabella Au-
    gusta)
Peshkov, Alexey Maximovich see
    Górky, Máxim
Pestalozzi, Johann Heinrich
  How Gertrude Teaches Her
    Children
Peterkin, Julia
  Black April
Peters, John Punnett
  Nippur
Peters, Paul and George Sklar
  Stevedore
Petersen, Donald
  Spectral Boy, The
Peterson, Louis
  Take a Giant Step
Petrakis, Harry Mark
  Dream of Kings, A
  Pericles on 31st Street
Petrarch, Francesco
  Canzoniere, Il
  On His Own Ignorance
  Rime of Petrarch, Le
Petrie, William Matthew Flinders
  Ten Years' Digging in Egypt
Petrie, William Matthew Flinders
    et al.
  History of Egypt, A
Petronius, Gaius
  Satyricon, The
Peyser, Ethel and Marion Bauer
  How Music Grew
Peyton, Thomas

Glasse of Time in the First
Age, The
Pfeiffer, Hans
Laternenfest (Lantern Festival)
Phelps, Elizabeth Stuart
Friends: A Duet
Singular Life, A
Philippe, Comte de Paris
History of the Civil War in
America, A
Phillips, David Graham
Deluge, The
Phillips, Montague, Alexander M.
Thompson and Gerald Dod-
son
Rebel Maid, The
Phillips, R. Hart
Cuba: Island of Paradox
Phillips, Stephen
Herod
Paolo and Francesca
Ulysses
Phillpotts, Adelaide see Phill-
potts, Eden and Adelaide
Phillpotts, Eden
Farmer's Wife, The
Saurus
Secret Woman, The
Sons of the Morning
Phillpotts, Eden and Adelaide
Yellow Sands
Phrynichus
Alcestis
Piaget, Jean
Grasp of Consciousness, The
Picard, Louis Baptiste
Petite ville, La
Picard, Max
World of Silence, The
Pick, Robert
Escape of Socrates, The
Pickering, Edgar
Dogs of War, The
In Press-Gang Days
Pico della Mirandola, Giovanni
Oration on the Dignity of
Man
Pidgin, Charles Felton
Blennerhassett
Quincy Adams Sawyer
Pieper, Josef
Belief and Faith
End of Time, The
Leisure the Basis of Culture
Pierce, Ovid Williams
On a Lonesome Porch
Piercy, Marge
Dance the Eagle to Sleep

Woman on the Edge of Time
Pigafetta, Antonio
Voyage of Magellan
Pijoan, Joseph
History of Art, A
Pilnyak, Boris
Naked Year, The
Volga Falls to the Caspian Sea,
The
Pincherle, A. see Moravia, Al-
berto
Pindar
Choral Lyrics
Epinicia, The
Odes
Pinero, Arthur Wing
Amazons, The
Dandy Dick
Enchanted Cottage, The
Gay Lord Quex, The
His House in Order
Iris
Magistrate, The
Mid-Channel
Notorious Mrs. Ebbsmith, The
Second Mrs. Tanqueray, The
Sweet Lavender
Thunderbolt, The
Trelawney of the Wells
Piñero, Miguel
Short Eyes
Pinget, Robert
Clope
Dead Letter
Fiston, Le
Pinski, David
Isaac Sheftel
King David and His Wives
Treasure, The
Zwie Family, The
Pinter, Harold
Birthday Party, The
Caretaker, The
Collection, The
Dumb Waiter, The
Homecoming, The
Landscape
Night Out, A
Old Times
Proust Screenplay, The
Room, The
Slight Ache, A
Three Plays
Piper, H. Beam
Little Fuzzy
Pipes, Richard
Russia Under the Old Regime
Pirandello, Luigi

In the Year '13
Old Story of My Farming Days
Reuther, Victor G.
Brothers Reuther, The
Rexroth, Kenneth
New Poems
Reyes, Alfonso
Visión de Anáhuac
Reymont, Ladislas
Peasants, The
Promised Land, The
Reynolds, Alfred and A. P. Herbert
Derby Day
Reynolds, Dorothy and Julian
Slade
Salad Days
Reynolds, Sir Joshua
Discourses
Rhodes, James Ford
History of the United States
from the Compromise of
1850
Rhoscomyl, Owen
For the White Rose of Arno
Rhys, Jean
Good Morning, Midnight
Wide Sargasso Sea
Ribeiro, João Ubaldo
Sergeant Getúlio
Ribman, Ronald
Journey of the Fifth Horse
Ricardo, David
Principles of Political Economy
and Taxation
Rice, Alice Hegan
Lovey Mary
Sandy
Rice, Anne
Interview with the Vampire
Rice, Elmer
Adding Machine, The
Cock Robin
Counsellor-at-Law
Cue for Passion
Dream Girl
Flight to the West
Grand Tour, The
Iron Cross, The
Left Bank, The
Not for Children
On Trial
Street Scene
Two on an Island
We the People
Rice, James and Sir Walter Besant
Chaplain of the Fleet, The
Golden Butterfly, The

Ready-Money Mortiboy
Rich, Adrienne Cecile
Diving into the Wreck; Poems,
1971-1972
Dream of a Common Language:
Poems 1974-1977, The
Necessities of Life; Poems,
1962-1965
Of Woman Born: Motherhood
As Experience and Institution
Poems: Selected and New
Richard, Adrienne
Pistol
Richard de Bury see Aungerville,
Richard
Richard of St. Victor
Benjamin Major
Benjamin Minor
Richards, I. A.
Principles of Literary Criticism
Richards, Laura E. and Maud Howe
Elliott
Julia Ward Howe
Richardson, Dorothy M.
Pilgrimage
Richardson, H. Edward
William Faulkner: The Journey
to Self-Discovery
Richardson, Henry Handel
Fortunes of Richard Mahony, The
Richardson, Howard and William
Berney
Dark of the Moon
Richardson, Jack
Gallows Humor
Richardson, Joanna
Enid Starkie
Sarah Bernhardt and Her World
Richardson, John
Wacousta
Richardson, Norval
Heart of Hope, The
Richardson, Samuel
Clarissa, or, The History of a
Young Lady
Pamela
Sir Charles Grandison
Richman, Arthur
Ambush
Richter, Conrad
Aristocrat, The
Awakening Land, The
Fields, The
Grandfathers, The
Lady, The
Sea of Grass, The
Simple Honorable Man, A
Town, The

K*A*P*L*A*N, The
Rosten, Norman
Come Slowly, Eden
Mister Johnson
Roswitha
Abraham
Roth, Arthur J.
Terrible Beauty, A
Roth, Henry
Call It Sleep
Roth, Philip
Goodbye, Columbus
Great American Novel, The
Letting Go
My Life As a Man
Portnoy's Complaint
Professor of Desire, The
When She Was Good
Rothenberg, Gunther E.
Art of Warfare in the Age
of Napoleon, The
Rothschild, Emma
Paradise Lost: The Decline
of the Auto-Industrial Age
Rotrou, Jean
Saint Genest (The True St.
Genesius)
Rotter, Fritz and Allen Vincent
Letters to Lucerne
Rousseau, Jean Jacques
Confessions
Creed of a Savoyard Priest,
The
Discourse on the Origin of
Inequality
Emile
New Héloïse, The
Social Contract, The
Roussin, André
Femme qui dit la vérité, Une
(A Woman Who Speaks the
Truth)
Figure of Fun
Glorieuses, Les (Saints in
Glory)
Little Hut, The
Rouvroy, Louis de see Saint-
Simon, Louis de Rouvroy,
Duke de
Rovere, Richard H.
Arrivals and Departures
Rovit, Earl
Far Cry, A
Player King, The
Rowe, Nicholas
Fair Penitent, The
Jane Shore, a Tragedy
Rowley, William

All's Lost by Lust
Birth of Merlin (attributed to)
Spanish Gipsy, The
Rowley, William, Thomas Dekker
and John Ford
Witch of Edmonton, The
Rowley, William and Thomas Mid-
dleton
Changeling, The
Rowley, William and John Webster
Cure for a Cuckold, A
Rowntree, Seebohm
Land and Labor
Poverty, a Study in Town Life
Rowse, A. L.
Churchills, The
Sir Walter Raleigh
Rowsell, Mary C.
Friend of the People, The
Monsieur de Paris
Rowson, Susanna Haswell
Charlotte Temple
Roy, Jules
Battle of Dienbienphu, The
War in Algeria, The
Royce, Josiah
Problem of Christianity, The
World and the Individual, The
Royle, Edwin M.
Squaw Man, The
Rozewicz, Tadeusz
Card Index, The
Rozov, Viktor Sergeyevich
In Search of Happiness
Vechno zhivye (Those Who Live
Forever)
Rubeanus, Johannes Crotus and
Ulrich von Hutten
Epistolae obscurorum virorum
Rubens, Paul A. et al.
Cingalee, The
Country Girl, A
Floradora
Rubens, Paul A. and Austen Hurgon
Miss Hook of Holland
Rubin, Louis
Golden Weather, The
Rubin, Theodore Isaac
David and Lisa
Ruddick, Sara and Pamela Daniels,
editors
Working It Out
Rudkin, David
Ashes
Ruffini, Giovanni
Doctor Antonio
Rufinus of Aquileia
Commentary on the Apostles'

Plain and Fancy
Stein, Joseph, Jerry Bock and
   Sheldon Harnick
   Fiddler on the Roof
Stein, Joseph, Fred Ebb and
   John Kander
   Zorba
Stein, Joseph and Will Glickman
   Mrs. Gibbons' Boys
Stein, Joseph, Robert Russell
   and Bob Merrill
   Take Me Along
Stein, Leo
   Appreciation: Painting, Poetry
   and Prose
Steinbeck, John
   Acts of King Arthur and His
   Noble Knights, The
   Burning Bright
   East of Eden
   Grapes of Wrath, The
   In Dubious Battle
   Moon Is Down, The
   Of Mice and Men
   Red Pony, The
   Sweet Thursday
   Travels with Charley
   Winter of Our Discontent, The
Steiner, George
   After Babel
Steiner, Jean-Francois
   Treblinka
Stella, Adorpan and Stefan Bekeffi
   Little Ladyship
Stendhal
   Charterhouse of Parma, The
   Lucien Leuwen
   Private Diaries of Stendhal,
   The
   Red and the Black, The
Stephen, Sir Leslie
   History of English Thought in
   the Eighteenth Century
   Hours in a Library
Stephens, Ann Sophia
   Fashion and Famine
Stephens, H. Morse
   History of the French Revolu-
   tion, A
Stephens, James
   Crock of Gold, The
   Deirdre
   Poetry of James Stephens
Stephens, John Lloyd
   Incidents of Travel in Central
   America, Chiapas and Yuca-
   tan
Stephens, Robert N.

Enemy to the King, An
   Gentleman Player, A
   Philip Winwood
Stephenson, B. C. and Alfred
   Cellier
   Dorothy
Stepniak, S.
   Career of a Nihilist, The
   Underground Russia
Stern, E. G.
   My Mother and I
Stern, Fritz
   Gold and Iron: Bismarck,
   Bleichröder, and the Building
   of the German Empire
Stern, Gerald
   Lucky Life
Stern, Gladys Bronwyn
   Debonair; the Story of Persephone
   Matriarch, The
Stern, Richard
   Other Men's Daughters
Sterne, Laurence
   Fragment in the Manner of
   Rabelais, The
   Journal to Eliza
   Political Romance, A (The His-
   tory of a Good Warm Watch-
   Coat)
   Sentimental Journey, A
   Tristram Shandy
Sternheim, Carl
   Pair of Drawers, A (The Under-
   pants)
   Snob, Der (The Snob; A Place
   in the World)
Stevens, James
   Paul Bunyan
Stevens, Leslie
   Marriage-Go-Round, The
Stevens, Sheppard
   Sign of Triumph, The
   Sword of Justice, The
Stevens, Thomas Wood
   Joan of Arc
Stevens, Wallace
   Collected Poems of Wallace
   Stevens, The
   Harmonium
   Letters of Wallace Stevens
   Opus Posthumous
   Poetry of Stevens, The
Stevenson, Burton E.
   At Odds with the Regent
   Heritage, The
   Soldier of Virginia, A
Stevenson, Charles Leslie
   Ethics and Language

Van Tine, Warren and Melvyn
  Dubofsky
  John L. Lewis: A Biography
Van Vechten, Carl
  Nigger Heaven
  Peter Whiffle
Van Vogt, Alfred Elton
  Slan
  Voyage of the Space Beagle,
    The
  Weapon Shops of Isher, The
  World of Null-A, The
Vanzetti, Bartolomeo and Nicola
    Sacco
  Letters from Prison
Varesi, Gilda and Dolly Byrne
  Enter Madame
Vari, John
  "Farewell, Farewell, Eugene"
Varley, John
  Ophiuchi Hotline, The
Varro, Terentius
  Agriculture
Varshavsky, Ilya
  Lavka snovidenyi
  Solntse zakhodit v Donomage
Vasari, Giorgio
  Lives of Italian Painters,
    Sculptors and Architects
Vaughan, Henry
  Poetry of Vaughan, The
Vauthier, Jean
  Capitaine Bada
  Personnage combattant, Le
    (The Struggling Individual)
  Prodiges, Les (The Prodigies)
Vazov, Ivan
  Under the Yoke
Veblen, Thorsten
  Theory of the Leisure Class,
    The
Vega Carpio, Lope Félix de
  Gardener's Dog, The
  King, The Greatest Alcalde,
    The
  Peribáñez and the Commander
    of Ocaña
  Sheep Well, The
  Star of Seville, The
Veiller, Bayard
  Thirteenth Chair, The
  Trial of Mary Dugan, The
  Within the Law
Venezis, Ilias
  Beyond the Aegean
Vercors
  You Shall Know Them
  Zoo ou l'assassin philanthrope

  (Zoo or The Philanthropic
    Murderer)
Verga, Giovanni
  Cavalleria Rusticana
  House by the Medlar Tree, The
  Malavoglia, The
  Mastro-Don Gesualdo
Vergerio, Pier Paolo
  On the Education of A Gentleman
Vergil
  Aeneid, The
  Ciris (attributed to)
  Copa (The Hostess) (attributed to)
  Culex (attributed to)
  Dirae (attributed to)
  Eclogues
  Georgics
  Lydia (attributed to)
  Moretum (attributed to)
  Priapea (attributed to)
Verhaeren, Emile
  Cloister, The
Verlaine, Paul
  Fêtes galantes and Other Poems
Vermigli, Peter Martyr
  Disputation of the Sacrament of
    the Eucharist, A
Verne, Jules
  Around the World in Eighty Days
  Begum's Fortune, The
  Clipper of the Clouds
  From the Earth to the Moon
  Journey to the Center of the
    Earth
  Master of the World, The
  Mysterious Island, The
  Twenty Thousand Leagues Under
    the Sea
Verneuil, Louis
  Affairs of State
Vernoy, Jules H., Jean François
    Alfred Bayard and Gaetano
    Donizetti
  Daughter of the Regiment, The
Vesalius, Andreas
  On the Structure of the Human
    Body (De humani corporis
    fabrica)
Veuillot, Louis
  Life of Our Lord Jesus Christ,
    The
Vian, Boris
  Empire Builders, The
  Generals' Tea Party, The
  Herbe rouge, L'
Viaud, Louis Marie Julien see
    Loti, Pierre
Vicente, Gil

517   WELTY

Welty, Eudora
  Bride of the Innisfallen, The
  Delta Wedding
  Eye of the Story: Selected
    Essays and Reviews, The
  Golden Apples, The
  Losing Battles
  Optimist's Daughter, The
  Ponder Heart, The
  Short Stories of Eudora Welty,
    The
Wendell, Barrett
  Barrett Wendell and His Let-
    ters. Edited by Mark
    Antony De Wolfe Howe
Wendell, Beth and Aldous Huxley
  Genius and the Goddess, The
Werfel, Franz
  Forty Days of Musa Dagh,
    The
  Goat Song
  Jacobowsky and the Colonel
  Juarez and Maximillian
  Man Who Conquered Death
  Paul Among the Jews
  Song of Bernadette, The
Werner, M. R.
  Barnum
  Brigham Young
Wertenbaker, Lael T.
  Gift of Time, A
Wertenbaker, Thomas Jefferson
  First Americans, The
Werth, Alexander
  Russia at War, 1941-1945
Wescott, Glenway
  Apartment in Athens
  Apple of the Eye, The
  Grandmothers, The
  Images of Truth
  Pilgrim Hawk, The
Wesker, Arnold
  Chicken Soup with Barley
  Chips with Everything
  I'm Talking About Jerusalem
  Kitchen, The
  Roots
Wesley, John
  Journal of John Wesley, The
  Plain Account of Christian
    Perfection, A
West, Anthony
  Heritage
West, Jessamyn
  Cress Delehanty
  Woman Said Yes, The
West, Mae
  Diamond Lil

West, Morris L.
  Daughter of Silence
  Devil's Advocate, The
  Shoes of the Fisherman, The
West, Nathanael
  Complete Works of Nathanael
    West, The
  Day of the Locust, The
  Miss Lonelyhearts
West, Paul
  I'm Expecting to Live Quite
    Soon
West, Rebecca
  Birds Fall Down, The
  Black Lamb and Grey Falcon
  Fountain Overflows, The
  Judge, The
  Train of Powder, A
Westall, William
  Birch Dene
  Red Bridal, A
Westcott, Edward Noyes
  David Harum
Westermarck, E. A.
  History of Human Marriage, The
Weston, R. P., et al.
  Girl Friend, The
Weston, R. P. and Bert Lee
  Shore Leave
Wetherell, Elizabeth
  Queechy
  Wide, Wide World, The
Wette, Adelheid
  Hänsel and Gretel
Wetzel, Donald
  All Summer Long
Wexley, John
  Last Mile, The
  They Shall Not Die
Weyman, Stanley J.
  Abbess of Vlaye, The
  Chippinge
  Gentleman of France, A
  House of the Wolf, The
  Red Cockade, The
  Starvecrow Farm
Whale, J. S.
  Christian Doctrine
Wharton, Edith
  Age of Innocence, The
  Custom of the Country, The
  Ethan Frome
  Fruit of the Tree, The
  House of Mirth, The
  Mother's Recompense, The
  Old Maid, The
  Old New York
  Reef, The

Spirit of the Service, The
Woods, George A.
   Vibrations
Woods, John
   Striking the Earth
Woods, Margaret L.
   King's Revoke, The
Woodward, Bob and Carl Bern-
      stein
   All the President's Men
Woodward, William E.
   George Washington, the Image
      and the Man
Woodworth, Samuel
   Forest Rose, The
Woolf, Leonard
   Beginning Again
   Journey Not the Arrival Mat-
      ters, The
Woolf, Noël and Sheila Buckley
   Bernadette
Woolf, Virginia
   Between the Acts
   Common Reader, The
   Contemporary Writers
   Diary of Virginia Woolf: Vol.
      I, 1915-1919, The
   Diary of Virginia Woolf, Vol.
      II: 1920-1924, The
   Flush
   Granite and Rainbow
   Jacob's Room
   Letters of Virginia Woolf, Vol.
      I: 1888-1912, The
   Letters of Virginia Woolf, Vol.
      II: 1912-1922, The
   Letters of Virginia Woolf, Vol.
      III: 1923-1928, The
   Literary Essays of Virginia
      Woolf, The
   Mrs. Dalloway
   Night and Day
   Orlando
   Room of One's Own, A
   To the Lighthouse
   Waves, The
   Writer's Diary, A
   Years, The
Wooll, Edward
   Libel!
Woollcott, Alexander and George
      S. Kaufman
   Dark Tower, The
Woolley, Bryan
   Time and Place
Woolman, John
   Journal of John Woolman,
      The

Woolson, Constance Fenimore
   Anne
   East Angels
Wordsworth, Dorothy
   Journals of Dorothy Wordsworth
Wordsworth, William
   Excursion, The
   Lines Written a Few Miles above
      Tintern Abbey
   Lyrical Ballads
   Ode on Intimations of Immortal-
      ity from Recollections of
      Early Childhood
   Poetry of Wordsworth, The
   Prelude, The
Wordsworth, William and Samuel
      Taylor Coleridge
   Lyrical Ballads
Wouk, Herman
   Caine Mutiny, The
   Caine Mutiny Court Martial, The
   Marjorie Morningstar
   Traitor, The
Wright, Anna Perrott Rose
   Room for One More
Wright, Austin Tappan
   Islandia
Wright, Constance
   Daughter to Napoleon
Wright, Harold Bell
   Winning of Barbara Worth, The
Wright, James
   To a Blossoming Pear Tree
   Two Citizens
Wright, Richard
   Native Son
   Richard Wright Reader
Wright, Richard and Paul Green
   Native Son
Wright, Robert et al.
   Kismet: A Musical Arabian
      Night
Wright, S. Fowler
   World Below, The
Wul, Stefan
   Niourk
   Temple of the Past, The
Wünsche, Konrad
   Adieux oder die Schlacht bei
      Stötteritz, Les (Les Adieux
      or The Battle of Stötteritz)
   Jerusalem, Jerusalem
   Über den Gartenzaun (Across the
      Garden Fence)
   Unbelehrbare, Der (The Unteach-
      able)
   Vor der Klagemauer (At the
      Wailing Wall)